MAGILL'S
SURVEY
OF
CINEMA

MAGILL'S SURVEY OF CINEMA

English Language Films

SECOND SERIES
VOLUME 5
PUT-THE

Edited by

FRANK N. MAGILL

Associate Editors

STEPHEN L. HANSON

PATRICIA KING HANSON

SALEM PRESS
Englewood Cliffs, N.J.

Library of Congress Catalog Card Number: 81-84330

Complete Set: ISBN 0-89356-230-0
Volume 5:   ISBN-0-89356-235-1

PRINTED IN THE UNITED STATES OF AMERICA

LIST OF TITLES IN VOLUME FIVE

MAGILL'S SURVEY OF CINEMA

PUTNEY SWOPE

Released: 1969
Production: Ron Sullivan for Cinema V
Direction: Robert Downey
Screenplay: Robert Downey
Cinematography: Gerald Cotts
Editing: Bud Smith
Running time: 84 minutes

Principal characters:
Putney Swope .... Arnold Johnson
Mrs. Swope .... Laura Greene
Elias, Jr. .... Allen Garfield
The Arab .... Antonio Fargas
Mr. Forget It .... Mel Brooks
President .... Pepi Hermine
First Lady .... Ruth Hermine

A decade before the zany, irreverent, and no-holds-barred farces, *Animal House* (1978) and *Airplane!* (1980), a thirty-one-year-old underground film-maker named Robert Downey wrote the screenplay and directed the film *Putney Swope*, a sophomoric, obscene, disjointed, and outrageously funny satire about race relations, money, and politics. The escapades presented by Downey in *Putney Swope* could have been described as "relevant" in 1969, the year in which the film was released. Putney (Arnold Johnson), the token black employee in an advertising agency, is accidentally elected chairman of the board of directors when the president suddenly dies during a promotional meeting. The elderly board members—greedy, corrupt, and capitalistic—are quickly replaced, except for a token white, by dashiki-clad, Afro-coiffed blacks. The agency name is then changed to Truth and Soul, Inc. Swope is idealistic in the manner in which he runs the agency. He refuses accounts for commercials dealing with alcohol, war toys, or cigarettes. He revolutionizes television advertising by creating shock-effect commercials for "Face-Off Acne Cream," "Lucky Airlines," "Get-Out-of-Here Mousetraps," and "Ethereal Cereal." The blurbs become so popular that nobody leaves the television set when they appear.

The President of the United States, a marijuana-smoking midget named Mimeo (Pepi Hermine), soon comes to regard Truth and Soul, Inc., as a threat to his authority as well as his vested interests. Swope is informed by Mimeo that the government will picket the agency if he does not advertise alcohol, war toys, and cigarettes, and particularly, the hazardous Borman Six, a German roadster. Meanwhile, money accumulates in the agency's basement, and some dissidents working under Swope threaten his authority. A white messenger boy attempts to assassinate him after being abused by the chairman and his staff. Dressed up as Fidel Castro, Swope attempts to abandon the agency with a sack of money. Finally, an Arab tosses a Molotov cocktail into the plexiglass vault in which the agency's money has been stored, and all of the cash assets of Truth and Soul, Inc. go up in smoke.

There is a message in *Putney Swope*: blacks may be equal to whites, but if so, they are also equally greedy and just as corrupt. This could be, and was, in fact, interpreted as a put-down of blacks by an insensitive, unintentionally racist white writer-director. The Harvard Lampoon placed the film third on its list of the Ten Worst Movies of 1969, and it received the Lampoon's "Twenty-Cent Token" award—"to that film which does the most fashionable injustice to a minority class."

Yet beyond any debate concerning the merits or lack thereof of Downey's depiction of blacks, *Putney Swope* is a marvelously manic satire. It is not a traditionally structured film but an illogical collage of comic vignettes, a collection of zany, weird characters inhabiting a surreal corporate landscape. Downey's directorial style can best be described as chaotic, with much of the footage devoted to Truth and Soul's commercial creations. For example, in the Face-Off Acne Cream ad, a white girl and black boy run arm in arm along the countryside to the tune of a ballad which begins: "It started last weekend, at the Yale-Howard game." Much of Downey's humor also depends upon the abrupt insertion of four-letter words in situations which are superficially proper.

Before *Putney Swope*, Downey had satirized motherhood and presidential assassinations in the underground films *Chafed Elbows* (1967) and *No More Excuses* (1968). The budget of the former (in which a young man marries his mother) was twenty-five thousand dollars, and the latter cost only twelve thousand. His budget for *Putney Swope* was two hundred thousand dollars, with shooting done in New York City office buildings after hours. In *Variety*'s list of "330 Films Above $100,000 in Rentals in the United States During 1970," *Putney Swope* was ranked sixty-first, with $1,439,826 in receipts—this was small, but still a profit over costs, which were kept low.

The reviews of *Putney Swope* were generally excellent except among more conservative critics. In 1969, the depiction of the President of the United States as a drug addict and a corrupt midget and the presence of four-letter words in a script was considered suspect. Wanda Hale, writing in *The New York Daily News*, awarded the film a no-star rating and described it as "vicious and vile, the most offensive picture I've ever seen. This one is retch-ed." Billed as the "Truth and Soul Movie" with an advertising campaign featuring a fist with its middle finger raised and replaced by a curvacious woman, *Putney Swope* broke box-office records when it opened at New York City's Cinema II theater. The film featured a huge cast of unknown talent, portraying characters with such outlandish names as Miss Redneck, New Jersey; Pittsburgh

Willie; Mr. Dinkleberry; Lady Beaver; Mr. Victrola Cola; Myron X; and Mr. O'Dinga. Comedian/director Mel Brooks is credited with an appearance as Mr. Forget It.

A pair of actors in the film have had successful careers in the 1970's. Three years after *Putney Swope*, Allen Garfield was supporting Robert Redford in *The Candidate* (1972); billed as Allen Goorwitz, he appeared in *The Brink's Job* (1979) and *The Stunt Man* (1980). Antonio Fargas, a versatile character performer adept at playing both vicious punks (*The Gambler*, 1974) and sensitive homosexuals (*Next Stop, Greenwich Village*, 1976), recently appeared in a cameo as a coach in the dismally unfunny *Mad Magazine's Up the Academy* (1980), one of the many films attempting to emulate the box-office success of *Animal House* and the popularity of television's *Saturday Night Live*. Downey followed up *Putney Swope* with *Greaser's Palace* (1972), a sometimes bright but mostly self-indulgent Jesus Christ parody with Jesus galavanting around in a zoot suit and the Holy Ghost garbed in a white sheet. He most recently directed *Up the Academy* but the jokes in that film are flat, and the plot, about boys in a military school who outwit their sadistic commanding officer, is predictable. Downey, who likes to refer to himself as a prince, has, artistically at least, become a pauper in the 1980's.

Rob Edelman

RACHEL, RACHEL

Released: 1968
Production: Paul Newman for Seven Arts/Warner Bros.
Direction: Paul Newman
Screenplay: Stewart Stern; based on the novel *A Jest of God* by Margaret
  Laurence
Cinematography: Gayne Rescher
Editing: Dede Allen
Running time: 101 minutes

Principal characters:
Rachel Cameron	Joanne Woodward
Calla Mackie	Estelle Parsons
Nick Kazlik	James Olson
Mrs. Cameron	Kate Harrington
Hector	Donald Moffat

Rachel, Rachel is a small, intimate film about a plain woman. The film succeeds in a monumentally difficult undertaking, that of dramatically portraying boredom without the work itself ever becoming boring. *Rachel, Rachel* is a character study, the exploration of a woman's inner life, her fantasies, her memories, and the sense and taste of her existence.

Rachel Cameron (Joanne Woodward) is a grade-school teacher approaching middle age. She muses to her schoolteacher friend Calla (Estelle Parsons) that it is her "last ascending year"—soon she will be headed downhill into her grave. It is the kind of observation that *Rachel, Rachel* handles with particular delicacy, which works to delineate Rachel's character without becoming falsely dramatic, maudlin, or self-pitying. Rachel is a woman who is above all sensible—her awareness of her mortality is simply part of being sensible. Rachel lives with her selfish and demanding mother (Kate Harrington), for whom she plays the dual roles of caretaker and infant, over the funeral home formerly owned by Rachel's father. Rachel grew up here, and the film's treatment of Rachel's childhood memories focus around death, the home, and Rachel's need for her father's affection and attention.

The film begins as the school year is drawing to a close. Rachel seems resigned to spending another boring summer, and we see her performing her usual activities of caring for her mother's bridge friends—making the sandwiches she has always made and serving her mother's friends politely in the way that she always has. *Rachel, Rachel* is a portrait of quiet stagnation.

It is the juxtaposition of the outward stagnation and frustration of Rachel's life with her vibrant inner mental life that gives the film its simple resonance. We see Rachel with her class, and then, when her favorite pupil is called down to the principal's office, there are sudden cuts of Rachel's fantasy of adopting him and taking him home with her to love and to nurture. The use of the fantasy sequences and the sound of Rachel voicing her thoughts weave Rachel's inner life with her outer one, creating a three-dimensional portrait of her. She fantasizes kissing the hairy knuckles of her school principal or jamming a handful of sleeping pills into her mother's mouth. Rachel Cameron is a picture of outward control and placidity and inward complexity and longing.

Rachel's friend Calla is a born-again Christian who has invited her repeatedly to come to prayer meeting and learn to "lean on the lord." Rachel is hesitant, fearing that she will make a fool of herself, but she finally accepts Calla's offer. They arrive at the prayer meeting, and Rachel enters reluctantly. She tries to sit through the meeting unnoticed, but the preacher singles her out during his preachings on "love." He begins to touch on the longing that Rachel has kept locked up, and she feels herself beginning to lose control. Cinematically the scene conveys Rachel's feeling of entrapment, claustrophobia, and lack of control. The crowd, seen from Rachel's point of view, is close, invasive, and passionate. She begins to weep, finally becoming hysterical. Outside the meeting, horrified, she tries to collect herself. Calla comforts her and begins to kiss her, leaving Rachel further emotionally distraught and confused.

Her life begins to change more radically when a childhood friend, Nick Kazlik (James Olson), whom she remembers in flashback from the time Nick's twin brother died, returns to town. He sees her and invites her out. At first she refuses, but then she makes a point of passing by the Kazliks' dairy farm. He asks her out again and this time she accepts. Kazlik is a high-school teacher and somewhat of a rogue. He asks Rachel if she is interested in a little "action," not realizing that "action" is the thing furthest from Rachel's life. One evening, they sit in front of the funeral parlor while Rachel decides whether to go home or to continue the evening with Nick and make love with him. He finally nudges her through her indecision and out to a deserted river bank where he lays out the blanket stashed in his trunk.

The scene is a pivotal one, and we hear Rachel's inner voice while we watch events take place. Nick, reacting to Rachel's sexual awkwardness, observes that "it's always hard the first time." Rachel asks him, "Is it that obvious that it's the first time for me?" Nick answers that there is no need for Rachel to "play virgin." Rachel's inner voice, however, reveals that she is not playing. Nick is her first lover and fills her with awe and romance. After their "first time," Rachel waits eagerly for him to call again, keeping the affair hidden from her mother. He does, and she spends a weekend with him, growing more attached, trying to tell him that she loves him and that she wants to bear his children—trying to be with him in a more committed way. Nick is uncomfortable with the turn of events. He deserts her and suddenly is gone from her life.

Rachel, still maintaining outward control, especially around her mother, is plunged into deep sadness. She waits for Nick to contact her and then begins to suspect that she is pregnant. She gets drunk with Hector (Donald Moffat), her friend and the owner of the funeral home, who claims that he has never seen her take a drink. Rachel is changing, loosening her controlled exterior. She begins to face some of her memories of her gruff, cold father. One powerful memory stands out among them.

Rachel as a little girl, played by Woodward and Paul Newman's daughter, stands before the cellar where her father embalms and prepares bodies for burial. The camera enters the cellar as if it were Rachel entering, passing a sign that reads "quarantine," then moves in on her father's preparation table. Her father is seen humming to himself, cleaning a dead child for its funeral. Rachel enters quietly, unnoticed by him, and lies down in one of the baskets used for dead bodies. As the basket closes Rachel's father sees her and in a panic tears off his medical gloves and coat and whisks her out of the quarantined area, screaming for her mother to come quick and wash her down. The most powerful image of the scene, however, is that of young Rachel being held by her father, her cheek against her father's, clutching him passionately, painfully. It is as though playing dead was young Rachel's only way to obtain her father's attention and affection. The scene is part of the film's strength, conveying the sense that Rachel's isolation is old and deep. It is a film about a character, the connection of present and past.

Rachel reconciles with Calla and decides that she will have her baby. She is now excited by the prospect, by the fact that she will finally be able to fulfill her love for children by giving birth to one and rearing it. She fantasizes about being in the park, watching schoolchildren go by and rocking her own baby in its pram. She goes to a doctor for prenatal care, but is shattered to find that her "pregnancy" is just a cyst. She submits to surgery, and, upon waking, hears the nurse tell her that she's "out of danger." She dryly comments, "How can I be out of danger if I'm not dead?"

Yet, Rachel is changed. She has decided to move. She offers her mother a place with her, if her mother wants to come. Even her mother's phony "heart attack" does not sway Rachel; she is now free of her mother's manipulation. The last scene finds Rachel finally moving, changing.

Woodward received an Academy Award nomination for her work in this film, and her rich portrayal of Rachel is surely one of the most finely honed and profound of her career. Undoubtedly, this performance was helped by her extraordinary rapport with the director and producer, her husband Paul Newman, whose handling of the story was extremely sensitive. *Rachel, Rachel* is a film that was allowed to be small, intimate, and closely observed. Stewart Stern's adaptation of Margaret Laurence's book *A Jest of God* reveals the kind of detail that makes this sort of smallness profound. A particular bit of dialogue illustrates the point. During Rachel's turmoil concerning Nick, we see her sitting and playing gin with her mother. Rachel is maintaining a surface control and yet the audience is aware of her deep emotion and confusion. Rachel's mother picks up a card saying, "I'm just going to take that nasty old queen, what do you think of *them* apples." The juxtaposition of Rachel's veneer of calm masking her turmoil and her mother's speech, so clichéd, so frustratingly small-townish and folksy, conveys the nature of their relationship with power and economy.

Hollywood's history seems to have been strongest in areas of spectacle and highly plotted storytelling. *Rachel, Rachel* is a successful exception to the rule, an intimate and fully fleshed character study.

Rebecca A. Bailin

RAGING BULL

Released: 1980
Production: Robert Chartoff and Irwin Winkler for United Artists
Direction: Martin Scorsese
Screenplay: Paul Schrader and Mardik Martin; based on the book of the same
  name by Jake La Motta, with Joseph Carter and Peter Savage
Cinematography: Michael Chapman
Editing: Thelma Schoonmaker (AA)
Running time: 129 minutes

> *Principal characters:*
> Jake La Motta .... Robert De Niro (AA)
> Vickie La Motta .... Cathy Moriarty
> Joey La Motta .... Joe Pesci
> Salvy .... Frank Vincent
> Tommy Como .... Nicholas Colasanto

Raging Bull is the story of the boxing career and decline of Jake La Motta,
who, for a short and not especially glorious time in 1949, was middleweight
boxing champion of the world. The film looks at La Motta's life in the ring,
re-creating his fights with Tony Janiro, Billy Fox, Marcel Cerdan (from whom
he won the title), and Sugar Ray Robinson (to whom he lost the title). It also
looks at his first and second marriages (the former very briefly), his stint as
a Florida nightclub owner, and his decline, during the late 1950's and 1960's,
into a second-rate club performer. La Motta's story seems almost to be modeled, with life following art, on any of a number of postwar Hollywood screen
biographies; one example is *The Set-Up* (1949), in which the boxing career
of the character played by Robert Ryan is compromised by the same Mafia
connections portrayed in *Raging Bull*. La Motta's own ghostwritten autobiography, on which the film was based, explicitly recognizes this parallel:
"I feel," he wrote, "like I'm looking at an old black-and-white movie of
myself . . . a string of poorly lit sequences with no beginning and some with
no end."

Martin Scorsese's film, however, could not be further from a Hollywood
"biopic." An initial screenplay by his frequent collaborator Mardik Martin
was apparently too directly biographical, concentrating heavily on the fight
scenes. Scorsese did not want to do a fight motion picture, and a second draft
in collaboration with Paul Schrader gave the film a structure and a tone which
bear the unmistakable hallmark of both Scorsese and Schrader, who had
previously worked with the director on *Taxi Driver* (1976). The final screenplay covers La Motta's life and career from 1941, when he was just beginning
to establish a reputation as a serious contender for the middleweight
championship, to 1964, when he was appearing in a New York nightclub

reciting extracts from William Shakespeare, Budd Schulberg, and Paddy Chayefsky. The film touches very briefly on his first marriage, but, in terms of personal life, focuses primarily on his second.

When La Motta first spots her at a Bronx open-air swimming pool, Vickie (Cathy Moriarty) is only fifteen. From the beginning, he is pathologically jealous at the slightest indication of her being interested in other men. For example, a chance remark by Vickie that Tony Janiro has "a pretty face" means that La Motta's only interest in his fight with Janiro is in destroying that face. Later, when he is out of town, he has his brother Joey watch over her. Joey subsequently becomes involved in a vicious fight with a small-time hood called Salvy (Frank Vincent), who, he thinks, is flirting with her. In the ensuing reconciliation organized by Salvy's boss Tommy Como (Nicholas Colasanto), Jake is also persuaded that, for obscure reasons, he will have to "throw" the fight with Billy Fox if he wants a chance at the title. He does so.

Then, in 1949, Jake gets his chance and beats Marcel Cerdan to become champion. His suspicions about Vickie's infidelity are, in the meantime, driving him almost insane. Finally, he even turns on his brother Joey, and, after he has physically assaulted both of them, the younger La Motta walks out. Jake is having weight problems and subsequently loses the title to Sugar Ray Robinson in a particularly brutal contest. Determined not to be knocked down, La Motta allows himself to be battered almost senseless until the referee stops the fight.

From this point on, La Motta's career goes into a sharp decline. Vickie leaves, taking the children. La Motta opens a smart Florida nightclub, but loses his license and is jailed when an underage girl is found in the place. In 1958, out of jail, he gets a job introducing strippers in a seedy New York bar. A chance encounter with Joey fails to bring about a reconciliation. When the film ends in 1964, La Motta's nightclub act is a little more respectable. He is doing recitations from great authors, including Marlon Brando's famous speech from *On the Waterfront* (1954), "I could have been a contender. . . ."

A great critical and commercial success, *Raging Bull* is something of a virtuoso film. Like La Motta in the ring, it moves in flurries of loud, hyperbolic activity, flinging off pearls of sweat and an occasional jet of blood. Superbly edited by Thelma Schoonmaker, it is relentless, violent (an aspect of the film which came in for a certain amount of criticism when it was first released), streetwise, and determined. Almost every sequence is a potential anthology piece, from the slow-motion credit shots of La Motta dancing around the ring in his hooded leopard-skin robe and Joey's sprawling fight with Salvy, to the "retired" La Motta's clumsy, disjointed nightclub act. Michael Chapman's cinematography is, as usual, flawless. Following a minor trend in 1980—and doubtless influenced by Scorsese's running battle with the color processing labs about the rate at which color prints deteriorate—it is shot in black-and-white, barring some color excerpts from Jake's home movies (scenes of happiness whose transitoriness and artificiality are underlined by the change of tone and texture). Elsewhere, the cinematography adapts seamlessly to the light values of the various locations: the bleak Bronx interiors, the smoky boxing arenas, the brittle Florida sunshine, and the seedy nightclubs of its final scenes.

In terms of performances, *Raging Bull* is one of those rare films in which a major actor decisively comes of age. Although most of the other 1981 Oscars went to Robert Redford's *Ordinary People*, there was never any real doubt that De Niro would get the Best Actor award. His is a phenomenal, once-in-a-decade performance. Although he went through a punishing training schedule for the boxing sequences and put on a staggering sixty pounds for the later scenes, it is not the externals but his inner intensity that makes the performance. Watching De Niro is exciting, compulsive, and even a little frightening. Pesci is likewise very fine as the volatile Joey; and, although she is not given much to do, Moriarty manages to bring both strength and dignity to the role of Vickie.

If there is one problem with the film, however, it lies in the sparseness of Schrader's screenplay. As in *Taxi Driver*, it is a strange dovetailing of Scorsese's Catholic background (the scene in which Jake brings Vickie back to a room complete with crucifix and family portraits is almost identical to one in Scorsese's earlier *Mean Streets*, 1973) and Schrader's Calvinist fatalism. Like the heroes of Schrader's own films as a director (Harvey Keitel in *Blue Collar*, 1978, and Richard Gere in *American Gigolo*, 1980), and above all like Travis Bickle in *Taxi Driver*, La Motta is not so much a man with a quest, as a man who *is* a quest. He wants the title; he wants to fight his way out of the ghetto; he wants to "make it on his own." In fact, it is not his fighting, but his experience of defeat and degradation which redeems him. La Motta is reduced—or elevated—to an almost symbolic figure, and as a result, psychology, motivation, and explanation are at a minimum. La Motta's career and private life (the two seem to impinge surprisingly little on each other) become like a series of personal stations of the cross, and the secondary characters, especially Vickie, become mere temptations, challenges, or obstacles along the way. Although this fragmented approach bears a fairly close resemblance to La Motta's own perception of his life story, there are times when the progress of the narrative and the development of the characters seem to be entirely subject to a schema of redemption that owes more to the structure of the screenplay than it does to the life of Jake La Motta.

Yet any sparseness in the screenplay, however intentional, is amply compensated for by the richness of Scorsese's cinematic vision and the power of De Niro's performance. *Raging Bull* is a film of great intensity, at times deeply disturbing as it portrays La Motta's self-destructive career, his jealousy, and his cruelty to himself and those around him. Occasionally, the film comes close to being a classical tragedy, since La Motta is destroyed by the very things that made him, briefly, world champion: his single-mindedness, coupled with his ability and maybe even his desire to take punishment.

Nick Roddick

RAIDERS OF THE LOST ARK

Released: 1981
Production: George Lucas and Howard Kazanjian for Paramount
Direction: Steven Spielberg
Screenplay: Lawrence Kasdan; based on an original story by George Lucas and Philip Kaufman
Cinematography: Douglas Slocombe
Editing: Michael Kahn
Music: John Williams
Running time: 115 minutes

Principal characters:

Indiana Jones	Harrison Ford
Marion Ravenwood	Karen Allen
Dietrich	Wolf Kahler
Belloq	Paul Freeman
Toht	Ronald Lacey
Sallah	John Rhys-Davies
Brody	Denholm Elliott

Delivered in the tradition of the Saturday matinee serials of the 1930's and 1940's, *Raiders of the Lost Ark* is a high-spirited escapist film which pits the hero, Indiana Jones (who greatly resembles Fred C. Dobbs in *Treasure of the Sierra Madre*, 1947), against the Nazis in a race to locate the powerful Ark of the Covenant. George Lucas and Steven Spielberg, as producer and director, respectively, created the film largely in response to their boyhood infatuations with Saturday matinee serials. "I wondered why they didn't make movies like that anymore. I still wanted to see them," Lucas has stated. Spielberg adds, "I've always wanted to bring a serial to life that blends Lash LaRue, Spy Smasher, Masked Marvel, and Tailspin Tommy with elements from Edgar Rice Burroughs. . . ."

In coming together, the creative talents of Lucas behind *Star Wars* (1977), *The Empire Strikes Back* (1980), and *American Graffiti* (1973), and of Spielberg behind *Jaws* (1975) and *Close Encounters of the Third Kind* (1977) deliver a film that showcases their sturdy technical capabilities, along with a decidedly gee-whiz demeanor. Production costs were twenty million dollars, which is a modest budget considering the overall appearance and scope of the film. *Raiders of the Lost Ark* opened in June, 1981, and was exceptionally well received at the box office, as indicated by the receipts. Within twenty-six days of the film's domestic release, it had grossed more than fifty million dollars, and, along with the popular *Superman II*, *Raiders of the Lost Ark* dominated the summer's theater business.

Purporting only to entertain, the film is delivered with great zest and is a fitting overture to the child that exists in most filmgoers. Pegged by many critics as a "popcorn picture," it typifies what the industry considers to be the perfect summer film, thereby joining the ranks of historically successful summertime releases including *Jaws* and *Star Wars*.

Nostalgic charm and delivery, however, are by no means the major reasons behind the film's sweep at the box office. Instead, it was the state of the industry itself which encouraged and fed that success. During the first five months of 1981, the industry was in the throes of a much-publicized slump. Of the spring releases, only John Boorman's *Excalibur* garnered critical praise and impressive box-office receipts. An Arthurian tale mixing sword, sorcery, and surrealism, *Excalibur* is most notable for being the first in a string of "sword and sorcery" (fantasy) films and for restoring Boorman, who had previously directed *Deliverance* (1972), to the industry's good graces. His reputation was put in jeopardy after he directed the much-ridiculed *Exorcist II: The Heretic*, the 1977 sequel to the wildly popular 1973 shocker, *The Exorcist*.

In addition to *Excalibur*, only the so-called "slasher" or "knife" films— such as the bloody *Friday the 13th Part II*—managed to make money. Unleashed by John Carpenter's legendary 1978 film, *Halloween*, the gruesome knife films (usually focusing on grisly murders executed with sharp-edged instruments) came to the screen in unsettling numbers throughout early 1981, to the dismay of most critics.

Along with a shortage of box-office successes, the industry was experiencing a writers' strike (which affected television production as well as feature films) and suffering the threat of a directors' strike (which was finally averted). The major studios were also hampered by uncertainty about the burgeoning video industry, a factor in the writers' strike. Also, Hollywood, as a whole, was still feeling the tremors of the unprecedented fiasco that was *Heaven's Gate* (1981), the costliest motion picture failure of all time. Given these conditions, as well as the nostalgic mood evoked by the adventure-laden *Raiders of the Lost Ark*, it is no surprise that audiences and critics eagerly rallied to the film.

The opening sequence establishes the tone for the breathlessly paced film. The time is 1936 and explorer-archaeologist Indiana ("Indy") Jones (Harrison Ford), on a mission to locate a gold idol, makes his way through a menacing Peruvian jungle. With bullwhip firmly in hand, Jones encounters a variety of obstacles including a turncoat guide, natives brandishing spears and blowguns, caverns filled with huge tarantulas, and gigantic cascading boulders. Even the temple enshrining the coveted statuette is brilliantly booby-trapped. Jones remains unflinching in the face of these dangers, however, and even manages to retain his composure when he encounters his nemesis, the crafty French archaeologist Belloq (Paul Freeman), who steals the hard-earned treasure. It is only after climbing aboard his getaway plane that Jones allows his heroic veneer to tarnish—a snake is aboard, and Jones absolutely hates snakes. To his yells of protest and fear the copilot snaps, "Show some backbone!"

The South American adventure is a prelude to the quest for the Ark. According to biblical legend, the gold-encrusted Ark is the chest which contains the broken tablets of the Ten Commandments, and whoever possesses the Ark will be infused with invincible powers. Thus, Hitler and the Nazis want the Ark. Because legend dictates that it was entombed by a pharaoh at the Well of Souls, located in the lost city of Tanis, Hitler has sent his agents to Egypt. There, under the direction of the unscrupulous Belloq, excavations are under way. In retaliation, United States Army Intelligence sends two men to visit Jones, at the college where he teaches, and enlist his aid, in the hope that he can somehow get to the Ark before the Nazis. The intrigue is compounded by the rumors that the Ark, similar to Pandora's Box, will bring disaster to those who tamper with it.

To begin his mission, Jones journeys to Nepal, where he hopes to be reunited with Professor Abner Ravenwood, an old friend who possesses the headpiece (which looks like a gold medallion) to the staff of Ra. According to legend, the headpiece is the key to discovering the exact location of the Ark. Once in Nepal, however, Jones learns that his colleague is dead, and that his daughter, Marion Ravenwood (Karen Allen), whom Jones loved and had left ten years earlier, now has the headpiece. Tough-talking, spunky, and hard-drinking (viewers meet her as she outdrinks a hardy Nepalese), Marion has not forgotten Jones. When first confronted by him in the bar that she owns, she unleashes a flying fist with the outburst, "I was a child. It was wrong!" Marion puts her hard feelings to rest, however, when her bar goes up in flames—the result of a grisly shoot-out induced by the appearance of Toht (Ronald Lacey), a treacherous and bespectacled Nazi spy (in the Peter Lorre tradition), who also wants the headpiece.

Now partners in adventure, Jones and Marion travel to Egypt—where the Ark is located and the film's action is centered. Here, Belloq, a Nazi captain named Dietrich (Wolf Kahler), Toht, and even a small, seemingly friendly monkey (actually a "spy" who raises his paw in a "Heil Hitler" salute) converge upon them. It is in the aftermath of a humor-laden chase through the streets of Cairo that a truck explodes, presumably killing Marion. Shaken by the loss, Jones seeks solace in drink. After a meeting with the cynical Belloq, who states, "I am a shadowy reflection of you. It would take only a notch to make you more like me," however, Jones is more determined than ever to locate the Ark.

He does locate it with the help of the rotund and amiable Sallah (John Rhys-Davies), and the headpiece, which provides the correct calculations. As the Nazis excavate in the wrong place, Jones, Sallah, and a small band of men carry out their own diggings nearby. When they, at last, unearth the historic tomb, Jones finds himself peering into an asp-ridden cavern. "Snakes. Why did it have to be snakes," he laments. When he manages to bring the

Ark to the surface, it is only to discover that Belloq and his men are waiting. Once again, Belloq relieves Jones of his treasure; but this time, the meeting of the adversaries carries a note of finality. Refusing to pull Jones from the tomb to safety, Belloq instead has Jones entombed alive. Before the lid is lowered on the tomb, however, Marion is shoved inside. Jones had learned during his excavations that Marion had been kidnaped, not killed, by Belloq and his men. Now the two are sealed inside the Well of Souls.

A vault of cascading mummies and literally thousands of snakes are among the horrors within the pharaoh's tomb. Once Jones and Marion miraculously make their way into the daylight, there are still other perils. For, as chance (in the tradition of the cliffhanger film) would have it, their escape to freedom occurs within sight of the airplane that will carry the Ark to Hitler. A fist fight follows and Jones's burly opponent is ultimately hacked to death by a whirling airplane propeller. When the entire plane explodes, in fiery pyrotechnics, Belloq quickly orders the Ark loaded aboard a truck. As the truck careens toward Cairo, the rumpled Jones follows—atop a white horse. "I'm just making this up as I go along," he admits, when Marion asks about his rescue plans.

Jones's impromptu chase, which is actually one of the film's most detailed sequences, also gives *Raiders of the Lost Ark* its most riveting moments. In a scene bringing to mind the classic Westerns, which found cowboys climbing aboard runaway stagecoaches, Jones clings beneath the fast moving truck and even gets dragged behind it, before he eventually overpowers the driver, and heads the truck away from the accompanying Nazi cars.

A tramp steamer is the next stop for the weary Marion and the wounded Jones. With the Ark safe in the steamer's cargo hold, the pair have a night in which to revitalize their romance. The bliss is short lived, however, for the next morning a German submarine overtakes the steamer. Again Belloq takes the Ark, along with Marion, whom he fancies. The undaunted Jones manages to hide during the search of the steamer, and it is only as the German submarine sails away that Jones is viewed clinging to the top of the vessel. Later, disguised as a Nazi soldier, Jones trudges alongside Belloq's men. Before sending the Ark to Hitler, it is to be opened in ceremonial splendor. Once again, Jones intercedes—this time by aiming a gun at the Ark, and threatening to "blow it back to God" unless Marion is released. "We are simply passing through history, but this is history," says Belloq, who will not be bluffed by Jones.

As *Raiders of the Lost Ark* mystically espouses, history is not always willing to be tampered with. When the Ark is finally opened, it unleashes sights and forces that are at first wondrous and later, deadly. With their eyes closed in order to withstand the hypnotic visions, Jones and Marion brace against each other (they are tied, back-to-back) as a flurry of technical wizardry, apparently summoning up God's anger, is released. They are the only ones who survive.

At the film's end, a concerned Jones is promised that some of the government's "top men" will probe the fascinating secrets of the Ark. Jones, however, now together with a beaming Marion, remains skeptical. His cynicism is well founded. In the closing scene, the Ark, packed inside a wooden crate, is summarily filed away, alongside thousands of similar cartons, in a massive government warehouse.

Like the final scene, which is reminiscent of the *Citizen Kane* (1941) warehouse sequence, *Raiders of the Lost Ark* brims with nuances of favorite films and genres. Jones himself is a battered hero who seems to be a mixture of Fred C. Dobbs and Errol Flynn. Moreover, when the film is not imitating old films (as in the films of the 1930's, an arrow across a map traces Jones's travels), it is poking gentle fun at them. Thus, when Jones hits a Nazi soldier, in order to get his uniform, the uniform does not fit.

Raiders of the Lost Ark was filmed in seventy-three days; a scant period, considering the film's many locales and the scope of the art direction. In order to facilitate a quick shooting schedule, Spielberg worked with a second unit director for the first time: the veteran action director Mickey Moore. "This is the fastest I've ever shot, next to my experience in television," said Spielberg, who averaged forty set-ups a day during location shooting. Spielberg came to the film following his work on the disappointing, unwieldy comedy, *1941* (1980).

In addition to amplifying the abilities of Spielberg and producer Lucas, *Raiders of the Lost Ark* echoes the talents of composer John Williams who had worked on *Jaws*, *Star Wars*, and *The Empire Strikes Back* and who provides the film with a rousing score. Newcomer Lawrence Kasdan, who wrote *Continental Divide* (1981), authored the screenplay.

Although *Raiders of the Lost Ark* was released to wide acclaim, some critics did express concern over the "PG" rating. With the film's penchant for violence including numerous deaths and the gory moments which follow the opening of the Ark (some of the Nazis literally melt into dripping ooze), several critics argued that the rating was too lenient. Still others worried that the film and the trend that it represents deviate too drastically from real life and actual concerns.

The critics were unanimous, however, in their admiration of Ford, the ruggedly handsome actor who portrays the rumpled hero Indiana Jones. Best known for his performances as space outlaw Han Solo in the *Star Wars* films, Harrison embellishes Jones with a more sardonic outlook. In one crowd-pleasing scene, Jones is challenged to do battle with a skilled swordsman. Without the slightest nod to nobility (or fair play), Jones pulls his gun and blasts the challenger. A one-time carpenter, Ford appeared in series television prior to achieving fame in *Star Wars*. Additionally, he has starred in films such as *Force Ten from Navarone* (1978), *Hanover Street* (1979), and *The Frisco Kid* (1979) mostly to lackluster critical reviews. Because Lucas has announced plans to film additional Indiana Jones exploits, Ford will probably continue the portrayal he launches in *Raiders of the Lost Ark*.

In the aftermath of its release, *Raiders of the Lost Ark* generated considerable press, including reports of Ford's stardom and the revitalization of the serial format. Also making headlines is a lawsuit involving an archaeologist who claims that Lucas stole his idea to create the film. The suit alleges that a screenplay by archaeologist-writer Robert L. Kuhn was to have been filmed by Stanley R. Rader, former treasurer of the controversial Worldwide Church of God. Rader and Kuhn reportedly planned to use the topic for a religious-oriented film.

Pat H. Broeske

THE RAIN PEOPLE

Released: 1969
Production: Bart Patton and Ronald Colby for Warner Bros.
Direction: Francis Ford Coppola
Screenplay: Francis Ford Coppola
Cinematography: Bill Butler
Editing: Barry Malkin
Running time: 101 minutes

Principal characters:
Jimmy Kilgannon (Killer) .... James Caan
Natalie Ravenna .... Shirley Knight
Gordon .... Robert Duvall
Mr. Alfred .... Tom Aldredge
Vinny Ravenna .... Robert Modica
Rosalie .... Marya Zimmet

"Perhaps the most unusually made pic ever financed by a U.S. major motion picture company . . . ," said *Variety* in its review of *The Rain People*, a film touted as one of Hollywood's new breed of "personal films." In retrospect, it was also one of the most important 1970's films to herald Francis Ford Coppola's daring experiments in new production techniques and in changing areas of production supervision. It is one of the first major American films to use techniques popularized by some of the more *avant garde*, European filmmakers such as Claude Lelouche with his hand-held cinematography, long takes, and penchant for photographing through windshields, telephone booths, windows, and mirrors.

Coppola also ventures into an investigation of a modified "improvisation" technique. Although a script was prepared and there were rehearsals first in New York, none of the locations was prescouted, and there was much improvisation on behalf of the principal actors in this American Odyssey about a housewife, Natalie Ravenna (Shirley Knight), who, unlike her successors in *Alice Doesn't Live Here Anymore* (1974) and *An Unmarried Woman* (1979), is not thrust from her comfortable marital state to fend for herself. Instead, she leaves her sleeping husband Vinny (Robert Modica) and upper-middle-class surroundings by choice to undertake a quest of self-discovery which includes involvements with a mentally crippled hitchhiker named Jimmy Kilgannon (James Caan) and a motorcycle cop named Gordon (Robert Duvall).

Coppola's style elicited mixed reviews, including those who claimed that Coppola ". . . overworks the hand-held camera and 'subliminal' flashback," and that "Someone responsible for follow focus either misses his mark or overshoots it." The majority of the more informed critics, however, were impressed with this feature-length example of *cinéma vérité* realism and spontaneity. Bill Butler's cinematography is actually quite successful. Coppola wanted to create a clear relationship between each image and each sound. This affected his decision to shoot much of the film with a zoom lens, which renders an out-of-focus background. "I saw it as a foreground movie—the relationship between two characters," said Coppola in an interview. Because he was doing so much with sound, he wanted ". . . only one thing to be happening in the image at any single time." The "subliminal" flashbacks which recall a traumatic episode from each of the three central characters' past— Natalie's wedding day; Jimmy's fateful game of football; and the fire in which Gordon's wife was burned to death—are very well devised.

The Rain People was shot cross-country from New York to Colorado, in eighteen states, on the low budget of $750,000, in three-and-one-half months. *Time* magazine commented that "*The Rain People* has such a strong sense of the U.S. as a dramatic character that Coppola's people tend to melt into the landscape." The mobility of Coppola and his crew allowed them to shoot such sequences as the mysterious and somber Amish people of Pennsylvania, who had to be filmed at a distance because of their religious views. This sequence was integral to Coppola's nervous directorial pace and his fascination with the topographic diversity of an often frightening rural America which he envisions as being populated with sterile, unfeeling people, a theme which is developed more fully in his subsequent films.

The performances of Knight, Caan, and Duvall, although criticized by some critics as being too influenced by the "method" school, are superb in this story of Natalie Ravenna. Early on a rainy morning, tearful and distraught, Natalie leaves her home and husband in a wealthy residential area of Long Island along with a note of explanation saying she will return soon. With no planned destination, she begins her flight, stopping briefly to visit her parents, with whom she argues, and then fleeing West on the New Jersey turnpike. After reflecting on her wedding and the trepidation she felt at the time, she stops to call her husband and explains that she is not sure if she knows she can be a good wife and that she does not like the feeling of being in servitude. "I used to wake up in the morning and it was mine, now it all belongs to you." He begs her to come home, and then she reveals the true source of her anxiety—she is pregnant and does not feel ready to become a mother. She explains that she is going to try to find herself, and then she hangs up.

Later, and after considerable hesitation, she picks up hitchhiker Jimmy Kilgannon, nicknamed "Killer" as a result of his college football heroism. He tells her he is no longer in school and that he is traveling to accept a job that the football-fan father of his former girl friend has offered him in West Virginia. When they stop at a motel for the night, she invites him to her room, where she taunts him mercilessly in a sequence in which Coppola employs an intricate play with mirrors. She finally realizes that his strange, childlike deference—"You are the most obedient man I've ever met in my life"—is due to mental incompetence. She discovers that the child-man has a metal plate in his scalp due to a head injury from a football game in which he incurred brain damage, and that this accounts for his simple behavior. Jimmy explains that the injury left him unable to study and play ball, so the school gave him one thousand dollars and asked him to leave. Natalie then sends him back to his room in a gesture of maternal concern.

The next morning she agrees to take him to his destination in West Virginia, but no farther, since she wants to travel alone. On the way to West Virginia, Jimmy tells Natalie that she is like the "Rain People," who "are made of rain and disappear altogether when they cry." When they arrive, Jimmy's girl friend, who had told everyone that they had slept together in college, is embarrassed by his condition and treats him so cruelly that Natalie, against her better judgment, drives him away. She explains to Jimmy that she is going to have a baby and can hardly take care of herself, much less him. She tries to leave him by the roadside but cannot. In Chattanooga, she again tries to lose Jimmy in a parade, but he reappears.

Natalie then finds a job listing for a handyman at a zoo on a post-office bulletin board and takes Jimmy to see about it. Mr. Alfred (Tom Aldredge), the zoo owner—a dishonest man who is cruel to the animals—seizes upon the opportunity to exploit Jimmy. As Natalie speeds away from the situation, she is stopped by a highway patrolman named Gordon, a widower with a twelve-year-old daughter, and they are immediately attracted to each other. He tells her that she has to go back and pay a fine for speeding at the local Justice of the Peace, who happens to be Mr. Alfred. They arrive at the zoo just as Jimmy is letting all the frightened and half-starved animals out of their cages to run free. To keep Jimmy from being arrested, Natalie once again assumes responsibility for him. Mr. Alfred keeps most of Jimmy's money in exchange for dropping the damage charges against him. As Natalie and Jimmy drive off, she explains that she has a date with Gordon that night.

Natalie calls her husband while Jimmy waits impatiently outside the phone booth tapping on the glass. At the point in the conversation when her husband agrees to an abortion, Jimmy symbolically severs the phone cord, which makes Natalie cry out angrily for him to get lost and stop bothering her. Deeply hurt, Jimmy shows up that night at Gordon's trailer home, where Gordon's sexual attentions to Natalie are constantly being interrupted by his unmanageable daughter Rosalie (Marya Zimmet). Gordon throws Rosalie out where she—the child with the mind of an adult—encounters Jimmy—the man with mind of a child. They pass time by peering into trailer windows and talking about their lives and the "Rain People," and end up peeking at Gordon and Natalie. When Natalie discovers that Gordon's wife and baby had been killed in a fire, she changes her mind about sleeping with him and wants to leave, but he forces her to make love. After Gordon throws her naked on the bed, Natalie grabs a gun, which he knocks on the floor. Natalie screams and Jimmy bursts through the door, violently tackling Gordon and throwing him outside, pummeling him all the while and evidently trying to kill him, as continual flashbacks of the football game in which he was injured are cross-cut with the present violence. Finally Rosalie picks up the gun and shoots Jimmy. Natalie, using all her strength, hysterically tries to drag Jimmy's body to her station wagon, promising that she will not leave him and that she and her husband will care for him. When someone shines a flashlight into the car, she finally realizes he is dead. The next morning, Natalie waits for her husband at the airport in a pouring rain reminiscent of the first day of her odyssey. When he arrives, they get into the station wagon and drive away.

Unlike other "road films" common to the late 1960's, the universality of Coppola's story and its psychological themes are still fresh today. On the first level, the film is a morality play depicting the evasion and eventual acceptance of responsibility. On a deeper level, however, it explores the compulsive quest for individual freedom versus the need for love, emotional commitment, and liaisons with other human beings. Coppola's central vision is not simply that one be aware of this inherent human dichotomy but that one must make a choice. Coppola's choice is love and commitment—it is better to feel and care at any cost, even if it leads to destruction. His protagonist discovers that being totally "free" is an unrealistic concept if one also accepts the need for love and meaningful encounters. When Natalie allows herself to feel, her fairy-tale odyssey comes to an end and her temporary world dissolves like the "Rain People."

As a footnote to *The Rain People*, another important director emerged from its production. Coppola, having perhaps an affinity with or sympathy for the precarious position of the graduate student in cinema (Coppola had studied at U.C.L.A., where his Master's production thesis, *You're a Big Boy Now*, 1967, became the first ever to be produced as a major feature) allowed George Lucas, a U.S.C. cinema graduate and production assistant on *The Rain People*, to make a documentary about the production of the picture. Coppola then produced *THX 1138*, a science-fiction drama, that Lucas wrote and directed, which became the predecessor of *Star Wars* (1977)—one of the biggest commercial successes and technical film achievements of all time.

Tanita C. Kelly

RANCHO NOTORIOUS

Released: 1952
Production: Howard Welsch for Fidelity Pictures/RKO/Radio
Direction: Fritz Lang
Screenplay: Daniel Taradash; based on the story "Gunsight Whitman" by Silva Richards
Cinematography: Hal Mohr
Editing: Otto Ludwig
Running time: 89 minutes

Principal characters:
Altar Keane .... Marlene Dietrich
Vern Haskell .... Arthur Kennedy
Frenchy Fairmont .... Mel Ferrer
Beth Forbes .... Gloria Henry
Baldy Gunder .... William Frawley

Rancho Notorious, like the later *Johnny Guitar* (1954), is a *film noir* Western from Fritz Lang, a director known for his films in the genre: *You Only Live Once* (1937), *The Woman in the Window* (1944), *Scarlet Street* (1945), *The Blue Gardenia* (1953), *The Big Heat* (1953), *While the City Sleeps* (1956), and *Beyond a Reasonable Doubt* (1956). Also like *Johnny Guitar*, it was misunderstood by contemporary reviewers, who saw it either as a lusty good time from a once-serious director or a contrived failure, a fake. Yet it too has become well-respected as a cult film and appears on a number of "Ten Best Westerns of All Time" lists, especially those of French critics (see *Le Western*, Union Générale de'Éditions, 1966). *Rancho Notorious* is a bit more difficult for modern audiences than *Johnny Guitar*, perhaps because it is not so obviously something other than a traditional Western. *Johnny Guitar* has an advantage (from a modern perspective) in being untraditional in its dialogue, characterization, visual style, and use of action. It also constitutes a fairly explicit commentary on its own historical period of the blacklist in Hollywood of the 1950's. Nevertheless, with a knowledge of Lang's other films, *Rancho Notorious* is recognizable as another film which undercuts its own genre expectations.

Originally called "Chuck-a-Luck," *Rancho Notorious* opens and closes with the song "The Legend of Chuck-a-Luck," which also provides transitions between many sequences. This device is so foreign to Westerns (except parodies of the genre such as *Cat Ballou*, 1965) that it is often greeted with hoots of laughter by modern audiences. Employed as a decoding device, however (and it is impossible to consider it it any other way when one is familiar with Lang's themes), as the score is used in musicals, "The Legend of Chuck-a-Luck" asserts that *Rancho Notorious* is about precisely the same themes of morality, guilt, and, above all, the uselessness of revenge for which Lang is lauded in his "serious" classics, such as *M* (1931): "Listen to the legend of Chuck-a-Luck/listen to the wheel of Fate/It spins the old old story of Hate,/ Murder, and Revenge."

Chuck-a-Luck is the name of a hideout run by an aging dancehall girl, Altar Keane (Marlene Dietrich). Vern Haskell (Arthur Kennedy) hears of it in his search for the man who killed his fiancée, and he masquerades as an outlaw in an effort to find it. A chance meeting in jail with Frenchy Fairmont (Mel Ferrer) gives Vern his opportunity. When they escape together, Frenchy takes him to the hidden outlaw ranch. Vern ingratiates himself with Altar, and eventually sees on her dress a pin that his fiancée was wearing when she was killed. The pin was a part of the share Altar has always collected from everyone as payment for the sanctuary of Chuck-a-Luck. Vern accuses her of harboring a murderer, but her own role of "no questions" prevents her from naming the man. Finally, Altar falls in love with Vern and betrays her own code for him. Vern then casts her aside and turns the murderer in to the sheriff. Altar's men return, accusing her of betraying them. Frenchy stands by her, but when Vern "saves" them from the men, Altar is hit by a bullet intended for Vern.

The plot of *Rancho Notorious* sounds like that of a fairly typical revenge Western, with the innocent girl dying to set the events in motion, the determined hero stopping at nothing to avenge his beloved, the sexy "bad" woman falling in love with him and dying because of it, and the revenge being accomplished. The influence of *film noir*, however, makes this a very different film. Instead of being a morally virtuous hero, Vern is an obsessed, neurotic *film noir* character whose motives are questionable and whose means are despicable. Altar Keane, as played by Dietrich, for whom this story was written, is not the wise and earthy "prostitute with the heart of gold" who understands the hero and is happy to die for him (the type perhaps best examplified by Katy Jurado in *High Noon*, 1952). She is, instead, the strong, sexy, and controlling heroine of *film noir*. She becomes the real hero as her integrity, based on the reality of the West instead of on the abstract principles which so often characterize morality in Westerns, is shown to be more admirable than Vern's.

Altar runs the hideout Chuck-a-Luck with a firm but fair hand. She takes ten percent of the outlaws' take, but many of the residents of the "community" have not "pulled jobs"—and therefore not contributed—for years. Altar deals with outlaws who would certainly cheat her, but without violence. Indeed, Chuck-a-Luck appears to be a little center of order and sanity as everybody works, things run smoothly, and Altar sings in the evening. Altar is the stable center of them all, strong, sexy, and smart. Obviously, these are not the characteristics, and this is not the role, of the traditional Western heroine. Even in the flashback sequences of the younger *femme fatale* Altar Keane of legend, she is her own woman. She is the solitary, self-sufficient character we expect in a hero, not like Vern, whose obsession eventually makes him a creature of pity.

Vern's methods of obtaining his information show a typical *film noir* contamination of the righteous pursuer by the unsavoriness which should be characteristic of the villain. He lies, misrepresents himself to the charming and honorable Frenchy, and, worst of all, makes love to Altar simply to get her to betray herself and her men. In a characteristic *film noir* inversion, the older woman is unable to resist the sexual attraction of the younger man, even though her loyalty is to Frenchy, who ironically has brought Vern to Chuck-a-Luck. The gentlemanly Frenchy comes to play a traditionally female role as opposed to Altar's traditionally male one, telling her that "time holds us together" when he sees her attraction to Vern.

In a particularly disturbing scene, Vern stretches his body out before Altar as he woos her; she tries to turn her back on him, but is obviously weakening. Vern sees his fiancée's pin on Altar, and redoubles his efforts to seduce her. The eroticism has a particularly unsavory flavor. Vern's only goal is to learn the name of the man who gave it to her, and when he finally does, Vern turns on Altar as though she had murdered the girl herself.

Vern's duplicity toward the real hero of the film is in contrast to Frenchy's; Frenchy saves Altar's winnings in a rigged saloon game, politely takes her home, and does not go in to her room for the payoff she is resigned to offering him. In the jail where he meets Vern, Frenchy is witty and such a gentleman that he provides a contrast to the corrupt politicians who are also locked up, awaiting the outcome of an election in which they will either be returned to office or hanged. This treatment of politicians is typical of Lang.

Rancho Notorious was made with a very limited budget, so most of the sets, even the exteriors, were shot in the studio. This gives Altar's hideout a slightly unreal look when we first see it, almost as if it were a magical kingdom in the hills. While Lang would have liked a larger budget, it is testimony to his talent that he was able to turn this potential weakness into an internally consistent element of the film. Indeed, Chuck-a-Luck is so far removed from the rest of the world that this visual presentation makes perfect sense.

Altar is very much a Lang hero: she lives by her own rules. They are not the same as society's, but they are shown to make as much sense, if not more; and she does live by them, unlike the vast majority of the characters in the film. Altar and Frenchy offer the only glimpse of honor and decency in the whole film, even though they are nothing more than an aging gunfighter and a dance-hall girl.

Janey Place

RANDOM HARVEST

Released: 1942
Production: Sidney Franklin for Metro-Goldwyn-Mayer
Direction: Mervyn LeRoy
Screenplay: Claudine West, George Froeschel, and Arthur Wimperis; based
on the novel of the same name by James Hilton
Cinematography: Joseph Ruttenberg
Editing: Harold F. Kress
Running time: 124 minutes

Principal characters:
Charles Rainier/
John "Smithy" Smith .... Ronald Colman
Paula/Margaret Hanson .... Greer Garson
Kitty .... Susan Peters

Random Harvest, although highly praised at the time of its release, has not
been acclaimed historically as an important film. While it is in no way a
milestone film, *Random Harvest* does epitomize the vast quantity of popular
romances produced during the war years at Metro-Goldwyn-Mayer. The film's
script was adapted from the novel of the same name written by James Hilton,
and in spite of the fact that the novel had not been widely read, Hilton's
reputation in Hollywood was enough to overcome the weaknesses of the
story. Frank Capra's version of Hilton's *Lost Horizon* (1937), starring Ronald
Colman, established the already popular novelist as a Hollywood success.
M-G-M, the next studio to film a Hilton novel with *Goodbye, Mr. Chips*
(1939), used that film to introduce their new British star, Greer Garson.

By the time M-G-M filmed *Random Harvest* in 1942, Colman and Garson
were established as the perfect Hilton stars. The novel was altered considerably, forfeiting a twist ending for a stronger narrative. Contemporary critics
unanimously hailed the film, finding it a deeply moving love story, and singling
out Garson's performance as her best, surpassing her Oscar-winning *Mrs.
Miniver* (for which James Hilton was one of the screenwriters).

Random Harvest received its premiere at Radio City Music Hall and ran
for a record engagement, proving to be one of the top twenty-five money-
makers of 1942. Both Colman and Susan Peters (for Best Supporting Actress)
were nominated for Academy Awards. The film even became a part of the
war effort. It was shown so frequently to servicemen that Colman's performance, along with his Red Cross service during the war, made him something
of a GI hero. Garson's Highland dance number in the film and her mini-
length kilt made the legs of the otherwise serious actress the object of much
publicity.

From a perspective of almost forty years, however, the film is dated.

Romance and the resolution of unrequited love, while attractive to World War II audiences, has more limited appeal today. Its implausible plot, depending heavily on coincidence, is possibly the basis for its failure with today's film audiences, although many of the details of amnesia and rediscovery of a past life are staples of television soap operas. What still works in spite of the contrived plot is the universal appeal of the struggle for true love: the film touches all of us who have known the dreams of impossible romance. Only in the most "unrealistic" circumstance could a chorus girl and a Lord fall in love and marry, but the charm of the actors makes us wish that they could.

The film's direction by Mervyn LeRoy is solid, but is not marked with the style of a strong directorial influence. *Random Harvest* is primarily a star vehicle, which is another reason it is ignored by today's critics who emphasize director's films. On the other hand, its 1942 success was primarily due to the attraction of the magnetic leading players. The script calls for Colman's character, Sir Charles Ranier, to age from twenty-nine to middle age. Colman, fifty-two years old when *Random Harvest* was filmed, is amazingly flexible in portraying both the youthful eagerness of a young lover and the despair of a lonely man. Garson's performance has equal vitality, especially in the first half of the film when her character, Paula, is an effervescent showgirl.

The film is designed to accommodate the personalities of the stars. It is a heavily plotted, talkie film which gives Colman and Garson plenty of dialogue in which to display their unique and beautiful British-accented voices. During its second half the film slows down considerably as the details of the very intricate story unfold. The characters are for the most part stereotypes, and themes are almost nonexistent. It is this lack of richness in characterization and theme and the development of plot alone that keeps *Random Harvest* from attaining the level of a classic film. The plot is both the essence of the film and its greatest flaw, with the story twisting on the most improbable coincidences.

The film opens in an asylum in the English countryside on a foggy November night in 1918. A war victim, an amnesiac, wanders away from the institution to nearby Melbridge, where the street is full of excitement and confusion. Armistice has just been signed with the Germans, and World War I is over. The announcement has brought the townspeople into the streets. John Smith (Ronald Colman), the amnesiac, wanders aimlessly amid the cheers and singing; he is a man without a past and apparently no future. Rescued from the crowd, he is befriended by Paula (Greer Garson), a singer with a traveling troupe. In love with John at first sight, Paula is rejected by her company for harboring an asylum inmate.

Thus Paula and "Smithy," as she calls him, start off on their own and settle in Devon, where Paula works while Smithy recovers his health but not his memory. Their love is idyllic, isolated from the realities of postwar Britain.

Smithy begins writing, and after his first sale, he proposes to Paula. They marry, buy a cottage, and start what should be a blissful life. Two years pass, a son is born, and Smithy is offered a permanent position on a Liverpool newspaper. At their first separation, he leaves her with a gift, a necklace of glass beads "the color of her eyes." With her battered vaudeville suitcase in his hand, Smithy crosses a rainy Liverpool Street, where he is hit suddenly by an unseen car, falls to the pavement, and rises again as Sir Charles Ranier, Captain in the Wessex Regiment, of Random Hall, North Random, Surrey. He has regained his distant past, but lost the memory of his recent interlude of happiness with Paula.

In 1920, Charles returns to Surrey. His father has just died and the family is gathered for the reading of the will. Charles inherits the old family business and begins his new life as the "Industrial Prince of England." Saddened by the three years missing from his life, he throws himself into his work. Four years pass, and Charles' niece by marriage, Kitty (Susan Peters), grows up and falls in love with her "uncle." Halfheartedly Ranier agrees to marry Kitty, but with the best part of him trapped in the missing past, he has lost his capacity to love. Ranier's only clue to those vital years is a door key that hangs on his watchchain, a key that could unlock the door to the past.

On the eve of his marriage to Kitty, Ranier's private secretary, Miss Margaret Hanson, is introduced; she is in reality Paula. Hiding her secret under a prim and efficient guise, "Margaret" has worked for Ranier for two years hoping desperately that his memory would return, that he would recognize her and love her once again. Resigned to the fact that it will not, and because their child has died, she remains silent, has her marriage annulled, and frees him to marry Kitty. Charles's lack of full commitment forces Kitty to cancel the wedding, however, leaving Ranier alone again with his work.

Suddenly a member of Parliament dies and the Conservative Party asks Ranier to step in. Now in need of a wife, he turns to his faithful secretary and suggests a "merger," a marriage of convenience. Heartbroken, but realizing that this is her opportunity to be near him always, Paula accepts. He promises never to make any "emotional demands," having only "sincere friendship to offer." They become the most envied couple in London, but Paula's existence is painful. Her unhappiness is typified in the scene of their third wedding anniversary. Charles has given her a dazzling necklace once worn by a Queen. The diamonds lie cold on her neck, and late into the night she cries longingly over the old glass beads which Smithy had given her.

Frustrated, Paula decides to take a sea voyage to get out of London and visit South America. Before her boat sails, however, she takes a few days to visit Devon and dream of the days she spent there with Smithy. Simultaneously Ranier is warned of strike agitation in Melbridge and goes to the factory personally to settle the dispute. The atmosphere is much the same as the opening scene; fog covers the street, and Ranier begins to see into his past.

Compulsively, he heads for Devon, unsure of his faint memory but determined to find his missing years. Just as Paula is leaving for her train, she takes one last walk past their old cottage. Charles finds Margaret at the gate and tries the door with his key. It opens ceremoniously, and the two, now Smithy and Paula again, fall lovingly into each other's arms.

Although the plot of *Random Harvest* sounds corny and melodramatic to today's audiences, it was extremely well received at the time of its initial release. It was one of the vast number of so-called "women's pictures" released during the 1930's and 1940's which relied heavily on star-crossed romance and self-sacrifice for plot development and which were financially successful. Another reason why this particular film was so successful can also be traced to the star magnetism of the principal actors. Colman and Garson seemed to make such a believable and attractive romantic couple that audiences cared little if their story was far-fetched. Especially during the years of World War II, this type of escapist romance with big-name stars had great popular appeal. Today, the film may elicit laughs in some quarters, but it is still worth viewing as good romantic escapist entertainment.

Joanne L. Yeck

REAR WINDOW

Released: 1954
Production: Alfred Hitchcock for Paramount
Direction: Alfred Hitchcock
Screenplay: John Michael Hayes; based on the short story of the same name by Cornell Woolrich
Cinematography: Robert Burks
Editing: George Tomasini
Running time: 112 minutes

Principal characters:
Jeff (L. B. Jeffries) .... James Stewart
Lisa Fremont .... Grace Kelly
Thomas J. Doyle .... Wendell Corey
Stella .... Thelma Ritter
Lars Thorwald .... Raymond Burr

Rear Window is one of five Alfred Hitchcock films which cannot be seen in the United States. A legal dispute concerning the estate of Cornell Woolrich, author of the original novella upon which the script is based, prevents any showing, commercial or nontheatrical. Like *Vertigo* (1958), however, which also cannot legally be screened, *Rear Window* is one of Hitchcock's very best films and maintains that reputation even under its legal restrictions.

Hitchcock is widely regarded as the best director of the English and American commercial cinema. He was the first of the *auteurs*, and has been honored in every conceivable way, from the large numbers of books and articles written about his works, the college courses centered about his *oeuvre*, and the critical and industry awards, to the box-office successes. No other director, with the possible exception of John Ford, has managed to combine artistic and commercial success so well, and Hitchcock certainly has done it with greater regularity. Perhaps the greatest tribute to the "master of suspense" is the number of films made which are attributed (or unattributed) homages to his films. Françoise Truffaut's *The Bride Wore Black* (1967) and *Mississippi Mermaid* (1969) are two of the best-known, but many French New Wave directors acknowledge their enormous debt to Hitchcock, as do such young American directors as Peter Bogdanovich.

Rear Window demonstrates beautifully what Hitchcock is so justly famous for: the perfect expression of emotions and themes in the visual style of the film. It is about Jeff (James Stewart), a free-lance photographer who is confined to his New York apartment in a wheelchair with a broken leg (sustained in a crash while he was photographing a car race) during a heat wave. He spies on his neighbors across the apartment courtyard (first with binoculars, then with the telephoto lens of his camera) and becomes convinced that one of them, Lars Thorwald (Raymond Burr), has killed his wife. He finally convinces his girl friend Lisa (Grace Kelly) and a detective friend Thomas Doyle (Wendell Corey) that he is on to something and gets them to help him prove it after they find evidence in the garden that has resulted in a curious dog being killed by Thorwald. Lisa gets bolder and goes into Thorwald's apartment, barely escaping when he returns unexpectedly. When Thorwald sees Jeff watching his movements and realizes that he is suspicious, he breaks into Jeff's apartment and throws him out the window, breaking his other leg. Thorwald is apprehended, and Jeff and Lisa seem to be closer to each other than at the beginning of the film.

Rear Window is about a *voyeur*. Jeff is more interested in other people's lives than he is in his own, as evidenced by his profession (which requires him to travel extensively, putting down few roots), his relationship with Lisa (in which she is far more committed than he, as evidenced by his unwillingness to consider any different life style or even pay her the attention he gives his subjects across the courtyard), and his neurotic avocation of spying on his neighbors. Jeff's alienation from his own surroundings is clear in the first shots: the moving camera of the opening cuts as it reaches Jeff, just before discovering him asleep in his chair, binoculars in his lap. He is thus separated from his surroundings; but in the last shot, the camera first shows him alone, then, without a cut, discovers Lisa's legs on the sofa beside him. Thus, they are joined in a way that they had not been in the first shots of the film.

Jeff names one of the people he watches "Miss Lonelyhearts," since she is lonely most of the time. Even when she gets up the courage to bring a man home, he turns out to be so crude that she throws him out of the house without carrying out her clear intentions. In a beautifully economical composition, Hitchcock shows us Jeff's greater involvement with her life than with his own; he raises a glass of wine in an answering (and unheeded) toast to her as Lisa prepares their food and wine in the background. She is just out of focus while he and Miss Lonelyhearts are in focus, thus separating her from Jeff and joining him with Miss Lonelyhearts. This also indicates Jeff's inability to show emotion and commitment: he requires great emotional distance which can be provided only in a *voyeur* situation where no demands are made on him. He resists Lisa, considering her "too perfect" in her high-style dress and manners. His insistence that she would not fit into his free-wheeling, traveling life seems to be an aspect of immaturity which is at least partially gone at the film's end.

Jeff's isolation is carried out visually as well as thematically in the film. That he becomes a *voyeur* might seem no more than an unhealthy extension of his profession, except that his relationship with Lisa makes it clear that he prefers to be on the outside of human emotions even in this aspect of his life. His physical relationship to the objects of most of his attention describes his isolation: each character is isolated in his/her own frame within the frame of the film. The kind of frame the characters have is an indication of their state of isolation from their own lives and from the rest of those in the apartment building. Lars Thorwald and his wife are separated by the two windows of their apartment, in a metaphor of their emotional separation. He occupies the first window, she the second, usually in her bed. When she is killed, that window becomes strangely vacant, even when he is in it. Miss Torso (so named because she exercises nearly nude in front of her window and entertains many young men) is often alone, framed by her one big window, isolated from the rest of the world but not from anything inside her own apartment. The newlyweds are very much together, and through their one big window we can see their door leading to the outside, through which they come into their own world. Miss Lonelyhearts is seen through one of two windows in her apartment, and her isolation is emphasized by the fact that there is no one with which to share it. Whichever window she is seen through, she seems a little dislocated.

Hitchcock uses still another kind of framing in *Rear Window*, this time to indicate the watching eye of Jeff and to emphasize his growing obsession with his neighbors and his further intrusion into their lives. First, he merely watches with his naked eye, which takes him only a little way into their apartments and lives. Next, he takes out his binoculars and we see his point of view through them: he is now much more involved with them by the simple device of his eye isolating the boundaries of their existence as we see them framed by the circle of the glasses. As his obsession grows still further, he takes out his long-lens camera in what is the most disturbing shot in the film except one. Before, his "Peeping Tomism" had a curious, innocent quality, but with the introduction of the long lens, it is almost as if he were pointing a weapon at them, entering and controlling their lives by his intrusion. The lens brings them closer to him, makes them appear larger in the frame, almost as big and important in his point-of-view angle as Lisa is when she is in his apartment. He has thus totally entered into their frames, and this has implications for his own isolation. It is usually a condition which indicates moral weakness and lack of emotional contact and which must be remedied; but in *Rear Window*, Jeff's intrusion into their privacy (especially in the case of Miss Lonelyhearts when he watches her humiliation in bringing home a one-night stand, then not having the fortitude to see it through) seems even worse than moral weakness. Since this is only one-way involvement, it is not healthy, and when it becomes two-way (when Lars Thorwald looks straight into the camera while the audience is looking with Jeff through his long lens) it is terrifying. It is as though Jeff were trying to play God and this is his subject turning on him. In trying to get inside their lives with no corresponding exposure of his own, he has put both Lisa (who acts as his legs and goes into Thorwald's apartment after more evidence) and himself in danger.

As Jeff intrudes more and more deeply into the lives of his neighbors, first through idle watching, then by using binoculars, and finally through his long lens, he is farther and farther detached from his own life. This is one reason why it is so disturbing when he first picks up the long lens: he is really confining his experience to that little lens while projecting his emotions away from his own apartment and Lisa. It is not until he sees Lisa through this device that he really knows that he loves her and is willing to commit himself to her.

There remains a question of how deeply Jeff does commit himself: in the last scene Lisa is finally in a costume that would seem to be suitable for his way of life—blue jeans—but she sneaks a look at her own magazine, putting down the one he would like to have her read as soon as she knows that he is asleep. Still, this seems like a gesture of assertion of her own personality: the panning shot from Jeff to Lisa joins them, and its manner of discovering first her feet, then her leg, and finally her entire body, places her very firmly in Jeff's apartment. As for her commitment, it would seem that the compromise indicated by the blue jeans is a necessary movement for her as well. Her life is so formally arranged in the beginning of the film that it leaves no room for surprise or romance of a deeply moving kind, and she must come out of her own social isolation through danger to reach him. The chaos and danger of the murder and its discovery is a device often used by Hitchcock to shake people out of their isolated, complacent lives and into contact with forces that are alive and volatile. Jeff and Lisa each must change in order for them to come together, and it is as significant that Jeff's back is to the window in the last scene as it is that Lisa is wearing blue jeans.

Janey Place

REBEL WITHOUT A CAUSE

Released: 1955
Production: David Weisbart for Warner Bros.
Direction: Nicholas Ray
Screenplay: Stewart Stern and Irving Shulman; based on an original screen
  story by Nicholas Ray
Cinematography: Ernest Haller
Editing: William Ziegler
Running time: 111 minutes

>   *Principal characters:*
>   Jim Stark .... James Dean
>   Judy .... Natalie Wood
>   Plato .... Sal Mineo
>   Jim's father .... James Backus
>   Buzz .... Corey Allen
>   Moose .... Nick Adams
>   Goon .... Dennis Hopper
>   Juvenile Officer Ray .... Edward Platt

Rebel Without a Cause is an interesting and valuable film in at least three
respects. First, in spite of its very stylized, perhaps glamorized, picture of
juvenile delinquency during the middle 1950's, it provides considerable sociological insight. Second, the film is not without aesthetic power, in part due
to its remarkably tight narrative structure. Finally, *Rebel Without a Cause* can
profitably be regarded as a springboard for a number of acting careers;
especially, it was the showcase that first presented and best preserved the
wonderful talent of James Dean, who was to die at the age of twenty-four
in an automobile wreck about the time that the film was released nationally.

Rebel Without a Cause was not the first Hollywood production to deal with
the subject of rebellious, actually criminal, youth. In 1954, Marlon Brando
and Lee Marvin starred in *The Wild One*, about a motorcycle gang's brief
domination of a small, helpless town. Earlier in 1955, the year when *Rebel
Without a Cause* itself was released, Glenn Ford and Sidney Poitier starred
in *The Blackboard Jungle*, dealing with a New York City school teacher's
struggles with rebellious and often violent students. *Rebel Without a Cause*,
however, probably constitutes the classic portrait of the troubled and misunderstood youth of the 1950's. The imitations that followed it, both in the
1950's and the 1960's, including the designed contrast of the Avalon-Funicello
"Bikini Beach" productions, are countless.

The portrait of delinquency in *Rebel Without a Cause* is at once stylized
and sympathetic. Stewart Stern's screenplay was based on Dr. Robert Linder's
case study, purchased by Warner Bros. studios as early as 1946, of a teenage

psychopath. Stern, in collaboration with Irving Shulman, transformed the Linder property into a "Romeo and Juliet" tale featuring the perhaps neurotic, but hardly psychotic, character of Jim Stark, which Dean was to infuse with so much life. Throughout the film, the various actions and events (some seriously criminal) that serve to distinguish the world of youth from the world of adults are largely seen through Jim Stark's experience and understanding. This singular characterization accounts for the film's break with the then current stereotypes of the adolescent's world; Dean's dominant performance in turn may help to account for the film's creation of new adolescent stereotypes that lasted well into the 1960's.

The story is brief and simple, and the structure of the plot is very tight. It begins in the predawn darkness of one day and ends precisely at dawn of the following day. This temporal unity is underscored by the telling sounds of sirens, symmetrically marking the opening and closing shots. The film opens with a drunk (and quite content) teenager named Jim Stark (James Dean) lying in a street with a clockwork animal, which he sets "sleeping" beneath a newspaper in a manner at once childlike and adult, as we hear the ominous approach of an unseen police car. The initial amalgam of Jim's "adult" dress (dark suit and tie) and prepubescent behavior set against the scream of the siren provides the perfect symbol for the thematic characterization which gives the film much of its aesthetic value. Appropriately, the sound of the actual siren yields to Dean's drunken imitation as we find him now in the lobby of the police station, sprawled upon a thronelike shoeshine chair.

From this point on, Director Nicholas Ray's ability to weave together a vast panoply of characters and events within a brief, twenty-five to thirty-hour frame comes to the fore. Before Dean even leaves the police station in the custody of his ineffectual father (James Backus), we meet the only truly responsible adult in the film (the detective Ray, played by Edward Platt), the Juliet-to-be, Judy (Natalie Wood), and the one adolescent closest to Linder's study of psychosis, Plato (Sal Mineo).

The following morning turns out to be Dean's first day at his new high school. Immediately he encounters the hostility of a local group, led by the leather-jacketed Buzz (Corey Allen), who is Judy's boyfriend, and including such characters as Goon (Dennis Hopper) and Moose (Nick Adams). This hostility comes to a peak later in the day, during a field trip to the Griffith Park Planetarium, where a knife fight between Jim Stark and Buzz sets the stage for a challenged "chickie run" later that evening. After talking briefly with the shy Plato, Jim returns home to prepare for the contest, which consists of driving two stolen cars at high speed toward a cliff, the winner being the last to jump from his vehicle. In part, this requires an important costume change to jeans, boots, and a red windbreaker, which significantly replace the white shirt and sportscoat of his first day at school.

The following events that occupy the night are filled with love and danger.

Buzz accidentally dies in the run; Jim and Judy are drawn together; Plato comes to view Jim and Judy as substitutes for his evidently uncaring parents and (since Buzz's gang seeks Jim, perhaps to avenge Buzz's death) takes an automatic pistol to help protect them. Jim, Judy, and Plato, all having left home in argument or anger, find refuge in a deserted mansion near the planetarium. Eventually Plato, fleeing from both the gang and the police, hides in the planetarium itself, where Jim bravely but vainly attempts to disarm the boy. Plato is killed by police bullets at dawn, and the film ends with the sound of an ambulance's siren. Plato is dressed in Jim's red jacket, while Jim again wears "adult" clothes, having borrowed his father's sportscoat,

Rebel Without a Cause was designed as a low-budget production. At the time of its casting, Backus was probably the highest-paid and best-known actor involved. While Wood and Mineo and others would go on to successful careers, Dean himself would die before half the year was out. His talent when the filming began in March of 1955 was hardly known; in fact, his real fame would prove to be posthumous. *East of Eden* (1954) had just been released, encountering mixed reviews of his performance. *Giant* (1956) was barely under contract. Still, even had Dean's death not fostered unusual audience interest in *Rebel Without a Cause*, it is difficult to believe that his wonderful work in the film would not have assured him of stardom.

Like the character of Cal in *East of Eden*, Jim Stark is perfect for the *persona* Dean had been carefully crafting from his theatrical and television apprenticeship to his Hollywood maturity. Generally regarded as a method actor, Dean's skill was always predicated upon his ability to downplay dialogue (often through inarticulate hesitations and incomplete, sometimes mumbled, phrases) for nonverbal communication: a glance, a stance, a gesture, a move-ment of the eye or mouth, an action smile, a walk. The result was a richly complex personality, at once shy and sly; kind, but capable of sudden violence; idealistic, but streetwise as well.

It is this same presence and actor's art that ultimately maintains audience enjoyment and critical interest in a film such as *Rebel Without a Cause*. Beyond its sociological and structural features, it is Dean's charisma—his puzzled, puzzling *persona*—that has repeatedly engaged audiences over the quarter of a century since its release. It was also probably Dean's best performance, and the one most closely associated with a man who died too early, on the threshold of a remarkable career. Dean's legend may have begun, ironically, with the wreck of his Porsche Spyder on Highway 466 on September 30, 1955. Clearly, however, it is his preserved performances in such films as *Rebel Without a Cause* which maintain and continue to transform that legend.

Edward S. Small

THE RECKLESS MOMENT

Released: 1949
Production: Walter Wanger for Columbia
Direction: Max Ophuls
Screenplay: Henry Garson and Robert W. Soderberg; based on Mel Dinelli and Robert E. Kent's adaptation of the short story "The Blank Wall" by Elizabeth Sanxay Holding
Cinematography: Burnett Guffey
Editing: Gene Havlick
Running time: 81 minutes

> *Principal characters:*
> Martin Donnelly .... James Mason
> Lucia Harper .... Joan Bennett
> Bea Harper .... Geraldine Brooks
> Tom Harper .... Henry O'Neill
> Ted Darby .... Shepperd Strudwick
> Nagel .... Roy Roberts

Max Ophuls is one of the cinema's great directors. His career had three phases spanning a quarter of a century and three countries. Ophuls was born in the Saar province of Germany, which passed twice from German hands to French occupation (1919-1935 and 1945-1957) and back again, in the plebiscites of 1935 and 1957. He was born a German national and worked in the German theater and cinema from 1930 to 1939, but became a French citizen in 1938. Ophuls was in Hollywood from 1941 to 1949, but was unable to get steady film work and made only four pictures here: *The Exile* (1947), *Letter from an Unknown Woman* (1948), *Caught* (1948), and *The Reckless Moment* (1949). He stayed in Paris after going there on a project for producer Walter Wanger which fell through, and, during this third phase of his career, made those films for which he is justly renowned: *La Ronde* (1950), *Le Plaisir* (1951), *Madame De . . .* (1953), and *Lola Montes* (1955).

Unlike many directors who were "discovered" only in the 1960's or whose reputations were limited to appreciation by the French New Wave critics and directors, Ophuls has been the subject of study in France and England for nearly three decades. Like Orson Welles, Ophuls is known for his spectacular *mise-en-scène.* He creates a multidimensional world of infinite texture and rich visual nuance through his use of space, light, and the moving camera.

Ophuls' American pictures are all genre films. They are "women's pictures," although not standard melodramas; they actually occupy a position between the mystery/thriller and the women's picture. They contribute to the aesthetic of *film noir* in their expressive visual style, dark shadows, and compositions, and their themes of entrapment and threat to the security of the stable home and family. The family unit rarely appears in *films noir* except to offer a vision of "normalcy," critiqued or simply presented, which is not within the grasp of the *film noir* characters, who live on the fringe of society. The intersection of the women's-picture themes of the primacy of family, the sacrificing mother, and the maintenance of values and behavior supportive of the family and the *film noir* themes and imagery of social personal breakdown and the resultant chaos is particularily effective in *The Reckless Moment*.

Lucia Harper (Joan Bennett) is an upper-middle-class housewife who lives with her family in Southern California, on Balboa Island, which comes to represent isolation from the crime, sleaziness, and chaos of Los Angeles. Her husband, never seen in the film, is in Europe building bridges. Bea (Geraldine Brooks), Lucia's seventeen-year-old daughter, has become involved with a seedy art dealer, Ted Darby (Shepperd Strudwick), who tells Lucia he would be willing to leave Bea alone in return for financial remuneration. Lucia refuses, thinking this information will cool Bea's interest. Bea does not believe her, however; she meets Ted that night in the Harpers' boat house and angrily hits him when he affirms that he needs money. Unknown to her, Ted falls through a railing after she leaves and is impaled on an anchor. Finding the body the next morning, Lucia disposes of it and tries to keep her family from finding out about the subsequent blackmailer, Martin Donnelly (James Mason), who wants to sell the letters Bea wrote to Ted which could implicate her in his death. Donnelly falls in love with Lucia, and in trying to protect her, kills his partner Nagel (Roy Roberts) and is himself killed in an ensuing car accident.

The Reckless Moment is brilliant in its use of parallel situations to illuminate each other. Lucia's life as a self-sacrificing wife and mother is shown to be a stifling cage, and the trap into which the "reckless moment" puts her has much in common with the life that she already leads. Her family, consisting of Bea, a younger son, David, and her husband's father (Henry O'Neill), who lives with them, confines her physically: she is constantly asked where she is going, where she has been, and what she has been doing. She is afraid to take the car to try to raise the blackmail money because she has promised it to David and her father-in-law and fears their questions, if she should change her mind. They confine her both psychologically and emotionally, continually telling her to eat and to sleep. More importantly, she finds herself cold, unemotional, and shut off from her own feelings in her efforts to main tain the veneer of normalcy. She is cold and unaffectionate toward Bea when the girl is hysterical and then depressed after learning about Darby's death. Lucia continually admonishes her to act normally and will not help Bea release the huge burden of guilt, fear, and shame that her daughter feels. Lucia's interaction with her son consists of telling the boy to button his shirt, roll down his pants, put on his shoes, and correct his table manners. Clearly, the substance of family life, with its expected nurturing of each member, has long ago been lost; all that remains is the hollow form. When Bea wants to go away for a few days after Darby's death, Lucia is worried about "how it will look" if Bea is away at Christmas, not about the girl's emotional health.

The Reckless Moment received mixed reviews, the poor ones probably resulting from the cold, unappealing character of its heroine. Cast against type in this film, Bennett was more often thought of in the 1940's as a sensuous woman. Similarly, Mason as a low-class blackmailer contradicts his usual image as the suave, aristocratic Englishman. The warmer reviews considered the film a tense, moody thriller.

Lucia's constricting role as the mainstay of her family is expressed in images of visual entrapment: shadows, staircases, actual bars (when she hears of the discovery of the body she has hidden, she is shot from inside a post-office cage, so that she appears to be behind bars), as well as compositions which constrict her physically. The blackmail is a further extension of her already existing situation, and when she is no longer in danger she is more trapped than ever. Her husband calls just as she arrives home after finding Martin dying in the car wreck, and as she talks to Tom the stair railing again puts her behind bars; her family crowds around her, further confining her.

Lucia's impoverished and suffocating life as a housewife is illuminated by exaggerating its worst aspects, signified by her entrapment by a blackmailer. There is, however, a further analogy which gives the film subtlety and depth: she and Martin play similar roles. Lucia tries to protect Bea, first from knowledge of the murder, then from all possible results, jeopardizing herself needlessly in the process. Martin does the same for Lucia. He tries to save her from his partner, Nagel, when she has decided to go to the police with the whole story; and in protecting her, he kills Nagel and dies himself. Earlier in the picture Lucia tells Martin, "You don't know how a family can surround you," and he answers, "You have your family, I have my Nagel." The connection between the two worlds is explicit.

Bea's attraction to Ted Darby sheds further light on the Harpers and their social milieu. Ophuls is concerned with questions of class, as are both *film noir* and women's pictures. Lucia's obsession with the appearance of normality, her objection to Ted as the "wrong kind of people," and her chastizing of Bea for not exercising proper discretion in her choice of friends all show a concern for maintaining class pretensions. Bea is fascinated with a less rigidly structured world and more spontaneous people, finding them in art school and in Ted Darby. She is much less repressed than Lucia, giving in immediately to her emotions of fear, hysteria, and depression. Martin comes from the same world, and although Lucia never returns his affection, she finally displays emotion when he lies dying. Realizing the results of her drive to preserve the veneer of respectability, she breaks down and stops crying only when her husband's call requires her to step back into her stifling role as wife and mother.

The Reckless Moment is a strange love story, but in Martin's death there are definite elements of the tragic, romantic, and transcendent ending. He is happy to die, having saved Lucia, whom he believes to be a murderess, from discovery, just as Lucia has risked everything to save Bea. Yet what each is saved for—the resumption of their alienated family life—throws both sacrifices into question. It is as a result of Mason's superb acting as well as Ophuls' sensitive direction that *The Reckless Moment* achieves the emotional uplift of the tragic love aspect of the story, and yet undercuts the social and class pretensions which required the sacrifices.

Janey Place

THE RED BADGE OF COURAGE

Released: 1951
Production: Gottfried Reinhardt for Metro-Goldwyn-Mayer
Direction: John Huston
Screenplay: John Huston; based on the novel of the same name by Stephen Crane
Cinematography: Harold Rosson
Editing: Ben Lewis
Music: Bronislau Kaper
Running time: 69 minutes

Principal characters:
The Youth	Audie Murphy
The Loud Soldier	Bill Mauldin
The Tall Soldier	John Dierkes
The Tattered Soldier	Royal Dano
The General	Tim Durant
The Cheerful Soldier	Andy Devine
The Lieutenant	Douglas Dick
Narration	James Whitmore

This black-and-white rendition of Stephen Crane's acclaimed and sensitive novel about the Civil War is remarkable in many respects. By all accounts, the film, written and directed by John Huston, embodies a great deal of Huston's personal vision of the story, despite a number of obstacles to his creative freedom. He portrays Crane's story of a naïve Yankee soldier's inner battles between cowardice and courage in the stark style of Matthew Brady's Civil War photographs. The major portion of the book consists of the Youth's thoughts as he joins the army with vague dreams of heroics; then, faced with war's reality, he deserts. Finally surmounting his fear, however, he leads a charge into battle. Huston's work bravely attacks the problem of conveying the Youth's internal states by a combination of beautifully appropriate visual symbols, meticulous cinematography, and spare, authentic dialogue.

The star of the film, Audie Murphy, was the most decorated hero of World War II. Although there was some talk of casting Montgomery Clift for the role, Huston pushed for Murphy and thus won the first of many arguments with M-G-M over the film. A legendary war hero, especially one of Murphy's elusive talent, may not necessarily have been the best choice of an actor to play a boy caught in the moral dilemma of desertion under fire. With the support of veteran actors Royal Dano as the Tattered Soldier and John Dierkes as the Tall Soldier, however, Murphy gets across his character's innocence and confusion. Bill Mauldin, creator of a famous wartime comic strip, *Willie and Joe*, performs admirably in the part of the Loud Soldier, the Youth's closest friend.

In scenes with Dano and Dierkes, such as that of the Tall Soldier's death, their portrayal of innate courage provides a good foil for the Youth's uncertainty. The Youth has deserted in the heat of a Confederate onslaught, but he has again rejoined his regiment. He is remorseful over his cowardly act. The Tall Soldier, wounded, breaks away from the rag-tag band of men who are marching away from the bloody battlefield. The Youth and the Tattered Soldier follow him up to the crest of a hill. He refuses their offers of help and squares his shoulders, only to suddenly drop dead. From this, and from scenes such as the one with Andy Devine as the Cheerful Soldier demonstrating his placid stoicism, the audience can infer the lessons that the Youth learns from his comrades. He enacts his newfound bravery when, at the end of the film, he proudly bears his wounds as he spurs on his fellows.

The battle sequence, patched together from the two separate battles Huston had intended, is seen from the Youth's frame of reference and is wonderfully portrayed. Difficult tracking shots providing a first-person point of view are managed expertly. The camera wends its way past dead men and through the woods as the Youth, in his terror, runs from the field of destruction. Added to provide realism are surprising yet accurate details: an injured soldier frantically searches for his lost eyeglasses, returns them to his face, and falls dead. The image of Murphy contemplating, in horror, an open-eyed corpse while the tree-filtered sunrays emphasize the gunsmoke is memorable for its beauty as well as for its statement about the incongruities of war.

The musical score by Bronislau Kaper enhances moods without seeming intrusive. The scene showing the Youth writing a letter home to his mother is accompanied by banjo music, which adds a carefree, down-home flavor. Many of Murphy's scenes alone are thus heightened.

The story behind the making of *The Red Badge of Courage* is almost as interesting as the film itself. The history of the film from inception to opening in New York, ironically detailed in Lillian Ross's book *Picture*, is an object lesson in the clash between art and business that is as old as the movie industry. Louis B. Mayer of M-G-M did not want the motion picture to be made because the Youth's cowardice did not match Mayer's idealistic notions of what the studio should show the American public. He was also, at the time, in a power struggle with Dore Schary over control of the studio, and Schary was in support of Huston. Huston's strong faith in the project and Schary's insistence finally won Mayer's grudging approval.

Gottfried Reinhardt, the producer and the son of the great German theatrical producer of the 1920's, Max Reinhardt, had the thankless job of trying to keep the excesses of Huston's creativity in line with financial restrictions. He also had to negotiate between Huston's and Mayer's differing concepts of the film. The compromises he effected were not good ones for the film. Because of the noisily adverse reaction of some teenagers at a preview in Pasadena and because of American involvement in the Korean War at the time, the film was severely edited, and in the process, its delicate sensibilities were seriously damaged. At the time of the editing, Huston was deeply involved in his next project, *The African Queen* (1951), and was unavailable and unwilling to fight for the integrity of *The Red Badge of Courage*. Reinhardt added a narrator, James Whitmore, and a short prologue showing the cover of the novel so that the viewer would know that the film was simply representing a classic novel, not striking out against war. The narration seemed to say that the opinions expressed in the film were not those of M-G-M. A month after Mayer resigned from his studio, the film opened to very good reviews but poor box-office returns.

The film Huston made before *The Red Badge of Courage*, *The Asphalt Jungle* (1950), won him Oscar nominations for writing and directing and the Screen Directors' Guild award for the year. The film he made after *The Red Badge of Courage*, *The African Queen*, gave him two more Oscar nominations and is universally recognized as a screen classic. He has said, however, that *The Red Badge of Courage* is his favorite film, although he has refused to see it in its released form. Even as it stands, it remains a distinguished entry in the career of a unique director as well as a fine example of a cinematic adaptation of a novel. Perhaps someday it will be restored to its original state and thus allowed to find its audience.

Stephanie Kreps

THE RED PONY

Released: 1949
Production: Lewis Milestone for Republic
Direction: Lewis Milestone
Screenplay: John Steinbeck; based on his short story of the same name
Cinematography: Tony Gaudio
Editing: Norman Colbert
Running time: 89 minutes

Principal characters:
Billy Buck .... Robert Mitchum
Tom Tiflin .... Peter Miles
Fred Tiflin .... Sheppherd Strudwick
Alice Tiflin .... Myrna Loy
Grandfather .... Louis Calhern

Following the success of such films as *Fury* (1936), *My Friend Flicka* (1943), and *The Yearling* (1946), animal stories appeared to be sure box-office hits in the late 1940's. Continuing this trend, Republic produced *The Red Pony* in 1949. Based on a series of short stories by John Steinbeck, the film attempted to transfer the popular horse story to the screen. The adaptation was written by Steinbeck himself, but much of the impact of the original version was lost on the screen. Produced and directed by Lewis Milestone, *The Red Pony* did not have the lasting power of previous Milestone works. Best-remembered for *All Quiet on the Western Front* (1930) and *The Front Page* (1931), Milestone did produce in *The Red Pony*, however, an interesting character study of a boy and his love for horses.

The film is set on a ranch in California. From the very beginning the audience realizes that the world of young Tom Tiflin (Peter Miles) revolves around horses. Although the family is obviously having a hard time financially, Tom's father (Sheppherd Strudwick) buys Tom a pony. The father-son relationship is not a close one, and this gesture is seen as an attempt by Fred Tiflin to gain his son's love. Billy Buck (Robert Mitchum), the laconic ranch hand, is more of an understanding father-figure to Tom. It is Billy who presents the boy with a saddle and guides him through the intricacies of training the pony, named Gabilan. Tom devotes his every waking thought to Gabilan and spends all his spare time training the horse.

Pleased with Gabilan's intelligence, Tom proudly shows Billy that the pony has been trained to open the barn door. As an omen of things to come, Billy looks disturbed and questions the wisdom of such a skill. Later, during a violent thunderstorm, Gabilan is frightened and lets himself out of the barn. When he returns home from school, Tom is frantic, for when Gabilan is found it is apparent that he has become ill from his wanderings in the storm. Told by his mother (Myrna Loy) that he must do his homework, Tom reluctantly leaves the pony in Billy's care. His mother later relents, however, and Tom spends the night with the worsening Gabilan.

The emotional impact of the story builds as Billy determines he must perform surgery to open the pony's windpipe. Tom's parents debate how much of the inevitable death Tom should be allowed to witness, finally deciding that he must be permitted to face the reality of death. Tom then helps Billy perform the bloody operation, but it is not successful and Gabilan walks off to die while Tom and Billy sleep. The next day when Tom discovers his pony's body being devoured by vultures, he savagely attacks the birds, even killing one with his hands. This scene, by far the most dramatic of the film, is also very graphic. At the time the film was released, this segment was criticized as too violent for a child's film. This scene also served to point out another contrast between Tom's father and Billy. Fred Tiflin makes Tom stop his frenzied attack, while Billy, realizing the value of such anger, criticizes the father's lack of empathy and carries the distraught Tom home.

Following this dramatic action, the film then proceeds to another crisis. Billy has promised Tom the foal of his own pregnant horse, Rosie, but as delivery time approaches, it appears that either the mother or colt will have to be sacrificed. Billy intends to live up to his promise to Tom and is preparing to kill Rosie. Now realizing the importance of a man's horse, however, Tom tries to stop Billy, but by the time they reach the barn, Rosie has delivered, and mother and colt are doing fine.

While the story of Tom, his horse, and the sage wisdom of Billy is the primary story line, there are various subplots in *The Red Pony*. One of these is the conflict between Tom's parents. Although it is never fully explained, Fred spends much of the film visiting his brother and trying to work out his problems. Summoned home when Gabilan becomes ill, Fred announces he is home to stay. While this underlying tension is never really explained, it does make believable his remote relationship with his son.

Another character study is developed around Tom's grandfather. One of the more likable people in the film, Grandfather (Louis Calhern) is a man living in the past. Having led a wagon train West, the old gentleman is full of "Did I tell you about the time . . ." stories. Fred's lack of patience is obvious, and even Alice Tiflin is brusque with her father. Tom, however, is close to his grandfather and enjoys the repetitious stories. Calhern's characterization of the old man is the most sympathetic portrayal of the film.

With the exceptions of Billy, Grandfather, and Tom in his one emotional outburst, the characters lack real feeling or humanity and provide few clues to their personalities. The original story of *The Red Pony* was acclaimed as an excellent story of a boy facing life. Much of this drama is unfortunately lost in the screen version, which seems to prove again the theory that the best works of literature fail to make the best films.

                                                    Elaine Raines

RED RIVER

Released: 1948
Production: Howard Hawks for Monterey; released by United Artists
Direction: Howard Hawks
Screenplay: Borden Chase and Charles Schnee; based on the novel *The Chisholm Trail* by Borden Chase
Cinematography: Russell Harlan
Editing: Christian Nyby
Music: Dmitri Tiomkin
Running time: 125 minutes

> *Principal characters:*
> Tom Dunson .... John Wayne
> Matt Garth .... Montgomery Clift
> Tess Millay .... Joanne Dru
> Groot Nadine .... Walter Brennan
> Fen .... Coleen Gray
> Cherry Valance .... John Ireland
> Buster McGee .... Noah Beery, Jr.
> Teeler Yacey .... Paul Fix
> Matt (younger) .... Mickey Kuhn

Red River has been widely acclaimed as the best of the cattle-drive Westerns. Like many of Howard Hawks's adventure films, its major themes are concerned with bravery, strength, and relationships among honorable men. Anchored to a well-developed script, these thematic concerns are further augmented by *Red River*'s visual beauty and the grandeur of its scope. Spanning a period of fifteen years, the film recounts the epic story of the founding of the Red River ranch and a subsequent historic cattle drive along the old Chisholm trail.

The action begins with a typically majestic shot of a wagon train passing through a sprawling valley. After one of the wagons has pulled out of line, Tom Dunson (John Wayne) informs the wagonmaster of his decision to leave the group in order to start his own herd. In the process, Tom abandons Fen (Coleen Gray), the woman he loves, because he feels that his present undertaking is simply "too much for a woman." After telling Dunson that she will join him later on, Fen then initiates one of *Red River*'s many recurrent motifs by letting him know that she believes he is "wrong." The accuracy of her judgment is confirmed shortly thereafter when the members of the wagon train are massacred by a band of hostile Indians. Consequently, when Dunson and his companion, Groot (Walter Brennan), encounter a young boy named Matt (Mickey Kuhn) wandering aimlessly through the prairie, Dunson's decision to take him under his wing can be seen as an attempt to compensate for the loss of Fen. Starting out with Dunson's lone bull and young Matt's single cow, the three soon claim a stretch of land north of the Rio Grande which Dunson decides to call the "Red River."

The rest of the film takes place fifteen years later, and the "Red River" has grown into a sizable enterprise. Because there is no local market for his cattle, however, Dunson is now faced with the arduous prospect of transporting his entire herd to Missouri. Once he sets out, the rigors of the journey begin to take their toll on both Dunson and his men. As he pushes them harder and harder, mutiny and desertion become a constant threat. Eventually this results in the forcible assumption of control by Matt (Montgomery Clift). Leaving Dunson behind, Matt reroutes the herd toward Abilene because a cowboy says that the railroad has already reached that part of Kansas. As he leads the men along the old Chisholm trail, Matt is now confronted with both the responsibility of bringing the herd safely to market, and the specter of Dunson's revengeful return.

Matt's two problems are further complicated when the cattle drive encounters a wagon train that is attacked by Indians. One of the members of the train is Tess (Joanne Dru), with whom Matt falls in love. A parallel to Fen, Tess tries to reunite Matt to Dunson when she meets Dunson after learning that Matt had taken the herd away from him. Although she is in love with Matt, she offers to bear Dunson a son if he will not seek revenge against his adopted son. Despite her role as an attempted peacemaker, Tess is only a minor interruption of the main focus of *Red River*, which is the tension between Dunson and Matt.

Beginning with their initial meeting, at which time Dunson takes away Matt's gun, the younger man is forced into a position of having to prove himself. This theme is motivated by Dunson's promise to add Matt's initial to the Red River brand as soon as he has "earned" it. Other sources of tension develop out of the contrasting personalities of the two men. For example, Dunson is repeatedly referred to as a "hard man" while Matt is accused of being "too soft." In spite of their differences, however, both men possess a sense of personal morality and rugged individualism which serves to endear them to each other, as well as to the audience.

The affection between the two makes Matt's decision to assume control of the herd an extremely difficult one. Thus, even though Matt's adoptive father's tyrannical ways have long since overstepped the bounds of rational behavior, it is not until Dunson is about to hang a group of deserters that Matt intervenes. From this point on the tension between the two is expressed conversationally, as Dunson vows to catch up with Matt and kill him. The irony of their opposition to each other is the fact that Matt's act of "betrayal" is the only way that he can ultimately earn his father's true respect.

The similarities and differences between Matt and Dunson are more fully developed in the scenes after they part. Unlike Dunson, Matt is not afraid to voice his own self-doubts. This is revealed during a brief scene in which Matt tells Groot that he knows Dunson is wrong, but that he hopes that he himself is right about the railroad in Abilene. Also, in an effort to placate the men, Matt drives the herd two days out of their way, which results in his subsequent decision to risk the herd in order to "save a bunch of gamblers and women." Like Dunson, however, he leaves Tess in order to finish the drive in much the same manner that Dunson left Fen nearly fifteen years before. Consequently, when the final confrontation occurs, Dunson cannot follow through on his threat to kill Matt. He has finally come to realize that Matt's actions have in fact earned him the right to have his initial added to the Red River brand.

In addition to the strength of its basic story construction, *Red River* profits from the skillful use of symbols. Among the most prominent of these symbols is the snake bracelet which Dunson had originally given to Fen when he first left the wagon train. This bracelet is later retrieved by Dunson from one of the Indians responsible for Fen's death, and is handed down to Matt. When it next appears it is on Tess's wrist, and it helps to make Dunson realize that Matt is virtually reliving his own series of earlier actions. In keeping with the consistency of Dunson's character, however, the symbolism of the bracelet as a link between the personalities of the two men is not recognized by him until the end of the film.

A good deal of the credit for the maintenance of believability in Dunson's megalomaniacal personality must be attributed to Wayne's completely convincing performance. In fact, without exception, the level of the performances of the entire cast is consistently excellent. Clift exudes just the right amount of sensitivity and inner strength required for Matt. Brennan, in a characteristic role, is also quite effective. Among the supporting players, John Ireland as Cherry, Noah Beery, Jr., as Buster, and Paul Fix as Teeler are all noteworthy. Only Dru's portrayal of the strong-willed Tess seems slightly flawed, although the blame for this rests more with her late appearance in the film than it does with her acting.

In visual terms, *Red River* is equally impressive. Using his locations to full advantage, Hawks repeatedly captures a feeling of adventure by thrusting the viewer into the center of the action. This is particularly evident during the scenes of the cattle stampede and the river-crossing, which make use of shots taken by a camera mounted inside one of the wagons. Another example of Hawks's impressive visual style occurs just before the men are about to embark on the drive. With a 360-degree pan over the men and the herd, their actual departure is prefaced by a series of quickly cut close-ups of the cowboys as they begin to "move 'em out." In addition to its visual beauty, *Red River* also evokes a real sense of what the West was like through its careful attention to such details as what it means to ride "point" or "drag." Combined with the skillful use of Dmitri Tiomkin's score, it is details such as these which help to make *Red River* one of the most emotionally effective Westerns ever produced.

Although it has been released in several different versions, *Red River* has been an object of critical admiration ever since its first showing in 1948. The principal difference in the versions has to do with the method of Groot's framing narration, which is either done in straight voice-overs or accompanied by the turning pages of a diary. Also deleted from several prints is the scene in which Cherry and Matt indulge in some highly competitive target practice. In this regard it is interesting to note that several have criticized *Red River* for its failure to develop the relationship between Matt and Cherry. Also subject to criticism is the fact that Dru's late appearance undercuts the credibility of her relationship with the two protagonists. *Red River* has nevertheless managed to survive the test of time and will long be remembered for both its visual beauty and excellent performances.

Alan Karp

THE REIVERS

Released: 1969
Production: Irving Ravetch for Cinema Films
Direction: Mark Rydell
Screenplay: Irving Ravetch and Harriet Frank, Jr.; based on the novel of the
  same name by William Faulkner
Cinematography: Richard Moore
Editing: Thomas Stanford
Running time: 107 minutes

> *Principal characters:*
> Boon Hogganbeck .... Steve McQueen
> Corrie .... Sharon Farrell
> Boss McCaslin .... Will Geer
> Ned McCaslin .... Rupert Crosse
> Lucius McCaslin .... Mitch Vogel
> Miss Reba .... Ruth White
> Uncle Possum .... Juano Hernandez
> Lucius Priest .... Voice of Burgess Meredith
> Otis .... Lindy Davis

The Reivers: A Reminiscence, William Faulkner's last novel, is a story about
the rapid changes in Southern society in the early twentieth century. The
novel is populated with old men with memories about older times, young
boys who dream about them, and families whose moral order will be forever
changed by the advent of the automobile and the encroachment of urban life.
Told primarily from the point of view of the narrator of the story, Lucius
Priest (voice of Burgess Meredith), a wizened and lovable old man, *The
Reivers* deals with Lucius' adventures as a boy in 1905 and of his relations
with his own grandfather. The story covers nearly one hundred years and
several generations of the boy's family.

Like so many other film translations of novels, this version of *The Reivers*
changes some of the original focus of Faulkner's tale. Directed by Mark
Rydell, with a screenplay by Irving Ravetch and Harriet Frank, Jr., the film
adaptation of Faulkner's story depicts a bittersweet set of memories of a life
forever vanished. Faulkner's story shows how his characters are products of
the unique ambience of rural Southern life, from the Civil War through
generations of changes. The challenge for the film's director and writers was
to reduce the novel's complexity and to make the film adaptation adhere
closely to the central idea of the novel: how a small boy comes to understand
himself through a very funny set of midadventures.

The action of the film takes place in 1905. The landscape is green, the
houses have a kind of lived-in scruffiness, and the front porches are all used.

Old Lucius tells the audience what 1905 was like. He does not mention what the present is like, the audience is led to understand that there was something special about the past that now is gone from Old Lucius' life. Young Lucius (Mitch Vogel) is approached by Boon Hogganbeck (Steve McQueen), a family retainer who talks the boy into riding with him in the new automobile owned by Boss McCaslin (Will Geer), a 1905 yellow Winton Flyer, all the way to Memphis. Boon wants Lucius to learn "a little something" about life, so he "borrows" the car, and, along with Lucius and Ned McCaslin (Rupert Crosse), the great joyride begins. Ned is a black man who is wiser than most people realize, getting his own way much of the time by talking and kidding around constantly.

As the three car thieves (reivers) make their way down dusty roads, the Winton Flyer becomes a symbol of change. Boon is not quite sure how to drive the puffing, dazzling vehicle, but he tries. Lucius is simply amazed at what he learns. Each passenger learns that the Winton is what the present is all about. As they pass by the landscape of the rural South, moving faster than they ever thought possible, each is aware that the old order has passed. Boon wants to be ready for the new age, Ned wants to have fun, and Lucius wants to determine how everything is changing so rapidly. Ned is also conscious of his race and proud to be a black man, and his pride is a hallmark of the new South. They go on to Memphis and visit the brothel run by Miss Reba (Ruth White). Ned knows most of the people, and Boon leaves Lucius in the hands of the lovable old matron. Lucius soon learns to love the women, grows attached to one of the girls, Corrie (Sharon Farrell), and winds up fighting over her with a character named Otis (Lindy Davis), who reveals the real nature of Corrie's profession. Lucius is then wounded, bandaged, and cared for by Corrie.

Lucius is wiser as a result of his experiences, and Boon is upset over this fact since he had not expected his young charge to discover quite so much about life. Both next learn that the conniving Ned has swapped the Winton Flyer for a horse that will not run. After a series of complications, the horse is entered in a race in a nearby town, populated by more benign, lovable types, and, after much praying and maneuvering, Lucius wins a few races with the newly acquired animal. The yellow Winton, always in the background, is finally reclaimed by Boss McCaslin, and after a sternly delivered lecture on virtue is given to young Lucius by Boss, the benevolent old man takes everyone back home. Boon marries Corrie, Ned continues to enjoy life, and the Hogganbecks eventually name their child after Lucius. The film ends with the former car-stealing trio happily playing in the Winton Flyer (with Lucius at the wheel), minus its tires, which have been removed by an always wary Boss McCaslin.

The novel was intended to be both humorous and instructive. The film version manages to capture this spirit, taking the audience on an amusing trip with three unique characters. Still, one notes the absence of much of Faulkner's original narrative: lost are the digressions about rural life, romance, and the complicated virtues of urban existence. McQueen is miscast as Boon, and does not come across well as a man half grown up, confused, and wanting to enjoy everything. His accent is wrong, as are his attempts to look concerned about Lucius. In the film, Lucius, Ned, and Boon are pictured as fun-loving scamps on the road to adventure and at least a bit of wisdom. At certain points, the audience may be at a loss to understand exactly what Lucius is feeling (Faulkner, however, was explicit in the novel). All that is known is that the young rural boy has to be learning something from everything that happens to him. The question is, what does the boy begin to understand about himself?

The film is well photographed. The colors of the Southern summer are captured in all of their lush warmth, with the color green everywhere mixed with the dust of the road and racetrack. As the Winton Flyer passes the emblems of the old order—farms, men working their small plots, the remnants of the old plantation life—the audience is introduced to the changes taking place in the South. It is in their vivid portrait of change, of the replacement of one way of life for another, of one set of rules for the less structured codes of urban existence, that the film's director and screenwriters are most successful. Old Boss McCaslin is part of another era; young Lucius is part of the new age; and Ned and Boon are caught in between. The settings filmed in *The Reivers* are lovely, and if the characters' motivations are often less than adequately treated, it is still enjoyable to watch the three reivers as they make their way into a new century.

Larry S. Rudner

REMBRANDT

Released: 1936
Production: Alexander Korda for London Films; released by United Artists
Direction: Alexander Korda
Screenplay: Carl Zuckmayer, Lajos Biro, and June Head, with dialogue by Arthur Wimperis
Cinematography: Georges Perinal and Richard Angst
Editing: William Hornbeck
Art direction: Vincent Korda
Costume design: John Armstrong
Music: Geoffrey Toye
Running time: 83 minutes

Principal characters:
Rembrandt ....Charles Laughton
Hendrickje Stoffels .... Elsa Lanchester
Geertja Dirx .... Gertrude Lawrence

Alexander Korda, producer and director of *Rembrandt*, was a Hungarian *émigré* who came to Britain in the early 1930's via Austria, Berlin, Paris, and Hollywood to revitalize the British film industry. Korda founded London Films, with their famous trademark of Big Ben striking solemnly, and surrounded himself with talented writers, designers, cinematographers, and other artists, many of whom were relations or refugees from Nazi Germany. He eventually acquired Denham Studios, where *Rembrandt* became the first film to be shot in its entirety.

Korda was an extremely cultured man who loved literature, music, and art, and he approached his new project with enormous respect for Rembrandt as an artist and with an intense desire to bring to the screen a perfect re-creation of his seventeenth century Dutch life. To achieve maximum authenticity, Korda's staff of designers, all of whom had just finished work on the futuristic *Things To Come* (1936), spent months in Holland collecting research material. As usual, the art direction was in the hands of Vincent Korda, Alexander's brother, and the costume design was to be done by John Armstrong. Korda spent money lavishly when preparing a film because he wanted every detail to be perfectly correct.

Early in the planning stages, the question of whether to film in color or black-and-white must have been a difficult one. Most subsequent biographies of artists have been in color, but *Rembrandt* was made in black-and-white. To try to capture the effect of Rembrandt's unique color effects would have been an awesome responsibility for a cinematographer. It must have been difficult enough to achieve Rembrandt's type of lighting, but the two cinematographers— Georges Perinal and Richard Angst—certainly succeeded in obtaining beautiful Dutch interior shots. Georges Perinal was an extremely gifted French cinematographer who worked on a number of now-classic French films of the early 1930's before *Rembrandt*, including *Le Sang d'un Poete*, *Sous les Toits de Paris*, and *Le Million*, and he worked with directors René Clair and Jean Cocteau before his contract with London Films.

Star Charles Laughton bore a striking resemblance to Rembrandt as represented in his self-portraits, but this was not the only reason for casting him. He was a brilliant actor who loved art and could easily understand and portray Rembrandt's difficulties with the bourgeois Dutch, who turned against his work after earlier successes. Laughton had studied acting under the Russian stage director Komisarjevsky while at the Royal Academy of Dramatic Art in London. He appeared in several plays in the West End after leaving the Academy and made a considerable success with *Dear Mr. Prohack* and *Alibi*, in which he played Agatha Christie's famed Belgian detective Hercule Poirot. His physical appearance was very different from that of the other young actors of the late 1920's and early 1930's, and he was painfully aware of this. He was certainly not a matinee idol, but he was too young and too intelligent to be confined to character parts and obviously had no desire to specialize in comedy roles. So Laughton left England for Hollywood, and although his career in the United States was uneven (owing somewhat to his own lack of judgment in choosing parts), he became a "character star."

Laughton's first film appearances were in a series of short experimental comedies, and his first major part was in the British film *Piccadilly* (1929). After the success of *The Private Life of Henry VIII* (1933) he wanted to work with Korda again, and, after one or two unrealized projects, they settled on *Rembrandt*. The scenario was written by Carl Zuckmayer, Lajos Biro, and June Head; the original scenario by Zuckmayer was not quite "English" enough, and Lajos Biro and June Head were added to the writing credit after alterations were made. Arthur Wimperis wrote the dialogue. The scenario consisted of a series of incidents in Rembrandt's later life and did not have any conventional linking scenes.

The story begins with the death of Rembrandt's first wife, Saskia von Vylenburgh (the character does not appear on the screen), and the disastrous reception of his commissioned portrait of the Civic Guard "The Night Watch," a combination of events that shattered Rembrandt. Aster Saskia's death the responsibility of running the home, studio, and even the finances fall to his housekeeper Geertja Dirx (Gertrude Lawrence). It was a difficult task in the face of Rembrandt's complete indifference to their rapidly disappearing income. Like so many artists, he would not compromise, and the paintings he did could not be sold for anything near their worth.

The most important love affair in the film is between Rembrandt and his young servant Hendrickje Stoffels (Elsa Lanchester). The painter is very happy to be loved again, and her simplicity of spirit illuminates the screen.

At their first meeting Rembrandt, always looking for new subjects to paint, makes the startled Hendrickje sit for him. She is very shy and implores him to let her return to the kitchen but he gently coaxes her to sit still and forget that he is there. Hendrickje's love, totally unselfish, makes him happy for the short time they have together. He marries her after the birth of their child, but she contracts a fatal illness and dies. At the end Rembrandt is an old man who works on his self-portrait, unmindful of the world around him, confining his attentions to his art.

All concerned in the production must have known that they were serving the artist well. Laughton's performance shows with great sensitivity the agony of a man constantly expected to compromise his talent. Laughton's total dedication to finding the character he was playing often made life difficult for his directors. Although Korda and Laughton shared the same enthusiasm for this very personal project, Korda found his technique of "character immersion" something of a trial, and they never made another film together.

Lawrence does her best with an unsympathetic part, but Geertja is a hard, shrewish woman, constantly reminding Rembrandt of her loyalty during hard times and demanding appreciation. Her attitude toward his painting is bourgeois; her endless nagging about his inability to pay their debts is a constant reminder of his dependence on the patrons he so much despises. Lawrence was primarily a stage star, and, like American actress Tallulah Bankhead, she never achieved the same success on the screen. It is difficult to understand why she accepted such an unsympathetic part—her forte was sophisticated comedy, which she played with immense style. The puritan-style costumes did not flatter her, and even cinematographer Perinal could not soften her features.

Lanchester, in real life Mrs. Charles Laughton, was already a successful stage actress in London when she met and married Laughton. They appeared in plays together, and the decision to go to America was a mutual one. She is a unique actress with a refreshing lack of vanity. It is her businesslike approach to her craft that makes her so successful in playing roles whose authenticity demands unflattering costumes, makeup, and hairstyles. Her playing of the simple peasant girl is touchingly sincere, and her scenes with Laughton in *Rembrandt* are exceptionally natural.

Unfortunately, *Rembrandt* was not a financial success. It received its premiere in Holland and all the critics liked it, but it did not have the ingredients to attract audiences. It must have been a tremendous disappointment for Korda, who cared so deeply for the subject, to realize that his beloved Rembrandt story was not going to achieve anything like the success of *The Private Life of Henry VIII*. In spite of the film's lack of box-office appeal, Korda had an affection for it; when warned about its rather highbrow subject he said "I know, but it's very beautiful."

Rembrandt was filmed again only six years later at the German UFA studios in Templehof and Babelsberg and in German-occupied Amsterdam and The Hague. This version also achieved remarkable "Rembrandt Lighting" effects, perhaps because the cinematographer was Richard Angst, who had also worked on the Korda version. The problem of successfully re-creating the artist's work for the screen was solved by UFA by releasing from prison one of the leading art forgers of the day. Hans Steinhoff directed and Rembrandt was played by Ewald Balser.

Elizabeth Leese

REPULSION

Released: 1965
Production: Gene Gutowski for Michael Klinger/Tony Tenser
Direction: Roman Polanski
Screenplay: Roman Polanski and Gerard Brach, with additional dialogue by
  David Stone
Cinematography: Gilbert Taylor
Editing: Alastair McIntyre
Music: Chico Hamilton
Running time: 105 minutes

> *Principal characters:*
> Carol Ledoux .... Catherine Deneuve
> Colin ....John Fraser
> Helen Ledoux .... Yvonne Furneaux
> Michael .... Ian Hendry
> Landlord ....Patrick Wymark
> Bridget .... Helen Fraser
> John ....James Villiers
> Reggie ....Hugh Futcher

"There's only one way to deal with men and that's to treat them as if you don't give a damn about them!" So says a venomous older client in the beauty salon where Carol Ledoux (Catherine Deneuve) works in *Repulsion*. The words constitute a gasp of disgust in a film reeking with sexual loathing.

Living with her sister Helen (Yvonne Furneaux) in a London flat, Carol appears to the world to be a shy "Cinderella." She could have any man, but the thought of sex secretly repels her. When her would-be boyfriend Colin (John Fraser) kisses her, she rushes upstairs to brush her teeth, then throws out the brush. After Helen goes off on a holiday with her married lover Michael (Ian Hendry), Carol is left alone in the apartment. Inevitably, her derangement flowers in the hothouse of solitude. When Colin, and then the landlord, try to intrude, Carol murders them both. By the end of the film, she has sunk into catatonia, unreachable by the men she loathes and fears— and wants so much.

Repulsion has some caustic dialogue and some wonderfully self-centered characters who fail utterly to see that something is *wrong* with Carol. It is a film without much *important* dialogue, however, and even Carol is used rather like a prop. Her nervous reactions and hallucinations express more than her few whispered words. The real interest of the movie is in Roman Polanski's mastery of "pure cinema"—staging, camera movement, sound effects, and editing—to create a claustrophobic madness. His skill is almost perversely sadistic, for it is all focused on showing how distasteful sex can be and how a personality can disintegrate.

The horror of the film is based on disgust, not a monster but a monstrous feeling, overpowering Carol with its intensity. She projects her disgust onto a perfectly "normal" shabby-genteel apartment and a perfectly "smooth" young man who wants to be her lover, until the man seems to her to be a rapist, like those in her fantasies, and the apartment becomes a trap where the walls yield like wet clay or crack to reveal holes in the universe.

Polanski creates visual and aural signals to dramatize Carol's madness: a molting rabbit, buzzing flies, a phone that rings with no one on the line, a razor in a tooth glass. Every image is developed to show growing disorder, decomposition, and death. The film has such visual energy that death has never seemed so lively. Consider the motif of eyes and circles: the first shot is of Carol's glassy eyes as she sits "daydreaming" at work. There are circular reflections of herself in various objects around the apartment. The front door has a round viewing glass which lets the dweller see who is knocking. There is a circular fixture for the light above Carol's bed; she stares at it while listening to her sister make love in the next room. By the end of the film, Carol imagines that ceiling fixture coming down to crush her in bed. The viewing glass in the front door is spattered with blood. Carol's eyes become a void, staring rigidly at nothing.

Another motif is one of recurring rape. It begins with the famous moment when Carol shuts a mirrored closet door and glimpses a reflected figure behind her, while the music makes a startling cry. When she turns, no one is there. Then, at night, a man pushes open her barricaded bedroom door and rapes her in a brutally suggestive fantasy. Still later, she opens the bedcovers to be surprised by another waiting attacker. When the (real) landlord tries to assault her, the fantasies have prepared us for Carol's fear and her flashing razor.

Sound effects heighten the fantasy. During the "rapes," Polanski drops all natural cries and scuffling. We hear only a loudly ticking clock. Again, when Carol realizes that she has bashed in her boyfriend's head, she opens her mouth to scream, but the only sound is the music shrieking.

In dealing with madness, Polanski has created what is possibly his most controlled film. Sequences are built of stunning contrasts: Carol sees potatoes sprout on a kitchen drainboard. Disturbed, she "sees" the wall crack. While watching it, she absentmindedly breaks a cracker. Suddenly the phone rings with a startling reality. Polanski's control extends beyond sequences to scenes, as when Carol's boyfriend tries to reason with her in her apartment. He has left the hall door open; a neighbor in the background watches the scene through that open door. In the foreground, Carol clutches a heavy candleholder behind her back. Our eyes dart from her weapon, out to the neighbor, and back to the weapon. The suspense is so great that we do not care what the boyfriend is saying.

In a deeper way, Polanski's film is unnerving because it links sex and disgust. It is rather like *Psycho* (1960) or *Frenzy* (1972), with their series of sexually motivated revenges. Carol's friends in the beauty shop have casual contempt for "bloody *men*." Her boyfriend's pals joke about his unsuccessful love affair, almost starting a fight. When one of them tells the boyfriend to cool off, and, still joking, kisses him on the lips, the boyfriend wipes his mouth in disgust. It is the same disgust that Carol has felt earlier. Even though she is offscreen then, we share her feelings for an instant.

Beyond its stunning technique and subtle shifting of our sympathies, *Repulsion* is a powerful portrait of the fragility of human personality—a constantly recurring theme of Polanski. In *The Tenant* (1976), another collaboration with scenarist Gerard Brach, Polanski himself plays a refugee overwhelmed by the personality of the prior tenant in his apartment. *Knife in the Water* (1963) and *Rosemary's Baby* (1966) also deal with the erosion of personality under siege. Even in *Chinatown* (1974) the detective's tragedy comes partly from not realizing the frailty of the Faye Dunaway character.

For Polanski, this view of human frailty is linked to the theme of exile. He himself has twice been displaced, once from his native Poland and once from the United States as a fugitive from justice. The character in *The Tenant* is an eastern European struggling in Paris. Carol in *Repulsion* is also displaced, a Frenchwoman in London. Paris, London, New York, or even Chinatown, to Polanski all of these places become, at times, the same limbo: a zone of exile where human sanity is forever under attack and tomorrow is always in doubt.

Ted Gershuny

RICHARD III

Released: 1956
Production: Laurence Olivier for London Films
Direction: Laurence Olivier
Screenplay: Laurence Olivier and Alan Dent; based on the play of the same
name by William Shakespeare
Cinematography: Otto Heller
Editing: Helga Cranston
Music: William Walton
Running time: 158 minutes

Principal characters:
Richard III .... Laurence Olivier
Anne Neville .... Claire Bloom
Clarence .... John Gielgud
Buckingham .... Ralph Richardson
Henry VII .... Stanley Baker
Edward IV .... Sir Cedric Hardwicke
Lord Hastings .... Alec Clunes

Beginning with Sam Taylor's *Taming of the Shrew* in 1929, the plays of
William Shakespeare have enjoyed an extensive and surprisingly rich history
of cinematic adaptation. As is to be expected, the great tragedies—*Hamlet*,
Macbeth, *King Lear*, and *Othello*—along with the popular *Romeo and Juliet*
are the plays that have been most frequently filmed, although Shakespeare's
comedies and Roman historical tragedies have also enjoyed successful film
productions. The most conspicuously neglected of Shakespeare's works are
the English histories—the Richard and Henry plays. Aside from Orson
Welles's brooding *Chimes at Midnight* (1967), in which Welles adapts some
of the Falstaff material from *Henry IV* and *Henry V*, only Laurence Olivier
has devoted any attention to these histories. Olivier produced, directed, and
starred in both *Henry V* (1945) and *Richard III*.

Just as *Henry V* is a more frequently studied play than *Richard III*, Olivier's
cinematic adaptation of *Henry V* is a much more widely known film than his
Richard III—doubtless owing to the fact that Henry is a much more appealing
character than Richard. If Henry is the mirror of all Christian kings, then
Richard is truly a satanic majesty. Whereas Prince Hal is a handsome young
hero rallying his countrymen to foreign conquest and glory, Richard is a
misshapen dwarf, twisted in mind and body. *Richard III* is set in fifteenth
century England. The War of the Roses has ended, and the House of York
has triumphed over the House of Lancaster. Edward IV (Sir Cedric Hardwicke) is King, but his brother Richard (Laurence Olivier), Duke of Glouces-

ter, has designs on the throne. Richard is deformed—a hunchback with a withered arm and leg—and feels destined by his deformity for villainy.

Richard falls to his task with a fiendish glee. He woos Anne Neville (Claire Bloom), whose husband and father in-law he has killed and sets his brother the King against their other brother, George (John Gielgud), Duke of Clarence. Although Edward eventually puts aside his rancor toward George, Richard has their brother murdered (hired assassins drown the unfortunate duke in a cask of malmsey wine). When the King dies, Richard imprisons and subsequently murders Edward's two young sons and contrives to have himself crowned in their stead. His lust for power unsated, Richard then turns on two of his most ardent supporters. He has Lord Hastings (Alec Clunes) executed on trumped-up charges of treason, and the Duke of Buckingham (Ralph Richardson) flees to avoid a similar fate. Buckingham makes his way to France, where Henry (Stanley Baker), Earl of Richmond, is preparing to launch an attack against Richard. The two armies meet on Bosworth Field, and Richard is killed. The victor is crowned Henry VII, the first of the illustrious Tudor dynasty.

In adapting the play for the cinema, Olivier made one significant addition to the script. He interpolated the coronation of Edward IV from the end of *Henry VI, Part 3* (the play that preceeded *Richard III* in Shakespeare's history cycle) into the beginning of the film. This accomplished two things: it gave the audience a bit of welcome background to the action commencing on the screen; and it also gave Olivier a framing device to use, much as he used the Globe Theatre to begin and end his production of *Henry V*. In *Richard III*, the framing device is the Crown of England. The Crown appears at three significant points in the film: at the beginning; in the middle, at Richard's coronation; and at the end, when, after Richard is killed in battle, one of Henry's followers lifts it reverently toward the head of the rightful occupant of the throne.

In additon, Olivier made a number of important deletions in the script. Most of these involved eliminating minor characters whose function was to parrot the Tudor political line—chief among these was Queen Margaret, widow of the deposed Lancastrian King Henry VI, who was given to uttering prophetic denunciations of Richard's villainy—but who did little to enhance the play's drama. Finally, many speeches were cut down, split up, or otherwise transposed to streamline the film. The resulting script, even more than Shakespeare's original play, focuses the audience's attention on Richard, and Richard alone.

The decision by Olivier the director to narrow the film's focus in this fashion puts an added burden on Olivier the actor; but no actor on stage or screen is better able to shoulder such a burden. Although his supporting cast includes some of the finest English actors of the day—Ralph Richardson as the pragmatic Buckingham and John Gielgud as the tormented Clarence, the film's most sympathetic character, are outstanding—Olivier thoroughly dominates the film.

Olivier's Richard is a thoughtful, even witty man, but he is unceasingly malevolent. During the first half of the film, Olivier concentrates on developing the witty side of Richard's character. He frequently addresses the audience directly, looking squarely into the camera with the ghost of a smile playing on his lips as he confides his fiendish machinations to us. Richard is clearly enjoying himself at this point, and he invites the audience to respond in like manner. His good humor can evaporate, however, without warning. When his young nephews make an innocent jest about his crooked back, Richard silences them with a wintry stare that puts a chill on the whole proceeding.

Gradually and subtly, Olivier shifts his emphasis from the witty to the sinister Richard. His mocking asides to the audience become less frequent as Richard gets closer to his goal. Indeed, the funniest scene in the film—the scene at Baynard's Castle in which Richard coyly pretends to decline the crown for which he has schemed and murdered, all the while surrounded by a notably unenthusiastic crowd of "supporters"—derives its humor at Richard's expense, not at his instigation. Instead, Richard's sadism, never far from the surface, takes over. Throwing aside all pretense of being reluctant to accept the crown, Richard suddenly hurtles down a bell rope from his balcony to the streets. With the bells pealing wildly, Richard forces Buckingham, his most loyal follower, to grovel at his feet.

The film goes from the bells at the castle to the bells at Richard's coronation, one of several effective cinematic devices used in *Richard III*. Olivier's Shakespearean films have been accused of being overly stagey, of being "mere" adaptations, with nothing particularly cinematic about them. While there is a kernel of truth to these allegations, Olivier has, deliberately and conscientiously, used a number of cinematic effects that lift *Richard III* beyond the category of a filmed stage play.

Most prominent among these effects is Olivier's use of shadow—the shadow of Richard himself. When Richard, planning his brother's murder, says to himself "Clarence beware! Thou keepest me from the light. But I will plan a pitchy day for thee," the camera moves from him to his shadow, which stretches over the steps on which he is standing. As Richard walks away, the shadow grows increasingly larger until it engulfs the entire screen. Similarly, Richard's shadow covers Anne Neville to symbolize his successful romantic conquest of his dead rival's wife. When Buckingham joins Richard's conspiracy, Olivier links the two visually by focusing on the shadows of the two men as they stride off to wreak their havoc. Such symbolism is not uncommon in films, to be sure, but Olivier never overplays his hand, and thus his use of shadow is dramatic rather than melodramatic. Such cinematic devices are, by some standards, rather pedestrian. It seems unlikely that such a charge would bother Olivier, whose purpose is to film a story, not to display a bravura flair with the camera.

The play *Richard III* is not in the first rank in Shakespeare's canon. It is, however, a good play, an interesting mixture of history and tragedy and a fascinating study of tyranny. Olivier's cinematic adaptation of the play, however, is a *tour de force*, a great film from a good play. Olivier is the cinema's finest adapter of Shakespeare, and *Richard III* both confirms and adds to his lofty reputation.

Robert Mitchell

RIO BRAVO

Released: 1959
Production: Howard Hawks for Warner Bros.
Direction: Howard Hawks
Screenplay: Jules Furthman and Leigh Brackett; based on an original story
 by B. H. McCampbell
Cinematography: Russell Harlan
Editing: Folmar Blangsted
Music: Dmitri Tiomkin
Running time: 141 minutes

Principal characters:
John T. Chance .... John Wayne
Dude .... Dean Martin
Colorado .... Ricky Nelson
Feathers .... Angie Dickinson
Stumpy .... Walter Brennan
Pat Wheeler .... Ward Bond
Nathan Burdett .... John Russell
Carlos .... Pedro Gonzalez-Gonzalez
Joe Burdett .... Claude Akins

Rio Bravo's critical reputation as both film and Western saga is unusually complex. At the time of its release, reviewers generally dismissed it as overlong, lacking in action, and poorly cast—with a good many jibes being directed at the acting of singing personalities Dean Martin and Ricky Nelson. In the ensuing years, however, first foreign and then American critics have discerned something else in the film's occasionally comic, but elaborate and unrelenting emphasis on the quarrelsome and difficult interrelationships of its protagonists. In fact, aside from the setting and the general plot outline, *Rio Bravo* has little, if any, common ground with other Western classics, from *The Iron Horse* (1925) to *High Noon* (1952). The traditional thematic preoccupations of the Western are American expansionism and the frontier conflict of order and lawlessness, but *Rio Bravo* merely uses its "Westernness" to assume the existence of this framework, then proceeds to concentrate on the moral dilemmas of the characters who exist within it.

The simple, straightforward plot of *Rio Bravo* is its most direct link to any Western tradition or framework. John T. Chance (John Wayne), the marshal of Rio Bravo, has arrested Joe Burdett (Claude Akins) for murder. His brother Nathan (John Russell), a wealthy and powerful landowner, is determined to secure his release through either bribery or violence. Chance, however, is equally determined to keep his prisoner in custody until the circuit judge arrives. Chance's resistance is aided by his current deputy, Stumpy

(Walter Brennan), a toothless, limping old man; a former deputy, Dude (Dean Martin), who is trying to recover from a long period of alcoholism; and a young gunman, Colorado (Ricky Nelson). In the course of his routine patrols of the town, Chance also becomes involved with an itinerant saloon girl named Feathers (Angie Dickinson).

For a film of its considerable length—141 minutes—the scope of *Rio Bravo*'s narrative is severely restricted and not devoted to detailed characterizations. All of the major characters are quickly defined in their first appearances. The screen *persona* of each actor, reinforced by the costuming and staging, is more than sufficient to invoke the appropriate Western archetypes and generate within the audience an expectation which is sustained through all the vignettes and set pieces until the film's conclusion. The most obvious example of this process is that of Wayne in the part of John T. Chance. The viewer anticipates through the mention of Wayne's very name in the opening titles a number of likely characteristics for the protagonist. He, like Wayne, will be physically large, laconic, and decisive. Various details of Wayne's posture and costume establish a graphic link with previous roles: from the yellow-handled revolver and single magnum-sized bullet in his gunbelt, to the "Red River D" belt buckle from an earlier collaboration with director Howard Hawks on *Red River* (1948), to the battered Cavalry hat from his work with John Ford on that director's Cavalry Trilogy. Hawks underscores Wayne's heroic posture in the first encounter with Dude in a bar, a place where the elements of law and order can meet in an uneasy truce. When Chance finds his former deputy groveling for a coin in a spittoon, he intervenes, and a tilting shot moves up his body until it reveals him, tight-lipped and resolute, seeming from the extremely low camera angle to tower over Dude (Dean Martin).

After such an introduction, the audience fully anticipates that Chance will be the major figure in *Rio Bravo*. He is, in fact, much more than that as he becomes both the narrative and thematic core of the film. He achieves the central narrative position because his arrest and continued imprisonment of Joe Burdett in the face of numerous antagonists motivate all the other actions. Dude knocks Chance unconscious and is then beaten up by Burdett, who then shoots a bystander attempting to help Dude. Chance recovers and tracks Burdett to another saloon where he takes him into custody. This sets the stage for the film's subsequent action. Thematically, Chance assumes a moral position which his fellow protagonists ultimately come to support, although they may initially vacillate.

This concept of Chance as a moral prototype and the related process of moral redemption of the other figures effectively fill out the long running time of *Rio Bravo*. The process, like the characters, is quickly defined and is emphasized through dialogue and stylistic motifs which prolong and elaborate it. For example, music, in the form of a trumpet phrase, *deguello*, originally played at the Alamo to symbolize "no quarter," haunts the lawmen who are barricaded in the jail. Initially, the protagonists become unnerved by listening to the eerie notes until their senses become immersed in the round-the-clock assault by the Mexican bugler. Only as they begin to adopt Chance's belief that their moral position is unassailable do they gain control of themselves. When Dude is about to succumb to his alcoholism by filling a shot glass and raising it to his lips, the renewed playing of the trumpet actually stops him. Defiantly, he pours the whiskey back into the bottle. Only after he does this does he realize that he did not spill any of the whiskey, proving that the uncontrollable shaking of his gunhand has finally abated. Eventually Dude joins Colorado and Stumpy in a musical interlude inside the jail, a sequence which breaks the spell of the *deguello* and its implicit threat that they will receive no quarter from Burdett's men.

Ironically, this particular sequence was most often singled out by reviewers as being arbitrarily inserted to exploit the presence of two singers in the film's cast. Hawks himself may have invited this criticism by remarking somewhat facetiously that for years he had seen Western series and singers on television, so he took two singers and put them in a Western. What such criticism overlooks is that *Rio Bravo*'s narrative organization, like that of almost all of Hawks's motion pictures, is designed to elucidate the director's personal view of human relationships. Although it is a genre film, *Rio Bravo* never attempts a purely generic statement; Hawks purposely denies many of the possibilities of the Western background. The typical image of daylight-illuminated landscapes is replaced by the enclosed space of the jailhouse and the menacing night exteriors of the town streets. Hawks does experiment with the analogy to the Alamo: that is the name of the town hotel, and the barricaded jail in which the outnumbered and besieged lawmen hold out is an obvious parallel. Hawks also expressed his conscious intention to rebut the pernicious view of Fred Zinnemann's *High Noon*. Hawks's distaste for the "hero" of that earlier production, a man who desperately tries to find help to face a band of outlaws, is expressed by John T. Chance. Both Chance's professionalism and his personal morality compel him to refuse help in doing the job he is paid to do, although he will not refuse help if it is offered. He just does not want well-meaning amateurs. Nevertheless, it is only the timely, unsolicited intervention of others which prevents him from being defeated.

In *El Dorado* (1966), an informal remake of *Rio Bravo*, the irony grew out of a mixture of nostalgia and pathos evinced by a pair of aged gunfighters. Hawks eschews any such sentiments in *Rio Bravo*. Unlike the two aging professionals in *El Dorado*, Chance is not defending a dying tradition but a living community. Unlike Dunson fighting for his land and cattle in Hawks's *Red River*, the motives behind Chance's actions are not self-serving. Chance fights for himself and his pride against ambiguous assailants, and that struggle is accomplished on a level beyond the considerations of genre. In a sense, *Rio Bravo* resembles a *bas relief* with all its figures thrust forward and with the Western background only incidental. Like a *bas relief*, carved only on one side, *Rio Bravo* is ideally viewed from one perspective: that of personal morality, not of genre.

Alain J. Silver

RIO RITA

Released: 1929
Production: William Le Baron for RKO/Radio
Direction: Luther Reed
Screenplay: Luther Reed and Russell Mack; based on Guy Bolton's and Fred
   Thompson's musical of the same name
Cinematography: Robert Kurrie and Lloyd Knetchel
Editing: William Hamilton
Song: Harry Tierney and Joe McCarthy
Running time: 135 minutes

Principal characters:
Rita Ferguson ....Bebe Daniels
Captain Jim Stewart ....John Boles
Chick Bean .... Bert Wheeler
Lovett .... Robert Woolsey
Dolly .... Dorothy Lee
Roberto Ferguson .... Don Alvarado
General Ravenoff .... Georges Renavent

   In less than six months after RKO released its first full-length talking feature, *Street Girl*, the studio had the premiere for its first musical based on the
extravagant Florenz Ziegfeld stage success, *Rio Rita*. By the end of 1929, *Rio
Rita* had put the new studio on solid financial ground. Producer William Le
Baron also quickly discovered that he had reclaimed a real star. In 1929, three
actresses from silent films found themselves, as a result of their appearances
as song stars, facing new careers that were to bring them more favor than
their work in silent films ever had. These actresses were Bebe Daniels, star
of *Rio Rita*; Bessie Love, of *Broadway Melody*; and Gloria Swanson, of *The
Trespasser*.
   Daniels first signed as a player with Paramount in 1919; ten years later she
was the studio's top female attraction. Paramount, however, was more interested by 1928 in promoting the career of the new Broadway players they were
signing than in fostering new careers in the talkies for their established silent
actors. The studio did not even bother giving Daniels a talking test and were
not very concerned when, in disgust, she bought up the remaining months
of her existing contract.
   William Le Baron, who had once been a producer at Paramount, was head
of production at the new RKO Studios, and he lost no time in signing Daniels
to a starring contract. They could not afford to pay her what she had been
getting weekly at Paramount, but she was willing to cut her salary to the bone
and take a percentage. She persuaded the studio to test her vocally, both
speaking and singing, for the lead role in *Rio Rita*, which RKO had purchased

from Ziegfeld. Nobody knew that Daniels had quietly been studying singing, and few remembered that before she had ever appeared in films, she had been a top child star on the Pacific Coast stage circuit, even playing Shakespeare, as one of the little princes killed in the Tower in *Richard III*. Nobody at RKO was prepared, however, for the results of Daniels' test. It made her a star all over again, and having settled for a percentage of the returns, she made a small fortune for herself. She sang two songs in particular that were immediate hits—"You're Always in My Arms" and "If You're in Love, You'll Waltz." These two melodies she recorded for Victor, and there was never any question that she herself sang them in the picture.

Rio Rita is set in a Mexican border town where reward signs are posted everywhere concerning the mysterious bandit known as the "Kinkajou." Also in the town there is a *gringo* named Jim (John Boles) who is very dashing and gallant; but nobody seems to know much about him. He wins the affections of Rita Ferguson (Bebe Daniels), belle of the Rio Grande, and thus gains the hatred of General Ravenoff (Georges Renavent), who controls the border town's politics. Rita refuses to believe the lies of the insidious Ravenoff about Jim until at a party given at his villa, he offers her proof that Jim is, in fact, a Texas Ranger Captain who has been assigned to arrest her brother Roberto (Don Alvarado) as being the bandit known as the "Kinkajou." With disdainful pride, Rita dismisses Jim, but later she saves his life from assassins whom Ravenoff has paid to lie in wait for him.

On the Mexican side of the Rio Grande, Ravenoff builds a magnificent barge, which he operates as a gambling resort. Again trying to win Rita's affection, he stages a huge party on the barge, hoping to impress her. Jim turns up at the party in disguise; he makes himself known to Rita, and his explanations renew her faith and love for him. Rita manages to divert Ravenoff's attention while Jim and the Rangers free the barge, guiding it gently through the river's current to float on the American side of the Rio Grande. There Jim exposes Ravenoff as the "Kinkajou." Ravenoff is taken into custody, and Rita's brother Roberto is freed. Rita becomes the bride of Captain Jim Stewart, and the Texas Rangers officiate at the big wedding.

The picture allowed for lavish staging of musical numbers, featuring the original songs from the Ziegfeld show written by Harry Tierney and Joseph McCarthy, plus two new ones by E. Y. Harburg and Harold Green. Dances were handsomely staged by Pearl Eaton. Boles was the ideal leading man for Daniels, their voices blending perfectly in the love duets they sang. Boles was soon a much-sought-after leading man, both in straight drama and in musicals. The comedy team of Bert Wheeler and Robert Woolsey was also introduced in this feature, and they were an instant hit with their patter and songs, as was the girl in their act, Dorothy Lee, a soubrette who could both dance and sing. Subsequently, RKO filmed a whole series of comedies costarring Wheeler and Woolsey, with pretty Lee nearly always on hand as feminine interest; the series included *Cracked Nuts* (1930), *Cockeyed Cavaliers* (1934), *Kentucky Kernels* (1935), and more than a dozen others.

After the smash hit of *Rio Rita*, Daniels starred in five other RKO features. She then played with Douglas Fairbanks in an Irving Berlin musical at United Artists, *Reaching for the Moon* (1931), and thereafter signed as a Warner Bros./First National star, where she appeared in five dramas and one show-stopping musical, *42nd Street* (1933). Her husband, Ben Lyon, and she then went to London, where they made new stage and film careers for themselves, and also appeared in several long-running radio and television series; and for one of the war years Daniels starred on the West End stage in *Panama Hattie*. The couple also served the Allied cause magnificently during World War II, with Daniels receiving the Medal of Freedom from the United States, an honor awarded only for service under fire.

RKO's *Rio Rita* opened at the Earl Carroll Theater in New York early in October of 1929, playing twice daily at a $2.50 top. Shortly thereafter, it opened in Los Angeles at Carthay Circle under much the same arrangement. It was constantly a sell-out at both theaters and at every other cinema house where it played. Daniels as the star of the singing romance was back before her public more beautiful than ever; *Rio Rita*, the beginning of the second half of her career, was the perfect vehicle to launch her on the road to new fame. In 1942, M-G-M remade *Rio Rita* into a vehicle for Kathryn Grayson and John Carroll with a wartime anti-Nazi theme, but it was not successful.

DeWitt Bodeen

THE ROBE

Released: 1953
Production: Frank Ross for Twentieth Century-Fox
Direction: Henry Koster
Screenplay: Philip Dunne and Gina Kaus; based on the novel of the same name by Lloyd C. Douglas
Cinematography: Leon Shamroy
Editing: Barbara McLean
Art direction: Lyle Wheeler and George W. Davis (AA)
Set decoration: Walter M. Scott and Paul S. Fox (AA)
Costume design: Charles Le Maire and Emile Santiago (AA)
Running time: 134 minutes

> *Principal characters:*
> Marcellus Gallio .... Richard Burton
> Diana .... Jean Simmons
> Demetrius .... Victor Mature
> Caligula .... Jay Robinson
> Pilate .... Richard Boone

With characteristic splash, Twentieth Century-Fox presented *The Robe* in gigantic CinemaScope and stereophonic sound in 1953 as one of Hollywood's answers to television and its growing control of America's entertainment. In many respects, *The Robe* was an ideal story with which to inaugurate the new large-screen process. It is Biblical fiction, a story which gave the filmmakers the opportunity to exploit the screen's dimensions by filling it with vast panoramic shots of Rome and of Jerusalem. Taken from the best-selling novel by the Reverend Lloyd C. Douglas, the story is more about the spread of Christianity and its effects upon the converts than about the life of Christ, who, in fact, figures only peripherally in the movie.

The film opens amidst the splendor of ancient Rome, ruled by the Emperor Tiberius. A human love story, as opposed to one of spiritual love, runs throughout the movie, revolving around Diana (Jean Simmons), a beautiful young Roman maiden who is the ward of the emperor. She is desired by Marcellus (Richard Burton) who will not accept defeat, whether in love or in the marketplace, and by the Prince Regent, Caligula (Jay Robinson), an evil, shrill, warped man accustomed to having his way in all things. Diana favors Marcellus, but must be discreet because of the power of Caligula.

For the Prince Regent, the final embarrassment comes when Marcellus outbids him for a servant offered for sale in the slave market. Demetrius, the slave, is a particularly strong Greek whose aloofness attracts the headstrong Marcellus. As revenge and as a way of removing Marcellus from competition for the favors of Diana, Caligula causes Marcellus and Demetrius to be banished to Palestine, where Roman troops support the rule of Pontius Pilate, Procurator of Judea, in Jerusalem.

With a particularly effective use of the wide-screen format, Marcellus is depicted as he approaches Jerusalem with Demetrius and a detachment of soldiers stretched across the landscape behind him. The low place that this assignment holds for the Roman conquerors is vividly expressed in this shot of the dry, dusty heat of Palestine, a poor land torn both politically and religiously by internecine struggles.

In Jerusalem, Marcellus lolls about in the baths, consumes a great deal of wine, and carouses with others who also have little to do to occupy their time. Routine legal and military matters are quickly dispensed with as Marcellus grows increasingly restless. In the meantime, Demetrius circulates among the inhabitants of the city and meets proponents of a new religious group, persons who call themselves followers of Jesus Christ. With his conversion, Demetrius steps up his struggle to gain freedom from his Roman master.

The events surrounding the betrayal, trial, and execution of the Messiah are presented with almost off-handed discretion. The entry of Christ into Jerusalem for the religious holidays is shown in a long shot, and the person riding the donkey is only a vague figure whose features cannot be distinguished among the crowd of followers. A few days later, a Roman official casually mentions the need to gather thirty pieces of silver for a routine political payoff to a Jewish informer.

The Pontius Pilate presented in *The Robe* is not the open-minded official often seen in Hollywood Biblical films, who attempts to persuade the crowd to free Jesus. Here, Pilate (Richard Boone) is an ill and tired bureaucrat who dislikes his job and its deadening sameness and fears that he never will be transferred out of this distasteful country. Mopping his brow of the sweat from a malaria attack, Pilate is so distracted that he forgets that he has already gone through his little show of washing his hands and starts to do it again as he hurries to finish with the unwelcome duty of pronouncing his verdict, a public humiliation of cross-bearing through the streets and death upon the cross. The journey to Golgotha by the cross-bearing prisoners is presented in a high-angled shot so that Christ is again a vague figure.

Marcellus is given the job of supervising what would normally be this routine execution of criminals. Bored with the duty, he passes the time by gambling with some soldiers for the robe they have taken from Jesus, whose feet are seen nailed to the cross. Marcellus wins the garment, but in the confusion following the earthquake which attends Christ's death, he loses both the robe and his slave.

Diana finally wields enough influence to have Marcellus returned to Rome, but she finds him ill-at-ease and seemingly not in control of his mental faculties. He has become convinced that he has been bewitched by the robe and by its crucified owner. Because of his feelings, the tribune willingly accepts an assignment to return to Palestine to investigate the activities of the religious sect called Christians. In Cana, he discovers Demetrius, the robe, and the Galilean Christians. He is calmed by his association with the religious persons and is impressed by their gentle, spiritual love.

Called back to Rome by Caligula, who is now emperor, Marcellus is charged by him with the job of finding and destroying the Christians whose influence has spread to the capital city. Marcellus has brought Demetrius with him, and Demetrius is tortured by soldiers who want him to reveal the names of the Christians in the city. Demetrius' strength under adverse conditions, along with the noble words and nonretaliatory actions of the Christians, soon brings Marcellus and Diana to the fold as converts. *The Robe* ends as Marcellus defends his new faith against the mad emperor and is executed by Roman archers.

Although in most cases the acting in *The Robe* is subservient to the film's story and scenery, most viewers were favorably impressed with the work of Burton, then relatively unknown in the United States. The smaller roles, such as Pilate, Peter, and Judas, are portrayed in nonpompous, unsentimentalized ways. Unfortunately, Mature as the slave, Demetrius, is saddled with the task of trying to show in his facial expressions all of the joys and agonies of early Christianity. When those exaggerated reactions are further distorted in wide-screen close-ups, they almost become caricatures, old-fashioned cartoons of the days of silent film overreaction. The pace of the film also seems at times to be held back by the need to stop occasionally so that the huge screen can be appropriately filled with awe-inspiring scenery and spectacle. Director Henry Koster does manage to move the action along as much as possible, however, and it was the action—or lack of it—and the screen size which occupied the comments of most critics in 1953.

Wide-screen CinemaScope, although first used in the United States for *The Robe*, was not a new process; it was invented by Henri Chretien in 1927 and was used in a French short by Claude Autant-Lara, *Construire un Feu* (1928). Unlike the Cinerama films, which used three projectors to throw three adjacent images upon an even larger, semicircular screen, or the 3-D films, whose two simultaneously projected images were separated by special glasses worn by the audience to give an illusion of depth, the CinemaScope motion picture required only an anamorphic lens to create its wide-screen feeling of audience involvement. When placed upon the camera, this special lens created tall, thin figures on the film, but when placed upon the projector, it produced normal images on a screen whose ratio was 2.55:1. Thus, by simply purchasing new lenses and modifying their screens, exhibitors were able to present films in the new format without the excessive costs of Cinerama, while viewers were able to feel more surrounded by the film without the awkward cardboard glasses of 3-D.

Both Cinerama and 3-D had come out in 1952 as ways to pull the public away from television and back into the theaters. Cinerama, however, was limited to a few metropolitan areas because of its cost, while 3-D was exploited only for its gimmickry, the novelty of which soon wore off. CinemaScope, even with its ratio later changed to 2.35:1, made a major impact upon commercial films and was quickly followed by other wide-screen processes, such as Todd-AO, Metrovision, and Panavision.

Thus *The Robe*, which was one of the top-grossing films of 1953 and which was nominated for an Academy Award as Best Picture (along with Burton as Best Actor), is more important today as the first film in CinemaScope than as a film whose content or directorial style make it memorable.

John C. Carlisle

ROBERTA

Released: 1935
Production: Pandro S. Berman for RKO/Radio
Direction: William A. Seiter
Screenplay: Jane Murfin, Sam Mintz, and Allan Scott, with additional dialogue by Glenn Tryon; based on the play of the same name by Otto Harbach and the novel *Gowns by Roberta* by Alice Duer Miller
Cinematography: Edward Cronjager
Editing: William Hamilton
Music: Jerome Kern
Choreography: Fred Astaire
Running time: 105 minutes

Principal characters:

Stephanie	Irene Dunne
Huck Haines	Fred Astaire
Scharwenka/Lizzie Gatz	Ginger Rogers
John Kent	Randolph Scott
Roberta/Aunt Minnie	Helen Westley
Sophie Teale	Claire Dodd
Voyda	Luis Alberni

Roberta was a crucial film in the development of Fred Astaire and Ginger Rogers as a dance team and as screen personalities. Released after *The Gay Divorcee*, their big success of 1934, it solidified the reputation they had established for charm, elegance, and exquisite dancing as well as proved their continuing popularity at the box office. Like *The Gay Divorcee*, *Roberta* was adapted from a hit Broadway show. The songs "Smoke Gets in Your Eyes," "Let's Begin," "Yesterdays," and "I'll Be Hard to Handle" were retained from the original Jerome Kern score, and Kern composed "Lovely to Look At" especially for the film. One other Kern song used in the film, "I Won't Dance," was not written for *Roberta*, but the lyrics were revised and adapted especially for Astaire by Dorothy Fields and Jimmy McHugh. Two essentially secondary roles in the play were augmented and expanded for the film to fit the screen personalities of Astaire and Rogers and to display their range and versatility as a dance team and as light comedians. The result has become a classic musical film.

John Kent (Randolph Scott), an ex-football player from the Midwest, is on his way to Paris to visit his Aunt Minnie (Helen Westley), who is the famous dress designer known as Roberta. He is accompanied by Huck Haines (Fred Astaire) and his band, the Wabash Indianians, who have a job in Paris at the Café Russe. The proprietor of the Café Russe, Voyda (Luis Alberni), however, meets them upon their arrival in France, takes one look at them after they disembark, and refuses to honor his contract with them: he wants "Indians" rather than "Indianians." John tries to help by forcing Voyda to listen to the band's novelty number. The band members put on gloves that resemble organ keys and stand close together, hands extended. As Huck "plays" this organ by pushing the keys, the band members vocally simulate organ sounds. Voyda is, however, unimpressed with their "organ number" and refuses to reconsider. Broke and with no immediate prospect of a job, the band boards the train to Paris with John, who takes them with him to visit his Aunt Minnie. While he goes to see her, they relax on the steps outside. Inside, John gets stuck in an elevator and is rescued by Roberta's assistant, Stephanie (Irene Dunne), an exiled Russian princess, who then conducts him to his Aunt Minnie.

John's reunion with his aunt is interrupted by shrill shouts from the next room, where the Polish countess, Scharwenka (Ginger Rogers), upset with a new gown, is making a scene. John, already protective of Stephanie, decides she might not be safe and goes to her assistance. Picking Stephanie up with one arm, he pushes the fiery Scharwenka down on to a couch with the other arm, repeating the action each time she tries to rise, so that she bobs up and down like a jack-in-the-box. Finally Scharwenka subsides, impressed by this "big, beautiful American" whom she now decides to captivate.

When Aunt Minnie reminds John that Scharwenka is the singing rage in Paris and might be useful in getting a job for Huck and the band, he enthusiastically signals Huck to play a number for the countess, and they strike up "Let's Begin." After the number Huck glimpses Schwarenka on the balcony and recognizes that she is his childhood sweetheart, Lizzie Gatz. He dashes excitedly inside, but she has also recognized him and turns her back on him because she does not want her true identity revealed. Once they are alone, however, she drops all pretense, including her fake Polish/French accent, and tells Huck that she is posing as a countess because "you've got to have a title to croon over here." They reestablish their old friendly relationship, and she agrees to try to get the band a job at the nightclub where she entertains.

Later, Aunt Minnie dies, leaving her business to John. At first appalled at the idea of running a high fashion salon, he tries to give it to Stephanie, but she persuades him to remain as her partner. Their growing friendship is interrupted by the arrival of John's former girl friend, Sophie Teale (Claire Dodd), a sophisticated, calculating woman whose interest in John is rekindled when she learns that he has inherited the salon. John thinks he is still in love with her and agrees to escort her to Huck's opening night, forgetting he has already promised to take Stephanie.

Huck, no admirer of Sophie, devises a scheme to separate John from her by persuading her to buy an evening gown that John dislikes so much that he has ordered it out of Roberta's collection. At Huck's opening night there is a final quarrel between Sophie and John when she shows him the dress.

He breaks off with her completely but is extremely angry with Stephanie for selling the dress to Sophie. When Stephanie enters later, regal and stately in tiara, cloak, and evening gown, accompanied by a retinue of loyal Russians, John, who has been drowning his sorrows in brandy, quarrels with her and leaves.

After this scene both John and Stephanie disappear, leaving an uneasy Huck to manage Roberta's. After Stephanie sees an outrageous newspaper interview with Huck and John about women's fashions, she returns in order to save the reputation of the salon. To help her out Huck decides to furnish music for the big fashion show which traditionally launches Roberta's new collection. After the show Lizzie tells a surprised Huck that she has decided to give in and marry him, and after a few misunderstandings, Stephanie and John are brought together again when Stephanie again rescues him from the stalled elevator at Roberta's. Overwhelmed when he learns that Stephanie loves him, John can only say, "Gee, that's swell," his all-purpose phrase for expressing approval or emotion. (Indeed, the phrase is used as a comic motif throughout the film.)

Although Astaire receives screen credit for choreographing the dances in *Roberta*, he was responsible for much more than the choreography, controlling every aspect of his dance numbers from initial conception through the final cutting and scoring of the number. In planning camera angles for a dance he was always guided by the principle that the audience should be unaware of the camera and that the flow of the dance should be uninterrupted. He believed the audience could follow complicated steps that would be lost on a stage because film presents dance from the ideal perspective. He avoided using reaction shots (showing other people watching the dancers), unusual camera angles, or close-ups showing just the head or feet of a dancer. His usual method was to film a dance without interruption, keeping the entire body of the dancer in the camera frame and the flow of the dance intact. He felt that in any dance, even tap, the movement of the upper part of the body was as important as that of the feet.

The first important musical number in the film, "Let's Begin," is sung by Huck as he directs the Wabash Indianians on the steps outside Roberta's to impress a prospective employer. It is a novelty number, with some members of the band helping Huck to supply the comedy: the banjo player gets his finger caught in the strings, a deep-voiced musician dons a wig and switches to shrill falsetto voice to join Huck in a musical exchange. At one point Huck dances briefly with his bewigged partner and another band member, but when they try to imitate his fancy steps, they fall down.

The most important musical number in the film, "I'll Be Hard to Handle," is sung by Lizzie in her fake accent for a rehearsal at the Café Russe (a later Astaire-Rogers film, *Follow the Fleet*, (1936), would also use a rehearsal number as well as the double romance plot structure). The song itself, as performed by Rogers, is one of the famous "wacky Ginger" routines which have become associated with her name. She stamps her foot fiercely, her eyes flash, she tosses her head emphatically, and she waves her hands about as she warns her listeners in song that she tells lies and is mean and selfish, finishing with a spirited series of nonsense syllables.

After the number she joins Huck, who has been listening on the steps below the stage, and they relax companionably, reminiscing about old times. As the conversation becomes more animated, she gets up and walks away, followed by Huck, who emphasizes his point with a staccato burst of taps. Soon their conversation is punctuated by brief dance breaks, and then they casually begin dancing, sometimes together, sometimes apart, with exaggerated, playful dips and turns, as if they are just kidding around. There is a bugle call, the music stops, and they begin a conversation carried on entirely by tap dancing, using their hands as well as their feet. He is obviously trying to explain his position to her and she, just as obviously, is growing more and more indignant. Finally, he taps completely around her, pleading his case, but her reply is so emphatic that he puts his hands to his ears. She appears to slap him and step on his foot. He staggers about until the bugle call fanfare that started the "conversation" ends it. The music now comes up in a faster tempo as they begin to tap and whirl madly and excitedly around. Finally they collapse slowly onto two chairs at the side of the dance floor.

The dance is electrifying to watch because it is so full of energy and verve, with unexpected changes in the mood, tempo, and rhythm that keep the audience a little off balance while wondering what the two will do next (and in fact the air of casual improvisation with which it begins is one of the chief delights of the dance). Although it is not closely integrated with the story, the dance does reveal and dramatize the progression of Huck and Lizzie's relationship. They begin it casually, grow more excited as it continues, have some misunderstandings, are reconciled, and end up in a flood of emotion before collapsing exhaustedly at the end. They begin the dance as friends, but when it is over their relationship has reached a new, more intense, level of feeling.

Another musical highlight of the film, "I Won't Dance," begins with Astaire playing "feelthy piano" (as Huck Haines has described it to Lizzie) with incredible style and flair. With a sweeping theatrical gesture he runs his hand along the keyboard and in one continuous smooth movement rises from the piano bench to direct the band. As they play animatedly, Lizzie comes bobbing into view, moving to the beat of the music. When Huck finally notices her, he stops the band, grabs her and stops her gyrations, then asks her what she wants. She mimes that she wants him to dance with her, but he refuses. She pouts and tries to cajole him by singing ingratiatingly that "When you dance, you're charming and you're gentle/'Specially when you do the Continental" and the band plays a few bars from "The Continental" (a song from *The Gay*

Divorcee in which the two had danced together). He refuses again by singing "I Won't Dance." As it ends he walks away from her and the band until he runs into two huge Cossacks in boots and fur hats who, one on each side, carry him down the steps and onto the dance floor. He scowls at them, then lets loose a volley of taps that chases them away. He begins the dance by shaking hands with some of the customers by the side of the floor, then gives a display of technical proficiency as he flails his arms about like a windmill, using his whole body in the dance.

In this solo dance, as in "I'll Be Hard to Handle," Astaire uses some of his favorite choreographic devices, especially "freeze and melt"—sudden transitions from abrupt stops to flowing movements. He felt that holding a pose for a moment before continuing with the next step gave dramatic emphasis and contrast. Astaire referred to his inimitable style as an "outlaw style" because it does not follow the rules of ballet, tap, or ballroom dancing but rather blends elements of all three.

The climax of the film is a musical fashion show with Huck, as master of ceremonies, providing a tongue-in-cheek commentary. After the models have paraded, Rogers walks slowly on stage and to her Astaire sings "Lovely to Look At." After the song ends, the two walk side by side, arm in arm, until they are casually gliding into a dance step as the music changes to "Smoke Gets in Your Eyes." Their graceful and beautiful dance conveys a delicate, tender moment. The two seem to be lost in a world of their own, as he gently presses her head to his shoulder. Just before the end of the film they charge back onstage to do a rambunctious, exciting reprise of "I Won't Dance." These last two dances are tantalizingly brief but powerful in their impact and whet the appetite for more Astaire and Rogers.

Dunne is charming and completely believable as Stephanie, the exiled Russian princess. Her sophistication is an excellent contrast to Scott's John Kent, described by his aunt as a "big, affectionate, blundering Newfoundland dog." In addition to her capable acting she displays her pure soprano voice in four Kern songs, the most notable of which is "Smoke Gets in Your Eyes." It is the presence of Astaire and Rogers, however, which makes *Roberta* so memorable. They animate every scene in which they appear, their freshness, vitality, and liveliness adding wit and charm to an otherwise inconsequential tale.

Julia Johnson

ROBIN AND MARIAN

Released: 1976
Production: Denis O'Dell for Ray Stark-Richard Shepherd; released by Columbia
Direction: Richard Lester
Screenplay: James Goldman
Cinematography: David Watkin
Editing: John Victor Smith
Music: John Barry
Running time: 112 minutes

Principal characters:
Robin Hood	Sean Connery
Maid Marian	Audrey Hepburn
King Richard	Richard Harris
Little John	Nicol Williamson
Sheriff of Nottingham	Robert Shaw
Will Scarlet	Denholm Elliott
Friar Tuck	Ronnie Barker
Sir Ranulf	Kenneth Haigh
King John	Ian Holm

Robin and Marian is a film about romance and about two people trying, in their own ways, to measure up to the legends that have grown up about them. It is a mature reflection upon the past and, at the same time, a fully developed eulogy on a long-abiding myth. As such, it beautifully complements and completes the progression of films that started with the fledgling *Robin Hood and His Merry Men* (1909) and continued through the adolescent exuberance of Douglas Fairbanks' *Robin Hood* (1922) and the youthful dash and vigor of Errol Flynn's *The Adventures of Robin Hood* (1938). *Robin and Marian*, unlike its predecessors, is not a traditional romance; instead, it is a study of the genre that attempts to comment upon the romantic myth even while celebrating it.

The most commonly accepted Robin Hood legend can be traced back as far as the Middle Ages to vague stories about a good outlaw who protected the poor while stealing from the rich. The first documentable reference to the character named Robin Hood occurs in the works of the Scottish chronicler John of Fordun in the late fourteenth century. The more well-known work *Lytel Geste of Robin Hood* by late fifteenth century printer Wynkyn de Worde describes many of the now-popular Robin Hood legends and has been widely read for centuries. In more modern times, Sir Walter Scott's historical romance *Ivanhoe* presents Robin Hood and his followers as minor characters in the action.

From Scott's time on there have been innumerable editions and variations of the Robin Hood stories both for adults and for children. The setting of an English forest and town in the early thirteenth century seemed to lend itself to illustrated editions of the stories, and eventually led to a number of popular films, cartoons, and two television series. The cinematic history of the Robin Hood legend began in the silent era with several versions of the story, going back to a 1909 British film. The most popular of the silents was the 1922 Fairbanks version which boasted spectacular stunts by its star and lavish production values. The first talking version of the legend, and the one which most critics consider to be the best, was Warner Bros.' 1938 *The Adventures of Robin Hood* starring Flynn and a number of popular contract players. Other films dealing with Robin Hood or his offspring proliferated in the late 1940's and 1950's, among them *The Bandit of Sherwood Forest* (1946) starring Cornell Wilde and the Walt Disney production *The Story of Robin Hood and His Merrie Men* (1952) starring Richard Todd. The latter film, although not particularly successful, was unique for its location shooting in the real Sherwood Forest, Robin Hood's legendary home. Perhaps the most successful screen Robin Hood next to Flynn was Richard Greene, who played the role for several years on British and American television, and in one feature film, *Sword of Sherwood Forest* (1961). There were other incarnations of the bandit, some cartoons, and even a parody television series produced in the late 1970's by Mel Brooks called *When Things Were Rotten*.

By 1976, when *Robin and Marian* was released, the principal figures of the legend had become so well known through books and films that it seemed impossible that a fresh approach could be taken, but this beautifully acted and directed film not only proves that it could be done but also creates some interesting new avenues bypassing the accepted approaches to the legend. In this version of the epic, director Richard Lester and screenwriter James Goldman actually demystify, to a great extent, the traditional story of the good-hearted bandit and his lady love. Their treatment intertwines realism and anachronism in such a manner as to resurrect a sense of the past that is possessed with a real vitality in its picture of the landscapes of long ago. Through the dichotomy of its vision, an impression is revealed of the stark canvas underlying the romantic tradition. Castles are grubby; the English countryside is sprinkled with toothless beggars and rotting shacks; and Robin's new followers, like the sheriff's, are boys who can hardly manage their weapons. Thus, the battles with the Sheriff of Nottingham and with the men of King John are not noble, quick, and clean; in the end, they are protracted, gory, and pointless. Yet Lester and Goldman are aware that modern man's romantic yearning for the past cannot be satisfied through such cynical allusions any more than it can by bland nostalgia. The result is a somewhat backhanded yet reasonable vision of history that accommodates the ironies of heroism but one that is also deeply cognizant of the burning hunger in the human heart that preserves the legend.

"When you are young you are too bashful to play a hero," Laurence Olivier was once quoted as saying, so "you debunk it." "It isn't until you're older that you can understand the pictoral beauty of heroism." Yet Lester and Goldman's Robin Hood as portrayed by Sean Connery also understands the fragility of heroes who possess human instincts. Their Robin Hood is a lion in autumn, a bright man and occasionally a reflective one, who has had a good life and yet cannot quite bring himself to call it a day. "I know him," the sheriff remarks at one point. "He's a little bit in love with death. He flirts, he teases. I can wait." Although Robin is old in body, a hero does not grow old in spirit, and that one last glory day always lies ahead in the crisp air of autumn if one flirts with death often enough.

Robin, with Little John (Nicol Williamson), has served Richard the Lion-Hearted (Richard Harris) faithfully for twenty years in the Holy Land, taking part in massacres and atrocities motivated by their sovereign's greed. Robin and John finally say "no," as the film begins, when Richard commands them to slaughter the undefended women and children at Chaluz, in France. They are imprisoned for their impudence, but Richard, mortally wounded by a mad old man, lets them be released before he dies. With nowhere left to go, Robin realizes that it is time to return home.

Arriving in England and making their way to Sherwood Forest, Robin and Little John encounter some of their old companions. During the course of conversation, Robin asks what happened to Marian. "I haven't thought of her in years," he adds. Although some critics have taken this statement as an attempt on director Lester's part to trivialize the legend, it also appears to resemble the casual kind of statement made by a person who does not want to reveal the true depth of his feelings, who is afraid to admit a weakness for the opposite sex that might lose him some credibility with his mates. Subsequent scenes in the film support this latter interpretation.

Marian, Robin learns, attempted to commit suicide when he left and was taken to Kirkly Abbey to recuperate. Eventually she took the veil and rose to become the Abbess. Now, twenty years after her affair with the outlaw, she is the one subject to arrest since King John has ordered the higher clergy out of England in reaction to a papal interdict against England at the time. Marian (Audrey Hepburn) is admittedly not a typical prioress and conducts the abbey's affairs with a certain wordly animation. She swears with an enviable expertise and puts up a heated battle when Robin arrives and insists upon saving her from the sheriff's clutches. As a principled woman, she would rather go to prison. She has virtually no choice in the matter, however, when Robin, who is determined to be a hero, slugs her, then slings her over a horse as if she were a saddle blanket.

Robin takes her to the forest where their romance rekindles itself in an alternately bickering and affectionate fashion. "My confessions were the envy of the convent," she tells her former lover. Then she chastises him with a sulk: "You never wrote." Robin replies: "I don't know how." Their feelings toward each other soon solidify and revolve around a single issue. The former outlaw, home again in his Sherwood Forest, finds his strength and spirits revived and looks forward to regaining his heroic niche in the legends and folklore. A daring rescue of the nuns from the sheriff's clutches and a sword-fight on the castle walls of Nottingham further inflame his ambitions. Yet this is exactly the type of escapade that Marian was hoping Robin had outgrown. He almost did not survive this swordfight, even though he will not admit it to himself, and Marian must look ahead to a day when he may not emerge victorious from one of his adventures.

Eventually, within the confines of the forest, Marian sheds her wimple and habit and, temporarily, her reservations. Then begins a sun-drenched court-ship of the reunited Robin Hood and Maid Marian in the setting of the lush English countryside. Soon, however, a whole new army of ragged farmers and young boys joins the remnants of Robin's original band and Marian's uneasiness again begins to grow. The new followers are inexperienced with weapons, and there is little time to train them before the Sheriff of Nottingham (Robert Shaw) arrives at the edge of the forest to lure the outlaws into combat. Robin, recognizing the weakness of his warriors, challenges the sheriff to a personal duel to settle their differences. Not surprisingly, the realistic sheriff, who had earlier bemoaned the inadequacy of his own soldiers' fighting ability, accepts the outlaw's challenge to a swordfight.

The fight begins in the middle of the battlefield. Although it is even at first, their age and the weight of the armor take their toll on both combatants; but the sheriff seems to be gradually gaining the upper hand. He wounds Robin seriously and begins to knock him about at will. He makes a mistake, however, and the outlaw thrusts his sword in under his guard and kills him. Suddenly the soldiers, seeing their leader slain, charge in to slaughter the ragged out-laws. Marian, who had threatened to leave Robin if he engaged in this combat, reappears and, with Little John's assistance, carries their wounded leader to the Abbey.

Lying in bed, Robin, now alone with Marian, brags about his feat of combat and looks to other such days ahead. He does not see Marian place the poison in the wine that she gives him to drink. Only after they have both consumed the potion and she has admitted that they are going to die does Robin face the truth and recognize that he would never have had another day like today. Even if he were to live, the next battle would undoubtedly be his last. Finally at peace with his legend, he calls for Little John and his bow. He shoots an arrow through the window and asks to be buried where it lands.

Although Marian makes the decision for the two of them—a quick, rela-tively painless death as opposed to the slow but no less suicidal path on which Robin has embarked—love transcends death, and the suicide scene is treated triumphantly. This has bothered some viewers who find Marian a little over-reliant on suicide to solve her problems. She is, however, more of a mythic handmaiden to a legend than a realistic woman with a number of options at her disposal. As critic Pauline Kael has pointed out, "Robin is a fool who loves to fight, and it doesn't matter who wins the war in Sherwood Forest—nothing good will come of anything." Marian has killed the man, but the legend survives, virile and intact; Robin, if left to himself, would have inevitably destroyed the legend along with himself. Thus, Robin's launch of his grave-seeking arrow into the infinity of myth and folklore fully sustains itself as a romantic image.

Although meager as a period spectacle, *Robin and Marian* provides, like no film before it, a realistic, wise, and occasionally witty response to our eternally childlike wonderment about how our heroes and heroines lived happily ever after. The film was not directed by Lester to be an old-fashioned, seductive melodrama in the tradition of *The Adventures of Robin Hood*; it was meant to be a bare frame supporting mosaic insets of exquisite beauty beneath a kind of intellectual veneer that completely suits its out-of-the-ordinary cast.

Ultimately, *Robin and Marian* must stand or fall on the strength of its stars. In Connery, Hepburn, Williamson, and Shaw, it has the best. Connery is one of the screen's last great charismatic masculine presences. A sex symbol as the ruthless James Bond early in his career, he has become more so in recent years by projecting a tenderness that had been unsuspected by other directors. Lester also encourages Connery and allows the actor to give expression to a rare zest for buffoonery that combines with the character's inherent qualities of romantic idealism and natural justice to create a portrayal of a man of rough-grained Anglo-Saxon nobility. Connery, now fleshy and gray, is the most realistic of heroic figures, and the placement of his rougher-hewn presence next to the silken Hepburn is theoretically a mismatch. They are perfect together, however, and their last scene in the film is one of the most effective tear-provoking scenes since Humphrey Bogart and Ingrid Bergman's final moments together in *Casablanca* (1942). As a couple, Connery and Hepburn are directly in the Bogart and Bergman mold of mismatched but perfectly suited lovers.

The moment that Hepburn first appears in *Robin and Marian* is a startling experience for theatergoers. She had not made a film in seven years after *Wait Until Dark* (1967), instead choosing marriage and retirement, and seeing her back on the screen with her delicate beauty undiminished reminds filmgoers of how long it has been since an actress so beguiled Americans and captured their imaginations. Like Connery, she now stands almost alone as a reminder of the traditional stars of yesterday.

Hepburn's professionalism is vividly demonstrated in one scene in which she drives a cart beside a stream. During the filming, the horse refused to stop and toppled into six feet of muddy water. Lester kept the cameras rolling, and Hepburn, rising from the water, turned the mishap into an effective scene. The director later wrote a scene in which Robin fishes Marian out and carries her lovingly to the bank. In another respect, the actress' professional sensibilities also helped to shape the finished product. Lester, in a quest for greater realism, kept cutting down on the love story between Robin and Marian, so Hepburn fought to retain some of the best lines between her and Connery. She defended her actions by saying, "With all those men, I was the one who had to defend the romance in the picture. Somebody had to take care of Marian." That is exactly what she accomplished. Her Marian is as lovely as legend has made us expect her to be. Her performance is a testimony both to passion and to the yearning for a real home and a bed with blankets.

Williamson's portrayal celebrates Little John as a faithful friend to Robin and defines his relationship as an unquestioning one that supports the wide-eyed, blunt heroism of Robin. He is to Robin what, in many respects, Robin is to Richard the Lion-Hearted. Robin follows Richard unquestioningly for more than twenty years, only to become disillusioned with his king's ruthless materialism. Little John, however, never questions Robin, and although his world comes to an end with Robin's death, he never feels betrayed, which is in itself a testimony to Robin's heroic stature. Shaw's performance as the Sheriff of Nottingham beautifully contradicts the legend and all that it has led us to expect. His sheriff is a realistic-minded, fair, and intelligent adversary. He is a prescient antihero who watches Robin flirt with death and waits for his chance. Although committing his life to be a foe of Robin's romantic idealism and sense of moral justice, he can still admire those qualities in his enemy. Like Robin, however, he is trapped by mythic forces beyond his control and must see his king's wishes through to their inevitable conclusion.

Some critics have found the pairing of Lester's television-honed directing style and Goldman's lofty dramatic lines to be less fortuitous than that of the pairing of Connery and Hepburn. Yet on the larger screen, Lester has not been a revolutionary creator of staccato scenes embodying marginally stylistic flourishes but has instead been a somewhat furtive romantic, as evidenced by his choice of subject matter in *The Three Musketeers* (1973), *The Four Musketeers* (1974), *Robin and Marian*, and more recently, *Superman II* (1981). He is as passionate and hot-blooded at times as his swashbuckling predecessors Michael Curtiz and George Sidney were in their more sentimental eras. Lester's device of possibly revisionist double vision fits him naturally. It may mitigate against the warm emotional rapport of the earlier, more richly textured versions of the Robin Hood legend, but it is appropriate to the modern period in cinema and at the same time is the only logical means to celebrate a legend even as it mourns its passing.

Robin and Marian is a flight of imagination as satisfying in its way as any that came before it. It is a temperate glance at history that is more intelligent and more pertinent than its predecessors because of the efforts of its writer, Goldman, who further demonstrates the abilities he revealed in *The Lion in Winter* (1967). The film is also, through the efforts of Lester, far richer in nuance and realistic detail than other treatments of the romantic genre. Its realism magnificently serves to frame and highlight the romantic and mythical aspects of the Robin Hood Legend. *Robin and Marian* is a contemporary companion piece and eulogy to the memories of Fairbanks, Flynn, and their fondly remembered movie traditions.

Stephen L. Hanson
Patricia King Hanson

ROCKY II

Released: 1979
Production: Irwin Winkler and Robert Chartoff; released by United Artists
Direction: Sylvester Stallone
Screenplay: Sylvester Stallone
Cinematography: Bill Butler
Editing: Danford B. Greene
Running time: 119 minutes

Principal characters:
Rocky Balboa .... Sylvester Stallone
Adrian .... Talia Shire
Apollo Creed .... Carl Weathers
Mickey .... Burgess Meredith
Paulie .... Burt Young

Rocky II is one exception to the rule that a sequel has less impact than the original. Sylvester Stallone was an unknown actor when he wrote and starred in the original *Rocky*, a sleeper which became the biggest hit of 1976. This box-office smash won an Academy Award for Best Picture as well as an Oscar for its director, John Avildson. In *Rocky II*, Stallone not only writes and acts but directs the film as well. The sequel, of course, lacks the novelty of the first film but it repeats the elements of Rocky's struggle to win which made the first film so likable and heightens them even more to become an entertaining second chapter in Rocky Balboa's life.

The film begins where the original ended with a review of the last round of the first boxing match between Rocky Balboa (Sylvester Stallone), "The Italian Stallion," and Apollo Creed (Carl Weathers), the current world heavyweight champion. The odds are against Rocky but he fights to the end and endears himself to boxing fans with a split decision whereby Apollo retains his crown. Rocky is catapulted to sudden fame, with which he has trouble coping, while Apollo loses credibility with boxing afficionados, most of whom believe that he fixed the fight.

After the match Rocky marries his girl friend Adrian (Talia Shire) and announces his retirement from boxing because the doctors warn him that more fights might blind him. He is deluged with offers to star in commercials, causing him to spend lavishly against future earnings. In his final and most expensive purchase, he buys a home in a situation which illustrates his ignorance of financial matters such as property taxes and mortgages and his innocent assumption that he and Adrian will never have a need for money.

Unfortunately, when Rocky begins shooting commercials he cannot read the cue cards and makes countless mistakes. After hours of retakes the director verbally abuses him so much that Rocky quits, thereby shutting himself out of future opportunities in television. He interviews for office jobs, but as the personnel officer questions him, it is revealed that Rocky does not have a high-school diploma, has no prior office experience, and has a limited vocabulary. The interviewer tactfully suggests that Rocky either take a manual labor job or return to boxing. After fruitlessly searching for other office work, Rocky finally accepts a job that Adrian's brother Paulie (Burt Young) finds for him at the meat packing plant where Paulie used to work. Rocky's working at the plant is an ironic turn of events because Paulie is now prospering in the loan shark collections work that Rocky used to do. Despite his fame, Rocky cannot exploit the moneymaking opportunities open to him because he has neither the business sense nor the broad education and experience needed to deal with these new circumstances.

In the meantime, Apollo broods over his hate mail, the consensus of which is that the match should have been awarded to Rocky. He argues with his trainer and business entourage about a rematch, refusing to listen to his manager's warning that he might lose. With his attention focused on repairing his battered reputation, Apollo initiates a humiliation campaign to shame Rocky back into the ring. The campaign opens with an advertisement in a Philadelphia newspaper calling Rocky "The Italian Chicken" and climaxes with a television interview in which Apollo insists that he would knock Rocky out in two rounds in a rematch.

Rocky accepts Apollo's challenge despite Adrian's disapproval and together with his trainer Mickey (Burgess Meredith), watches the first fight on film. Analyzing Apollo's weaknesses, Mickey devises a strategy to win in which Rocky must learn to fight right-handed in order to confuse Apollo and then in the last round switch to his strong left. Rocky begins training but loses heart when Adrian discourages him and he discovers that boxing right-handed is nearly impossible for him. During Rocky's training, Adrian delivers a premature baby who is healthy, but the birth causes Adrian to slip into a coma. Rocky refuses to train until Adrian regains consciousness even though the fight is very close. When she recovers, Rocky tells her he will give up boxing for her, but she changes her mind and now fully supports his decision to box. Rocky enthusiastically resumes training, this sequence shown in a montage ending with a repeat of Rocky's triumphant run around Philadelphia as seen in the earlier film.

The promoters dub the rematch "Superfight II," but Rocky surprises and then disappoints fans with his right-handed boxing. He survives the first fourteen rounds but is knocked down twice and is losing badly. In the last round he switches suddenly and catches Apollo off guard. He knocks Apollo down and then stumbles and falls himself. As both struggle to stand, the referee calls out the count. Apollo almost regains his balance but falls at the ninth count and Rocky, in the nick of time, stands and thereby takes the heavyweight championship away from Apollo. He shares his triumph with Adrian when he announces over television in typical "Rocky" fashion, "Yo, Adrian. I did it." Weathers and Stallone, both excellent actors, perform well together, especially in the well-choreographed fight sequence. All the moves are executed well and are very realistic: the punches, the pain, and the determination to win are reflected in their faces and bodies.

Stallone as a director performs adequately; he tries nothing new but does succeed in repeating successful scenes from *Rocky* and, by adding new twists, achieving a sense of expectation. For example, in the training sequence, Mickey uses new techniques to train Rocky especially since he is training right-handed. In the powerful jogging scene around Philadelphia, Rocky leads hundreds of young fans who shout and cavort around him as he again sprints throughout the city, in direct contrast to the first film's picture of the lone man running through the streets.

In knowing Rocky's character intimately because he parallels Stallone's own ups and downs, Stallone is adept in displaying him to his greatest advantage. This emphasis on Rocky, however, seems to leave little energy to develop the characters around him. Shire and Young are noted actors, but their performances are always in Rocky's shadow. Meredith, however, is shown well although too briefly as Rocky's trainer, spitting out boxing expertise and growling at his protégé, albeit with affection. The film might not be well rounded in character development, but Rocky's own personality is enough to carry the film alone.

The screenplay is well done although there are sluggish moments in the plot. If Rocky accepted one manual labor position, why could he not accept others? With his strong will, Rocky is uncharacteristically weak in giving up so easily after he is laid off. Also, when Adrian is unconscious in the hospital, the incident is dwelt upon too long, stalling the action rather than showing Rocky's devotion to his wife. Otherwise the dialogue is vibrant with the essence of Philadelphia street slang and spotlights gripping moments in boxing and the anguish as well as triumph behind the matches. Stallone has given film audiences a glimpse of the boxing world and has utilized the "rags to riches" formula well to produce an entertaining and highly successful sequel to the lovable *Rocky*. The financial, if not critical success of *Rocky II* has led to the development of another sequel, *Rocky III*, which will begin production in 1981.

Ruth L. Hirayama

THE ROCKY HORROR PICTURE SHOW

Released: 1975
Production: Michael White for Twentieth Century-Fox
Direction: Jim Sharman
Screenplay: Jim Sharman and Richard O'Brien; based on the play of the same name by Richard O'Brien
Cinematography: Peter Suschitzky
Editing: Graeme Clifford
Running time: 100 minutes

Principal characters:
Dr. Frank-N-Furter .... Tim Curry
Janet Weiss .... Susan Sarandon
Brad Majors .... Barry Bostwick
Riff Raff .... Richard O'Brien
Dr. Everett Scott .... Jonathan Adams
Columbia .... Little Nell (Nell Campbell)
Rocky .... Peter Hinwood
Eddie .... Meatloaf
Magenta .... Pat Quinn
Criminologist (Narrator) .... Charles Gray

The Rocky Horror Picture Show serves as a strong reminder that the word "fan" is an abbreviated form of "fanatic." For nearly as long as there have been motion pictures, of course, there have been fans, but in earlier days most fan adulation was directed toward individual personalities; the films themselves were, in a sense, only vehicles through which movie stars were presented to their adoring public. The phenomenon of the so-called "cult movie"—where a particular film is itself the primary object of devotion—did not really appear until the 1970's. *The Rocky Horror Picture Show*, while not the first such film, is certainly the most prominent (and profitable) example— a sort of *The Birth of a Nation* of cult movies.

The film originated as a stage musical, *The Rocky Horror Show*, glittery, tongue-in-cheek, highly theatrical spoof of science-fiction/horror films. The play opened at London's Royal Court Theatre in 1973 and was subsequently brought to Los Angeles by record producer Lou Adler. On the basis of the show's highly successful ten-month run at the Roxy Theater on the Sunset Strip, Adler secured backing for a film version. Jim Sharman, director of the original, was engaged to direct the adaptation and to cowrite the screenplay with Richard O'Brien, author and costar of the play. Most of the original cast, including O'Brien, re-created their roles for the film.

Except for the kind of "opening-up" common in stage-to-film transitions, *The Rocky Horror Picture Show* did not alter the play's basic structure. The film relates the strange adventures of Brad Majors (Barry Bostwick) and Janet Weiss (Susan Sarandon), a clean-cut, sexually repressed young couple. Inspired to become engaged by the wedding of two friends, they set out to visit the man who introduced them—Dr. Everett Scott (Jonathan Adams), their old science teacher. On a dark and stormy night somewhere in Ohio, their car breaks down and they are forced to seek refuge in a mysterious old castle. Greeted at the door by a hunchbacked handyman, Riff Raff (Richard O'Brien), and a strange domestic (later revealed as Riff Raff's sister), Magenta (Patricia Quinn), Brad and Janet are ushered into the castle, where they find themselves in the midst of the Annual Transylvanian Convention, a gathering of aliens from another galaxy. Before the couple can use the phone and be on their way, the Transylvanians' leader appears—Dr. Frank-N-Furter (Tim Curry), a "mad scientist" who is also a transvestite. He announces that he has discovered "the secret to life . . . itself," and insists that Brad and Janet stick around to witness the results of his latest experiment. His creation turns out to be Rocky (Peter Hinwood), a muscular blonde sex object created exclusively for the gratification of the bisexual Frank. No sooner has Rocky come to life than Eddie (Meatloaf), a greasy-haired throwback to the 1950's who had come to the castle as a delivery boy and remained to become one of the doctor's unsuccessful experiments, bursts from the "deep freeze" on his motorcycle. He wreaks havoc on the assemblage until Frank dispatches him with an icepick, much to the dismay of Frank's assistant and ex-lover Columbia (Little Nell), who had a crush on Eddie.

Brad and Janet spend the night at the castle—in separate rooms—and during the night Frank seduces them both; meanwhile, Riff Raff sadistically torments Rocky with a torch, driving him out into the darkness. Janet, wandering around in an excited state following her sexual awakening with Frank, stumbles across Rocky and seduces *him*. The next day, Frank is outraged to discover that Rocky has undergone heterosexual initiation; just as he begins to punish Riff Raff for his complicity in Rocky's defloration, Dr. Scott, in his wheelchair, shows up at the castle. Ostensibly searching for his nephew Eddie, Dr. Scott is recognized by Frank as a government investigator of UFO's. Fearing a conspiracy among his visitors, Frank immobilizes them, Rocky, and the rebellious Columbia. He dresses Brad, Janet, Rocky, and Columbia in costumes identical to his own—outrageous facial makeup, black stockings, garter belts, and high heels and reanimates them in a bizarre stage spectacle, starring himself. At the climax of their performance, Riff Raff and Magenta burst into the theater; Riff Raff announces that he has been promoted to leadership of the Transylvanians because of Frank's extreme decadence. Frank's attempts to explain are in vain, as Riff Raff kills him and Columbia with a laser gun. The aggrieved Rocky lifts Frank's lifeless body and, in a parody of the climactic moments of *King Kong* (1933), climbs with it to the top of the radio tower in the RKO/Radio logo which serves as the stage backdrop. Riff Raff then shoots him down and proceeds to beam the entire castle back to their home planet of Transexual in the galaxy of Transylvania. Brad, Janet, and Dr. Scott are left behind. (Interwoven throughout the above narrative are fourteen musical numbers, and an on-camera narration by a criminologist, played by Charles Gray, who explains the events as a sort of case history.)

Upon the film's initial release in the fall of 1975, critics familiar with the original play were virtually unanimous in declaring the inferiority of the adaptation. "Lacks the excitement and theatricality of the stage version," said one; typical comments were "self-consciously slick," "heavy-handed, unimaginative," and "labored." Other observers, lacking the perspective of comparison, were simply bewildered or actively offended by the film's blatant extolment of the joys of transsexuality and total pleasure. The critical reaction, coupled with Twentieth Century-Fox's half-hearted distribution of the film, resulted in an unsurprisingly tepid box-office performance, and the film seemed destined for oblivion. In spite of what the critics thought, however, an "underground" audience was developing, made up of a relatively small number of people who came to see the film again and again. The breakthrough came in April, 1976, when it was booked as a midnight show at the Waverly Theater in New York City.

Midnight exhibition on weekends was not a new concept, but most of the fare in previous years had been oddball, often aggressively tasteless films such as *Pink Flamingos* (1972) and *El Topo* (1971). The latter is often credited as initiating the practice, which was generally limited to major urban centers. *The Rocky Horror Picture Show* was different: more conventional in many ways than earlier "midnight films," it was nevertheless too bizarre for general audiences. In what can only be seen as a fortuitous blending of social, historical, and artistic circumstances, *The Rocky Horror Picture Show* established the phenomenon of the full-fledged "cult movie." The film was an immediate success at the Waverly, and other theaters across the country followed as the film began to build a wider audience. As word spread, the distributors took notice and put more prints into circulation; eventually, seeing *The Rocky Horror Picture Show* became a weekend "must" for people in hundreds of locations, from New York to Los Angeles to such unlikely spots as Bozeman, Montana, and Denton, Texas. At the end of 1979, Twentieth Century-Fox reported that the film had taken in the amazing sum of five million dollars in rentals for the year—five times the production cost, and five times the rentals accrued in the original release—for a total of nine million dollars to date; at that time, approximately two hundred prints were in use, compared to thirty-five only two years before, with each grossing at its full potential within the midnight-show format.

The real significance of *The Rocky Horror Picture Show*, however, is not to be found in its profit/distribution statistics—however remarkable—but in the nature of the response it elicits from its audiences. The basis for the "cult" is the fact that its fans return to see the film again and again, even (in extreme cases) hundreds of times; this practice breeds a total familiarity with the events and characters. In this respect, except perhaps for the frequency of repeat viewings, it is not very different from *The Wizard of Oz* (1939) or *Gone with the Wind* (1939). There is another factor, however: fans of *The Rocky Horror Picture Show* call it "the first audience-participation movie," and they go all-out to prove it. It is an understatement to say that half the show at any given screening of the film is not on the screen at all. Some people regularly attend the midnight shows dressed as their favorite character—which, considering the extremely bizarre nature of most of the film's characters, requires a great deal of effort. Costumed or not, however, once the film is under way, audience members abandon themselves completely to an uninhibited celebration; they sing along with the characters, toss objects at the screen and at one another (rice during the wedding scene and slices of toast when Frank proposed "a toast," for example), rush into the aisles to dance the "Time Warp," the Transylvanians' favorite dance, answer questions asked by characters in the film (or, more often, shout out questions which are then "answered" by the characters), and so on. For example, when Janet implores Brad "Where will you go? We're in the middle of nowhere!," the audience roars "Try the castle!"; Brad, "on cue," replies: "Didn't we pass a castle back down the road a few miles?" There is a "script" of sorts for the audience response, the basics of which are fairly easy to master even with a single viewing; the result is a sort of chaotic unison, like a drunken glee club. Those in costume position themselves beside and sometimes in front of the screen, and during the course of the film mimic the dialogue and mannerisms of their corresponding characters with remarkable fidelity. The more conservative-minded may find such behavior—not to mention the film itself—tasteless, disgusting, and perverse; the cultists, with a trace of irony, call it "good clean fun."

The media reports on *The Rocky Horror Picture Show* phenomenon tend to stress the pseudoreligious aspects of audience behavior. ("If I don't come to see it I feel guilty," one devotee is quoted as saying; another declares: "It's a way of life.") Although the emphasis on the word "cult" may conjure up visions of a unified spiritual experience, *The Rocky Horror Picture Show* exhibition is in fact more akin to a sporting event—closer to a riot than a ritual. The so-called "hard-core" fans—those who know and faithfully follow the "script"—constitute a minority; for many, the occasion is an excuse to scream epithets at the screen with little rhyme or reason. "Don't dream it. Be it" sing the characters in the final scene, and appropriate to that message (echoed throughout the film) of personal liberation, much of the audience response is blatantly and aggressively sexual. Also common is the type of "wise-guy" commentary which flows naturally in such an atmosphere. To their credit, however, the cultists are not close-minded about this sort of uninhibited improvisation; a particularly clever remark will be greeted with laughter and applause, and may eventually find itself incorporated into the ever-changing script. It is generally acknowledged that the exact nature of *The Rocky Horror Picture Show* audience varies widely from location to location, and even from one show to the next. These observations are evident if one attends showings at one of the film's longest-running engagements, the Tiffany Theater in Los Angeles—also the home of some of its wildest audiences.

With a film as insistently weird as *The Rocky Horror Picture Show*, questions of "art" are difficult at best, and the audience antics make an objective appraisal of the film's merits nearly impossible. This is due to the constant distraction from the screen and the audience's refusal to allow any dead space; the revelry severely hinders the viewer's perception of such matters as the film's pacing and, to some extent, simple comprehension of the plot. The mere existence of the cult (to say nothing of its tenacity) has rendered the initial negative critical reaction virtually irrelevant. Much of the criticism may have been justified, but the critics were obviously overlooking the qualities which have enabled the film not only to find an enthusiastic audience, but also to entertain it with great success for more than five years to date. In addition, the nature of the film's reception makes sociological analysis as fruitful and necessary as aesthetic evaluation.

It is fairly easy to identify the sources of the film's appeal. As is apparent from the opening song—"Science Fiction Double Feature," the lyrics mouthed by a gigantic pair of lips—*The Rocky Horror Picture Show* is both a tribute to and an affectionate send-up of science-fiction/horror films—not the sophisticated technological marvels of the 1970's, but the more basic mad scientist/rampaging creature potboilers of the 1930's, 1940's, and (especially) 1950's. These are films which, in spite of (or perhaps because of) their incredible lack of sophistication, hold a great fascination for children and adolescents, and many adults as well. Psychologists have observed that the most sympathetic characters in these films are often not the ostensible heroes, but the "monsters"—hounded by "civilization" (usually shown at its paranoid worst) and invariably losing out to the combined forces of Good and Science. *The Rocky Horror Picture Show* infuses this sentiment with a kinky sexuality and a youth-oriented antiestablishmentism, and turns the generic formula upside down. All the basic elements are present, but each is a little different: old dark castle (in Ohio), mad scientist (an alien transvestite), Transylvania (a distant galaxy), evil, scheming servants (who sing and dance a lot), a "monster" (who just happens to be a beautiful blonde sex-toy), and so on. Numerous scenes directly ape specific film moments, and the initiation of Brad and Janet into the joys of transsexuality is a sort of naughty variation on the familiar theme of innocents unlocking forbidden secrets—with the innocents in this case made the butt of all the jokes. With a generous dash of rock 'n' roll, the resulting concoction has something for everyone (or perhaps just everyone under thirty), questions of cinematic quality aside.

Neither the concept nor its filmic execution are particularly sophisticated, but the filmmakers more than make up for the shortcomings of the material with sheer imagination. The direction and cinematography are sometimes pointlessly flashy, but occasionally inspired; much reliance is placed on odd angles and distorting lenses, effectively complementing the bizarre goings-on. The somewhat pedestrian staging of the many musical numbers is balanced by the generally high quality of the music, the cleverness of the lyrics, and the exuberance of the performers.

It is with the performers, in fact, that much of the film's appeal lies. Bostwick and Sarandon are particularly good as symbolic embodiments of the repressed 1950's meeting the uninhibited 1970's, and eventually letting themselves go completely. The major contributions to the film, however, are those of Curry and O'Brien. O'Brien must be acknowledged not only for his portrayal of Riff Raff, but also as the primary creative force behind the film—author of the original play, music, and lyrics, and coauthor of the screenplay. The film's formidable central figure is Curry's Dr. Frank-N-Furter, however, an outrageous, perverse, splendidly theatrical *tour-de-force*. Curry, who originated the role on the London stage, plays his broad character with exquisite control; he has been called, variously, "half Auntie Mame, half Bela Lugosi," "a hybrid of Sophie Tucker and Mick Jagger," "a cross between Greer Garson and Steve Reeves," and "part David Bowie, part Joan Crawford, part Basil Rathbone." Each of these descriptions is entirely appropriate—it is a star turn to rank with the best. It is impossible not to quiver with "antici . . . pation" at his sultry invitation to "come up to the lab . . . and see what's on the slab." If and when *The Rocky Horror Picture Show* cult dies out—not an imminent prospect—Curry's incarnation of Dr. Frank-N-Furter will remain, an unforgettable memory in the minds of thousands.

Howard H. Prouty

ROMAN HOLIDAY

Released: 1953
Production: William Wyler for Paramount
Direction: William Wyler
Screenplay: Ian McLellan Hunter and John Dighton
Cinematography: Franz Planer and Henri Alekan
Editing: Robert Swink
Running time: 119 minutes

> *Principal characters:*
> Joe Bradley .... Gregory Peck
> Princess Anne .... Audrey Hepburn (AA)
> Irving Radovich .... Eddie Albert

Roman Holiday has the distinction of being simultaneously one of the most charming comedy-dramas of the 1950's, one of Audrey Hepburn's best roles, and one of eminent director William Wyler's best films. It had a successful combination of romance, comedy, drama, and beautiful location shooting which makes it popular still as a late-night television feature. The story, which is in part a romantic comedy, concerns a bored princess who leaves the stultifying confines of her royal guardians to find her prince charming in the outside world. It is the opposite of the usual Cinderella story. In this case the princess prefers to see how Cinderella lives, rather than the other way around.

For the role of the princess who must be equally believable as royalty and a street girl, Wyler chose British actress Audrey Hepburn, who was then virtually unknown in films. She combined at the same time the qualities of both a princess and a waif, a combination which appealed to Wyler and to audiences as well. After making *Roman Holiday*, for which she won an Academy Award as Best Actress, Hepburn remained a major star for almost fifteen years before her self-imposed retirement in 1967. (This retirement lasted until she reentered films in 1975 with *Robin and Marion*.) The other leading character, or, more accurately, prince charming, is played by Gregory Peck, already an established star, equally at home in heavy drama or light, romantic stories. The chemical blend of these two stars, combined with Wyler's talents, made an extremely popular film.

As the story begins, the audience learns that Princess Anne (Audrey Hepburn), who is the daughter of a King of an unnamed European country, is touring the capital cities of Europe. The lovely young princess is constantly being ordered about by her guardians, and even the maids, who all want her to act decorously and to be exposed only to things that are suitable for a princess. Anne, on the other hand, wants to experience life. She would like to meet some of the "real" people in Europe, so while in Rome, she sneaks out of her palatial quarters to experience life for herself. Unfortunately, her maid has put a sleeping powder in her nightly glass of warm milk, and the drowsy Anne is barely able to walk around. Taking pity on the girl, American reporter Joe Bradley (Gregory Peck), who is assigned to Rome and is perpetually broke, brings her back to his apartment to spend the night. The next day he discovers who she is, but hoping to get a big story that will help him with his career, he goes along with her subterfuge and convinces his photographer friend Irving Radovich (Eddie Albert) to loan him money so that he can entertain the princess.

The events of the next day prove exciting for Anne, who does not suspect that Joe knows her real identity. She spends the day doing exactly what she wants—not what others want her to do. She goes touring with Joe, has her hair cut, gets arrested over a minor incident, and winds up the evening dancing on a barge in the Tiber River. While on the barge some of the men charged with finding the princess spot Anne, and she makes up a story to Joe and Irving so that they will fight the men off. In a wonderfully funny scene all of the people on the barge engage in a melee which is highlighted by Anne's hitting one of the men over the head with a guitar. Meanwhile this, as well as other incidents of the day, has been photographed by the ever-present Irving. During the course of the day, Joe, who initially had only a mercenary interest in Anne, begins to fall in love with her. As he is becoming closer to her, however, Anne realizes that she must return to her other life, the only one that is real for her, that of a princess. She sadly leaves Joe and returns to her entourage, which has been keeping the news of her disappearance secret from the press.

On the next day, Princess Anne is scheduled to give a press conference. Now, feeling more confident and free than before, Anne overrules her advisers and invites the press to come closer to her. She sees Joe and Irving in the group. When it is their turn to be presented to the Princess, Irving presents the Princess with some "souvenier" photographs of her trip to Rome. As she looks through the pictures of her drinking, dancing, and fighting, she tells Irving that she will treasure them. For Joe and Anne, the only words are polite and seemingly impersonal. Although the ending of the film seems sad, it was a more realistic ending than the sort which is usually given in this type of story. In real life people usually realize, as Anne and Joe did, that a Royal Princess and a down-and-out reporter cannot marry and live happily ever after. The very impossibility of the situation makes the brief day of happiness shared by the two people all the more romantic and their parting more bittersweet.

There have been innumerable stories and films about commoners and royalty involved in love affairs, usually in a similarly light vein. In the 1940's, two film comedies concerned this subject, *Her Highness and the Bellboy* (1944) and *Princess O'Rourke* (1942), both of which ended with the princess running away and marrying her commoner lover. In *Roman Holiday*, Anne's brief experiences in the world outside of her insulated palace enable her to see her duty more clearly and to realize finally that in order to be a true princess she must be able to command and direct. Before her "escape" she had been a timid, complaining girl, frightened to oppose even the maids in their desire to make her do her duty. At the end she is a woman, self-confident and able to accept her position as a future ruler; she knows her duties and her rights. Thus, when she opposes her advisers and says "Rome" when asked what her favorite city of the tour is, she is asserting not only herself, but also her prerogative as a princess. For Joe, however, the story does seem sad. His situation shows no more improvement at the end of the story than it did at the beginning because his affection for Anne has made him give up the thought of selling her story to the newspaper. He is no richer and no better off in his career, and he has lost the girl he loves.

Although *Roman Holiday* is more a comedy than a drama, like some of Wyler's other films, it beautifully blends the two genres. This blending is also evident in Wyler's *Friendly Persuasion* (1956) and *Funny Girl* (1968), among others. The hopelessness of the love between Anne and Joe may be apparent, but it is the poignant way in which their brief love affair ends that makes it so human. A "happy" ending in the more traditional sense, in which the two lovers go off together, would have been much less effective.

Wyler's films consistently attempted to show down-to-earth characters faced with real-life situations, even when, as in *Roman Holiday*, the circumstances may on the surface seem out of the ordinary. *The Best Years of Our Lives* (1946), one of the greatest films of all time and one which brought an Academy Award to Wyler for Best Picture, certainly is an example of Wyler's own brand of "realism." His characters there, as well as in *Roman Holiday*, were multidimensional, not only serious or comic. Wyler was at his best when showing depth in his characters, from *Dodsworth* (1936) to *Funny Girl*. He was one of the most eminent directors of the twentieth century, although he is not usually mentioned in the same vein as the more celebrated *auteurs* Alfred Hitchcock and John Ford. Wyler, who died in July, 1981, received both the Irving Thalberg Memorial Award from the Academy of Motion Picture Arts and Sciences and the American Film Institute Life Achievement Award.

Patricia King Hanson

ROMEO AND JULIET

Released: 1936
Production: Irving Thalberg; released by Metro-Goldwyn-Mayer
Direction: George Cukor
Screenplay: Talbot Jennings; based on the play of the same name by William Shakespeare
Cinematography: William Daniels
Editing: Margaret Booth
Art direction: Cedric Gibbons
Interior decoration: Oliver Messel and Cedric Gibbons
Costume design: Oliver Messel and Adrian
Dance direction: Agnes De Mille
Music: Herbert Stothart
Running time: 127 minutes

Principal characters:

Romeo	Leslie Howard
Juliet	Norma Shearer
Mercutio	John Barrymore
Nurse	Edna May Oliver
Tybalt	Basil Rathbone
Lord Capulet	C. Aubrey Smith
Paris	Ralph Forbes
Friar Laurence	Henry Kilker
Benvolio	Reginald Denny
Lady Capulet	Violet Kemble Cooper
Peter	Andy Devine
Prince of Verona	Conway Tearle
Lord Montague	Robert Warwick
Lady Montague	Virginia Hammond

The 1936 film *Romeo and Juliet* was the third talking film based upon the plays of Shakespeare and the first reasonably successful one aesthetically. There had been numerous silent films from Shakespeare, but these made no attempt to deal with the language and relied solely upon condensed retellings of the plots. Theda Bara had played Juliet in a silent film, and Beverly Bayne and Francis X. Bushman had portrayed the lovers in another, but these are forgotten relics of an earlier age. Then in 1929, Douglas Fairbanks and Mary Pickford made *The Taming of the Shrew* as their first talking film. Pickford, America's Sweetheart, was hardly a convincing shrew, however, and Fairbanks played Petruchio as an athletic adventurer in the tradition of his Zorro, Robin Hood, and d'Artagnan. The film ran only sixty-five minutes but had "Additional Dialogue by Sam Taylor," hardly a collaborator equal to Shakespeare. In brief, the film was an unsatisfactory vehicle to launch Fairbanks and Pickford into sound; Shakespeare was subordinated to their images.

In 1935, Warner Bros. made a film of *A Midsummer Night's Dream*, based upon the celebrated stage version directed by Max Reinhardt. Reinhardt and William Dieterle shared the direction of the film, which in its efforts to be prestigious was merely pretentious, overblown without being entertaining. It is notable for some monumental miscasting: James Cagney plays Bottom like a gangster, Mickey Rooney's Puck is closer to Peck's Bad Boy, Dick Powell (then a baby-faced crooner) is clearly out of his element as one of the young lovers, Victor Jory (noted for playing carpetbaggers and stubble-bearded villains) is a strange Oberon, and most of the other performers were contract players with little or no experience in Shakespeare. Only Olivia de Havilland as Hermia and Joe E. Brown as Flute emerge with any credit.

So far, it looked as if film was the wrong medium for Shakespeare and as if the Bard could not be successful at the box office. M-G-M, however, had been remarkably successful in filming other classics, such as *David Copperfield* (1935) and *A Tale of Two Cities* (1935), and producer Irving Thalberg decided to make *Romeo and Juliet* with his wife Norma Shearer in the lead. Shearer had successfully portrayed Elizabeth Barrett Browning on screen in *The Barretts of Wimpole Street* (1934), and although she was now thirty-five years old, hardly the teenager of the Shakespearean play, Thalberg was certain that she could be a convincing Juliet and that the film would bring prestige to both of them. To direct, he picked George Cukor, who had done outstanding work with *Little Women* (1933) and *David Copperfield*. Not only did Cukor have a feeling for period films, but he excelled in getting outstanding performances from his players. After a career as a stage director, he had started in films as a dialogue director, and he was particularly noted for his subtle skill with actresses.

Robert Donat, then the preeminent romantic star of British cinema following his success in *The 39 Steps* (1935), was offered $100,000 to play Romeo but declined, in part because of his reluctance to work in Hollywood. The part then went to forty-six-year-old Leslie Howard, who had just played Hamlet on the New York stage. Forty-four-year-old Basil Rathbone, who had recently alternated played Romeo and Tybalt on stage opposite Katherine Cornell, was cast as Tybalt. Playing Mercutio was fifty-four-year-old John Barrymore, returning to the screen after a two-year absence during which he had had a physical and mental breakdown as a result of alcoholism. Cukor had directed Barrymore in two of his most memorable films, *A Bill of Divorcement* (1932) and *Dinner at Eight* (1933), and now gave him a chance for a comeback, although no longer as the star. Although Mercutio dies halfway through the play, the role can let the right actor steal the show up to that point. Laurence Olivier and John Gielgud were alternating playing Romeo and Mercutio on the London stage while the M-G-M film was in production.

The rest of the cast were M-G-M stock players, but the studio had a remarkable company of outstanding character actors who were better suited to Shakespeare than those Warners had cast in *A Midsummer Night's Dream*. The role of the nurse went to Edna May Oliver, who excelled at playing sharp-tongued but warm-hearted spinsters, such as Aunt March in *Little Women*, Aunt Betsy Trotwood in *David Copperfield*, and Miss Pross in *A Tale of Two Cities*. The venerable Sir C. Aubrey Smith, then seventy-three years old, brought an impressive authority to the role of Lord Capulet. Ralph Forbes, best-remembered as the youngest brother in the silent *Beau Geste* (1926), was an ardent Paris. Even adenoidal Andy Devine, who later made a career of playing comic sidekicks in Westerns, was effective as Peter, the Capulets' comic servant.

Talbot Jennings, who had received an Academy Award nomination as collaborator on the screenplay for *Mutiny on the Bounty* (1935), did the adaptation. This time there was no additional dialogue. The language is all Shakespeare's; Jennings simply adapted the play to the screen and made some judicious cuts. M-G-M thought so highly of his adaptation that the studio published it, together with notes on the production.

The story is so well known to all students of Shakespeare that a brief synopsis can suffice. In Renaissance Verona, the two leading families—the Montagues and Capulets—have long been engaged in a blood feud. No one remembers its origins, but members of each household engage in combat whenever they meet. The story opens with a brawl between them which is stopped by the Prince (Conway Tearle), who threatens death to any further violators of the peace. The heir to the house of Montague, young Romeo, has no concern with the feud; he has been enamored of the fair Rosaline, who does not requite his love. To divert him from his gloom, his companions Benvolio and Mercutio persuade him to accompany them in disguise to a masked ball being held by Capulet. There he sees Capulet's thirteen-year-old daughter Juliet and is instantly smitten with love for her. As they dance together, he tells her of his passion, and she responds in equal measure. Tybalt, Lady Capulet's fiery nephew, discovers the masquerade and wishes to kill Romeo, but Capulet forbids him to harm their uninvited guest. From Juliet's nurse, Romeo learns that the lady he loves is the daughter of his family's leading enemy; the nurse also informs Juliet that the man she danced with is a Montague.

After the ball, Romeo hides from the mockery of his friends and climbs the wall into the Capulet garden. When Juliet comes out onto her balcony, Romeo makes his presence known, proclaims his love, and plans with her to meet the next day and marry in secret. To this end Romeo enlists the aid of Friar Laurence (Henry Kilker). Juliet finds an excuse to go to his cell, and there they are wed. Returning alone to his household, however, Romeo encounters Tybalt, who challenges him to fight. Romeo declines to quarrel with his wife's kinsman, but Mercutio has no such qualms and takes up the challenge instead. As Romeo tries to break up the swordplay, Tybalt thrusts under his arm, gives Mercutio a mortal wound, and then flees. Enraged at the death of his dearest friend, Romeo encounters Tybalt again, engages him at sword's point, and kills him. Now it is Romeo's turn to flee, before the Prince can decree his death. Since the death of Tybalt was repayment for the death of Mercutio, however, the Prince merely banishes Romeo from Verona.

Before departing, Romeo spends one night of love in Juliet's chamber and then goes into exile. Juliet has not yet recovered from her grief when her parents, ignorant of her secret marriage, announce that she is to marry Paris, a young nobleman. When she refuses, her father goes into a rage and vows to disown her unless she will bow to his will. In this dilemma, Juliet consults Friar Laurence, who advises her to agree to the marriage. On the night before it, she is to take a drug that he gives her, which will make her appear to be dead for forty-two hours. When she is laid in the Capulet vault, he will send for Romeo, who will be with her when she awakens and will take her with him to safety. Overcoming her fears, Juliet drinks the potion. The messenger sent to Romeo miscarries, however; he is quarantined in a plague-stricken house and cannot deliver the letter. Meanwhile, Benvolio (Reginald Denny) has told Romeo that Juliet is dead. The grief-stricken husband buys a poison and returns secretly to Verona to have a last look at his wife and then kill himself. As he opens the tomb, the grieving Paris comes upon him; they fight, and Paris is slain. In the tomb, Romeo finds Juliet seemingly dead. He drinks the poison, kisses her, and dies. Friar Laurence then arrives, a few minutes too late. When Juliet awakens, the friar attempts to lead her from the tomb, but she sees Romeo. The noise of the approaching watch frightens Friar Laurence away, and Juliet, alone with her dead husband, kills herself with his dagger. The death of their children draws Montague and Capulet together in their grief, the feud is ended, and the star-crossed lovers are buried together.

The adaptation is faithful to Shakespeare's text, and the cuts are unobtrusive. Cukor and his cast treat the poetry with respect and create the most lyric of all film versions of *Romeo and Juliet*. The production values are outstanding and free the story from the limitations of the stage. Although the picture was filmed at Culver City, M-G-M re-created Verona on an opulent scale. The opening fight sprawls over a vast cathedral square, the masque at the Capulets' is colorful, with lively choreography, the Capulet garden is parklike, and the fights are spirited. Herbert Stothart's score contains authentic Renaissance music which adds to the period flavor.

Despite their ages, Leslie Howard and Norma Shearer are plausible, although obviously not the teenagers that Shakespeare intended. Shearer has a pre-Raphaelite look, and her costumes are copied from Botticelli paintings. Howard, although a lyric lover, seems a bit ethereal as the hot-blooded Romeo; he seems better-suited to a drawing room. As Mercutio, Barrymore is much too jaded, but he performs flamboyantly, perhaps delivering the bawdry a bit too broadly. As the butt of his humor, Oliver is more effective as the Rabelaisian nurse. Rathbone is the very devil of an insolent, fire-eating Tybalt. His is the definitive performance in the role, for which he was nominated for an Academy Award.

Although the acting is never less than good and is sometimes splendid, the casting suffers from the ages of the principal players, especially by contrast to two later films of *Romeo and Juliet*. In his autobiography, Errol Flynn claims that he wanted to play Romeo but could not get out of his contract to Warners. He would have looked perfect in the role, being only twenty-seven at the time, but Cukor doubted that Flynn could have handled the language.

Laurence Olivier, also in his twenties, would have been an ideal choice for Romeo, a role he was then playing on the London stage. Three months after Cukor's film opened, Olivier made his own debut in a Shakespeare film as Orlando in *As You Like It* (1936). He gave an admirable performance as the young lover, but the German accent of Elizabeth Bergner's Rosalind flawed an otherwise fine film. Olivier was disappointed with the production and said at the time that Shakespeare should not be filmed; nor was Shakespeare filmed again until Olivier's monumental production of *Henry V* (1944), which opened the way for subsequent films of Shakespeare by Olivier and others.

Among them were four films of *Romeo and Juliet*. Two of these were versions of the Prokofiev ballet, one made in Russia on location in the Crimea, with Ulanova as Juliet, the other a filming of the stage production with Nureyev and Fonteyn. In 1954, a British film of the play starred Laurence Harvey and Susan Shentall, with Flora Robson as the nurse and Sebastian Cabot as Capulet. This time, the lovers were in their early twenties, and the production benefited by being shot on location in Italy with superb color cinematography. Unfortunately, the script was less well preserved, and Mercutio's part was cut to practically nothing. By far the most popular film of *Romeo and Juliet* was directed by Franco Zeffirelli in 1968. This version too was enhanced by Italian locations and color, plus a fine score by Nino Rota. Zeffirelli directed the film in a fiery Mediterranean fashion that kept it moving at a headlong and passionate pace. Part of the film's popularity arose from the fact that actual teenagers played the leads. John Whiting as Romeo was eighteen; Olivia Hussey as Juliet was sixteen. Accordingly, the picture was immensely popular with teenage audiences. Indeed, Zeffirelli was so intent upon youthful casting that most of Romeo's companions look like a band of Cub Scouts.

Cukor admired the energy of Zeffirelli's version and its ability to engage young people but thought that many of the performers in it spoke their lines badly; he told Gavin Lambert that "Somebody said that Zeffirelli's Juliet sounded like a chemist's daughter from Wimbledon. . . . I didn't believe either Romeo or Juliet as coming from the nobility. They were just nice, sexy kids who carried on like mad. But then maybe *our* lovers were too stodgy."

Lambert suggested that Cukor's version had been inhibited by the idea of "cultural prestige" and that it was "short on passion." Cukor agreed that Shearer and Howard were not "really passionate actors" and concluded that if he were to remake *Romeo and Juliet*, he would "get the garlic and the Mediterranean into it" and give it the quality of desperation that Zeffirelli captured. Nevertheless, Cukor has maintained that he thinks his version is the best in terms of Shakespeare's poetry, and he is probably right. He never made another Shakespearean film, but in *A Double Life* (1947) he directed Ronald Colman and Signe Hasso in several key scenes from *Othello*, and Colman won the Academy Award for his performance.

As for *Romeo and Juliet*, it received admiring notices when it first appeared. Frank Nugent, reviewing it for *The New York Times*, found it "in perfect taste" and called it "a dignified, sensitive, and entirely admirable Shakespearean—not Hollywoodean—production." It made him conclude that "the screen is a perfect medium for Shakespeare"; certainly, it was the first satisfactory filming of Shakespeare, and on that ground it deserves acclaim. Seen today, it is still an impressive film, more traditional and less innovative than later Shakespeare films, but a solid work of cinematic art.

Robert E. Morsberger

ROOM FOR ONE MORE

Released: 1952
Production: Henry Blanke for Warner Bros.
Direction: Norman Taurog
Screenplay: Jack Rose and Melville Shavelson; based on the novel of the same name by Anna Perrot Rose
Cinematography: Robert Burks
Editing: Alan Crosland, Jr.
Music: Max Steiner
Running time: 97 minutes

Principal characters:

George "Poppy" Rose	Cary Grant
Anna Rose	Betsy Drake
Miss Kenyon	Lurene Tuttle
Jane	Iris Mann
Teenie	George Winslow
Jimmy-John	Clifford Tatum, Jr.
Trot	Gay Gordon
Tim	Malcolm Cassell
Ben Roberts	Larry Olson

Room for One More is a warm and witty comedy, adapted from the book of the same name by Anna Perrott Rose, that deals with her experiences in rearing foster children. A judicious selection from and condensation of Rose's book was made by screenwriters Jack Rose and Melville Shavelson to indicate the trials and triumphs of caring for disturbed and unwanted children while keeping essentially within the genre of the Hollywood family comedy.

We first see, however, not a family but a nursery full of infants and then find that a welfare worker, Miss Kenyon (Lurene Tuttle), is giving a talk to a women's group about how easy it is to find homes for little golden-haired girls but how much trouble it is to find foster homes for older children, many with physical or emotional problems. She finally directly asks the women in the group to accept some of the older children in their own homes and immediately receives a flurry of excuses. Only Anna Rose (Betsy Drake) is receptive to her plea, and Miss Kenyon takes immediate advantage of the situation to prevail upon her to accept Jane (Iris Mann), a thirteen-year-old who has been beaten and abused and has tried to commit suicide.

Before Jane enters the Rose household, however, we see what the household is like in a madcap scene. George (Gary Grant) the father, who is called "Poppy" by everyone in the family, is preparing a birthday cake for their youngest child, Teenie (George Winslow), while the other two children, Tim (Malcolm Cassell) and Trot (Gay Gordon), supervise the birth of a litter of kittens underneath the kitchen stove. Capping the confusion is the fact that a stray dog gets in and eats the birthday cake.

When Anna enters this scene with the idea of bringing another child into the family, George points out to her that as a city engineer on a fixed income ("and they fixed it good"), he is just able to provide for the family they have. Miss Kenyon and Anna, however, virtually force George to accept Jane for two weeks. George finds Jane so difficult and hostile that he is sure she is a lost cause and only wants to send her back to the home. "I've been trying to figure out who her parents might have been," he says. "Was John Dillinger ever married?"

Anna, however, thinks that Jane needs trust and self-confidence and arranges for her to baby-sit for the neighbors. Jane proves herself in a crisis when the parents are unexpectedly late getting home, and she gains self-confidence as well as some love and respect from the Rose family. When the two-week period is up and Miss Kenyon comes to take Jane back to the home, George changes his mind about wanting to get rid of her and silently carries her suitcase back up to her room.

Jane is not, however, the last addition to the Rose family. Just before a long-planned vacation at the beach, Anna informs George that they are going to take along a boy from the home. George is determined to do no such thing. He is told that the child is sullen, mean, and the worst student in summer school, but the moment George sees that the boy, Jimmy-John (Clifford Tatum, Jr.), wears braces on his legs, he does not hesitate and takes him along. He and the rest of the family soon have good reason to regret that decision. Jimmy-John will not talk to or play with anyone. Anna finally gets him to talk, but he fails to win much sympathy from the other children, especially when he kicks out the spokes of Tim's bicycle in frustration at not being able to ride it. The parents decide that it will be up to the children whether Jimmy-John stays in the family. Each child writes his or her decision on a slip of paper, and no one wants the problem child to stay in the family— until they find he cannot read. They then immediately take pity on him and change their minds, telling him they all voted for him to stay with them.

Each of the new children faces one major crisis during the rest of the film, and each overcomes it successfully. Jane is invited to the New Year's Prom by Ben Roberts (Larry Olsen) and is completely thrilled except that she has no suitable dress. Anna remakes one of her dresses to fit Jane, but Teenie's verdict is that the made-over dress "stinks." The other children, seeing that Jane must have a new dress, give up their Christmas presents so that there will be money to buy her one. When the problem has been overcome, however, they suddenly find that Ben will not take her to the prom because his parents do not think a foster child is good enough for their son. Tim has to take her to the dance while George goes to the Roberts' house and lectures the parents on bigotry. He then takes Ben to the dance, but Jane is already the most popular girl there, with all the boys eager to dance with her.

Jimmy-John, meanwhile, has taken an interest in the Boy Scouts and is determined to earn a Merit Badge in hiking to become an Eagle Scout. His final test for the badge is a ten-mile hike. Despite his crippled legs and a below-freezing day he manages to accomplish the task; the next to the last scene is the Boy Scout ceremony in the high school gymnasium in which he is made an Eagle Scout. To the assembled crowd he says, "I had a head start over most of you fellows; I had a chance to pick my own parents." The film ends with George and Anna alone together, having left the children with neighbors. "I won't know what to do with myself," says Anna. "*I* will," her husband replies.

Two main elements keep this film from being merely an oversimplified, sentimental story: the comedy and the sexual theme. The comedy ranges from the slapstick, such as a self-inflating raft suddenly inflating inside George's desk at work while his boss is talking to him, to sophisticated wit. Indeed, George has a witty remark for nearly every situation, but that certainly does not make him seem in control of these situations. Underlying the whole film is the sexual theme: Anna's continual concern for the children keeps her from having any free time to be alone with George. He mentions this throughout the film, and we see several times that George's plans for a romantic evening are interrupted by such incidents as Jimmy-John demanding a reading lesson so he can read the Boy Scout manual. George's reaction, however, is usually witty and good-humored.

The couple's main discussion of this problem is not in private but in a very public setting. Anna, George discovers, is lecturing to a civic group on the joys of rearing foster children, so George attends and—pretending to be just another member of the audience—rises and asks if she is not likely to neglect her husband. "In what way?" she asks. "How many ways are there?" he replies. She then responds that her husband should not feel neglected because he has the undying love and affection of every member of his family, including his wife, and George accepts this. His delight, however, is undisguised at the close of the film when he finally has his wife entirely to himself, having arranged for a neighbor to babysit with the children. The theme is handled lightly enough that it is never offensive but strongly enough to give another realistic dimension to the film.

Some present day viewers have remarked that Anna is too well-groomed to be a mother of five children who is living on a limited income, but one must realize that the Hollywood film of the 1930's, 1940's, and early 1950's was generally bound by a set of conventions that were accepted by its audience and insisted upon by its producers. In addition to the censorship of sexual matters, there were rules almost as rigid about the depiction of women and of family life. Virtually every actress, for example, unless she was playing a character part, was lighted attractively and always appeared with her hair and makeup in perfect order no matter what sort of physical or mental ordeal her character might be undergoing. Within these conventions a great many cinema masterpieces were produced as well as an even greater number of lesser but still enjoyable and entertaining works, such as *Room for One More*, that can be appreciated for their considerable virtues if their conventions are accepted.

Director Norman Taurog's skill in mixing comedy and sentiment is well demonstrated in this film, as is his great ability with child actors. They are neither too stiff nor too cute. Especially memorable because of his deep, fog-horn voice is Winslow (who was five years old at the time) as Teenie. As the parents, Grant and Drake (who were married to each other at the time) give excellent performances, even though the part was somewhat unusual for Grant, who generally played urbane characters without children. The entire film is well served by a surprisingly light score by Max Steiner.

Room for One More, incidentally, is called *The Easy Way* when it is shown on television, to avoid confusion with a television series, unrelated to this film, entitled *Room for One More*.

Julia Johnson

ROXIE HART

Released: 1942
Production: Nunnally Johnson for Twentieth Century-Fox
Direction: William A. Wellman
Screenplay: Nunnally Johnson; based on the play *Chicago* by Maurine Watkins
Cinematography: Leon Shamroy
Editing: James B. Clark
Choreography: Hermes Pan
Running time: 75 minutes

Principal characters:
Roxie Hart .... Ginger Rogers
Billy Flynn .... Adolphe Menjou
Homer Howard .... George Montgomery
Jake Callahan ....Lynne Overman
E. Clay Benham .... Nigel Bruce
Babe .... Phil Silvers
Mrs. Morton ....Sara Allgood
O'Malley ....William Frawley
Gertie ....Iris Adrian
Amos Hart .... George Chandler
Mary Sunshine .... Spring Byington

"This picture is dedicated to all the beautiful women in the world who have shot their men full of holes out of pique," announces a title at the beginning of *Roxie Hart*. The film rapidly proceeds to demonstrate what happened in 1927 when women did just that in Chicago. Newspaper headlines tell the lurid tales of many a murderess getting off lightly, provided she has a sharp lawyer, a tear in her eye, and an all-male jury. Roxie's is such a story as told by Homer Howard (George Montgomery) from a vantage point some time in the future to a bar full of listeners eager to hear about Cook County in the good old days.

In 1927, Homer, a neophyte reporter, teams up with old pro Jake Callahan (Lynne Overman), to cover yet another murder. It seems that Roxie Hart (Ginger Rogers) did or did not shoot a man, depending on who is talking and who is listening. Convinced by Jake that the road to fame lies in pleading guilty and getting a theatrical lawyer such as Billy Flynn (Adolphe Menjou) to take her case, Roxie goes to jail. There, while the matron Mrs. Morton (Sara Allgood) reads the paper and the ladies in the women's section stalk around in high heels and slinky black dresses, Roxie battles an old-timer for the unofficial "Queen of the Killers" title. Once successful, she is waited on by Mrs. Morton and the reporters, who hang on her every word. Suddenly Roxie leaps to her feet and begins an impromptu "Black Bottom" to show

how she used to make her living. The reporters join in, and soon Roxie has captivated Homer, who becomes her biggest fan and protector. Roxie's position in the jail is threatened by a real criminal, gravel-voiced Two Gun Gertie (Iris Adrian), who almost succeeds in winning her unofficial title. Roxie cleverly decides she might be pregnant, however, and Flynn demands that her trial start on Mother's Day.

The proceedings are a three-ring circus. Jake comments on the radio from the courtroom that Roxie is a "game little sharpshooter"; Flynn rehearses Roxie and orders her to act "demure" when she hikes her skirt above her knees; and Flynn affects a rumpled appearance to demonstrate that he is merely a "simple barefoot mouthpiece." The judge jumps from his bench to include himself in the pictures being taken of Roxie when she takes the stand; the jury sways in unison to get a better look at her legs; and Roxie conveniently passes out, leaving Flynn to conclude his summation with her in his arms, intoning "The defense rests!"

"You're yesterday's news!" a reporter tells Roxie as he rushes from the courtroom to cover the story of her ex-husband, Amos Hart (George Chandler), who has confessed to the crime of which she has been acquitted. For the last time the narrative switches to the tavern where bartender O'Malley (William Frawley, who also plays the jury foreman) toasts Roxie—"What a dame!"—and Homer lifts his glass "To the bad old days." Homer exits to find his wife and six children waiting for him in the car. He has married and tamed Roxie, who informs him in a deadpan manner that they will need a bigger car next year: she is expecting again.

One of the most telling sequences of the film depicts Roxie's parents back on the farm learning on the telephone of their little girl's plight. "They're going to hang Roxie," her father tells her mother. "Good," she rejoins, to which her father responds, "What did I tell you?" The scene encapsulates both Roxie's relationship with her family and the notion that these occurences were so commonplace that many people were not shocked when faced with a loved one's demise.

Roxie Hart is a satire on soap-opera themes, the sort of spoof director William Wellman had done so expertly before in *Nothing Sacred* (1937) and the kind of film other directors had done even better: for example, Howard Hawks in *His Girl Friday* (1942, from *The Front Page*, made in 1931). Both of these films were written by Ben Hecht; however, Nunnally Johnson's adaptation of Maurine Watkins' play *Chicago* is not nearly as adroit or acerbic as Hecht's originals. Neither is it as well cast, except for Menjou (who played editor Walter Burns in the first film version of *The Front Page*) as a fast-talking mesmerizer and something of a comic genius, and Overman, who makes Jake a cynical jokester of relentless practicality.

Montgomery is pleasant enough as Homer, but his role requires more than a firm jaw line and an emphatic manner of delivering lines. Rogers is both more and less than she should be. She is cute and snappy as the gum-chewing floozy, but Roxie would have benefitted from the vulgarity Rogers gave the part of Anytime Annie in *42nd Street* (1933). She tries to be appealing and to some extent she succeeds, but she also wants to be liked as an actress. Her acting is calculated, so that she becomes a comment on the film she is in. Rogers is not really a raunchy hell-raiser, nor is she as decorous as the last scene would have the audience believe—she is something in between.

Wellman is willing to go all out in attacking corruption, the scandal-mongering media, and even naïve young women like Roxie whose only real sin is that they want attention. He does not go far enough, however; *Roxie Hart* would be more successful as a fast, no-holds-barred farce in the style of *Twentieth Century* (1934) and *His Girl Friday*, with characters developed by exposition rather than by slowing down the film to make points about individual eccentricities. Still, the movie is enjoyable and definitely has some memorable moments, such as Rogers hiking her skirts and tap dancing on the metal staircase of the jail for Montgomery while she figures out what her next ploy will be.

It seems that Wellman wanted *Roxie Hart* to be a ferocious parody, but he was constrained by Johnson's somewhat timid script. Wellman is best with brassy, low-life material—*Public Enemy* (1931), for example—or more socially aware topics—such as *The Ox-Bow Incident* (1942) and *The Story of G. I. Joe* (1944)—but he often allows a wide streak of sentimentality to creep into even his toughest movies. Unfortunately, in *Roxie Hart* it weakens the thrust that should be this film's chief virtue.

Judith M. Kass

RUGGLES OF RED GAP

Released: 1935
Production: Arthur Hornblow, Jr. for Paramount
Direction: Leo McCarey
Assistant direction: A. F. Erickson
Screenplay: Walter de Leon and Harlan Thompson; based on Humphrey
   Pearson's adaptation of the novel and play of the same name by Harry
   Leon Wilson
Cinematography: Alfred Gilks
Editing: Edward Dmytryk
Art direction: Hans Dreier and Robert Odell
Costume design: Travis Banton
Music: Ralph Rainger and Sam Coslow

Principal characters:
Marmaduke Ruggles	Charles Laughton
Effie Floud	Mary Boland
Egbert Floud	Charles Ruggles
Prunella Judson	Zasu Pitts
Honorable George Van Bassingwell, The Earl of Burnstead	Roland Young
Nell Kenner	Leila Hyams
Ma Pettingill	Maude Eburne
Mrs. Belknap-Jackson	Leota Lorraine
Charles Belknap-Jackson	Lucien Littlefield
Lisette	Alice Ardell
Clothier	Armand Kaliz
Barber	Rolfe Sedan
Jeff Tuttle	James Burke
Jake Henshaw	Clarence Wilson

Americana as a genre has been well served by the various versions of
Ruggles of Red Gap, originally a novel and a 1915 play by Harry Leon Wilson.
In it, a British and very proper gentleman's gentleman is both humanized and
Americanized in the not so wild West just after the turn of the century. The
definitive version is the 1935 production starring Charles Laughton. Preceding
it were a 1918 silent directed by L. C. Windom with Taylor Holmes and a
1923 silent directed by James Cruze starring Edward Everett Horton. The
fourth screen adaptation was rewritten for Bob Hope and Lucille Ball and
turned into a musical Western, *Fancy Pants* (1950), directed by George Marshall.

For the Laughton film, at least two of the characters are combined—the
Earl and the Honorable George—into one role, played by Roland Young.

Also, Ruggles is made to recite Lincoln's Gettysburg Address in such a stirring manner that the scene had no comic climax, and the native-born Americans stood in awe before being offered free drinks. Director Leo McCarey, who had worked early in his career on the comedies of Stan Laurel and Oliver Hardy and Charley Chase and who would go on to make both sophisticated comedies and sentimental dramas, knew how to blend the comic and dramatic elements of this scene. Another outstanding interlude occurs late in the film when hostess Nell Kenner (Leila Hyams) teaches the Earl how to accompany her on "Pretty Baby." This scene was not ad-libbed by its participants, but it works so well that it seems as if it were.

A title reads "It was Paris—In the spring of 1908." The hungover Earl of Burnstead, the Honorable George Van Bassingwell (Roland Young), is awakened by his very efficient manservant, Marmaduke Ruggles (Charles Laughton). After asking him how he is, the Earl informs Ruggles that he is to go to America, since the Earl has lost him in a poker game with wealthy lumber-cattle baron Egbert Floud (Charles Ruggles). Ruggles, taking the news with little emotion, remarks that North America is quite an unclaimed country. Egbert, "Sourdough" to his friends, enters and shakes Ruggles' hand, explaining that it is the idea of his social-climbing wife Effie (Mary Boland) to bring him back home with them. Egbert is an easy going man who can be pushed only so far, except by his overbearing spouse.

The Earl sadly says it should be fun dressing himself as he bids Ruggles goodbye. Effie, determined to make Egbert a gentleman, has Lisette, a French maid (Alice Ardell), take out all of his unfashionable plaid suits and burn them. When she brings Ruggles along to a clothier (Armand Kaliz) to advise Egbert on the proper attire, the newly won servant first explains to the salesman that Egbert was forced to run out of his burning building "in the altogether" and had borrowed his suit from bystanders. Egbert almost runs off after he is decked out in morning clothes, complete with top hat. Next, however, he is taken to a barber (Rolfe Sedan) who clips the tips of Egbert's mustache, who retaliates with the same procedure on his tormentor.

Once Effie is out of sight, Egbert tells Ruggles to forget about going to an art gallery and to accompany him to his favorite outdoor café. Ruggles informs him that he cannot sit with a superior, but Egbert declares that they are equals and dubs him "Colonel." An old pal from back home, Jeff Tuttle (James Burke), is driving by in a carriage and gets an enthusiastic greeting from Egbert, who begins riding on his back. The stuffy Ruggles retreats from this scene and has to be coaxed back by Egbert. Showing off his French, Jeff orders "viskey sodah" and soon all three are drunk, with a smiling Ruggles letting out a loud "yahoo" and a "yip-yip-yippy." Egbert and Ruggles get in and out of a hansom cab because neither wants to be first, and the three wind up on a merry-go-round, with the two Westerners pretending to be riding wild broncos and a grinning Ruggles sitting it out.

Approaching the Flouds's apartment, Ruggles is still yahooing and attempting to ride Jeff's back. Egbert explains to Effie that drink brings out the beast in Ruggles, who forced him and Jeff to imbibe by threatening them with a long knife. Effie attempts to berate Ruggles, who grabs her as he sinks, chuckling, to the floor. Next morning, Effie voices her disappointment in Ruggles, who imagines the West to be full of wild Indians (courtesy of superimposed stock footage) as he pours another drink.

On the train to the Floud home in Red Gap, Washington, Ruggles carefully folds Egbert's breast pocket handkerchief, which the latter uses to blow his nose. Effie's sister (Leota Lorraine) and her husband, aristocratic Charles Belknap-Jackson (Lucian Littlefield), greet them at the station, but Egbert saves his affection for his earthy mother-in-law, cigarette-smoking Ma Pettingill (Maude Eburne). Despite the division in the family, they all live in a huge mansion, with Ma and Egbert putting up with the snobbish members of the family. On the way to give editor Jake Henshaw (Clarence Wilson) the story of Effie's reception to show off their new servant, Egbert and Ruggles stop off at a beer party given by pretty Nell Kenner.

Jake is at the "bash" and gets an exclusive story of "Colonel" Ruggles of the British Army, while Ruggles turns his attention to widow Prunella Judson (Zasu Pitts) and the two dance. Belknap-Jackson interrupts them, orders Ruggles to return home, and kicks him when the servant says he had better stay with Egbert. In kicking him back, Ruggles makes an enemy. Effie is ready to fire Ruggles when Ma gleefully shows her Jake's story about their "honored house guest," and the society women arrive to meet the colonel.

Now behaving in a manner to which he is unaccustomed, Ruggles rides over to Mrs. Judson's and attempts to jump her picket fence. Once inside her ranch house, he deals with her dog and then offers tips on cooking, one of his many talents. When Ma and Egbert leave for awhile, Belknap-Jackson fires Ruggles, but at the Silver Dollar Saloon, he is rehired by Egbert and Ma. Mrs. Judson is happy to learn of Ruggles' true identity, as she had felt inferior to him when she thought he was a Colonel. Egbert attempts to recite the Gettysburg Address in defense of Ruggles' rights; but when he falters the servant continues, delivering it in such a beautifully moving way that the patrons are almost speechless.

Ruggles decides to open a restaurant, The Anglo-American Grill, with his friends' help. Egbert attempts to assert himself with Effie, and Ruggles is dismayed to learn that the Earl is coming to reclaim him. The Earl prefers to miss Effie's dinner party in his honor and winds up at Nell's, where he is completely charmed by her. Ruggles' decision to run the Grill meets with skepticism from the Earl when he arrives late for the opening with Nell, to whom he is now engaged. Moved to throw out the nasty Belknap-Jackson, Ruggles feels he has failed. He then joins in the singing of "For He's a Jolly Good Fellow" before realizing it is for him. Misty-eyed, he thanks the patrons and then is pushed into Prunella's arms.

McCarey used the best talent in all departments, with Alfred Gilks as cinematographer, Walter de Leon and Harlan Thompson as scenarists, and Humphrey Pearson doing the adaptation. Ralph Rainger and Sam Coslow oversaw the production of the musical numbers, which consisted of renditions of such old favorites as "By the Light of the Silvery Moon" and "Pretty Baby." Travis Banton did the costumes, while the art direction was executed by Hans Dreier and Robert Odell. Two directors also worked in other capacities on the production: A. F. Erickson as assistant director and Edward Dmytryk, beginning his own directorial career that year with a low-budgeted Western called *The Hawk* (or *Trail of the Hawk*), as editor.

Winner of the Academy Award for Best Actor for *The Private Life of Henry VIII* (1933), Laughton really grows into the Ruggles' character and appears to be having as good a time acting it as we are watching it. He begins in a very stiff fashion as the unruffled Ruggles, servant to the Earl, neatly underplayed by Young. From there, he progresses to tipsy and pixilated drunk, loyal friend and eventual lover, a bogus colonel, a man torn between duty and freedom, and finally, someone in charge of his own affairs, crying at a display of true friendship toward him. Laughton may steal the film, but he has plenty of competition from an expert assortment of comics in Young, Ruggles, and his frequent costar Boland (in a number of marital comedies), Pitts, Eburne, and Littlefield, and a wide sampling of familiar character actors, including Burke, Sedan, Wilson, Victor Potel, Frank Rice, Dell Henderson, and Sarah Edwards. Not as well remembered as the other leads, Hyams shines as the good-hearted hostess Nell. An M-G-M ingenue, Hyams was featured in films as early as 1924 and had leads in *The Big House* (1930), *Freaks* (1932), *The Big Broadcast* (1932), and *Island of Lost Souls* (1933) before winding up in independent films and "B"-features.

John Cocchi

THE RULING CLASS

Released: 1972
Production: Jules Buck and Jack Hawkins for Avco Embassy
Direction: Peter Medak
Screenplay: Peter Barnes; based on his play of the same name
Cinematography: Ken Hodges
Editing: Ray Lovejoy
Running time: 154 minutes

> *Principal characters:*
> Jack, 14th Earl of Gurney ....Peter O'Toole
> Bishop Lampton .... Alastair Sim
> Tucker .... Arthur Lowe
> 13th Earl of Gurney ....Harry Andrews
> Lady Claire Gurney ....Coral Browne
> Dr. Herder .... Michael Bryant
> McKyle .... Nigel Green
> Sir Charles Gurney .... William Mervyn
> Grace Shelley .... Carolyn Seymour

One of the most outrageous, offensive, and magnificent film satires was unleashed upon the public in 1972, in *The Ruling Class*. The British feature merrily exposed the depravity of the English aristocracy, the hypocrisy of organized religion, and that heinous animal that is man. Flamboyantly directed by Peter Medak and starring Peter O'Toole, it became one of the most controversial films of the 1970's and one of the most wicked satires in cinema history.

The film opens to expose the favorite nocturnal perversity of the 13th Earl of Gurney (Harry Andrews). Relaxing after thundering a law-and-order speech in London, he returns to the bedroom of his magnificent estate; dons long underwear, a ballet tu-tu, and a three-cornered hat; puts his head in a silk noose; and swings about his bedroom. On this night, however, he tips over the ladder on which he usually alights and hangs himself. There is shock when Bishop Lampton (Alastair Sim) reads the will. To the Earl's brother Sir Charles (William Mervyn), Charles' spouse Lady Claire (Coral Browne), and their feebleminded son Dinsdale (James Villiers), he leaves nothing. Aside from thirty thousand pounds for the butler Tucker (Arthur Lowe)— who promptly begins drinking and insulting the family—the title and estate will pass entirely to the Earl's son Jack (Peter O'Toole), who has spent the past eight years in a lunatic asylum.

Jack arrives at the estate sporting a beard, flowing blonde hair, monk's robes, and tennis shoes. He is convinced that he is Jesus Christ. To the family's horror, Jack soon places a huge wooden cross in the living room upon which he habitually hangs. He also preaches love, rides a tricycle, claims he is wed to the Lady of the Camellias, and plans to give away the Gurney fortune.

Sir Charles takes action. Hoping to institutionalize Jack again after he has fathered a new heir, he schemes to wed Jack to his own mistress, socially ambitious Grace Shelley (Carolyn Seymour). When she first meets her proposed bridegroom, she is dressed as Camille and singing a selection from *La Traviata*. Grace soon falls in love with Jack, however, and informs him of Sir Charles' plot. Jack forgives her, rides his tricycle into her marriage boudoir, and impregnates her. On the night their son is born, psychiatrist Dr. Herder (Michael Bryant) brings to the estate McKyle (Nigel Green), a raving lunatic who believes he is the "Electric Christ." Claiming that the true God is a God of wrath for "strong stomachs," the "High Voltage Messiah" chews glass bottles, horrifies Jack with a terrible repertoire of electronic shocks, and traumatizes the heir until he no longer believes he is Jesus Christ.

Instead, Jack now believes he is Jack the Ripper. As the Ripper, he knifes Lady Claire and blames the murder on Tucker; drives Sir Charles, Dr. Herder, and Bishop Lampton to an asylum; takes a seat at the House of Lords, where he delivers a speech in praise of bigotry and vengeance that wins a standing ovation from his peers; and returns to the estate, where he promptly kills his loving wife Grace. The baby, obviously inheriting the family curse, cries out "I AM JACK!" as the film ends.

The Ruling Class was Britain's official entry at the 1972 Cannes Film Festival. United Artists secured rights for release in the United States, but when that corporation announced plans to edit extensively the 154-minute feature, the producers balked, and Avco Embassy obtained the rights. In the fall of 1972, *The Ruling Class* had its premiere in the United States (trimmed of only six minutes and rated "R") and created enormous controversy. *Newsweek* condemned the film as "sledgehammer satire" and "odious," while *Variety* lauded it as "brilliantly caustic"; *New York* praised it as "fantastic fun," and the *Los Angeles Times* derided it as ". . . snail-slow, slag-heavy, shrill and gesticulating."

Indeed, *The Ruling Class* is more than satire; it is a celluloid nightmare, absurd, horrible, fascinating, and disturbing. Director Peter Medak crams the picture with riveting nonsense: a gorilla crashes through a window to tip his hat; O'Toole bursts into a duet of "My Blue Heaven" with Seymour or leads fox hunters in an evangelistic rendition of "Dem Bones." The film rampages from silly humor to repellant spectacle to true horror. Yet the film is saved from total distaste by the artistry of the cast: the beautifully "bitchy" Browne, who caustically portrays Lady Claire; Lowe as the ever unruffled Tucker; and Mervyn as the glowering Sir Charles. Sir Charles delivers the film's most outrageous line: finding the corpse of his slain wife on the floor, he looks into the camera and intones, "Very well. Who is the impudent clown responsible for this?" with the controlled wrath of a schoolmaster.

The Ruling Class

The most outstanding performance is O'Toole's. As "Jesus Christ," out-fitted with a girlishly curly blonde wig, he is both divinely mad and poignantly heartbreaking; as Jack the Ripper, shorn of his locks and icily austere, he is a bloodthirsty, terrifying obscenity. *Time* praised O'Toole's 14th Earl of Gurney as "a performance of such intensity that it may trouble sleep as surely as it will haunt memory—funny, disturbing, finally devastating." For his incredible performance that was miraculously free of blasphemy and awesomely filled with bravado, O'Toole received his fifth Academy Best Actor nomination, but the 1972 Oscar went to Marlon Brando for his performance in *The Godfather*.

The Ruling Class did not prove to be an exceptional box-office success. It employs a type of satire not to all moviegoers' liking. At times it demands audience attention in the manner that a snake enraptures a doomed bird, and its statement that a Jack the Ripper would be more assured of success in the contemporary world than would Jesus Christ is by no means a comfortable one. Yet for its excesses, the picture has more than its share of creativity, imagination, and flair. *The Ruling Class* remains an unforgettably chilling cinema lampoon, perhaps best described by O'Toole as "a comedy with tragic relief."

Gregory William Mank

THE RUSSIANS ARE COMING, THE RUSSIANS ARE COMING

Released: 1966
Production: Norman Jewison for United Artists
Direction: Norman Jewison
Screenplay: William Rose; based on the novel *The Off-Islanders* by Nathanial Benchley
Cinematography: Joseph Biroc
Editing: Hal Ashby and J. Terry Williams
Running time: 126 minutes

Principal characters:
Walt Whittaker	Carl Reiner
Elspeth Whittaker	Eva Marie Saint
Lieutenant Rozanov	Alan Arkin
Link Mattocks	Brian Keith
Norman Jones	Jonathan Winters
The Russian Captain	Theodore Bikel
Fendall Hawkins	Paul Ford
Luther Grilk	Ben Blue
Kolchin	John Phillip Law
Alison Palmer	Andrea Drome
Alice Foss	Tessie O'Shea
Muriel Everett	Doro Merande
Airplane Mechanic	Michael J. Pollard
Pete Whittaker	Sheldon Golomb
Annie Whittaker	Cindy Putnam

A zany contemporary comedy about a Russian submarine that runs aground off the coast of a New England island, *The Russians Are Coming, The Russians Are Coming* was produced at a time when America was still feeling the effects of the Cold War years and the Cuban missile crisis. It was from the severe tension and paranoia of these years that Norman Jewison's spoof of Soviet-American relations created a much-needed fresh perspective and comic relief.

Set during the balmy September end-of-summer days in Gloucester, Massachusetts, the farcical film deals with the riotously funny chaos and confusion that occurs when a Russian submarine, manned by a Captain (Theodore Bikel) eager to get a closer look at America in his telescope, gets stuck on a sandbar four hundred feet off the coast of the sleepy vacation island. Leading a nine-man party in search of a boat to help free the vessel, the petrified Lieutenant Rozanov (Alan Arkin) at first ludicrously pretends to be Norwegian. He and his team surround an isolated old beach home inhabited by a lovable but irascible New York comedy writer, Walt Whittaker (Carl Reiner), his pretty and intelligent wife Elspeth (Eva Marie Saint), their two world-weary children, Pete (Sheldon Golomb) and Annie (Cindy Putnam), and their beautiful eighteen-year-old babysitter Alison Palmer (Andrea Drome).

Leaving Kolchin (John Phillip Law), a handsome and romantic but tense young sailor, to watch over the half-curious, half-frightened Whittaker group, Rozanov and his men steal an old beat-up car from the town's postmistress, Muriel Everett (Dora Merande), who in turn telephones the gossipy switch-board operator Alice Foss (Tessie O'Shea), who makes sure everyone in town knows about the arrival of the Russians. With the lack of communication and the escalated rumors and suspicions, the terrified town soon expects a full-scale invasion. Meanwhile, Walt Whittaker escapes from the timorous Kul-chin, finds Rozanov and the other sailors, and finds them a boat. Rozanov then goes back to the Whittaker house to get Kulchin, who has fallen in love with Alison.

In the confusion, the Russian Captain (who has taken his submarine into the small harbor) threatens to blow up the town unless Rozanov and Kulchin are returned to him; the tension in the town builds as the crowds of villagers stand around the harbor. Suddenly, a small boy slips from his "lookout" position high up in the church steeple and precariously hangs over the ledge. All at once, in the interest of the frightened and crying boy, political riffs are dropped and humane values take over; the islanders and the Russian sailors unite, form a huge human pyramid, and rescue the small child. A new spirit of love and goodwill abounds, and to protect the Russians from the United States Naval aircraft circling overhead, a group of villagers in their small boats accompany the submarine into safe waters at Elspeth's suggestion. The movie ends on an uplifting and upbeat note, with a feeling of mutual coop-eration and peaceful coexistence.

The Russians Are Coming, The Russians Are Coming was based on the 1961 novel *The Off-Islanders*, written by Nathanial Benchley, the son of humorist Robert Benchley and the father of novelist Peter Benchley (who later wrote his own famous story, *Jaws*, about a group of isolated islanders fearful of an outside threat). The screenplay, however, was written by William Rose, who wrote the equally zany *It's a Mad, Mad, Mad, Mad World* (1963) as well as *The Secret of Santa Vittoria* (1969) and *Guess Who's Coming to Dinner?* (1967).

What really makes this Cold War comedy work, however, are the excellent performances. Arkin is superb as Lieutenant Rozanov, the nervous Russian sailor; indeed, with his Russian accent and multinuanced facial expressions, Arkin incorporates humor, cunning, charm, and compassion all at once into his characterization. *The Russians Are Coming, The Russians Are Coming* was Arkin's film acting debut, and the versatile performer went on to create a variety of interesting roles—the proud Puerto Rican papa in *Popi* (1964), the psychopathic killer in *Wait Until Dark* (1967), the lonely deaf-mute in *The*

Heart Is a Lonely Hunter (1968), and the timid dentist in *The In-Laws* (1978). His versatility has made him an equally effective villain or buffoon, and he has wisely chosen to go from film to film without being categorized as either a comic or a straight dramatic actor. Perhaps because of his success initially here, however, most people tend to think of him as a comedian, or comic actor, most often playing ethnic parts.

There are numerous other actors in the film who add to the fun. Jonathan Winters plays nutty Norman Jones, the dithering deputy under the command of Link Mattocks (Brian Keith), the level-headed, if dour, sheriff. Paul Ford plays the blustery war veteran Fendall Hawkins, a sword-swinging legionnaire who appoints himself civil defense leader. Ben Blue plays the drunk Luther Grilk, the village's erstwhile Paul Revere, and Michael J. Pollard plays a goofy airplane mechanic. Such characters lead Rozanov to the inescapable conclusion that "Everybody on American island is complete and utter not sane."

The Russians Are Coming, The Russians Are Coming satirizes American invasion hysterics in a way that no other film has been able to do. It is a healthy look at East-West relations in the same vein as such films as Billy Wilder's *One, Two, Three* (1961), Peter Ustinov's *Romanoff and Juliet* (1961), and Peter Sellers' *The Mouse That Roared* (1959), without taking sides, or making one group any more redeeming or ridiculous than the other. In fact, Jewison's film is one of the few that actually makes the Soviets "nice," rather than ridiculous or monstrous. At the end of the film, all of the people are shown to be caring, down-to-earth people.

The film was nominated for four Academy Awards, including Best Picture, Best Editing, Best Screenplay, and Best Actor for Arkin. It did not win any awards, but it did do very well at the box office and is occasionally revived on television. Although the Cold War theme may be dated, the comic performances are still highly enjoyable.

Leslie Taubman

SABOTEUR

Released: 1942
Production: Frank Lloyd and Jack H. Skirball for Universal
Direction: Alfred Hitchcock
Screenplay: Peter Viertel, Joan Harrison, and Dorothy Parker; based on an
  original story by Alfred Hitchcock
Cinematography: Joseph A. Valentine
Editing: Otto Ludwig
Running time: 108 minutes

Principal characters:
Barry Kane	Robert Cummings
Patricia Martin	Priscilla Lane
Fry	Norman Lloyd
Charles Tobin	Otto Kruger
Mrs. Van Sutton	Alma Kruger
Mr. Freeman	Alan Baxter

"The Wrong Man" is the hero of many Alfred Hitchcock films. In *Saboteur*,
Barry Kane (Robert Cummings) is not guilty of sabotage, yet he is pursued
as though he were the man who set a murderous fire at a munitions plant.

The usual police or detective story is a plot of crime, pursuit, and punishment. The crime creates an imbalance in the world which can be remedied
only by reversing the original aggression. Order is restored at the end, when
the detective confronts the criminal. The one who has victimized others is
now the detective's victim—the victim of justice. In *The 39 Steps* (1935),
North by Northwest (1957), *Saboteur*, and, of course, *The Wrong Man* (1957),
Hitchcock complicates this classical pursuit and justice plot through the introduction of a third party—the innocent man falsely accused of a crime. Because
the representatives of official justice—the police or the FBI—are uninformed,
slow, or absent, the "wrong man" must do their job for them; the amateur
must replace the professionals. The wrong man has no choice but to play the
role of detective, pursuing the real criminal in order to prove his innocence.
Legal justice is distant, only at the edge of the plot. In contrast, the hero
lives at the heart of the dangerous ground, threatened by both the real criminal
and the police.

Critics who stress the influence of Hitchcock's Jesuit education upon his
work point out the Catholic overtones of the victim-hero plot. The persecution
and suffering of the guiltless Jesus is probably the "wrong man" story most
central to our culture. Although Hitchcock is clearly not filming an explicit
imitation of Christ, he has tapped the dark power of this ancient theme,
brightening it considerably in the process.

As Hitchcock told French director/critic François Truffaut, Robert Cummings "belongs to the light-comedy class of actors." The director wanted an actor of more "stature" to play his wrong man, perhaps Gary Cooper. The lightness that Cummings brings to the role of the accused saboteur, however, is displayed by almost all the Hitchcock heroes in the so-called picaresque films. Like Robert Donat in *The 39 Steps* and Cary Grant in *North by Northwest*, Cummings projects a resilience and a clever opportunism. The picaresque hero is essentially a charming rogue, never at a loss for words or action. Indeed, he is something of a chameleon—an actor quick to assume whatever role will get him out of the jam. Barry Kane first masquerades under the name of his dead friend, then pretends to be the *real* saboteur in order to infiltrate the Nazi ring. He acts spontaneously, not by plan. In his most audacious performance, Kane poses as a member of the upper classes at a charity ball, temporarily evading his pursuers by auctioning his rich hostess' jewelry to the highest bidder. Confronted with such a nefarious character, it is small wonder that the heroine, Patricia Martin (Priscilla Lane), refuses to believe that Kane is the innocent man he claims to be.

Scenes similar to the charity ball are screened in a number of Hitchcock films. Paradoxically, the hero is most alone when he is surrounded by a crowd. In the wings, his enemies wait to close in, but he is safe as long as he remains in the gaze of the anonymous public. Barry Kane can survive only by pretending to be one of "the others"—the normal men who are ignorant of the plot being played before their very eyes. Kane cannot cry out that the ballroom is filled with Nazis; the situation is too absurd—no one would believe him. Only three parties know the true situation—the hero, the villains, and ourselves, the spectators. The average man on the screen remains blissfully ignorant. It is impossible to communicate with them; futile to try to wake them to the danger. As in a nightmare, Kane dances with increasing anxiety, knowing himself to be irrevocably cut off from the rest of humanity by his terrible knowledge. The greatest terror comes not in solitary, dark places of mystery, but in the brightly lit public world of dances, concerts, and carnivals.

The charity ball isolates and magnifies a principle of Hitchcock's method which guides so many of the scenes in *Saboteur* and other films of its type. It might be called the principle of irony: characters within the same scene perceive the situation in opposing ways. One character, or group of characters, possesses no knowledge, true or false; face to face with the truth, they are unable to recognize it. In contrast, the hero, the villains, and/or the spectator know exactly what is happening. Early in *Saboteur*, for example, the heroine refuses to believe Kane's protests of innocence, just as the charity ball dancers later casually dismiss the truth. These scenes draw their suspense (and often their comedy) from a false perception of the real situation, and they serve the additional purpose of more closely cementing our identification with the hero. When we alone share the hero's knowledge, we are isolated with him, apart from the crowd. The emotional links between us are bound more tightly as, together, we face the nonbelievers. The ironic method establishes a complicity between spectator and hero by setting us both against an indifferent or hostile public world.

The story's climax at the Statue of Liberty (filmed in the studio, *not* on location) will immediately remind the spectator of the chase across the faces of the Mount Rushmore presidents at the end of *North by Northwest*. Hitchcock seems fascinated by the surreal or fairy-tale image of a tiny human figure against the face of a giant. In his early British film, *Blackmail* (1929), a man dangles by a slender rope in front of the gigantic stone face of an Egyptian pharaoh in the British Museum. The national monument climax is a specific form of a more general Hitchcock scene featuring another kind of public spectacle—a music hall, a movie, or an amusement park. In these places of entertainment, Hitchcock can stage two stories simultaneously. While the ignorant crowd enjoys the public amusement on stage or screen, hero and villain are locked in their own desperate plot. Yet the real, private story is masked by the crowd's reaction to the spectacle. *Saboteur* offers one of the most brilliant of these public/private scenes when Fry (Norman Lloyd) the real saboteur, is pursued across the stage at Radio City Music Hall during the screening of a movie. As his tiny figure darts across the screen a comic murder scene arouses peals of laughter from the audience. The "real" gunshots of Fry and his pursuers are believed to be only a hilarious part of the show, since guns are also being fired in the film. Perceptions are confused; reality is thought to be illusion. Once again, the scene is built on irony—reading the same message in two different ways.

Saboteur was the fifth film Hitchcock made in the United States after he left England in 1939. Like *Foreign Correspondent* (1940), it was intended to influence American opinion against Nazi Germany. Although *Saboteur* was not released until April, 1942, production began before Pearl Harbor, when the United States was still officially neutral in the war. Given the timing of the film, it is not far-fetched to see the Lane character as representing the "official" United States attitude. It is difficult for the committed hero to convince this all-American girl who was a billboard model that the Nazi menace is real, but once she is "shamed" by the circus people with whom Kane takes refuge, she enlists in the anti-Nazi fight. Unable to ignore the evidence of evil, the girl moves from initial doubt through a passive partnership with the hero to a final active pursuit of Fry, the saboteur. The extent of her political conversion is signaled at the end when Fry sarcastically calls her "Little Miss Liberty, carrying the torch." Presumably, her journey to action is intended as a shining example for America, the nation.

Although *Saboteur* resembles *The 39 Steps* and *North by Northwest*, its reputation has suffered in comparison to these Hitchcock classics, perhaps because it is a less unified film. According to Hitchcock, "the script lacks discipline." Brilliant episodes such as the fire in the first scene and the film-within-a-film near the end stand as a series of set-pieces, each with its own suspense and resolution. Hitchcock believed, in retrospect, that this loosely organized "mass of ideas" should have been considerably "pruned" before the film was shot. The director said he committed "a serious error" at the end because the audience would have been more anguished if the hero, not the villain, were in danger of falling from Liberty's torch.

Hitchcock ignored the beauties of *Saboteur* in order to denounce its faults. As he so often explained, Hitchcock preferred filmmaking to be the precise application of a previous plan, stating, "I wish I didn't have to shoot the picture. When I've gone through the script and created the picture on paper, for me the creative job is done, and the rest is just a bore." *Saboteur* is a film which refused to be tamed in the scripting stage, thus denying Hitchcock's passion for total control. It remains wild and undomesticated; the images overpower the logic in scenes as bizarre and sometimes as surreal as the images of a dream. To contemporary critics, the most fascinating qualities of *Saboteur* may be precisely those which, like Frankenstein's monster, escaped the director's authority.

Dennis L. Giles

SANDS OF IWO JIMA

Released: 1949
Production: Edmund Grainger for Republic
Direction: Allan Dwan
Screenplay: Harry Brown and James Edward Grant; based on an original
story by Harry Brown
Cinematography: Reggie Lanning
Editing: Richard L. Van Enger
Music: Victor Young
Running time: 109 minutes

Principal characters:
Sergeant John M. Stryker .... John Wayne
Pfc. Peter Conway .... John Agar
Allison Bromley .... Adele Mara
Al Thomas .... Forrest Tucker
Corporal Robert Dunn .... Arthur Franz
Mary .... Julie Bishop
Pfc. Frank Flynn .... Richard Jaeckel
Private "Ski" Choynski .... Hal Fieberling
Pfc. Benny Regazzi .... Wally Cassell

During and immediately following times of war the public wants to be
comforted and assured of its country's cause and power; it wants to see and
to hate the enemy. During World War II, war pictures containing that kind
of nationalism and vengeance scored big hits at the American box office. As
the postwar years passed, however, there was an increasing interest in films
dealing with an individual's problems, rather than in those of the country.
Sands of Iwo Jima, released in 1949, is more a social drama than a political
statement. The United States Marine Corps' landing on Iwo Jima and the
training and preparation that led up to it serve as a backdrop for the drama.
The film is actually a display of young, popular actors exemplifying romanticized wartime ideals: courage, camaraderie, love, and honor. This approach
is suitable to director Allan Dwan, a prolific, commercial American filmmaker.

The story, written by Harry Brown, concerns a hard-nosed sergeant who
tries to mold a group of greenhorn Marines into a tough-fighting rifle squad.
The action begins in New Zealand where the various characters are introduced
in the course of their vigorous military exercises: Peter Conway (John Agar),
son of a colonel who was killed ten months earlier; Benny Regazzi (Wally
Cassell), the Italian jokester who plans to be everyone's manager once state-
side; Ski (Hal Fieberling), the burly Pole; Thomas (Forrest Tucker); the
brawling brothers; and many other young types. Above all, there is Sergeant

John Stryker (John Wayne), who is hard on them and who suffers their wrath while he teaches them how to survive. As the story unfolds we become more familiar with the characters, but our attention is especially focused on Sergeant Stryker and Peter Conway. The conflict between these two men surfaces as the major interest of the story.

We learn early in the film that Conway's father, the Colonel, was Stryker's former commanding officer. Stryker has patterned his own behavior after the Colonel and, to the young Conway, he represents the father who had always considered his son to be a coward—not tough enough to be a United States Marine. Conway is the sensitive type, outspoken on the topic of morality and at odds with Stryker's gung-ho, soldierly attitudes. Conway, however, is unaware that Stryker also suffers. We learn of Stryker's drinking problem, which developed after his wife left him and his son failed to write to him.

Although the Sergeant feels some affinity for the Colonel's son and offers him advice from time to time, Conway never hesitates to rebuke his gestures of friendship. On leave in New Zealand, Conway falls in love with a girl named Allison (Adele Mara). Stryker warns him about the problems of falling in love during a war, but Conway does not listen and marries Allison. In a later scene, when they are again on leave, their ongoing war of words increases. Stryker tries to congratulate Conway on the birth of his son, but Conway cuts him off, declaring that his son will be intelligent and cultured, as opposed to a Marine Colonel or another Sergeant Stryker. In an earlier scene with Allison, Conway told her that he must prove his bravery to a man (his father) who is already dead, so we are privy to Conway's shame and lifelong feelings of inferiority. Conway proves that he is not cowardly through the rather predictable irony of saving Stryker's life during combat. He earns the respect of Sergeant Stryker, and he comes both to understand and to admire him as a decent, tragic person. In fact, Sergeant Stryker gains the respect of all of his men before, as irony would have it, he is killed by a Japanese sniper just as the American flag is about to be raised on Mount Suribachi.

Aside from this intimate, human story. *Sands of Iwo Jima* is a war picture, part of the genre of American war films which reached its peak in the wake of World War II. A fundamental of this genre is that it uses the atmosphere of war to intensify everything that happens. There is an existential desperation within the charcters' interaction, since each interaction concerns a life-and-death situation. Normally, taking a leisurely coffee break does not determine the fate of one's friends. During combat, however, when Thomas stops for coffee before getting ammunition back to his buddies, their bunker is over-taken and one man is killed by the enemy. Similarly, separaton of lovers in a wartime situation is magnified and more strongly felt because it could be the final separation.

Dwan employs a number of devices which are often associated with the war picture genre. The film opens with the Marines' Hymn, which is followed by a printed tribute to the exploits and valor of the Marine Corps. There are the familiar battle scenes interspersed throughout the film. These thundering, action-packed scenes are used not only to depict the war accurately, but also to offset the quieter scenes of intimacy. The battle scenes in *Sands of Iwo Jima* are first-rate, gripping, and especially well edited. Dwan and cinematographer Reggie Lanning often frame a picture in which the machinery of war dominates the soldiers. Some scenes open out from the barrel of a rifle or machine gun. In one particular shot, a rifle barrel in the foreground shadows a column of marching soldiers.

Today's audiences have become so familiar with these war picture standards that even the story line is predictable. We know that Conway will prove his heroism and that he and the Sergeant will eventually become friends, and we are pretty sure that Sergeant Stryker will die at the end. These inevitabilities put more than the usual weight on an individual actor's ability. Wayne stands out among the cast. His Sergeant Stryker, harsh and heroic on the outside, is inwardly proud and compassionate. Wayne's acting overcomes many of the dramatic clichés that are built into the film. He makes a heavily romanticized character almost believable, and we are dependent on that ability to sustain our interest. Agar is well cast as Conway but, finally, seems only as good as his character. The other members of the cast give adequate performances as well; however, Dwan is interested in what characters stand for more than the complexities of their personalities. He likes to study expressions and faces rather than gestures or dialogue, and is therefore fond of close-ups.

It is not difficult to see how *Sands of Iwo Jima* was a precursor to Dwan's Westerns of the 1950's. Like the later films, this film romanticizes characters and history. It is also the story of two men in conflict, with love as a subplot. Dwan's commercial popularity issues from his ability to adapt to the spirit of the times. That affirmation in itself is a kind of optimism which he has carried from his early days working on silent films through the light comedies of the 1930's and 1940's and the Westerns of the 1950's and into his most recent work for television. *Sands of Iwo Jima* is certainly a document of its time in American cinematic history, testimony to the sense of relief in the victorious years that followed a costly, although cohesively fought war. There are no bad guys in this flag-waving motion picture and the good guys simply get better. Dwan and Wayne are both good guys in American film history, which may explain why this 1949 film is continually revived on television and in the smaller revival theaters.

Ralph Angel

SARATOGA TRUNK

Released: 1945
Production: Hal B. Wallis for Warner Bros.
Direction: Sam Wood
Screenplay: Casey Robinson; based on the novel of the same name by Edna Ferber
Cinematography: Ernest Haller
Editing: Ralph Dawson
Running time: 135 minutes

Principal characters:
Colonel Clint Maroon .... Gary Cooper
Clio Dulaine .... Ingrid Bergman
Angelique .... Flora Robson
Bart Van Steed .... John Warburton
Cupidon .... Jerry Austin

On February 22, 1943, Sam Wood finished directing *For Whom the Bell Tolls* starring Gary Cooper and Ingrid Bergman. On May 26 of that same year, the three began filming again with a very different type of film, *Saratoga Trunk*. The picture's release, however, for some unknown reason was held up for more than two years. During these two years, *Saratoga Trunk* was shown in service club theaters to Armed Forces' audiences all over the world. When it finally opened to the general public in November, 1945, in Hollywood, it was a sensation. By the fourth week after its release, *Saratoga Trunk* had been seen in Los Angeles by an audience equal in number to one quarter of the city's entire population. *Look* magazine ran a special publication on the Hollywood film industry hailing *Saratoga Trunk* as an exemplary film. The critics' only complaint, in fact, was the film's length; the "epic" was over two hours long. On the other hand, none of them could suggest which scenes to cut. Bosley Crowther's review for *The New York Times* stands out as a lone negative vote, calling the film "grand, flashy, empty Hollywood style."

Audiences, however, disagreed with his evaluation. They accepted, for example, the naturally blonde Bergman as the glamorized Clio Dulaine, a saucy brunette. This had been one of the film's inconsistencies noted by critics. The studio hype was exceeded only by that for *Gone with the Wind* (1939). Before the film was cast, ballot boxes were placed in theaters all across the country asking moviegoers to choose the film's leading man. Cooper's name was selected as the unchallenged choice for the role of Clint Maroon.

The story by Edna Ferber had first been serialized in W. R. Hearst's *Cosmopolitan* magazine. The extremely popular novelist, author of *So Big*, *Showboat*, and *Cimarron*, had for years provided perfect stories for Hollywood. Once *Saratoga Trunk* was published in book form it almost was a guaranteed screen success. There is no doubt that Warner's hoped for a box-office gross the size of *Gone with the Wind*. Warner Bros. was confident that the character of Clio Dulaine would match the popularity of Scarlett O'Hara. Unfortunately, the lack of both talent and budget kept *Saratoga Trunk* from approaching the epic grandeur of *Gone with the Wind*. As Bosley Crowther observed, the style was there, but it was empty.

Nevertheless, the film is far above average. Cooper and Bergman give charming performances and are both convincing in their parts. Cooper plays his established *persona*, a longlegged, monosyllabic cowboy who is not as dumb as he looks. Bergman, on the contrary, plays a coquette who is quite unlike the unassuming natural girls she had been typecast as before. Her performance transcends much of the character's superficiality. In black wig and heavy makeup, Bergman is transformed into a worldly woman. She also would have ample opportunity for histrionics as the sometimes neurotic and delirious Clio. This type of acting became important to her in *Gaslight* (1944), for which she received her first Oscar.

The film opens as Clio Dulaine (Ingrid Bergman) arrives in New Orleans from Paris. Clio, a stunning Creole (half Spanish, half French), is accompanied by her maid Angelique (Flora Robson) and her dwarf coachman Cupido (Jerry Austin). She has vowed not to be a suffering mistress like her dead mother; instead she will marry an American and he will be wealthy. Clio arrives on New Orleans' Rampart Street determined to settle her "mama's" score with "papa's" New Orleans wife and children.

Shortly after her arrival Clio encounters a handsome Texan in the French Market. Clint Maroon (Gary Cooper) amuses her with his backwoods' cunning and American gaucherie. Their second meeting occurs in an amusing scene in a famous New Orleans French restaurant. Clint complains that the menu is not in "American," and Clio boldly offers to order for him. "They say everything here is licking good," Clint says, making conversation. "Kinda steamy in New Orleans." "New Orleans," Clio corrects his pronunciation. Clint's response is sharp, "You fixin' to learn me English?" Seeing through her Parisian coyness, Clint warns, "I was born in Texas, but it weren't yesterday."

They are an odd couple and do not see eye to eye on a great deal. Clint has a "little lady in Texas" who embroiders forget-me-nots on his ties, and Clio jealously teases him about her. In Texas it seems there are only two kinds of women—good and bad—so, consequently, figuring Clio out proves quite a challenge for Clint. Clio's capriciousness, for example, is summed up when she declares, "Sometimes I'm my mother—who gave everything for love. And sometimes I'm grandmama who gave everything too, but not for love. And sometimes I'm my great-grandmama who was an actress. . . ." Despite the differences in their natures, Clint and Clio have a strong common purpose: revenge. Together they set out to embarrass Clio's father's family.

She shocks New Orleans when she announces that her mother's house will be turned into a brothel. Clint, however, becomes fed up with her schemes finally and leaves for Saratoga to take care of a little business of his own. He has an account to settle with the railroad barons who overran his Texas property.

Clio succeeds in blackmailing her father's family. She achieves her mother's wish, a Christian burial, with a tombstone reading: "Rita beloved *wife*. . . ." Clio burns the Rampart house and the last memories of her mother. With New Orleans behind her, she heads for Saratoga ready for phase two of her plans—a rich husband. Clio's story parallels Clint's as they set their cap for the same man. She succeeds in capturing the attention of Bart Van Steed (John Warburton), the bachelor. Clint on the other hand, is interested in Bart Van Steed, the railroad baron. Van Steed is fighting against Maroon's railroad enemies.

The two story lines collide at the film's climax. Clint, although in love with Clio, leaves her and Bart behind to lead the fight for the Saratoga Trunk Line. Alone with Clio, Bart proposes marriage. Faced with the decision between Clint and Bart, Clio sees for the first time that money and security are not everything. Her heart goes to Clint, who fights his own battles, instead of to a weakling like Van Steed who pays others to fight for him.

Her realization comes too late, however, as Clint is seriously wounded in the railroad skirmish. The grief-stricken Clio sits by his "deathbed," embroidering forget-me-nots on a white tie. Yet, well aware of what he is saying, Clint talks "deliriously" about the virtues of that "little woman in Texas." Desperately hoping that he will live, Clio swears that she loves only him and promises to let Clint "wear the pants." That is all he needs to hear. Clint drops the pose of delirium and announces that he won the railroad battle and a fortune as well. Clio now has both the man she loves and the financial security of which she has dreamed. She falls into his arms.

Today *Saratoga Trunk* stands as one of Warner Bros.' most lavish films. The music by Max Steiner, direction by Sam Wood, screenplay by Casey Robinson, and commendable performances by Cooper and Bergman represent the tradition of fine "stock company" pictures that made Hollywood the film capital of the world.

Joanne L. Yeck

SATURDAY NIGHT AND SUNDAY MORNING

Released: 1960
Production: Tony Richardson and Harry Saltzman for Woodfall Productions
Direction: Karel Reisz
Screenplay: Alan Sillitoe; based on his novel of the same name
Cinematography: Freddie Francis
Editing: Seth Holt
Music: John Dankworth
Running time: 90 minutes

Principal characters:

Arthur Seaton	Albert Finney
Doreen	Shirley Anne Field
Brenda	Rachel Roberts
Aunt Ada	Hylda Baker
Bert	Norman Rossington

In 1960, documentary film director Karel Reisz made his first full-length movie, *Saturday Night and Sunday Morning*. Adapted from Alan Sillitoe's novel set in his native Nottingham, it was considered a step forward by most British critics. Although Tony Richardson's company, Woodfall Productions, had already filmed two plays by John Osborne, heralding the start of the new British school of realism, *Saturday Night and Sunday Morning* was felt to be the first authentic look at the British working class.

The film is basically a character study of one young man working in a Nottingham factory. In his novel and screen adaptation, Sillitoe explores the choices open to his hero, Arthur Seaton (Albert Finney), and by doing so, charts the course of his daily life. Reisz's direction is solid, shows much restraint, and avoids bravura. The film is like Arthur's life—low-keyed and naturalistic. What emerges is not a glum picture of a tedious, dull person, for Arthur has a bounce and a rebelliousness that one feels will survive his commonplace factory job, even if he has no more than a wife, children, and a council flat. His character contains many unpleasant elements. He is callous in speech to those around him, he feels little responsibility toward the society in which he lives, and his motto in life is "Don't let the bastards grind you down." Such a hero under less skilled hands could be loathsome, yet Finney never allows Arthur to become negative. Finney is so talented an actor that he seems to make Arthur's life stand for something, however vague, and he makes it clear that he will never be made to act and think like a machine.

The dialogue in the film is extremely important. Local accents are freely used, and the slang and unique expressions of England's industrial North are utilized for the first time in film. Yet its regional setting does not detract from the universality of *Saturday Night and Sunday Morning*. Here is the story of a man who lives the same life as most working men, but feels that more is waiting down the road for him than for his mates. When marriage looms large and life looks predictable, Arthur resigns himself to the inevitable. Yet Sillitoe has endowed this character with such tenacity that a feeling remains at the climax of the film that Arthur is still not quite beaten down. As he looks out at the new housing estate he will probably live in with his bride-to-be, he throws a stone and murmurs "It won't be the last one I'll throw." This act of defiance, small as it may seem, hints that the young working class need not completely give way to conformity and sit home watching television every night. More than any other film of the British realists who flourished between 1959 and 1963, *Saturday Night and Sunday Morning* embodies working-class attitudes without condemning them or ennobling them. Sillitoe has created characters of flesh and blood, and the story he tells is enthralling from the first moment to the last.

The film's action is seen through the eyes of Arthur Seaton, a twenty-two-year-old factory worker in Nottingham, the sprawling industrial city of the British midlands. All week Arthur works hard at his lathe for his weekly pay, living for Saturday night when he can go with his buddies to the local pub and spend the evening drinking and brawling. Here a comparison can be made with the character John Travolta plays in *Saturday Night Fever* (1977), in which the hero lives for his weekly appearances on the dance floor. In *Saturday Night Fever*, however, a tribute is made to American mobility, for Travolta is allowed to escape into Manhattan, perhaps to lead a more satisfying life than his parents did. Arthur Seaton is bound by class and tradition to stay in Nottingham and repeat the life of generations of Seatons. The film is really about his attempts to escape this fate. He has a devil-may-care personality and soon gets involved with Brenda (Rachel Roberts), the wife of a fellow worker. At the same time, he meets Doreen (Shirley Anne Field), a girl with rigid ideas about sex and marriage who will not settle for a casual affair. As Arthur seeks to satisfy both women and continue his boisterous life with his friends, events crowd in on him.

Brenda becomes pregnant, and Arthur takes her to his Aunt Ada (Hylda Baker) in hopes she can help him procure an abortion. The attempt fails. Arthur quickly comes to the realization of his own responsibility toward another human being and offers to marry her. Brenda, sensing their affair is over, decides to have the baby and take the consequences, hoping her husband will not find out. Brenda, as Roberts portrays her, seems almost to shrink as her self-confidence vanishes once she learns of her pregnancy. In a truly marvelous performance, Roberts plays a woman trapped by circumstance with little or no resources at her disposal. Arthur eventually puts the situation with Brenda out of his mind and continues to court Doreen. Events catch up with him at a local fair where Brenda's husband and his soldier brother waylay Arthur and beat him senseless. This is the turning point of the film as well as the turning point of Arthur's life, for he realizes that he has earned this punishment. He agrees to marry Doreen and settle on a new housing estate. Already it is obvious that Doreen has within her the personality of a nagging wife as she goes on at Arthur while they look at the new estate. He knows within himself, however, that he will remain the same obstinate Arthur Seaton.

Saturday Night and Sunday Morning tells its story through a series of incidents that together build a life. What comes out of them is a portrait of Arthur Seaton as a true contemporary character, with a practical self-interest that finds nothing to respond to in the conformism of his parents and work-mates. Yet he knows all along that conformism is his inheritance. Some critics found Arthur's attempts to deal with life in ways that gave him pleasure immoral. They balked at the fact that all Arthur really wanted out of life was a good time—the rest, as Arthur was fond of saying, "is propaganda." Sillitoe explained in interviews that he did not want audiences to judge Arthur as either moral or immoral, but rather to understand how a man like him thinks and acts. He stated, "I wanted to show certain people as I thought them to be, not as I imagined other people wanted to see them."

In this amazing film, Reisz, Sillitoe, Finney, and the excellent supporting cast all collaborated to create a milestone in British film history. Helped greatly by John Dankworth's music and Freddie Francis' remarkable camera-work, the film succeeds on every level. This group at the newly organized Woodfall Films showed the world that it was possible to make a serious and intelligent film about working-class life in England. *Saturday Night and Sunday Morning* was to be followed by films of a similar nature directed by John Schlesinger and Tony Richardson. *A Kind of Loving* (1962), *A Taste of Honey* (1961), and *The Loneliness of the Long Distance Runner* (1962) all contributed to the brief but brilliant flowering of the British cinema between 1959 and 1963.

Joan Cohen

SATURDAY NIGHT FEVER

Released: 1977
Production: Robert Stigwood for Paramount
Direction: John Badham
Screenplay: Norman Wexler; based on an original story of the same name by
   Nik Cohn
Cinematography: Ralf D. Bode
Editing: David Rawlins
Music: Barry Gibb, Robin Gibb, and Maurice Gibb
Running time: 120 minutes

Principal characters:
Tony Manero	John Travolta
Stephanie	Karen Lynn Gorney
Annette	Donna Pescow
Bobby C	Barry Miller
Joey	Joseph Call
Double J	Paul Pape
Gus	Bruce Ornstein
Frank	Martin Shakar

By late 1977, disco music in one form or another had been around for at least three years. It was just another musical genre then, and music critics were touting punk rock as the next big thing. The release of *Saturday Night Fever* in December of that year, however, had as galvanic an impact on popular music as did the appearance of Elvis Presley in 1956 and the Beatles in 1964 on Ed Sullivan's television show. An entire nation, like it or not, sat up and took notice. Within the space of a year, *Saturday Night Fever* had become one of the ten highest-grossing films of all time, and the film's soundtrack became the best-selling record album of all time, with more than twenty million copies sold. Disco established itself as the preeminent musical mode of the late 1970's, and John Travolta, the film's young star, was hailed as a new Marlon Brando. Clearly *Saturday Night Fever* was more than a film—it was a phenomenon.

The film had its origins in a brief sketch about the disco subculture in Brooklyn by English rock critic Nik Cohn, who specialized in writing about teenage epiphanies—that one moment of uncomplicated ecstasy that makes the drudgery of the rest of the week seem bearable—in a phrase, "Saturday Night Fever." Norman Wexler's screenplay takes Cohn's basic idea and gives it a story line, albeit a bumpy one. Ironically, Wexler manages to subvert Cohn's basic theme in the process, suggesting that no ecstasy is uncomplicated and that every Saturday night is necessarily followed by a Sunday morning.

Tony Manero (John Travolta) is *Saturday Night Fever*'s teenage hero, and the film opens with a shot of him strutting down the street, a young man full of himself. His everyday life, however, is uninspiring. A nineteen-year-old Italian-American from the Bay Ridge section of Brooklyn, he clerks in a paint store by day and lives with his parents. His job is boring and unremunerative, and his home life is suffocating. The strut in his step comes from the one night a week when Tony transcends the drudgery of his workaday life. On Saturday night, Tony Manero is the king of 2001 Odyssey, a local discotheque.

Tony and his friends Joey (Joseph Call), Double J (Paul Pape), Gus (Bruce Ornstein), and Bobby C (Barry Miller) enter 2001 like a conquering army, with Tony in the lead. Some traditional social roles are reversed inside the disco. Women become sexually aggressive, even predatory. This is fine with Tony's retinue, a loutish and generally unsympathetic lot revved up by alcohol, pills, and teenage lust. Tony's feelings, however, are more ambivalent. He clearly revels in the admiration, verging on worship, that he inspires in the girls in 2001. Yet to Tony, dance is a spiritual and physical discipline, almost a sacrament, and he resents the fact that others regard the activity as little more than a mating ritual. For him, fornicating and dancing are two distinctly separate activities. "You make it with some of these chicks, they think you gotta dance with them," he complains, giving an unintentionally ironic twist to the old cliché.

Tony's most ardent admirer is Annette (Donna Pescow), a chunky girl who has a hopeless crush on him; but Tony's eye is caught by a girl in a white dress who is dancing rings around her partner. Suddenly it is Tony Manero who is in the throes of a hopeless crush.

The disco announces a city-wide dance contest with a five-hundred-dollar prize for the winning couple. Tony seeks out the girl in white, Stephanie (Karen Lynn Gorney), and persuades her to be his partner. She is unlike any girl Tony has ever known, independent, aggressively (sometimes pretentiously) intelligent, and intent upon bettering herself. This, for Stephanie, means moving from Brooklyn to Manhattan. She is willing to dance with Tony, but has no interest in seeing him socially, which is, of course, a precise reversal of the role in which Tony usually finds himself.

Their dance practice/courtship proceeds by fits and starts, since Tony is as awkward socially as he is graceful on the dance floor. By the time the big dance contest rolls around, however, Stephanie begins to develop an affection for the smitten Tony.

The film's musical climax occurs at the dance contest. In a scene in which Wexler once again underlines Tony's belief in the sacredness of the dance, Tony and Stephanie watch nervously as the top dancers from all over the city compete for the prize. 2001 is Tony's turf, however, and he is clearly the crowd favorite. The routine that he and Stephanie have painstakingly worked out proceeds without a hitch until toward the end of the song, when their eyes meet. They pause and kiss for a long moment, until, realizing where they are, they wind up their routine. Tony is dejected, certain that their moment of passion has cost them first place. Nevertheless, he and Stephanie, cheered on by his friends, are awarded the prize.

To everyone's astonishment, however, Tony is furious. His sense of propriety and honor has been violated. Even if his friends and the judges are too blind to tell the difference, he knows that he does not deserve the prize. He hands the check to the Puerto Rican couple who placed second and stalks out of the disco, dragging Stephanie with him. He takes her to his car, virtually throws her into the backseat, and begins pawing her. Startled and angry, she leaves him in the car and heads for home.

At this point, Tony is at a crossroads. Dancing, formerly his one sure solace, has temporarily turned to ashes. Saturday night has betrayed him, and he must choose between his old life or an uncertain future in Stephanie's world. His first impulse is to return to the safety of his old friends. Tony, Joey, Bobby C, Double J, and the hapless Annette drive off into the night looking for adventure, trouble, or whatever comes along. In a long and overly graphic sequence, the security of Tony's former life dissolves. His friends drug Annette into a stupor and then have sex with her. Next, they park near the Verrazano Narrows bridge, where Bobby C, troubled by his girl friend's pregnancy and afraid of marriage, commits suicide by leaping to his death.

His life in shreds, Tony boards a subway and rides all night, trying to decide what to do. Finally he reaches a decision and goes to see Stephanie. They talk, and both apologize. Stephanie wants to continue their relationship, but not on a sexual basis. "Do you think you could be friends with a girl?" she asks. "I don't know," he replies. "I'll try." The film thus closes with Tony's promise to look beyond Saturday night to the world of adulthood.

It should be said at the outset that there are a number of serious flaws in this film. It was almost certainly conceived as an exploitation film, designed to cash in on the disco fad and the popularity of Travolta, who had achieved prominence as one of the juvenile leads in the television series *Welcome Back Kotter*. Perhaps because they knew that they had a sure moneymaker on their hands, the filmmakers neglected to come up with an entirely coherent and believeable plot. There is a lengthy and largely extraneous subplot involving Tony's brother Frank (Martin Shakar), a priest who loses his vocation, and there is a brief and entirely extraneous subplot about a miniature gang war between Tony's friends and a group of Puerto Ricans. Nevertheless, director John Badham makes the best of the uneven script, and where the script is strong, Badham's direction shines. The film's best moments occur inside the disco, where, under Badham's guidance, the flashing lights and drifting fog of 2001 Odyssey turn into a combination of Disneyland and Sodom and Gomorrah.

Most of the cast is also at the mercy of the script. Gorney tries her best, but has trouble coping with a script that treats her by turns as the Ideal

Woman and as a posturing simpleton. She is also a bit too old to be playing a girl of twenty, and despite attempts to make it appear otherwise, she is an average dancer at best. More affecting is Pescow as Annette, the girl whose love Tony spurns in his quest for Stephanie. Among the male supporting cast, Miller stands out. As Bobby C, he turns in a fine performance as a boy whose nervousness slowly turns into hysteria as everyone around studiously ignores him.

Two other factors lift *Saturday Night Fever* above the level of its plot: the music on the soundtrack (particularly the Trammps' "Disco Inferno" and the songs by the Bee Gees) and the acting of Travolta. Much to everyone's surprise, Travolta turned in a stunning performance which earned him an Oscar nomination as Best Actor, and made him the youngest man to be nominated in that category in the Academy's history. His dance sequences are alive with a kinetic energy that fairly leaps off the screen. Yet, fine as these moments are, they are the least of his accomplishments, for Travolta is an actor before he is a dancer. The part of Tony Manero could easily have been turned into a caricature; on paper, the role lacks substance. Travolta, however, with no apparent effort, not only breathes life into Tony Manero; he also turns Tony, who is self-centered, misogynistic, and not overly bright, into a character who is more than merely sympathetic. In Travolta's hands, Tony Manero is downright lovable. His performance is a *tour de force* and is reason enough to believe that *Saturday Night Fever* will be remembered long after disco has gone the way of the turkey trot.

Robert Mitchell

THE SAVAGE INNOCENTS

Released: 1959
Production: Maleno Malenotti for Paramount
Direction: Nicholas Ray
Screenplay: Nicholas Ray; based on the novel *Top of the World* by Hans Ruesch
Cinematography: Aldo Tonti and Peter Hennessy
Editing: Ralph Kemplen
Running time: 110 minutes

Principal characters:
Inuk	Anthony Quinn
Asiak	Yoko Tani
Trooper	Carlo Giustini
Trooper	Peter O'Toole
Powtee	Marie Yang
Hiko	Anna May Wong
Missionary	Marco Guglielmi

Anthony Quinn, an Academy Award-winning (Best Supporting) actor (*Viva Zapata!*, 1952, *Lust for Life*, 1956), has a remarkable ability to portray realistically a variety of ethnic types. The actor, a native of Chihuahua, Mexico, has played such diverse characters as Paul Gauguin (*Lust for Life*), Mountain Rivera (*Requiem for a Heavyweight*, 1962), Kiang (*East of Sumatra*, 1953), Portugee (*The World in His Arms*, 1952), Alexis Zorba (*Zorba the Greek*, 1964), and Italo Bambolini (*The Secret of Santa Vittoria*, 1969). In Nicholas Ray's *The Savage Innocents* (1960), he even portrays an Eskimo.

The Savage Innocents is a sensationalized although not unapt title for the film. Quinn stars as Inuk, a powerful but childlike Eskimo hunter who for years has borrowed the wives of other men, a normal custom in a land with few women. At the beginning of the film, he has decided to marry and becomes the husband of Asiak (Yoko Tani). The pair, along with Asiak's aged mother Powtee (Marie Yang), travel hundreds of miles to a trading post to obtain a rifle for fox skins. Asiak, however, does not take to "civilization"; Inuk builds an igloo for his wife and mother-in-law a distance from the post. They are soon visited by a missionary (Marco Guglielmi), who is outraged when Inuk offers him Asiak as a token of his hospitality. The hunter, angered by what he takes to be an insult, accidentally kills the missionary. In one of the more touching sequences in the film, the couple flees, leaving Powtee, who realizes she will be a burden, to die alone in the snow.

Shortly after the birth of their son, Inuk is arrested by a pair of Canadian troopers (Carlo Giustini and Peter O'Toole) for the murder of the missionary. As they travel south to take in Inuk to be tried, one of the troopers freezes to death; the other survives only because Inuk takes him back to his igloo. The trooper explains that, out of gratitude, he will allow Inuk to escape. The Eskimo will not run, however; confused, the trooper insults Inuk, spits in Asiak's face, and disappears into the snow. Inuk and Asiak are bewildered by the actions of white men and the requirements of white society, so they return to their home in the wilderness.

Ray, director of *The Savage Innocents*, has been hailed by *auteur* critics for his cinematic individualism. His films are filled with social consciousness, with characters who are either physically, emotionally, or spiritually isolated. His characters, harassed because they live outside the mainstream of society, include alienated teenagers James Dean, Natalie Wood, and Sal Mineo in *Rebel Without a Cause* (1956) and fugitives/lovers Farley Granger and Cathy O'Donnell in *They Live by Night* (1949). According to Ray, there is no universal moral code, and his Inuk and Asiak are consistent with his cinematic vision. The Eskimos are isolated nomads who are content with hunting and fishing. They are unable to comprehend the white man's laws and moral code and should not be judged as "savages" because of their life style.

The sequences in *The Savage Innocents* in which Inuk hunts are fascinating; those which depict his simple living conditions are eloquent. As a quasi-documentary, the film works quite nicely, and perhaps it should have been filmed as a documentary in the spirit of Robert Flaherty's *Nanook of the North* (1924). Aldo Tonti and Peter Hennessy's color cinematography is particularly striking, with sequences lavishly shot on location in Greenland and around Hudson Bay (the igloos, however, were constructed in England's Pinewood Studios). In fact, much of the film's one-hundred-ten-minute running time is concerned solely with the details of Eskimo life. The best sequences are of Quinn hunting seals, foxes, bears, and walruses, and of the Eskimos' surviving the cold, hard winters. They eat raw seal meat; animals die bloodily and painfully; life is simple, but also crude.

Overall, *The Savage Innocents* is an average film because the scenario and dialogue intrude on its documentary aspect. The plot twists are not believable, and Ray's screenplay is far too verbose. Quinn, however, offers an excellent performance as Inuk. His career has been uneven; his *Zorba the Greek* is as captivating as his *Greek Tycoon* (1978) is overblown. As Inuk, however, he delivers his lines in pidgin English and is thoroughly believable as the Eskimo. Japanese Tani, a fine actress, gives Quinn solid support as Asiak, although her career in American films was limited.

The Savage Innocents is also of interest for the appearance of a pre-*Lawrence of Arabia* (1962) O'Toole; in that Academy Award-winning film, O'Toole received billing over Quinn and became a star. Here, he is seen only briefly as one of the troopers. His voice is dubbed, however, and he requested that his name be removed from the credits. *The Savage Innocents* is one of the final screen appearances of Anna May Wong, who is cast in a small role.

The Chinese-American actress is familiar to audiences from *The Thief of Bagdad* (1924), *Shanghai Express* (1932), and other films of the 1920's and 1930's.

The Savage Innocents is an Italian/American/British coproduction, with the $1,500,000 budget evenly divided between England's J. Arthur Rank, America's Paramount, and Italy's Maleno Malenotti, the producer. The film cannot be referred to as "American" or "British" or "Italian." The Pinewood Studios and a British crew were utilized in the filming; the director/screenwriter is American; the cinematographers are Italian and British; and the cast is made up of Americans, Japanese, Chinese, and British. As the Hollywood studio system was dying, *The Savage Innocents* portended the "internationalization" of future film production. The film was a financial failure; it was not mentioned on *Variety*'s list of high rental films for 1959, earning less than one million dollars at the box office. It has become a favorite of Ray's followers in ensuing years, however, and is certainly the finest talking film on Eskimo life.

Rob Edelman

SAVE THE TIGER

Released: 1973
Production: Steve Shagan for Filmways/Jalem/Cirandinha; released by Paramount
Direction: John G. Avildsen
Screenplay: Steve Shagan
Cinematography: James Crabe
Editing: David Bretherton
Running time: 100 minutes

Principal characters:
Harry Stoner	Jack Lemmon (AA)
Phil Greene	Jack Gilford
Myra	Laurie Heineman
Fred Mirrell	Norman Burton
Janet Stoner	Patricia Smith
Charlie Robbins	Thayer David
Meyer	William Hansen
Rico	Harvey Jason
Ula	Liv Von Linden
Margo	Lara Parker
Jackie	Eloise Hardt
Dusty	Janina

At some point between the golden days when he followed Dolph Camilli's career as first baseman for the Brooklyn Dodgers and the days spent under golden skies in Los Angeles, where his dress factory is about to go bankrupt, Harry Stoner (Jack Lemmon) has allowed himself to romanticize history and to renegotiate fundamental moral precepts in order to survive. *Save the Tiger* offers a two-day expedition into the life of this man. As the film begins, he is preparing for the fashion showing that he hopes will solve his financial problems and help save his fifteen-year investment in the garment business. On the way to his factory he meets Myra (Laurie Heineman), a hippie hitchhiker who spends her life admittedly "going nowhere," hitchhiking up and down Sunset Strip all day. She offers to have sex with him, but he declines and instead goes to see Ula (Liv Von Linden), his Danish mistress. He begins reminiscing with her about 1940's jazz bands, Dodger at bats, and the landing of American troops on the beach at Anzio, thoughts into which he will slump deeper and deeper in the space of his two-day crisis.

Harry arrives at the factory late, but with apologies and a kind word for everyone. It immediately becomes apparent that more than a successful fashion show is going to be necessary to compensate for last year's "ballet with the books" that has kept Capri Casuals solvent during the current season.

Phil (Jack Gilford) is Harry's partner and moral counterpoint. He wants to ask the mills and unions to carry them for another year on the strength of their history, but Harry's position is that history no longer buys loyalty. He counters with the proposition that they call in Charlie Robbins (Thayer David), a professional arsonist, check to see that the insurance on their Long Beach factory is paid up, and talk business. Faced with the knowledge that their books will not stand up under an audit, Harry reminds Phil that the issue is survival on any terms necessary, both for themselves and their employees. Then another dilemma presents itself in the person of Fred Mirrell (Norman Burton), a buyer from the East Coast who wants Harry to arrange an afternoon with two prostitutes as a condition of his order. Phil does not approve of pimping and arson as ways to guarantee his retirement, but Harry negotiates an afternoon for Fred with two prostitutes, Margo (Lara Parker) and Dusty (Janina); he arranges a meeting at a downtown porno house with Charlie Robbins for himself and Phil after the showing.

Over lunch, Harry and Phil allow themselves to grow nostalgic in order to obscure the focus of what they are about to do. Phil "was going to join the Lincoln Brigade . . . going to defend Madrid . . . save the world. I never got out of New York." Harry lapses into the merits of *Casablanca* (1942), John Garfield, and the 1939 Dodger lineup. We are, somehow, expected to accept Harry's facile defense that his former idealism has been corrupted by a world in which "there are no more rules," and Lemmon's performance is so driven and intense that it almost works. In the end, however, invoking the muses of Lena Horne at the Cotton Club and Freddie Fitzsimmons' knuckle ball and announcing that he always used to stand up when the "Star Spangled Banner" was played does not have sufficient moral weight to legitimize Harry's position. Screenwriter Steve Shagan mistakenly tries to vindicate Harry's materialism and corruption through a sentimentalized evasion of responsibility.

When Phil and Harry arrive at the hotel for the show, they receive a frantic call from Margo telling them that Mirrell has collapsed and she is afraid he is dead. Harry's angry response is that they should have gotten the order up front. At this point his terms for survival do not include any considerations beyond the parameters of self-interest. Then the show opens with the song "Isle of Capri," and the audience gets a capsule summary of the significance of Capri, Anzio, and the scars on Harry's back. He begins to introduce the collection to the buyers, but when he looks up he sees a wounded soldier in the audience. He begins to run together a commentary for the fashion show, his recollections of Anzio, and his recuperation at Capri. Each time he looks up, more dead and wounded soldiers replace the buyers in the audience; Harry becomes incoherent and is eased off stage. By the time he and Phil meet with Robbins, he is back in control of himself. Phil gives Charlie the down payment, the address of the Long Beach factory, and the key. In an obtuse defense of arson that parallels Harry's own thinking, Charlie advises Phil not to confuse morality with technology. In this closed world of technology, pimping, and arson, the only minor attempt to balance the conflicting values is given by Meyer (William Hansen), an old Jewish cutter in Harry's factory whom Harry visits after the show. He gently and reasonably argues that survival is worth nothing if you do not have a dream. By putting this idea in the voice of an elderly immigrant, Shagan offers it as a poignant, almost anachronistic moment rather than a moral option in the film. Meyer's version of the American dream has limits of its own, as we learn when he complains to Harry that he will not work with Rico (Harvey Jason), a homosexual designer.

Later that evening Harry picks up Myra and drives her out to the beach where he spends the night smoking marijuana and engaging her in a game called "names": his litany of public figures of the 1940's pitted against Myra's disconnected recall of 1960's rock groups. When he and Phil go back to the porno theater the next day, they learn that they are in violation of too many fire ordinances to collect on the insurance unless the fire is started on the floor below in another factory. Harry gives Charlie the go-ahead to start the fire anyway. The action ends as Harry stops by a baseball field after the meeting with Charlie. A group of children is playing and Harry picks up a ball that has bounced toward him. He effects a grand wind-up in the style of Johnny Vandemeer as the sounds of Ebbetts Field and the voice of Red Barber mount in his mind. The children demand the ball back, however, and tell him that he cannot play; they "have their rules." The camera pulls back and leaves Harry staring off as the sounds fade and the yellowing gloom of Los Angeles dulls the screen.

Lemmon was awarded the 1973 Academy Award for Best Actor for his portrayal of Harry Stoner, and Gilford as Phil was nominated for Best Supporting Actor. Shagan was nominated for an Academy Award for Best Story and Screenplay (based on factual material or material not previously published) and received the 1973 Writers Guild of America Award for Best Drama Written Directly for the Screen.

Joyce Olin

SAYONARA

Released: 1957
Production: William Goetz for Warner Bros.
Direction: Joshua Logan
Screenplay: Paul Osborn; based on the novel of the same name by James Michener
Cinematography: Ellsworth Fredericks
Editing: Arthur P. Schmidt and Philip W. Anderson
Art direction: Ted Haworth (AA); set decoration, Robert Priestley (AA)
Sound: George R. Groves (AA)
Running time: 147 minutes

Principal characters:

Major Lloyd Gruver	Marlon Brando
Hana-ogi	Miiko Taka
Airman Joe Kelly	Red Buttons (AA)
Eileen Webster	Patricia Owens
Nakamura	Ricardo Montalban
Katsumi	Myoshi Umeki (AA)
Captain Bailey	James Garner
General Webster	Kent Smith
Mrs. Webster	Martha Scott

In the middle 1950's, any film which starred Marlon Brando was an event. The actor had become one of the screen's most interesting personalities both off screen and on. It is true that with *The Godfather* (1972) and *Last Tango in Paris* (1973), Brando has again built up a well-deserved following, but when he was young, even the announcement that he had signed to do a role for a particular film was enough to create enormous interest in the picture for both the American and the European public. With *Sayonara*, Brando started trying to use his box-office popularity to get some moral satisfaction out of his film roles. He felt that this particular story, dealing as it did with the consequences of interracial marriage, would give him a platform to say something important about prejudice in its many guises. Although Brando was encouraged by director Joshua Logan to help revise the screenplay to suit himself, the revisions were not used because Logan had to gain the cooperation of the Air Force and felt that Brando's version might offend. This displeased Brando, and relations between the two men were somewhat strained throughout shooting, but Brando's performance in *Sayonara* did not suffer and remains one of his most restrained pieces of acting.

Set in Japan during the Korean War, *Sayonara* deals with the consequences of romance between American servicemen and Japanese women. Brando thought his role was ill-defined in the screenplay by Paul Osborn and decided to make Major Lloyd Gruver a bigoted Southerner, thus giving him a longer road to travel in terms of ridding himself of the ideas of race with which he had been born. Red Buttons plays an important role in the film's subplot as the American flyer Joe Kelly who marries a Japanese girl named Katsumi (Myoshi Umeki) and suffers greatly for it. A Japanese-American woman with no previous acting experience named Miiko Taka was cast as the lovely actress with whom Major Gruver falls in love, Hana-ogi. The film was sumptuously photographed on location in Kyoto, Kobe, and Osaka, and the beauty and color of Japan in the changing seasons give the film some of its grace and charm.

Director Logan, long a man of the theater, had definite ideas about the project. He insisted that the film be a study in contrasts. For the exterior scenes shot on location, he used natural lighting and rather stark colors; for the indoor studio scenes, warmer colors of red, yellow, and tangerine were employed to accentuate the warmth and beauty of the love scenes between Brando and his Japanese sweetheart. Logan had a long-time interest in the Far East that stemmed from his first visit to Japan in 1951. He had run into his old friend, author James Michener, there, and Michener had promised to write him a play set in Japan. After some rather complicated legal machinations, however, the project became a film adapted from Michener's novel. Logan was still very anxious to direct it, so he prepared carefully and paid special attention to every detail of the production.

Sayonara deals with the clash of rigid American military customs and prejudices against the calm of traditional Japan. Major Lloyd Gruver of the United States Air Force is said to be suffering from "combat fatigue," an excuse invented to allow him to be with his fiancée, Eileen Webster (Patricia Owens), who is the daughter of General Webster (Kent Smith), an important member of the American high command stationed in Tokyo. There he reluctantly agrees to act as best man at the wedding of one of his men, Joe Kelly, who is marrying Katsumi, a Japanese girl. By doing this, Gruver incurs the disapproval of General and Mrs. Webster (Martha Scott). They believe that Gruver approves of marriages between American servicemen and Japanese women, but nothing can be further from the truth. Gruver is a Southerner, and although a decent man, he is subject to the racial ideas he was brought up with.

As he grows to know Japan and its people, however, Gruver begins to change. He becomes fascinated with the country, and, through his continuing friendship with Joe and Katsumi and his love for a beautiful actress, Hana-ogi, he becomes a different person, able to accept and understand a good deal more. Ironically enough, Gruver finds himself involved in a fierce campaign on the part of military authorities to discourage and even disrupt marriages between Japanese and Americans. Unable to persuade General Webster to countermand an order posting Joe Kelly back to the United States without his wife, he formally breaks off his engagement to General Webster's daughter Eileen. When Gruver goes to the Kellys' house to tell them the bad news, he finds the couple dead: they have carried out a joint suicide pact rather than be separated. This event completely marks the end of the old Gruver. He is devastated and tells Hana-ogi of the tragedy as she is about to leave for Tokyo for a theatrical engagement. She tearfully leaves him, supposedly for good, but Gruver follows the acting troop to Tokyo and persuades her to marry him. The fate of Gruver's fiancée is also tied in with Japan. Ironically she, too, has become very attached to Japanese culture and at the end of the film has begun a romance with a famous Japanese actor named Nakamura (Ricardo Montalban).

Within the framework of this simple story, Logan manages to make the film contain a specific Japanese feeling. Kyoto is the principal location and contains the huge temples, the giant Buddhas, the famed Geisha training schools, and the theaters of Bunraku and Kabuki. Warner Bros. also received permission to film in the ancient Imperial Gardens of Kyoto, never before filmed by either Japanese or American companies. It is against the backgrounds of these gardens that the spectacles of the film take place—the Tanbata festival with fireworks and the parade of the All Girl Maytsubayashi Troupe. Counterpoised against the Japanese flavor of the film is the acting of Brando, playing an individual who slowly but visibly reacts to all of the beauty and charm that the audience is seeing on the screen, and who changes forever because of it. It is truly a marvelous performance and one of Brando's most underrated ones.

The film received mixed reviews, for some critics found it corny and overly romantic, while others felt that Brando went too far in his impersonation of a Southerner. It was nominated for nine Academy Awards, however, including Best Picture, Best Actor, and Best Director, and won in three categories— Art Direction, Best Supporting Actor (Buttons), and Best Supporting Actress (Umeki). Brando was not immensely proud of the way the picture turned out, but he was not ashamed either. In an interview he remarked: "There's a lot of hearts and flowers in it, but beneath the romance it attacks prejudices that exist on the part of the Japanese as well as on our part."

Joan Cohen

SCARAMOUCHE

Released: 1952
Production: Carey Wilson for Metro-Goldwyn-Mayer
Direction: George Sidney
Screenplay: Ronald Miller and George Froeschel; based on the novel of the same name by Rafael Sabatini
Cinematography: Charles Rosher
Editing: James E. Newcom
Art direction: Cedric Gibbons and Hans Peters
Set decoration: Edwin P. Willis and Richard Pefferie
Special effects: A. Arnold Gillespie, Warren Newcombe, and Irving C. Ries
Costume design: Gile Steele
Music: Victor Young
Running time: 118 minutes

Principal characters:
Andre Moreau .... Stewart Granger
Lenore .... Eleanor Parker
Aline de Gavrillac .... Janet Leigh
Noel, Marquis de Maynes .... Mel Ferrer
Chevalier de Chabrillaine ....Henry Wilcoxon
Marie Antoinette .... Nina Foch
Gaston Binet .... Robert Coote
Philippe de Valmorin .... Richard Anderson
George de Valmorin .... Lewis Stone
Dr. Dubuque .... John Litel
Pierrot .... Dan Foster
Punchinello .... Owen McGiveney
President .... Douglas Dumbrille

Two of the most popular novelists whose works were adapted as motion-picture swashbucklers were Alexandre Dumas and Rafael Sabatini, often billed as "the modern Dumas." Four of Sabatini's novels were made into silent films, among them *Scaramouche* (1923), with Ramon Novarro, Alice Terry, and Lewis Stone. In 1935, Sabatini's *Captain Blood* was remade as Errol Flynn's first starring vehicle and helped revive the swashbuckler as one of the most popular film genres for the next thirty years. Subsequently, *The Sea Hawk* (1940) used a Sabatini title but has an entirely different plot and cast. *The Black Swan* (1942) kept only one episode from Sabatini's novel; the leading character was changed, and all the rest of the plot was new. For some reason, *Scaramouche*, Sabatini's best and most enduring novel, was not remade until 1952.

In the meantime, Stewart Granger, an up-and-coming British film actor, had been making a name for himself in Gainsborough and J. Arthur Rank productions, where he cut a dashing figure in such costume adventures as *The Man in Gray* (1943), *Caesar and Cleopatra* (1945), *Caravan* (1946), *Captain Boycott* (1947), *Blanche Fury* (1948), and *Saraband for Dead Lovers* (1948). When, in 1950, Flynn, on loan from Warners', chose to star in *Kim* rather than *King Solomon's Mines* at M-G-M, Metro imported Granger to take his place. *King Solomon's Mines* became the studio's biggest hit of 1950 and made Granger an instant Hollywood star. M-G-M promptly put him in *Soldiers Three* (1951), an inferior Kiplingesque adventure-comedy, and then in *The Light Touch* (1952), a comedy of manners about an art thief. Neither of these advanced Granger's image, so the studio looked around for a suitable vehicle to showcase the new star before he lost his luminosity. Fortunately, they hit upon *Scaramouche*.

It is curious that certain genres flourished at particular studios and not at others. The gangster film was mainly a Warners' product. Swashbucklers flourished chiefly at Warners', with Flynn; at Fox, with Tyrone Power; at Edward Small's independent company, and briefly after World War II at Columbia, with Cornel Wilde and Larry Parks. M-G-M, specializing in musicals, family dramas, and soap operas, had rarely done a Western and only two swashbucklers prior to 1950. Perhaps the reason was the contract player system that kept most stars working for one studio rather than free-lancing, and M-G-M did not have any swashbuckling stars in its stable. Its chief adventurer was Clark Gable, who was too obviously American to fit into period costumers, although he was successful in *Mutiny on the Bounty* (1935).

With Granger, M-G-M finally had its swashbuckler, and he became the leading practitioner of the genre in the 1950's, when Flynn was going into decline, Douglas Fairbanks, Jr., had retired from films, and Power was seeking more diverse roles.

Scaramouche is probably the best swashbuckling novel of the twentieth century. Set in the years before the French Revolution, it tells of Andre-Louis Moreau, an illegitimate young Frenchman, who begins as an idealistic lawyer. When the arrogant aristocrat the Marquis de la Tour d'Azyr forces his best friend into a duel and coolly kills him, Moreau dedicates himself to revenge. He uses his power of oratory to inflame the populace against aristocratic power and privilege and helps light the fire of forthcoming revolution. Driven into outlawry, he takes refuge with a band of traveling players and quickly becomes Scaramouche, the star comedian in the Commedia del'Arte company. When the Marquis tries to seduce his girl at the theater, Moreau causes a riot that almost destroys his enemy. Forced to flee again, he goes to Paris, where he apprentices himself to a fencing master and soon becomes the finest swordsman in France. He then becomes a delegate to the Third Estate of the Estates General, where aristocratic swordsmen have been challenging unskilled plebeians into duels and murdering them. Moreau reverses this trend, however, by killing the aristocrats. Eventually, his wish to fight the Marquis is gratified. He runs him through the arm but fails to kill him. Later, he learns that the Marquis is his father.

The 1923 film followed the novel closely; but the 1952 version, written by Ronald Millard and George Froeschel, while following the main outline, takes considerable liberties with the details. As *The New York Times* critic Bosley Crowther noted, they "decided right off that they weren't in the same league with historians. Whatever solemn intimations of the French Revolution may have been in the original Sabatini story were cheerfully simplified by them." Thus the political aspects and episodes of the novel were discarded and replaced merely by a general allegiance to the cause of liberty, equality, and fraternity. Moreau does not serve as a delegate from Nantes, or make speeches, or become a member of the Estates General. Neither does he become master of a fencing salon. Whereas Sabatini relies upon ironic wit and repartee, the film goes in more for slapstick humor, especially in the theater scenes, and takes, as Crowther put it, "a cheekier attitude toward romance." In the film, the aristocratic villain is not Moreau's father but his brother, here called Noel, Marquis de Maynes (Mel Ferrer). The Marquis does kill Philippe de Valmorin (Vilmorin in the book), and Moreau does learn to master the sword in order to get revenge. Discarding the rhetoric and politics of the novel, however, the film version becomes a spirited, energetic romp, mostly in the theater, where Moreau performs as a masked clown while dallying with the vaudeville troupe's red-haired, amorous, devil-may-care leading lady, Lenore (Eleanor Parker). In both novel and film, Moreau's true love is the aristocratic lady Aline (Janet Leigh); it is a film cliché for the noble hero to have two loves, one a lively gamin or guttersnipe, the other an elegant lady. The former is invariably more appealing, but the caste system always seems to demand that the hero marry the latter. Usually, the gamin dies saving his life, but in *Scaramouche*, which never takes itself very seriously, she ends up as the mistress of young Napoleon Bonaparte. As the fiery actress, Parker almost steals the show; certainly she is more engaging than either the decorative but bland Leigh or Nina Foch, who is worked into the plot as Marie Antoinette.

Essentially *Scaramouche* is Granger's film. The novel opens with the line, "He was born with a gift of laughter and a sense that the world was mad." Granger, with his reckless grin and sardonic manner, fits the role admirably. Originally, it was planned for Granger to play both the lead and the villain, with Elizabeth Taylor as Aline and Ava Gardner as Lenore, but the revised cast left Granger only with the role of Moreau/Scaramouche. In it, he avoids the more intense and grim aspects of the novel's hero; and except for the scene in which his best friend is killed, he performs with great panache as a light-hearted adventurer. He seems to be enjoying himself immensely and communicates that enjoyment to the audience. The theater scenes are much more slapstick than in the novel; in the latter, Moreau is a brilliant comic actor, whereas in the film, he plays more broadly and relies mainly upon pratfalls. This approach is a bit disappointing to fans of the novel, but the film is great fun in its own right.

The climactic swordfight, performed not at dawn on a duelling ground, as in the novel, but in the theater, with Moreau in full Scaramouche costume, is the longest and most spectacular ever filmed. In preparation for it, Granger had eight weeks of training with a fencing master. The duel, which takes place all over the theater, lasts eight minutes and is at least twice the length of any preceding movie duel. According to M-G-M, Granger and Ferrer had to memorize eighty-seven individual passes and perform twenty-eight stunts. In terms of academic fencing, the duel is often preposterous, as the adversaries thrust and parry while balancing themselves on the theater seats and balcony rails, swinging on curtains, and sliding down sashes. It is all extremely agile and athletic and visually exciting, however, even if technically silly.

The cast all perform ably, but top honors go to Granger and Parker for their spirited, good-humored characterizations. It is worth noting that Lewis Stone, the wicked marquis of the 1923 version, has a small role as Georges de Valmorin.

With its slapstick and flippant attitude toward romance, *Scaramouche*, as *Variety* observed, "never seems to be quite certain whether it is a costume adventure drama or a satire on costume adventure dramas." Director George Sidney had used a similar approach when directing Gene Kelly in *The Three Musketeers* (1948). Both films are fun, but neither takes itself very seriously. *Cue* magazine may have been most accurate in calling *Scaramouche* "a roaring romantic spectacle." It was one of the big hits of the year, and in consequence, M-G-M became one of the main producers of swashbucklers in the first half of the 1950's, with *Ivanhoe* (1952), *Knights of the Round Table* (1953), and *Quentin Durward* (1955), all starring Robert Taylor, and with a sequence of other Granger costume epics, such as a remake of *The Prisoner of Zenda* (1952), *All the Brothers Were Valiant* (1953), *Young Bess* (1953), *Beau Brummel* (1954), and Fritz Lang's *Moonfleet* (1955). After 1956, Granger began to get inferior roles, and his career declined. His last swashbuckler was *The Swordsman of Siena* (1962); thereafter, he appeared mainly in low-budget European productions. *Scaramouche* is not his best film (*Saraband for Dead Lovers*, *King Solomon's Mines*, and *Moonfleet* are better in some ways), but it is one of the highlights of his career and established him as the preeminent swashbuckler of the 1950's.

Robert E. Morsberger

THE SCARLET EMPRESS

Released: 1934
Production: Paramount
Direction: Josef von Sternberg
Screenplay: Manuel Komroff; based on a diary of Catherine the Great
Cinematography: Bert Glennon
Editing: no listing
Interior decoration: Hans Dreier and staff headed by Peter Ballbusch and
    Richard Kollorsz
Costume design: Travis Banton
Running time: 110 minutes

Principal characters:
Sophia Frederica/Catherine II .... Marlene Dietrich
Count Alexei ....John Lodge
Grand Duke Peter .... Sam Jaffe
Empress Elizabeth .... Louise Dresser

Perhaps *The Scarlet Empress* was best described by its director, Josef von Sternberg, when he called it "a relentless excursion into style." Ostensibly the film is about Catherine the Great, the eighteenth century Russian Empress, but the story of her life is not so much told as used as a point of departure for an audaciously extravagant film which is essentially a comedy. Loosely based on Catherine's diaries, it shows her youth as a German Princess, her journey to Russia to marry the Grand Duke Peter (whom she discovers is insane), and her marriage and disillusionment in a decadent court. It ends with the murder of her husband and her seizure of the throne.

Although some regard film as a collaborative art while others think that the director should be given credit for the overall result, about *The Scarlet Empress* there should be no argument. It definitely is the creation of its director. Sternberg claims to have dominated everything—scenery, sets (including the statues and paintings used), costumes, script, cinematography, music, and "every gesture by a player." The result is a work in which the visual impact is stunning and dominates all the rest.

Other films may be aimed at the emotions or the mind, but this one is aimed at the eye. Everything else in *The Scarlet Empress* is subordinated to the visual aspect, which is especially true of the narrative. The film does tell a fairly clear story, but it is simple and straightforward with few nuances to complicate things. Impatient with the necessity of advancing the narrative, Sternberg frequently uses written titles to explain what is happening or what is going to happen. Thus there is never any confusion about the plot to distract the viewer from the images.

The acting, too, is subordinated by being stylized. The viewer soon realizes that Sternberg is using acting in a quite different way from that of most directors. Instead of trying to evoke performances from his actors and actresses which would make their characters three-dimensional, credible creations, he has them, for the most part, keep their portrayals and delivery of lines flat and unemotional. This flatness of delivery and deliberately constrained style is used for both comedic and serious scenes, and in both cases it distances the viewer from the content and gives more emphasis to the visual style. Marlene Dietrich as Catherine does more acting than the others, but even her performance is a limited, stylized one, especially in the first part of the film, in which she indicates her innocence by a wide-eyed, open-mouthed look. Then, after we learn from a title that she has become disillusioned and decides to exploit her sexuality, she abandons that look.

The fact that the film is a comedy is beyond question, but it is such a strange one that it has confused many viewers. Comedies are usually set in the present, but this seems to be a film about actual historical characters. Also, it does not maintain a distinctly comic tone throughout. Instead, it sometimes slips in a funny line in what otherwise seems to be a serious scene. For example, when the old Empress (Louise Dresser) receives Catherine and her mother, she gives them each a medal and then says, "May you wear it in good health, and be careful it doesn't scratch you." Not all the humor is verbal. One of the early scenes shows the young princess Catherine ostentatiously kissing the hand of each person in the room. The effect is comic but again disconcerting because of its ambiguity. Sternberg has used slight ridicule rather than complete burlesque to achieve his effect. With the character of the Grand Duke Peter (Sam Jaffe), however, the comedy is more obvious. Described by the titles as a half-wit, he is always accompanied by elaborately costumed black servants, one a hunchback and another a boy with wolfhounds. His blond wig, bulging eyes, and foolish grin make him look somewhat like Harpo Marx, and his main activities are playing with toy soldiers and boring holes in the walls so he can spy on Catherine. Even Peter is not a completely comic figure, however, for when he becomes Czar, he orders tortures, murders, and floggings and threatens to get rid of Catherine.

The sets and costumes are as elaborate as the narrative and acting are simplified; in fact, they frequently dwarf and almost overpower the characters. The Russian court is filled with large, gargoylelike statues, many of which hold candles. We are introduced to the old Empress by a shot of a grotesque sculpture of an eagle, which we find—as the camera tilts down—is the back of her throne and is much larger than she is. Later we see Catherine's face nearly lost amid the misshapen faces of the statues around her. Only the lighting gives her any emphasis. The costuming, too, can only be described as extravagant. All characters are dressed ornately with great attention to detail, but Catherine is dressed most lavishly and never wears the same costume twice. As the young princess she wears an elaborately beruffled white dress and a bow in her hair, while in Russia, she wears dozens of different costumes, including one which features pearls from wrist to elbow, around her neck, and in several rows on her tiara. Another is trimmed in feathers, and several use furs; one has a huge fur muff which matches her fur hat. In the final scene she wears a white hussar's uniform as she rides through the palace to claim the throne.

The sets, costumes, and actors are further stylized and made visually stunning by the lighting. It is dramatic and effectively uses shadow and darkness, not to convey a mood, but for aesthetic effect. Each composition, each shot, is beautiful in itself as well as in relation to the rest of the film. In general there are dark shadows or figures in darkness in each scene, with lighter shadows on the faces of the principal characters. Adding to the patterns of light and shadow are the large candles held by the grotesque statues throughout the palace. The overall effect is a visual richness in which each frame is lavishly filled with detail and lighted dramatically. The use of the camera and editing is also expressive. The camera sometimes lingers on one detail; at other times it moves through a scene or tilts up or down to reveal more details. With such a wealth of detail the pace of the editing is generally measured, with many long dissolves between scenes.

In such an opulent film, no sequence is uninteresting, but particularly noteworthy are two: a montage of torture scenes near the beginning of the film, and the wedding. In the first, the young princess is read stories of Czars and Czarinas who were hangmen and we see a series of fantastic and grotesque images of torture, ending with a huge bell in which a man hanging upside-down is the clapper, helplessly swinging as the bell is rung. Sternberg ends the sequence with a dissolve from the swinging man to the princess happily playing on a swing. The wedding scene begins by showing the huge, ornate chamber filled with flags, hanging tapestries, priests, and candles. As the ritual proceeds, we see Catherine and a handsome courtier exchange looks; then the sequence concentrates on Catherine's veiled face and the candle she is holding, its flame wavering as she breathes.

Another sequence embodies all the various aspects of the film. Having discovered that Count Alexei (John Lodge), who has been pursuing her and has given her a locket with his picture in it, is the lover of the old Empress Elizabeth, Catherine throws the locket out the window. It catches on one branch of a tree, stops momentarily, then drops to another, then another, before falling into a snowdrift. The camera lingers on the beauty of the locket hanging in the moonlight at each step of its slow descent. Then Catherine regrets her impulsive action and runs out to retrieve the locket. She is stopped by a guard who does not recognize her. Unable to convince him who she is, she lets herself be seduced, saying, "Well, Lieutenant, you are fortunate— very fortunate." The sexual intrigue, the comedy, and emphasis on the visual (in the depiction of the locket falling) are characteristic of *The Scarlet Empress* from start to finish.

The Scarlet Empress is, then, a masterpiece of visual stylization. It is not to everyone's taste, especially since it purposely tries to keep the viewer slightly off balance by mixing comedy and historical drama. It is a film in which almost nothing is subtle but every effect is carefully planned. Sternberg shows himself to be truly a poet of shadow and light.

Timothy W. Johnson

SCARLET STREET

Released: 1945
Production: Walter Wanger for Diana Productions; released by Universal
Direction: Fritz Lang
Screenplay: Dudley Nichols; based on the play *La Chienne* by Georges de la Fourcharliere
Cinematography: Milton Krasner
Editing: Arthur Hilton
Running time: 103 minutes

> *Principal characters:*
> Christopher Cross .... Edward G. Robinson
> Kitty March .... Joan Bennett
> Johnny .... Dan Duryea

Fritz Lang's *Scarlet Street*, a remake of Jean Renoir's *La Chienne* (1931), captures the fatalistic tone of French poetic realism and the more cynical spirit of the American *film noir*. The film begins after a dinner honoring twenty-five years of faithful service by Christopher Cross (Edward G. Robinson), a middle-aged clerk. Chris accidently stumbles into a web of intrigue which ultimately causes his downfall when he defends the "honor" of a woman who is being slapped around on a street corner. Chris's dream is to be loved by a young woman, someone who can see his artistic soul hidden beneath years of gray hair and wrinkles. His marriage, generated out of loneliness, is a fiasco. He cannot live up to the memory of his wife's first husband, and out of desperation he turns to his new found friend, Kitty March (Joan Bennett), for companionship.

Unknown to Chris, Kitty and her lover Johnny (Dan Duryea) think that he is a rich artist and plan to blackmail him for some easy money. Chris rents a studio apartment with funds embezzled from his job, and he supports Kitty while he pursues his art. Johnny tries to peddle some of Chris's surrealistic paintings and starts a sizable commotion in the art world. The paintings are considered the work of a genius, and attempts are made to find the painter. Johnny convinces a famous critic and an art dealer that Kitty is the person who painted them, and she becomes an instant celebrity. Chris approves, wanting Kitty to be linked to him in a symbolic marriage—her name on his paintings.

His wife's first husband then resurfaces, which frees him for Kitty's love. When Chris stumbles on Kitty and Johnny in a compromising situation, his entire world is shattered. Returning to the studio later he murders Kitty with an ice-pick. Chris is not suspected of the murder because he has kept his relationship discreet, and Johnny is sought as the murderer instead. Chris's embezzlement meanwhile is discovered and he is fired.

During the trial Johnny tries to explain his innocence and convince the jury that Chris Cross was the real artist who created the paintings attributed to Kitty. He fails, is sentenced to death in the electric chair, and dies for a crime he never committed. Chris is now a broken man; he has gone through a moral crisis and emerged a homeless bum. He cannot accept his guilt, nor can he convince anyone that he murdered Kitty and condemned an innocent man to death for cheating him out of an improbable love affair.

Lang had been a major filmmaker for nearly twenty years prior to making *Scarlet Street*. He was one of the most important directors during the golden age of the German cinema, and he directed such silent classics as *Siegfried* (1924), *Metropolis* (1927), *Spies* (1928), and the innovative sound film *M* (1931), starring Peter Lorre. Lang left Germany when Hitler rose to power and eventually settled in Hollywood in 1935. There he began a new career that would last for thirty years.

His first American film, *Fury* (1936), concerns a man who is wrongly accused of murder and experiences the violence of an uncontrollable lynch mob. He survives and goes underground, driven by the spirit of revenge to see the leader of the mob persecuted for his assumed death. After an emotional trial of the mob's ringleaders, he appears and symbolically ameliorates them. They are freed but can never live down the brutal truth of their heinous deeds. In many ways *Fury* is similar to *Scarlet Street*, except that in the latter film, Chris Cross, guilty of a crime of passion, places the blame on an innocent man and watches him be sentenced and executed for loving the woman of his dreams. The cynicism of this film is unrelenting. In *Fury*, by contrast, the principal character is able to see the dilemma and move beyond revenge; his outlook is jaded, but he remains morally true. Chris Cross is weak and is driven by revenge. Although his crime is never recognized by the institutions of justice, he pays for his crime internally. His conscience will not let him rest, and his life becomes a nightmare, a living hell from which there is no escape.

Robinson captures the essence of Chris Cross with great dramatic skill. He is the perfect embodiment of a man hungering for affection, an innocent man trapped by his dreams. Lang had used Robinson, Bennett, and Duryea for his previous film, *Woman in the Window* (1944), which can be seen as a sort of blueprint for the more cynical *Scarlet Street*. In *Woman in the Window* Robinson is also put into a sexual triangle which ends in murder. That film, however, is constructed as a dream and presents a world of fantasy. *Scarlet Street* takes the same dream and turns it into reality.

The use of songs such as "Melancholy Baby" creates themes for the characters. These, combined with its straightforward filmmaking style, give *Scarlet Street* an unusual power. The most underrated factor in the film is the creation of a Greenwich Village environment. This studio environment is a throwback to the German cinema's famed "street films." The buildings and rain-slicked pavement come alive in *Scarlet Street*; one of Chris's paintings even shows the street interpreted surrealistically with a huge serpent threatening the two-dimensional environment. The one thing that characterizes both his artwork and his life is his lack of perspective.

Lang is able to put the elements of plot, acting, and surface environment together to create a portrait of hopelessness and shattered dreams. *Scarlet Street* is the cinematic equivalent of a nightmare, with Lang becoming the master of dreams.

Carl F. Macek

THE SCOUNDREL

Released: 1935
Production: Ben Hecht and Charles MacArthur
Direction: Ben Hecht and Charles MacArthur
Assistant direction: Lee Garmes
Screenplay: Ben Hecht and Charles MacArthur (AA)
Cinematography: Lee Garmes
Editing: no listing
Running time: 75 minutes

Principal characters:
Anthony Mallare ....Noel Coward
Cora Moore ....Julie Haydon
Paul Decker ....Stanley Ridges
Carlotta .... Rosita Moreno
Julia Vivian .... Martha Sleeper
Margie ....Hope Williams
Jimmy Clay .... Ernest Cossart
Mildred Langwiter .... Everley Gregg
Maurice Stern .... Edward Cianneli
Mrs. Rolinson .... Helen Strickland
Rothenstien ....Lionel Stander
Slezack .... Harry Davenport
Luigi .... William Ricciardi
Scrub Woman ....Isabelle Foster
Fortune Teller .... Madame Shushkina

The Scoundrel marked Noel Coward's first appearance in a sound film and, in fact, his first film since a "bit" part in D. W. Griffith's 1918 production of *Hearts of the World*. Coward had come to America to direct his play *Point Valaine*, starring Alfred Lunt and Lynn Fontanne, and when it proved to be a critical and commercial failure, he agreed to do the film for a salary of five thousand dollars on the assurance that his leading lady would be codirector and screenwriter Charles MacArthur's wife, Helen Hayes. As it transpired, Hayes was not available, and the leading lady was the relatively minor stage and screen actress, Julie Haydon.

Ben Hecht and Charles MacArthur had begun their independent producing program with *Crime Without Passion* (1934), which was followed by *Once in a Blue Moon* (1936) and *The Scoundrel*, but because the last was considered such a prestige effort, not only because of the presence of Coward but also because it had obvious literary links to New York's famed Algonquin Hotel Round Table, *The Scoundrel* was released as the second Hecht-MacArthur production. It cost $190,000 to produce, which was nothing by Hollywood standards, and was shot at Paramount's Astoria Studios on Long Island. The film might have been written for Coward, whose acid tones were perfect for such lines as, in answer to a proposed walk in Central Park, "On a Sunday? It's full of butlers!" or in response to his copublisher's query "Are we interested in the workingman's woes?" "Only vaguely." Hecht, however, has written, "I never cared too much for Coward. Vaudeville patter with an English accent. And a superiority complex that went over big with sofa-cushion menders."

The Scoundrel, whose working title was *Miracle in 49th Street*, was based in part on an earlier novel by Hecht, while the character of Anthony Mallare was supposedly based on theatrical producer Jed Harris. The leading character's name comes from a privately published pornographic novel of the 1920's, *Fantasius Mallare*. Both Hecht and MacArthur appear, uncredited, in the film, as two bums in a flophouse to which Cora Moore (Julie Haydon) goes, looking for Paul Decker (Stanley Ridges).

Anthony Mallare (Noel Coward), the scoundrel of the title, is an elegant, arrogant New York publisher, ever ready with a witty quip to impress the crowd of authors who gather around him (all of whom despise and ridicule him when he is not there), his partner, and his secretary. "He is Mr. Hecht's favorite hero," wrote Andre Sennwald in *The New York Times* (May 3, 1935), "a thing of evil who destroys everything he touches." Among the literary crowd ever present in Mallare's outer office are many caricatures of members of the famed Algonquin Round Table, including, uncredited, Alexander Woollcott playing a character similar to himself: Vanderveer Veyden, a literate sophisticate familiar with every piece of New York literary society gossip. Every member of the Mallare literary set is as phony as Mallare himself. As for Mallare, his true character is soon revealed when he refuses a miniscule advance to a starving professor-author and sends him away knowing he will commit suicide.

Into this group comes Cora Moore, a young, innocent, and unspoiled poetess who grows to love Mallare, despite his warning her, "I am never nice." She breaks up with her boyfriend, Paul Decker, on Mallare's account, but eventually Mallare ditches her for a concert pianist, the only woman who seemed shallower than he, whom he pursues when she leaves for Bermuda. Cora Moore tells him, "Not a single human being will cry for you," and she hopes his plane will crash. That very thing happens when bad weather brings down the plane in the ocean, and Mallare and his fellow passengers are presumed dead.

No one grieves for the dead Mallare. His partner is moving into his office when he is shocked to discover Mallare sitting at his desk. A strangely quiet and brooding Mallare tells his partner that he is not dead, but both the partner and Mallare's secretary are confused and frightened when, after the publisher's departure, they find seaweed lying on his desk.

During a scene in Mallare's apartment that night, the audience learns the truth. Mallare is indeed dead, but because there is nothing but everlasting night for those for whom no tears are shed to save them, Mallare has been allowed to return to earth for one month to find someone to cry for him. As a member of his literary circle puts it, however, "When a man dies, people weep. When an attitude dies, people shrug." No one weeps for Mallare.

Desperately, Mallare searches for Cora Moore, the one real woman in his life. She is living in a slum room with Paul Decker, who has lost his job for embezzling funds. When Mallare eventually finds them on his last day of hope, Decker, in anger at what Mallare has wrought, shoots Mallare and then himself. Bullets cannot harm a dead man, however, and Mallare is unhurt. For the first time showing any sign of any emotion, Mallare begs God not to punish these two innocent people for his sins. A miracle occurs and Decker's wounds are healed. In joy, Cora Moore falls at Mallare's feet, crying. Mallare's soul is saved. God's voice, perhaps ominously, is also the voice of Coward.

The film's chief appeal lies in the witty, brilliant, and caustic dialogue—one must admire a screenwriter who describes the streets of New York in the summer as looking like a socialist picnic—and in the brilliant performance of Coward. No one in the cast comes close to Coward's brilliance, least of all Haydon as Cora Moore, who is too much of an actress to lose herself in the role. The special effects are minor but well handled, such as the scene in which Coward stands with his back to the camera looking at the storm outside his apartment and those windows open as Coward walks forward to be drowned in a superimposed ocean.

The critics liked *The Scoundrel*, although the film was really too literate to be a commercial success. It did, however, open in New York at the Radio City Music Hall, a theater which usually runs potentially "commercial" films. *Photoplay* (July, 1935) described the film as "An exceptional, magnificently executed character study. . . . It's arty, but if this is art, let's have more of it!" "Filmgoers who fail to see *The Scoundrel*," commented *The New York Times*, "are likely to be frozen out of after-dinner conversations for the next few weeks." Abel Green in *Variety* (May 8, 1935) wrote, "It'll appeal to the palates of the pseudo, near- and full-fledged sophisticates but it'll leave the average film fan bewildered. It's not box-office in the accepted sense."

Of the four independent Hecht-MacArthur productions, *The Scoundrel* is the most impressive, and the one that has remained popular to the present time. Coward certainly never had a better vehicle to bring out his ascerbic wit, even including those written by himself.

Anthony Slide

THE SEA WOLF

Released: 1941
Production: Hal B. Wallis for Warner Bros.
Direction: Michael Curtiz
Screenplay: Robert Rossen; based on the novel of the same name by Jack London
Cinematography: Sol Polito
Editing: George Amy
Art direction: Anton Grot
Special effects: Byron Haskin and Nathan Levinson
Music: Erich Wolfgang Korngold
Running time: 100 minutes

Principal characters:
Wolf Larsen	Edward G. Robinson
George Leach	John Garfield
Ruth Webster	Ida Lupino
Humphrey Van Weyden	Alexander Knox
Doctor Louie Prescott	Gene Lockhart
Cooky	Barry Fitzgerald

The first screen adaptation of Jack London's *The Sea Wolf* appeared in 1913, within the author's lifetime and only ten years after the novel was written. Since then, six other versions have been filmed, the last being *Wolf Larsen* in 1957. Of all of these versions, the most memorable remains the 1941 Warner Bros. production directed by Michael Curtiz and starring Edward G. Robinson as Wolf Larsen, the tyrannical and amoral captain of the *Ghost*.

Throughout the 1930's, Warners' turned out a cycle of socially relevant dramas, such as *I Am a Fugitive from a Chain Gang* (1932), *Wild Boys of the Road* (1933), *Marked Women* (1937), and *They Won't Forget* (1937). These films were peopled with working-class characters that appealed to a Depression-era audience, and they combined realism with melodramatic action. In a quest for greater prestige Warner Bros. also searched for scripts adapted from literary classics. *The Sea Wolf* must have seemed like a good choice, since it contains plenty of excitement and has something of a literary reputation. London's primary thematic intention in the novel had been to attack Friedrich Nietzsche's philosophy of the superman through the allegorical figure of Wolf Larsen. In 1941, with the Fascist powers acting upon their concept of the "Master Race," threatening to swallow up a large portion of the globe, the analogy of the story to the atmosphere of the 1940's must have impressed the film's screenwriter, Robert Rossen.

Although several of Hollywood's wartime propaganda efforts may appear simplistic or even elementary to modern viewers, it seems rather presumptuous to judge from the critically safer vantage point of hindsight. In fact, some of the trendier films of the more recent 1960's also seem naïve by today's standards. In the 1940's, however, it was not difficult to be affected by the thinly disguised propaganda in films such as *The Sea Wolf* or Alfred Hitchcock's *Lifeboat* (1944). In the latter film, for example, a lifeboat serves as a microcosm containing all of the conflicts that the war imposed on society at large. The sealing-ship *Ghost* functions in a similar manner in *The Sea Wolf*, and it is not difficult to note certain resemblances between Walter Slezak's character of the Nazi captain in *Lifeboat* and that of Wolf Larsen as portrayed by Robinson in *The Sea Wolf*.

The Sea Wolf is an adventure film with overtones of sadism and grandiose delusions. The plot itself is simple and little changed from the novel. The survivors of a ferry crash are picked up by a freighter commanded by a psychopathic captain, Wolf Larsen (Edward G. Robinson), who holds them captive. The characters include a writer, Humphrey Van Weyden (Alexander Knox), two young and rather tough escaped convicts, George Leach (John Garfield) and Ruth Webster (Ida Lupino), a drunken doctor named Louie Prescott (Gene Lockhart), and a cook (Barry Fitzgerald), in addition to a crew played by a number of Warner Bros. stock "heavies."

Larsen's death ship is little more than a pirate schooner on which the captives suffer through beatings, a suicide, and finally a mutiny during which the survivors attempt to escape. Finally, Van Weyden, Leach, and Webster, who have escaped in an open boat but are adrift aimlessly in the fog, are pursued by Larsen on the *Ghost*. The malevolent captain suffers from severe headaches, however, and is overcome by a seizure accompanied by blindness. When the small boat finally comes alongside the *Ghost* in the fog, the three escapees stumble back onboard to find the captain alone and blind in his mutiny-ruined ship, evil to the end.

In his adaption of the London novel, Rossen made some important changes in the characters. London had narrated his story from the point of view of one Humphrey Van Weyden, an effete intellectual who, although a weakling at the beginning, gradually becomes stronger, outwitting Larsen in the process. The film adopts an omniscient view, and the character of Van Weyden is eased from the center of the story. The primary result of this change is that Larsen looms as a much more dominant figure in the film than he was in the novel. Also, one of the novel's minor characters, George Leach, who had drowned midway through the book, is shifted to a leading role in opposition to Larsen in the film version. It is ultimately Van Weyden who drowns along with Larsen in order to save Leach. With this shift in the plot, the character of Van Weyden's romantic interest, Maud Brewster, is eliminated. In her place is substituted a new female character, Ruth Webster, who is the type of good-bad girl ideally suited to the character of Leach as portrayed by Garfield. Although she serves a similar function to that of London's Maud, she is more directly pivotal to the conflict between Leach and Larsen. Both of these lovers are on the run from the law. Leach, in fact, volunteered for service on the *Ghost* while several other crew members had to be shanghaied.

Despite the changes and the compressions necessary to bring the story to the screen, a good deal of the original novel, including its central theme, remains completely intact. One could even argue that the film has made some improvements. For example, in London's treatment, it takes a certain amount of willpower on the part of the reader to generate much sympathy for Van Weyden. In the film, audience identification with Garfield's Leach is made immediately, and the conflict between him and Larsen is structurally better balanced. Essentially, the role of Van Weyden is the same in both versions— he is an onlooker. Ruth Webster is also a much more convincing character in the film than is the rather bloodless and idealized Maud in the written version. She also helps get things going sooner, in a dramatic sense, by entering the story at the beginning rather than halfway through.

Whether all of these changes reflected Rossen's own ideas or were demanded by the studio's front office is unverifiable and ultimately unimportant. Intellectual characters such as Van Weyden rarely figured centrally in the themes of films of the 1940's. Ideologically, the film fits well within the Warners' mold of socially conscious thrillers, several of which Rossen himself had written. It also bears certain similarities to several of the writer's later films made when he was a director, notably his version of novelist Robert Penn Warren's *All the King's Men* (1949).

Stylistically, the film's authorship is even harder to resolve. From his first Hollywood feature, *The Third Degree*, in 1926, until 1953, the Hungarian-born Curtiz dutifully filled his contract at Warner Bros. to every one's mutual satisfaction. After the collapse of the studio system, when Curtiz was free to go elsewhere, his career ironically went into a precipitous decline. A competent rather than inspired director, even his best films, such as *Casablanca* (1942) and *Mildred Pierce* (1945), seem successful only partially as a result of his direct responsibility and appear more visibly dependent in varying degrees upon other hands as well as choice casting. None of these films is without directorial flair, but Curtiz could never imbue his films with any consistent personality as did Raoul Walsh in similar circumstances. Apart from a detectable tendency toward expressionism, which seems endemic of many films of the 1940's, it is difficult to discern his stylistic signature from other middle-of-the-road stylists such as Jean Negulesco or George Sherman.

In the case of *The Sea Wolf*, Curtiz is ably abetted by Sol Polito's low-key cinematography, Anton Grot's art direction, and the special effects of Byron Haskin and Nathan Levinson. For long shots, miniatures were used, since the entire film was shot in the studio. This was probably a matter of thematic necessity. The setting is almost continually fogbound, creating a claustrophobic atmosphere. The expressive use of back-lighting, as, for example, when

Ruth Webster goes to meet Larsen in his cabin, imparts an oppressively Germanic flavor to the film. Erich Wolfgang Korngold, departing from the style he established in the Errol Flynn "swashbuckler" films, composed an excellently moody score.

The casting is particularly appropriate, although at times it verges close to stereotyping, particularly in the case of Fitzgerald as the reptilian Cooky. Garfield and Lupino create some chemistry between them, balancing their hard-bitten roles with a degree of vulnerability. As Van Weyden, Knox is intelligent and quietly courageous and not at all weak like the character in the novel. Dominating all of the scenes, however, is Robinson as Wolf Larsen. There is always some danger of Larsen's becoming a mere abstraction of evil, but Robinson makes the character credible and human. This is particularly true in the film, when the nearly insane and blind Larsen staggers around the *Ghost*. Robinson fully realizes the tragic dimension of the role. For all of the film's many contributions, it is Robinson's performance that stays in the mind longest.

Mike Vanderlan

SÉANCE ON A WET AFTERNOON

Released: 1964
Production: Richard Attenborough for Allied Film Makers
Direction: Bryan Forbes
Screenplay: Bryan Forbes; based on the novel of the same name by Mark McShane
Cinematography: Gerry Turpin
Editing: Derek York
Running time: 115 minutes

Principal characters:
Myra Savage	Kim Stanley
Bill Savage	Richard Attenborough
Amanda Clayton	Judith Donner
Mrs. Clayton	Nanette Newman
Mr. Clayton	Mark Eden
Walsh	Patrick Magee
Plainclothesman	John Lees

Séance on a Wet Afternoon is an odd masterpiece that would seem, on the face of it, to be in a genre by itself, just as many masterpieces seem to create their own categories. The plot concerns Myra Savage (Kim Stanley), a professional medium who coerces her timid husband Bill (Richard Attenborough) into kidnaping a small child. The object is, she feels (or believes she is told, by the spirit of their dead son), to provide her parents and the police with the right clues at the right time and thus enhance her reputation. The child and the ransom money would eventually be returned intact.

Bill is terrified of the illegalities involved, but he is equally terrified of his wife. Whenever he protests, if only to interject a note of sense, Myra either ignores him or makes it sound like his failure. Sometimes she pretends to be helpless, or, if she can get away with it, she persuades Bill to claim (although he knows better) that he is, in fact, the one who is helpless. The dead son whose spirit is allegedly guiding this conspiracy has died at birth, but if Bill brings this up, the discussion invariably ends with his assuming the blame even for that occurrence. The elusive nature of this consuming interdependence, much more than the kidnaping, is what generates the film's suspense.

The kidnaping is accomplished cleanly. Bill shows himself to be quite capable when he is out of his wife's clutches. He distracts the chauffeur of the car carrying the child, drives away with the child, and takes her to a remote field in order to switch vehicles. The child, Amanda Clayton (Judith Donner), is also resourceful, however; out in the countryside, she manages to seal herself completely inside the family limousine. Bill eventually uncovers a key, but not before he is reduced to pounding on the window, begging her to come out.

Once she is brought to Bill's house (knocked out with ether), the couple install her in an upstairs room made over to look like part of a hospital. When she comes to, they tell her that she was sick, and when she asks about the kidnaping, they tell her it was just a dream. The child is nevertheless suspicious since her room does not look at all like the one in the hospital where she had her tonsils out. At that time, there was more than one Doctor and Nurse, and they did not wear masks all the time, like Myra and Bill. Bill, for his part, finds her all the more endearing for being so shrewd. They develop a rapport, in spite of his mask, and their relationship brings out the father in him. Myra, on the other hand, for all of her talk of understanding children, can develop no rapport at all with the little girl. Whenever she speaks about her one gets the idea (confirmed in Bill's facial reaction) that she is actually speaking of herself as a child. When forced to confront a child as a real and separate entity, she is frightened and even a little appalled.

The child drives a wedge deeper between her captors in their marriage. The plan, however, is going like clockwork. Myra visits the child's parents, Mr. and Mrs. Clayton (Mark Eden and Nanette Newman), and manages, successfully, to console the mother with news that she received "in a dream." Bill collects the ransom in a harrowing chase through a subway. Yet on an emotional level, things are going terribly wrong. The spirit of their dead son, Myra tells Bill, is urging them to keep the little girl. Bill, as usual, tries to inject some degree of sense into the situation, but it is no use.

Wednesday afternoon rolls around and with it Myra's weekly séance. The mother of the kidnaped girl is among the small group of regulars. Myra could not be more pleased since this will be the making of her reputation. During her trance, she begins to lose control. The little girl, half conscious beyond the wall and suffering from a mild fever, begins to call out for her mother. Her cry is completely muffled by the wall, but the mother reacts as if to a presence in her subconscious. Bill, seeing this, recognizes that there is a disturbance going on in the child's room and rushes out to attend to her. In his absence, Myra's trance becomes a communication with the spirit of her dead son, incoherent to the others but alarming in the context of the kidnaping. She collapses. After the others have gone and Bill revives her, she relates the message: their son wants them to send him the spirit of the child—in other words, to kill her. Bill is stunned into silence at this request. Since the ransom escapade, he has had no compunction about talking back. It is he who is taking the direct risks now. He is not a killer and has grown to love the child, so when Myra charges him with carrying out the deed, he only does what she commands up to a point. He carries the girl, sleeping and warmly bundled, to a place in the forest where she will be easily found by a scout troop.

The denouement comes that evening. Two detectives, who have been circling around the Savages ever since Myra visited the parents, pay a call. Detective Walsh (Patrick Magee) believes strongly in psychic phenomena and asks if Myra can stage a séance, on the chance that it might provide helpful information. Bill is aware that the inspectors are looking them over as possible suspects, but says nothing. Myra, either unaware of this or (more likely) fearing it but unable to avoid the inevitable, agrees, and in her trance she gives a symbolic but unequivocal confession. Walsh and the other plainclothesman (John Lees) look over at Bill, who nods. They are sympathetic to the couple even as they have to arrest them. Myra is barely out of her trance as they are led away.

There would seem to be no weakness whatever about this film; it accomplishes exactly what it set out to do. The situation and the relationships between the characters ring true because of the splendid performances of every actor in the production. Stanley and Attenborough in particular provide such a strong sense of pathos and dignity that the story, although it describes an extreme situation, never becomes preposterous.

Ambiguity plays a strong role in this film, as the exact nature of the crime Myra and Bill are planning is not revealed until the kidnaping is under way. Similarly, Myra is portrayed as both mad and quite potentially clairvoyant (certainly intensely sensitive), and the razor's edge balance of this dimension multiplies the story's internal conflicts. Everything is in a state of transference. For example, Bill's relationship with Myra deteriorates throughout the course of the crime as she deteriorates mentally. By taking the risks and caring for the child, Bill is restored to potency and a mastery of his own will. The child's cry in the next room becomes, in the minds of the séance participants, a psychic phenomenon and is seen, in the omniscient view of the story, as an ironic misinterpretation on their part. Yet did the child simply call for her mother in her delirium or did her delirium place her in a receptive state? The answers to all of these things is approached and yet left to its mystery.

The intricacies of this twisting plot are kept in firm grasp by the screenplay and the direction of Bryan Forbes. The cool, rainy-day look of suburban London dominates the conscious levels of the film, but it is the dramatic structure, both in plotting and execution, that finally prevails. The grey chilliness provides an exact antithesis to the nervous heat generated by the actors, Stanley in particular. No move in the film is superfluous, yet the surface details—the bric-a-brac filling the Savages' house, Bill's motorcycle with its side car, and the cloaks Myra wears—all lead outward in a kind of spiral of superfluity, suggesting universes existing both within and without the characters, their house, and their story.

The film received almost unanimously good reviews when it first opened, although many of these took the vaguely defensive tone of trying to promote it as "unusual entertainment." It seems to have done decently at the box office, but has survived with greater tenacity on late-night television and through occasional showings in small art theaters.

F. X. Feeney

SECONDS

Released: 1966
Production: Edward Lewis for Paramount
Direction: John Frankenheimer
Screenplay: Lewis John Carlino; based on the novel of the same name by David Ely
Cinematography: James Wong Howe
Editing: Ferris Webster and David Webster
Running time: 105 minutes

Principal characters:
Antiochus "Tony" Wilson	Rock Hudson
Norma Marcus	Salome Jens
Arthur Hamilton	John Randolph
The Old Southern Gentleman	Will Geer
Mr. Ruby	Jeff Corey
Davalo	Khigh Dhiegh
Charlie	Murray Hamilton
John	Wesley Addy

The fantasy of beginning life over again and doing everything differently comes true for Arthur Hamilton (John Randolph) in *Seconds*. He is contacted by an old acquaintance, Charlie (Murray Hamilton), and literally seduced into an organization which specializes in total makeovers of the human body. Suddenly, stodgy, bored, middle-aged businessman Arthur becomes the handsome and successful California artist Antiochus Wilson (Rock Hudson), who looks twenty years younger. Revitalized, he is encouraged to luxuriate in the new life found for him by the organization, but soon he is plagued by guilt and loneliness.

The initial portions of the film have a cloak-and-dagger suspense about them, beginning with Charlie's telephone calls and hurried meetings which are overtly suspicious. Arthur must go through several "way-stations" before finally meeting an "Old Southern Gentleman" (Will Geer) who encourages him to look on him as a "father." This man quickly gets Arthur to confess to feelings of dissatisfaction. The Old Gentleman sympathizes and hints he may have an alternative to Arthur's current malaise. After a few meetings, he presents a program developed by his organization that promises to alleviate Arthur's unhappiness by providing him with a new body and new life. Arthur is tempted to purchase this service but balks when it comes time to make the final agreement. Blackmail is then used to secure his signature on the contract.

This sequence is especially interesting in its montage. Ushered into the Old Gentleman's office, Arthur is surprised to receive hostile treatment when he refuses the company's services. He is forced to watch a film which they say will change his mind. A small projector and screen appear, and the room's lights are extinguished. Arthur is shocked to find himself treated to a home-made pornographic film starring himself that was made while he was drugged and believed himself to be under the care of the company's counselor. The intercutting between Arthur watching his performance and Arthur performing is dynamic because of the contrast and juxtaposition of the two activities. The stag film is shot all with a wide-angle lens mounted high on the wall near the ceiling but able to pivot somewhat and look down upon the bed as well as off to the other areas of the room. This placement gives a distorted appearance to Arthur and the woman, which is the appropriate style for a film which distorts the facts. This distortion is further enhanced by the fact that Arthur does not appear to be drugged or intoxicated by anything other than the supposed excitement of the sexual encounter. The only noise during this scene is the even metronomic clicking of the film projector which sounds ominously like a time bomb. At the same time, the juxtaposition of an elegant low-angle close-up of Arthur's stunned face haloed by the backlighting of the projection lamp while he watches the coarsely lit pornographic film further underscores the manipulation of reality produced by the organization. The sequence is a complete visual exposition of the organization's power over its clients. Arthur weakly agrees to undergo a change of life and accepts the rationale offered to him by the Old Gentleman that it is, after all, what he really wants to do.

The next several minutes of the motion picture are an interesting series of scenes of the rejuvenation process. These are shot in a documentary style to add verisimilitude to the scientific techniques which will change Arthur into Antiochus, or "Tony." *Seconds* received criticism because of its use of Hudson to portray the "new" Arthur Hamilton. This was because Hudson's motion picture *persona* was so well-established that it seemed unrealistic that character actor Randolph could be so far transformed. This is a problem that has diminished since the film's premiere because the motion picture is less affected now by Hudson's star status. The film justifies the transformation by numerous realistic scenes of the medical techniques used to effect the change. Hamilton is shown consulting with plastic surgeons who have graphed his current face from all angles to decide what structural changes can be made with it. He is shown struggling to regain physical fitness with a therapist, and he even undergoes complete orthodonture.

His current life is simultaneously being disposed of with discretion. The Old Gentleman's secretary, Mr. Ruby (Jeff Corey), assures Arthur there will be no problems in acquiring a corpse to stand in for Arthur's presumed death in a fiery car crash. Arthur is too preoccupied with becoming Tony Wilson to pry into the processes which provide that service. Mr. Ruby escorts the "new" Tony Wilson to the life of his dreams as an oil painter in Malibu. A member of the organization, John (Wesley Addy), is introduced to function as his butler and help him adjust to his new surroundings.

It is not long however, before the strange reality of his new situation oppresses him. Appropriately, he meets an exotic foreign woman, Norma Marcus (Salome Jens), who seems to share his *angst*. They see each other frequently and life becomes more exciting. The sequences of Tony Wilson's new life are shot in a romantically soft, low-contrast style. Everything appears very normal and pleasant, and Tony is only mildly chastized by John and Norma for not enjoying himself more. She encourages Tony to attend a wild wine-making party, and he in turn plans to give a house-warming party and invite his new neighbors. The orgy and the party both begin slowly but soon grow in intensity as the alcohol flows freely. The controlled movements of the camera and slow pacing of the editing begins to speed up until both employ dizzying angles and abrupt cuts to exemplify the perceptions of the merry-makers. This effect is more severe in the sequences of Tony's party as it primarily illustrates his drunken alienation from the identity of Tony Wilson. Finally, he confesses to being a "reborn" as if it were some kind of party joke. Suddenly all clarity is restored to the film's image, and the chilling revelation is made that all of his guests have been similarly reborn, including Norma.

The extent to which his new life has been manipulated is too much for Tony Wilson, and he runs away from Malibu. He nostalgically returns to his old home and visits his widow, but he is naïvely disappointed to discover that the distances between them have not been erased by his death. Their "reunion" is filmed in such a way as to emphasize the static coldness of his previous existence. The house is insipidly perfect, the living room formal and stiffly arranged. The wife receives his visit with officious politeness, but she is clearly not interested in discussing her late husband and is only mildly intrigued by Tony's wistfulness about him. Hudson's performance in this scene is a good example of his understated approach to acting. He blends the emotions of nostalgia, disappointment, and bewilderment while he struggles to conceal the motives for his visit and seems on the verge of admitting his true identity to her. The wife's suspicions over the reasons of his visit are aroused but she is not sufficiently interested in any facet of her late husband's life to question seriously Tony Wilson's mysterious behavior.

The film's conclusion answers the questions that Hamilton/Wilson failed to ask in the beginning about how the organization acquires its new clients and finds their stand-ins for the staged deaths. Tony Wilson is recaptured by the organization and escorted backward through the company with brutally cold, businesslike hostility. The father figure of the Old Gentleman reviles him for his ingratitude, and Mr. Ruby is no longer sympathetic to his problems. Wilson is amazed by their behavior. Through all his trials, he has remained unaware of their ultimate power and is completely unprepared for the denouement of his fantasy life. The final scenes are not filmed in the pseudodocumentary style that had previously marked the exposition of the company's internal affairs. These sequences are filmed principally with wide-angle lens in medium-close and tight-close shots taken from unusual angles. The editing is jumpy, as is much of the cinematography, to intensify visually the anxiety that grips Wilson. Despite his increasing paranoia, Tony Wilson remains naïve enough to doubt that all this could be happening to him and refuses to consider the true reality of his situation.

In this respect, Tony Wilson is an example of an average man who fails to realize the extent to which he is manipulated. He readily accepts other people's versions of facts as "truths" and their images as "reality." *Seconds* could be seen as a fantasy extrapolation of the dangers of conformity and socialization. It is as if *The Man in the Gray Flannel Suit* (1956) had a nightmare. Arthur Hamilton vaguely realizes in his middle-age that his life has been one of conformity to the successive and accepted authority of his parents, teachers, wife, family, and business, but he never actually rebels against it, although he does grumble occasionally. When presented with the opportunity to buy his way into "freedom" (another concept he accepts without question), he childishly accepts the stick of candy. Although he never realizes that he has just traded himself in to a life under a different set of tyrants, it is obvious that the film intends its characters to represent these stages of societal authority. The Old Gentleman is a father, Mr. Ruby a teacher, Norma and John a surrogate family, and the career of a painter supplants that of a successful business. In addition, the film makes the statement that Tony Wilson's new life fails because it is already complete and perfect when he is grafted to it. Ultimately, the film's lessons are that manipulation is alienating and that Mephistopheles, even in the guise of an organization, always collects his debts.

Elizabeth Ward

SECRETS

Released: 1933
Production: United Artists
Direction: Frank Borzage
Screenplay: Frances Marion, with additional dialogue by Salisbury Field and Leonard Praskins; based on the play of the same name by Rudolph Besier and May Edington
Cinematography: Ray June
Editing: Hugh Bennett
Costume design: Adrian
Music: Alfred Newman
Running time: 85 minutes

Principal characters:
Mary Marlow/Mary Carlton .... Mary Pickford
John Carlton .... Leslie Howard
Mr. Marlow .... C. Aubrey Smith
Mrs. Marlow .... Blanche Frederici
Susan Channing .... Doris Lloyd
"Sunshine" .... Ned Sparks
Señora Martinez .... Mona Maris

Mary Pickford's first talking feature, *Coquette* (1929), had been a pronounced financial success, which also brought her new recognition as an actress when the Motion Picture Academy named her Best Actress of the year. After breaking the mold of the young ingenue, she was determined to maintain her stride and hoped to rise to even further heights. To try something different again, her husband, Douglas Fairbanks, persuaded her to costar with him in a screen version of William Shakespeare's *The Taming of the Shrew*, released later in 1929. Despite their great personal popularity as a couple offscreen, as an acting team Pickford and Fairbanks left something to be desired. It was not a happy production, and worse, it did not make a large profit, probably because there was a public resistance to Shakespearean films at the time. Furthermore, United Artists (partially owned by Pickford) was in a precarious situation: forced to find a buyer for their chain of theaters because of a new governmental regulation, they were going to be dependent on the sale of their product in order to continue as a releasing company.

Pickford, more than ever aware that her third talking venture must be both financially and artistically successful, bought a property that had been one of silent star Norma Talmadge's most memorable film achievements, *Secrets*. It was a romance; it would allow her a wide scope of characterization, permitting her to progress from youth to old age. She signed Marshall Neilan to direct because he had directed some of her best silents, and she selected Kenneth

MacKenna from Broadway to be her leading man. As production continued, however, watching the dailies closely, Pickford realized that this version of *Secrets* could not even compare with the old Talmadge silent, and, even more disappointingly, she herself was not very good in it. With six reels completed she halted production, sought the advice of a few trusted friends, and came reluctantly to an expensive decision: abandonment of this production of *Secrets*. She retained her faith in the property, however, and signed Frances Marion, who had written the scenarios for some of her best silents and was now the most successful and highest paid of screenwriters, to come to her rescue. Marion had written the silent version for Talmadge; she was very familiar with the play and was the best possible person to redesign it to suit the new film image that Pickford wanted for herself as a screen star.

While Marion worked and preproduction plans for the new *Secrets* were begun, Pickford realized that she could not afford to be offscreen for so long a time merely waiting. She owned another property she had bought from Talmadge, the play *Kiki*, which had also been a success for Talmadge as a silent and before that had been a memorable stage hit for David Belasco starring Lenore Ulric. Moreover, it was a sophisticated comedy, and as a comedienne Pickford felt that she was on sure ground. Production started immediately on *Kiki*, with Sam Taylor directing and an expert *farceur*, Reginald Denny, signed to be leading man. *Kiki* was made quickly and released in 1931, and although most critics found it an amusing diversion proving that as a film comedienne Pickford was tops, it was not regarded as important in a day when film attendance was experiencing more than a mild recession. *Kiki*, like *The Taming of the Shrew*, was not a big box-office winner.

Now more than ever Pickford realized how vital it was that she have a hit, and she still hoped she could get it with the new version of *Secrets*. Marion devised a remarkably fluid script. The stage play by Rudolph Besier and May Edington had enjoyed a run of 168 performances on Broadway in 1922 and was fondly remembered as one of the most distinguished offerings of its popular stage star, Margaret Lawrence. Marion's screenplay, like the play, was divided into three parts: the first act was set in New England during the nineteenth century (rather than England, as in the play), and introduced the youthful romance between John Carlton (Leslie Howard) and Mary Marlow (Mary Pickford), who disregard parental disapproval of their love and run away to build a new life together in California (rather than in Montana, as it had been in the play); the second act was immediately arresting as an action-filled melodrama of pioneer life; and the third act dealt with John and Mary Carlton as old, successful, and the parents of grown children who do not understand them. It was just the formula Pickford wanted, because her own marriage was having difficulties. She felt that if her husband could recognize the parallel between the fictional Carltons and the living Fairbanks and Pickford, their own personal love story might be revived.

Pickford, a frugal person who had always liked cutting production expenses, spared nothing to make *Secrets* her very best. To direct, she hired Frank Borzage, who had a reputation for making sensitive romance believable, and who also had a reputation for being expensive. She had wanted Gary Cooper as her leading man, but he could not be borrowed, so she not only paid Leslie Howard a munificent sum to play opposite her, but also guaranteed him separate featured credit directly under the film's title, something she had never before conceded. The supporting cast was the most distinguished she had ever hired; to play the four children when they are grown in the last sequence, she engaged four real ex-stars of the silent screen—Ethel Clayton, Bessie Barriscale, Huntley Gordon, and Theodore von Eltz—who gave the production added class and real dimension. Ray June was cinematographer, and Pickford was never more lovingly photographed. Hugh Bennett, film editor, did one of his smoothest jobs on *Secrets*. She borrowed Adrian from Metro-Goldwyn-Mayer to design the costumes, and Alfred Newman was picked to write an excellent musical score. She was determined that *Secrets* would turn the tide in her favor.

The film, which spans a fifty-year period, was made with style and great taste. It did not, however, have the scope and powerful drive of *Cavalcade*, which had enchanted the Academy members in 1932-1933 into naming it Best Picture. *Secrets* is a romance of a rich girl, Mary Marlow, who falls in love with one of her father's employees, John Carlton. Her family forbids them to marry, but they are young and adventurous, and their love is strong. They elope and run off to homestead in California, settling down to build a cattle ranch with a home where they may rear their own family. Their happiness is complete when they become parents, but they are then beleaguered by desperados, and in a stirring sequence, the two, with only the help of a hired man (Ned Sparks), defend their home with guns. Unhurt themselves, they drive off their wounded attackers and relax in weary pride. Mary goes into an adjoining room, where her baby rests in a cradle, and finds the child dead, a victim of the battle.

With the echoes of the final shooting fading outside, Mary gathers the child into her arms and simply sits in a rocking chair, huddled over the dead baby, the tragedy of life etched upon her face as she realizes what has happened. It is a long scene, played with no dialogue. It had been the high point, too, of Talmadge's silent performance, but played by Pickford, the tragedy was acute and almost unbearable. Talmadge, in playing the scene, had held a small mirror to the baby's mouth, but there was no living breath to cloud the glass. Mary plays it beyond tears of her own, with no business, aware of the tragedy, forced to accept it, just clinging to the child and gently rocking.

The last third of the story has John and Mary Carlton fifty years older, and rich parents of other children, who are now middle-aged, obsessed with security, and demanding further concessions from their parents. John has broken off a relationship with the beautiful Señora Martinez (Mona Maris), which he has secretly maintained over a period of time, and he confesses his adultery to Mary, who forgives him, saying that she has known of it all along, but it had been her secret. The children want their parents to sign a paper which would put them in charge of the family wealth. John locks the door, and he and Mary escape by the garden window just as they had when they eloped in California. As they drive away together in an automobile, the music of "Oh, Susanna!" begins, and double-exposed over the shot of their old, happy faces as they drive Westward is a vision of them as they were when young driving in a covered wagon across the continent into California, seeking a new life together.

Secrets had its premiere in the East and got good notices, and Pickford was commended for her splendid work. The year was 1933, however, and the recession had changed into a new depression. President Roosevelt closed the banks temporarily, and some did not reopen. United Artists had no theaters of its own in the West, especially in the Los Angeles area, where it might exhibit its product. The studio's current films piled up, waiting release. The big United Artists theater in downtown Los Angeles was exhibiting motion pictures from other studios, and eventually United Artists was forced to rent a smaller downtown playhouse, the Tower and it was there that *Secrets* had its belated premiere.

Unfortunately, this film failed to bring the popular success which Pickford needed to help her failing career, and as a result she retired unhappily as a film star. She had been a motion picture actress for nearly a quarter of a century, since 1909, when she started work at Biograph with D. W. Griffith. There were several false starts on new projects that drew her interest temporarily after her retirement, but none materialized. She had always trusted her mother's judgment in business affairs, and when Mrs. Pickford died, Mary was at a loss. She would express enthusiasm on something, then lose interest and back out of a deal, sometimes on the first day of production. Lillian Gish advised her to buy the long-running Broadway hit *Life with Father* for herself, but Mary felt that the asking price was too high, and the film was eventually made with Irene Dunne in 1947. Later, she admitted that she had made a mistake.

Secrets also proved to be a personal failure as well. She and Fairbanks were separated and then divorced shortly thereafter. It was a pity that her career as a great star ended when it did, after only four appearances as a star of talking films, and at the age of forty. If she had searched, however, for a film on which to bow out, she could not have chosen a more fitting one than *Secrets*. It contains some of the most memorable of all Pickford scenes and is a vivid testimony to her excellence as a screen star.

DeWitt Bodeen

SEND ME NO FLOWERS

Released: 1964
Production: Harry Keller for Universal
Direction: Norman Jewison
Screenplay: Julius J. Epstein; based on the play of the same name by Norman Barasch and Carroll Moore
Cinematography: Daniel L. Fapp
Editing: J. Terry Williams
Running time: 99 minutes

Principal characters:

George Kimball	Rock Hudson
Judy Kimball	Doris Day
Arnold Nash	Tony Randall
Bert Power	Clint Walker
Mr. Akins	Paul Lynde
Winston Burr	Hal March
Doctor Ralph Morrisey	Edward Andrews
Linda Bullard	Patricia Barry

In the late 1950's and early 1960's Doris Day made a series of three films with Rock Hudson exemplifying the comedy style which would become synonymous with her name. Those films also sum up the feeling of the majority of American situation comedies during that era. Enormously popular at the box office, the Hudson-Day domestic comedies were echoed by a number of similar films and television series. The television situation comedies of those years—*I Love Lucy, I Married Joan, Ozzie and Harriet,* and others—evoked the same world of middle-class domestic hilarity portrayed by the Hudson-Day films, and later Day films with other leading men.

The team extended (and ended) their string of successes in 1964 with *Send Me No Flowers.* It is a simple comedy of errors, milking hypochondria and the medical profession for all the laughs that they can supply. Hudson is George Kimball, a hypochondriac, married to bubble-headed Judy, played with breathy enthusiasm by Day. George goes to the doctor for a check-up, and the doctor assures him that nothing is wrong, but by chance, George overhears a phone call in the doctor's office which seems to contradict that prognosis. The patient that his doctor is talking about on the phone has only weeks to live. Of course, that patient is not George, but George goes home convinced that he is dying. He wants to spare Judy the news, but does confide in his buddy Arnold Nash (Tony Randall, the mainstay sidekick in all three Day-Hudson films).

The rest of the movie exploits all the possibilities of George's misunderstood diagnosis. Arnold, always ready with a new draft of the eulogy, is full of advice for George, the most important of which relates to George's wife. Judy will want to remarry, he tells the soon-to-be-deceased. When George has a nightmare imagining a bongo-playing cad who will seduce Judy for her money, he begins to eye possible choices for Judy's respectable second husband. When none of their country-club friends seems right, Judy's college sweetheart shows up. Bert Power (Clint Walker) is a bachelor millionaire with the build of Mr. America, and he has a beaming, bearhugging affection for Judy. Bert is the obvious choice, but George cannot stand it. Eventually, prodded by Arnold, George does the noble thing and prepares a will bequeathing Judy to Bert; then he suggests the three of them go dancing at the country club.

At the club, George decides to do another good deed. He talks to a neighbor woman, Linda Bullard (Patricia Barry). Linda is separated from her husband and has gotten a call from George's friend Winston Burr (Hal March) offering to "help." George knows Winston is a no-good wolf and warns Linda, whereby she gives him a big, grateful kiss. Judy sees the kiss and, incensed, accuses George of having an affair. To prove his innocence, George reveals the "truth" that he is dying. Judy, tearstricken, comes up with a wheelchair and a trip to the Mayo clinic to save her husband's life, but then George's doctor stops by and Judy learns that her husband is in the best of health. She is furious, believing once again that he is having an affair. In a wonderful piece of slapstick, she manages to trick George into his wheelchair in the kitchen, then shoot him out the backdoor, where he ricochets around the garage.

George then talks to the doctor and learns that he is really not dying. Now he has to convince Judy that he is not having an affair. Arnold has more advice. Women never believe denials, he tells George, so confess to an affair and promise never to do it again. George, although dubious, takes the advice. He confesses to Judy that he is all through with a mythical "Dolores Yellowstone" and, in a stroke of genius, produces a check made out to "cash" for one thousand dollars, which, he says, paid Dolores off, whereby Judy promptly leaves him. At the last minute, the marriage is saved when Judy gets a visit from an enthusiastic mortician, played by Paul Lynde. He has come to give a receipt for the one-thousand-dollar check George gave him. The money reserves three plots at Green Hills mortuary—for George, Doris, and her second husband. Judy realizes George has been lying about "Dolores" and otherwise telling the truth, and the movie ends as Judy and George are about to relive their honeymoon.

The plot of *Send Me No Flowers* is obviously a simple frame on which to hang a series of comedy bits, such as Judy in an out-of-control golf cart or George hung up in his wheelchair. Day, Hudson, and Randall had been teamed in this sort of comedy before, and all were adept at playing the light comedy required. The movie actually depends at least as much upon the Hudson-Randall team as Hudson-Day, and the supporting cast of morticians, doctors, bachelors, and wives is similarly well-cast, all actors familiar from many comedy roles.

Norman Jewison, who had directed a Day-James Garner comedy, *The Thrill of It All*, the preceding year, directed *Send Me No Flowers*. His style for both films is straightforward and unobtrusive. If anything, this picture is less flashy than *The Thrill of It All*, whose plot about producing television commercials allowed Jewison to play with shooting techniques then popular in commercials. Jewison used the same flashy, highly edited, and glossy style slightly later, in *The Cincinnati Kid* (1965), *The Thomas Crown Affair* (1968), and *In the Heat of the Night* (1969); but that style is absent from *Send Me No Flowers*.

Hudson and Day began their comedy partnership in 1959 with *Pillow Talk*. Critics referred to it, and succeeding movies, as "sugar spun gloss." The movies are obviously light material, with slim plots and characters of less than overwhelming intelligence, but critical sniping at the films never seemed to affect their success at the box office. Eventually Hudson bowed out of the partnership, and Day continued to make comedies modeled on her successes with Hudson. Eventually, referring to a picture as a "Doris Day film" was similar to using the term "John Wayne film," in the sense that the name of the star alone reveals something of what such a movie is about. In fact, Day's image was so firmly conventionalized that by the late 1960's the actress began to parody it in movies such as Frank Tashlin's *Caprice* (1967). *Caprice* was not a big success, but the public affinity for Day comedies, weakened as she toyed with self-parody, was at full strength in the Hudson-Day years.

Leslie Donaldson

SERGEANT RUTLEDGE

Released: 1960
Production: Patrick Ford and Willis Goldbeck for Ford Productions; released by Warner Bros.
Direction: John Ford
Screenplay: Willis Goldbeck and James Warner Bellah
Cinematography: Bert Glennon
Editing: Jack Murray
Running time: 111 minutes

Principal characters:

Lieutenant Tom Cantrell	Jeffrey Hunter
Mary Beecher	Constance Towers
Sergeant Braxton Rutledge	Woody Strode
Mrs. Cordelia Fosgate	Billie Burke
Colonel Otis Fosgate	Willis Bouchey
Sergeant Matthew Luke Skidmore	Juano Hernandez
Captain Shattuck	Carleton Young
Lucy Dabney	Foley Richards
Chandler Hubble	Fred Libby
Chris Hubble	Jan Styne

At the end of his life, John Ford's critical reception suffered because many liberals chose to dismiss his films as jingoistic and reactionary. Supported, perhaps, by Ford's close association with John Wayne, a self-proclaimed conservative, these attitudes are disproven if one examines the films themselves. Ford had grave doubts about the thrust of American society, doubts which are explored in such works as *The Man Who Shot Liberty Valance* (1962). With the exception of Stanley Kramer, Ford was also the only major director in the 1950's-early 1960's to deal overtly with racism in his films. In *The Searchers* (1956), *Two Rode Together* (1961), and *Cheyenne Autumn* (1964), miscegenation and prejudice directed against the Indians are major themes. In *Donovan's Reef* (1963), a raucous, brawling comedy, the presence of the children of a marriage between a Polynesian princess and an Anglo Navy doctor considerably deepens and darkens the otherwise light-hearted mood. In *Sergeant Rutledge* (1960), Ford straightforwardly considers the effects of racial prejudice in the context of a black cavalry trooper in the old Southwest.

The story is told through the testimony of witnesses during the court martial of Sergeant Braxton Rutledge (Woody Strode), the first sergeant of the Ninth Cavalry Regiment. On trial for the rape and murder of a white girl, Sergeant Rutledge is defended by his commanding officer and friend, Lieutenant Tom Cantrell (Jeffrey Hunter). The first witness is Mary Beecher (Constance Towers), to whom Cantrell is attached. Mary describes the events at Spindle

Railroad Station when she expected to meet her father. Instead she found
the dead station master and was rescued by Sergeant Rutledge when the
Apaches attacked again. When Cantrell arrived the next morning and arrested
Rutledge, she was confused and indignant.

The next witness is Mrs. Cordelia Fosgate (Billie Burke), the wife of the
court martial's presiding officer, Colonel Otis Fosgate. She establishes the
friendship between Sergeant Rutledge and Lucy Dabney (Foley Richards),
daughter of the post commandant. She also describes hearing shots the night
of the murder, in the process revealing herself as a snobbish, bigoted woman
excited by the prurient aspects of the trial. The post doctor then describes
the murder scene, and tells the court that the cross Lucy wore was torn from
her neck.

Lieutenant Cantrell is then called to the stand as a prosecution witness,
and he relates the arrest of Rutledge and the pursuit of the Apaches. The
troop is attacked by the Indians, and Rutledge is permitted to fight with the
unit. One of his soldiers is shot, so Rutledge rides out to rescue him. Asked
by the dying trooper why they are fighting a white man's war and what will
become of his little girls, Rutledge replies that the actions of the regiment
will give his daughters something to be proud of someday. The soldier dies,
and Rutledge escapes from Lieutenant Cantrell.

Captain Shattuck (Carleton Young), the prosecuting attorney, next calls
Rutledge to the witness stand. Shattuck goads Rutledge with increasingly
racist remarks to say why he returned to the regiment. The top sergeant
responds by saying that he felt he must warn the troop of an ambush because
the regiment was his home, his source of self-respect. If he left, he would be
just another "swamp-running nigger, but I'm not. I'm a *man*."

Mary Beecher is recalled to the stand, where she describes how Lieutenant
Cantrell found a coat on an Indian marked with the initials CH. Cantrell then
finds the cross on another Indian, and asks Mary to witness his find. Cantrell
had earlier told of finding the body of Chris Hubble (Jan Styne), the settler's
son, killed by Indians in the desert. Cantrell now attempts to build a case
implicating the young Hubble in the murder, but he has doubts because the
coat is too large for the slightly built teenager. Cantrell then calls the settler,
Chandler Hubble (Fred Libby), to the stand where he positively identifies the
cross Cantrell found on the Indian as Lucy's cross. Through more questioning
and physical threats by Cantrell, Hubble breaks down and confesses that he
raped and murdered Lucy, not his son, who had grabbed his father's coat
when he dashed off to fight the Apaches. With the confession the trial is over,
Sergeant Rutledge is redeemed, and Lieutenant Cantrell and Mary Beecher
are reconciled.

Although *Sergeant Rutledge* does not prove that Ford was a liberal, it does
demonstrate that in matters of race he was concerned with the quality of a
man and not with the color of his skin. In an era when few films considered

race relations, Ford made five in an eight-year period that neither preached to nor pummeled the audience. Instead, by showing the effects of prejudice on a community in *Two Rode Together* and *Donovan's Reef*, and by exhibiting what the black soldier was capable of achieving, as in *Sergeant Rutledge*, Ford spoke to an audience not generally considered to be very receptive to antiracist themes and undoubtedly changed some people's attitudes about racial minorities. Ten years before *Shaft* (1971) and *Super Fly* (1972), Strode was able to portray a black hero the equal of Wayne in a film directed by the man who had virtually created the heroic myth which Wayne embodied.

The apotheosis of the black hero is readily apparent in the film. More subtle and more telling (the mark of Ford's genius) is the way in which he implicates the audience in the prejudice demonstrated by the white characters on the screen. Cordelia Fosgate represents white society at the trial. Silly, shallow, and snobbish, Mrs. Fosgate is also sexually stimulated by the lurid aspects of the court martial, by Sergeant Rutledge's physical magnificence, and by his blackness. Ford allows the audience to laugh at Mrs. Fosgate, but he forces them to share her feelings in the scene in which Mary Beecher is alone at Spindle Station. Mary runs screaming from the station when she discovers the body of the stationmaster. In close-up, she is grabbed by the powerful black hand of Sergeant Rutledge, who urges her not to scream. Ford then tightens the close-up to a shot of the black hand on the white throat. He then gives the audience time to dwell on the implications of that shot by cutting back to the trial. Only after a lengthy argument between Cantrell and Shattuck does the audience learn that Rutledge is trying to save Mary from the Indians, not attack her himself. By then the audience has had ample time to consider its own prejudices and not be quite so condescending to the overt prejudice of Mrs. Fosgate.

Sergeant Rutledge is certainly not one of Ford's masterworks; only Strode's personification of the noble Rutledge and Burke's superb performance as the flighty Mrs. Fosgate are of much interest. The film is worthy of attention, however, because it is a personal favorite of America's foremost director and because it deals courageously with a problem as old as America itself. Racial fear and hatred have been a part of the American experience since Jamestown was settled in 1607 and are still with us; they can only be eradicated if we are willing to deal with them as honestly and forthrightly as Ford does in *Sergeant Rutledge*.

Don K Thompson

THE SERVANT

Released: 1963
Production: Joseph Losey and Norman Priggen for Warner Bros.
Direction: Joseph Losey
Screenplay: Harold Pinter; based on the novel of the same name by Robin Maugham
Cinematography: Douglas Slocombe
Editing: Reginald Mills
Running time: 115 minutes

Principal characters:

Barrett	Dirk Bogarde
Vera	Sarah Miles
Susan	Wendy Craig
Tony	James Fox

Joseph Losey, a filmmaker with an erratic track record, is an expressionistic director who eschews the narrative film's obligatory story line for what he defines as motion pictures with "theme" or which go "beyond theme" in his effort to have the audience "think" about his films rather than sit back and follow a preconceived plot line. A few of his films—*The Servant, Modesty Blaise* (1966), *Accident* (1967), and *The Go-Between* (1971)—have captured this cinematic quality with, arguably, varying degrees of success.

Losey, a native of Wisconsin, had a modest career as a director in Hollywood during the 1940's and 1950's, with his best-remembered film being *The Boy with Green Hair* (1948), a mixture of fantasy and realism about a war orphan who becomes a social outcast when his hair turns green. When Losey's alleged Marxist leanings caused him to be blacklisted in the 1950's, he took up exile in England where he continued to make films of a most personal nature—films replete with the various aspects of and criticism of "hypocrisy."

The Servant, which Losey directed from Harold Pinter's screenplay based on the novel by Robin Maugham, came on the heels of a renewal of interest in English filmmaking. England's post-World War II film production was sporadic in nature to say the least, but with such films as *Room at the Top* (1959), *Look Back in Anger* (1959), and *The Loneliness of the Long Distance Runner* (1962), British films took on a renewed significance in world cinema, a significance critical of traditional values and society. Films, novels, and plays which criticized English society and the class struggles inherent therein had become the acceptable norm in British culture. In addition, *The Servant* likewise came on the heels of the scandalous Profumo case involving sexual misconduct among high-ranking British officials. Regarded as a fascinating and devastatingly unpleasant view of the British social structure, *The Servant* became a *cause célèbre*.

While the screenplay was based on Maugham's structured novel, Pinter fashioned an enigmatic, surreal script to which Losey added his own cinematic *Grand Guignol* flair to produce a psychological horror story. The plot around which the film evolves is simpler than Losey's intentions imply.

Tony (James Fox) is a rich, indolent, young upper-class Englishman who returns to London from abroad and purchases a large Georgian house in which to establish himself as a gentleman. Holding to anachronistic convention, he hires a manservant named Barrett (Dirk Bogarde), a so-called gentleman's gentleman from a long line of gentlemen's gentlemen. Barrett is a man of extraordinary finesse and ability, and the ramshackle home is soon put into immaculate order. Tony wallows in the unstinting attention of the indispensable Barrett, but Tony's fiancée, Susan (Wendy Craig), a fellow aristocrat, senses something amiss. To further enhance Tony's comfort, Barrett brings into the household his "sister" Vera (Sarah Miles), passing her off as a maid.

Tony becomes increasingly dependent upon Barrett and also becomes intimately involved with Vera. When he discovers Barrett and Vera to be lovers and not relatives, Tony dismisses them both, after which his life falls apart. Finally, Barrett and Tony meet in a pub, Tony reengages the manservant whom he needs so badly, and the final ironic twist is complete: the master has become the servant and the servant the master.

The plot is little more than a melodrama, but as Losey is never interested in plots *per se*, he gives the film his own personal, cinematic style, the result being a provocative, repelling story of the destructiveness of power and debauchery. The story line of *The Servant* is a twist of Edward Chodorov's 1934 play, *Kind Lady*. M-G-M brought it to the screen in 1951 and cast Maurice Evans as the duplicitous artist, who, with Angela Lansbury as his Cockney maid-accomplice, unscrupulously endeavors to fleece a dowager, played by Ethel Barrymore, of a valuable art collection. What makes the Pinter/Losey version more than a mere psychological melodrama is Losey's remarkable ability to create an atmosphere of psychological terror.

This mood is established from the very opening credits of the film, in which we see Barrett walking through the London streets in the rain to keep the job interview with Tony. The audience immediately assesses Barrett's fastidious, arrogant, slightly bent image. As he enters Tony's newly acquired home, we not only see that the house is in a state of disrepair, but we also see a Tony who is voluptuously resigned to the good things in life. It is an atmosphere which not only is ripe for the devious intent of Barrett, but also one which claustrophobically foreshadows imminent doom.

Tony's interview queries are perfunctorily tossed at Barrett, who prissily answers with precise yet unrevealing answers. He explains that he has impeccable credentials as a manservant, and to the question, "Can you cook?" he responds, "My soufflés have always received a great deal of praise." We see at once that the spoiled, self-indulgent Tony will be no match for Barrett, whose control of the situation is instantly established.

Barrett sets about putting Tony's residence in order, from the selection of paint and wallpaper to the arranging of fresh flowers, all with an efficient, imperious, and solicitous sense of control. Losey's camera follows Barrett's actions in long, flowing arcs and extremely perverse close-ups—two techniques which are indicative of Losey's style—creating a black-and-white quality of voyeuristic distortion. When Barrett enters the living room without knocking to find Tony and Susan romantically embraced, it is the camera and the audience as well as Barrett that become the intruders.

As Barrett's power play is put into effect, there is an overpowering sensuality to the master/servant relationship from which surfaces an obvious homosexual undertone. At another point, when Barrett and Tony quarrel and Tony sulks on the staircase, the staircase railings become prison bars in Losey's camera lens. When Barrett brings his "sister" Vera into the house as a maid, Losey's camera catches their three reflections in a mirror through a brandy snifter, predicting the entanglement of their three lives and psyches.

As Barrett intends, Vera seduces Tony, and only when Tony and Susan return home to find Barrett and Vera in bed does Tony realize that he has been duped. Tony dismisses the two of them, but left on his own he sinks further into emotional dependence on the absent Barrett. When Barrett and Tony meet by chance in a local pub, their conversation is that of a pair of lovers making up after a quarrel, and of course Tony acquiesces and rehires Barrett. The role reversals are now complete—Barrett is the master and Tony the servant—and their life together is one of constant husband-wife bickering, at once infantile and grotesque.

The film's much-discussed ending—the orgy scene—was a daring device in 1963. With his characters fully clothed, Losey creates an erotic atmosphere of complete degradation with a further irony: now that Barrett has complete control of Tony, and Susan and Vera as well, he himself has become so corrupted by power that he is no longer the master at all.

Basically a four-character plot, the acting throughout is excellent. Bogarde makes a sublimely unctuous Barrett, and Fox is sensually dissolute and vulnerable to the insidious debauchery. Miles is striking as the conniving tart, and Craig brings the proper genteel balance to this motley quartet.

The film has been criticized as being both a remarkable breakthrough in nonnarrative film form and a pretentious allegory about English society in particular and modern society in general. However one reacts to this and other works by Losey, there is always the underlying and very important fact that Losey's view of the world is that of a misanthrope, and all of his film outings contain a self-conscious effort to be "significant"—two characteristics which invariably work against any artist. A message without heart is soon forgotten.

The British Film Academy bestowed acting honors on Bogarde as Best

Actor of the Year and Fox as "the most promising newcomer to leading roles," and also gave an award to Douglas Slocombe's black-and-white cinematography. In addition, Pinter's script received the British Screen Writer's Award for Best Screenplay of 1963.

Ronald Bowers

THE SET-UP

Released: 1949
Production: Richard Goldstone for RKO/Radio
Direction: Robert Wise
Screenplay: Art Cohn; based on the poem of the same name by Joseph Moncure March
Cinematography: Milton Krasner
Editing: Roland Gross
Music: Constantin Bakaleinikoff
Running time: 72 minutes

> *Principal characters:*
> Stoker Thompson .... Robert Ryan
> Julie Thompson .... Audrey Totter
> Gus .... Wallace Ford
> Tiny .... George Tobias
> Little Boy .... Alan Baxter

The Set-Up is an unusually powerful film directed by Robert Wise. It tells the story of Stoker Thompson (Robert Ryan), a second-class boxer with the grit and determination to transcend his marginal talent as a prizefighter. The "set-up" of the title comes when Stoker's manager Gus (Wallace Ford) agrees to have him take a dive. Stoker is unaware of the initial agreement and is under the impression that he is going to box a clean fight. It is when he is eventually told to lose the match that a conflict arises. Stoker's wife Julie (Audrey Totter), who realizes the consequences of not complying with the mob's dictates, is worried and confused. Julie cannot stand the idea of Stoker's taking any more physical punishment, yet she understands his need to assert his independence. The fight is presented with gritty realism, and the crowd is depicted as a vicious mob driven by blood-lust; the physical abuse is unrelenting in the film. During the fight, Julie leaves ringside to collect her thoughts and decide if she should leave her husband, and during her absence, Stoker wins the fight. His elation quickly is shattered, however, when he is pursued by a number of strong-arm boys. Stoker's panicked flight through the deserted auditorium leaves him cornered in a blind alley, where he is savagely beaten as a warning to anyone foolish enough to disregard the directives of the mob. Julie finally comes back and finds the bruised and bloody Stoker lying in the gutter.

The Set-Up is an experimental film in many ways. First, it is one of a very few films to have been adapted from a poem. Written in 1928, *The Set-Up* was itself an experiment in the dramatic use of the poem. The rhythm and imagery of Joseph Moncure March's poetry is approximated in Wise's film. The violence, the anger, and even the sweaty environment of a second-rate boxing stadium is captured with incredible precision. The characters are both grotesque and interpretive. Wise is able to suggest a great deal of the emotional content of the poem through elements of pure cinematic technique in a way that enhances the threadbare screenplay. Another successful experiment in *The Set-Up* is the use of "real time"; in other words, the events that take place on the screen take up the same amount of time that they would if they occurred in real life—there is no condensation or extension of time. This technique enhances the tension of Stoker's decision not to accept the set-up. "Real time" was used with excellent results by Fred Zinnemann in *High Noon* (1952), but few other directors have used the device.

Ryan as Stoker embodies the spirit of an idealist unable to see his obvious limitations. Ryan never got the recognition he deserved as an actor; his consistent quality and intense screen *persona* highlighted many films, from *Crossfire* (1947) to *The Wild Bunch* (1969). His naturalness and intrinsic cynicism captured perfectly the postwar angst presented in many Hollywood films. The physical abuse that Stoker endures is typical of the problems encountered by his other screen characters. His ability to project weakness, pain, and a sense of defeat made Ryan an important figure in the *film noir* genre. Wise began his career in filmmaking as an editor, and his early work for Orson Welles on *Citizen Kane* (1942) and Val Lewton on *The Body Snatcher* (1945) led to his career as a director. Moving from horror films, to crime-melodramas, to musicals such as *The Sound of Music* (1965), Wise brought a sense of atmosphere and an attention to detail to films, from *The Curse of the Cat People* (1944) to *Star Trek—The Motion Picture* (1979).

The Set-Up can be seen as part of a cycle of boxing films which were released during the late 1940's. Along with this film, Robert Rossen's *Body and Soul* (1947) and Mark Robeson's *Champion* (1949) are the most significant, with each film analyzing a particular aspect of prizefighting. While most boxing films concentrate on the entire milieu of the boxing world, *The Set-Up* is much more intimate. There are none of the typical clichés associated with boxing films; instead, this film functions on a level of iconography and experimentality that overshadows the structural limitations of the genre. Many critics consider *The Set-Up* the best boxing film ever made. The overwhelming pessimism of *The Set-Up* is cathartic; the film is emotionally draining yet uniquely satisfying. The strong direction and intense performances give it a remarkable sense of realism, while the intimacy of the characterizations and the use of "real time" help make it a shattering exposé of professional boxing.

Carl F. Macek

SEVEN DAYS IN MAY

Released: 1964
Production: Edward Lewis for Paramount
Direction: John Frankenheimer
Screenplay: Rod Serling; based on the novel of the same name by Fletcher Knebel and Charles W. Bailey II
Cinematography: Ellsworth Fredericks
Editing: Ferris Webster
Running time: 120 minutes

Principal characters:

General James M. Scott	Burt Lancaster
Colonel Martin "Jiggs" Casey	Kirk Douglas
President Jordan Lyman	Fredric March
Eleanor "Ellie" Holbrook	Ava Gardner
Senator Raymond Clark	Edmond O'Brien
Paul Girard	Martin Balsam
Admiral Barnswell	John Houseman
Colonel "Mutt" Henderson	Andrew Duggan

John Frankenheimer's *Seven Days in May* accomplishes a great deal in 120 minutes. As a thriller, it builds up an irresistible tension; as a fictional documentary, it almost convinces the audience that military coups lurk in the heart of the Pentagon; and as a political statement, it warns against dictatorship and upholds the values of democracy. It is as a thriller that *Seven Days in May* achieved its popularity at the box office. Beginning as early as the credits, the film establishes a dramatic tension that continues until the last moment of the film. Rod Serling, a master at creating excitement and suspense, adapted the script from Fletcher Knebel's and Charles Bailey's very popular, melodramatic novel. Director Frankenheimer's earlier film, *The Manchurian Candidate* (1962), established his reputation as a high-paced filmmaker, and this film helped him maintain it.

Seven Days in May begins with a protest march in front of the White House in which some demonstrators are protesting the President's recent signing of a nuclear arms treaty with Russia, while others are protesting against the protesters. Soon the demonstrators begin to fight. The camera then goes inside the White House to reveal a troubled President (Fredric March) whose blood pressure is up and whose Gallup public opinion ratings are down.

Next the camera switches to the Pentagon, where, with appropriate restraint, Colonel Martin "Jiggs" Casey (Kirk Douglas) tells his boss, General James M. Scott (Burt Lancaster), how much he admires him. This admiration will soon change. At first, a few small questions begin to arise in Jiggs's mind. When Jiggs first sees a top-secret paper that contains some horse-racing bets, he is amused. Later, however, when Colonel "Mutt" Henderson (Andrew Duggan), a friend of his and an assistant commander of a military base in Texas, describes his latest assignment as a large-scale, top-secret operation called "ECOMCON" (one of the horse-racing names), Jiggs is very upset. He starts connecting these strange bits of related information to the important secret alert planned for the following Sunday. A Marine for eighteen years, he wants to believe in his boss and in the value of the military. General Scott, who is in charge of the alert, tells Jiggs that no newspapermen or Congressmen will be present at the Sunday event. Later Jiggs goes to a cocktail party given by a prominent Washington hostess, Ellie Holbrook (Ava Gardner), Scott's former mistress. At the party, a right-wing senator ominously warns Jiggs to "stay on the alert on Sunday." When Jiggs drives to the General's house late that night, he finds the same senator's car there.

Jiggs is beginning to piece together the elements of an ugly and frightening puzzle. His fears increase when General Scott lies about what he was doing the night of the party. Next, after a staff meeting, Jiggs finds a note about "ECOMCON," and someone tells him that, of all those invited to participate in the horse betting, only an Admiral Barnswell refused to bet.

Later a confused and worried Jiggs watches a political rally on television and sees a superpatriot introduce General Scott. No longer able to be silent, Jiggs reluctantly calls the President and asks for a late-night meeting at the White House. There he finally reveals his worst fears: he suspects that the country is in danger of a military coup, led by General Scott. It will take place next Sunday during the secret alert. At first, the President and his press secretary, Paul Girard, (Martin Balsam) are very skeptical, but as Jiggs describes each piece of evidence, the President decides to investigate the awful possibility. He must work fast, as there are only four days left before the alert.

The investigation must be done in complete secrecy; if the accusation is wrong, any news about the investigation would discredit the already unpopular administration. If the accusation is true, the general alarm might threaten the entire country. The President quickly establishes investigative procedures. His close friend, Georgia Senator Clark (Edmond O'Brien), is to go to Texas and find the hidden base. Girard will travel to Gibraltar and get Admiral Barnswell (John Houseman, in a small role which belies the almost universal contention that he made his film acting debut in his Academy Award-winning performance as Kingsford in *The Paper Chase*, 1973) to give a written confession of his knowledge of the plot. Jiggs is to act as informer against General Scott.

Jiggs's assignment changes quickly, however; when he criticizes Scott's ultraconservative political backing, the General tells Jiggs to take the rest of the week off. Before he leaves for Texas, Senator Clark insists that Jiggs must instead get Ellie Holbrook to tell all she knows about her former lover, Scott.

Although Jiggs hates to hurt this proud and sensitive woman whom he admires, he reluctantly feigns a romantic interest and thereby obtains a packet of Scott's letters to her.

To build up a sense of action, the camera switches back and forth between the men on the investigative team and shows the troubled President telling Scott that he has decided not to participate in the alert. Meanwhile, Girard gets a signed statement from Admiral Barnswell, slips the statement into a cigarette case, then calls the President and tells him about the statement. The President is shaken to realize that the conspiracy is a fact, but he is also relieved that at least his people have solid evidence against the conspirators. The relief is short-lived, however, when a messenger informs the President that Girard has died in a plane crash.

In Texas, Senator Clark is also soon in danger. Talking with a customer at a local bar, he learns about the base and drives out to it. There, unidentified military personnel lock him into a small room, and, until the assistant base commander visits him, his fate looks almost as bleak as Girard's. When Clark describes the plot to Jiggs's friend Mutt, the assistant commander, the officer helps him escape from the base.

Back in Washington, the President's team has reached a stalemate, and time is running out. Girard is dead, the signed statement is lost, and Admiral Barnswell now pretends that he has never heard of any coup. As yet, the President's team has not heard from Clark, and they fear for his safety. The President's only real proof against Scott now is in Ellie's letters, and he does not want to use them and ruin her reputation. Under great stress, the President makes some critical decisions. He calls Scott into the Oval Office and cancels the alert. Then he confronts Scott with evidence of the planned coup and asks for the General's resignation. An unruffled Scott refuses to resign and says he will take the issue to the public. Confidently aware of his popularity with the American people, Scott plans to go on television and expose the President as "a weak sister." In spite of this threat, the President decides not to use Ellie's letters, and instead asks Jiggs to return them to their owner.

Finally, however, at the last moment, the luck begins to change. Clark telephones to say he is safe and to tell what he has learned. Soon he is back in Washington. When the President begins a press conference to announce that he has asked for the resignations of the Joint Chiefs of Staff, a messenger interrupts him and hands the President Girard's cigarette case, which has been discovered in the rubble of the plane wreckage.

In a dramatic moment, Jiggs confronts Scott with the signed statement which reveals the plot. Furious but still undaunted, the General at first plans to use his "ECOMCON" network to break in on the President's televised press conference, but then he changes his mind, realizing that his political allies will all desert him, and he resignedly rides home in his staff car. Jiggs returns the letters to Ellie, and, addressing the American people on television, the President gives a rousing speech about the values of democracy.

Serling's script has all of the ingredients of a good Hollywood thriller: tension, fast-paced action, a bit of romance, and characterizations which make clear distinctions between the good guys and the bad guys. Both the camerawork and the music help to reinforce the script's tension: for example, two scenes are shot in a darkened room, and another shows only the back of Scott's head. The editing itself is fast-paced, and the scenes become shorter and faster as the plot develops. Close-ups and stills of the actors' stressful faces and of objects such as Girard's cigarette case emphasize the serious nature of the investigation. At the end of many scenes, heavy, percussive instruments warn the audience that the danger is building. At times the percussion becomes a little too predictable, and there are a few too many serious close-ups, but for the most part, the cinematic effects keep the audience anxiously awaiting the next development.

To add to the film's success as a thriller, Frankenheimer has selected an expensive cast of box-office favorites. Douglas and Lancaster play the roles they play in most all of their films, but since the script essentially calls for a square-jawed, level-headed Douglas and a cool, calculating Lancaster, the casting works rather well. Gardner's acting shows some depth and variety, while March, Balsam, and Houseman give still better performances. O'Brien's performance, however, is the only truly notable one. In contrast to the other actors, he manages to create a multidimensional character. He makes the boozing Senator Clark a weary and rumpled man who frequently surprises the audience with his humor and even more with his ultimate efficiency and courage. For this performance, O'Brien was nominated for an Academy Award for Best Supporting Actor.

Seven Days in May gained box-office success as a thriller, but it is most interesting as a fictionally based "documentary." The script and particularly the camera help to create the documentary effect. In the script, the action is quick, and people are almost always on the move. The dialogue has a clipped, efficient quality suggestive of newsreel interviews. Rarely lingering on any one scene, the camera's quick movements enhance this effect. At times, the film seems awkwardly self-conscious as a fictional documentary—its close-ups and its cutting techniques become rather methodical—but in its script and in its camerawork, it seems to set the way for later, somewhat more sophisticated fictionalized documentaries, such as *Z* (1969) and *State of Siege* (1973).

The most notable aspect of Frankenheimer's documentarylike film is its emphasis on television. Frankenheimer began his career as a television director for *Playhouse 90* and other live drama series and has been moving toward use of television in films ever since. Serling also had considerable success with television script writing.

At the beginning of the film, the film camera, like a television news camera, seems caught up in the violence of the protest in front of the White House. It unsteadily focuses on a policeman's back and a protester's angry face, and then it is tossed about and the screen is almost blacked out. Grainy textures and hurried shots through top-secret corridors further suggest the television news camera. Throughout the film, in fact, the audience spends a great deal of time looking at television sets. The rim of a set frames the entire scene of Scott's political rally. During the President's television-phone calls, the camera again shows Scott on a television screen. In a number of scenes, the audience sees close-ups of television cameras and broad shots of a wall of television monitors.

One of the themes of Frankenheimer's documentary is, in fact, the power of television. Much of General Scott's dangerous power seems to stem from his potential use of television and other communication networks. When the President asks him to resign, Scott says he will take the issue to the people— and the audience knows this means television viewers. Later, the General threatens to break in on the President's televised press conference. Shots of the enormous wall of television monitors, and the fact that so many of the characters are watching on their home sets, emphasizes the danger of Scott's power.

There is something especially credible about television. Many people have learned to believe in the evening news, and the extraordinary things they see on it have become their measure of reality. This popular belief in television is a strong thematic point in the film, and it also enables Frankenheimer to camouflage some of the script's problems. The script makes a number of demands on the audience. It pretends to be accurate, yet it presents an extremely simplistic view of Washington politics. It asks the audience to believe that someone as clever and cunning as General Scott would reveal his political secrets in love letters to a mistress. Jiggs is rather openly spying on the General, yet the script suggests that in spite of their extremely careful planning, the coup's organizers never have him followed. Most seriously, it tells the audience that the coup leaders have established a very large military base and are training one hundred officers and thirty-six hundred men without anyone's knowledge except that of a few small-town Texans who live nearby. The flimsiness of these plot details is offset, however, by the fact that the audience has already seen things just as unbelievable on the evening news, and is thus more susceptible to believing them in a television-style movie. Also, the increasing pace and tension of the action give the audience little time to worry about nuances of plot.

Most criticisms of *Seven Days in May*, however, concern not the credibility of its script but rather its attempts to make a political statement, something evident in the novel as well. The film warns the public against the dangers of ultraright-wing superpatriots, especially those in the military, and it praises the values of an open, liberal democracy. When these ideas are an integral part of the acting, camerawork, and script, they are successful; but when March as the President issues platitudinous speeches about democratic values, the film becomes overly preachy. Even though the viewer may agree with the ideas in these speeches, the movie is least significant when it propagandizes.

In spite of some unlikely elements in the plot and the heavy-handed attempts to instruct the audience, *Seven Days in May* is still interesting and very entertaining. As a thriller, it keeps the viewers on the edge of their seats; as a fictional documentary, it creates a pathway for similar films that follow; and as a political statement, its criticisms are as appropriate today as in 1964.

Elaine McCreight

SEVEN DAYS TO NOON

Released: 1950
Production: John Boulting and Roy Boulting for London Films
Direction: John Boulting
Screenplay: Frank Harvey and Roy Boulting; based on an original story by
  Paul Dehn and James Bernard (AA)
Cinematography: Gilbert Taylor and Ray Sturgess
Editing: Ray Boulting
Running time: 94 minutes

> *Principal characters:*
> Professor Willingdon .... Barry Jones
> Goldie .... Olive Sloane
> Superintendent Folland .... André Morell
> Ann Willingdon .... Sheila Manahan
> Mrs. Peckett .... Joan Hickson
> The Prime Minister .... Ronald Adam
> Stephen Lane .... Hugh Cross

On August 6, 1945, the Enola Gay, a B-29 Superfortress, dropped the first atomic bomb ever to be used in warfare on the city of Hiroshima, Japan. The bomb exploded in midair above the city killing and maiming tens of thousands of people. More than two-thirds of Hiroshima was destroyed, and the world was abruptly thrust into the atomic age. World War II ended, but the possibility now existed that, should there ever be a World War III, combatants would not battle one another merely with tanks or submarines or guns. The result would not be a battlefield strewn with corpses, but the total obliteration of mankind.

To this day, debate about the utilization of atomic energy, from the construction of nuclear power plants to the necessity of nuclear proliferation, has been unceasing. Filmmakers have not ignored the subject. In *The China Syndrome* (1979), an accident in a nuclear energy plant comes close to rendering an area the size of Pennsylvania uninhabitable. Other films have dramatically (*Fail-Safe*, 1964) and satirically (*Dr. Strangelove, Or: How I Learned to Stop Worrying and Love the Bomb*, 1964) treated the crisis resulting from an unwarranted nuclear attack by the United States on the Soviet Union.

Seven Days to Noon, a British film produced five years after Hiroshima and almost thirty years before *The China Syndrome*, is a straightforward, absorbing, thought-provoking account of a city faced with the threat of an atomic bomb blowing up its center.

In *Seven Days to Noon*, the pacifistic Professor Willingdon (Barry Jones), a brilliant scientist, fears that his research and discoveries in atomic energy will ultimately be utilized for the destruction of mankind. He steals an atom bomb and threatens to blow up the central part of London unless bomb production is ceased. Willingdon issues an ultimatum to the Prime Minister of England (Ronald Adam), giving him until noon on Sunday—seven days' time—to comply with his wishes. If the conditions are not met, the professor will explode the bomb.

Scotland Yard is called into the case, with Superintendent Folland (André Morell) in charge. Willingdon becomes the object of a nationwide manhunt as he roams around London with the bomb in his suitcase. At first, in order to prevent panic, the government does not report the impending danger to the people. When Scotland Yard is unable to apprehend the elusive scientist, the Prime Minister declares over the radio that a state of emergency exists. A portion of London may soon have to be evacuated, and a workable plan of action must be drawn up. Days pass, and the professor is still not captured. In a massively detailed maneuver filmed on location in the London streets, the evacuation plan is set in motion. It is Sunday morning, just hours before noon, and the military combs the deserted evacuation area for Willingdon. In a tense climax, he is captured while praying in a church and the bomb is defused seconds before it is scheduled to go off.

As a straight suspense film, *Seven Days to Noon* is an exciting, pulsating drama. The story easily builds to a heightening of tension as the seconds tick away and the clock creeps toward noon Sunday. Predictably, Willingdon is caught, but he has the power of life and death over thousands. The film is endowed with a scary reality which, cinematically, is its major strength. Thus, the sequences of the mass evacuation of London and the shots of the deserted city are particularly eerie.

Director John Boulting, whose twin brother and frequent collaborator Roy penned the screenplay with Frank Harvey, does not overly stress the pro- or antinuclear possibilities inherent within the scenario. The film is not political. It is clear that atomic bomb production will not be halted and that Willingdon's request will not even be considered. These were not the issues when the film was released in 1950, during the Cold War. Willingdon, as impressively portrayed by Jones, is a man who has lost all reason even though his motives may be noble. Perhaps he is, in his way, trying to force the government and people of England, and the entire world, to face up to the threat of nuclear power. He is, in essence, a man who, in his zeal, has lost all sanity. Willingdon may be a scientist and pacifist, but he is depicted as an irresponsible individual. At the finale, the British government still continues a policy that might cause the demise of the entire country.

Seven Days to Noon features no major stars; none of its actors was well known before or after the film's release. Willingdon is easily the biggest and best role in the career of Jones, a fine character actor who began performing on the stage during the early 1920's. Jones eloquently depicts Willingdon's confusion, isolation, and frustration. In his mind, he is being logical. To the government and everyone else, however, he is a lunatic. Jones is nicely supported by Sheila Manahan (as the professor's daughter), Morell and Adam (representing the British authorities), and, most impressively, by Olive Sloane as Goldie, an aging music-hall performer who befriends Willingdon and unknowingly harbors him.

The earliest films of the Boulting brothers, including *Seven Days to Noon* and *The Magic Box* (1952), are highly regarded by critics. Paul Dehn and James Bernard's story for *Seven Days to Noon* won an Academy Award, although the competition was generally weak, consisting of *The Bullfighter and the Lady*, *The Frogmen*, *Here Comes the Groom* and *Teresa*. The Boultings went on to produce, direct, and write light-hearted satires dealing with contemporary issues. These include *I'm All Right Jack* (1960) about trade unions and *Heaven's Above* (1963), about British clergy life. Both starred Peter Sellers.

Seven Days to Noon did not do well financially—according to *Variety*, it earned less than $1,250,000—but its premise is as timely today as in 1950.

Rob Edelman

THE SEVEN-PER-CENT SOLUTION

Released: 1976
Production: Herbert Ross for Universal
Direction: Herbert Ross
Screenplay: Nicholas Meyer; based on his novel of the same name
Cinematography: Oswald Morris
Editing: Chris Barnes
Costume design: Alan Barrett
Running time: 113 minutes

Principal characters:
Sigmund Freud .... Alan Arkin
Lola Deveraux .... Vanessa Redgrave
Dr. Watson .... Robert Duvall
Sherlock Holmes .... Nicol Williamson
Professor Moriarty .... Laurence Olivier
Lowenstein .... Joel Grey
Mary Watson .... Samantha Eggar
Baron von Leinsdorf .... Jeremy Kemp
Mycroft Holmes .... Charles Gray

Nicholas Meyer is a man noted for his highly imaginative stories. In his delightful comedy/mystery/fantasy *Time After Time* (1979), which he scripted and directed, H. G. Wells invents a real time machine that is stolen by Jack the Ripper. The novelist then travels through time from Victorian England to 1979 San Francisco in pursuit of the killer. Meyer also wrote the screenplay for the film version of his best-selling novel, *The Seven-Per-cent Solution*, with Herbert Ross directing the 1976 release. Its premise is just as unusual as *Time After Time*; a famous fictional character (Sir Arthur Conan Doyle's Sherlock Holmes) and a real-life personality (Vienna's Sigmund Freud) meet and solve a mystery. The result is a stylish, witty, and fascinating film.

The plot of *The Seven-Per-cent Solution* is elaborate. In 1939, an aged Dr. John Watson (Robert Duvall), friend and chronicler of the late private detective Sherlock Holmes, reads that Dr. Sigmund Freud, pioneer psychoanalyst, has passed away. He then dictates an account of what really happened almost fifty years before, when Holmes was missing for three years and presumed to have plunged into the Reichenbach Falls during a confrontation with his nemesis, Professor Moriarty. In the spring of 1891, according to Watson, he was summoned to 221B Baker Street by Mrs. Hudson, Holmes's landlady. The detective had barricaded himself in his room, and was refusing to eat.

Watson finds Holmes (Nicol Williamson) bored, deeply depressed, obsessed with the evil Moriarty, and high on cocaine, which he mixes in a "seven-percent solution" with water; Watson can do nothing for his friend. When he arrives home, he is greeted by a shy little man (Laurence Olivier) who declares that he is Moriarty. The professor says that he is no criminal mastermind but a harmless mathematics tutor who taught Holmes and his brother Mycroft (Charles Drake) at their father's estate in Sussex when they were youngsters. He complains that Holmes has been harassing him unnecessarily, refers to a "tragedy," and then disappears.

Watson feels that only one man can assist Holmes: Sigmund Freud (Alan Arkin), a young Viennese doctor. Watson, Mycroft, and Moriarty trick Holmes into traveling to Vienna in pursuit of the professor. The detective expects to trap Moriarty in an apartment, but instead finds Dr. Freud. Holmes realizes Watson's motives for the fraud, and agrees to undergo a cure for his addiction.

Several days later, after Holmes's painful withdrawal from the drug (presented in an interesting sequence highlighted by jerky camera movement) Freud receives a message requesting him to visit the beautiful musical comedy star Lola Deveraux (Vanessa Redgrave), a patient whom he has treated for drug addiction and who has just attempted suicide. Freud, accompanied by Holmes and Watson, visits Lola in the hospital. The woman explains that she was kidnaped and forcibly injected with drugs, and tells them that her abductor was a thin little man wearing a bowler hat. The trio notices such a man outside the hospital. His name is Lowenstein (Joel Grey), and he is employed by Baron von Leinsdorf (Jeremy Kemp), who soon kidnaps Lola with the intent to pass her over to the wealthy Amin Pasha who, in turn, has promised to settle the baron's gambling debts. After a narrow escape from death in a horse-riding arena and a trip to a Viennese brothel, they learn that the pasha and the baron are about to depart by train for Istanbul—with Lola. Holmes, Watson, and Freud hijack their own train, and, after an exciting locomotive chase, catch their foes. Holmes jumps the train and defeats the baron in a sword fight, and he and Freud rescue Lola from the pasha.

Holmes is by now cured of his drug addiction, but, under hypnosis, he remembers that as a child his father killed his mother when he discovered her making love with Moriarty. This explains his loathing for the professor. In the final scene, Holmes takes off for a relaxing river cruise and discovers that the beautiful Lola is his companion.

Prior to *The Seven-Per-cent Solution*, Sherlock Holmes had been presented on screen as a brilliantly eccentric super-sleuth. In cinema, the detective dates back to American-made one-reelers in 1903, 1905, and 1908. Other actors to play him from the silents to the 1970's were William Gillette, John Barrymore, Clive Brook, Raymond Massey, Christopher Lee, Peter Cushing, Christopher Plummer, Robert Stephens, and, of course, Basil Rathbone, in the Universal series from the late 1930's to the mid-1940's. Meyer's characterization of the detective is no godlike good guy, but a typical hero of the 1970's: neurotic, drug-addicted, and in desperate need of psychiatric care.

The Seven-Per-cent Solution is an intriguing mystery-adventure, rife with the whimsical "elementary, my dear Watson" spirit that is the tradition of Conan Doyle's characters. There is wit—a duel between Freud and the baron that occurs just after Holmes undergoes his cure ends up as a tennis match—and there is action—the train chase is particularly exciting. Meyer, however, has added a new dimension to the proceedings. Moriarty is no cunning cut-throat but a timid old man unjustifiably picked on by Holmes. Watson is no bumbler, unlike the inimitable Nigel Bruce, who played the character opposite Rathbone, but a forceful young man with a beautiful wife (Samantha Eggar). The idea of Holmes under the psychiatric care of Sigmund Freud is as out-rageous yet as cinematically enjoyable as that of H. G. Wells driving a car or dining in McDonald's in contemporary San Francisco.

Oswald Morris' cinematography gives the film the look of a daguerrotype, and brilliant production designer Ken Adam's turn-of-the century settings are pleasingly authentic. Alan Barrett's costumes are elegant; he earned an Acad-emy Award nomination for his work, but lost to Danilo Donati for *Fellini's Casanova*. Meyer's screenplay was also Oscar-nominated; however, the win-ner was William Goldman for *All the President's Men*. *The Seven-Per-cent Solution* is more a Meyer's film than Herbert Ross's, even though the latter is credited as director. Ross, a former musical comedy and ballet choreog-rapher, has directed comedies (1970's *The Owl and the Pussycat*; 1975's *The Sunshine Boys*) and musicals (1969's *Goodbye Mr. Chips*; 1975's *Funny Lady*). His most personal works, however, are the ballet films *The Turning Point* (1977) and *Nijinsky* (1980).

Arkin and Duvall offer solid performances. Arkin does not overplay his Hungarian-Jewish accent; his Freud is effectively understated. Duvall, in an odd bit of casting, is believably British as Watson, and is much better in the part than one might expect. Redgrave and Olivier are their usual superb selves in what are little more than cameo roles. Williamson, perhaps the least well-known of all the principals, is brilliant as Holmes. His delivery is excellent and his mannerisms perfectly timed. His Holmes is no one-dimensional detective hero but a troubled, impatient, agonized human being.

The Seven-Per-cent Solution received mixed reviews and was no box-office blockbuster. Filmed on a budget of four million dollars, it was forty-ninth on the *Variety* list of top rental pictures for 1977, with a box-office take of only $5,472,000. It did receive two Oscar nominations, however, and was also on the ten-best lists of *The New York Times* and the National Board of Review.

Rob Edelman

SHAFT

Released: 1971
Production: Joel Freeman for Metro-Goldwyn-Mayer
Direction: Gordon Parks
Screenplay: John D. F. Black; based on the novel of the same name by Ernest Tidyman
Cinematography: Urs Furrer
Editing: Hugh A. Robertson
Music: Isaac Hayes
Song: Isaac Hayes, "Theme from Shaft" (AA)
Running time: 100 minutes

> *Principal characters:*
> John Shaft .... Richard Roundtree
> Bumpy Jonas .... Moses Gunn
> Ellie .... Gwen Mitchell
> Ben Buford .... Christopher St. John
> Lieutenant Victor Androzzi .... Charles Cioffi
> Sergeant Tom Hannon .... Lawrence Pressman
> Marcy Jonas .... Sherri Brewer

Sam Spade and Philip Marlowe are the quintessential Hollywood private eyes: tough, resilient, fearless, cynical, even heroic loners. During the 1940's, when those detectives were portrayed by Humphrey Bogart, Dick Powell, and Robert Montgomery, blacks in these same films were relegated to roles as mammies, janitors, cleaning ladies, and piano players with dialogue consisting of little more than "yes, boss." By 1971, however, Martin Luther King, Jr., Hilda Parks, James Meredith, and Sidney Poitier had made America receptive to private eye John Shaft, portrayed by handsome Richard Roundtree, the first authentic black film superhero. The film is titled, simply, *Shaft*.

The character of John Shaft was the creation of Ernest Tidyman, who received an Academy Award for his screenplay for *The French Connection* (1971). His Shaft is suave, romantic, brave, streetwise, and indestructible in the best tradition of the Hollywood private detective. Shaft dresses in turtleneck sweaters and expensive leather pants and jackets. As the advertisements proclaimed, Shaft is "Hotter Than Bond, Cooler Than Bullitt." His appeal is that he is fundamentally a good guy, as well as a resourceful private eye who takes no orders from the police force. He is as appealing to women as he is intimidating to wiseguys. The attraction of *Shaft* is not merely to black audiences. It is not a black exploitation film; its bad buys are both blacks and whites. The film is not a reverse racist diatribe, as is Melvin Van Peebles' bitter, angry *Sweet Sweetback's Baadasssss Song*, which had been released a few months earlier. Shaft takes no guff from whites, however; for example, when a thug calls him a nigger, he responds by calling the mobster a wop and later breaks a bottle across his face. Shaft's girl friend Ellie (Gwenn Mitchell) is black, but he is not averse to picking up a white girl in a bar and sharing a nude embrace with her in a shower. Ultimately, the main purpose of *Shaft* is to entertain. There is no message in the film; it is simply one hundred minutes of good, old-fashioned, upbeat, professionally packaged escapism. Its hero just happens to be black, and he also happens to win.

John Shaft (Richard Roundtree) lives in a Greenwich Village brownstone and works out of an office in Times Square, but his main contacts remain uptown in Harlem, where black underworld boss Bumpy Jonas (Moses Gunn) dispatches two of his henchmen to bring the detective to him. It is not an easy assignment. One dies in a three-story fall and the other confesses to Shaft after a scuffle that "Bumpy sent us to bring you uptown." The police also harass Shaft. Lieutenant Victor Androzzi (Charles Cioffi) warns him that his detective's license will be revoked unless he informs the police on the racketeer Jonas' activities. Jonas, however, just wants to hire the detective to find his daughter Marcy (Sherri Brewer), who has apparently been kidnaped by a group of black militants headed by Ben Buford (Christopher St. John), an old friend of Shaft. The girl has actually been abducted by some Mafia racketeers, however, who are plotting to take over Jonas' operation. Shaft traces Marcy and her captors to a Harlem hotel. He rescues her at the finale by hanging from a rope and bursting through a hotel window like Tarzan swinging across the jungle to rescue Jane from the clutches of an evil witch doctor. In the process, he wipes out the entire squad of kidnapers.

Shaft is directed by Gordon Parks, who, as a craftsman and storyteller, is not John Huston or Howard Hawks, but whose work here is slick and professional. Parks is a black American pioneer. A former fashion and society photographer, he was the first black staff photographer at *Life* magazine. In 1968, he directed, wrote, and composed the musical score for *The Learning Tree*, an autobiographical novel published five years earlier. The film is a sensitive, perceptive account of growing up black in America during the 1920's. *The Learning Tree*, the first major film directed by a black man for a major studio in the United States, did poorly at the box office. In 1972, Park's son, Gordon Parks, Jr., directed *Super Fly*, one of the most popular and controversial black films of the era. The film's hero, Priest (Ron O'Neal), is no private detective or police lieutenant but a cocaine dealer whose activities are glorified and romanticized. John Shaft may be unconventional, but he is most assuredly on the side of "right"; Priest is merely a drug pusher, a hero hardly fit for emulation by impressionable ghetto youth.

Shaft has an outstanding music score. Isaac Hayes's throbbing, rock/soul-oriented background music adds immeasurably to the pace of the film. His score won a Golden Globe Award but lost out to Michel Legrand's *Summer of '42* for the Academy Award for Best Original Dramatic Score. His "Theme from Shaft" did become a "Top 40" hit, however, and was awarded an Oscar for Best Song—no minor accomplishment, since the Academy members have traditionally ignored "new" music. For example, six years after the release of *Shaft*, the Bee Gees's outstanding disco score for *Saturday Night Fever* did not even receive an Oscar nomination. Hayes's nomination and award is, in retrospect, that much more impressive. Although Hayes went on to star in such low-grade black exploitation films as *Truck Turner* (1974), his talents are far better utilized in the recording studio.

Roundtree's career has never matched the popularity and promise indicated by *Shaft*. He was introduced in the film, and his good looks and better-than-average acting ability (he had appeared with the Negro Ensemble Company in New York and in a road company production of "The Great White Hope") portended a bright screen career, which has not as yet materialized. During the 1970's, he appeared in such films as *Charlie One-Eye* (1972), *Earthquake* (1974), and *Man Friday* (1975), which were far less worthy efforts than *Shaft*.

Shaft was a tremendous box-office success. Filmed at a cost of $1.2 million, it earned $6,100,000 in the first year of its release and was ranked twelfth on *Variety*'s list of top-grossing films. *Shaft*, along with *Sweet Sweetback's Baadasssss Song* and Ossie Davis' *Cotton Comes to Harlem* (1970), confirmed that there was indeed a viable market for films in which blacks starred and portrayed heroes. The film was followed by two adequate but undistinguished features: *Shaft's Big Score* (1972), directed by Parks, in which the detective solves the murder of a friend and tangles again with Bumpy Jonas; and *Shaft in Africa* (1973), directed by John Guillermin, in which the hero helps an African nation halt slave-trading. *Shaft's Big Score* made a small profit, but *Shaft in Africa* took a loss. In 1972, the original film was optioned by CBS television as a pilot for an hour-long television series, which enjoyed a brief run.

Rob Edelman

SHAKE HANDS WITH THE DEVIL

Released: 1959
Production: Michael Anderson for United Artists
Direction: Michael Anderson
Screenplay: Ivan Goff and Ben Roberts; based on the novel of the same name by Reardon Conner
Cinematography: Erwin Hillier
Editing: Gordon Pilkington
Running time: 100 minutes

Principal characters:

Sean Lenihan	James Cagney
Kerry O'Shea	Don Murray
Kitty	Glynis Johns
Jennifer Curtis	Dana Wynter
Lady Fitzhugh	Sybil Thorndike
Paddy Nolan	Ray McAnally
Colonel Smithson	Christopher Rhodes
Sir Arnold Fielding	Clive Morton

"Those who shake hands with the devil often find they have difficulty getting their hands back." Thus does folk wisdom remonstrate against the temptation to do good by doing evil. Michael Anderson's *Shake Hands with the Devil*, which takes its title from this old saying, is about two men who are tempted to let the end justify the means. Both succumb to the temptation, but one man extricates himself. The other is destroyed.

This drama is set in Ireland in 1921, and Kerry O'Shea (Don Murray), a young American of Irish parentage, finds himself caught up in "the troubles" while pursuing a medical degree at Dublin's Royal College of Surgeons. Although pressed by his fiercely nationalistic friends at the college to join the guerrilla movement against the British forces occupying their homeland, O'Shea professes his neutrality. Even the fact that his father, once a high-ranking official in the Sinn Fein (the rebel army), had been killed by the British Black and Tans fails to move him. Violence, he says, never solved anything. "Ah, it must be a grand thing to be an American, with your war for independence already won," is his friend's sardonic rejoinder.

O'Shea is drawn into the conflict against his will, however, when, despite his neutrality, the British troops subject him to the same brutal harassment that characterizes their treatment of all Irish citizens. Indeed, this is a key to understanding the film. Anderson does not give his protagonists easy choices. The Black and Tans are presented as nothing more than thugs; it is a given in the film that the British occupation of Ireland is odious and ought to be ended. The question that Anderson and his writers Ivan Goff and Ben Roberts pose is the morality of accomplishing this end by violent means. The turning point for Kerry O'Shea comes when he and his friend Paddy Nolan (Ray McAnally) stumble into the middle of a shootout between an Irish terrorist and the Black and Tans. Nolan is wounded, and in carrying his friend to shelter, O'Shea leaves behind a book with his name in it. There are no innocent bystanders in the minds of the Black and Tans: like it or not, Kerry O'Shea is now a wanted man.

Anderson uses this incident to introduce the film's second protagonist, Sean Lenihan (James Cagney). Lenihan is a brilliant surgeon—he appeared briefly in an earlier scene as one of O'Shea's professors—and also, it is revealed, second in command in the Sinn Fein hierarchy. Kerry learns of Lenihan's political activities when the doctor is summoned to the home of a Sinn Fein sympathizer in an unsuccessful attempt to save Paddy Nolan's life. Lenihan represents the militant wing of the Sinn Fein. He believes in refusing to compromise, or even to negotiate, with the British; and he heads the rebels' military unit. Lenihan is a hard man, and his hardness extends beyond the British. He is also intensely misogynistic, and it is his hatred of women, of all his many hatreds, that will eventually prove his undoing.

Anderson reveals all this gradually, however; during the first half of the film, Lenihan is a sympathetic character. After Nolan's death he offers Kerry O'Shea, who still declines to join the Sinn Fein, safe passage out of the country. Before this can be effected, however, O'Shea is captured and tortured by the Black and Tans. By the time Lenihan and his men come to the rescue, O'Shea is ready to join. "You'll see blood flow," warns Lenihan. "I can taste my own right now," replies his new recruit. Thus O'Shea, like Lenihan before him, embraces violence as a legitimate tactic. Both men have shaken hands with the devil.

Things begin to unravel when Lady Fitzhugh (Sybil Thorndike), an elderly Sinn Fein sympathizer, is captured while attempting to smuggle a wounded terrorist leader out of the country. Lenihan and O'Shea respond by kidnaping Jennifer Curtis (Dana Wynter), daughter of Sir Arnold Fielding (Clive Morton), the leader of English forces in Ireland. She is to be held until Lady Fitzhugh is released. Ultimately, it is the women in the film who occasion its decisive plot turns. Lenihan, the woman hater, is uncomfortable around Jennifer Curtis; the arrival at their hideout of Kitty (Glynis Johns), a barmaid, and friend of several of Lenihan's gang, only serves to further arouse his ire. Lady Fitzhugh also complicates things by going on a hunger strike in an English prison, where she eventually dies. Capping everything, Kerry O'Shea and Jennifer Curtis fall in love.

Things come to a head during a dockside assassination attempt on Colonel Smithson (Christopher Rhodes), the British officer who captured and tortured O'Shea. Kitty, banished from the Sinn Fein hideout and ignorant of the planned attack, walks into the middle of the ambush and inadvertently gives

Lenihan's men away. A shootout follows, with Lenihan, O'Shea, and a few others finally escaping. Maddened by what he perceives as this female perfidy, Lenihan resolves to execute Jennifer Curtis. Meanwhile, Kerry O'Shea and his friends receive word that the moderate faction of the Sinn Fein has negotiated a truce with the British. They are ordered to cease their violence and release Jennifer Curtis unharmed.

The film's climax occurs on a rocky beach outside the lighthouse where Jennifer has been kept. A defiant Lenihan rejects the possibility of a truce and vows to keep fighting. One by one, however, his followers desert him. "You've forgotten what you're fighting *for*," cries O'Shea. "It's all just killing now." Anderson emphasizes Lenihan's physical and mental isolation from his erstwhile comrades in the film's final shot. Lenihan stands on the shore, a solitary figure, halfway between the men and Jennifer Curtis. Despite the desertion of his followers, however, Lenihan's corrosive hatred—by now little more than simple bloodlust—will not be denied. He turns to shoot his captive, but before he can do so, he himself is killed by a quick shot from the gun of Kerry O'Shea. In horror and disgust, O'Shea hurls his gun onto the rocks along the shoreline. At great cost, he has extricated his hand from the devil's grasp.

Throughout the film, Anderson and his writers compare and contrast their four principal characters—Lenihan, the brilliant but bloodthristy Irishman, with O'Shea, the humane Irish-American, and, in lesser roles, Kitty, the earthy, ingenuous Irishwoman, with Jennifer Curtis, the genteel and calculating English woman. Although on paper the two sets of parts are roughly equal, on the screen the Irish characters stand out. The Irish subject of the film may have something to do with this, but an even more important factor is the acting of the people playing these characters.

Murray as Kerry O'Shea and Wynter as Jennifer Curtis give good, competent performances, but these performances are overshadowed by those of Cagney and Johns as Sean Lenihan and Kitty, respectively. Johns, in a minor role, brings an incredible amount of warmth to the character of the simple barmaid, who has a more profound (although totally intuitive, rather than intellectual) understanding of the Irish question than do any of her swaggering Sinn Fein boyfriends. Cagney is simply Cagney. He inhabits the character of Sean Lenihan with such verve and zest that Lenihan becomes the focus of the film. In the beginning, he is all charm and twinkle. Slowly, however, Cagney reveals the canker in Lenihan's heart, and by the end of the film, we have no sympathy left for Sean Lenihan—only pity.

Anderson uses his cast well. A number of the smaller roles were played by actors from the Irish Abbey Theatre, and they lent a good deal of authenticity to the film. *Shake Hands with the Devil* is tightly paced. Although it is a film with a moral, Anderson never stops to moralize. His conclusions about the ultimate immorality of violence are manifested through the workings of the plot, not through windy sermons that slow down the action. *Shake Hands with the Devil* is a taut, compelling study of the Irish question with universal lessons as relevant today as they were in 1959, or in 1921.

Robert Mitchell

SHAMPOO

Released: 1975
Production: Warren Beatty for Rubeeker
Direction: Hal Ashby
Screenplay: Robert Towne and Warren Beatty
Cinematography: Laszlo Kovacs
Editing: Robert C. Jones
Running time: 109 minutes

Principal characters:
George .... Warren Beatty
Jill .... Goldie Hawn
Jackie .... Julie Christie
Felicia .... Lee Grant (AA)
Lester .... Jack Warden
Lorna .... Carrie Fisher
Johnny Pope .... Tony Bill

The appearance of Warren Beatty's *Shampoo* early in 1975 met with widespread media attention which was to continue throughout the year. *The New York Times* featured the film in two reviews, the first by Walter Goodman in which he lambasted the film as heavy-handed, obvious, and a general disappointment. Several months later, however, Vincent Canby followed with an article praising the film as the best contemporary American farce in recent years. Such disparity of response was characteristic of the film's reception with the public as well, with many viewers remaining uncertain of their final judgment. Yet this mixed response did not dampen the film's success or lessen its impact on subsequent films.

A Don Juan/Casanova story, choosing, suprisingly, a Beverly Hills hairdresser as the sexual hero, the film illuminates contemporary mores through observation of social as well as political behavior. Many critics fell prey to the possibilities this opened for comparison with Beatty's own much-publicized personal life. Like the character he portrays, Beatty reportedly had been leading an active sex life, playing Romeo to numerous Hollywood Juliets; in spite of his virile image, he remained single. When he chose to portray a hairdresser, a profession often depicted as being practiced largely by homosexuals, many critics chose not only to analyze the film character's behavior and psychology channels, but also to extend the analysis to Beatty himself. In so doing they neglected the impact, humor, and overall effect of the film.

The story resembles, if not in particulars, at least in tradition, its literary antecedents. George (Warren Beatty) is a simple fellow, quite naïvely giving his best to each situation which presents itself to him. That at which he succeeds is providing others with pleasure. When he attempts to plan his own success, however, he ends up the loser. The story takes place on Election Eve, 1968, and occupies less than two days in George's life. He is involved with a rather complicated network of individuals. Jill (Goldie Hawn), a would-be actress, is his current girl friend and the best friend of his former lover Jackie (Julie Christie). He has also attracted the attention of his client, Felicia (Lee Grant), whose wealthy husband, Lester (Jack Warden), could provide George with the financial backing he needs to acquire his own salon. This already complicated group of people is further complicated by the fact that Jackie has become Lester's mistress, having found her talents better rewarded in this arrangement than in any other she has undertaken.

The convergence of crises for all of the principal characters in the film moves the story forward. George wants to open his own beauty salon, hoping that Lester will finance his venture after the banks have turned him down. Because he has never saved any money or done anything more than setting hair and sleeping with many of his clients, George has no credit rating. Felicia tries to convince Lester to back George's venture, vaguely implying that George is a homosexual so that Lester will not suspect her of ulterior motives. At the same time that George is having problems getting his financial backing, Jill is also giving him trouble. She has become fed up with his philandering and has started to see someone new: Johnny Pope (Tony Bill). Jackie also brings added pressure on George when seeing her again convinces him that he is still in love with her.

In the background to all of these complicated relationships are scenes of George on his motorcycle, racing around town with his hair blower in his belt like a gun in a holster, going from woman to woman. Yet it is not George who comes off without sympathy in the end; it is the women. While at first he appears to be using them (or at least deceiving them), in the end, it is the women who seem to benefit the most. This becomes particularly obvious as the election night party at The Factory comes closer and George must not only satisfy the sexual and emotional needs of the women, but also do their hair. In the end, all of the women give George up, although only Jackie seems to have any regrets. George wants to "take care" of her, but she realizes that the security that Lester offers is more important than any emotional feelings she has for George.

What lends these two days in 1968 the power to expose contemporary social and sexual values is the balance with which the personal and political events are blended. 1968 saw the election of Richard Nixon to the presidency; Lester is a hearty contributor to Nixon's campaign, and as the election occurs, the story unfolds. Businessmen are depicted as political supporters of their own best interests, not those of the nation. Constant reminders—campaign posters, election night parties, speeches on television—keep the political activities present as a backdrop for George's sexual adventures.

The story is appropriately set in Beverly Hills, California, home of affluence and excess. While women pamper themselves, and in this case bed the hairdresser, their husbands are off making money. Meanwhile, an election with serious future consequences takes place. The film defines with humor the social conditions which make such an election possible: each character is so set on satisfying his or her own needs that there is no vision left for the national situation.

The film, written by Robert Towne and Warren Beatty, is a tightly plotted, calculated comedy of manners. The Los Angeles setting offers those elements necessary in such a contemporary farce. There is affluence, allowing the characters to pursue sybaritic ends. The distances between one location and another provide obstacles to potential encounters, which must be worked in between the comings and goings of various characters. The eventual delays allow situations to arise such as George's going to bed with Lorna (Carrie Fisher), Lester and Felicia's seventeen-year-old daughter, while he waits for Felicia to arrive. When Felicia arrives home she realizes that she must take advantage of the situation at hand and hops into bed with the exhausted George, who must give her a comb out after they are done.

The script also provides the cast with realistic dialogue, which lends believability to characters who could easily have become stereotypes. Without extensive exposition to develop characters, the audience believes the words and actions and understands the motivations. Director Hal Ashby complements the script with an excellent and appropriate cast. Beatty is convincing as the handsome hairdresser who cannot say no; he might be compared to the familiar female prostitute with the heart of gold. George's naïveté results in his being the loser, however, since he cannot even feel good about sacrificing for someone else's benefit. As the film ends, George stands alone watching Jackie and Lester drive away, incapable of understanding what went wrong. He is left without his stable of lovers, although his salon may become a reality because of a change of heart by the surprisingly forgiving Lester.

Hawn, whose career in films began in 1968, shows the ability that audiences have come to recognize in her performances. She has succeeded in turning the dumb blonde into a character with dimension. Christie, who has played a diversity of roles in her career, gives a convincing performance as the foulmouthed yet caring Jackie. Grant won the Academy Award for Best Supporting Actress for her role as Felicia. She, like the other female performers, has the ability to portray believably a wide spectrum of characters. The casting of these three women offers an interesting portrait of the successful modern female in film and of the challenge of maintaining a long and successful career through careful selection of roles.

Despite the success of *Shampoo*, it has remained, from its release to the present, controversial. Bernice Mann, a retired manicurist, brought a lawsuit against Beatty and Towne, claiming that she had submitted a treatment, "Women Plus," which became the premise for *Shampoo*. In the Los Angeles

Superior Court, she was awarded $185,000 in damages. A month later, the decision was reversed and the award nullified. The second decision is now being appealed. On close examination, the events appear cloudy at best. Mann had written merely a sketchy outline, a series of scenes. The outline ended up in the hands of a reader for an independent company on the Columbia lot. The reader claims to have found in an envelope a treatment for a novel about nurses entitled "Two Weeks." This was the title mentioned in the rejection notice. Those who have compared Mann's "Women Plus" with Towne's *Shampoo* find only the most general similarities: a beauty shop and a womanizing hairdresser. Perhaps the greatest interest in the case lies in the precedent which the decision could set. There are innumerable "writers" who would gladly pursue a lawsuit against a major studio over a script they felt had been pirated. In addition to the pending decision in the *Shampoo* case, a similar suit has been filed against the makers of *Raiders of the Lost Ark* (1981). The charge concerns a novel presented to the company and rejected which the author claims provided the premise for the film. One can be sure that both would-be screenwriters and filmmakers will watch the outcome of these cases with a serious eye.

Kenneth T. Burles

SHANGHAI EXPRESS

Released: 1932
Production: Adolph Zukor for Paramount
Direction: Josef von Sternberg
Screenplay: Jules Furthman; based on an original screen story by Harry Hervey
Cinematography: Lee Garmes
Editing: no listing
Costume design: Travis Banton
Running time: 84 minutes

Principal characters:
Shanghai Lily .... Marlene Dietrich
Captain Donald Harvey .... Clive Brook
Henry Chang .... Warner Oland
Hue Fei .... Anna May Wong
Sam Salt .... Eugene Pallette
Reverend Carmichael .... Lawrence Grant
Mrs. Haggerty .... Louise Closser Hale
Eric Baum ....Gustav von Seyffertitz
Major Lenard .... Emile Chautard
Li Fung .... Neshida Minoru
Albright ....Claude King

German-born Marlene Dietrich built her early career on playing women of the world in exotic stories usually directed by Josef von Sternberg. The producer-director-writer guided her in seven films, from the German-made *The Blue Angel* (1930) to *The Devil Is a Woman* (1935), all of which were noted for their erotic content as much as for their stories. With Oscar-winner Lee Garmes's fluid cinematography and Travis Banton's impressive costuming, *Shanghai Express* can easily stand as one of the best films made by the Dietrich-Sternberg collaboration. It came at exactly the halfway point, having been preceded by *Morocco* (1930) and followed by *The Scarlet Empress* (1934), both of which can be considered classics. The others, *Blonde Venus* (1932) and *Dishonored* (1931), fall into the entertaining-but-less-memorable category.

Set in 1931, when China is in a state of civil war, *Shanghai Express* introduces a group of people of varying backgrounds journeying from Beijing (Peking) to Shanghai. They enjoy first-class compartments while the natives are crowded into other cars. Hui Fei (Anna May Wong), a Eurasian whose background is suspect, arrives at the station in a sedan and boards the train in a manner suggesting that she is running away from something. Mrs. Haggerty (Louise Closser Hale), a boardinghouse-keeper concerned only with her dog's welfare, encounters the Reverend Carmichael (Lawrence Grant) as they both buy tickets.

Also in first class are the lady known as Shanghai Lily (Marlene Dietrich); Captain Donald Harvey (Clive Brook), a British medical officer on a mission; Henry Chang (Warner Oland), a supposed merchant who has little regard for anyone; American Sam Salt (Eugene Pallette), a man who will bet on anything; a German invalid named Eric Baum (Gustav von Seyffertitz); and French Major Lenard (Emile Chautard). The Reverend refuses to share space with two such undesirable women as Lily and Hui, while Harvey is learning from a fellow officer of Lily's reputation as a "coaster," a woman who travels up and down the coast for illicit reasons.

People and animals have to be cleared from the tracks and the Reverend grows impatient as a cow feeds her calf in the path of the train. "Time and life have no value" in China, Chang tells him. Casually meeting Lily, Harvey recognizes her as his long-ago love, Madeline. She addresses him sarcastically as "Doc," but knows exactly how long they have been apart—five years and four weeks. He has thought of nothing but her and remarks as to how much she has changed. When she says that her name has been changed, he asks if she is married, and she utters that famous line, "It took more than one man to change my name to Shanghai Lily," then adds her billing as "The White Flower of China."

As the train departs, soldiers sitting on top of the cars spear food with their bayonets. Lily plays a jazz record while Harvey leaves and Mrs. Haggerty walks in to get acquainted. When she says that she takes only respectable people at her Shanghai boarding house, Lily counters with "Don't you find them dull?" and "What kind of a house?" Mrs. Haggerty, realizing her error, retreats, and the Reverend discusses Lily with Harvey, who insists that she is a friend. Lily comes by in a white-feathered black hat, modifying the all black outfit in which she boarded the train. Although polite to her and Hui, Harvey manages to avoid the latter's handshake.

Government troops stop the express, examine passports, and take away a spy, Li Fung (Neshida Minoru). At this, Chang sends a message to his troops to stop the train at Te-Shan at midnight. After trying to force himself on Hui, Chang reveals to Sam that he was born of a white father and a Chinese mother but is not proud of his white blood. Lily approaches Harvey on the observation car and asks, "Do you vant to be alone, doctor?" The answer is clear when she sees her picture in the watch she once gave him. Without her, he has kept active, but he has no wish to be hurt again. Lily admits she made him jealous to test his love but lost him instead. The two kiss passionately, but she continues to tease.

Chang watches as the train stops to take on water and his soldiers steal aboard and proceed to kill the government troops. Revealed as Commander in Chief of the revolutionists, Chang is recognized finally by Hui, who says there is a twenty-thousand-dollar reward for him. He questions his prisoners, Baum being exposed as an opium dealer and not a coal banker. Chang brands him for the insolence he showed on the train. Translating for the Major, Lily declares that the officer has been disgraced but wears his uniform for the sake of his sister, whom he is to meet. Since Harvey will operate on the Governor General of Shanghai for a blood clot, Chang announces that he has found the perfect hostage to bargain for the return of his "right hand," Li Fung.

Asked to accompany Chang to his palace, Lily insists that she has reformed. Harvey breaks in and knocks Chang to the floor, prompting the war lord to have Lily dragged back to the train and Hui dragged to him. The Reverend caustically tells Lily to pray for Harvey's life and is impressed when she does so. In the morning, Division Superintendent Albright (Claude King) arrives by train with Li for the trade. When Lily protests her love for Harvey, Chang threatens to blind him until she gives her word of honor to accompany the rebel leader. Hui stabs Chang to death for her night of dishonor, however, and Harvey takes Lily back to the train.

Hui is to receive the reward for Chang, and the Reverend now defends Lily to Harvey. In a negligee, Lily enters Harvey's compartment but insists she would have prayed for anyone, not just him. All depart at Shanghai, where the Major tearfully introduces his sister to Lily. Spying on her buying him a new watch to replace the one he had lost, Harvey asks Lily's forgiveness and they engage in a long embrace.

Facing death, dishonor, and the loss of her lover, the Dietrich character remains a strong and resourceful individual, rarely showing her true emotions and masking sentiment with sarcasm. The actress makes it seem so effortless that many, including Sternberg, could accuse her of not acting at all. The smoldering passion she reveals in this film is nicely offset by Brook as the Stiff British medical officer torn between a desire to forgive her indiscretions and a long-suppressed need for her love. Oland displays his usual skill as a despicable villain, and Wong plays the Oriental equivalent of Shanghai Lily, although she appears to be misunderstood rather than immoral. This actress had an international career from the late silent days until her death in 1961, appearing in British, French, and American films. The comedy is in the hands of Hale and Pallette, although Dietrich does much of her emoting in a tongue-in-cheek style, as if to show that she is fully aware of the absurdity of the situations in which she sometimes finds herself.

Sternberg uses a very slow dissolve effectively to emphasize the action. The confining atmosphere of the train, on which most of the story takes place, and the setting of the rebel headquarters support his ability to keep the dramatics flowing smoothly. There is little in *Shanghai Express* which could be called excessively lavish, so Sternberg's use of his sets and backgrounds compensates for any lack of production values.

In 1951, Paramount released a remake called *Peking Express*, directed by

William Dieterle, as more of an action feature. It had Joseph Cotten as the doctor, Corinne Calvet as the Shanghai Lily equivalent, a Frenchwoman of dubious past, and Marvin Miller as the villain. Most of the secondary characters were eliminated, and Edmund Gwenn had a costarring role as the man of the cloth played in the original by Grant as a supporting part. The direction of the train was changed so that it headed from Shanghai to Peking, and the action was updated to the Chinese Communist era.

John Cocchi

SHE WORE A YELLOW RIBBON

Released: 1949
Production: John Ford and Merian C. Cooper for Argosy Pictures; released
  by RKO/Radio
Direction: John Ford
Screenplay: Frank S. Nugent and Laurence Stallings; based on the short story
  "War Party" by James Warner Bellah
Cinematography: Winton C. Hoch (AA)
Editing: Jack Murray
Running time: 103 minutes

Principal characters:

Captain Nathan Brittles	John Wayne
Sergeant Quinncannon	Victor McLaglen
Sergeant Tyree	Ben Johnson
Lieutenant Flint Colhill	John Agar
Lieutenant Pennell	Harry Carey, Jr.
Olivia Dandridge	Joanne Dru
Major Allshard	George O'Brien
Mrs. Allshard	Mildred Natwick
Pony That Walks	Chief Big Tree

Of the fourteen Westerns John Ford filmed in the sound era, nine dealt
with some aspect of the United States Army's cavalry regiments. In five
films—*Fort Apache* (1948), *She Wore a Yellow Ribbon* (1949), *Rio Grande*
(1950), *The Horse Soldiers* (1959), and *Sergeant Rutledge* (1960)—the cavalry
unit is the central concern of the director. It is also present in four other
films—*Stagecoach* (1939), *The Searchers* (1956), *Two Rode Together* (1961),
and *Cheyenne Autumn* (1964). Ford's opinion of the cavalry changed through
the years. In *Stagecoach*, the horse soldiers perform the traditional rescue,
saving the civilians under attack by the Indians. By 1964 in *Cheyenne Autumn*,
the Indians are the protagonists, and the cavalry has become the enemy. *The
Horse Soldiers*, set in the Civil War, portrays the cavalry as the instrument
effecting the restoration of the Union, but also destroying the gallant, gracious
society of the South which Ford admired. The effects of hypocrisy and racial
prejudice within the cavalry family are examined in The Searchers, *Two Rode
Together*, and *Sergeant Rutledge*. The latter film is especially noteworthy
because it portrays the experience of black soldiers in the Ninth Cavalry
regiment.
    Ford's most positive views of the horse troopers, however, are delineated
in what film critics refer to as the cavalry trilogy: *Fort Apache*, *She Wore a
Yellow Ribbon*, and *Rio Grande*. Similarities of theme and mood as well as
chronological proximity set these films apart from the others dealing with the

cavalry. All three films are based on stories by James Warner Bellah, all star John Wayne, all were filmed in Monument Valley, Utah, and all concentrate on the white trooper's experience, in contrast to *Sergeant Rutledge*. These three films combine two of Ford's favorite themes—civilization versus the wilderness and the individual versus society—in a unifying metaphor. The results of Ford's reflections on these themes in the context of the cavalry are three films of power, beauty, and artistry that are important in the context of Ford's career as well as being significant contributions to American film history.

The middle film, *She Wore a Yellow Ribbon*, is both the most nostalgic and the most celebratory of the three films. It looks to the past as a happier time when the cavalry was confident of its abilities. The film takes place in 1876, just after Custer's death on the Little Big Horn River, a period when the cavalry's future was very much in doubt. Captain Nathan Brittles (John Wayne) is retiring from the Army. As he prepares to conduct the morning inspection of the troop, he is interrupted by the arrival of a patrol bringing in the stagecoach, which has been attacked by Indians. The driver is dead, and the payroll is missing. Sergeant Tyree (Ben Johnson) identifies an arrow as one made by the Southern Cheyenne. Even though Brittles only has six days remaining, Major Allshard (George O'Brien) orders him to conduct one last patrol in order to push the Indians further north and away from the settlements in the area of the fort. Allshard also orders the Captain, in spite of Brittles' written protest, to escort Mrs. Allshard (Mildred Natwick) and her niece, Olivia Dandridge (Joanne Dru), to the nearest stagecoach station.

The patrol is unsuccessful. Because of the presence of the women, the troop cannot prevent the Indians from gathering to buy rifles with the stolen payroll. Because the wagons slow them down, the troop arrives at the stage junction too late to prevent the massacre of the stage master, his family, and a small unit of soldiers. One of the dead soldiers, known as Trooper Smith, is actually a former Brigadier General in the Confederate Army. Other former Confederate soldiers, including Tyree, pay their last respects to the General with a small Confederate flag hastily sewn together by Mrs. Allshard.

On the return march to the fort, Brittles must split the patrol, leaving Lieutenant Colhill (John Agar) with a troop guarding a river crossing. Once the civilians are safely returned to the fort, Lieutenant Pennell (Harry Carey, Jr.) is ordered to rescue Colhill and his soldiers. Captain Brittles cannot go, however, because his retirement will be effective before the troop can return to the post. The soldiers give Brittles a watch as a token to mark his retirement, then leave without him. Brittles sneaks out of the fort, however, rejoins the unit, and assumes command again. He and Sergeant Tyree go into the Indian camp under a truce flag, and Brittles talks to the old chief, Pony That Walks (Chief Big Tree). The Indian says he can no longer command the young warriors, just as Brittles has also lost his command. He invites Brittles to get drunk with him, and together they will watch the coming war. Brittles returns to the waiting soldiers and that night orders the troop to stampede the Indians' horses, thereby preventing the battle.

Brittles is now officially retired, and he rides toward the West, intending to spend his retirement in California. Tyree overtakes him, however, and tells him to return to the fort. There Brittles receives orders promoting him to Lieutenant-Colonel in command of the civilian scouts. After receiving the congratulations of the Allshards, Miss Dandridge, and the young lieutenants, Brittles goes to his wife's grave to tell her the news as the film ends.

Nathan Brittles is a man who lives in the past. When the film's action begins, wife and daughters are dead, he is aging, and he must leave the army, his only other love. In a bleak present, the past of happier, more vigorous days is infinitely preferable. In his role as Brittles, Wayne gives a performance that is subtle, moving, and restrained. Critics who doubt Wayne's abilities as an actor should study the scene in which Brittles receives the watch from his troop. Wayne skillfully portrays the character's conflicting emotions—regret, embarrassment, pleasure, the struggle to remain composed and disciplined—in a scene that is both moving and comic, but never false. Wayne's performance in this film equals the artistry he demonstrates in two other Ford films, *The Searchers* and *The Man Who Shot Liberty Valance* (1962).

Other actors who contribute noteworthy performances include many of the members of Ford's favorite group of character players, such as Victor McLaglen as Sergeant Quinncannon, the comic, boozy alter ego of Nathan Brittles; Natwick as Mrs. Allshard, the tough, no-nonsense Army wife who offers compassion and understanding to the lonely troopers fighting the Indians; and Johnson in his first screen role as a competent soldier alienated from the present and living in the past like Captain Brittles. It is the presence offscreen of Winton C. Hoch and Ford, however, which is most responsible for the visual beauty and the tone of the film. Hoch won an Academy Award for his color cinematography in *She Wore a Yellow Ribbon*. Ford has said that he was trying here to re-create the colors in the cavalry paintings of Frederic Remington. Hoch's Oscar and the beauty of the film attest to the success of those attempts, There is a glow like firelight in much of the film, a glow that enhances its sense of nostalgia. Hoch's scenes of the patrol moving through Monument Valley in a thunderstorm is a technical marvel as well as a stunning artistic achievement.

It remained for Ford, however, to bring the disparate elements together into a cohesive whole, both within the film and within the context of his career. While the characters in the film look back longingly to a past now lost to them, the film celebrates their efforts in the present to extend the benefits of civilization to the wilderness. There is no sense, unlike in future Ford films, that those efforts are not positive contributions. The Indians pose a real threat to the settlers, and the protection provided by the cavalry is both necessary and correct. By means of a combination of Irish immigrants and former Confederates, groups deeply admired by Ford, Yankee civilization is spread to the frontier. In the other two films of the trilogy, there are divisions within the cavalry family, but in *She Wore a Yellow Ribbon*, that family is united. This film, then, is Ford's most positive examination of one of his favorite subjects, the United States Cavalry.

Don K Thompson

THE SHINING

Released: 1980
Production: Stanley Kubrick for Warner Bros.
Direction: Stanley Kubrick
Screenplay: Stanley Kubrick and Diane Johnson; based on the novel of the same name by Stephen King
Cinematography: John Alcott
Editing: Ray Lovejoy
Running time: 146 minutes

Principal characters:

Jack Torrance	Jack Nicholson
Wendy Torrance	Shelley Duvall
Danny Torrance	Danny Lloyd
Dick Hallorann	Scatman Crothers
Ullman	Barry Nelson
Bartender	Joseph Turkel
Waiter	Philip Stone

Stanley Kubrick's *The Shining* is an attempt to do for horror films what his *2001: A Space Odyssey* (1968) did for science fiction: to expand the genre to its fullest dimensions, to invest it with rich thematic import, and to make it into a vehicle for the recurrent idea in his own work as a director. *The Shining* manifests several similarities to Kubrick's other films. For example, as in *2001*, the narrative pace crawls, taking more than two hours to recount a relatively simple plot. As he did in *Barry Lyndon* (1975), Kubrick again lingers over panoramic scenes, creating picture postcards out of the interior of the vast hotel which provides the major setting for *The Shining*. As he has done previously in such films as *Dr. Strangelove* (1964) and *2001*, Kubrick takes his background music from the work of noteworthy composers to create the desired dramatic effect. For *The Shining* he has used the music of Béla Bartók, Gyorgy Ligeti, and Krzysztof Penderecki. Finally, the fundamental assumptions about human nature which underlie this horror film recall the view articulated by Kubrick in *Dr. Strangelove*, *2001*, and *A Clockwork Orange* (1971). This film clearly bears its director's characteristic mark.

Based on the best-selling novel by science-fiction author Stephen King, *The Shining* deals with the disintegration of Jack Torrance (Jack Nicholson), an ex-teacher-turned-writer who agrees to serve as winter caretaker for the Overlook Hotel in the Colorado Rockies. During his interview for the position, the hotel manager Ullman (Barry Nelson) reveals some of the hotel's disturbing history. A previous winter caretaker had brutally murdered his family on the premises. Moreover, Torrance is cautioned about the deleterious psychological effects of the long winter isolation at the hotel. Since he is eager for the solitude in order to do some writing, however, Torrance is unperturbed by Ullman's warnings. Packing up his wife Wendy (Shelley Duvall) and son Danny (Danny Lloyd), Torrance sets up housekeeping in the Overlook Hotel. Danny Torrance possesses psychic power. When he arrives at the hotel, he finds some kinship with Dick Hallorann (Scatman Crothers), who also possesses this power, which he calls "the shining." Before leaving the hotel for the winter, Hallorann advises Danny about the use of his power and warns him to avoid Room 237 in the hotel.

The Torrances are now alone, and Jack's descent into madness begins. He becomes irritable, he neglects his duties as caretaker, he spends all his time typing feverishly, and he fraternizes with a ghostly crowd in the hotel's bar. When Wendy discovers that his typing has resulted only in reams of paper covered with "All work and no play make Jack a dull boy" in various typographic configurations, Jack begins to stalk the family with an ax, perhaps reenacting the crime of the earlier caretaker. Jack's pursuit of Wendy and Danny continues through the empty halls of the hotel and through the snow-encrusted maze built of hedges on the grounds, despite the efforts of Hallorann, whose psychic sensibilities have summoned him to the hotel from his Florida vacation. By the end of the film, the seemingly mild-mannered Jack Torrance has become maniacally homicidal.

The film does not clearly indicate what causes Jack's metamorphosis, although it may result from the influence of the ghosts. A spectral bartender (Joe Turkel) panders to Jack's weakness for alcohol. A ghostly waiter (Philip Stone), whose name is the same as that of Jack's murderous predecessor as caretaker, encourages him to "correct" his wife and child when they offend him. Jack's transformation could also stem from the pervasive influence of the past. Not only is there the hotel's history of violence, but also in his personal background Jack has a history of brutality, having injured his son while in a drunken rage—an incident which corresponded with the beginning of Danny's psychic power. Furthermore, the film suggests the possibility of reincarnation. The ghostly waiter tells Jack that the ex-teacher has always been present in the hotel, perhaps in previous lives, and the film's last shot focuses on a photograph of a group of people taken at the hotel in 1921 with Jack's face prominent in the scene. A third explanation for Jack's change may arise from the bleak view of human nature which pervades much of Kubrick's work. The Overlook Hotel, snowbound for the winter, loses almost all touch with civilization. As social influences recede, the veneer of civilization disappears from Jack's character, leaving a raw human nature which is violent and brutal. Uncontrolled by the restrictions of society, man is worse than an animal. Living at the Overlook Hotel has stripped Jack Torrance down to his bloodthirsty heart of darkness.

In addition to this negative view of humanity, another theme in *The Shining* involves the ambivalence between illusion and reality. This confusion becomes evident in several ways. First, Jack—and the viewers of the film—may be only imagining the ghosts at the Overlook Hotel. No one else seems to encounter them in the crowded bar until right at the film's end, when the terror of the situation can account for any illusion. At a point earlier in the film, Jack has visited the mysterious Room 237 to find a beautiful, seductive bather who becomes a wrinkled crone in his embrace before disappearing altogether; the illusory loveliness yields to another illusion, that of a hag, before it evaporates into the reality of nothingness. After the experience Jack is unsure what, if anything, has happened.

Another way in which the problem of illusion and reality emerges occurs in the visionary life of the psychic Danny. He sees a pair of young girls, perhaps the murdered daughters of the previous caretaker, witnesses a torrent of blood spilling from an elevator, and is lured into Room 237. Are these visions part of the hotel's past, of its future, or of the fevered imagination of a young boy who has been mistreated by his father? Still another way in which the film explores this theme is its emphasis on the effects of the mass media. On the way to the hotel, for example, Jack and Wendy discuss the Donner Party, a group of early American pioneers reduced to cannibalism by the rigors of the wilderness. Wendy is afraid that young Danny will be upset by their reference to this ugly episode in American frontier history, but the boy claims that he knows all about cannibalism from television. His reality is apparently shaped by that medium, at least in part. Moreover, it is television that remains the only real link between the isolated Overlook Hotel and the outside world, and the Torrance family spends a good deal of time in front of the screen. Perhaps the fact that their impressions of outside reality come through the illusory medium of television contributes to the malaise which comes to infect them.

Although *The Shining* is Kubrick's film, it also owes much to the performance of Nicholson. Much of the horror may come from special effects such as the elevator filled with blood, but the most horrifying effect of all is Nicholson's mobile face. As Jack Torrance gradually loses control, Nicholson's expressions frenetically shift from rage to gloom. During the film's climax, the pursuit of Danny through the maze, Nicholson creates an animalistic characterization as Jack snarls, spits, and hunches into the chase. Using some of the characteristics which he employed for positive effect in his portrayal of McMurphy in *One Flew Over the Cuckoo's Nest* (1975), Nicholson creates in Jack Torrance a crazed maniac bent only on brutality and reminds the viewers of the potential for violence and horror present in everyone.

The Shining elicited mixed reviews after its long production schedule created much interest on the part of the press and the theatergoing public. The film was faulted for its excessive length, its failure to meet the expectations of the horror genre, and Kubrick's overemphasis on technical flourish at the expense of narrative development. It was praised, however, for its magnitude

The Shining

of scope. Historically, the horror film has been a low-budget affair, often hastily put together to provide cheap thrills for a young audience. *The Shining*, however, three years in production, employs no cheap tricks and leaves much for adults in the audience to think about.

Frances M. Malpezzi
William M. Clements

SHIP OF FOOLS

Released: 1965
Production: Stanley Kramer for Columbia
Direction: Stanley Kramer
Screenplay: Abby Mann; based on the novel of the same name by Katherine
  Anne Porter
Cinematography: Ernest Laszlo (ΛΛ)
Editing: Robert C. Jones
Art direction: Robert Clatworthy (AA); set decoration, Joseph Kish (AA)
Running time: 149 minutes

Principal characters:
Mary Treadwell	Vivien Leigh
La Condesa	Simone Signoret
Rieber	José Ferrer
Tenny	Lee Marvin
Dr. Schumann	Oskar Werner
Jenny	Elizabeth Ashley
David	George Segal
Glocken	Michael Dunn
Lowenthal	Heinz Ruehmann
Pepe	Jose Greco

Throughout his career, Stanley Kramer has consistently dealt with explosive, controversial themes. His choice of subject matter as both producer and director cannot be faulted. His films have examined race relations and racism in *Guess Who's Coming to Dinner?* (1967), *Pressure Point* (1962), *The Defiant Ones* (1958), and *Home of the Brave* (1949); nuclear fission in *On the Beach* (1959); the rehabilitation of paraplegics in *The Men* (1950); the Scopes Monkey Trial in *Inherit the Wind* (1960); the postwar trial of Nazi war criminals in *Judgment at Nuremberg* (1961); mental disturbance in *The Caine Mutiny* (1954); corruption in the medical profession in *Not as a Stranger* (1954); and the rebellion of youth in *The Wild One* (1954).

Kramer has often explored these subjects, however, in a splashy, exploitative, clichéd manner which belies serious analysis. In *Guess Who's Coming to Dinner?*, for example, white, beautiful Katharine Houghton's choice for a mate is not an average, working-class black man but a handsome, respectable, educated doctor, played by Sidney Poitier, a candidate for the Nobel Prize, *The Wild One* glorifies its sullen young motorcycle-riding protagonist, portrayed by Marlon Brando. The "where-it's-at" dialogue and stock university establishment versus campus radicals setting of *RPM* (1970) is ludicrous and laughable. *Not as a Stranger* is glutted with adultery and fornication and is a crass, gaudy tearjerker. *Ship of Fools* is no different. As a reflection of the human condition, the film is not without social significance, but it is mostly a glossy, classy soap opera, a *Grand Hotel* (1932) set on the ocean.

Katherine Anne Porter's highly praised fifty-character, five-hundred-page novel ranked first among fiction best-sellers the week after its publication in 1962. Her characters, curiously, were not the tragic, heroic, misunderstood human beings depicted in the film, but were mostly bigots, pimps, and other assorted weaklings. Kramer and screenwriter Abby Mann compressed and modified the book into a preachy, clumsily symbolic, two-and-one-half-hour soap opera. Both the film and its source have no neatly ordered plot, but are more concerned with actions and interactions between characters than with story line and drama.

The film is set in 1933 as the Nazis are taking power in Germany—two years later than the setting of the novel. The *Vera*, a fictional ship, departs from Vera Cruz on a twenty-six-day voyage to Bremerhaven, stopping in Havana to take on several hundred Spanish sugar plantation laborers and a Spanish countess, a political prisoner en route to exile in Tenerife. Among those on board are a cross-section of humanity including Mary Treadwell (Vivien Leigh), a pathetically coquettish, decaying forty-six-year-old Southern American divorcée; Tenny (Lee Marvin), a drunken, lecherous, broken-down baseball player, a failure because he "could never hit a curve ball on the outside corner," who is teased and then shunned by Mary Treadwell; and the drug-addicted, world-weary La Condesa (Simone Signoret), who has a poignant but brief love affair with Schumann (Oskar Werner), the ship's disillusioned but compassionate doctor who dies of heart disease before the *Vera* reaches it destination; there is also Jenny (Elizabeth Ashley) and David (George Segal), a pair of quarrelsome American artists who are unable to define their emotions in relation to their sexual atttraction; Pepe (Jose Greco), the sneering head of a Spanish dance troupe, who acts as procurer for some of his dancers; Rieber (José Ferrer), an obnoxious, Jew-baiting German publisher; and Lowenthal (Heinz Ruehmann), an optimistic German Jewish salesman who blurts: "There are nearly a million Jews in Germany. What are they going to do, kill us all?" Their connecting link is Glocken (Michael Dunn, replacing Lewis Stone, the physician in *Grand Hotel*), a puckish, knowing dwarf who acts as both catalyst and Greek Chorus. "This is a ship of fools," he tells us at the onset, and "if you look closely you may even find yourself on board."

While these characters are all well-defined within the framework of the narrative, all are nevertheless clichéd "types": the Nazi is the incarnation of inhumanity; the Jew is saintly and naïvely hopeful that reason will win out over injustice; the sad, helpless lovers are destined to part. The supporting roles are no different: a prostitute is kindly; a schoolboy is fumbling in the presence of the prostitute; a young girl, repressed by her parents, blossoms into womanhood. Mann's script is mostly ponderous ("You know how frus-

trating it is to reach out for something, and then you find it isn't there."
"You're strange—sometimes you're so bitter—yet you're so soft and warm,
like a child." "She's the only real thing that ever happened to me").

What heightens the effect and power of *Ship of Fools*, however, is the
bravura acting. Kramer has a knack for offbeat casting and for eliciting fine
performances from his actors. Spencer Tracy, Kirk Douglas, Katharine Hepburn, Tony Curtis, Julie Harris, Beah Richards, Maximilian Schell, Sidney
Poitier, Cara Williams, Cecil Kellaway, Judy Garland, Montgomery Clift,
Gary Cooper, and Tom Tully are among the performers who earned Oscars
or Oscar nominations in Kramer films. Such diverse actors as Ava Gardner,
Arthur Franz, Steve Brodie, Hans Conried, Bobby Darin, Lloyd Bridges,
Ruth Roman, James Edwards, and Fred Astaire—the latter minus his dancing
shoes and Ginger Rogers—have done some of their best work in his films.

In *Ship of Fools* Kramer again draws superior performances. Signoret and
Werner are no less than superb; the relationship between Schumann and La
Condesa is as sad as it is tender, and their scenes together stick in the gut as
well as the mind. In both her addiction and exile, La Condesa can sense her
oncoming doom; with merely a glance and an inflection, Signoret movingly
conveys the feeling of a woman who has wearily accepted her fate. Schumann
has been so defeated by life that he can only die once La Condesa departs
the ship, and Werner acts the part with a perfect mixture of poignancy and
introspection. At the time of the film's release, the actor was known to
American audiences primarily for his work in François Truffaut's *Jules and
Jim* (1962) and Anatole Litvak's *Decision Before Dawn* (1951). Among his
other films are *Interlude* (1968), *The Spy Who Came in from the Cold* (1965),
and *Fahrenheit 451* (1966). *Ship of Fools*, however, remains his most popular
success.

Leigh, Marvin and Dunn also offer strong characterizations. Leigh, in a
part not unlike that of Scarlett O'Hara and Blanche DuBois, is appropriately
coy and contemptuous in the final performance of her distinguished although
unhappily short career. After more than a decade of fine supporting parts,
including work in Kramer's *The Wild One*, *The Caine Mutiny*, and *Not as a
Stranger*, Marvin became a star in *Ship of Fools* and his other 1965 release,
Cat Ballou. In competition against Werner, Rod Steiger for *The Pawnbroker*,
Richard Burton for *The Spy Who Came in from the Cold*, and Laurence
Olivier for *Othello*, Marvin won an Academy Award as Best Actor of the
year for *Cat Ballou*. Dunn's Glocken is the best role and performance of his
career. Although the acting of Segal and Ashley is easily the weakest in the
film, their performances are not poor; they simply pale in comparison to the
work of their costars.

Ship of Fools was nominated for eight Academy Awards, including one for
Best Picture. Signoret and Dunn along with Werner were cited in the acting
categories, but none won. The film was a winner in the categories of Best

Black-and-White Cinematography (Ernest Laszlo) and Best Black-and-White Art Direction (Robert Clatworthy) and Set Decoration (Joseph Kish).

Ronald L. Bowers

THE SHOP AROUND THE CORNER

Released: 1940
Production: Ernst Lubitsch for Metro-Goldwyn-Mayer
Direction: Ernst Lubitsch
Screenplay: Samson Raphaelson
Cinematography: William Daniels
Editing: Gene Ruggiero
Running time: 97 minutes

Principal characters:
Klara Novak	Margaret Sullavan
Alfred Kralik	James Stewart
Hugo Matuschek	Frank Morgan
Vadas	Joseph Schildkraut
Pirovitch	Felix Bressart
Pepi	William Tracy
Detective	Charles Halton

The plot of *The Shop Around the Corner* is based upon a decidedly unlikely coincidence, but expert direction by German émigré Ernst Lubitsch, accomplished performances from a distinguished cast that features James Stewart and Margaret Sullavan, and an artful script by Samson Raphaelson (from a play by Nikolaus Laszlo) concentrate upon the interplay of characters rather than on the plot. The film is, therefore, an entertaining and humorous example of the solidly crafted work that Hollywood produced during the 1930's and 1940's.

The film opens with a low-key scene that establishes the personalities of the employees of the shops of Matuschek and Company, which is in Budapest, without giving any indication what direction the plot will take. All the employees are careful to be waiting at the door when the owner arrives to open up the store. In his presence they are deferential to the point of servility, even though before he arrives they were full of gossip.

The main characters we meet are the head clerk, Alfred Kralik (James Stewart), who tells the others about the seven-course meal he had at the home of the owner the evening before; Pirovitch (Felix Bressart), an especially subservient clerk who leaves the room every time the owner asks for an expression of opinion; Pepi (William Tracy), the errand boy with his eye on bigger things; and the owner himself, Hugo Matuschek (Frank Morgan), a blustery autocrat.

After the business of the day begins, Kralik reveals to Pirovitch that he has an anonymous pen pal, a woman with whom he has been corresponding on intellectual subjects. They have not exchanged any personal information, not even their names. They open their letters "Dear Friend" and address them to box numbers. According to his correspondent, the personal details do not matter "so long as our minds meet."

Then Mr. Matuschek asks his staff's opinion of an item he wants the shop to sell, a musical cigarette box. Only Kralik will disagree with the owner's obvious enthusiasm for the item. The issue has not yet been resolved when a young woman, Klara Novak (Margaret Sullavan), comes into the shop. Although it takes her a while to come to the point, she tells Kralik that she wants a job. Kralik assures her that it is impossible, but Matuschek, who overhears only the last part of the conversation, interrupts to say that nothing is impossible at Matuschek and Company. Then he has to reverse himself when he hears what she wants. Klara, however, is undaunted. She pretends to be a salesperson and sells one of the musical cigarette boxes to a woman customer even though the woman does not know exactly what it is. This tactic wins her a job but not the friendship of Kralik. They work together, but they are hostile and argumentative with each other.

Then one evening the life of nearly everyone in the shop is changed. Kralik has arranged to meet his pen pal in person, but he is quite nervous about it, espcially when Matuschek says that everyone must work overtime to redecorate the windows. Then Matuschek calls Kralik into his office and unexpectedly fires him. This makes Kralik feel too dispirited to go to the café where he is to meet his anonymous correspondent. Instead he sends Pirovitch with a note, but when Pirovitch reports that the young woman is Klara, Kralik decides not to send the note. He goes into the café and begins talking with Klara as if he had met her by chance. She is so upset with his annoying her when she is awaiting her "dear friend" that she refuses to converse with him. She calls him a "little insignificant clerk" who could never understand the kind of man for whom she is waiting.

Meanwhile we also learn why Matuschek fired Kralik when a private detective (Charles Halton) comes into the office to tell Matushek that the anonymous letter he had received is true: his wife is having an affair with one of his employees. To Matuschek's surprise, however, the culprit is not Kralik, as he suspected, but Vadas (Joseph Schildkraut). After the detective leaves, the despondent shop owner is about to commit suicide when Pepi returns from an errand just in time to thwart the attempt.

Soon the picture brightens. Kralik visits Matuscheck in his hospital room and is rehired, made manager of the shop, and given a raise, and Pepi takes advantage of the situation to get himself promoted to clerk. The next day we see that they both enjoy their new positions, but Klara is not at all happy. Not only did her pen pal fail to keep his appointment but also her worst enemy (Kralik) has been elevated to the position of manager and she must take orders from him.

It is not until the end of the film that she learns the identity of her secret correspondent. Meanwhile, Kralik visits her home when she misses work because of her "psychological" problems. She tells Kralik more about her pen pal and says that it is difficult to explain "a man like him to a man like you." Finally, however, he reveals his identity on Christmas Eve. The shop has been crowded all day, and the totaling of the accounts is a joyous occasion for all. Then Klara and Kralik are left alone in the shop and begin conversing as Kralik extinguishes the lights. Kralik has one last bit of fun with her as he tells her that her correspondent came to see him and he is a fat, balding man who is mainly interested in her salary. Then he says "Box 237," and she realizes that Kralik is her "dear friend." The film ends with the couple happily embracing.

This story is a quite popular one. It has been produced as a stage play, filmed twice (the 1949 remake was called *In the Good Old Summertime*), and most recently on television by the BBC as a musical called *She Loves Me* (1979). It is built upon an interesting variation of a plot that is fairly common in romantic comedy: two people fall in love while fighting with each other— *It Happened One Night* (1934) is one of the best examples of the use of this plot. *The Shop Around the Corner* makes the irony of the situation explicit through the coincidence of the two happening to work together without knowing they have a separate and quite different relationship in letters. This emphasizes an important theme—the difference between the face people present to the outside world and the way they view themselves. Both Klara and Kralik think that their true character is revealed only in letters they write, but at the shop they fail to consider that the other workers may also have interesting personalities that are not revealed at work.

The success of *The Shop Around the Corner* is due primarily to the planning, work, and talent of one man: Lubitsch. He personally bought the story and agreed to work for M-G-M only if they would let him produce and direct it. He also chose Stewart and Sullavan to star in the film, and when he found that they were not then available, he waited until they were. (In the meantime he directed *Ninotchka*, 1939.) Under his direction the two splendidly played their roles to focus upon the interplay of character rather than the artifice in the plot.

Sharon Wiseman

SILVER DOLLAR

Released: 1932
Production: First National
Direction: Alfred E. Green
Screenplay: Carl Erickson and Harvey Thew; based on the book of the same
name by David Karsner
Cinematography: James Van Trees
Editing: George Marks
Running time: 84 minutes

> *Principal characters:*
> Yates Martin .... Edward G. Robinson
> Lily Owens .... Bebe Daniels
> Sarah Martin .... Aline MacMahon
> Poker Annie .... Jobyna Howland
> Mine Foreman .... DeWitt Jennings
> Col. Stanton .... Robert Warwick
> President Chester A. Arthur .... Emmett Corrigan
> General Grant .... Walter Rogers
> William Jennings Bryan .... Niles Welch

In the first decade of the talking film, some vivid pieces of Americana were brought to the screen. One of these that adhered closely to the story as it really happened was First National's *Silver Dollar*, which was a fictionalized story of Colorado's "Silver King," Horace A. W. Tabor, about whom it was said, "Follow him and you'll be buried in a silver casket." He became a United States Senator and was responsible for building some of Denver's and Leadville, Colorado's most magnificent edifices, including the opera house in Denver bearing his name.

In the film story, Tabor becomes Yates Martin (Edward G. Robinson), at first seen as a shiftless adventurer like so many others seeking silver in the Colorado hills. He marries a woman from Kansas named Sarah (Aline MacMahon), and with her at his side his luck changes. He strikes it rich, with a deep, seemingly endless silver vein that makes Colorado the silver state of the Union and him its king. He lavishes his wealth upon the mining towns, turning them, with the profligacy of a Roman emperor, into shining cities. He tries to live up to his wealth, but Sarah, who has labored long under Protestant poverty, holds him down. She advises against any wild speculation he considers, but he disregards her, and rides the wave of riches and popularity to become Mayor of Denver, then Lieutenant Governor of Colorado, and finally, United States Senator.

Yates loves opera and all musical extravaganzas, and out of his vast wealth he constructs a wonderfully baroque opera house which is so elegant that

General Grant (Walter Rogers) comes as a guest to its gala opening. Yates moves in the company of the famous—not only Grant but President Chester A. Arthur (Emmett Corrigan) and an ambitious young man, William Jennings Bryan (Niles Welch). Sarah warns him that he is inviting disaster, but he turns a deaf ear to her Cassandralike prophecies. He meets a beautiful adventuress with a talent for the theater named Lily Owens (Bebe Daniels). Lily is not only a rare beauty, but she has a taste for anything that is beautiful, no matter how expensive. Yates falls in love with Lily and lavishes his wealth upon her as he has never been able to do with Sarah, who thought silks and diamonds inventions of the devil. Lily is not only impressed, but she falls in love with this simple-hearted Colorado emperor. He abandons Sarah, and a divorce is arranged. Lily and he go to Washington, where they are married in the presence of President Arthur.

The Washington scene changes when Grover Cleveland comes to the presidency. One of the first things Cleveland does is demonitize silver, putting the country on the gold standard. Overnight, Yates Martin is wrecked financially. He tries to clutch to some security, but silver has lost its power, and everything he has built drifts away from him on the wave of gold supremacy. Lily tries to help him, but her wealth is small in comparison to what he needs and cannot stem the tide of disaster. Back in Denver, broke and sickening, he wanders like a ghost amid the greatness that was once his. One night, he slips into the great opera house he built with his silver wealth. He is an old, tired, dying man, and now as he steps out onto the great performance stage, he looks about him in wonderment, hearing unforgettable melodies that had once been sung from this stage. His head filled with song that has suddenly turned to cacophony, he slips to his knees, overcome by the stroke that seizes him, and dies there on the shadowed stage.

There is only one scene to be played out as a finale. His funeral, at least, is deserving of him. The two principal mourners are the two women he married—Sarah, in her sober, plain, dark, sturdy clothes, and grieving Lily, lovely in black silk and midnight chiffon. It is such a scene as artist Grant Wood might have fancied, as the silver coffin is lowered into the earth and the two women who had loved him, each in her way, lament his passing from the earthly scene.

Robinson plays Yates Martin with a kind of heroic realism, an extraordinary accomplishment in some ways, because not until the end is Martin in the least way the stuff of which heroes are made. Martin, like Tabor, upon whom his character is fashioned, is a good-hearted vulgarian whom luck has touched but not refined. In the midst of his growing power, he remains a simple, loud-mouthed wanderer, perplexed, like a child, when his wealth vanishes, and he becomes nothing and nobody. Daniels is an enchanting Lily Owens, the character drawn from the real-life Elizabeth "Baby" Doe. It was the best acting role Daniels had at Warner Bros. First National, and she makes Lily a sympathetic and lovely figure. In real life, the character of "Baby" Doe quickly became legendary, a familiar figure in Denver and Leadville everyday life, and then as she moved up into the mining country, confident that the wealth she had lost would be returned to her, she became a pathetic creature, an old lady dying one winter in her unheated cabin, frozen to death. MacMahon plays the completely contrasting role of the first wife, Sarah, with a granite calm. Sarah is a prophetess of doom that becomes all too real in its total tragedy because no one will listen to her, just as the characters in the *Iliad* failed to heed the voice of Cassandra.

In its day *Silver Dollar* was much appreciated; it had the mark of truth upon it, and its highlights were praised as being as vividly atmospheric as the more epic moments of the silent film *The Covered Wagon* (1923). It has a vivid relentlessness in its story construction, and the three principals of the triangle become living, breathing people who loved and lost when their grandeur of living tarnished overnight like the silver upon which it was based.

DeWitt Bodeen

THE SIN OF MADELON CLAUDET

Released: 1931
Production: Irving Thalberg for Metro-Goldwyn-Mayer
Direction: Edgar Selwyn
Screenplay: Charles MacArthur; based on the play *The Lullaby* by Edward
  Knoblock
Cinematography: Oliver T. Marsh
Editing: Tom Held
Running time: 73 minutes

Principal characters:

Madelon Claudet	Helen Hayes (AA)
Carlo Boretti	Lewis Stone
Larry	Nell Hamilton
Dr. Jacques Claudet	Robert Young
Rosalie	Marie Prevost
Victor	Cliff Edwards
Dr. Dulac	Jean Hersholt
Alice Claudet	Karen Morley

Irving Thalberg was determined to make M-G-M's products truly presti-
gious during the first years of the talking picture, and to that end he lured
some of the brightest stars from the Broadway stage to try their luck in
Hollywood; only one major star resisted him—Katharine Cornell. The three
Barrymores graced M-G-M products regularly, however, and so did Alfred
Lunt and Lynn Fontanne for a single but brilliant appearance in *The Guards-
man* (1931). In that same year, M-G-M, at Thalberg's instigation, brought
Helen Hayes to their Culver City lot. They signed her to an attractive contract,
and her first picture was announced as the film version of an Edward Knoblock
play, *The Lullaby*, in which Florence Reed had successfully starred on Broadway during the 1923 season. Edgar Selwyn wrote the screenplay adaptation
and also directed it, following fairly closely the play's story line. The original
premise of the play was a mother-love narrative, reminiscent in a way of
Madame X (1929), as most self-sacrificing mother-and-son dramas are by the
time they get to the screen.

In the story Hayes played an innocent young peasant girl from Normandy
named Madelon Claudet who is captivated by an American painter. They fall
in love, and she runs away with him to Paris, where they set up housekeeping
in Montmartre. He is called home for an emergency, however, and promises
to return to fetch her; but of course he never does, instead marrying a rich
girl from his own class whose wealthy family had always wanted him to wed
their daughter. Madelon finds herself pregnant and is befriended by an elderly
gentleman, Carlo Boretti (Lewis Stone), who sees to it that Madelon has the

best of care. She gives birth to a son, whom she pays her good friends, Rosalie (Marie Prevost) and Victor (Cliff Edwards), who live outside of Paris in the country, to bring up as their own.

Boretti loves Madelon, and they become a familiar pair in Parisian night life, an aging man of the world adoring a pretty young protégée. Boretti, however, unknown to Madelon, is a very clever jewel thief and is eventually caught by the police. He commits suicide, but Madelon is convicted as his accomplice and sent to prison. When Madelon is freed, she goes to see her son Jacques Claudet (Robert Young), who does not know that she is his mother. Nor, as she tells Rosalie and Victor, does she ever want him to learn that his mother has been in jail. She learns that although he is only a young boy, he has shown a definite interest in medical science, and she determines that he will be a great doctor, no matter what her sacrifice.

In order to send him to medical school, Madelon becomes a prostitute, gradually becoming a pathetic old hooker. She faithfully sends Rosalie and Victor money, and her son, who believes his mother to be dead, receives the best medical education possible, eventually opening his own offices and gaining recognition as a brilliant young doctor. One day an old woman, a stranger, comes to him; it is, of course, Madelon, who knows that her days are numbered and wants to see her son once more. He examines her, and comments that he is not surprised she has sought him out, for it is obvious that she has done a great deal of living in her time. He leaves the office for a moment; she looks around proudly and then slips out into the streets, never letting him know that she is his mother.

This high-class Thalberg production was a failure when it was previewed in Huntington, a town not far from Los Angeles. Hayes crept from the theater with bowed head, fearful that someone might recognize her. Thalberg was going to Europe, and he ordered the picture shelved until his return. Unfortunately, some of the press had caught the picture's preview. *Photoplay* magazine reviewed it as *The Lullaby* in its September, 1931 issue, praising the Hayes performance, but noting that the picture was tired and cliché-ridden. When Thalberg returned from Europe, he looked at the picture himself again, and decided that it needed a careful rewrite. He called in a capable craftsman, Charles MacArthur, a playwright who in real life also happened to be recently married to Hayes.

MacArthur constructed a frame for the story. Alice (Karen Morley), the unhappy wife of young Dr. Claudet, goes to a Dr. Dulac (Jean Hersholt), to whom she confesses that she is leaving her doctor husband, who is too devoted to his profession. She has sacrificed enough, she says, and Dr. Dulac tells her that she knows nothing of real sacrifice, and thereupon launches into the story of Madelon Claudet. MacArthur threw away scenes, writing out entirely such characters as Suzette, Boretti's love before Madelon came into his life, and also eliminating scenes involving such actors as Claire McDowell, Bradley

Page, and Tenen Holtz. MacArthur wrote in new characters such as Dr. Dulac and Alice, and created new scenes and montages for his wife to play.

In the meantime, Hayes went out on loan to Samuel Goldwyn to play opposite Ronald Colman in *Arrowsmith* (1931). The added scenes for *The Lullaby* were put into production, and Hayes secretly worked on the scenes in which she was involved on Sundays. Eventually, Goldwyn found out what was going on and protested, so that any further reshooting requiring Hayes had to be postponed to be filmed as soon as her Goldwyn assignment was completed.

Retitled *The Sin of Madelon Claudet*, a second preview of the reclaimed film was held in Glendale, and the audience responded enthusiastically. Hayes was despondent about the picture, however, and did not even attend the preview. Later that night she was called upon by two friends, actresses Ruth Chatterton and Lois Wilson, who had seen it and were as enthusiastic about her work as the audience had been. Hollywood, they were confident, had gained a new star in Hayes. The picture was premiered and was an instant smash hit. *Photoplay* reviewed it again, raving about the Hayes performance, naming the film as one of the six best of that month. The Academy voted her Best Actress for their 1931-1932 season, and her film career became the most enduring of all the careers of the stalwarts that M-G-M had enticed from the Broadway stage. She remained a movie star for M-G-M for more than two years, playing in at least a half-dozen more features and going once more on loan-out, this time to Paramount for *A Farewell to Arms* (1932) with Gary Cooper. Then she returned to the theater, confessing that she had let herself be persuaded into a screen career only for the money paid her. Over the years she remained a top Broadway star, and although she eventually returned to Hollywood, it was essentially as a supporting player in character roles. She captured another Oscar as Best Supporting Actress with *Airport* in 1970 and still does an occasional film, principally for Walt Disney Productions, and sometimes makes a notable television appearance, but her true love as an actress remains the theater.

The credit for the success of *The Sin of Madelon Claudet* belongs to Thalberg for believing in Hayes, but mostly to Charles MacArthur, who had revised and rewritten the screenplay even while it was in postproduction, and who quite rightly has sole credit as screenwriter. *The Lullaby* as a play had been one of those dramas enjoying a Broadway success during the 1920's because it had some daring sex scenes. In the play, Madelon, after serving a twenty-year term in prison, takes to the streets again when she is freed, but she has learned that the son she bore has become a sailor in the French Navy, and so she will have nothing to do with navy men. When a sailor tries to force his attentions upon her, she shoots him, returning to prison to serve a new term. It was highly censorable material, and MacArthur, in turning the son into a doctor and adding the frame for the story, gave it a legitimate dimension, assuring it a favorable reception with the film public and also giving Madelon a sympathetic reason for taking to the streets.

Soon the mother-love story was enjoying a new popularity as film fare. Actresses such as Elissa Landi, Constance Bennett, Claudette Colbert, Barbara Stanwyck, and even Tallulah Bankhead and Clara Bow were pounding the pavement to get money for their babies' welfare. M-G-M remade *Madame X* (1937) with Gladys George and borrowed Irene Dunne to do a talking version of *The Lady*, a onetime silent success in which Norma Talmadge had starred, calling the new treatment *The Secret of Madame Blanche* (1933), a title that was more than vaguely reminiscent of *The Sin of Madelon Claudet*.

Thalberg surrounded Hayes with the best available talent, notably Stone, who gave one of his customary sympathetic portrayals as the jewel thief who loves and befriends Madelon. The last sequence provided an introduction to feature films for Young, very young indeed as Jacques, the boy for whom Madelon sacrifices everything. Young is very believable as a medical man, and he is still playing that role on television in reruns of his successful *Marcus Welby, M.D.* series. At no time, however, has he ever had so talented a patient as he did when Hayes played his unacknowledged mother in *The Sin of Madelon Claudet*.

DeWitt Bodeen

SINCE YOU WENT AWAY

Released: 1944
Production: David O. Selznick
Direction: John Cromwell
Screenplay: David O. Selznick; based on the novel of the same name by
  Margaret Buell Wilder
Cinematography: Stanley Cortez and Lee Garmes
Editing: Hal C. Kern and James E. Newcom
Music: Max Steiner (AA)
Running time: 180 minutes

Principal characters:
Anne Hilton	Claudette Colbert
Jane Hilton	Jennifer Jones
Bridget Hilton	Shirley Temple
Lieutenant Tony Willet	Joseph Cotten
Corporal Bill Smollett	Robert Walker
Colonel Smollett	Monty Woolley
Emily Hawkins	Agnes Moorehead
Fidelia	Hattie McDaniel
Clergyman	Lionel Barrymore
Woman Welder	Nazimova
Harold Smith	Guy Madison

Since You Went Away could be seen as a 1940's updating of *Little Women* (1933). It was a production of David O. Selznick, who was still looking for a blockbuster that would match the success of the phenomenal *Gone with the Wind*, which he produced in 1939. He thought he had found the perfect vehicle when he purchased Margaret Buell Wilder's book about her experiences on the home front while her husband was overseas during World War II. The book is in the form of moving letters which tell of Mrs. Wilder's life with her children at home, coping with the emotional and financial frustrations of being left behind. Like *Little Women* (which Selznick also had adapted as a film), the action centers around a mother and her daughters: their romances, their jobs, their anxieties, and their triumphs. It is a long film stitched together by a series of vignettes about the Hilton family, but all the pieces form a complete whole as home-front events parallel the progress of the war.

Selznick hired veteran filmmaker John Cromwell to direct. The two men had worked together on *David Copperfield* (1935), *The Prisoner of Zenda* (1937), and *Made for Each Other* (1938), and relations between them were extremely sympathetic. Selznick had a reputation for trying to take over his films regardless of what the director wanted, but Cromwell had Selznick's absolute trust and as a result, met with little interference. Selznick did write the script, however, and took charge of casting.

Claudette Colbert plays Anne Hilton, the mother and wife of the family. Colbert was known for her warmth and sincerity and was convincing as a woman who was both intelligent and beautiful, but always aware that her main jobs in life were those of a wife and mother. Shirley Temple, in her first important role after a childhood of stardom, makes a smooth transition to young adulthood as Bridget, the youngest Hilton daughter. Jennifer Jones, who plays Jane, the older daughter, was closely coached by Selznick; she was shortly to become his wife, and he paid careful attention to all her roles. To add to the emotional temperature of the film, Jones's estranged husband Robert Walker is cast as Corporal Bill Smollett, the man with whom Jane falls in love. Joseph Cotten, who appeared in several Selznick films, plays Tony, the "friend of the family" and long-time admirer of Anne. He is the detached observer who continually remarks on the effect of the war. With the addition of Monty Woolley, Agnes Moorehead, and the young, unknown Guy Madison, *Since You Went Away* was cast to perfection. The long (three-hour) film is quite sentimental, but always gripping and emotionally moving because it is based on honest feeling. The camera movements and Max Steiner's beautiful Oscar-winning score are understated, allowing the performers the fluidity, natural warmth, and conviction that is always apparent on the screen.

The film begins by introducing the Hilton family at the start of World War II. Tim Hilton, father of the adolescent Bridget and twenty-one-year-old Jane and husband to Anne, has just gone off to war. To emphasize the detachment of the father from his home and family, he is never actually seen in the film. Only a photograph of actor Neil Hamilton serves as a visual reminder of his existence. Anne realizes that with her husband gone, they cannot quite make ends meet, and she is forced to make some changes. The long-time maid Fidelia (Hattie McDaniel) is let go, but she insists on working for them free of charge. Even with their frugality, however, the family is driven to advertise for a lodger, who appears in the person of Colonel Smollett, a crusty old gentlemen to whose temperament they take a while to adjust. Lieutenant Tony Willet, a naval officer and Anne's old beau, comes to stay with the family while on leave, and Jane, the oldest Hilton girl, soon develops a romantic crush on him, which Tony treats with great tenderness while teasingly flirting with Anne. The film focuses on the activities of the family to help the war effort; a dance is organized at a nearby air hangar, Jane decides to forgo college in order to become a nurse's aide, and Anne goes to work in a war parts factory as a welder.

Romance also plays its part in the lives of the Hiltons. Jane falls in love with Colonel Smollett's grandson Bill, a sensitive young man basically opposed to war and soldiering, and eventually helps effect a reconciliation between Bill and his estranged grandfather. Bridget develops an interest in a young sailor named Harold, beautifully played by Madison, another Selznick discovery, in a small but memorable part. Friends and neighbors drop in on the family constantly, some with news of loss of sons and husbands. As the film winds up, there is heartbreak for Jane and Colonel Smollett as a telegram arrives announcing that Bill has been killed in action. As always, Tony is there to comfort the family, and the film ends with the glad news of Tim's imminent return.

The plot is deliberately undramatic and ordinary, a true tale of millions of Americans during the war. Although the women in the Hilton family went out to work, they would return to their homes when their men came back. The war changed the direction of women's lives as portrayed in American films from the 1930's and early 1940's, when Joan Blondell and Glenda Farrell were newspaper reporters and Rosalind Russell could run an office. In the traditional 1950's films, women were glad to have their men back again and thought their primary job was to make a comfortable home for them.

Audiences loved *Since You Went Away*, feeling that the players were real and voiced their own concerns. The script does not dwell too much on the war itself, paring down the unpleasant incidents of such a conflict to a minimum. There are nevertheless some poignant moments, as when a boy asks Anne at a dance if her husband will help him find a job after the war, which she promises he will. The next scene tells of the boy's death in a training flight. Although *Since You Went Away* was not another *Gone with the Wind* and critics gave it only faint-hearted praise, the American public flocked to see the film. Both the film and Colbert were nominated for Academy Awards, and Max Steiner was awarded one for his musical score. Certainly, the film stands as one of the best films made in America to deal in such an honest manner with the home front. Not until *The Best Years of Our Lives* (1946), which told of the problems of returning soldiers after the war, was a film to show so truthfully the effects of the war on American civilian life.

Joan Cohen

SKIPPY

Released: 1931
Production: Paramount
Direction: Norman Taurog (AA)
Screenplay: Joseph L. Mankiewicz, Norman Z. McLeod, and Don Marquis;
  inspired by Percy Crosby's comic strip of the same name
Cinematography: Karl Struss
Editing: no listing
Running time: 88 minutes

Principal characters:
Skippy Skinner	Jackie Cooper
Sooky Wayne	Robert Coogan
Eloise	Mitzi Green
Sidney	Jackie Searl
Doctor Herbert Skinner	Willard Robertson
Mrs. Ellen Skinner	Enid Bennett

Fifty years ago, children on screen were no preteen prostitutes (*Pretty Baby*, 1978), nor did they accidentally find in their homes strange, nude ladies with whom their daddies were sleeping (*Kramer vs. Kramer*, 1979). Cinematic kids were cute, mischievous, and innocent; Hal Roach's "Our Gang" comedies had long been a popular film series; and *Tom Sawyer* (1930) and *Huckleberry Finn* (1931), starring Junior Durkin and Jackie Coogan (who was *The Kid* opposite Charlie Chaplin in the wonderful 1921 comedy feature), had just been immortalized on screen. One of the most endearing film children of the era was *Skippy* (1931), the title character in a poignant, unabashedly cute and sentimental comedy.

Skippy is based on the adventures of Percy Crosby's popular syndicated comic-strip character Skippy Skinner (Jackie Cooper), and his friends Eloise (Mitzi Green), Sidney (Jackie Searl), and Sooky Wayne (Robert Coogan, five-year-old brother of Jackie), all of Shanty Town. Six-year-old Skippy (created by Crosby in 1913) is not allowed by his parents to play in Shanty Town, but the boy cannot ignore its "other side of the tracks" allure. The vacant lots and garbage piles make a marvelous playground. The stray dogs are friendly companions, and Sooky, Shanty Town's most pitiful urchin, is Skippy's best pal.

The sequence of events in the story is very simple—Dr. Herbert Skinner (Willard Robertson), Skippy's father and the town health officer, has condemned Shanty Town. Skippy is upset to hear that his favorite haunt might soon be leveled. During a brawl in which Skippy and Sooky are pitted against a bully, the son of the town dog catcher, the window of the dog catcher's truck is broken; soon, Sooky's dog Penny is carted off to the pound. The pair must raise three dollars in three days for a dog license; otherwise Penny will be destroyed.

When they crack open Skippy's small iron savings bank, the money pays for the broken windshield, but the merciless dog catcher demands more for the license. Skippy removes his father's pet formula from several bottles and earns sixty-eight cents from the sale of the empty containers. Another $2.03 is raised from the production of an amateur show in which the tomboyish Eloise recites her poetry. The kids bring the money to the dog catcher, only to learn that Penny has been put to sleep. A city ordinance justifying the act is signed by Skippy's father.

Sooky is heartbroken, but Skippy is angry and has a tearful showdown with his father. The remorseful Dr. Skinner buys a bicycle for his son. Although Skippy has long coveted the bike, he promptly trades it in for a mangy puppy for Sooky. When he rushes to present it to his friend, he discovers that Dr. Skinner has already purchased a bulldog for the boy. He also has found work for Sooky's mother, and ordered that Shanty Town be cleaned and painted. Finally the good doctor socks the dog catcher, and everybody lives happily ever after.

Skippy is far too idealistic about the ethics and behavior of children. Skippy and his pals are basically good-hearted little angels; in reality, most children are not as moralistic as Skippy, and would keep their bicycle rather than trade it in out of pity for a friend. Dr. Skinner may seem like a villain to Skippy, a man who heartlessly sentences puppies to death, but the doctor is really a man of compassion, sympathetic to the problems of six-year-olds. At the finale, he rights all the wrongs committed by the dastardly dog catcher and wins the everlasting admiration of his son.

Skippy is a character in the tradition of Andy Hardy, an idealized spirit of the model all-American boy. He is unusually human for a comic strip character; his pugnacious demeanor is transcribed to the screen via the engaging performance of ten-year-old Cooper, nephew of the film's director, Norman Taurog. Young Cooper had appeared in Lloyd Hamilton and Bobby Clark comedies at age three, and was in eight "Our Gang" episodes. His button nose, blonde hair, and perpetual pout endeared him to audiences; he earned an Academy Award nomination for his work (to this day the youngest Best Actor nominee ever), losing to Lionel Barrymore in *A Free Soul*. Cooper became Metro-Goldwyn-Mayer's number-one child star. He played the adoring son of broken-down boxer Wallace Beery in *The Champ* (1931), and also appeared with Beery in *The Bowery* (1933) and *Treasure Island* (1934). He grew up to become a television star in the popular series *The People's Choice* and *Hennesey*, sometime film actor (he was Perry White in 1978's *Superman*), and director of such superficial feminist propaganda films as *Stand Up and Be Counted* (1972) and the made-for-television *Rodeo Girl* (1980).

The other child actors did not fare as well professionally as Cooper. Searl, whose Sidney is as high-strung as his Sid Sawyer in *Tom Sawyer* and *Huckle-berry Finn*, played adult supporting roles during the 1940's and later character parts on television. Sid Sawyer is easily the best role of his career. Robert Coogan, eleven years younger than Jackie, debuted in *Skippy* and had a limited career as a juvenile and character actor. Green played Becky Thatcher in *Tom Sawyer* and *Huckleberry Finn*, and in 1932 was *Little Orphan Annie*. She retired in 1934, at age fourteen, and returned to the screen eighteen years later in supporting roles in the undistinguished Runyonesque comedy with music, *Bloodhounds of Broadway* (1952), and the tepid Bud Abbott and Lou Costello comedy, *Abbott and Costello Lost in Alaska* (1952). In addition, silent star Enid Bennett, who retired from films in 1925 as the wife of director Fred Niblo, returned to the screen to portray Skippy's mother. She had renewed her career once before, in a 1929 Los Angeles stage production of *The Streets of New York* with Edward Everett Horton.

Taurog received an Academy Award as the Best Director of 1931-1932 for his work on *Skippy*. Taurog is perhaps the least-remembered of all Oscar-winning directors; that year he topped Josef von Sternberg (*Morocco*), Lewis Milestone (*The Front Page*), Clarence Brown (*A Free Soul*), and Wesley Ruggles (*Cimarron*). It is an ironic commentary on the measure of the Academy Award as an accurate indicator of cinematic talent that Taurog was cited for his work, while Alfred Hitchcock, D. W. Griffith, Howard Hawks, Orson Welles, Ernst Lubitsch, and Charles Chaplin never once earned Best Director statues.

Taurog was a competent craftsman, however, adept at directing young performers. He handled Coogan, Junior Durkin, Green, and Searl in *Huckleberry Finn*, as well as Tommy Kelly and Jackie Moran (*The Adventures of Tom Sawyer*, 1938), Mickey Rooney (with Spencer Tracy in *Boys' Town*, 1938, Rooney starring in *Men of Boys' Town*, 1941, Rooney and Virginia Weidler in *Young Tom Edison*, 1940, Rooney and Freddie Bartholomew in *A Yank at Eton*, 1942), and George Winslow (*Room for One More*, 1952).

Skippy was partially filmed on location in San Bernardino, California, with local schoolchildren cast in bit parts. The film received excellent notices, did well at the box office, and was cited by *The New York Times* as one of the ten best films of the year. It also received Oscar nominations for Best Picture (losing to *Cimarron*) and Screenplay Adaptation (for Joseph L. Mankiewicz, Norman Z. McLeod, and Don Marquis, who were beaten by Howard Estabrook, also for *Cimarron*). *Skippy* was quickly followed up by an entertaining Taurog-directed sequel, *Sooky* (1931), a chronicle of the further escapades of Crosby's comic-strip creations.

Rob Edelman

SLEEPER

Released: 1973
Production: Jack Grossberg for United Artists
Direction: Woody Allen
Screenplay: Woody Allen and Marshall Brickman
Cinematography: David M. Walsh
Editing: Ralph Rosenblum
Art direction: Dale Hennesy
Special effects: A. D. Flowers
Running time: 86 minutes

Principal characters:
Miles Monroe ....Woody Allen
Luna Schlosser ....Diane Keaton
Erno Windt .... John Beck

Woody Allen travels two hundred years into the future in *Sleeper*, a homage to slapstick that combines effective visual gags and frequently hilarious one-liners with a disciplined delivery. Although the film is filled with now-standard Allen trademarks, including a character derived from the filmmaker's *nebbish* alter ego and New York-inspired neuroses, *Sleeper* is distinguished by its sustained story line, its futuristic setting (previous Allen films had contemporary settings), and its well-defined characters. In straightforward fashion, *Sleeper* tells the story of a Rip Van Winkle-like character who reawakens in the future in a totalitarian society similar to that portrayed in Charles Chaplin's *Modern Times* (1936).

The Allen-Marshall Brickman screenplay first introduces Miles Monroe (Woody Allen), proprietor of Greenwich Village's Happy Carrot Health Food Store, reawakening after a two-hundred-year "sleep." Emerging from cryonics with his feet encased in Reynolds Wrap, he finds himself in the year 2173. Quizzed by the scientists who have saved him (two hundred years earlier, a seemingly simple ulcer operation went wrong), Monroe later discovers he is to be brainwashed. He escapes and disguises himself as a robot in the home of a beautiful, trendy poetess named Luna Schlosser (Diane Keaton). After she discovers his identity, however, she is compelled to turn him in. Following a series of misadventures, Monroe is eventually captured and reprogrammed. Later, Schlosser—who has since joined the now-fashionable revolutionary underground—kidnaps Monroe and deprograms him. With plans to overthrow the existing government, the two disguise themselves as doctors in order to foil an intricate operation that could save the life of The Leader. In the aftermath of an attempt on his life, all that remains of The Leader is his nose, so there are plans to clone him from that nose. Monroe and Schlosser steal the nose, however, and in the chase that ensues, it is flattened by a steamroller. Their mission accomplished, Monroe and Schlosser declare their love for each other.

Although the story line is a decidedly simple one, *Sleeper* differs from earlier Allen films in that the humor of each scene works to enchance and sustain the story. In contrast, films such as *Take the Money and Run* (1969) and *Bananas* (1971) were dominated by erratic delivery, which made them look like nonstop parades of joke-laden skits; likewise, *Everything You Always Wanted to Know About Sex But Were Afraid to Ask* (1972) was only a series of skits. With the quality of these films in mind, and with highly polished works such as *Annie Hall* (1977) and *Manhattan* (1979) still to come, it is not surprising that critics welcomed *Sleeper* as Allen's most even work to that time. True to its name, the film proved a sleeper at the box office; the $3,100,000 production (filmed in a fourteen-week period) more than held its own, critically and commercially, in a year dominated by big-name films such as *The Sting* (budgeted at eight million dollars) and *The Exorcist* (budgeted at twelve million dollars).

Highlighted by its zany tribute to slapstick, *Sleeper* includes moments with Allen as a Chaplinesque robot battling a gigantic chocolate mousse with a broom. After stumbling (literally) over a vegetable garden filled with man-sized vegetables, Allen becomes involved in a madcap chase, complete with an enormous banana. If the film's story line seems more earnest and more smoothly delivered than earlier Allen films, the humor remains pure Allen. Although some of the jokes are self-indulgent (particularly one involving a man named Albert Shanker who destroyed civilization when he acquired a nuclear warhead—a private joke for New Yorkers familiar with Shanker as a key figure in a much-publicized teachers' strike during the 1960's) the majority of the humor has widespread appeal. In discussing contemporary personalities, Monroe tells the scientists that Norman Mailer has "donated his ego to the Harvard Medical School." In quizzing Monroe about one Richard M. Nixon, of whom no known records (or tapes) exist, the scientists declare, "We have a theory that he might once have been President of the United States, but that he did something horrendous." (Interestingly, *Sleeper* was released before the impeachment panel had begun the hearings stemming from the Watergate scandal.)

Equally amusing is the film's view of the future, which includes McDonald's hamburgers (750 Million Zillion Burgers Sold), sexual advances such as the Orgasmitron machine (participants need not remove their clothes), and amazing medical discoveries such as the fact that heavy fats, cream pies, and tobacco are good for one's health. *Sleeper* also includes hilarious sight gags involving Allen—notably his foray into the robot world, which finds him made up in white face with what appears to be a bottle-stop in his mouth (his glasses, of course, set him off from the rest of the robots). There is also a scene in which a special space suit inflates, sending him dangling in the air.

Sleeper is further highlighted by the teaming of Allen and Keaton. Although they played opposite each other in the Herbert Ross-directed *Play It Again, Sam* (1972), *Sleeper* marks the first time Allen directed the comedienne, who later became his favorite leading lady. Essentially a two-character film, with the exception of John Beck as a muscle-bound revolutionary, *Sleeper* underlines Keaton's comedic range. Her poetess character delivers Rod McKuenish "deep" verse, along with heavy-handed observations (such as the fact that "God" spelled backward is "dog"). The Keaton scene that most delighted critics involves her parody of Marlon Brando as Stanley Kowalski in *A Streetcar Named Desire* (1951). She plays the role opposite Allen's Blanche DuBois (the improbable scene occurs following a brainwashing). Keaton also displays a flair for one-liners. (Keaton: "You haven't had sex in 200 years?" Allen: "204—if you count my marriage.") She is also party to one of the film's funniest discoveries: upon finding a rusted-over two-hundred-year-old Volkswagen, Monroe and Schlosser find that it starts on the first try.

In addition to the disciplined story line and the teaming of Keaton and Allen, *Sleeper* is marked by the special effects of A. D. Flowers, who worked on *The Poseidon Adventure* (1972), and the art direction of Dale Hennesy, best-known for the 1966 film journey inside the human body, *Fantastic Voyage*. The rousing score is by Allen (a clarinetist by avocation) and The Preservation Hall Jazz Band of New Orleans, and Allen's own group, The New Orleans Funeral and Marching Orchestra.

Pat H. Broeske

THE SNAKE PIT

Released: 1948
Production: Anatole Litvak and Robert Bassler for Twentieth Century-Fox
Direction: Anatole Litvak
Screenplay: Frank Partos and Millen Brand; based on the novel of the same
  name by Mary Jane Ward
Cinematography: Leo Tover
Editing: Dorothy Spencer
Sound: Thomas T. Moulton (AA)
Running time: 108 minutes

> *Principal characters:*
> Virginia Stuart Cunningham ...... Olivia de Havilland
> Robert Cunningham .... Mark Stevens
> Doctor Mark Kik .... Leo Genn
> Grace .... Celeste Holm
> Doctor Terry .... Glenn Langan
> Nurse Davis .... Helen Craig
> Mrs. Stuart .... Natalie Schafer
> Mr. Stuart .... Damian O'Flynn

With the end of World War II in 1945, American life—disrupted in the 1930's by the Great Depression and then in the 1940's by World War II—returned to what was generally considered to be normal, and the film moguls in Hollywood made sincere attempts to provide the filmgoing public with intelligent works which were designed to be more than merely escapist entertainment. As the wildly implausible cinematic fantasies of the 1930's and 1940's lost their appeal, Hollywood answered the dilemma by offering generous helpings of "real life." A concerted effort was made to bring important social issues to the screen: the readjustment of returning war veterans in *The Best Years of Our Lives* (1946); anti-Semitism in *Gentlemen's Agreement* (1947); and mental illness in *The Snake Pit* (1948).

Released by Twentieth Century-Fox and directed by Anatole Litvak, *The Snake Pit* was a daring and controversial film for its day. The frank and sincere treatment of Mary Jane Ward's forceful novel won support from the critics for its excellence, but many felt compelled to include a warning that the film was not for all tastes and that its realistic depiction of life in a mental institution might prove unsettling to children and those with weak stomachs. Even today, after many subsequent films have traversed the same ground, *The Snake Pit* remains the definitive work in examining the life of a seriously disturbed personality.

The film opens with young Virginia Cunningham (Olivia de Havilland) confined in large Juniper Hill State Hospital, where she is withdrawn and uncooperative, exhibiting the symptoms of the true psychotic. Only Dr. Mark Kik (Leo Genn) seems capable of giving her proper understanding and treatment. Once he is able to make Virginia talk, he arranges private sessions with her in hopes of curing her illness. Through a series of flashbacks, we learn of Virginia's bittersweet childhood; of her cold, unsympathetic mother (Natalie Schafer); and of her loving but strict father (Damian O'Flynn). Little Virginia longs for a more loving mother, but she is consistently robbed of the feeling that she desperately wants, particularly after her mother becomes pregnant for a second time. Her father is devoted and caring, and Virginia worships him like no other man, yet even he is lost to her when he sides with her mother against her. After one scolding, Virginia becomes infuriated with her parents and destroys a little doll that has come to represent her father. Not long after that, her father dies from uremia, leaving a void in the child's life and creating a feeling of guilt within her subconscious mind.

Years later (as we learn from other flashbacks), Virginia, a withdrawn, slender girl, is attracted to Gordon (Leif Erickson), the eldest son of a fatherless family whose members depend upon him completely. She becomes enamored of him for his strong paternal qualities, yet when Gordon asks her to marry him, her reaction is one of revulsion, and she becomes so upset as to be physically ill. While riding with Gordon in his car, she is stricken, and he races her home. Paying too much attention to Virginia and not enough to the road, Gordon smashes the car into a truck and is killed—which, as Dr. Kik subsequently explains, adds to Virginia's feelings of guilt.

Virginia's husband Robert (Mark Stevens) feels that under Dr. Kik's care his wife is making great progress, and he arranges for Virginia to have a hearing with the hospital staff to determine whether she can be allowed to go home. Kik, feeling that Virginia needs additional care, is reluctant to allow the examination but sits in on it anyway. He attempts to question her very gently, but when she exhibits strong symptoms of paranoia, another doctor takes over. His demeanor proves too unsettling for Virginia, and she loses control completely, biting the doctor and flying into a rage which leads to her confinement in a large ward to which severe cases are committed.

Time passes, and Virginia regains her senses and resumes her struggle for sanity within herself. During a visit from Robert, she learns that it was his idea rather than Kik's for her to go in front of the staff. This reassures her, since she has had doubts about the doctor.

Soon Dr. Kik has Virginia transferred to Ward 1, where all the "best" patients are sent. The young lady sees this as the final step before her release and vows to keep herself in full control at all times to prove her sanity. Before long, however, she has a run-in with tyrannical Nurse Davis (Nancy Craig), who is infatuated with Dr. Kik and feels that Virginia is manipulating him. Fearful that she will be expelled from the ward, Virginia hides in a bathroom and is soon the object of a frantic search. Davis finally discovers the girl's hiding place and tricks her into the open by claiming that her husband Robert has arrived to see her. As Virginia steps out of the bathroom, she realizes that she has been tricked and reacts violently. Davis then has her put into a straitjacket and thrown into the "snake pit," an overcrowded ward where the most serious cases with little hope of recovery are confined. Because of Dr. Kik's intervention, however, Virginia is given the proper treatment. She finds that her surroundings give her a frame of reference she did not have before. Confined with those who seem much more sick than herself, Virginia begins to feel that she is not as bad off as she thought. Some time later, when she is quite lucid, Dr. Kik reveals what he believes to be the cause of her illness: her feelings of guilt at the loss of her father and Gordon. He explains that while it might be difficult to pinpoint any one incident as a trigger, Virginia can now arm herself with the knowledge of her general condition and how it may have come about. Later on, at a hospital dance for patients, Dr. Kik informs a happier Virginia that he has recommended a return visit with the hospital staff. Apprehensive but confident, the girl convinces the staff that she is well on the road to recovery, and Robert comes to take her away.

Much of *The Snake Pit*'s success derives from the fine performances of the cast. De Havilland is a standout; nominated for that year's Academy Award for Best Actress, she lost a close race to Jane Wyman for *Johnny Belinda*. British newcomer Genn won exceptionally good notices from the critics for his sensitive, sincere interpretation of Dr. Kik. Stevens (whom Fox had hoped to make a big star, but had failed to do) is effective as Robert Cunningham; and a truly superlative cast of seasoned character actors—some of them in unbilled roles that amount to little more than cameos—round out a group of pleasing performances, aided by the steady direction of Anatole Litvak, whose treatment of Frank Partos' and Millen Brand's script is letter-perfect. The scenario itself is one of those rare examples of an adaptation which rigidly adheres to its source. Nominated for five Academy Awards, including one for Best Picture, *The Snake Pit* won only for Best Sound Recording. De Havilland fared somewhat better with the New York Film Critics, who awarded her their Best Actress Award.

Ed Hulse

SO BIG

Released: 1953
Production: Henry Blanke for Warner Bros.
Direction: Robert Wise
Screenplay: John Twist; based on the novel of the same name by Edna Ferber
Cinematography: Ellsworth Fredericks
Editing: Thomas Reilly
Costume design: Milo Anderson
Music: Max Steiner
Running time: 101 Minutes

Principal characters:
Selina DeJong	Jane Wyman
Pervus DeJong	Sterling Hayden
Dallas O'Mara	Nancy Olson
Dirk DeJong	Steve Forrest
Julie Hempel	Elizabeth Fraser
Paula Hempel	Martha Hyer
Roelf Pool	Walter Coy
Roelf (younger)	Richard Beymer
Dirk (younger)	Tommy Rettig
Klaas Pool	Roland Winters
August Hempel	Jacques Aubuchon
Mrs. Pool	Ruth Swanson

The late novelist Edna Ferber, undeniably an arresting yarn-spinner, often seemed to be reworking the same genealogical sagas over and over again. Her gently bred but indomitable heroines of an earlier America were always being carried away to long, hard lives by well-meaning but flawed husbands, and begetting children who grew up to give them little peace. *So Big*, Ferber's Pulitzer Prize-winning novel, is no exception to this formula. It has been filmed three times: in 1925, with Colleen Moore; in 1932, with Barbara Stanwyck; and in 1953, with Jane Wyman. The last version, with Robert Wise sensitively directing for Warner Bros., is a touching, neglected Wyman gem that, while imperfect, still gives a lovely light. The star's deeply felt characterization of a selfless, idealistic mother—which sees her mature from schoolgirl days to middle-age with her usual quiet grace—is responsible for most of the glow. Her turn-of-the-century, refined character, named Selina Peake, never expected to wind up in life as "wheat." Her wealthy father always told her that there were only two kinds of people in the world who really counted: "wheat"—those who provided life's necessities; and "emerald"—those with creative talent. When he suddenly dies the motherless girl loses their elegant Chicago home and is forced to leave finishing school to take a teaching job in rugged New Holland, a nearby community of farmers. She rents the icy attic of a churlish farmer, Klaas Pool (Roland Winters), whose artistically inclined adolescent son Roelf (Richard Beymer) is encouraged by Selina. The poetic-minded, unconventional city girl is looked on as peculiar in the area— an impression that even passing decades will not dispel.

At a box supper she meets big, good-looking Purvis DeJong (Sterling Hayden), an uneducated poor farmer, and decides to give him mathematics instruction to prevent him from being cheated at the market. They fall in love and marry. She wears an old-fashioned Dutch bridal outfit as the groom whirls her around his parlor to a sprightly old-country waltz actually composed by Hollywood's Max Steiner, the creator of many beautiful Warner Bros. scores.

Selina joins her new husband in the fields, where she will remain for the rest of her life. A few years later after the birth of their son Dirk (Tommy Rettig), whom she nicknames "So Big," her husband dies, without ever really understanding his wife and her book-inspired ideas about topics such as irrigation to combat their lowland soil problems. Now Selina—determined to make the farm pay for "So Big's" sake—has to drive to the rowdy Chicago Haymarket herself, something which no other farm woman in that area has ever done before. This earns her more local scorn. When no one buys their vegetables, Selina and "So Big" set off in their wagon to peddle them in the suburbs. There, she runs into her old school friend Julie Hempel (Elizabeth Fraser), whose rich hog-butcher father (Jacques Aubuchon) subsequently advises Selina and helps her make the farm successful.

"DeJong Asparagus" becomes famous, allowing her to send Dirk (now played by Steve Forrest) to study architecture in college. After graduation, he disappoints his mother—long convinced that her son is "emerald"—by forsaking creativity to take up with grasping Paula Hempel (Martha Hyer), Julie's daughter, and succumbing to the lure of "big money" in the business world. Selina has some consolation when her protégé Roelf Pool (now played by Walter Coy) grows up to be a celebrated composer. Dirk, meanwhile, vows to return to architecture, after falling in love with pretty artist Dallas O'Mara (Nancy Olson), who thinks as his mother does. "So Big" dances his now happy mother around the parlor of their old farmhouse just as his father had on their wedding night many years before. Charming though this ending is in John Twist's screenplay, it still plays somewhat inconclusively. Does Dirk finally win Dallas, who looks for awhile like she might be interested in Roelf? Does he follow through on his sudden resolution to listen to his creative urge? These questions are left unanswered.

Next to Wyman, Hayden exhibits the most presence among the actors as the Dutch-accented husband and makes a short role seem longer. Through him, Purvis DeJong becomes a flesh-and-blood creation, a stalwart man frustrated at the only work he knows how to do by limited intellect. He is a family head who also can be overbearing at times with his simple beliefs. By dint of his sincerely projected affection for his odd "little Lina," however, Hayden's

DeJong becomes predominantly a sympathetic and attractive character. Forrest is a strapping, fair, realistic appearing son of Hayden; Olson, who is used sparingly, is briskly appealing; Hyer is appropriately shallow; and young Beymer, later to star for Wise in the film of *West Side Story* (1961), is convincing as the incipient composer who worships Selina.

Wyman sets the pace, however, never relying on the makeup, never straining to affect the aging process as so many contemporaries did (some in this very film), but letting it come naturally as in life. The gradual weathering of her sweet face, in particular, is smoothly done. In the beginning, it is crowned by flowered bonnets, but before too many harvests go by they are replaced by eccentric-looking old fedoras. Olson, as Dallas O'Mara (who signals the flashback by investigating Selina's trunk of mementoes), states the effect accurately after meeting the dedicated mother coming in from the fields: "That funny, gorgeous, battered old hat! And those eyes—they're all lit up from inside!" Helping this inner light to surface is Ellsworth Fredericks' perceptive camera, which understands that the motion picture's prime asset is Wyman's photogenic face. An especially poignant moment occurs after the premature death of Roelf's young mother (Ruth Swanson), who once had confided to the new schoolteacher that she had run away several times from Roelf's harsh father but had never been able to run far enough. "She ran far enough this time," Selina murmurs pensively to no one in particular, with a moving combination of irony and compassion.

The rural scenes in *So Big* contain a seasonal lyricism a couple of notches below those in Wyman's earlier *Johnny Belinda* (1948), and the story's statements concerning the real values of life, while thought by some to be rather dated in 1953, now may have become relevant again. *So Big* can still be enjoyed on many levels as an example of polished moviemaking.

Doug McClelland

SO ENDS OUR NIGHT

Released: 1941
Production: United Artists
Direction: John Cromwell
Screenplay: Talbot Jennings; based on the novel *Flotsam* by Erich Maria Remarque
Cinematography: William Daniels
Editing: William Reynolds
Production design: William Cameron Menzies
Running time: 120 minutes

Principal characters:
Josef Steiner .... Fredric March
Ruth Holland .... Margaret Sullavan
Marie Steiner .... Frances Dee
Ludwig Kern .... Glenn Ford
Lilo .... Anna Sten
Brenner .... Erich Von Stroheim

In 1940-1941, with Nazi Germany on the march, a series of films appeared which depicted contemporary events in Europe as they led relentlessly toward another world war. These films presented highly personal dramas; *The Mortal Storm* (1940) and *The Man I Married* (1940) are two examples. Today such dramas are rarely shown, audiences being more interested in the spectacular *Götterdämmerung* that soon swept the world into World War II.

The personal dramas, however, that occurred daily in Europe among those who were persecuted and were forever on the move from one beleaguered country to another were far more touching film subjects than the explosion of combat that ensued worldwide. *So Ends Our Night* is the story of such a group, seeking a safety that is theirs for only a brief time before they must move on away from the enemy on its constant march. The most precious possession such runaway people can have is a passport. Without it their attempt to move on can be thwarted, and they will be thrown into temporary detention camps and then moved on toward destruction in the big concentration camps. Passports become life-savers for refugees, and the market for the precious commodity is one wherein any price can be demanded. Without credentials, even though they are false, those who are running toward freedom are running blindly, certain to be trapped and exterminated.

Erich Maria Remarque, author of *All Quiet on the Western Front*, wrote a novel about such people, calling it, appropriately, *Flotsam*. David L. Loew and Albert Lewin bought it, hired Talbot Jennings to make a screenplay out of it, and then engaged the estimable director, John Cromwell, to direct it for United Artists release. The picture, which was retitled *So Ends Our Night*, was tremendously moving, as acted by a large cast of notable players.

One of those on the run is Joseph Steiner (Fredric March), a onetime officer in the German army who has become a political refugee from Germany. He is married to a beautiful girl, Marie (Frances Dee), who is ill, and he is forced to leave her behind when he flees from Vienna. He urges her to divorce him so that there can be no basis for persecution, but she refuses to do this. He is caught with no passport or work permit and thrown into jail, where he meets another young political refugee named Ludwig Kern (Glenn Ford). Eventually, they are released from prison and escorted to the border of Czechoslovakia, from which Kern heads for Prague, hoping to find his father, while Steiner slips back into Austria.

In Vienna, Steiner manages to buy a forged passport and gets work as a barker in the Prater, the big amusement park. He meets a beautiful Russian refugee named Lilo (Anna Sten), and she falls in love with him, but quickly realizes that there is only one woman in his life—Marie, whom he cannot endanger by trying to see. They can only meet in the cathedral square and do no more than look at each other furtively. Steiner is relentlessly pursued by a Gestapo officer named Brenner (Erich Von Stroheim), who suspects that Steiner is an escaped refugee of importance.

Meanwhile, Ludwig Kern, thwarted in finding his father and living in fear of being arrested again, meets a charming girl named Ruth Holland (Margaret Sullavan), who is drawn to him, but she resists falling in love, and leaves Prague for Vienna. Ironically, Kern also returns to Vienna to rejoin Steiner, who gets him a job in the Prater. Ruth goes to the amusement park because she has been advised to leave Vienna, and wants to see Kern before she goes. She fully intends leaving a good-bye note for him, but when she encounters him, she realizes that she finally loves him and cannot abandon him. The police come to the Prater checking on passports, and Kern is forced to flee. He later finds Ruth in Switzerland, however, and they are able to get across the French border and travel toward Paris.

Hitler's Nazis have marched into Austria, and Steiner is almost trapped by a company that invades the Prater. Lilo helps him to escape, although she loses her own life in the effort. Steiner manages to make his way to Paris, and although he gets a job on a construction crew there, it is obvious that this is only a brief respite. The Nazis will themselves be in Paris soon. When Kern learns that a French professor has fallen in love with Ruth, he advises her to marry him, but she will have none of it; she loves Kern more than ever and is determined to stay by him.

Steiner receives word that his wife is desperately ill in Germany and is not expected to live. He decides to go to Berlin, which he does, relentlessly followed by Brenner. Steiner makes a deal with the police, promising to turn his friends over to them if he may stay with his wife until she dies. The agreement is made, and when she dies, he is handcuffed to a triumphant

Brenner and led to his enemy's chambers. As they mount the huge staircase, Steiner sees his chance and jumps through a large glass window, killing himself and also carrying the cruel Brenner handcuffed to him to death. In Paris, Kern is arrested and sent to the border for deportation. Ruth manages to get passports for both herself and Kern through the professor who had wanted to marry her. She finds Kern before he is shipped over the border, and, together, with their new valid passports, they head west, hoping to get passage on a ship bound for America.

With his genius for understatement and his fidelity to complete realism, the late John Cromwell turned out one of his most moving studies of human beings in the grip of mortal fear. The picture is fraught with a feeling of restlessness as the characters seek to run from persecution toward freedom, and it is a relief when at least two of them who are in love are able to do so. *So Ends Our Night* got good bookings and reviews, but in spite of a star-filled cast, it did not make money. Today, although prints do exist, especially in television vaults, it is an extremely difficult picture to find.

Both March and Ford were highly praised for their work as two men on the run. March's eyes are haunted as he seeks the one woman he loves, played beautifully by Dee, and the scene in which they find each other but cannot show any sign of recognition or emotion is fraught with longing as well as suspense. Dee, with only two sequences in the entire picture, manages to make an unforgettable impression.

This was a very early appearance for Ford, and he reveals a sensitivity that he was not often allowed to convey in his subsequent larger roles. *Variety*, however, did term him "one of the best juvenile finds of the year," and indicated that "he can run in the fastest company and generate widespread public following." Sullavan is lovely as Ruth, the girl he loves, and their romantic scenes have a memorable lyric quality. Sten is excellent as the carnival girl who gives her life for March, and Stroheim contributes another of his inimitable portraits of "the man you love to hate."

All the production values are outstanding, particularly the work of William Cameron Menzies, who created an extraordinarily faithful set of the Prater, known as the "Coney Island of Vienna." He designed 130 sets for the picture, and they all lend dramatic authority as background for the tragic story that is told.

DeWitt Bodeen

SOME CAME RUNNING

Released: 1958
Production: Sol C. Siegel for Metro-Goldwyn-Mayer
Direction: Vincente Minnelli
Screenplay: John Patrick and Arthur Sheekman; based on the novel of the same name by James Jones
Cinematography: William Daniels
Editing: Adrienne Fazan
Music: Elmer Bernstein
Running time: 127 minutes

Principal characters:
Dave Hirsh	Frank Sinatra
Bama Dillert	Dean Martin
Ginny Moorhead	Shirley MacLaine
Gwen French	Martha Hyer
Frank Hirsh	Arthur Kennedy
Raymond Lanchak	Steven Peck
Agnes Hirsh	Leora Dana

The film version of James Jones's *From Here to Eternity* had been an enormous artistic and commercial success in 1953. When Jones's second novel, *Some Came Running*, was published five years later, Metro paid the author handsomely for the screen rights, feeling that, with the casting of Frank Sinatra, who had won an Oscar for his work in *From Here to Eternity*, the film would assuredly be a hit. Vincente Minnelli, an M-G-M director known chiefly for his dazzling musicals, was assigned the picture, and shooting began on location in Indiana.

The film opens with a shot of a Greyhound bus crossing the rolling green Midwestern hills and halting in the small town of Parkman. Two passengers debark: Dave Hirsh (Frank Sinatra), a hungover soldier and failed novelist just back from overseas, and Ginny Moorhead (Shirley MacLaine), a young drifter who attached herself to Dave during a drunken evening in Chicago where he was mustered out. Dave is horrified to find that during the course of his binge he mentioned that Parkman was his hometown, and that as a consequence, his drinking buddies deposited him on a bus headed back to the town he had run away from sixteen years before. He shakes off Ginny, registers in the best hotel in town, and deposits a large sum of money, gambling winnings, in the bank.

Word spreads fast and soon he is face to face with his older brother Frank (Arthur Kennedy), a successful jeweler and a pillar of the community. A longstanding bitterness exists between the two brothers since Frank, the head of the house after their father deserted them, had placed Dave in a home for boys. Putting his feelings aside, Dave agrees to have dinner at Frank's home, where he meets Gwen French (Martha Hyer), an instructor at the local college who knows Dave through the stories and novels he wrote before the war. Dave tries to seduce Gwen, but she insists that she is interested in him solely as a writer. In frustration, he asks her to drop him off at Smitty's bar, where he has been invited by Bama Dillert (Dean Martin), an easygoing gambler whom he had met earlier that day, to sit in on a poker game. Ginny has stayed on in Parkman. Dave makes a date with her for after the game, even though she is with an obviously disturbed man named Raymond (Steven Peck) who has followed her from Chicago. After the game, Dave, Ginny, and Bama leave the bar only to be accosted by Raymond. Dave knocks him out, but the police arrive, and Dave's latest brawl makes the papers much to the horror of Frank and his wife Agnes (Leora Dana).

After Dave and Bama rent a house and go into partnership as gamblers, Dave pays a visit to Gwen, hoping to seduce her by bringing along one of his old, unfinished manuscripts. Gwen finds the story compelling and insists on sending it to an editor that she knows. Overwhelmed by the story, she lowers her guard and allows herself to be seduced. Ginny, meanwhile, desperately in love, goes to Gwen to persuade her to give up Dave. Gwen is horrified, recognizing that Ginny must be the girl over whom Dave had the fight on his first night in Parkman. When Dave next tries to see Gwen, she lashes out at him, telling him that she is disgusted by his violent and dissolute life style.

Defeated and lonely, Dave marries Ginny, and the two of them plan to leave Parkman. Before they can do so, however, the psychotic Raymond tracks them down and attempts to kill Dave. Ginny throws herself in front of Dave, and Raymond empties his gun into her. At the funeral, Bama, honoring Ginny, removes the lucky stetson which throughout the film has never left his head. The main characters stand at the site of Ginny's grave listening to a minister reciting the Lord's Prayer by the edge of the river. We are left with no clear idea as to what Dave will do: stay in Parkman and try to win Gwen back; continue writing; or drift.

Minnelli is so well known and respected as a director of musicals, that the occasional "serious" Minnelli film, such as *The Clock* (1945), is generally either overlooked or panned as being somewhat dull or overblown. One of the hallmarks of his work is that he uses bold strokes. Some find this technique melodramatic, but the outcome is always arresting. There is a hurried quality to *Some Came Running* which is absent from Fred Zinneman's fine adaptation of *From Here to Eternity*, but Minnelli and his actors do the best they can with an inferior script. Sinatra is his usual capable self, but as in so many of his films, one regrets that he did not bring more to the role than his standard portrait of a hipster. MacLaine became a major star on the strength of her performance as Ginny. Martin and the rest of the cast all perform ably, and Hyer deserves special notice for making her portrayal of Gwen French believable despite the fact that her character's motivation, either through censorship or negligence, was sketchily treated. *Some Came Running* is an excellent melodrama, one which plays much better if one has not read the book and is not an ardent fan of James Jones.

Michael Shepler

SOMEBODY UP THERE LIKES ME

Released: 1956
Production: Charles Schnee for Metro-Goldwyn-Mayer
Direction: Robert Wise
Screenplay: Ernest Lehman; based on the book by Rocky Graziano and Rowland Barber
Cinematography: Joseph Ruttenberg
Editing: Albert Akst
Technical adviser: Johnny Indrisano
Running time: 112 minutes

Principal characters:

Rocky Graziano (Rocco Barbella)	Paul Newman
Norma Graziano	Pier Angeli
Irving Cohen	Everett Sloane
Romolo	Sal Mineo
Mrs. Barbella	Eileen Heckart
Nick Barbella	Harold J. Stone
Benny	Joseph Buloff
Whitey Bimstein	Sammy White
Frankie Peppo	Robert Loggia

Somebody Up There Likes Me was Paul Newman's third film, Pier Angeli's sixth, and director Robert Wise's twenty-third. Wise had previously put Robert Ryan and Audrey Totter through their paces in *The Set-Up* (1949), so he was no stranger to either gritty realism or the boxing arena. *Somebody Up There Likes Me* is a film that positively relishes its grimy authenticity, its sweat, its muscle, and its slums.

The film is basically a true story that charts the rise of Rocky Graziano from a Lower East Side tenement to a Lower East Side development apartment. Along the way he picks up the Light Heavyweight title (1947-1948), a wife, and a family. Rocky, as played by Newman, is dumb about life and dumb about book learning, but he is also street-wise and has an absolutely tenacious belief, once he has accepted the idea, that he is destined for greatness. The man who convinces him, Irving Cohen (Everett Sloane), becomes his manager, and the woman who supports him throughout is Norma, his Jewish wife, played very sweetly and convincingly by Pier Angeli. The two others who have the most influence on him are his father, a drunken, frustrated, ex-third-rate boxer (Harold J. Sloane), and his mother (Eileen Heckart), who tells him that he must help himself. Since she is visiting him in an Army prison where he has been sent for going AWOL, a continuation of the rebellious behavior that kept him in reformatories throughout most of his youth, her words carry a certain validity.

It is in the Army that Rocky first learns that he can fight, but he does nothing with the notion until Cohen sees him and persuades him that he can be not just good, but possibly great. Even then he resists the idea. With characteristic ambivalence, he procrastinates and makes Cohen convince *him*. Similarly, Norma has to force him into admitting he loves her and wants to marry her. Seated across from City Hall, where they have gone to get married, she has to drag Rocky into the building. There are several scenes between Rocky and his parents which echo this inability to confess his emotions, his helpless inarticulateness about his feelings, and the choked up frustration he experiences whenever he has to say "I need you, help me," or "I love you." Rocky does have to say these words, since life will not let him get away with anything. He is even reminded of the petty criminal he almost became by the continued presence of his friend Romolo (Sal Mineo), a kid much like himself except that he did not happen to get the breaks.

The comparisons between Newman's Rocky Graziano and Marlon Brando's Terry Malloy in *On the Waterfront* (1954) are obvious and numerous. Like Terry, Rocky could have gotten "a one-way ticket to palookaville" and become a bum. Like Terry, Rocky is helped both by women and by understanding older men who believe in his ability to overcome the seemingly insurmountable obstacles in his way. Newman followed Graziano around for a week, learning how to move and fight like a boxer; earlier Brando had done the same thing. (Ironically, Newman was criticized for imitating Brando, when in fact both actors were imitating the same teacher.)

Rocky has a number of insightful confrontations with people from the old neighborhood, among them Benny (Joseph Buloff), the proprietor of the local candy store. At one point, lamenting the unfulfilled prospects of youth, Benny declares, "You should be sued for breach of promise!" He is railing at Rocky for his habitual half-criminal behavior, behavior echoed continually by his peers. Frankie Peppo (Robert Loggia), the crook who knew him in the Army prison, threatens to get him in trouble with the Boxing Commission if he does not throw a fight. Rocky himself talks to the Commission and is suspended, but, of course, he regains his license and a shot at the title.

Somebody Up There Likes Me is a film of confession, a category that almost became a subgenre in the films of the 1950's, in which one character after another confesses to a crime, a sin of omission or commission, or a slight transgression. Confessing was the rage from about 1947 to the 1950's; Elia Kazan had to make an entire film (*On the Waterfront*) to justify the fact that he had named names before the House UnAmerican Activities Committee. Others excused themselves more obliquely by inserting references to confessing without making it the subject of the film. Director Sam Fuller built his career around a series of films which had as their central theme a virulent, crude anti-Communism, and Leo McCarey directed another "confessional" film, *My Son John* (1952), in which the hero, Robert Walker, is treated like a leper because he has been a Communist.

Somebody Up There Likes Me is therefore much more than a film about a dumb man who achieves success with his fists, sees the error of his ways, and becomes a model citizen. Once the 1950's arrived, Metro-Goldwyn-Mayer stepped into the arena of social consciousness, where studios such as Warner Bros. and Twentieth Century-Fox had been operating all along, and began making films with some social content. Instead of gilded trash such as *The Hucksters* (1947) and *Susan and God* (1940), they made *Blackboard Jungle* (1955) and *Intruder in the Dust* (1951), films that gloss over the real horrors of juvenile delinquency and discrimination, but which still manage to inform the audience about a problem.

Somebody Up There Likes Me is grand entertainment. It is long, but it moves; director Wise keeps the pace up while cinematographer Joseph Ruttenberg makes both the location scenes and the studio sets seem real without being blatant. Newman plays an enjoyable "dumbbell," raffishly charming as he shuffles and mumbles his way through his courtship of Norma. His title bout with Tony Zale is as exciting as the fights Wise staged for *The Set-Up* or those Robert Rossen directed for *Body and Soul* (1947). When he tours the "nabe" with Norma, pushing a baby carriage, his mouth clamped around a huge, ugly cigar, smiling and shaking hands with his old friends, Newman is a joy to watch. He has a light in his eye that seems to say "Acting's fun; look at me, you're going to get a charge out of this." *Somebody Up There Likes Me* did not make Newman a star, but it earned him good reviews and made a great deal of money; it took two subsequent successes, *Cat on a Hot Tin Roof* (1958) and *Exodus* (1960), to make him a star.

Judith M. Kass

SOMETIMES A GREAT NOTION

Released: 1971
Production: John Foreman for Newman-Foreman/Universal
Direction: Paul Newman
Screenplay: John Gay; based on the novel of the same name by Ken Kesey
Cinematography: Richard Moore
Editing: Bob Wyman
Running time: 113 minutes

Principal characters:
Hank Stamper	Paul Newman
Henry Stamper	Henry Fonda
Viv Stamper	Lee Remick
Leeland Stamper	Michael Sarrazin
Joe Ben Stamper	Richard Jaeckel
Willard Eggleston	Lee de Broux
Floyd Evenwrite	Joe Maross

The chief virtue of *Sometimes a Great Notion* is its presentation of three interesting and compelling characters as they interact with one another, other people, and the forces of nature. All three are creations not only of the author of the novel upon which the film is based, Ken Kesey, and the scriptwriter, John Gay, but also of the actors who portray the characters. Two of the characters are larger than life, but that does not protect them from defeat or ambiguous victory.

Henry Stamper is an almost legendary character played by an almost legendary actor—Henry Fonda, in his seventy-second film role. In *Sometimes a Great Notion* Fonda lets his age (sixty-five) show in his portrayal of the colorful, cantankerous, and individualistic patriarch of an Oregon logging family. When we first see him, he is still active although a recent fall from a tree has left one arm in a cast that holds the arm perpendicular to his body. He is also very much in charge of his clan, especially the family members who live under his roof. It includes his son Hank (Paul Newman) and nephew Joe Ben (Richard Jaeckel), both in their thirties or early forties, and Hank's wife Viv (Lee Remick) and Joe Ben's wife Jan (Linda Lawson). Henry dominates everything. He awakens everyone for work at 4:30 in the morning, directs the breakfast table conversation, and is the first one to tell off anyone who wants to change the family's ways. He states that the purpose of life is "to work and eat and sleep and screw and drink and to keep on goin'—that's all there is."

Hank Stamper is a close relative of the characters Newman played in *Hud* (1963) and *Cool Hand Luke* (1967)—tough, independent, and macho. He defers to no one except his father. Like Henry, Hank lives a physical life, adhering to the Stamper code: "Never Give an Inch" (the title of the film in Britain and occasionally on American television).

After a long, evocative shot of the Oregon coast under the credits we are quickly introduced to a central conflict of the film; it is between the Stampers and the logger's union. The union, which has the backing of the entire town except for the Stampers, is striking in order to get a higher price from the lumber companies. Within the first few minutes of the film we see the head of the union, Floyd Evenwrite (Joe Maross), who has gone across the river to try to talk the Stampers into joining the strike, chased back to his boat by the family and hurried along by sticks of dynamite thrown in the water by Hank.

After the conflict between the Stampers and the rest of the town is established, the third major character—who provides an additional conflict—is introduced. He is Leeland Stamper (Michael Sarrazin), the only child of Henry's second marriage. When he unexpectedly arrives at the Stamper house, he surprises everyone. Gradually, throughout the film, we learn his story. As a small child he saw his mother in bed with Hank and has bitterly resented his half-brother ever since. Later his mother left Henry and the whole atmosphere of the Stamper clan, taking Lee with her. When she committed suicide by jumping out of a window, Lee became more angry at the Stampers, and Hank in particular. He has not, however, been able to decide what to do with his life. Therefore, after a failed suicide attempt of his own, he arrives at the Stamper house with a college education, long hair, and a quite different view of life from that of the other male Stampers.

Lee does not pretend to accept the family's way of thinking, and Henry and Hank deride his appearance and his education. When Lee begins working with them, however, they find a common ground in the work of logging. It demands strength, courage, and skill—all of which are conveyed remarkably by the camera.

As the days pass, the Stampers (including Lee) continue logging, the townspeople continue to be hostile, and Lee discovers that he has more in common with Viv, Hank's wife, than he does with any of his family.

The other loggers try to stop the Stampers by killing Henry's favorite hound dog, by cutting a cable to cause a potentially fatal "accident," and by destroying a brand new truck belonging to the Stampers. Willard Eggleston (Lee de Broux), the owner of the local movie theater, tries to talk Hank into supporting the strike because his own business will fail if the strike does not succeed. Finally, Willard tells Hank that he will kill himself and make it appear to be an accident so his insurance money can be collected.

In the next two days each of the threads of the plot comes to a climax. First we see Willard fall off a ladder after putting up the words "Closed Thanks to Hank Stamper" on the marquee of his theater. The next morning at breakfast the Stamper clan hears the news of his death on the radio. Viv, who is the only one besides Hank who has heard Willard's threat, urges Hank to stay home from work, to "give an inch." Hank, however, refuses to listen to her. Since Henry has removed his cast during the night, all the men—Henry, Hank, Joe, Ben, and Lee—go off to work together. It is a catastrophic decision.

One of the trees they are cutting down suddenly splits and falls in the wrong direction. The accident severs Henry's arm and causes a huge log to roll down a hill and pin Joe Ben underneath it in shallow but rapidly rising water. Lee takes Henry to the hospital while Hank tries to rescue Joe Ben. The rescue attempt is the most powerful single scene in the film. Joe Ben is sitting up in the water with the log in his lap. He is not injured, but he cannot move. Hank tries sawing the log with his chain saw, but it dies. He tries prying it off Joe Ben's legs, but it is too large. As the water continues to rise, the only hope is that the log will float enough to free Joe Ben, who keeps cheerfully wisecracking about his situation. When the water begins to cover Joe Ben's face, Hank ducks under the water to breathe air into Joe Ben's mouth. This works until Joe Ben, thinking the sight of the two men seemingly kissing is funny, bursts out laughing underwater and drowns. Hank stands up screaming his cousin's name; it is the first time we have seen him show emotion. The poignant power of the scene comes from its mixture of peril and cheerfulness.

Next Hank goes to see Henry in the hospital. The father is still defiant and has had his severed arm put into the freezer at the Stamper house, but he soon dies. Hank then returns home and finds that Viv has left him. Neither of these events evokes any display of emotion.

Only Hank and Lee are left. They finally seem to reach a sort of truce when Hank tells Lee that Hank's "affair" with Lee's mother happened when Hank was only fourteen and Lee's mother was thirty, so that Hank was hardly taking advantage of her. He also tells Lee, "The old man said you really cut it today." Then, when it appears that Hank is going to forget everything in an alcoholic stupor, a telephone call from one of the strikers goads him into deciding to float the Stamper logs down the river singlehandedly. Lee joins him, and as the two pilot the tugboat and four large "rafts" of logs past the unbelieving townspeople, Hank affixes Henry's arm—with all fingers but the middle one tied down—to the tugboat in a gruesome expression of Stamper defiance.

Sometimes a Great Notion does suffer from a somewhat confusing point of view, as does the novel upon which it was based. The determination of the Stampers to fulfill their contract regardless of the cost to anyone else raises, but does not actually try to answer, many questions about individualism and social responsibility. The film is sympathetic throughout to the Stampers even though we see the human cost of their actions.

The production of the film was plagued by problems. During the filming the original director was replaced and the costar (and new director) Newman broke his ankle. After a delay, the filming was finally finished, but difficulties emerged in the editing, reportedly causing some important scenes to be removed. Although the film that emerged from these tribulations is somewhat uneven, it is well worth watching for its virtues—strong performances by Fonda, Newman, and Sarrazin, the powerful and moving scene between Newman and Jaeckel, and a beautiful filmic presentation of Oregon scenery and the work of lumberjacks.

Sharon Wiseman

SONS AND LOVERS

Released: 1960
Production: Jerry Wald for Twentieth Century-Fox
Direction: Jack Cardiff
Screenplay: Gavin Lambert and T. E. B. Clarke; based on the novel of the same name by D. H. Lawrence
Cinematography: Freddie Francis (AA)
Editing: Gordon Pilkington
Music: Mario Nascimbene
Running time: 103 minutes

Principal characters:
Mr. Morel .... Trevor Howard
Paul Morel .... Dean Stockwell
Mrs. Morel .... Wendy Hiller
Miriam Leivers .... Heather Sears
Clara Dawes .... Mary Ure
Mrs. Leivers .... Rosalie Crutchley
Art buyer: .... Ernest Thesiger

In contrast to the film fare of the 1950's, much of which consisted of garish musicals, mindless Westerns, and brash black-and-white science-fiction thrillers, a serious mood piece exploring personal dilemmas was a refreshing digression to begin the new decade and was thus well received by critics. Although not a great financial success, *Sons and Lovers* was highly acclaimed and received six Academy Award nominations, winning one for the black-and-white cinematography by Freddie Francis.

As a somber, explosive story of the interplay among disturbed lives in the English Midlands industrial town of Bestwood, the screen adaptation of D. H. Lawrence's novel *Sons and Lovers* requires of its audience a particular sensitivity and perception, a discernment of the unseen, and especially an appreciation of the nuances of light and shadow created in Francis' black-and-white cinematography. It is, in fact, the pictorial qualities of the film which continue to elicit praise, even from those critics who consider the characterizations and story somewhat dated. Because it presents Lawrence's concern with the liberation of the individual from parental and childhood constraints, the film does not hold a wide popular appeal for today's audiences because of the obsession of films throughout the 1960's with adolescents leaving home to "do their own thing." The fact that later filmmakers and novelists overworked the theme of growth into adulthood, however, should not detract from the intrinsic merits of either Lawrence's novel or the film.

Renaming his hometown of Eastwood and updating the story to 1910, Lawrence related in the novel the story of his wretched early years, during which he was caught between and nearly destroyed by bitter and incessant parental conflict. The film picks up the story midway and deals only with Lawrence's attempt to extricate himself from his background. Lawrence is represented in the person of Paul Morel (Dean Stockwell). With this heavy brows, dark, brooding eyes, and boyish build, Stockwell elicits sympathy as Paul, the sentimental, artistic youngest son unknowingly restrained by an overly attentive mother (Wendy Hiller) from becoming a lover. Mrs. Morel's excessive solicitude stems from a long-unmet need to love and be loved by her churlish coal-miner husband (Trevor Howard). Unable to accept the reality of her son loving someone else, she is threatened by his friendship with young women and subtly maintains an apron-string hold on his affections of which he is unaware.

Warmly maternal-looking Mrs. Morel is perpetually scandalized or disgusted, admonishing all around her, sometimes with good humor, but more often with true consternation. While she appears martyred and long-suffering at the hands of her husband and sons, we recognize that she is the agent of her own despair. Her protective veil of indignation is drawn aside only to receive Paul's affections and to praise the portraits he draws. It is his aesthetic inclinations which remind her of what she might have tapped in herself had she not given way to the girlhood passion aroused in her by a swaggering, handsome suitor from the coal pits who was socially not her equal.

For her last son she has planned a life of collar and tie, clean hands, and cultivated ways. She does not intend, however, that these goals be achieved at any distance from her. Having lost one son, William, to the allure of London and one of its women, and another son, Arthur, to the mines, her psychological grip on Paul tightens as the story progresses. Her encouragement of a London education for him appears to be uncharacteristically selfless, but she too readily accepts his insistence to stay behind with her for us to believe that she truly desires the best for him. Paul believes his mother to be helpless against his drunkenly abusive father and fears that in his absence she will be harmed during the man's violent outbursts. He does not realize that it is actually she who is in control of her husband, whom she has weakened and demoralized over the years through her fault-finding. She is the cause of his anguish, as she taunts and provokes his rages, thus victimizing herself. Through anger and frustration at her bleak existence and failed marriage, she has emasculated her husband; and in attempting to retain something of beauty in life, she is emasculating her only remaining son as well.

An opportunity for Paul to study art in London under the patronage of a buyer (Ernest Thesiger) of one of his drawings (oddly enough, one of his father) is lost due to Paul's concern for his mother's safety.

Upon learning of Paul's decision to take a job near Bestwood in the office of Jordan's corset factory, his father is enraged because it represents a repudiation of coal mining as a living. His mother is angry outwardly because of the compromise of his talents, but she is also distressed that Paul's relationship with his friend Miriam Leivers (Heather Sears) might flower, thus depriving herself of Paul's attentions. She would much prefer that his distance from her be measured in geographic distance rather than the emotional distance that an involvement with another woman would create. Miriam is a simple farm girl who shares Paul's passion for poetry and beauty in nature. Her passion reaches no further, however, because of the fear and shame of sex instilled in her by her Calvinist-bred mother (Rosalie Crutchley). The excessive religiousity of Miriam's nature enables her to love Paul only spiritually, but since his spirit is concerned with other things, he can love her only physically. Despite her sexual surrender to him as a means to win him wholly, she drives him from her by her aversion to sex and by her claims on his soul. Sears is not persuasive as the ethereal Miriam. Her gamin features make her appear too impish for the role of a girl so possessed of moral severity as to believe "This thing between men and women is ugly" and is to be endured only for the sake of having children.

Later, at Jordan's, Paul meets the more worldly Clara Dawes (Mary Ure), who is in charge of a workroom full of mindless young girls. Her estranged husband, also employed by the factory, witnesses the evolution of an affair between them. Intrigued by her street-corner feminist proselytizing and her beauty, Paul learns of her marriage too late to slow his sensual longing for her. On a holiday together, Clara possesses him, but only sexually, because of his inability to love beyond his mother. He must nevertheless be credited with escaping his mother's company, however briefly, for a seaside tryst with Clara. Miriam's opposite, Clara can offer only the sexual. Ure's portrayal of Baxter Dawes's faithless wife is only slightly less assuring than Sears's characterization. The distance and detachment with which she plays the role is disappointing. Her appearance and enigmatic manner would have better suited her for the part of Miriam.

Paul returns to Bestwood and is beaten up by Dawes, himself a philanderer. He returns to see his dying mother, who forbids her husband to see her in her powerless state. She succumbs to a heart attack in the film, although in the original story she dies from cancer and Paul's euthanasia. The elder Morel can at last give up the fight in his wife's absence. He turns uncharacteristically philosophical for Paul's benefit, but the two remain unreconciled. Later, at his mother's grave, Paul encounters Miriam, who is ready to bestow her brand of maternal affection on the troubled Paul. He will have none of her, however, vowing never to belong to anyone again. He is not moved by her impending trip to London to become a teacher despite his similar destination in search of himself. It is there, he expects, that he will discover how to love.

Such an inconclusive ending is highly unsatisfactory even to the viewer who prefers personal interpretation to a neatly packaged story. The unfathomable final scene, however, is in keeping with this largely directionless, unfocused film. Early scenes find Paul lauding the nineteenth century poet Shelley and celebrating art, never to be mentioned again, which lead to the unsatisfactory impression that he has given up aesthetic pursuits for sensual ones. The screenplay has captured the mood and feeling of Lawrence's prose and has taken much dialogue from the novel itself, but the story is not so much that of the author's early life as it is strung-together incidents. These sketches are beautifully illustrated by the brilliant cinematographer-turned-director, Jack Cardiff, but they do not coalesce in the end. A minor criticism also can be made of the music of Mario Nascimbene, which is intrusive; too many scenes are heralded with heavy chords or loud, rhapsodic violins. *Sons and Lovers* is a film of promised but unrealized potential.

Nancy S. Kinney

SORRY, WRONG NUMBER

Released: 1948
Production: Anatole Litvak and Hal B. Wallis for Paramount
Direction: Anatole Litvak
Screenplay: Lucille Fletcher; based on her radio play of the same name
Cinematography: Sol Polito
Editing: Warren Low
Running time: 89 minutes

Principal characters:
Leona Stevenson	Barbara Stanwyck
Harry Stevenson	Burt Lancaster
Sally Lord	Ann Richards
Doctor Alexander	Wendell Corey
Waldo Evans	Harold Vermilyea

Sorry, Wrong Number is the story of Leona Stevenson (Barbara Stanwyck), a domineering woman, bedridden and isolated, who is gradually made helpless by the unfolding of her own history. While trying to locate her husband, Henry (Burt Lancaster), Leona reviews their relationship in flashbacks prompted by various phone calls to people who know them both. Gradually she realizes that Henry is not the obedient, loving company man that she and her father have encouraged him to be. The phone calls reveal another Henry, an amateur thief in trouble with professional thieves, who is about to sacrifice his wife's life to raise the money which could save his own. Leona, horrified, sees her life spread out before her, with every step of the process which has driven Henry to plan her death clearly traceable to her own blind will.

Leona is an invalid alone in the house, with Henry out of town and her nurse given the night off. A chance wrong connection on her phone has allowed Leona to overhear two men planning a murder for that night. As she dials other numbers in an effort to identify the original wrong number, Leona learns enough about Henry to cause her to think that the murder may be her own. The development of the murder plot parallels her developing awareness of her husband's other life as a frustrated businessman and husband, corporate thief, and finally would-be murderer.

Sorry, Wrong Number had been an extremely successful radio play. The problem in making the film centered on how to open up a play about an invalid confined to her bed and telephone. The solution was to have the camera escape Leona's room during a series of flashbacks narrated by telephone informants. As Leona receives or places call after call, the flashbacks show us the gradual erosion in her health which has left her an invalid. The change in her health is clearly a change in the way Leona conceives of her power over Henry. At first an active and dominant woman who snares her handsome husband away from a simpler small-town girl, Leona gradually takes on the role of a victim, stricken by heart illness in order to maintain her hold over Henry. Every time he challenges her authority, she has a heart seizure which plays upon his guilt, and she has her way. The strategy has finally left her an invalid.

Anatole Litvak directs the film with a tightly constructed counterpoint of fluid, moving cinematography and images of confinement. Although Leona is trapped in her sickroom, the camera roams her room and the first floor below, conveying to us a menace which she must conjecture. The flashbacks which "open up" the film are usually initiated by people speaking within narrow phone booths, alcoves, or curtained rooms. The freedom of space promised by the flashbacks, opening onto various times and places, is underscored by their settings: a rainy night, cluttered laboratory, noisy subway platform, car interior, or cramped study. Even the beach is dark and confining, with silhouettes of fishing nets and pilings blocking the frame. These characters cannot escape events which carry them along to inevitable conclusions, all grim. Thus the camera's movement is one of discovering obstructions and barriers in a generally dark world.

After Leona's first phone call in which she overhears the murder plan, she becomes frightened and places succeeding calls in an effort to locate her husband. A call to her husband's secretary reveals that Henry was visited by an old girl friend at the office. In flashback, Leona relives her wooing and winning of Henry, a high-school dropout from a small town. She was an heiress to a drug company fortune, and with a combination of money and predatory determination, she took Henry away from Sally Lord (Ann Richards), a straightforward and easily dominated blonde. It is Sally who has visited Henry at the office, seemingly out of the blue. Sally, however, is now married to a federal investigator who is building a case against Henry. Sally tries to warn Henry but he leaves before she can explain and now Sally tries to tell Leona what she knows of her husband's investigation. Leona gets her first concrete evidence of Henry's criminal activities as Sally reports an exchange of money on a deserted beach.

More flashbacks show us Henry's frustration with his job as a decorative vice president in his father-in-law's company. Leona is blind to his frustration and manages to win all of their arguments. One of the calls Leona places is to her doctor (Wendell Corey). He reveals that Henry has been told that Leona's disease is psychological and can be cured, but Henry has kept the news, and the doctor's advice, from her. Suddenly Leona realizes that Henry may not want her to recover.

Another shock is a call from Henry's partner-in-crime at the drug company, who reveals the history of their crimes to Leona. He reveals that he and Henry have been stealing drugs from the company and selling them to gangsters. When Henry began to fence the drugs himself, to make more money, the gangsters decided to take action. They are demanding a share of Henry's profits, money Henry does not have. The gangsters have a suggestion, however: Henry can raise the money by cashing his wife's life insurance policy— but, of course, Henry cannot collect until Leona dies.

Leona, hysterical but still partially disbelieving, makes another call, trying to have a hospital send her a nurse for the night. The call gets her nowhere, however, and Leona is finally beside herself with telephoning. When the phone rings again, she grabs it and wildly tells the operator that she is too sick to take the call, but this time, the call is from Henry.

Leona tries to calm herself; she now knows that Henry is not the man she believed him to be hours earlier, but she still is not ready to believe he is her murderer. She tearfully tells Henry that she knows he is in trouble and will give him any money he needs. She repeats her love for him and apologizes for not having seen his troubles before. Finally, she remembers a message which his partner has left for him. Leona does not quite understand what the message means, but she repeats it for Henry. The police have captured the gangsters who want the money and have also discovered Henry's beach hideaway. As she talks, a frantic Henry realizes that the police know all about him and that a financially unnecessary murder is about to be committed. As Leona speaks, we see the shadow of her assailant on the landing. As her murderer reaches the bedroom door, Henry shouts at Leona to go to the window and scream. Leona, however, is afraid to leave her bed; terrified, she begs Henry to protect her. Henry can only listen helplessly as he hears Leona's scream and the sound of objects falling off the nightstand. Shortly, an anonymous male voice comes on the line to tell Henry, "Sorry, wrong number."

Leslie Donaldson

SOUNDER

Released: 1972
Production: Robert B. Radnitz for Twentieth Century-Fox
Direction: Martin Ritt
Screenplay: Lonne Elder III; based on the novel of the same name by William
   H. Armstrong
Cinematography: John A. Alonzo
Editing: Sidney Levin
Music: Taj Mahal
Running time: 105 minutes

Principal characters:
David Lee Morgan .... Kevin Hooks
Nathan Lee Morgan .... Paul Winfield
Rebecca Morgan .... Cicely Tyson
Ike .... Taj Mahal
Sheriff Young .... James Best
Mrs. Boatwright .... Carmen Mathews
Camille Johnson .... Janet MacLachlan

Sounder is a simple, but not simplistic, film made by white urbanites about black country folk without, surprisingly, patronizing either the subject or the audience. It deals with an aspect of American life in a historical context in the manner of *The Grapes of Wrath* (1940) and *To Kill a Mockingbird* (1962). These films focus on one family during a period of stress, but they are also about the larger issues that confront the characters. In *Sounder* the content is very understated and concerns a young boy's maturation and how he reconciles his love for his family with his aspirations for an education.

It is 1933 in the Louisiana countryside where Nathan Morgan (Paul Winfield) ekes out a meager living for his wife and three children. He and his eldest son, David Lee (Kevin Hooks), go raccoon hunting with Sounder, their hound, but miss their target. In the morning, mysteriously, there is meat for breakfast. The sheriff (James Best) arrests Nathan for stealing and he is sentenced to a year at hard labor at a distant work camp. Through the intercession of a kindly white woman, Mrs. Boatwright (Carmen Mathews), who employs Rebecca Morgan (Cicely Tyson) to do laundry and who lends David books, David learns where his father has been taken. He sets off to see him, but although he locates the camp, he cannot find Nathan. A white overseer injures David's hand, causing David to ask for help at a schoolhouse. The schoolteacher, Camille Johnson (Janet MacLachlan), binds his wound and takes him temporarily into her home, inviting him to attend her school in the fall. David returns to his family, and together they manage to bring in their crops. One day a limping Nathan returns. He was hurt in a dynamite blast and his time was shortened when it was obvious he was no longer fit to work. With the family reunited, David does not want to leave his father to go to school; but Nathan makes David see that an education is the way to leave behind the harsh sharecropper's life, and he and David, with Sounder in the wagon, set off for Miss Johnson's school.

Sounder is a film of quiet faith, not a religious movie, but one that believes in people's ability to triumph over adversity and in the idea that life, no matter how hard, must eventually yield its riches to the deserving. Without stating it directly, *Sounder* says that David's journey to see his father matures him. He becomes the man of the family by asking Mrs. Boatwright about Nathan's whereabouts, and later by setting out to find him. The foundation for David's assurance and competence is his warm, supportive family and his close relationship with his father. These are the bases for his growth, a process that begins when he starts on his trip, develops in the home of Miss Johnson, who tells him about black heroes about whom he has never heard, and culminates with David's return to her school to continue his education. A shot that encapsulates this family feeling occurs toward the end of the film. The Morgans race down the road to greet Nathan, they hug and kiss and hold one another, then the five turn with their arms around one another and head back to the house. Their arms stretched across one another's backs symbolize their unity and their strength.

The rest of the production is as visually compelling as this scene. The Panavision frame is ideal for the long country vistas and the endless horizons. Director Martin Ritt and his cinematographer, John A. Alonzo, pause lovingly, but not overlong on these views. They have a tendency to sentimentalize their subject somewhat, but one facet of rural life they do not gloss over is its grinding poverty. The Morgans' farm is a ramshackle affair without paint or window glass. It is falling to pieces, a place to get away from and for which never to be homesick. As David says when he leaves, "I'm gonna miss this old raggedy place, but I sure ain't gonna worry about it."

Equally unsentimental is Ritt's treatment of David's journey, the events that lead up to it, and Nathan's reunion with his family. The whites are not completely unsympathetic. The sheriff may patronize the Morgans, but Mrs. Boatwright does not. A timid, well-meaning Southern lady, she violates her principles by rifling the sheriff's files to help David locate his father. In lending David books, she is, in fact, the white counterpart of Miss Johnson by virtue of her attempts to broaden the young boy's horizons.

Sounder is the antithesis of the black exploitation films that were made in the early 1970's, including *Super Fly* (1972), *Shaft* (1971), and *Blacula* (1972). It refuses to deal in racial stereotypes and instead presents fully rounded human beings. The performances match the serious intent of the director and of writer Lonne Elder III, who developed the rather spare William Armstrong novella which had won the prestigious Newbery Prize for children's fiction.

Tyson, bony and rangy inside her floppy, faded print dresses, plays Rebecca as a woman with unexpected reserves of strength and a ferocious desire to keep her family together. Tyson is an intelligent performer, and she endows Rebecca with a dignity and tenderness which earned her an Oscar nomination for Best Actress. Winfield is hearty in the opening scenes, but in the climactic sequence with Hooks by the river, he is subdued; although still a loving, vigorous man, he is now touchingly concerned with helping his son get on in the world. Hooks himself is amazing, a totally self-possessed teenager who is wide-eyed, respectful, but determined to have his way. The son of actor Robert Hooks, he does an absolutely solid job, at once eager and alive, yet reticent and watchful. He gives a performance of great variety and intuition. MacLachlan is equally fine in her small part, but there is a problem with the character she plays. One cannot help wondering why Miss Johnson does not try to help David find his father, especially since she lives near the labor camp.

Another problem is the film's title, since Sounder is hardly a leading character. This is not a typical boy-and-his-dog drama, so there is no particular reason to name the film after the dog. Sounder's toughness and stamina, which might be linked to Nathan's, are not explored by the filmmakers. The title survives, somewhat pointlessly, from the book.

Prejudice is not a major theme of *Sounder*, but it is a recurring part of the subtext. The "justice" that white men mete out to blacks, as exemplified by Nathan's sentence of a year at hard labor, is doubtlessly disproportionate compared with that imposed on whites. Such facts as exploitation by landowners and store proprietors and unequal education are all a part of the world in which David Morgan must grow up and from which Nathan wants him to escape. Nathan has no choice, but David does. The exercise of his options, his coming to maturity, and his eventual liberation through education are the real themes of *Sounder*.

Sounder is a touching and inspiring film, and although it may err by staying on the safe side of the issues it raises, it is nevertheless an ambitious and insightful film. The success of *Sounder* led to a sequel entitled *Part 2, Sounder* in 1976. Although that film was well received critically, its principal actors were different and it was not as financially successful as its predecessor.

Judith M. Kass

SPARTACUS

Released: 1960
Production: Kirk Douglas for Bryna/Universal-International
Direction: Stanley Kubrick
Screenplay: Dalton Trumbo; based on the novel of the same name by Howard Fast
Cinematography: Russell Metty (AA)
Editing: Robert Lawrence
Art direction: Alexander Golitzen and Eric Orbom; set decoration, Russell A. Gausman and Julie Heron (AA)
Costume design: Valles and Bill Thomas (AA)
Music: Alex North (AA)
Running time: 196 minutes

Principal characters:
Spartacus	Kirk Douglas
Marcus Licinius Crassus	Laurence Olivier
Varinia	Jean Simmons
Lentulus Gracchus	Charles Laughton
Lentulus Batiatus	Peter Ustinov (AA)
Antoninus	Tony Curtis
Julius Caesar	John Gavin
Draba	Woody Strode
Glabrus	John Dall

When *Spartacus* was filmed, it was reported to be the most expensive motion picture ever produced in Hollywood. Filmed in Technicolor and Super Technirama 70, it sported a cast of thousands, with the leads played by some of the biggest names in the business. It was reputedly filmed at a cost of more than four million dollars, a modest amount today when budgets are significantly higher.

Spartacus (Kirk Douglas) is the name of a third-generation Thracian slave who is sold to Lentulus Batiatus (Peter Ustinov), the operator of a gladiator school at Capua. The early scenes at the gladiatorial school are the best in the film; once the slaves escape and begin to gain power throughout the empire, it is not easy to top the initial interest they generate. A great Roman general, Marcus Licinius Crassus (Laurence Olivier), on his way to Rome, pauses at Capua and orders as entertainment a gladiatorial battle to the death. The two women of the general's party select the two slaves who will fight to the death to entertain them. They choose the two strongest and most virile men in the slaves' quarters: Draba (Woody Strode), a giant black man, and the Thracian Spartacus. The two men are despondent because they have been friendly in the compound and have only admiration for each other, and now one must kill the other. Spartacus had earlier been given Varinia (Jean Simmons), a slave, to be his woman, and she watches the gladiatorial battle in dread horror, for Spartacus is obviously no match for the superhuman Draba. The black man gains the advantage over Spartacus, but when given the sign to kill, Draba refuses to do so, and instead charges on the spectator's box in an insane rage. A guard spears him in the back, and Crassus finishes him off with a knife thrust in the neck.

Spartacus broods over the murder of his friend and is comforted by Varinia who reveals her love to him. Spurred into open revolt, he awaits his chance and leads the gladiators in a bold rebellion, slaying the guards and escaping with a band of slave warriors into the open country. Varinia goes willingly with Spartacus, and they vow never to part. Word spreads of the revolt, and slaves from all over the empire leave their masters to join the army of slaves, who march upon the Roman camps, scattering them and killing those who would force them into a new bondage. In their struggle to maintain their freedom, the growing band of slaves develops a feeling for the right of all people to fight for freedom.

In Rome, the Senate is in a turmoil of revolt itself, for Crassus loathes the mob which Lentulus Gracchus (Charles Laughton), a political leader, attempts to control. He is absent from the Senate on one occasion, and Gracchus seizes the opportunity to suggest that Glabrus (John Dall), a young protégé of Crassus, who is commander of the Roman garrison, be sent to destroy Spartacus and his army. Crassus, learning of this treachery, has his Roman legions march out of the city by a secret route. In Crassus' household is an attractive slave, Antoninus (Tony Curtis), whom he covets sexually; but before he can make known his desires, Antoninus quietly escapes and joins the army of Spartacus, bringing him information that the Roman legions are on the march. Spartacus ambushes and slaughters Glabrus' legion and then leads his men to the southern coast, where he has bribed Arabian pirates for ships in which the escaped slaves hope to sail for their homelands. The Roman bribes are more generous, however, and the pirate ships never show up.

The only alternative now open to Spartacus is to attack the Roman legions commanded by Crassus. In the battle that ensues, the three armies of Crassus destroy the slave army of sixty thousand men. Batiatus is hired to search the dead and wounded slaves and find Spartacus, so that all will know for certain that he is dead and no longer to be feared. Varinia is found with her new born baby, and she tells Batiatus that Spartacus has been slain. Actually, Spartacus has been captured as an anonymous slave and is being marched to Rome with six thousand other captives who have survived, only to be crucified as they march. The crucifixes erected by the Roman army line both sides of the road to Rome. Only Spartacus and Antoninus reach the city, where they are taken into Crassus' household as slaves. Varinia has also been taken into the house of Crassus with her baby. Crassus is puzzled and angered over this beautiful woman whose love he desires but cannot possess. In spite of all his power and wealth, she remains loyal to her husband and lover. Crassus is certain now that one of the two new captive slaves in his household is Spartacus, and he orders a fight to the death between the two, followed by crucifixion of the winner. Not wanting Spartacus to hang upon a cross, Antoninus attempts to kill his friend, but Spartacus in the struggle manages to slay Antoninus out of mercy. The victor, Spartacus is crucified on a cross outside the gates of Rome.

Gracchus, knowing that his own power has ended because Crassus has saved the empire, makes a deal with Batiatus to kidnap Varinia and her child from the house of Crassus. Batiatus brings them to Gracchus, who sets them free and orders Batiatus to take them by cart and horse to some land where they may start a new life. Gracchus then takes his own life. Spartacus, hanging still alive on the cross outside the gates of Rome, sees Varinia, and she holds up their son for him to look upon before the guard drives the horse and cart on. He then dies, knowing that he has triumphed in life because he has been given a love that not even Crassus, with all his power, could buy, and knowing that his own son will be free.

The three-hour-and-sixteen-minute story of *Spartacus* is a magnificent pageant of the ancient world and commands attention wherever it is shown in its original release form. Douglas, who not only played Spartacus but also was head of Bryna, which produced the picture, was wise in his choice of young Stanley Kubrick, who had directed only four previous features, to direct *Spartacus*. Kubrick has made it a film of exciting stature and power. He was given the right to supervise the first editing to his own satisfaction, but when Douglas viewed that version in the studio, he ordered the film back into production to reshoot scenes that featured him in addition to a number of close-ups of himself that Kubrick had not ordered. Word also leaked out that Kubrick had been so captivated by Olivier's performance as Crassus that the major footage in the Kubrick-approved version had favored him, rather than the title character. Even in the film's final form, Olivier's Crassus, the handsomest, cruellest, most intelligent general of pagan Rome, dominates, perhaps because as an actor Olivier cannot be dominated or suppressed. Douglas commands sympathy in the title role, and his love for the exquisite Varinia is completely believable. The supporting cast also contributes superlative performances. Ustinov won an Academy Award for his supporting performance as Batiatus, owner of the gladiatorial school, while Laughton is superb as Gracchus, the plebeian political leader of Rome. There are outstanding performances by Curtis as Antoninus, the singer of songs, and by John Gavin, extremely attractive and aristocratic as a young Julius Caesar.

Douglas is also to be applauded for employing Dalton Trumbo to write the screenplay from the Howard Fast novel. In the McCarthy era, both Trumbo and Fast had suffered blacklisting; in fact, it took Trumbo many years to get his name back on the credits of films he wrote. Having purchased the film rights to a novel written by a politically suspect novelist, Douglas engaged a screenplay writer who was even more suspect and boldly insisted that Trumbo have his proper credit under his real name. The Fast novel was virtually presold as an interesting film property; it had already sold more than three million copies and had been translated into no less than forty-five languages when Douglas acquired the movie rights.

It is true that there is a great deal of wanton cruelty and violence shown in *Spartacus*, but the story is based upon historical fact, and describes an age when slavery was part of the way of life and slaves were victims of the most inhuman and abusive kind of treatment. *Spartacus* is a moving drama of one man's search for his rights, his struggle to establish himself and those he loves as human beings, and his fight to maintain freedom of thought and action. The film is a dramatic plea for mercy, for the right of every man to achieve human dignity in his way of life. Seen today, its impact is still strong, and the story it tells remains inspiring and engrossing.

DeWitt Bodeen

SPITFIRE
(THE FIRST OF THE FEW)

Released: 1942
Production: Leslie Howard for Misbourne-British Aviation
Direction: Leslie Howard
Screenplay: Anatole de Grunwald and Miles Malleson; based on an original story by Henry C. James and Katherine Strueby
Cinematography: Jack Hilyard
Editing: Douglas Myers
Running time: 117 minutes

Principal characters:
R. J. Mitchell	Leslie Howard
Geoffrey Crisp	David Niven
Diana Mitchell	Rosamond John
Commander Bride	Roland Culver
Lady Houston	Tonie Edgar Bruce

Although he was born in England, Leslie Howard first achieved great success as an actor—on both stage and screen—in the United States. He is today probably best remembered for his roles in three American films, *Of Human Bondage* (1934), *The Petrified Forest* (1936), and *Gone With the Wind* (1939), as well as for one British film, *Pygmalion* (1938). Indeed, he never lost touch with England, and when World War II broke out, he volunteered to do anything he could for England's war effort. At forty-six, he was too old to serve in the military, but he was soon busy making propaganda films and weekly radio broadcasts in England. Then, on May 21, 1943, he was killed when the Germans shot down a passenger airplane in which he was returning to England from Lisbon. The Nazis had never before molested such passenger planes, but apparently they believed that Winston Churchill was aboard that flight. Howard's covert war activities have been the subject of much speculation over the years, both in print and popular legend, but his exact role has yet to be satisfactorily explained.

Spitfire marked Howard's last appearance on film and is a fine example of his war effort as well as a good film in itself. It is the story of Reginald Joseph Mitchell (Leslie Howard), the man who designed the Spitfire fighter plane that was instrumental in England's turning back the Nazi aerial assault.

After an opening montage that shows the early German conquests and the predictions of the Nazi leaders that Britain will be conquered in a short time, the film shows an English fighter station on September 15, 1940, the day that will see the Royal Air Force down 185 Nazi planes. A group of fighter pilots is talking about the Spitfire plane and its inventor, but no one knows much about the inventor, although they have unrestrained admiration for the aircraft itself. Their station commander, Geoffrey Crisp (David Niven), informs them that he knew Mitchell, the man who designed the plane, well. As he begins to tell Mitchell's story, the film flashes back to 1922.

We see Mitchell and his wife Diana (Rosamond John) enjoying a seaside holiday. Mitchell spends much of his time studying the flight of seagulls through binoculars. He thinks that an airplane should be designed to look more like the streamlined body of a bird than the almost boxlike shapes with many supporting struts that were used at that time. After his holiday, however, he finds that his superiors at Supermarine Aviation have no enthusiasm for his new ideas. In fact, they think he should go back to working in the assembly shop for a while to get some practical experience.

It is at this point that Crisp enters Mitchell's story as he comes looking for a job. He had gone to school with Mitchell and had been a pilot in World War I. Mitchell accepts him warmly and explains his ideas for a new type of airplane; Crisp volunteers to fly the plane as soon as it is built. Mitchell, however, still cannot convince the Supermarine board of directors that his ideas are sound.

Then, at a meeting called for Supermarine to plan its entry for the next Schneider Cup race, an annual international seaplane race that was an important factor in aircraft design and national prestige in the 1920's and early 1930's, Mitchell tells the board that he can build a plane that will win, but it must be completely his own design; otherwise he will resign. The board members cannot accept this; so Mitchell leaves the room with his plans under his arm and faces the prospect of having to find a job outside aviation, a prospect which he describes as giving up something he was "meant to do." His wife supports his decision and tells him that his designs will be accepted someday. That day comes sooner than expected, when, only one week after his resignation, he is called by Commander Bride (Roland Culver), his only supporter on the Supermarine board, and invited back to build his plane.

Mitchell's problems are not over, however; his first plane crashes when Crisp, who is flying it as he had hoped, faints as he rounds a turn in the Schneider Cup race. Then, in 1927, Mitchell gets his first Schneider Cup victory. The speed trial of his next plane kills the pilot, but Mitchell is roused from his depression over this event when he finds that the Vickers armaments company has bought Supermarine for 500,000 pounds just to acquire Mitchell's services. Given virtual *carte blanche* by Vickers, the designer responds with another Schneider Cup-winning plane. In 1931, beset by economic hard times, the English government decides not to enter the Schneider competition because of the 100,000 pounds it will cost. Only the intervention of Lady Houston (Tonie Edgar Bruce) with a 100,000 pound check enables Mitchell to enter and win another Cup race, posting the then-unheard-of speed of 340 miles per hour.

After that victory, Mitchell feels that he has done all he can do in aviation until a 1933 holiday in Germany with Crisp leads to the most important job of his life. In Germany he meets some boastful men in the aircraft industry who tell him that they have forgotten the Versailles Treaty, which does not allow them to build military airplanes. They will not be underdogs for long, they tell him; they will be overlords.

Upon returning to England, Mitchell puts all his energy into designing the "fastest and deadliest" fighter plane possible and convincing the authorities that it is vitally necessary. It will be, he says, "a bird that spits fire . . . a spitfire bird." The night-and-day effort takes its toll on his health, however, and he is told by a doctor that only a year of rest will enable him to live more than a year. Mitchell decides that his work is more important than his life and strives to finish his work in eight months. When his wife finds out the seriousness of his illness, she persuades him to go away with her for a rest. At just that moment, however, he sees a newspaper headline: "German Bombers Wipe Out Spanish Town," and both of them then realize that he cannot stop.

Finally the first Spitfire is built. By now Mitchell is confined to a wheelchair, but when Crisp tests the new plane, he flies by Mitchell's house and gives him the thumbs up sign. His only remaining concern is whether the British government will decide to build more of the planes. Soon after he gets the affirmative word from the government, R. J. Mitchell falls asleep and dies.

For its closing sequence, *Spitfire* returns to September 15, 1940. Crisp tells his men that Mitchell died a happy man and then accompanies them as they take to the air against the attacking German planes. After they defeat the attackers, Crisp turns his face up to the sky and says, "They can't take the Spitfires, Mitch." The film ends with Winston Churchill's famous quotation about the Royal Air Force: "Never in the field of human conflict was so much owed by so many to so few." This is, of course, the source of the British title of the film, *The First of the Few*.

To some extent *Spitfire* is a standard cinematic story of an inventor overcoming opposition and setbacks to achieve success and vindication. It rises above the ordinary, however, largely because of the low-key approach in its writing, acting, and directing, which gives it a realistic rather than melodramatic tone. Howard must be given most of the credit for this effective means of presentation because he not only played the lead role but also produced and directed the film. Several montage sequences effectively convey such processes as the building of the Spitfire, and Howard is well supported by John as his wife and Niven as Geoffrey Crisp, the only major character who has an outgoing personality. *Spitfire* must have been inspiring in wartime, and it is still moving today.

Marilynn Wilson

SPLENDOR IN THE GRASS

Released: 1961
Production: Elia Kazan for Warner Bros.
Direction: Elia Kazan
Screenplay: William Inge (AA)
Cinematography: Boris Kaufman
Editing: Gene Milford
Running time: 124 minutes

Principal characters:
Wilma Dean Loomis (Deanie)	Natalie Wood
Bud Stamper	Warren Beatty
Ace Stamper	Pat Hingle
Mrs. Loomis	Audrey Christie
Ginny Stamper	Barbara Loden
Angelina	Zohra Lampert
Doc Smiley	John McGovern
Del Loomis	Fred Stewart
Mrs. Stamper	Joanna Roos

The films of Elia Kazan frequently break new ground in terms of thematic content. *Gentlemen's Agreement*, made in 1947, took a stern look at anti-Semitism; *Pinky*, featuring Jeanne Crain, was a 1949 film about a "colored" girl passing for white; and *On the Waterfront*, made in 1954, examined the corrupt harbor unions of New York. Alongside these Kazan titles, *Splendor in the Grass*, although richly atmospheric with sturdy performances, has a story line that, viewed in the 1980's, appears weak, particularly when compared to contemporary motion pictures with explicit sexual themes. In 1961 when *Splendor in the Grass* was released, however, it was the year's most controversial film. Its themes of parental domination, moral codes, young love, and sexual frustration all come into conflict against the setting of a small Kansas town during the late 1920's.

The relatively simple story line follows high-school sweethearts Wilma Dean Loomis (Natalie Wood), known as Deanie, and Bud Stamper (Warren Beatty), who are in love and want to progress beyond the hand-holding stage. Although sexually frustrated, they are nevertheless bound to conventional moral standards. When they turn to their parents and other adults in authority, such as the family doctor (John McGovern), for advice, they are confronted with hypocrisy. In confusion, Deanie and Bud ultimately part without even physically consummating their love. Consequently, their sexual desires have not subsided, and, as a result, Deanie suffers a mental breakdown while Bud has a moral one. At the film's end, after some passage of time, the two meet again. Their once-shattered lives have been patched up. Something was lost, and something was gained.

Splendor in the Grass is the first story written directly for the screen by Pulitzer Prize-winning playwright William Inge, who received an Oscar for the screenplay. The story line is actually based on a fragment from Inge's own youth, which he had told to Kazan when Kazan was directing Inge's *The Dark at the Top of the Stairs* on Broadway. The film's title comes from William Wordsworth's "Ode on Intimations of Immortality." The full quotation reads: "Though nothing can bring back the hour, / Of splendor in the grass, / Glory in the flower, / We will grieve not, rather find / Strength in what remains behind." When called upon to decipher the passage's meaning in a scene in the classroom, Deanie is moved to tears and runs from the class. The film itself then becomes an illustration of Wordsworth's lines as Deanie and Bud live them out.

Deanie is the daughter of a meek but well-meaning butcher named Del (Fred Stewart). Her domineering mother (Audrey Christie), who has always been physically repelled by men, has tried to instill her own fears into Deanie, and she is appalled when she learns that her daughter is having sexual conflicts. Bud is the son of Ace Stamper (Pat Hingle), a self-made millionaire whose own moral code is ambivalent. There are good girls, and there are loose girls—and the latter, he tells Bud, are "fair game." Bud's confusion is compounded because, although Deanie is a "good" girl, she also arouses his sexual passion.

Bud also faces pressures concerning his future. Although he wants to attend an agricultural college, his father wants him to go to Yale and excel in sports. Bud's mother (Joanna Roos), a weak woman continually overruled by her husband, can do little to help her son. When Bud's older sister, Ginny (Barbara Loden), returns home from college a failure, Bud is pressured even more to attend Yale and to become a success. Ginny has also returned home with a bad reputation—which she lives up to during a Christmas country-club dance. She has a sexual escapade with a group of rowdy locals in a sordid scene that begins with heavy drinking, pawing, and mauling inside the dance hall, then erupts into passion in parked cars outside. Bud witnesses the whole thing and, in anger, tries to fight off some of the men. A bloody melee ensues. For Bud the sexual scene has increased his own torment, but now he does not want to turn to Deanie for comfort.

Instead, he makes a point of ignoring her, and also succumbs to the advances of a promiscuous girl at school, and the two make love under a waterfall. Deanie is aware of what Bud is doing, but, unable to comprehend fully his reasons, she begins to suffer from melancholia. Her parents are advised to take her to a psychiatrist, but they fail to heed the warnings and Deanie's troubles continue. Particularly effective is a bathtub sequence in which Deanie goes into a hysterical fit, flailing about, laughing and crying uncontrollably, while her mother helplessly watches. Later, she pulls herself together enough to attend the school prom. Seductively dressed, she seeks out Bud and begs him to make love to her, but, insensitive to her mentally frail state, he balks, thinking that it is not what Deanie really wants. Deanie's breakdown then becomes complete and she tries to kill herself by jumping into the river. She is placed in a Wichita sanatorium, where she begins to pick up the pieces of her broken life. Bud, meanwhile, goes to Yale, which is not what he wants, although he puts up with it for his father. Ace continues to dominate his son's life and, at one point, during a visit, even sends a prostitute to Bud's room in order to raise his son's spirits. When the stock market crashes in 1929, Ace jumps from a hotel window to his death, and Bud at last finds a kind of peace.

Deanie is also finding peace at the sanatorium. She knows she is getting better when her parents visit and she is able to shrug off her mother's complaints and attempts at domination. Her father is also revealing a new sense of strength and concern. A young medical student, who was also a patient at the sanatorium, falls in love with her, and when Deanie finally returns home she is contemplating a future with him. First, however, she is anxious to see Bud, and when several girl friends drop by the Loomis home to welcome her home, Deanie expresses this desire. Her mother is insistent that she must not see Bud again, but Deanie finds an ally in her father, who tells her where Bud is now living. With her girl friends, Deanie drives down a dusty road to Bud's ramshackle house and farm. What Deanie does not know is that Bud has married a New Haven waitress and now has a family. After a brief conversation alone with Bud, they are joined by Angelina (Zohra Lampert), Bud's simple but earnest wife. When Deanie finally leaves, she and Bud have reached an unspoken understanding. It is as if they are each now entirely different people. Happiness, she tells her friends, is no longer what she thinks about. Like Bud, she is reconciled to the life ahead of her.

Splendor in the Grass is marked by its vivid atmosphere. The story line takes place between the years 1928 and 1932, and Kazan is particularly effective in delivering the feeling of changing time periods, moving from the upbeat Jazz Age of the 1920's to the Depression-filled 1930's. The film also marks the first screen appearance of Beatty, in the role of Bud; Kazan brought Beatty to the screen after just one Broadway stage appearance, in Inge's *A Loss of Roses*. A number of critics thought that Beatty displayed some of the moody, brooding qualities of James Dean (who was also directed by Kazan, in *East of Eden*, a 1954 film about a youth in conflict with parents and surroundings. Wood as Deanie delivers one of her finest performances and one for which she was nominated for an Oscar.

As originally filmed, *Splendor in the Grass* caused some concern among Hollywood's censors. They disliked the original bathtub sequence, in which Wood runs naked away from the camera, from the tub and down the hall to her room. Although nudity was emerging in European productions, the *Splen-*

dor in the Grass sequence marked the first time that the star of a feature-length American film was naked, but at the insistence of the censors, the studio ordered the scene cut.

Pat H. Broeske

STAGE DOOR

Released: 1937
Production: Pandro S. Berman for RKO/Radio
Direction: Gregory La Cava
Screenplay: Morrie Ryskind and Anthony Veiller; based on the play of the
same name by Edna Ferber and George S. Kaufman
Cinematography: Robert de Grasse
Editing: William Hamilton
Running time: 92 minutes

Principal characters:
Terry Randall (Sims)	Katharine Hepburn
Jean Maitland	Ginger Rogers
Anthony Powell	Adolphe Menjou
Kaye Hamilton	Andrea Leeds
Judy Canfield	Lucille Ball
Eve	Eve Arden
Linda Shaw	Gail Patrick
Catherine Luther	Constance Collier
Stringbean	Ann Miller
Henry Sims	Samuel S. Hinds

Stage Door is about the dreams and aspirations of a group of struggling
actresses in a theatrical boarding house in New York. The film is a brisk,
brilliant, and funny comedy with a star-studded cast well directed by Gregory
La Cava. In the opening scene, the living room of the Footlights Club, a
slightly seedy Manhattan boarding house, is filled with women, all of whom
seem to be talking or arguing loudly. Into this turmoil comes Terry Randall
(Katherine Hepburn), a rich, well-dressed, and cultivated young woman who
takes the theater very seriously and wants to live in a theatrical atmosphere.
Terry's wealth and superior attitude, however, provoke immediate antipathy
from the other residents, particularly Jean Maitland (Ginger Rogers). Terry's
complete opposite temperamentally, Jean is flippant and earthy, often using
wisecracks and insults to hide her feelings. Jean's acid comments when she
finds that Terry has been assigned to be her roommate are shrugged off by
Terry with the remark that such insolence is probably the result of an "inferior
upbringing."

As the other boarders are discussing what is wrong with Terry, Kaye Hamilton (Andrea Leeds) returns tired, depressed, and hungry from a fruitless
day spent in producers' offices. She is obviously well liked by all the boarders,
especially by Jean, to whom she confides her disappointments and her burning
desire to be cast in the lead of a new play, *Enchanted April*. High-strung and
acutely sensitive, Kaye does not have enough money to pay her rent at the

boarding house and does not eat meals there in hopes that they will not ask her for the money she owes. To save her pride she pretends she eats elsewhere, although the others suspect the true state of things. Like Terry, Kaye takes herself and her profession very seriously, but unlike Terry she is gentle, kind, and unpretentious.

Terry's attempts to discuss William Shakespeare at dinner are ridiculed and greeted with wisecracks. Eve (Eve Arden), the resident needler, comments that Terry seems to have "an awful crush on Shakespeare," provoking Terry to remark scornfully that they are all trying too hard to be comic and do not take anything seriously. One of the strengths of the film is the deft way it interweaves the stories of the various residents of the boarding house, using the contrasting personalities to add variety to what is essentially the well-worn story of young people trying to break into show business.

One main character who does not live at the Footlights Club is the Broadway producer Anthony Powell (Adolphe Menjou). He immediately becomes interested in Jean when he sees her rehearsing a tap-dance routine with her lanky partner Stringbean (Ann Miller). Jean, however, is made uneasy by his attention and responds sarcastically to his questions. Powell is not discouraged by Jean's lack of enthusiasm, however, and uses his influence to get her and Stringbean a job in a nightclub. At first Jean does not realize that Powell got them the job and wants to avoid any entanglement with him, but when she learns the truth, she reluctantly agrees to go out with him, feeling she must protect her job. Soon, however, she succumbs to his practiced charm and believes herself in love with him despite the warnings she gets from Linda Shaw (Gail Patrick), a cast-aside girl friend of Powell who also lives at the Footlights Club.

We soon see Powell in his penthouse trying to seduce Jean in just the way Linda had previously described to her. Displaying photographs of his wife and son, he tells Jean his wife will not divorce him. Then, after his butler serves them champagne, he lowers the lights to create a more romantic mood and promises to put Jean's name in lights on a marquee on Broadway. We can only be amazed that the practical, knowledgeable Jean is taken in by all this, but Powell's plans go awry when Jean becomes upset and begins to cry, and he quickly sends her home in his car.

Meanwhile, Terry has bet Eve and Judy (Lucille Ball) that she will be able to see Powell at his office. The next day they are waiting in the reception room to see if she succeeds when Kaye arrives, expecting to read the part of the lead in *Enchanted April*. When Powell's secretary cancels the appointment, Kaye faints just as Terry arrives. Enraged, Terry storms into Powell's office and gives him a stern lecture about not seeing people. Later, Powell invites Terry to his penthouse and tells her he wants her to play the lead in *Enchanted April* (which the money of a mysterious backer has now made it possible for him to produce). Knowing that Jean is still infatuated with Powell, Terry decides to open her eyes to his true character. When Jean arrives at the penthouse, Terry contrives to be found in a compromising position. After Jean's angry departure, Powell proceeds to try out his usual routine on Terry, who believes none of it. She informs him that she does not want to be molded and believes in acting with her brain. She also tells him that she recognizes the photographs and knows that his supposed wife and son are fakes he uses to protect himself against entanglements. Although she antagonizes Powell by constantly arguing with him, he inexplicably still offers her the role coveted by Kaye. When Kaye hears that Terry has gotten the role, she is brokenhearted but generously insists that Terry deserves her chance in the theater too.

Rehearsals for *Enchanted April* do not progress smoothly. Terry pays little attention to the director, arguing constantly with him and the author of the play and delivering her lines woodenly and amateurishly. On opening night Kaye, now very weak and supposed to be in bed, comes to wish a nervous Terry good luck, offering at the same time some thoughtful suggestions on interpreting the role. Then, overwrought after her visit with Terry, Kaye jumps from an upstairs window and is killed.

At the theater, a heartbroken Jean goes backstage and tells Terry that she blames her for Kaye's death. Shattered, Terry at first refuses to go on, but in the best tradition of the theater pulls herself together, goes on, and gives a moving performance. She is immediately acclaimed as an important new actress. After the performance Powell learns that his mysterious wealthy backer is Henry Sims (Samuel S. Hinds), the "Wheat King," who also happens to be Terry's father. Opposed to her career in the theater, he had backed *Enchanted April* in hopes that Terry would be a failure and would then return home to pursue a more conventional career.

In the final scenes we learn that Terry, now referred to as an "eccentric debutante" by the newspapers, is still living at the Footlights Club and still rooming with Jean, now her close friend. As life goes on at the Footlights Club a new arrival comes to inquire about a room, and the cycle begins again, unaffected by Terry's triumph or Kaye's tragedy.

To attribute the wit and brilliance of *Stage Door* to its director, La Cava, is perhaps to overstate the case only slightly. La Cava (who also directed one of the best screwball comedies of the 1930's, *My Man Godfrey*, 1936), demanded and received more control of the film than was usual for directors in Hollywood at that time. He selected the cast and approved the sets, costumes, and musical score for the film. Perhaps his most important contribution besides directing the film, however, was reworking and rewriting the script. It is based on the hit Broadway play by George S. Kaufman and Edna Ferber but was significantly changed in the adaptation by Anthony Veiller, Morrie Ryskind, and La Cava. Not only did they eliminate many sarcastic references to Hollywood, but they also sent stenographers to casting offices and reception rooms in Hollywood to obtain much of the dialogue used in the film. The result is a screenplay more distinguished, many believe, than the play upon which it was based. La Cava's philosophy of directing was "If you can't be good, be quick." In *Stage Door* he is both. The film never loses momentum or interest as he deftly interweaves and balances the contrasting personalities and stories of the women living at the Footlights Club.

The cast is uniformly excellent, a fine example of ensemble playing, but Rogers as Jean Maitland and Hepburn as Terry Randall must be singled out for special praise. In one of her best performances, Rogers—who already had shown her ability as a fine light comedienne—proved that she could handle a dramatic role as well. Hepburn, whose career was in the doldrums at the time, is impresssive as the serious aristocrat (a role reminiscent of her earlier, Oscar-winning performance in *Morning Glory*, 1933). Indeed, some of the incidents in the film are loosely based on Hepburn's past theatrical experiences. The scenes in the film from *Enchanted April*, for example, recall scenes from *The Lake*, a disastrous Broadway play in which Hepburn had appeared a few years earlier. The line "The calla lillies are in bloom again," which we hear her speak several times as she rehearses for *Enchanted April*, became part of the Hepburn legend, and has been used by mimics for more than forty years to identify her.

Leeds as the sensitive Kaye Hamilton is also outstanding, bringing warmth and credibility to a somewhat hackneyed role, and Arden and Ball are both perfect as the wise-cracking philosophers of the Footlights Club. Menjou is convincing as the cynical Broadway producer, a role he had already perfected in *Morning Glory*. *Stage Door* was not only critically acclaimed, but was also a hit at the box office.

Julia Johnson

STAGE FRIGHT

Released: 1950
Production: Alfred Hitchcock for Warner Bros.
Direction: Alfred Hitchcock
Screenplay: Whitfield Cook, with additional dialogue by James Bridie; based on Alma Reville's adaptation of the short stories "Man Running" and "Outrun the Constable" by Selwyn Jepson
Cinematography: Wilkie Cooper
Editing: Emard Jarins
Costume design: Milo Anderson and Christian Dior
Music: Leighton Lucas
Running time: 110 minutes

Principal characters:

Eve Gill	Jane Wyman
Charlotte Inwood	Marlene Dietrich
Inspector Wilfred Smith	Michael Wilding
Jonathan Cooper	Richard Todd
Commodore Gill	Alastair Sim
Nellie	Kay Walsh
Mrs. Gill	Sybil Thorndike
Bibulous gent	Miles Malleson
Freddie	Hector MacGregor
Shooting gallery attendant	Joyce Grenfell
Inspector Byard	André Morell
Chubby	Patricia Hitchcock

If *Stage Fright* had come from a less luminous director than Alfred Hitchcock, its sophistication probably would have looked very impressive. From the master of suspense, however, it was received as a somewhat tepid mystery with its real merit in some quiet British humor. The filming took place in England, Hitchcock's home ground, after a decade's work in America, and the director uses such top stars as Jane Wyman, fresh from her Academy Award-winning performance in *Johnny Belinda* (1948); Marlene Dietrich; Richard Todd, who had just been nominated for an Academy Award for *The Hasty Heart* (1949); Michael Wilding; Sybil Thorndike; Kay Walsh; Joyce Grenfell; and Alastair Sim, who plays Wyman's gabby, theatrical, would-be rascal father.

Wyman portrays American-educated (hence her accent) Eve Gill, a student at London's Royal Academy of Dramatic Art who, it becomes apparent, has a tendency to overdramatize everything rather naturally. She gets a real-life chance at character acting when her boyfriend, Jonathan Cooper (Richard Todd), confesses to her that he also has been involved with a musical comedy star named Charlotte Inwood (Marlene Dietrich), who has just implicated him in the murder of her husband. He claims Charlotte did it, although her maid Nellie (Kay Walsh) glimpsed him leaving the scene of the crime, which he tells Eve he had visited only to fetch a dress for Charlotte to replace her blood-stained one. With the help of her father, Eve hides Jonathan and sets out to prove him innocent and Charlotte guilty. The denouement finds the opposite to be unastonishingly true. Luckily, in the meantime Eve has fallen in love with the detective on the case, Smith (Michael Wilding).

Hitchcock has been quoted as professing no affection for *Stage Fright*, although he has made far worse films (such as the immediately preceding *Under Capricorn*, 1949, starring Ingrid Bergman). One of the reasons he has given is that Wyman does not go far enough in her plot masquerade as a Cockney maid, and, while overall Wyman makes a pretty, endearingly willful heroine, there is some foundation for Hitchcock's thesis. To get close to Charlotte, Eve manages to bribe the actress' regular maid Nellie to be ill and takes her place as her cousin. Adopting dowdy clothes, Eve slicks back her bangs, removes her make-up, and puts on thick glasses. The finishing touch is a cigarette dangling from pallid lips. She leaves her house, and then, to audience-test the disguise, rings her own bell. "I . . ." Her mother (Sybil Thorndike) interrupts, exclaiming, "Oh, there you are, Eve darling. Help me find my glasses. I can't see a thing." Obviously, less extreme measures will do, and Eve modifies her "cover," returning the glasses and fluffing her bangs a little. Wyman's accent is weak, however; this probably is what disturbed Hitchcock. Her Cockney surfaces mostly when she addresses Dietrich as "Mattam." Charlotte, in turn, absentmindedly beckons her as everything but Doris, the name she has taken for the ruse: "Phyllis . . . Elsie . . . Mavis."

Dietrich's characterization of Charlotte is that of an amusingly self-absorbed, gaudy figure. "Couldn't we let it plunge a little?," she asks her dressmaker, donning her new black mourning dress. When it is mentioned that the murderer might come to the theater, she scoffs, "The only murderer around here is the orchestra leader." Reportedly, Cole Porter wrote her big number, "The Laziest Girl in Town," especially for Dietrich, and it remained in her nightclub repertoire for many years. It serves, but nevertheless gives the feather-festooned singer lyrics not always consonant with her glamorous Teutonic image—"My heart is achin'/To bring home the bacon," for example. When the mystery is almost over, Dietrich, wearing a costume by Christian Dior, sadly reminds the drably dressed Doris, whom she seems to take pains never to have to look at, "We may never see each other again. . . ."

Sim, one of the finest character comedians England ever produced, has—if not exactly a fieldday—one of his best American exposures to that date. His sly, rakish touch does much to sustain interest. When the Commodore gives sanctuary to his daughter's homicide-suspected lover, he blurts after him that there are some good murder mysteries in his room, then quickly realizes his gaffe and adds, "Ah, beg your pardon." He and his drolly vague wife live apart—"I never could be bothered with your mother," he blithely tells Eve. Introduced to Smith, Mrs. Gill muses, "Smith. That name sounds familiar. . . . This is Eve's father. We see him now and again."

Wilding, whose mumbled dialogue Wyman later said had to be almost totally redubbed, is still unintelligible at times. With no help from the Whitfield Cook script (adapted by Mrs. Hitchcock, Alma Reville), Todd achieves some sympathy as the boyish-appearing but unbalanced, hair-trigger killer. Walsh displays an impressive repertoire of lower-working-class mannerisms as the pub-crawling, soon blackmailing maid. Toothsome Joyce Grenfell has an eccentrically amusing cameo in a shooting gallery—"Do come and shoot lovely ducks heah for half a crown"; while Hitchcock's daughter Patricia also has a few less funny moments as Wyman's school friend Chubby.

Stage Fright is far from a disaster. There are the seductive performances, and here and there an unmistakable Hitchcock touch: a field of shiny umbrellas in the rain, recalling the assassination scene from his *Foreign Correspondent* (1940) a decade earlier; a defiant corpse pressing against the closet from which a dress must be purloined quickly; the "hero's" escape from police into his car, which he locks, then finds stalled as his pursuers begin pounding on "safety glass" windows which break just as the car finally starts; a bribed child's walk down the aisle and up on the stage to deliver a blood-stained doll to the performing Dietrich; and Hitchcock himself, in his trademark flash, turning to look at Wyman talking to herself as he passes her on the street.

Hitchcock must have been impressed by his star's darkly expressive eyes so widely praised in *Johnny Belinda*; he makes good use of them in *Stage Fright* via innumerable close-ups. (She is much better photographed than most actresses in the less-than-lush British-made films of the day.) They are best utilized near the end when the well-meaning but meddling Eve and Jonathan are hiding in a theater prop room. A voice suddenly booms out to proclaim that Jonathan, the murderer after all, might now kill her. She plays almost this whole scene with him in close-up, shadows enveloping all but her great eyes, now an almost poetic mixture of sorrow, pity, and terror. She humors him until they come to the door, which she then bolts between them, screaming for help. Frantic, Jonathan is quelled when an iron curtain drop falls on him.

Stage Fright is not very frightening, but it has a bit of civilized wit and a group of skilled as well as likable troupers who mesh together to make an enjoyable, if not great, example of Hitchcock's artistry.

Doug McClelland

STAIRWAY TO HEAVEN
(A MATTER OF LIFE AND DEATH)

Released: 1946
Production: Emeric Pressburger and Michael Powell for J. Arthur Rank; released by Universal
Direction: Emeric Pressburger and Michael Powell
Screenplay: Emeric Pressburger and Michael Powell
Cinematography: Jack Cardiff
Editing: Reginald Mills
Production design: Alfred Junge
Special effects: Douglas Woolsey and Henry Harris
Running time: 104 minutes

Principal characters:
Peter D. Carter	David Niven
Doctor Frank Reeves	Roger Livesey
June	Kim Hunter
Abraham Farlan	Raymond Massey
Conductor 71	Marius Goring
Bob Trubshaw	Robert Coote
Judge/Surgeon	Abraham Sofaer
Young dead flyer	Richard Attenborough

Stairway to Heaven is one of the most successful fantasy films of all time. Made just after the close of World War II, it successfully combined the postwar feelings of hope with romance, special effects, and a philosophical belief in the innate justice of a good cause. The 1940's produced a number of very good fantasies which had supernatural themes. *Here Comes Mr. Jordan* (1941), *Heaven Can Wait* (1943), *It's a Wonderful Life* (1946), and *The Ghost and Mrs. Muir* (1947) were all successful films which had major sections of their plots devoted to life in the hereafter. *Stairway to Heaven*, like *Here Comes Mr. Jordan* and *Heaven Can Wait* (and *The Devil and Daniel Webster*, 1941, to a certain extent), has a main character whose fate is decided by celestial beings during the course of the action.

In *Here Comes Mr. Jordan* and in its remake, *Heaven Can Wait* (1978), a man who is wrongly taken by a representative from heaven convinces the higher authority to find him a suitable body in which to come back to life until his actual death date, some years in the future. In the 1943 *Heaven Can Wait* (whose only relationship to the 1978 film of the same name is the wording of the title), an old man who has died must wait at the gates of heaven, reviewing his whole life, in order to see if he will be sent to heaven or hell. *Stairway to Heaven* takes some aspects of these earlier films and has the main action of the story culminate at a heavenly trial, in a vein similar to *The Devil and Daniel Webster*.

Each of these films, dispite general similarities, is very different, and each, in its own way, is an excellent film. *Stairway to Heaven* is the only one of all of these, however, to rely extensively on special effects and lavish sets depicting heaven. The sets and special effects alone would have set it above the others, but not content to rely on gimmicks, filmmakers Emeric Pressburger and Michael Powell, "The Archers," who coproduced, codirected, and cowrote the film, created a marvelously well-written and well-acted drama as well.

After the film's credits, there is a short "disclaimer" which describes briefly what we will see: "a story of two worlds." One of these worlds is real, and the other exists in the mind of a young flyer. The last line of this disclaimer states, "Any connection between this world and any other world is purely coincidental." Then a narrator discusses the planets and the stars, and the vivid blue atmosphere gradually focuses in on a map of Western Europe where a city is in flames, having been attacked by a thousand bombers. The date is May 2, 1945 (two days before the end of World War II), and a young flyer who had participated in the airstrike is desperately calling for contact on his radio.

The flyer is David Niven, in his first nonwar-related film since his entrance into the British army in 1939. The plane is in a dense fog, and the only person that the flyer, whose name is Peter D. Carter, can contact is an American radio operator stationed in England named June (Kim Hunter). He tells her that he is going to jump from the plane and he will certainly die because there are no functional parachutes and he is running out of gas. All of the crew are dead, including his "sparks," Bob Trubshaw (Robert Coote), whom we see staring in a death gaze. In this brief conversation which takes place at a desperate moment, Peter and June fall in love, even though they realize that there is no hope. Then Peter jumps from the plane.

The next scene shows an unconscious Peter floating in the water as he is washed ashore. He gets up, looks at the deserted beach, and thinks that he is in heaven. When he sees a naked young boy sitting on the dunes playing an eerie tune on a pipe, the sight seems to confirm his suspicions. He feels euphoric, especially when he sees a dog and happily concludes that there must be animals in heaven, too, until the boy casually informs him of his whereabouts, Leighwood, England. When Peter realizes that this is the town where June lives, he sets off immediately to find her, only to have her ride by on her bicycle that very moment. When they realize who they each are, they are in love immediately. June cannot believe that Peter is still alive, and neither can Peter. They both conclude that it must be a miracle, and do not want to think about it anymore.

Now the action switches to a huge set that looks roughly like an airline terminal with numerous busy clerks wearing uniforms and a number of airmen. We realize that this is heaven because Bob is waiting for Peter to join him. One of the clerks assures him that if Peter were to die, he would surely be along at any moment, but Peter does not show up. Bob inquires whether there could be a mistake, but the clerk sternly tells him that there are no mistakes *here*. Then an alarm rings which confirms Bob's suspicions: there has been a mistake, and the person responsible is Conductor 71 (Marius Goring). As it happens, Conductor 71 (who is a Frenchman in eighteenth century dress) got lost in the English fog and was not able to find Peter. His superiors admonish him and instruct him to return to earth immediately and bring Peter, if it is not too late.

These two parallel actions are interesting photographically because, unlike the vast majority of films, which are either all color or all black-and-white, *Stairway to Heaven* has considerable portions of each. Whereas *The Wizard of Oz* (1939) was distinguished by black-and-white "real" action and color dream action, the real action of *Stairway to Heaven* is in color, but the dream world, heaven, is in black-and-white. This may seem to be a missed opportunity for some fantastic cinematography and colorful sets, but it goes along with the psychological aspect of the film. If, as the disclaimer states, the other world exists only in Peter's mind, then it would be more likely to be in black-and-white, as more dreams are in black-and-white than color. This would be true especially of a pragmatic type of person such as Peter.

Conductor 71 comes down to earth, looks directly at the audience, and jokes, "We are starved for Technicolor up there," then approaches Peter. Peter is just asking June if she wants another drink when time stops. They are in the countryside, having a picnic, and June, who is lying down, appears to be sleeping until Conductor 71 tells the incredulous Peter who he is. Peter does finally believe Conductor 71, but he refuses to leave because he has fallen in love with June. It would not have mattered yesterday, he says, but the extra time has brought him a love which he will not give up. Thus the main action and problem of the film is established. Peter will not leave June and life, while Conductor 71 must correct his error in the record books of heaven. A few days pass, and now we see that Peter, who has been suffering from extreme headaches, is staying at a military hospital. June is worried about him so she brings a friend from the village, Dr. Frank Reeves (Roger Livesey), to meet him. The two men get along well immediately, and after a few questions about peculiar odors or tastes which Peter is experiencing, Frank convinces Peter to come and stay with him for a few days. Frank soon discovers that Peter suffered a minor concussion two years before, and, as an expert in neurological disorders, he is certain that Peter has developed a tumor which must be removed.

While Peter is staying with Frank, his headaches become worse and his visits from the tenacious Conductor 71 become more frequent. (No one else ever sees Conductor 71, even though Frank and June try to be with Peter at all times.) Peter finally convinces Conductor 71 that he wants a "trial" in which to plead his case. The trial seems to be stacked against him, however, because Conductor 71 informs him that Abraham Farlan (Raymond Massey), one of the men killed at Lexington in 1775, will be the prosecuting attorney. Farlan hates the English, so Peter must find a defense attorney who will plead his case in the strongest manner possible.

The next few days become increasingly difficult for Peter. He spends most of his waking hours reading, trying to select a defense attorney from history. One day he tells Frank that the case is scheduled for that night, but that he has failed to get anyone to take his case. He desperately wants to live, but his exhaustion grows and his mental state is rapidly deteriorating. Frank realizes that Peter's operation must be that very night, and he makes all of the arrangements, even giving the surgeon extensive notes on other similar cases. As the time for the operation approaches, Frank calls for an ambulance, then leaves June and Peter at his home so that he will be able to get to the hospital first and prepare for the operation. In the blinding rain, however, the ambulance hits Frank's motorcycle and he is killed instantly. June at first does not want to tell Peter, who has come to depend on Frank almost completely during his illness, but when she finally does tell him, Peter decides that it is Frank who will now be his defense attorney at the trial.

Once this is resolved, we see the parallel action of Peter being prepared for surgery just as the celestial court is being convened. As Peter is wheeled into surgery and placed under the anesthetic, we see things from his point of view, literally in his head, as his eyelids close out the activities in the operating room. Now, on a seemingly endless stairway, Peter, dressed in his airman's uniform, ascends to heaven and the trial. Frank will be his attorney, and Bob is his chief witness. The one thing they lack, evidence, is taken from June in the form of a tiny tear rolling down her cheek which is proof of her love for Peter.

The trial is set in a massive, stadiumlike courtroom. There are groups representing every country of the world and every period of history, with most seats taken by English and American soldiers who have died in World War II. Farlan is smug and stern. He plans to base his case on the corruption of a young American girl by an Englishman, and he has selected a jury of several nations, each member of which has every reason to hate the English. When Frank objects, the judge (Abraham Sofaer) allows him to select a new jury, and he replaces them with naturalized American citizens. He hopes to show that the very fairness and justice of the American way of life will not allow his client to be punished for something which was beyond his control.

Through the course of the trial Farlan and Frank banter back and forth, each making salient points about the other cultures. There are a number of lofty yet meaningful speeches with suitable applause and scoffing from the audience. Finally the trial seems to be at a stalemate, and the only way to help Peter is to bring another witness, June, to the trial. Because she is still alive and cannot come to them, the principals of the trial descend the huge staircase and go into the operating room in which time again has been suspended. There they cross-examine June and discover that she loves Peter so much that she is willing to give up her own life for his, thus making the record books even. Peter is restrained from stopping her from walking onto the staircase, and she starts her ascent to heaven. Just then the staircase stops, however, and June is allowed to come back to earth. The jury finds unanimously for the defense and gives Peter a very generous new death date.

In the final scene, Peter wakes up in the hospital and tells June that he has won his case; the operation has also been a success. Thus we are left with the feeling that all of the heavenly scenes took place only within Peter's mind— except that a book on chess falls out of Peter's suitcase, a book which Conductor 71 had taken out of Frank's library.

When *Stairway to Heaven* opened during Christmas week in 1946 (coincidentally the same week that another film about heavenly intervention, *It's a Wonderful Life*, opened), *The New York Times* film critic Bosley Crowther gave it rave reviews, saying that it was the best film of the Christmas season, traditionally an important release time for films. Other critics on both sides of the Atlantic agreed with him. The film was first shown in England, where it was made, before King George VI, as the first Royal Premiere. As a lavishly produced, multistar film, it was one of the first British big-budget films after the war.

The film excels on almost every level. The script, one of many collaborative works by Pressburger and Powell, is complex yet easy to follow. At one point in the film when Frank is discussing Peter's case with another doctor, he says that Peter never steps out of the realm of possibilities of his fantasy. This could also be said of *Stairway to Heaven*. Within the context of a fantasy, everything is orderly and logical. All of the action could take place within Peter's imagination and, because of his tumor, seem just as real as Frank or June. The only loose end of the script is perhaps the explanation of Peter's miraculously safe return to earth from his plane. Frank says, more than once, that this might be the key to Peter's sanity, yet there is never an attempt to find an answer. This unanswered question, as in the book, may have been a deliberately placed loose end, however, included to make the fantasy more believable. Although it seems almost impossible that a man could bail out of an airplane over the English channel without a parachute and live, it is not totally impossible. One logical explanation could be that the fog, combined with the breakdown of the plane's instruments, shrouded the fact that the plane may have been gradually losing altitude and that when Peter jumped he was not far enough away from the water to cause his death.

The film's dialogue, which easily could have fallen into platitudes in the trial scenes, does not. What Frank and Farlan say is true and universal. In Frank's talk of love, he goes to the very core of man's desire for freedom and tolerance. Farlan seems pompous and Puritanical at first, but in the end, even he is shown to be a just man and someone worthy of a place in heaven. Unlike most films in which foreigners are portrayed, *Stairway to Heaven* is not populated with stereotypes and buffoons. Except for Conductor 71, who is something of a stereotyped film Frenchman, the Americans, Englishmen, and people of other nationalities portrayed are individuals, real and down-to-earth.

The film's special effects are especially noteworthy. The sequences in heaven with the long descending staircase are very imaginative, but the earthly sequences have some even better effects. In one scene Frank is in his *camera obscura*, and June comes to visit him. In a darkened room, Frank opens the camera and the entire village is seen in an oval space which looks like a movie screen. Frank and June are separated from the action of the village and placed above it in a parallel to what will happen when Frank is up in heaven defending Peter.

Jack Cardiff's cinematography is used for great effect when it shows Peter's point of view. A number of scenes are shot on angles so that the audience gets the feeling that they, too, are lying down, looking up at people standing over them. This technique was used quite frequently in the 1930's and 1940's, but it has since gone out of fashion. While it is tiresome to watch, in a film such as this, the technique definitely adds to the aura which the directors are trying to create.

The production design makes the celestial sequences particularly interesting. While the sets and properties of the earthly sequences are very ordinary and of a typically English vintage, the sets for heaven are grandiose. There is a feeling of massive space that pervades these scenes and dwarfs the actors. There are literally hundreds of actors in some of the scenes, yet they are never huddled together. As one of the heavenly authorities says, "there will be room for everyone," and in the courtroom this fact comes to life. The picture of a huge stadium or theater-in-the-round in which the spectators watch as someone's life hangs in the balance is an antecedent of a similar scene in *All That Jazz* (1979). The latter film is more lavish in its music and dancing, but it contains a definite parallel of the scene in *Stairway to Heaven*.

The acting by all of the principals is first-rate. Although Niven was the leading man of the film, its real hero is Livesey. He is not handsome or romantic, but his performance is both powerful and subdued. It is difficult to recite long speeches without appearing stuffy, but Livesey gives every line of Peter's defense feeling. Niven, too, is good in his role as Peter, although by the nature of the story, he must give up almost every scene, except the first, to others. Goring, an actor who frequently plays foreigners because of his facility with different accents and languages, is an enjoyable pixie as

Conductor 71. The powdered face and curly hair hide his rather severe features and enable him to play a sympathetic character. Conductor 71 is sneaky but also lovable, and we sense that he would like Peter to win his case. This is probably the only role which Goring has ever had in which he was not evil or sadistic, which is unfortunate, because he definitely has a flair for scene-stealing comedy.

The other members of the cast are also good both collectively and individually. Massey gives a typically stern performance, the type of thing on which he has based his career, but the typecasting does not detract from his excellence in the role. Hunter is good as June, but with the great actors in the film, she is somewhat overshadowed in a more subdued role. Coote has the only other reasonably large part in the film and is also characteristically good. The final well-known name in the film is Richard Attenborough, who is merely seen and not heard. He is billed as a dead flyer, above several other members of the cast with speaking parts without apparent reason. He had made a few films before this, most notably *In Which We Serve* (1942), but his career was yet to flourish as it did in the 1950's.

Stairway to Heaven is frequently shown on late-night television; but it has been critically glossed over since its premiere. This is unfortunate because it is a masterpiece. There are plans to remake the film, possibly with John Travolta and Olivia Newton-John as the young lovers, but a new production would have to work extremely hard to keep pace with the older version.

Patricia King Hanson

STALAG 17

Released: 1953
Production: Billy Wilder for Paramount
Direction: Billy Wilder
Screenplay: Billy Wilder and Edwin Blum; based on the play of the same name by Donald Bevan and Edmund Trczinski
Cinematography: Ernest Laszlo
Editing: Doane Harrison
Running time: 120 minutes

Principal characters:
Sefton	William Holden (AA)
Lieutenant Dunbar	Don Taylor
Oberst Von Scherbach	Otto Preminger
"Animal" Stosh	Robert Strauss
Harry	Harvey Lembeck
Hoffy	Richard Erdman
Price	Peter Graves
Duke	Neville Brand
Schulz	Sig Rumann
Cookie (Narrator)	Gil Stratton

There is something intrinsically appealing about a reluctant hero, a cynic who insists that he is only looking out for his own interests, but who ultimately reveals a need for solidarity with others. This kind of hero always redeems himself by confronting a given situation which has effectively defeated the energies of more selfless individuals. When such a hero suffers for his self-proclaimed callousness, he becomes even more sympathetic, as is effectively demonstrated by *Stalag 17*, a film about a group of American prisoners during World War II. It is a work by Billy Wilder, a writer and director who has often been considered as cynical as Sefton, the hero of his film, but who has increasingly revealed a sometimes repressed romanticism which has more recently forced a reconsideration of his entire body of work. *Stalag 17* is one of his most simple films, but it is also one of his most dramatically compelling. The major reason for this is that Sefton, a prisoner of war, becomes increasingly isolated from the other prisoners in a confined situation, and Wilder, who sees no other character deserving of the audience's identification, invests this isolation with precise emotional shadings which create so much tension that the audience yearns for Sefton's vindication.

Sefton (William Holden) draws attention to his apparent alienation from the other prisoners at the very outset of the story by betting cigarettes against the chances of two of the men surviving an escape attempt. When they are shot, the others become scornful of his apparent lack of sensitivity. Actually,

Sefton is not inhumane, as is made evident by his expression when the shots are heard. His fault lies in his lack of judgment in not realizing how his actions will be interpreted. A man's character might be complex, but in war, unambiguous solidarity against the enemy is expected. When later events convince the prisoners that there is a traitor in their midst, Sefton is the natural suspect. He trades with the enemy for favors such as visiting the neighboring camp of Russian women prisoners and his trunk contains riches that he only possesses through being a prisoner of war. Up to a point, it is difficult not to feel ambivalent toward him. When his fellow prisoners give him a savage beating, believing him to be the traitor more out of resentment than as a result of tangible evidence, this feeling of ambivalence changes. Sefton vows to uncover the real spy, who is actually a German passing as an American named Price (Peter Graves). After he succeeds and reveals the spy to the others, he makes a successful escape with Dunbar (Don Taylor), a war hero in danger of death from the Gestapo and a man whom Sefton dislikes on account of his inherited wealth in America. Sefton maintains as attitude of mock disdain for the other prisoners in the final scenes, which leaves them properly chastened in his absence.

The essentials of *Stalag 17* are brilliantly realized and its structure cannot be faulted. Within this structure, however, there are flaws, most evident in the first half of the film, when sympathy for Sefton can only develop gradually, and Wilder must make something interesting out of material in which the hero is not directly involved. There are several badly realized characters, notably the prisoner who delivers the mail and who is presented as a leader but is so ridiculously comic that he can never be taken seriously, and Dunbar's companion, a self-satisfied and conceited fellow who does imitations of movie stars. More damagingly, there is the character of Cookie (Gil Stratton), who narrates the story. In his narration, he comes across as intelligent and self-reliant, but in the story, he is presented for no apparent reason as Sefton's lackey and stooge, remaining loyal to Sefton for most of the film without giving an explanation for this inexplicable behavior.

In the role of the German commandant, Wilder cast Otto Preminger, himself a major director, and a man whose physical appearance and manner are perfect for the role. After a promising introduction, however, in which the commandant wryly apologizes to the prisoners for not giving them "a white Christmas . . . just like the ones you used to know," the character ceases to develop and is seen very little. Sig Rumann's Schulz ultimately becomes the German antagonist the story requires, which does a great deal to make up for the deficiency in the Preminger characterization.

The visual monotony of a film set mostly in a barracks, with a few well-placed exterior sequences, is overcome by Wilder, however, through imaginative camera placement and resourceful groupings of actors. Most of the characters do contribute positively to the telling of the story. Wilder is adept at concealing the identity of the real villain, and the script provides a perfect moment to reveal him. None of the barracks leaders—Hoffy (Richard Erdman), Price, and Duke (Neville Brand)—are notably sympathetic, but Duke registers strongly as Sefton's principal tormentor, and for that reason, he might reasonably be expected to be the spy. Appropriately, he is the first to admit his wrongheadedness when Sefton reveals the identity of the spy, who turns out to be Price. Low-comedy relief is provided by two inseparable characters, "Animal" (Robert Strauss) and his pal Harry (Harvey Lembeck). Some of the humor involving these two characters is strained, but the comic payoff works perfectly and is superbly placed during the Christmas celebration sequence, the finest in the film. Animal has throughout the film been tortured by thoughts of women, and of Betty Grable in particular. As the men dance, Harry approaches Animal in crude drag, and the drunken Animal believes he is dancing with Grable. Harry regrets the deception and reveals his identity, and Animal, previously seen only as a figure of fun, reacts with genuine anguish which is at once funny and unexpectedly moving.

Earlier in the Christmas sequence, which owes its excellence to richness of tone, Wilder creates the film's most dramatically moving moment. Sefton is alone on his bunk, recovering from the beating. His alienation is at its most intense as the other prisoners dance in a line up and down the barracks singing the stirring "When Johnny Comes Marching Home." The audience has just learned Price's true identity, and Sefton, by virtue of his isolation from the group, notices the shadow of a swinging light cord, part of Price's communications system. The patriotic spirit aroused by the song is something in which all of the men except Sefton may share as a group, and the visualization of the scene, enhanced by expressive lighting, gives quiet force to the hero's lonely resolve. As a result, when the Christmas sequence later reaches a climax at the moment in which Sefton emerges from the shadows after having witnessed a meeting between Price and Schulz and the camera closes in to reveal his pleasure of discovery, that pleasure is felt equally by the audience.

In all of his scenes, Holden is perfect as Sefton. He is credible in his cynicism but never far from having the audience's total sympathy. Even if it is conceded that Bryan Forbes's *King Rat* (1965) is a deeper and more moving treatment of a similar subject, it is fair to say that George Segal's interpretation of his role in that film owes something to Holden's in *Stalag 17*. Holden himself played another cynical prisoner-of-war in *The Bridge on the River Kwai* (1957), directed by David Lean, but his performance was overshadowed by Alec Guinness' powerful Oscar-winning role in the same film.

Holden ranks close to Jack Lemmon as an ideal Wilder player, having appeared in four films for the director, the first of which—*Sunset Boulevard* (1950)—effectively changed his screen image, which had previously been that of a bland romantic lead. It is likely that he won an Academy Award for his performance as Sefton because it is the kind of role in which an actor can make a strong impression, but that does not take away from the fact that he is central to the film and the key to its effectiveness.

Blake Lucas

THE STAR

Released: 1952
Production: Bert E. Friedlob for Twentieth Century-Fox
Direction: Stuart Heisler
Screenplay: Katherine Albert and Dale Eunson
Cinematography: Ernest Laszlo
Editing: Otto Ludwig
Running time: 90 minutes

Principal characters:
Margaret Elliot	Bette Davis
Jim Johannson	Sterling Hayden
Gretchen	Natalie Wood
Harry Stone	Warner Anderson
Peggy Morgan	Barbara Woodel
Margaret's sister	Fay Baker
Roy, Margaret's brother-in-law	David Alpert
Barbara Lawrence	Herself

In the short period of time between December of 1952 and August of 1953 two notable films were released that begin with the same crisis—a film star fears that his or her career may be over. One is *The Band Wagon* (1953) featuring Fred Astaire, and the other is *The Star* (1952) featuring Bette Davis. In both films the plight of the fictional character portrayed bears the same resemblance to the life of the actual person playing the part. In addition, both films begin with the same emblem of the star's decline in popularity—an auction of the star's personal effects at which the bids are pitifully low. Beyond these similarities, however, the two films are quite unlike, with different emphases, different themes, and different resolutions of the initial crisis.

In *The Star*, Margaret Elliot (Bette Davis) is a woman who was once rich, young, and famous, but now she is none of these. Her wealth is so depleted that she is forced to auction her personal effects, her fame reduced to the tentative recognition of one waitress, and her age passing the point at which Hollywood consigns its former leading ladies to secondary or character roles. We first see Margaret meeting her agent, Harry Stone (Warner Anderson), and pleading with him to get a film contract for her to revive her financial and professional fortunes. "One good picture is all I need," she tells him, but he tells her that the public wants a "fresh, dewy quality."

Margaret gets little reassurance from anyone else. She goes to see her daughter Gretchen (Natalie Wood) at the house of her ex-husband, John Morgan. Although Gretchen still adores her mother, John's new wife Peggy (Barbara Woodel) lectures Margaret on how John now gets the love and support that Margaret could never give him, and Gretchen innocently tells her that girls at her day camp say Margaret is washed up. When she returns to her modest apartment, she is asked for her back rent and then finds that her sister (Fay Baker) and her sister's husband, Roy (David Alpert) have come to demand money. Their only response to her financial plight is to criticize her for being extravagant, but Margaret points out that she bought them a house, set Roy up in business, and paid thousands of dollars of their expenses. In a rage she finally throws them out of her apartment and then turns to her last reminder of her days of glory, her Academy Award statuette, and says the film's most memorable line, "Come on Oscar, let's you and me get drunk."

With the Oscar on her dashboard she drives drunkenly past the houses of now successful stars and pauses to gaze at the large mansion that was once hers, but the ride ends when she wrecks the car and is arrested and jailed for drunken driving. This proves to be both the low point of her life and the event that begins her recovery. She is mortified by the publicity, especially because of her daughter, but she is bailed out of jail by Jim Johannson (Sterling Hayden).

Many years before, we find, Margaret got Jim a leading role in one of her films and was determined to make him a star (partly as revenge against another star who refused to be in the film). The film, however, was a failure, and Jim left Hollywood to become a happy and successful ship owner. When he finds that Margaret cannot return to her apartment, the owner having finally locked her out because she was so far behind on the rent, Jim takes her to his unassuming but comfortable shipyard quarters.

Jim is sympathetic to Margaret but not to her obsession with regaining her stardom. At one point he loses his patience and tells her, "I once thought you were a woman; I was wrong, you're nothing but a career." After an enjoyable and relaxing day sailing with Jim and Gretchen, Margaret begins to accept the idea of giving up Hollywood for something else. She agrees to apply for a job as a salesperson at a Los Angeles department store, the May Company. After the job interview, she tells Jim that she gave one of her best performances to get the job. When she actually begins working at the store, however, she finds that she cannot abandon her former self so easily. When she overhears two dowagers talking about whether she is Margaret Elliot, she explodes, telling them "I am Margaret Elliot and I intend to stay Margaret Elliot" before stalking out of the store more than ever determined to be a star again.

She manages to get a screen test for the part of the older sister of the lead in an upcoming film, and she is convinced that the right sort of performance in the test will win her the lead. She makes herself look younger than she should be for the role in the test, and despite the director's instructions, she plays the scene flirtatiously instead of sullenly, as it is written. After the test she is sure that she has succeeded and wants to celebrate at a famous Hollywood restaurant, but Jim offers to take her to a quiet restaurant in unfashionable Long Beach instead. "Why do you keep torturing yourself with all this," he says. "You must know by now you could stay here with me."

The next day all her illusions crumble. She sees the screen test and is humiliated, screaming "Oh, it's horrible, it's horrible" at her image on the screen. Afterwards at a Hollywood party she finds that someone else has been given the part for which she tested and cannot help but notice that the center of attention is a "fresh, dewey" young actress (Barbara Lawrence playing herself). Finally, when a writer describes to her a script he would like her to do, about an ambitious star whom the audience can only pity because she is "denied her birthright—the privilege and glory of just being a woman"— Margaret runs from the party, picks up Gretchen, and flies to Jim. The film ends with a shot of Gretchen watching as Jim and Margaret embrace and then a shot of just the two.

The Star invites comparison with *All About Eve* (1950), which also starred Davis and also was about an older actress in a milieu that prizes youth, but Davis herself has pointed out one essential difference: *All About Eve* is about an actress, but *The Star* is about a "motion picture star."

The greatest strength of *The Star* is undoubtedly Davis' performance. The film is not by any means based upon the life of Davis, but it gains some resonance from the fact that Davis' career a few years earlier (just before *All About Eve*) had reached much the same stage as that of Margaret at the opening of the film, and like Margaret she had, in some of her best years, had trouble getting the studio to give her good scripts and good parts. Davis' acting in *The Star* is highly charged and emotional, but always believable and never excessive. Perhaps the most affecting scene is the one in which she confronts her own ridiculous performance in the screen test and begins to realize that she will never be a young movie star again.

Hayden also plays a role that bears some resemblance to his own life, since he began acting in order to finance his seagoing ambitions and periodically abandoned his acting career to return to the sea. In this film, however, he is often stilted or stiff, mainly because of the script by Katherine Albert and Dale Eunson, which requires him to be a solid, sensible character in contrast to Davis' more emotional one.

Stuart Heisler directed with good attention to actual locations as well as to the performances of the actors.

Clifford Henry

THE STARS LOOK DOWN

Released: 1939
Production: Isadore Goldsmith for Metro-Goldwyn-Mayer
Direction: Carol Reed
Screenplay: J. B. Williams and A. J. Cronin; based on the novel of the same name by A. J. Cronin
Cinematography: Mutz Greenbaum
Editing: Reginald Beck
Special effects: Henry Harris and Ernest Palmer
Running time: 104 minutes

Principal characters:
Davey Fenwick .... Michael Redgrave
Jenny Sunley .... Margaret Lockwood
Joe Gowlan .... Emlyn Williams
Martha Fenwick .... Nancy Price
Robert Fenwick .... Edward Rigby
Richard Barras .... Allan Jeaves
Stanley Millington .... Cecil Parker
Laura Millington .... Linden Travers

It is surely a tribute to the all-pervasiveness of the influence of the British documentary movement in the 1930's, led by men such as John Grierson and Paul Rotha, that the first major film of a director with a totally different background should at times be so reminiscent of government-sponsored documentaries such as *Coal Face* and *Night Mail*. *The Stars Look Down*, a realistic mining drama, was Carol Reed's ninth film, but his first to receive international acclaim. It is adapted from a novel by A. J. Cronin, another of whose novels, *The Citadel*, had been successfully brought to the screen the previous year. The screenplay necessarily compresses Cronin's novel, and even to some extent alters its emphasis and flavor, notably in removing almost completely the character of the mine-owner's pacifist son, and in discreetly toning down the socialist overtones of Davey Fenwick's career. It does not obscure the very real anger of the original, however, and the film is an example almost unique in the commercial cinema of a tradition of British realism which was to be swallowed up entirely in the bland, all-pull-together populism of wartime dramas such as *Millions Like Us* (1943) and *Waterloo Road* (1944), not to mention the excellent although reactionary *This Happy Breed* (1944). *The Stars Look Down*, despite its moments of melodrama and despite the mystical idealism which mars the ending (the camera pans up into the sky and a portentous voice talks about going "into the light of the world that would and must be"), remains a brilliant realist drama, excellently acted (particularly by Michael Redgrave and Emlyn Williams) and powerfully filmed (by Mutz Greenbaum, with location and special effects work by Henry Harris and Ernest Palmer). For its time, it pulls very few punches.

The story is set in the northeast of England (not Wales, as most American sources claim) in the mining village of Sleesdale. When Richard Barras (Allan Jeeves), owner of the Paradise Mine, announces plans to reopen the notoriously unsafe Scupper Flats workings, Robert Fenwick (Edward Rigby), a pitman for more than forty years, persuades the men to strike. He gets little support from his dour, hardworking wife Martha (Nancy Price), who also resents the plan of their eldest son Davey (Michael Redgrave) to better himself and go to Tynecastle University. A sudden refusal of credit by the Sleesdale butcher leads to an outbreak of looting in the course of which Joe Gowlan (Emlyn Williams), a contemporary of Davey, helps himself to a handful of notes from the till and sets off for Tynecastle. Davey's father is jailed for the theft, while Joe builds up a prosperous career as a none-too-honest bookmaker. Two years later, Davey, now a student in Tynecastle, runs into Joe (whom he takes for a friend) at a cinema, and the latter is only too happy to pass on to him his attractive girl friend Jenny Sunley (Margaret Lockwood), an usherette whom he wants to ditch for a more prestigious affair with Laura Millington (Linden Travers), wife of a powerful businessman. Angered, Jenny throws herself at Davey, sweeps him off his feet, and they marry.

Jenny's petulant desire for the good life (in a characterization which Lockwood would perfect in *The Wicked Lady*, 1945) leads Davey to give up his college and political ambitions and take a job as schoolmaster in Sleesdale. She is bored, and he feels he has let his friends down. In the meantime Joe, now a business associate of Millington, returns to Sleesdale to do business with Barras, and visits his old flame Jenny. Davey becomes involved once more in the affairs of the mine when it becomes clear that Joe's contract with Barras will mean reopening the treacherous Scupper Flats, and he goes to Tynecastle to plead for Union help. When he gets back to Sleesdale he finds his house dark except for a bedroom light, and meets Joe coming out. A fight ensues, and Joe is beaten, but he uses the whole affair against Davey, suggesting to the Union that his opposition to the Scupper Flats plan is a personnel vendetta. The old workings are reopened, and a disaster inevitably ensues: a pick breaks the wall between Scupper Flats and the old workings beyond, flooding the mine. Many of the miners are killed outright, but some survive for a number of days—among them Davey's father and his brother Hughie, who is due to leave the mine for a career in professional soccer, and one of Davey's pupils whose parents would not let him stay in school—before dying from lack of air. Davey determines to return to his original ambition of politics in order to fight for the miners' future and the nationalization of the mines.

The Stars Look Down inevitably invites comparison with Ernst Pabst's 1931 masterpiece *Kameradschaft*, as well as with John Ford's almost contemporary

How Green Was My Valley (1941), a film whose heavy promotion and runaway success, which led to five Oscars, somewhat overshadowed *The Stars Look Down* in the United States. In both cases, the British film stands up well in comparison. The film was launched in February, 1939, when producer Goldsmith announced plans for a £100,000 budget (about $425,000 at that time), but location work did not begin until June 15, 1939, at St. Helen's Siddick Colliery, Workington, County Durham, with studio work in July and August at Twickenham and Shepperton Studios. Shooting was completed on a day generally remembered for other events—September 1, 1939—and the film was premiered on January 22, 1940 at the Odeon, Leicester Square. Certain of the grimmer scenes of the mine disaster were cut after the outbreak of war, but Reed had few reservations about its being suitable wartime entertainment: "plenty of people paid to see it," he said, "which is the only definite answer to that question." Reviews in the daily press were excellent, and the film broke records at the Odeon. Only Rotha in the *Documentary Newsletter* roundly attacked it for being inauthentic and sentimental. Almost all the performances received acclaim, although there were some suggestions that Lockwood was miscast, and special mention was made of Nancy Price as Davey's mother. Reservations were expressed about the love story at the film's center, but unreserved praise was lavished on the realistic background and the terrifying special effects of the flood. *The Stars Look Down* was not released in the United States by M-G-M until July, 1941. "Now and again there comes along a film that seems to have been struck off at white heat," wrote Theodore Strauss in *The New York Times*, going on to praise the film's sincerity, the performances, and above all the scene of the miners' wives' pithead vigil, "one of the magnificent passages of screen realism."

If the "white heat" of *The Stars Look Down* is somewhat cooled by the unctuousness of its final voice-over, the film is nevertheless explicitly—and, for a British movie of the time, untypically—concerned with the plight of the working class: not the usual sentimentalized band of cheerful, cheeky Cockneys, but a real mining community with a genuine hero of the people, albeit played by a well-educated, middle-class actor. The film's stance—typical enough of Cronin but extremely untypical of Reed, one of the least "committed" of British directors—is made clear in Davey's speech to the University debating society in favor of nationalizing the mines: "I resent that this great buried treasure should be dispensed to this man or that to use as a pabulum of self-aggrandizement." Flowery, perhaps, but unequivocal. The socialist-capitalist theme is nicely dramatized in the conflict between Joe and Davey, as much over political as over personal matters; and Davey's progressive ideas are neatly indicated in a row with his conservative headmaster. Davey has taught his students to draw Scandinavia on a map by showing them the similarity of its shape to something they see every day of their lives: a pit pony. The headmaster is furious at this departure from established practice:

"Scandinavia is a bear, Mr. Fenwick, a bear." Stupidity and greed, then, are Davey's chief enemies.

The film does not sentimentalize the miners, showing them in a strikingly realistic light through the use of real locations, with low-angle, documentary-style shots of the workers leaving the colliery at the end of a shift, giving way to a series of dissolves on their barracklike cottages and back laneways. At times Reed departs from this realism to a shadow-dominated expressionism strongly anticipatory of two of his best-known films, *The Third Man* (1949) and *Odd Man Out* (1946). At times, too, he departs from the strict line of narrative to include almost surrealistic touches such as the child reaching up in ecstasy during the looting of the butcher's shop to steal a cardboard display lamb. Such touches serve only to inflect the grim realism of a film which gives the kind of unflattering picture of social conditions in Britain not really found again until the work of the new generation of filmmakers, particularly Lindsay Anderson and Karel Reisz, in the late 1950's. Like these later films, *The Stars Look Down* is a realist drama, not a documentary. Its finest scenes, such as Davey's mother stonily watching him leave for Tynecastle and refusing to say good-bye, and the trapped miners dying of asphyxiation in Scupper Flats, rely primarily on emotion. They are among the most powerful in the British cinema and among the best that Reed has ever done.

Nick Roddick

STARTING OVER

Released: 1979
Production: Alan J. Pakula and James L. Brooks for Paramount
Direction: Alan J. Pakula
Screenplay: James L. Brooks; based on the novel of the same name by Dan Wakefield
Cinematography: Sven Nykvist
Editing: Marion Rothman
Music: Marvin Hamlisch
Running time: 105 minutes

Principal characters:
Phil Potter	Burt Reynolds
Marilyn Holmberg	Jill Clayburgh
Jessica Potter	Candice Bergen
Michael Potter	Charles Durning
Marva Potter	Frances Sternhagen
Marie	Mary Kay Place
Paul	Austin Pendleton

Starting Over was 1979's answer to *An Unmarried Woman* (1978), giving the man's point of view. Like another of the year's successful films, *Kramer vs. Kramer*, *Starting Over* tells the story of a husband who loses his wife because she wants to "find herself." While *Kramer vs. Kramer* won Oscars for Best Picture, Best Actor (Dustin Hoffman), and Best Supporting Actress (Meryl Streep) for its sometimes poignant, sometimes funny treatment of a man and his son facing life without a woman, *Starting Over*, although in a more deliberately comical vein, is as realistic and poignant as the better-known film.

In this story, Phil Potter (Burt Reynolds), who is apparently a writer (although this is never explained very well in the film), is being sent away from his New York penthouse apartment by his rich wife Jessica (Candice Bergen) because she wants to go it alone and try to make a success of her budding singing and songwriting career. The opening voice-overs are serious and touching as Phil tries to make jokes about their parting while he suggests that they go to bed together. Jessica is adamant, however, and Phil realizes that he must leave when he finds a letter written to Jessica by a former lover in one of his drawers. The first comic note of the film occurs when Phil wonders how Jessica could have an affair with someone who signs a letter "Evermore, Neil." When he closes the door of their apartment behind him, the audience realizes that the film is indeed a comedy, because we see Phil wince as Jessica plays the piano and sings in wonderfully offkey tones, "It's Easy for You."

Phil then goes to the Boston home of his psychiatrist brother Michael (Charles Durning) and his wife, Marva (Frances Sternhagen), who make tender but ultimately humorous attempts to comfort him. His brother wants Phil to join a divorced men's encounter group at the local church, and Marva feels that this will be an "enriching experience" for him.

When Phil finds an apartment in a modest walk-up building in Boston, he furnishes it with the bare essentials from the local discount department store and begins setting up house. The euphoria of furnishing his apartment is very short-lived, however, and in a spell of deep loneliness he calls Michael and Marva, only to find out that it is the middle of the night. They do invite him for dinner the next evening, however, and it is from this point that Phil begins his new life.

At Michael and Marva's house he meets Marilyn Holmberg (Jill Clayburgh), a thirty-ish elementary schoolteacher who mistakes him for a molester on her way from the bus stop. Once the initial embarrassment is over, they realize that they like each other, and Phil eventually asks Marilyn out. She turns him down at first and fixes him up with one of her girl friends, Marie (Mary Kay Place), instead. While Phil is having a disastrous first date with Marie, we learn that Jessica's song is a hit when Marie sings it happily while she is getting ready to go out. After the date, Phil calls Marilyn and asks her out again, hoping that she will not mind "getting involved" up to a point.

They date, have fun together, and eventually become lovers. Everything seems to be going wonderfully for them until Jessica calls Phil during Thanksgiving dinner, just as he and Marilyn and Michael and Marva are happily sitting down to a turkey dinner in Phil's apartment. Phil later tells Marilyn that he does not still love Jessica, and they decide to live together. When they are shopping for furniture in Bloomingdale's, however, Phil begins to hyperventilate, and when Michael comes to get him, it is obvious that Phil's hyperventilating is a reaction to his impending arrangement with Marilyn. Phil's predicament is complicated even further when Jessica comes to Boston and asks Phil to come back to her, in a particularly funny scene in which a song of seduction is parodied in a Boston hotel room. Marilyn lets Phil go when he tells her that he is going back to Jessica, but makes him promise that he will never try to see her again. He promises, but leaves her very sadly.

Two different patterns of action occur now. In New York, Phil is returning with Jessica to the old life, while in Boston, Marilyn is being fixed up by Michael and Marva with a new boyfriend who is an extremely tall basketball player. After only one day with Jessica, Phil realizes that it is Marilyn he wants, and he leaves New York, this time for good. Marilyn does not want to see him, however, and continues seeing the basketball player. Eventually, Phil corners Marilyn after her boyfriend's team has finished practicing and convinces her to take another chance with him and this time marry him. She finally agrees, and the film ends.

The story is a 1970's updating of many old films of the boy-meets-girl variety, but with humor and sensitivity that uplift it from being just another copy of an old movie. Neither Jessica, Phil, nor Marilyn is one-dimensional. Each, in turn, is hurt by love and reluctant to try again. At first Phil turns to Marilyn as a refuge, oblivious to the fact that she has been hurt before and does not want to be hurt again. Although Marilyn realizes that Phil cannot commit himself to her until he is totally over Jessica, she still gets hurt when he returns to his wife. Jessica, on the other hand, begins as a very unsympathetic, even ludicrous character, but gains the audience's sympathy at the end because when she finally does realize that she loves Phil, it is too late to keep him.

The problems encountered by these characters are presented in a very funny way. There is no attempt at real jokes or deliberate pratfalls in the film, but the very human situations are in themselves humorous. Phil's surprise at Marie's throwing herself at him, followed by his quick, pleading telephone call to Marilyn, is one example. Reynolds is a straight man throughout the film, and much humor is derived from his deadpan reactions to the absurd situations which surround him. The scenes of the divorced men's encounter group are particularly effective. There is only one character, Paul (Austin Pendleton), who has an unbelievable story: he keeps marrying and divorcing the same woman over and over. When each of the other men reveals his own story, however, the audience realizes that each member of the group has a story similar to Phil's. This comes to light satirically in a scene in which the divorced men's encounter group coldly passes the divorced women's encounter group on the stairs; everyone is hurt and bitter and no one wants to forgive any member of the opposite sex. Later, when the men's group's Christmas party is a disaster of chips and packaged dips, they join the feast prepared by the women's group and seem to break the ice in another funny scene.

Many critics consider the ending which brings Phil and Marilyn together trite, but it is actually a welcome change from many other films of the era which simply have the characters go their separate ways. The film makes the point from the beginning that Phil is not the wandering type, but the marrying type. The independence which Jessica seeks, and which causes the breakup in the first place, is not a problem with Marilyn. Marilyn is already independent and does not "need" a man to bring her happiness; Phil is merely bringing her a new dimension of happiness.

Reynolds, who is usually associated with the "Good Ole' Boy" roles that he has played in such films as *Smokey and the Bandit* (1977) is very good as a rather shy, insecure Easterner. His drawing power as one of the top box-office stars of the late 1970's and early 1980's is undoubtedly the principal reason that *Starting Over* was such a great financial success, earning more than thirty-one million dollars in the first ten weeks of its release in the United States. The film is good apart from Reynolds, but with no other potentially big box-office stars, no stunts, and no special effects, the film would not have done as well without him. Clayburgh, who had just been nominated for an Oscar for her role as a woman starting over in *An Unmarried Woman*, gives a very believable performance. Her role is totally unglamorous, and the character of Marilyn is almost devoid of sophistication. Clayburgh wears little or no makeup in the film, yet she has an inner beauty which transcends the plasticized beauty of many other actresses.

Perhaps the stand-out performance of the film, however, is that of Bergen. Playing totally against type, she satirizes her own beauty, distorting her face dramatically as she sings (terribly) Jessica's ridiculous songs; her singing is the most purposefully funny thing in the film. She was given her first Oscar nomination, for Best Supporting Actress, for her performance. The others in the cast—Durning, Sternhagen, and especially Pendleton—all add to the film to make it an enjoyable whole. Aside from Bergen, who excels, all of the characters give journeymenlike performances. It is the interplay among the characters that gives the film its flavor, something which is built into the script by screenwriter James L. Brooks. Brooks was one of the creators of the successful television series *The Mary Tyler Moore Show*, which also derived much of its humor from poking mild fun at the human foibles of its familiar characters.

Pakula's direction reinforces the comfortable relationships among the characters. Although not of the *auteur* status as yet, Pakula has directed a number of varied yet successful films, including 1976's second-highest-grossing film, *All the President's Men*. Beginning his career as a producer with *Fear Strikes Out* (1957), Pakula went into partnership with director Robert Mulligan in 1962 with *To Kill a Mockingbird* and made five more films with him. Pakula's first film as a director was *The Sterile Cuckoo* (1969), and from that time on, Pakula has been a very successful director as well as producer.

Patricia King Hanson

THE STEEL HELMET

Released: 1951
Production: Samuel Fuller for Lippert
Direction: Samuel Fuller
Screenplay: Samuel Fuller
Cinematography: Ernest W. Miller
Editing: Philip Cahn
Running time: 84 minutes

Principal characters:
Sergeant Zack .... Gene Evans
Private Bronte .... Robert Hutton
Lieutenant Driscoll .... Steve Brodie
Corporal Thompson .... James Edwards
Sergeant Tanaka .... Richard Loo
Joe, Second GI .... Sid Melton
Private Baldy .... Richard Monahan
Short Round .... William Chun
The Red .... Harold Fong
First GI .... Neyle Morrow
Second Lieutenant .... Lynn Stalmaster

The Steel Helmet, an exciting, gritty, realistic, and skillfully depicted drama, was the third film directed by Samuel Fuller, and his first set on the battlefield. It was also the first American film to portray the Korean War. His previous films were *I Shot Jesse James* (1948) and *The Baron of Arizona* (1949).

The Steel Helmet is no massive war epic of battleships and bombs and battalions of soldiers. Rather, it features a small cast in a modest production. Short Round (William Chun), a twelve-year-old Korean orphan, despises the Communists because they have murdered his parents. While wandering in a field, he encounters Sergeant Zack (Gene Evans). Zack's company has been decimated by Korean guerrillas and he has been wounded. His hands are tied behind his back, and he is crawling through a field of corpses when he is found by the boy. Short Round frees him and, despite the soldier's protests, insists on following the sergeant. The boy tells Zack that, according to an old Buddhist saying, the sergeant's heart is now in his hands. The boy's knowledge of the countryside does, however, quickly prove to be an asset to the soldier.

The pair is soon joined by Corporal Thompson (James Edwards), a black medic, another survivor of a platoon of soldiers that has been massacred. Their immediate goal becomes one of heading back to American-occupied territory. They soon come upon a patrol, headed by the insecure, inexperienced Lieutenant Driscoll (Steve Brodie), which is attempting to establish a radio outpost to observe and select enemy targets for American artillery strikes. Among those under Driscoll's command are Private Baldy (Richard Monahan), who is, appropriately, completely bald; Sergeant Tanaka (Richard Loo), a Japanese-American; and Private Bronte (Robert Hutton), a former conscientious objector. Zack recognizes Driscoll and recalls that he had used some influence to avoid combat during World War II. Driscoll enlists Zack's aid in his project, and the survivors join the Patrol.

With Short Round's help, the patrol finds a Buddhist temple and establishes an outpost with radio communications to headquarters. A Communist soldier (Harold Fong), a North Korean major, is discovered hiding in the Temple; he stabs one of the American soldiers to death and breaks the radio. After a frantic search, Zack captures him. The men refer to their prisoner as "The Red." Driscoll assumes charge of The Red since all prisoners are supposed to be taken in for interrogation. Next, Short Round is killed by a sniper. Zack finds a note that the boy had written in Korean in which he prays that Zack will like him. When The Red laughs at the boy's words and spits in Zack's face, the sergeant shoots and kills him, for which he is chastized by Driscoll.

The North Koreans soon begin a furious attack on the temple. Baldy finally fixes the radio and broadcasts the patrol's dilemma to headquarters. American artillery and machine gun fire from the patrol kill most of the enemy, but most of the Americans are also dead; the only survivors are Zack, Baldy, and Thompson. American reinforcements finally arrive, and the three men rejoin the main body of GI's.

Fuller's films, from *The Steel Helmet* to *The Big Red One* (1980), are not as graphically bloody as those of Sam Peckinpah, or as many of the Westerns, crime dramas, and horror films released during the 1970's; but they are filled with enough butchery and violence to realistically and effectively depict the effect of combat on soldiers. To Fuller, war is literally hell. He certainly does not gratuitously glorify battle, and his soldiers do not die bloodlessly, with the "Stars and Stripes Forever" pounding patriotically on the sound track; but he does portray his GI's as adventurous, larger-than-life stereotypes. His films are in no way indictments of the inhumanity of war, and Sergeant Zack and his comrades could easily be found on the pages of comic books.

As befitting the time of its release, *The Steel Helmet* is unabashedly anti-Communist. The American presence in Korea is not questioned. The film is a reflection of its era, containing dialogue that might resemble a hysterical editorial of the *New York Daily News*. For example, Zack asks The Red (who has no name): "Where are the rest of your Russians?" The major's response— "I'm not a Russian, I'm a North Korean"—is irrelevant. There is a parallel between *The Steel Helmet* and John Wayne's hawkish *The Green Berets* (1968), the only major American Vietnam film released during the war years. In both, an American soldier develops a fondness for an Asian boy. In *The Steel Helmet*, the child dies; in *The Green Berets*, it is the man, Sergeant Peterson, played by Jim Hutton, who is killed in a boobytrap. The image is one of

Americans fighting in Asia to "save the children." The actual issues in both wars were, of course, far more complicated than the films describe.

As a genre film, *The Steel Helmet* is filled with suspense and action. Fuller is a master of getting the most out of the least; he shot the film in the remarkably short period of ten days, on a miniscule budget. Evans gives a brilliant and sensitive performance as Zack. On the surface his Zack is rough and heartless, a veteran at the kill-or-be-killed game of war. He is intelligent and sensitive, however, and develops feelings for Short Round. When the boy is killed, Zack almost—but not quite—loses control of his emotions. The scenes with Evans and Short Round and the confrontation, after Short Round's death, between Evans and The Red are the most compelling in the film. Before *The Steel Helmet*, Evans had appeared in minor roles beginning in 1947 with *Under Colorado Skies*. He later appeared in Fuller's *Shock Corridor* (1963), *Hell and High Water* (1954), *Park Row* (1952), and *Fixed Bayonets* (1951). In *Fixed Bayonets* he plays Rock, essentially the same character as Zack.

The Steel Helmet is an important film historically because of the manner in which two of its characters are presented. Thompson may not be a full-fledged soldier—he is a medic—but he is no shuffling janitor or pullman porter. He is black, and a survivor. Edwards is fine as Thompson; he excelled in a bit part as a boxer in *The Set-Up* (1949), and starred in *Home of the Brave* (1949) as a soldier maligned and ignored by his white buddies (one of whom was played by Brodie) while on patrol on a Japanese-held island during World War II. If it were not for Sidney Poitier, Edwards might have become the star of Hollywood's "integration" films of the 1950's. *Home of the Brave* was unfortunately the only film in which he played the lead; his final screen appearance was in *Patton* (1970), in which he plays the general's valet. Loo's Sergeant Tanaka, the Nisei bazooka specialist, is no "Nip" or "Jap" stereotype but a good American soldier. *The Steel Helmet* is, in fact, exemplary in that its American GI's are not all white, whether they be farm boys from Kansas or cabbies from Brooklyn. *The Steel Helmet* may be unsophisticated politically, but Fuller should be lauded for depicting all of his soliders as equals.

According to *Variety*, *The Steel Helmet* did poorly at the box office, earning less than one million dollars, but it received generally good reviews, and Fuller deservedly won the Writers Guild of America Award for "Best-Written American Low Budget Film."

Rob Edelman

THE STERILE CUCKOO

Released: 1969
Production: Alan J. Pakula for Paramount
Direction: Alan J. Pakula
Screenplay: Alvin Sargent; based on the novel of the same name by John Nichols
Cinematography: Milton Krasner
Editing: Sam O'Steen
Running time: 107 minutes

> *Principal characters:*
> "Pookie" Adams ....Liza Minnelli
> Jerry Payne .... Wendell Burton
> Schumaker .... Tim McIntire

The wide-screen appeal of Liza Minnelli, daughter of Judy Garland and Vincente Minnelli, had yet to be determined in 1969. She had already won a Tony Award several years earlier for her work on Broadway in *Flora the Red Menace*, but had appeared only once on film, in a twenty-minute role opposite Albert Finney in *Charlie Bubbles* (1967). Any questions about her abilities were dispelled, however, by her performance in *The Sterile Cuckoo*, her first starring effort. Although the film is far from flawless, her performance won her an Oscar nomination and made her a star.

College freshmen Mary Anne "Pookie" Adams (Liza Minnelli) and Jerry Payne (Wendell Burton) meet on a bus as they travel to their respective schools in Upstate New York. While Pookie is verbose and outspoken, Jerry is naïve and reserved. They visit each other and develop a friendship. Jerry is able to adapt to his new surroundings, but Pookie defensively makes fun of her schoolmates; to her, the world is inhabited by "weirdos." She is also neurotically preoccupied with death, and she and Jerry first kiss while visiting an old cemetery, after which they fall in love.

Pookie is too immature to handle the relationship, however; she is overly jealous when Jerry wants to spend a week skiing with his roommate or even visiting his parents for vacation. She is often cloying to an obnoxious degree; at one point, Jerry must tell her to "settle down," and it soon becomes obvious that he will outgrow her. At one point, Jerry tells Pookie that he thinks "we've been seeing too much of each other" and that he'll call her in a month. Pookie gallantly smiles and says okay, but as she drives away, she almost wrecks her car. At this point, the two have parted and the film should end. Yet Jerry does call her, only to learn that she has quit school and disappeared. She later turns up, and Jerry finds her registered in a boarding house, reclusively staring off into space. He suggests she visit her father, and the film ends as she leaves. It is unclear if their affair is truly over, or if they will see each other again later; the necessary finality to the relationship is not established.

The Sterile Cuckoo is an affecting portrait of first love. The relationship between Pookie and Jerry may be transient, and may be barely recalled by either in later years, yet it is a special moment in time for both. Most appealing is a sequence in which the couple awkwardly rent a motel room in order to sleep together for the first time. Pookie must be reassured that Jerry has registered them as "Mr. and Mrs." As Jerry nervously takes Pookie's clothes off, her sweater catches hold of her chin, and Jerry must fish her glasses out as if he has just dropped them into a fish bowl. Pookie ultimately completes the removal of her garments herself. When she is finished, Jerry is more awestruck than overcome with lust. The film is also eloquent when Pookie tells Jerry that their relationship is "too perfect," and that she is nervous because it probably will not last. Jerry tells her, simply, that he loves her, and they embrace.

The Sterile Cuckoo is the first directorial effort of Alan J. Pakula. Previously, Pakula had produced films which Robert Mulligan directed, such as *Fear Strikes Out* (1957), *To Kill a Mockingbird* (1962), *Love with the Proper Stranger* (1963), and *Up the Down Staircase* (1967). Pakula had taken an option on *The Sterile Cuckoo* in 1964, a year before the John Nichols novel was published, but was unable to proceed with the film because he and Mulligan were involved with other projects. Minnelli, who became interested in making the film, persuaded Pakula to direct and turned down the lead role on Broadway in *Promises, Promises* and a concert tour to star in the film.

Pakula's lack of experience behind the camera is evident. *The Sterile Cuckoo* often lags and is episodic: as one sequence ends, the next begins without any transition. An obtrusive song, "Come Saturday Morning," drones on the sound track as Pookie and Jerry walk arm in arm through the country. After their relationship has been established, there are too many montage sequences of the two "falling in love." Alvin Sargent's screenplay needs to be opened up; *The Sterile Cuckoo* is virtually a two-character film, with Jerry's beer-guzzling roommate Schumaker (Tim McIntire) the only other character with any appreciable dialogue. University life is also idealized beyond believability. Pookie and Jerry are ludicrously unaware of sex or drugs or Vietnam—an incredible stance for a 1969 film about "contemporary" college students to take.

Overall, though, *The Sterile Cuckoo* is a worthy debut for its novice director. The film is basically a practice run for Pakula. He has gone on to direct three of the better films of the 1970's: *Klute* (1971), *The Parallax View* (1974), and *All the President's Men* (1976).

Minnelli has not become the cinema superstar her mother was, but she did win an Academy Award in 1972 for her dynamic performance as the "divinely decadent" Sally Bowles in *Cabaret*. While the critics were divided about *The Sterile Cuckoo*, all were unanimous in their praise for Minnelli. Her best scene is a telephone conversation with Jerry as he explains that he must stay on campus by himself and study for exams over the Easter holiday. Pookie smiles valiantly and makes small talk, yet she conveys her fear and desperation over the belief that Jerry is really cutting her out of his life. Finally, she breaks down and begs him to allow her to keep him company. Pookie is maddeningly immature, yet Minnelli still manages to keep her lovable and interesting.

The film career of Burton has not been as successful as his costar's and director's. Two years after *The Sterile Cuckoo*, he starred in *Fortune in Men's Eyes*, a drama about homosexuality in prison, and has since virtually vanished from major motion pictures. His performance is no less eloquent than Minnelli's, however; his Jerry is an appropriately understated characterization, just as Jerry is a low-keyed, understated individual.

Rob Edelman

STORM BOY

Released: 1980
Production: Matt Carroll for South Australia Film
Direction: Henri Safran
Screenplay: Sonia Borg; based on the novel of the same name by Colin Thiele
Cinematography: Geoff Burton
Editing: G. Turney-Smith
Running time: 88 minutes

Principal characters:
Mike Kingsley .... Greg Rowe
Fingerbone Bill .... Gulpilil
Tom Kingsley .... Peter Cummins
Ranger .... Tony Allison
Miss Walters .... Judy Dick

One of the most refreshing films to come out of the renaissance of the national cinema of Australia in the late 1970's was Henri Safran's *Storm Boy*, released in Australia in 1976 and in the United States in 1980. It seems to have been typed as a children's film, but it is, in fact, a mature (although nonsensational) look at one ten-year-old boy as he comes to understand the cycles of nature and of life.

Storm Boy is set in the Coorong, an eighty-mile-long finger of lake and marshland near Adelaide, close by Australia's southern shoreline. The land is wild (a portion of it is a sanctuary for waterfowl) and has an eerie beauty. Safran and cinematographer Geoff Burton transform the scenes of sunrise and sunset into magical vistas. The Coorong is an important part of the film— a presence as important as any actor—and, along with three characters, it acts out *Storm Boy*'s story. Tom Kingsley (Peter Cummins), known locally as Hide-a-Way Tom, lives with his son Mike (Greg Rowe) in a shack on the edge of the Coorong. By Tom Kingsley's choice, theirs is an extremely isolated existence. Kingsley makes a subsistence living as a fisherman and is content with his lot, but ten-year-old Mike is reaching the age at which he is becoming curious about the outside world. When a transistor radio washes ashore amid the other flotsam and jetsam of the day, Mike is intrigued, but his father makes him throw it away.

The tension between wilderness and civilization remain unresolved until the end of the film. Indeed, one of the delights of *Storm Boy* is the way in which the filmmakers (Safran and writer Sonia Borg) play upon this tension in ways that turn many contemporary clichés upside down. One thing that the filmmakers suggest is that their young protagonist cannot truly appreciate what civilization has to offer until he better understands the wilderness.

Mike's "instructor" in this undertaking is Fingerbone Bill (Gulpilil), an aborigine who has camped in the Coorong a few miles from the Kingsleys' shack. Mike stumbles onto him quite by accident one day, and his first reaction is sheer terror. He runs home to tell his father about the man with the gun (Fingerbone Bill carries an ancient-looking hunting rifle), but when a visit to the aborigine's supposed campsite turns up no evidence of human habitation, Kingsley concludes that Fingerbone Bill is a figment of his son's imagination. The two meet again when a horrified Mike, poling his raft through the marshes one morning, comes upon a pair of hunters (or "shooters," as they are called in *Storm Boy*) blasting away at the pelicans in the wildlife reserve. He is powerless to stop them, but Fingerbone Bill is not. Fingerbone Bill fires a warning shot in the shooters' general direction, and the two men leave in panic.

This incident is the beginning of a deep friendship between Mike and Fingerbone Bill. The aborigine names Mike "Storm Boy" (the death of a pelican at the hands of the shooters is the harbinger of a storm) and leads his new friend to a nest where three motherless pelican chicks are fluttering helplessly. Storm boy resolves to raise them himself. It is the process of raising the pelicans that enables Mike to comprehend truly the wilderness in which he has lived most of his life. *Storm Boy* is much more than an exotic variation on the "boy and his dog" theme, however; Safran and his associates refuse to descend into the melodrama that cheapens many American and British versions of stories of children and animals.

Tom Kingsley, for example, undoubtedly would be the villain of the film in the hands of a less subtle group of artists. In *Storm Boy* he is nothing of the sort. He has his faults, but his love for Mike is apparent at all times. Furthermore—and against our preconditioned expectations—he gets along fine with Fingerbone Bill once they finally meet. There is no resentment between the two men, either as the shared objects of Mike/Storm Boy's affection, or on racial grounds.

Similarly, Fingerbone Bill might have been turned into "the noble savage." In *Storm Boy*, he has his faults too. He has been exiled by his tribe (indeed, he is under a death sentence) for a violation of their marriage and courtship customs. Additionally, it is Fingerbone Bill, the very spirit of the wilderness, who gives Storm Boy his first book, who urges him to learn to read, and who ultimately suggests a plan that will enable Tom and his son to move back to town where the boy can go to school.

This evenhanded attitude extends to the film's two important supporting roles. The Ranger (Tony Allison) who patrols the Coorong and is looking for Fingerbone Bill, and Miss Walters (Judy Dick), the schoolteacher from town who insists that Tom Kingsley see to Mike's education, are not presented as ogres; they are human beings who have Mike's best interests at heart. Indeed, the only real villains in *Storm Boy* are the shooters and their ilk, wanton destroyers of the way of life in the Coorong.

Although *Storm Boy* is not an "action film" by any means, it has moments of excitement and conflict. A scene in which young Mike, alone in the Kingsley shack on the beach at night, is terrorized by a bunch of drunken kids in dune buggies, is particularly powerful; and the "storm at sea" sequence, wherein Mr. Percival, the brightest of Mike's pelicans, effects the rescue of three men by flying out to their boat with a tow line in his beak, is also dramatic and shot for maximum effect.

Storm Boy concludes with Mike's final lesson on the nature of life in the wilderness. He has learned about life; now he must learn about death—and rebirth. Shooters reappear in the Coorong. Shots are fired, and Mr. Percival is nowhere to be found. Fingerbone Bill locates Mr. Percival's body and leads Mike to the spot where he buried it, right next to a nest with a newly hatched pelican in it. "Perhaps Mr. Percival starting all over again," smiles Fingerbone Bill. "Birds like him never die." The scene is handled very tastefully, without an attempt at tearjerking. We see and share the boy's grief, but the filmmakers never ask us (or him) to wallow in it.

Thus are the film's theme and plot brought together. Just as Mike has participated in the birth/death/rebirth cycle of nature, so his own life is undergoing a change. As the film ends, Mike and his father are about to move into town so that Mike can go to school (at Fingerbone Bill's suggestion, Tom Kingsley has accepted a reward from the three men whose lives were saved by Mr. Percival to finance the project). After weeks of ambivalence, Mike at last feels ready, and even eager, for the transition.

Safran made good use of his small cast. Outside his own country, Gulpilil may well be the best-known actor in all of Australian cinema; his most prominent roles have been in Nicholas Roeg's *Walkabout* (1971) and Peter Weir's *The Last Wave* (1979). He specializes, of course, in playing aborigines, and in *Storm Boy*, as in his other performances, he offers a fascinating, richly textured portrayal. Fingerbone Bill is nobody's stereotype; he comes across as a complex and fully rounded character, filled with dignity, wisdom, and the joy of life.

Cummins is similarly excellent as Hide-a-Way Tom Kingsley. Beneath his stolid exterior, we can always sense his love for his son. Kingsley is a man of few words, but Cummins uses gestures and facial expressions to supplement his dialogue, and his character is developed sympathetically and effectively. Rowe as Mike/Storm Boy lacks the subtlety of Gulpilil and Cummins, but as a child actor, he is far from bad. He clearly enjoys himself with the pelicans, and portrays with conviction the maturation process that is at the core of the film. His performance is quite believable.

Safran melds the acting of Gulpilil, Cummins, and Rowe and the lovely cinematography of Burton into a subtly powerful film. *Storm Boy* was his first (and, as of 1981, only) feature film, although one of his short subjects, *Listen to the Lion* (the story of the death of a Sydney derelict), was named the year's

best short film in Australia in 1977. On the evidence in *Storm Boy*, Safran
is a director with a gift for subtlety and understatement, as well as a willingness
to subvert stereotypes.

The fact that *Storm Boy* is less widely known outside Australia than its
flashier (and deservedly popular) cousins such as *My Brilliant Career* (1980),
The Last Wave, and *The Chant of Jimmy Blacksmith* (1978) does not, of
course, indicate that it is inferior to them. It was marketed, to its disadvantage,
as a children's film in an age when such films are not greatly esteemed—
perhaps rightly, given the general debasement of the genre in the 1960's and
1970's. If *Storm Boy* is a children's film, however, it is a children's film that
steadfastly refuses to be childish. It is a mature and reflective film about
childhood, and as such, it merits our serious attention.

                                                              Robert Mitchell

THE STORY OF ALEXANDER GRAHAM BELL

Released: 1939
Production: Darryl F. Zanuck for Twentieth Century-Fox
Direction: Irving Cummings
Screenplay: Lamar Trotti; based on a story by Ray Harris
Cinematography: Leon Shamroy
Editing: Walter Thompson
Running time: 97 minutes

Principal characters:
Alexander Graham Bell .... Don Ameche
Mabel Hubbard Bell .... Loretta Young
Thomas Watson .... Henry Fonda
Gardner Hubbard .... Charles Coburn
Thomas Sanders .... Gene Lockhart
Gertrude Hubbard .... Sally Blane
Grace Hubbard .... Polly Ann Young
Berta Hubbard .... Georgiana Young
George Sanders .... Bobs Watson
Queen Victoria .... Beryl Mercer

The biographical film used to be a staple of Hollywood, particularly at Twentieth Century-Fox and Warner Bros. These films usually featured inventors or scientists and concentrated on the subject's difficulty in solving a scientific or technical problem as well as difficulty in gaining public support. Quite often, in order to make the film more entertaining, the story of a romance was involved with the person's work. *The Story of Alexander Graham Bell* is a prime example of this genre. Made by Twentieth Century-Fox, it selects out of the long life of Alexander Graham Bell two intertwined events, his invention of the telephone and his romance with Mabel Hubbard. The film was quite popular, and the title role remains the one for which Don Ameche is best remembered.

In the first part of the film, Alexander Graham Bell (Don Ameche) is a poor young inventor and teacher of the deaf, apparently supporting himself on a small stipend he receives from Thomas Sanders (Gene Lockhart). Sanders' young son, George (Bobs Watson), is deaf and mute, and Bell is teaching him to speak and also to understand messages by using a glove that has letters on it. Bell first meets Mabel (Loretta Young) when he goes to the house of Gardner Hubbard (Charles Coburn), a man who has asked Bell to see his "little girl" who has been deaf since she was four years old. Bell is more interested in getting Hubbard's financial support for his experiments in telegraphy than in working with his daughter because he has no time for more pupils, but when they meet and Bell finds that Mabel is a beautiful young woman they fall in love with each other at once. True to the conventions of romantic comedy, Bell and Mabel first "meet cute." As Bell is on his way to the Hubbards' house, he is almost hit by Mabel as she goes sledding down the sidewalk. Neither knows who the other is, and Bell is quite indignant. This incident provides a moment of embarrassment when the two are introduced soon afterward.

Bell soon becomes so engrossed with Mabel that he begins losing enthusiasm for his experiments and thinks about getting a regular job so that he can marry. Mabel, however, tells him to finish his work first because the wife will wait. Then he tells her his newest idea, which he says is either his biggest or his craziest—the telephone. "When are you going to start work on it, Mr. Bell?" she responds. Bell begins work immediately, with the help of Thomas Watson (Henry Fonda), an electrician. Watson's sardonic wit and his concern for such commonplace items as food and a social life provide a counterpoint to the idealism of Bell throughout the rest of the film. He recognizes that Bell is a genius while he is "just a plain ordinary man," but nevertheless he quickly becomes tired of subsisting on cheese and apples and living in cheap housing so that Bell can continue to be creative. Fonda is effective and entertaining in this role, which immediately preceded his portrayal of Abraham Lincoln in *Young Mr. Lincoln* (1939) and Tom Joad in *The Grapes of Wrath* (1940)—the two films that firmly established him as a star of the first magnitude.

Success does not, of course, come easy for Bell. Besides his lack of money, he has to overcome his own occasional discouragement and the opposition of Mabel's father, who forbids him to see Mabel for a while. On March 10, 1876, however, he achieves success in the laboratory. He spills some acid on his leg and says, "Mr. Watson, come here, I want you." Watson, who is half-dozing in another room, hears Bell's voice through the instrument that they are preparing to test. He rushes in excitedly yelling "It talked," and the two nearly forget the acid burn in their exhilaration. They immediately begin determining how the feat was accomplished.

This realization of his goal proves to be only the beginning of another series of battles for Bell. He demonstrates the device in a public hall to attract investors, but no one will take the invention seriously or invest in it. He is left with only Sanders and Hubbard as his backers. An indication that Queen Victoria is interested in the telephone causes him to decide to go to England to demonstrate it to her. Mabel decides she must go with him, so they marry and soon depart for England, hoping that the approval of the Queen will make the telephone popular.

Bell is successful in persuading the Queen (Beryl Mercer) to install telephones in Buckingham Palace, but the same day he receives word from the United States that a competing telephone company threatens to ruin the New England Bell Telephone Company that he has established. Soon he finds that the giant Western Union Company is suing him for an infringement of patent.

Almost all the rest of the film is devoted to the trial. At first the situation looks bleak for Bell because another man applied for a patent on the basic telephone device on the same day that Bell did and Bell has no records to show when he first developed the essential idea for the device. He finally emerges victorious after Mabel presents to the court—against Bell's wishes—a personal letter that proves his claim, and Bell follows with an emotional speech defending the right of a genius over those with money and power. Western Union admits it was wrong, blames one of its engineers for "misrepresenting" certain facts, and offers to unite with Bell. The film ends with Bell describing to Mabel his latest idea—that a device could be made to enable men to fly. "When are you going to start work on it, Mr. Bell?" she replies.

The Story of Alexander Graham Bell, until the overly sentimental and melodramatic courtroom sequence, is a solid and engrossing drama. Ameche and Young play their idealized parts well, but Fonda, who has a more rounded and entertaining character to portray, gives the most interesting performance. The direction by Irving Cummings is sound and never ostentatious. Incidentally, Mabel's three sisters are played by Loretta Young's real-life sisters, Sally Blane, Polly Ann Young, and Georgiana Young.

As is usual in Hollywood biographies, the attention to accuracy is inconsistent. For example, the research department at Twentieth Century-Fox found out exactly what a pawn ticket looked like in 1875 in order to make authentic a scene in which Bell pawns some of his possessions, but completely ignored the fact that it took Alexander Graham Bell more than fifteen years, much litigation, and an appeal to the Supreme Court to win his patent suit. Nevertheless, *The Story of Alexander Graham Bell* soon became part of American popular culture. In a 1941 film, *Ball of Fire*, a character played by Barbara Stanwyck calls the telephone the Ameche "because he invented it."

Sharon Wiseman

THE STORY OF LOUIS PASTEUR

Released: 1936
Production: Henry Blanke for Warner Bros.
Direction: William Dieterle
Screenplay: Sheridan Gibney and Pierre Collings
Cinematography: Tony Gaudio
Editing: Ralph Dawson
Running time: 85 minutes

Principal characters:
Louis Pasteur	Paul Muni (AA)
Marie Pasteur	Josephine Hutchinson
Annette Pasteur	Anita Louise
Dr. Jean Martel	Donald Woods
Dr. Zaranoff	Akim Tamiroff
Joseph Meister	Dickie Moore
Dr. Charbonnet	Fritz Leiber
Dr. Emile Roux	Henry O'Neill

Paul Muni received the 1936 Academy Award for Best Actor for his performance as the French scientist in *The Story of Louis Pasteur*. He won this honor despite strong competition including Gary Cooper in *Mr. Deeds Goes to Town*, Walter Huston in *Dodsworth*, William Powell in *My Man Godfrey*, and Spencer Tracy in *San Francisco*. Ironically, Warner Bros. did not originally want to make *The Story of Louis Pasteur*, but Muni insisted that he wanted to do the film, and after six rewrites, production began. The budget, which was less than $400,000, was so small that several standing sets had to be used. The palace of Napoleon III, for example, was actually a redressed Warner Bros. set once used in a Busby Berkeley musical.

The biographical drama begins when the eminent scientist Louis Pasteur (Paul Muni) is already established in his profession rather than presenting any details of his early life. Married to Marie (Josephine Hutchinson), Pasteur also has a grown daughter, Annette (Anita Louise), who is engaged to Pasteur's assistant, Dr. Jean Martel (Donald Woods). Although a dedicated chemist, Pasteur is forever in conflict with the French Academy of Medicine and also with Dr. Charbonnet (Fritz Leiber), who is his chief critic. Specifically, Pasteur is convinced that microbes are the cause of disease. He is further convinced that sterilization of doctors' instruments during childbirth is absolutely necessary to prevent birth-related disease.

When the medical community opposes and ridicules this position, Pasteur and his family move to the French countryside. There he pursues the treatment of a disease called anthrax in sheep and cattle. After evolving an antitoxin, he tests the serum by vaccinating twenty-five sheep while leaving another twenty-five untreated. As a result only the treated sheep survive. Next, he becomes convinced that he must find a cure for rabies (hydrophobia). Pasteur develops a serum from the saliva of a rabid dog and tries the unproven vaccine on a young boy named Joseph Meister (Dickie Moore) who has been bitten by such a dog. The child survives. In the end, Charbonnet and the French Academy of Medicine must acknowledge Pasteur's invaluable contributions to mankind.

First entitled *Enemy of Man*, retitled *The Fighter*, then *Death Fighter*, and then *The Story of Louis Pasteur* in its final form, the film is a highly engrossing drama which achieves much of its impact through its superb cast. Outstanding are Hutchinson, who is extremely credible as Pasteur's wife, and Leiber as Dr. Charbonnet. Henry O'Neill as Dr. Emile Roux (another of Pasteur's assistants) is strong in his role, and child star Moore is believable as the sickly Joseph Meister. Louise as Annette and Woods as Dr. Jean Martel lend the right touch of romance, although their presence adds little to the story.

Muni, wearing heavy makeup and a beard which make him almost completely unrecognizable, is superb in the title role. Called "an actor's actor" and "a prestige actor," Muni sensitively portrays the courageous and unflinching scientist/scholar, and repeated his role as Pasteur with Leiber in Cecil B. De Mille's Lux Radio Theater adaptation on CBS on November 23, 1936. To prepare for the film role, Muni (as was his usual practice) did much research. He studied medical journals and documents, read numerous books on Louis Pasteur and other great scientists such as Paul Ehrlich and Martin Lister, and even visited the Pasteur Institute outside of Paris. Interestingly, the brilliantly talented Muni never had a formal acting class in his life.

Born in 1895 in Lemberg, Austria (now part of Poland), Muni, the son of traveling actors, came to Hollywood at the start of the talking picture era following a successful career in the Yiddish Art Theatre and on the Broadway stage. After the success of *I Am a Fugitive from a Chain Gang* (1932) and some routine Warner Bros. melodramas, Muni began making several films of social import with director William Dieterle, who himself was a former matinee idol in Berlin and a disciple of famed director Max Reinhardt.

A versatile actor, Muni nevertheless did not achieve the enormous popularity of such fellow actors as Humphrey Bogart, Edward G. Robinson, and Spencer Tracy. Perhaps because he never repeated a character and did not incorporate his own personality into his roles, he did not develop a distinctive screen *persona* with which audiences could identify. In an ironic sense, Muni's very talent and versatility kept him from the great success attained by other actors with less talent.

The Story of Louis Pasteur opened in 1936 without much studio promotion or publicity, but received excellent reviews and good "word-of-mouth" advertising by excited moviegoers; Muni won the Academy Award for Best Actor, and the film went on to become a box-office success as well. Despite some dull stretches which sound like lectures on science, this intelligent production remains a moving and informative film. It is another example of several fine science biographies popular in the late 1930's and early 1940's, among them *Dr. Ehrlich's Magic Bullet* (1940), *Madame Curie* (1943), and *Yellow Jack* (1938). This type of film, which brought high production values and acting talents to intellectual subjects, had unfortunately all but disappeared from the screen by 1950, and has never returned.

Leslie Taubman

THE STORY OF VERNON AND IRENE CASTLE

Released: 1939
Production: George Haight for RKO/Radio
Direction: H. C. Potter
Screenplay: Richard Sherman; based on Oscar Hammerstein II and Dorothy Yost's adaptation of the book *My Husband* by Irene Castle
Cinematography: Robert de Grasse
Editing: William Hamilton
Dance direction: Hermes Pan
Running time: 90 minutes

Principal characters:
Vernon Castle	Fred Astaire
Irene Castle	Ginger Rogers
Maggie Sutton	Edna May Oliver
Walter	Walter Brennan
Lew Fields	Himself
Papa Aubel	Etienne Girardot
Emile Aubel	Rolfe Sedan

The Story of Vernon and Irene Castle was chosen to climax the series of nine films that Fred Astaire and Ginger Rogers made for RKO in the 1930's. The film was based on the lives of a phenomenally popular dance team in the era before World War I, Vernon and Irene Castle, who popularized the art of ballroom dancing and set fashions in clothes and hairstyles. In many ways, the success and popularity of Astaire and Rogers in the 1930's was reminiscent of the popularity of the team of Vernon and Irene Castle some twenty years earlier, and the similarities between the two dance teams gives an added resonance and poignancy to the film.

As the film opens, Vernon Castle (Fred Astaire) is playing second comic in slapstick vaudeville skits, but when he meets the youthful Irene (Ginger Rogers), this situation soon changes, as she encourages him to pursue a career as a dancer. After their marriage they audition for a dancing job with Vernon's mentor, comic Lew Fields (playing himself), but he turns them down, saying that no one "would pay to see a man dance with his wife."

By a stroke of luck, two French theater producers, the Aubels (Etienne Girardot and Rolfe Sedan), are watching the Castles audition and offer them a job in their new Paris show. After waiting for weeks in Paris for the show to open, they discover that the Aubels want only Vernon, and they want him only as a comedian, not as a dancer. Despondently, they go back to their rooms to dance quietly together, not knowing what to do next. Fortunately, they are discovered by theatrical agent Maggie Sutton (Edna May Oliver), who gets them an audition at the Café de Paris, where they are overwhelmingly successful. Their popularity leads to their clothes as well as their dances being copied by the Parisians.

A montage then depicts just how popular and influential the Castles have become, lending their names to candies, toiletries, cigars, and shoes, while setting fashions in clothes, hats, shoes, and hairstyles. When Irene decides to bob her hair, she immediately starts a whole new fashion. In an imaginative depiction of their successful whirlwind tour across the United States, "thirty-five cities in twenty-eight days," they are shown dancing their way across a huge map of the United States, followed by dancing throngs of people who spring up wherever they go. This scene was accomplished by painting the map on a floor mat and shooting it from a forty-foot tower.

By the time the tour ends, World War I has begun, and Vernon, despite Irene's almost hysterical protests and forebodings, enlists in the Royal Flying Corps. He survives many dangerous missions in France only to be killed in an accident at a Texas airfield in 1918. In the poignant ending, Irene watches herself and Vernon as ghosts dancing down a long path into eternity. Vernon's epitaph in the film is pronounced by the Castles' old servant and friend, Walter (Walter Brennan), who tells Irene that her husband will be remembered for "the way he laughed, the way he danced, the way he made other people want to dance." This line could also serve as the epitaph for the dance team of Astaire and Rogers.

Although RKO had purchased Irene Castle's story for Astaire and Rogers in 1936, it was not until it was scheduled to be filmed that everyone knew it would be their last film together at RKO. A great deal of care was therefore taken to ensure that it would be a high-quality finish to the series. In addition, Astaire's casting as Vernon Castle gave him an opportunity to pay tribute to a man who had greatly influenced his own career. Astaire and his sister, Adele, had seen the Castles perform at the height of their fame and had even used, according to Astaire, "some of their ballroom steps for our vaudeville act."

Irene Castle had script approval as well as approval of the cast, costumes, and director for *The Story of Vernon and Irene Castle*. She proved to be difficult to please. Although she approved of Astaire playing her husband, she took exception to Rogers, criticizing her makeup, hairstyles, and costumes. She also severely criticized the finished film in her autobiography, *Castles in the Air*. Actually, however, for a Hollywood film biography the film was remarkably faithful to the major facts. Many details of the life of Vernon and Irene Castle were altered or rearranged, and the costumes and hairstyles were not *exactly* like the ones the Castles wore, but the overall outline of their story was preserved, and the costumes were closely modeled on the original ones.

The Story of Vernon and Irene Castle is the only period musical that Astaire and Rogers did together. In it they gave up their own dances and to a certain extent their own style to re-create dances from another era. There are no great dances of courtship or seduction or passion. Instead, the dances are nostalgic re-creations—polished, technically sophisticated, smooth, and effortless—but they lack the power to evoke moods and emotions as had the dances in their earlier films. Astaire and Rogers would make one more film together (*The Barkleys of Broadway*, 1949), but since Rogers was only a last-minute substitute for Judy Garland in that film, *The Story of Vernon and Irene Castle* marks the true end of the team's creative partnership.

Julia Johnson

THE STRANGE LOVE OF MARTHA IVERS

Released: 1946
Production: Hal B. Wallis for Paramount
Direction: Lewis Milestone
Screenplay: Robert Rossen
Cinematography: Farciot Edouart and Victor Milner
Editing: Archie Marshak
Running time: 117 minutes

Principal characters:
Martha Ivers	Barbara Stanwyck
Sam Masterson	Van Heflin
Walter O'Neil	Kirk Douglas
Toni Marachek	Lizabeth Scott
Mrs. Ivers	Judith Anderson
Martha Ivers (younger)	Janis Wilson
Sam Masterson (younger)	Darryl Hickman
Walter O'Neil (younger)	Mickey Kuhn
Mr. O'Neil	Roman Bohnen

The Strange Love of Martha Ivers is many stories. It is a murder story about concealing the crime; a misspent love story about choosing the wrong man; a *film noir* story about a compelling past which cannot be escaped; and a small-town intrigue about outsiders who disturb the community.

When we first see the title character Martha Ivers (Janis Wilson) she is a young girl, running away from home. Martha lives in Iverstown and it is 1928. Iverstown is Americana, but the story is also Dickensian because Martha has a rich, hardhearted aunt (Judith Anderson) who runs the town from her mansion, and an independent young ruffian, Sam (Darryl Hickman) who helps her run away from the mansion and hide in a boxcar. There is also Walter (Mickey Kuhn), the frightened, prim, bespectacled boy who is, above all, obedient to his father. When Martha is caught in the boxcar and brought back to her aunt's mansion, Walter promptly apppears in his father's tow at her aunt's doorway. He has come to claim responsibility for her capture by informing on her whereabouts. His father is hoping for a reward from the old lady, but all she offers the boy is a glass of milk and piece of cake. Walter goes upstairs to see Martha, who has smuggled her kitten into the house while she plans her next escape. Sam appears at the window and Martha cajoles him into taking her away again, and Walter, standing by, is sworn to silence. When the kitten escapes down the stairs, Sam is sent after it. The aunt hears it mewing and climbs the stairs in pursuit; Sam hides. With Gothic cruelty the aunt finds the kitten and beats it to death on the stairs with her walking stick. Martha rushes down to its defense, grabs the stick, and brings it down on her aunt's head. Walter looks on as the aunt tumbles down the stairs, dead.

At that moment the strange love of Martha Ivers really begins. Her love is based on obsession with denial and betrayal. From then on, all her references to the murder make it seem inevitable and compelling. All the sacrifices and bargains she makes to conceal her crime are, therefore, inescapable. Immediately after she kills her aunt we see Martha deny her own involvement in the murder. She tells Walter's father that a man did it, and then ran away. Walter and his father support her story, in an unspoken deal. Walter will have part in Martha's inheritance—and in Martha.

From the scene on the stairs the film dissolves to Iverstown twenty years later. Sam (Van Heflin) is passing through town, now a grown man. He notices the Iverstown sign on the highway, and runs his car into a tree while looking at it. After he puts the car in the shop, he meets a woman named Toni Marachek (Lizabeth Scott) who is young, sexy, available, and worldly-wise. She picks him up, and they go to his hotel. Next day she is arrested for violating probation—she was supposed to have left town. In a predictable ironic twist, Walter (Kirk Douglas) is now the town District Attorney. Sam goes to look up his old friend to get his new girl out of jail. That is the way he meets Walter's wife, Martha (Barbara Stanwyck), again.

Although the plot has been fairly predictable, the strength of *The Strange Love of Martha Ivers* is that it twists ordinary plot points to give all of Martha's actions a centrifugal force. What Martha has told herself all these years is that she cannot have what she wants, because she will be betrayed by her past. Now she learns that she cannot have what she wants because she will not be betrayed. Both Walter and Martha always have assumed that Sam was a third witness to the murder. When he shows up in town and asks Walter for a favor, they conclude that he is threatening blackmail. This is not the case, however. First of all, he did not see the murder. Second, after Martha tells him that she did it, he does not want to blackmail her for either love or money. Walter in actuality has blackmailed her for both, but even though the threat of betrayal is Walter's hold on Martha, he admits that he could never betray her. By betraying her, Walter would betray himself as both an accomplice and a lover, because Walter is truly in love with Martha. The combination of Sam's and Walter's reactions shows Martha that her every fear of betrayal by someone else is an echo of her own solicitation of those betrayals. It is an echo loudest in the sound of the pistol she aims for Walter, at the end, pulling its trigger as she holds it at her side.

Since the murder, Martha has metaphorically lived her life on those stairs which helped her to commit the crime, and the camera places her there at important moments. The first time we see Martha as a grown woman, she is walking back up the stairs. The movement signals a return to her past. In the same way, the adult Sam drives back into Iverstown in the opposite screen direction that he took as a boy leaving town on the train. Sam will be able to escape his past, however, eventually leaving town again with Toni. Their departure is one of the few daylight, open scenes in the movie. Toni also walks away from a past which would mark her as a promiscuous woman and a thief who has done time in prison.

Martha differs from them. She has promised herself that, in a way, only her past gives her control of the present, as well as a reason not to live in it. As long as the crime in her past is a secret, it gives her the money and power to run the town, buy her husband the governorship, and run up and down those stairs in the mansion. To keep the murder a secret, however, she must live with the "bargain" of Walter, living with a man she is convinced she does not want. She lives in the "past" by sleeping with a series of men who represent Walter's alternatives and Sam's substitutes, all the while playing the D.A.'s wife and pillar of the community. She and Walter share only their crime. The only close shots she shares with him, in a composition implying togetherness and mutual dependency, occur when they discuss the murder, which is the basis of their relationship. Her kiss is perfunctory, and the camera backs away from the cold embrace she offers her husband. As murderers, however, the two are passionately involved.

When Sam asks Walter for a favor for Toni, Walter acts to protect himself from what he assumes is blackmail. He has Sam beaten; Sam returns to threaten Walter's life if he tries that again. Martha, on the other hand, figures her past can be seduced. She takes Sam to the hill where they used to meet as kids. By a campfire she relives the moment of the murder, not hearing Sam when he says he was not there. When he says it again, she realizes that she has revealed the secret. Worse than that, she realizes that Sam does not share in her past or guilt. Martha tries to attack Sam, this time grabbing a branch rather than a walking stick, but Sam grabs the stick and forces her attack into an embrace which Martha soon accepts passionately.

Now Sam has the idea he will go away with Martha and be reclaimed by her passion. Walter gets drunk as he waits for Sam to arrive at the mansion. When Sam gets there, Walter tries to tell him how Martha has ruined his life by making him an accomplice. Drunk, he walks away from Martha and Sam and rolls down the stairs, fracturing his skull. Martha sees him lying on the stairs and sees a way to "replay" her aunt's murder and then be rid of it. "Set me free," she urges Sam—by just killing Walter. Sam walks down the stairs towards Walter. As the camera stays on an uncomfortably close shot of Martha's face, we watch her expression as she hopes for the murder; then her face becomes impossible to read. From her point of view, we see Sam carry Walter into the study. There is no murder.

Her plea for Walter's murder has changed Sam's attitude toward her to pity. Martha, realizing he will leave her, points the gun at what she cannot have anyway. "You're not going away," she tells Sam. At that moment, the camera looks down on both Walter and Martha. They are so rarely together, and always over murder, that the shot helps Sam's precarious position hit home. "I'm sorry for both of you," Sam says, and walks out the door. Walter crosses with Martha to the window, and both watch Sam cross the lawn. Walter knows Martha just tried to kill him; he has the gun at her side. Martha tells Walter she could not be without him, and, coming full circle, repeats what she said about Sam the night of the murder. "He'll never tell." Walter brings the gun up; then the camera frames the two in close shot. As always, they are together over a murder. Walter cannot pull the trigger, however, and Martha guides the gun closer to her side, and pulls the trigger for him. It is a romance based on murder.

The story, in retelling, seems overly dramatic, but the acting and direction raise what could have been a mediocre film to the level of a classic. Eminent director Lewis Milestone, perhaps best-rememberd for his masterpiece *All Quiet on the Western Front* (1930), for which he won an Academy Award, lets the mood of the film dominate the action. The actors, especially Stanwyck and Douglas, also enhance the mood. There is a good transition from the early segment of the film to the later due in large part to the similarities of character between the child and adult actors. When Stanwyck emerges as the adult Martha, she is the same basic character that she was as a child—not evil, but twisted. Douglas and Heflin also convey the transition to adulthood well, although in Heflin's case Sam's character is not as deep as the others, and therefore his performance does not shine as do Stanwyck's and Douglas'.

Leslie Donaldson

THE STRANGER

Released: 1946
Production: Sam Spiegel for International; released by RKO/Radio
Direction: Orson Welles
Screenplay: Anthony Veiller; based on Victor Trivas and Decla Dunning's
    adaptation of an original story by Victor Trivas
Cinematography: Russell Metty
Editing: Ernest Nims
Running time: 95 minutes

> *Principal characters:*
> Wilson .... Edward G. Robinson
> Mary Longstreet (Rankin) .... Loretta Young
> Charles Rankin/Franz Kindler .... Orson Welles
> Judge Longstreet .... Philip Merivale
> Mr. Potter .... Billy House
> Noah Longstreet .... Richard Long
> Konrad Meinike .... Konstantin Shayne
> Sara .... Martha Wentworth

Like *Citizen Kane* (1941), *The Stranger* features and was directed by Orson
Welles. For the earlier film, Welles was given great freedom as well as control
over the filming and editing, and the result was a masterpiece. Because *Citizen
Kane* was not, however, a commercial success, Welles began having trouble
with the administrators of the studio. He was therefore able to make *The
Stranger* for producer S. P. Eagle (who later became known as Sam Spiegel)
only by agreeing to adhere closely to the script and to an editing plan drawn
up in advance. The resulting film is a satisfactory suspense thriller with a few
indications of Welles's talent, but it naturally is not on the same level as
Citizen Kane. Ironically, it was the most profitable of all the films that Welles
has directed. This film has no connection with *L'Étranger*, the famous novel
by Albert Camus which was coincidentally published in the United States
under the title *The Stranger* in the same year that the film was released, 1946.
Camus' work was filmed later, in 1967, by the Italian director Luchino Vis-
conti.

The opening scenes of Welles's film establish the premise, the style, and
a recurring motif. At the Allied War Crimes Commission hearings one man,
Wilson (Edward G. Robinson), demands, "This obscenity must be destroyed!"
In order to accomplish this, he says, a criminal must be set free. Then we see
that the criminal, Konrad Meinike (Konstantin Shayne), after being set free,
is followed by Wilson, who unaccountably makes little attempt to keep Meinike from knowing that he is being followed. After we learn that Meinike is
looking for a man named Franz Kindler, he leads Wilson to Harper, Con-

necticut. Welles and his cinematographer, Russell Metty, make good use of low-angle shots and shadows throughout the sequence, and they also concentrate on Wilson's ever-present pipe. Indeed, we see Wilson's pipe before we see his face.

The elements of the mystery concerning why Meinike is seeking Kindler and why Wilson is following him are revealed slowly during the first half of the film. Kindler (Orson Welles) was the mastermind behind the Nazi atrocities, and Meinike was his executive officer. Kindler has gone to the small Connecticut town of Harper and become a history teacher there, using the name Charles Rankin. He is engaged to the daughter of a justice of the Supreme Court and thinks that his camouflage is perfect. He can remain "hidden" in his role as a model respectable citizen "until the day when we strike again." In contrast to the unrepentant Kindler, Meinike has become religious and has searched out his old boss to persuade him to confess and repent.

When Meinike finds Kindler disguised as Rankin and tries to talk to him, Rankin realizes that Meinike was purposely freed to lead the authorities to himself. As Meinike kneels to lead Rankin in a confession of guilt, Rankin strangles him and quickly covers the body with leaves. He has to hurry so that he will not be late for his marriage to Mary Longstreet (Loretta Young). Indeed, there is a direct cut from Rankin covering his trail in the woods where he committed the murder to Rankin being married. Immediately after the ceremony Rankin leaves and buries the body.

At this point Wilson, who has been a somewhat obscure figure usually only observing the action, becomes a central figure in the film. He engages the proprietor of the local drugstore, Mr. Potter (Billy House), in conversation in an effort to learn who in the town might be Kindler, since Meinike has disappeared and can no longer lead him to the man. Indeed, Potter also becomes an important figure in the film because he knows everyone and sees and talks with most of them as they visit his store. Besides a source of information, Potter functions as the voice of collective small-town consciousness of Harper. In order to explain his own presence in the town Wilson says that he is a dealer in antiques.

When Rankin and Mary return from their honeymoon, Wilson joins them at her father's house for a dinner. During the conversation at the table, Mary's brother Noah (Richard Long) makes a statement about Germans that provokes a monologue on the German psyche by Rankin, who says that Germans are lovers of war. When Noah attempts to answer one of his points by quoting Karl Marx, Rankin replies that Marx was not a German, that he was in fact, a Jew. After the dinner, Wilson goes back to his room and telephones Washington D.C., to report that he is leaving Harper because he is convinced that Rankin is not Kindler. He then goes to sleep. Meanwhile, Rankin has taken Mary's dog out for a walk. When the dog begins digging in the dirt, Rankin realizes that he is digging at the spot where Meinike is buried and gives the animal a savage kick. The film then cuts immediately to Wilson sitting up in bed, not because he had heard Rankin but because he had suddenly realized that no one "but a Nazi would deny that Karl Marx was a German because he was a Jew."

Now Wilson is sure that he has found the right man and that he must make him reveal himself somehow, for there are no pictures of Kindler, and with Meinike gone, there is no one who can identify him. At this point Mary begins to find out damaging things about her husband, but she remains loyal to him. Finally he tells her that he killed Meinike and also killed her dog to keep him from revealing the grave, but he explains this as being a result of a blackmail attempt by Meinike and reveals nothing of his Nazi past. Mary immediately promises to stand by him and to keep his secret from everyone. Only a momentary shudder when he embraces her reveals any hesitancy on her part.

Wilson has decided that Mary must be told the whole story. He has her father (Philip Merivale) telephone and invite her to his house alone. There Wilson shows Mary some films of victims of the Nazis and explains to her who Rankin really is. She refuses to believe him. After she leaves, Wilson explains to her father that the facts are too horrible for her to face. Rankin then begins suspecting that Mary may reveal something about him and plans to kill her.

Incidents come quickly after this point. Throughout the film Rankin has been repairing the large ornate clock in the church tower. His plan now is to saw in half some of the rungs of the ladder to the clock and telephone Mary to meet him there. Meanwhile he will be at the drugstore playing checkers with Potter and will thus have a perfect alibi. All goes according to plan except that Mary's maid Sara (Martha Wentworth) pretends to have a heart attack to keep her from leaving the house. When Rankin returns to the house and finds Mary there, he reveals enough in his surprised reactions that she understands that he tried to kill her.

A quick series of events then leads to the conclusion with Rankin in the clock tower and Mary going up to kill him. Then Wilson joins them as a crowd of citizens of the town gather below. Rankin protests that he only followed orders, only did his duty, but Wilson and Mary are understandably unmoved. Mary then shoots and wounds him, causing him to stagger and fall onto the outside platform of the clock. The clock is an elaborate one with lifesized figures that circle around it. As Rankin tries to stand up on the platform, one of the figures impales him on a sword it is holding. It is a gruesome image. Then Rankin falls to his death below as the hands of the clock spin wildly. The film ends with Wilson saying to Mary, "Pleasant dreams."

Reportedly, John Huston wrote most of the script for *The Stranger*, and

Welles also worked on it, although the screen credits give Anthony Vieller credit for the screenplay from a story and adaptation by Victor Trivas and Decla Dunning. As is obvious from the summary there is a certain amount of melodrama and improbable behavior in the script, but neither is excessive for a thriller. Indeed, it is the acting and directing in such a film that must keep the viewer's emotional involvement high enough that questions of the credibility of the plot do not arise.

In *The Stranger* both the acting and directing are up to this challenge. Robinson is particulary effective as the determined but quiet sleuth, and Young portrays well the psychological turmoil of a person who has just learned that a crucial part of her life is exactly the opposite of what she believed it to be. Welles's acting is credible, and as director he added many stylistic touches that have been mentioned even though he did not have the opportunity to make the film as personal a statement as he would have liked. All in all, the film is an entertaining thriller and an interesting look at one aspect of the career of Welles.

Marilynn Wilson

STRANGERS ON A TRAIN

Released: 1951
Production: Alfred Hitchcock for Warner Bros.
Direction: Alfred Hitchcock
Screenplay: Raymond Chandler and Czenzi Ormonde; based on the novel of
the same name by Patricia Highsmith
Cinematography: Robert Burks
Editing: William Ziegler
Running time: 101 minutes

Principal characters:

Guy Haines	Farley Granger
Bruno Antony	Robert Walker
Anne Morton	Ruth Roman
Barbara Morton	Patricia Hitchcock
Senator Morton	Leo G. Carroll
Miriam Joyce Haines	Laura Elliot
Mrs. Antony	Marion Lorne
Bass Fiddler	Alfred Hitchcock

Alfred Hitchcock's *Strangers on a Train* illustrates clearly the filmmaking characteristics which earned the director his reputation as the "master of suspense." In addition, it offers an interesting lesson in understanding the medium as one distinct from literature, theater, television, or any other art form to which one might attempt comparison. By examining the film as an adaptation of a novel, a total synthesis of elements, and a manipulator of its audience, one can recognize some of the elements which set film apart, as well as the skill with which Hitchcock practiced his art.

The adaptation of a novel to film presents numerous problems. A novel, by nature, requires more scenes to develop the characters and involves the reader in a more plausible plot than does a film. Not only does the novel require pages of description to create a physical impression of people and places, but it also must describe the psychological aspects which motivate the action of the story. The physical is easily achieved in a visual medium, but the degree to which motivation is established may vary depending on the aim of the director. Too often, the film version of a novel alienates the person who has first read the book by offering a different interpretation or by representing characters in a way which differs from the impressions in the reader's mind. The reverse can also be true: the book might alienate those persons who first see the movie, for similar reasons. A more serious problem is the "bookish" film, one which fails to involve and excite the filmgoer by relying on literary rather than cinematic devices.

In adapting the first novel of young writer Patricia Highsmith, Hitchcock wisely chose to accept only the basic premise of the book. The psychological complexity of the novel, that which had so fascinated the novelist, would have proved an overwhelming task to translate to the screen. Hitchcock's selection of tough-guy novelist Raymond Chandler as one of the screenwriters further indicates his intention to shift the novel's emphasis from the psychological confusion which afflicts Guy Haines to the imbalanced psychological state of Bruno Antony, placing Guy in the familiar Hitchcock situation of an innocent man who circumstantially falls under suspicion of a crime he did not commit.

Guy Haines (Farley Granger), an amateur tennis player, lives in Washington, D.C., where he works for Senator Morton (Leo G. Carroll). Guy loves the senator's daughter Anne (Ruth Roman), whom he hopes to marry as soon as he can obtain a divorce from his estranged wife, Miriam (Laura Elliot), who is still living in their hometown of Metcalfe. As Guy travels to a tennis match, he plans to interrupt his train journey to discuss the divorce with Miriam. On the train he meets Bruno Antony (Robert Walker), an affluent good-for-nothing who seems to know everything about Guy, information gleaned from the society pages of Washington, D.C., newspapers. When Guy finds the dining car full, he has no choice but to accept Bruno's invitation to lunch in his compartment. During lunch, Bruno proposes a bizarre scheme: he will kill Guy's wife, and Guy will kill Bruno's father, a wealthy man who disapproves of his son's frivolous and costly life style. Based on the assumption that only the criminal with a motive is caught, Bruno is certain that their motiveless crimes will escape detection. When Guy disembarks at Metcalfe, he dismisses Bruno as an eccentric.

In his conversation with Miriam, Guy learns that she is pregnant by another man. Rather than simplifying his situation, however, this news complicates it. Miriam plans to join Guy in Washington, taking full advantage of his newly acquired social standing for herself and "their" child. Furious, Guy leaves the music shop in which Miriam works. Before boarding the train, he calls Anne, and in his frustration he says that he could kill Miriam.

Unknown to Guy, Bruno has taken their conversation very seriously. He travels to Metcalfe and follows Miriam and her two male companions to an amusement park. On an island accessible only by small boats which first pass through the Tunnel of Love, Bruno confronts Miriam alone and strangles her. When Guy returns to Washington, Bruno is waiting for him in a shadowy street. He naïvely confesses his act to Guy, fully expecting Guy now to act out his part of the plan, but Guy, caught totally off guard by this confession, is both insulted and confused. The arrival of the police confirms the truth of Bruno's statement and places Guy in the web of suspicion surrounding a crime with which he had nothing to do.

Bruno persists in holding Guy to his part of the plan, waiting for him to kill Mr. Antony. He hounds Guy with telephone calls and appearances. When

Guy makes it clear that he wants nothing to do with the plot, Bruno threatens to implicate him further in Miriam's murder by placing the cigarette lighter which Guy inadvertently left in Bruno's train compartment at the scene of the murder. As Bruno travels to Metcalfe, Guy competes in a tennis tournament, hoping to complete the match and escape the police guard which watches his every move.

Successful in his escape, Guy travels to Metcalfe, but unknown to him, he is followed by the police. When he arrives at the amusement park, he confronts Bruno near the small boat concession which will give him access to the island. In the ensuing chase, Bruno and Guy find themselves on the carousel, which runs wildly out of control. As they struggle, the carousel flies apart, and Bruno is trapped under the debris. Before he dies, Guy attempts to extract a confession from him, but Bruno dies clutching the lighter in his hand. When the boat operator tells the police he had seen Bruno the night of the murder and they see the lighter, they are convinced that Guy is innocent. Guy is free to pursue his political career and to marry Anne, conveniently free not only of Bruno, but also of Miriam.

The acting in the film is generally undistinguished, a quality which underscores the synthesis of cinematic elements rather than detracts from the production. The minor characters show the professionalism of their years, allowing themselves to be directed toward achieving a total film effect. Carroll, one of Hitchcock's favorite actors, gives a credible performance as the senator. Marion Lorne, employing her familiar befuddled manner, adds not only humor but also credence to the character of Bruno—with her as his mother, his distorted mind is understandable. Granger and Roman offer one-dimensional performances in line with the flat characters they portray. Patricia Hitchcock, Hitchcock's daughter, plays the senator's younger daughter Barbara broadly, providing frequent spirit and comic relief in the bland relationship between Guy and Anne. As is appropriate, it is Walker who provides a strong portrayal as Bruno. The pivotal character in the story, Walker's Bruno is mannered, dispicable, and truly horrifying. His character combines with the elements of the film to heighten tension and advance the story to those suspenseful moments which maintain the film's pace.

Hitchcock holds the other elements of the film in balance as well. The cinematography and editing are skillful, always aimed at achieving the desired effect. They never call too much attention to themselves. The goal, as with the acting, is to maintain suspense and pace. The murder scene, the crosscutting from Bruno reaching for the fallen lighter to Guy playing tennis against the clock, and the final confrontation between Bruno and Guy are all timed to drive the tension to the point where it must be relieved. A scene achieving the same effect occurs when Guy goes to Bruno's house according to the plan. Instead of going to kill Mr. Antony, however, he goes to warn him. The audience, given no knowledge of this, is led to believe that Guy might have broken under the pressure. The tension is finally relieved, and the story line remains unbroken.

In spite of the simple plot, Hitchcock successfully captures the audience and leads it along with no time to question events, relationships, or emotions. The opening scene begins this process. Without the aid of dialogue, the audience observes the lower legs and feet of two men hurrying through a train station. One man is athletic, solid, respectable: the other is extravagant, high-strung, effete. The characters of Guy and Bruno are immediately established, and the urgency of their situation sweeps the viewer into the story. Hitchcock continues to rely on visual images to hold the audience and sustain the suspense and pace of the film. When Bruno returns to Metcalfe to place the cigarette lighter at the scene of the crime, Guy is engaged in a tennis match. As he leaves the station, Bruno drops the lighter through a grate in the street, and while he attempts to retrieve it, Guy attempts to complete the match and arrive in Metcalfe before Bruno completes his plan. The cross-cutting creates in the audience the same anxiety felt by the characters.

These visual images make use of two related yet different situations. One interesting use of the dual image presented in separate scenes concerns strangulation. When Bruno strangles Miriam, her glasses fall to the ground, and the murder is filmed as a reflection in the lenses. Hitchcock's indirect presentation of violence has become one of the best known in cinema, and it effectively instills a feeling of terror in the viewer. The image is mirrored at a society party to which Bruno obtains an invitation. As Bruno speaks with an elderly lady, the topic flirtatiously turns to the hypothetical murder of her husband. Bruno playfully demonstrates strangulation as a method. When he sees Barbara, who wears glasses similar in shape to those Miriam wore, his hands tighten on the lady's neck, and he almost strangles her. Barbara's terror comes from behind the glasses, as had Miriam's when she first realized that Bruno intended to kill her.

Hitchcock's manipulation of the audience to feel the anxiety of the innocent man wrongly accused is heightened by the clues placed throughout the film which later hinder Guy's attempt to establish an alibi. The audience observes Bruno finding Guy's lighter, Guy's argument with Miriam to which there are observers but not listeners, Guy's call to Anne when he says he could kill Miriam, Guy's conversation with a drunk on the train the night Miriam is murdered: all of these situations establish in the viewer's mind Guy's alibi, yet the circumstances thwart Guy's effort to clear himself. The audience, placed in an all-seeing position, feels the frustration which Guy feels. This gradual manipulation draws the viewer into the dilemma from the film's beginning, advances the story without delay, and never releases its hold on the audience, creating an experience which is completely self-contained.

The cohesiveness of the elements of *Strangers on a Train* underscores Hitchcock's expertise as a director. By fully utilizing the devices peculiar to cinema, allowing no one to overshadow the others, he creates a fast-paced, suspenseful thriller with a happy ending. The film becomes a unit, an effective piece of entertainment, and a lesson in the art of filmmaking. The success of the film with audiences is evidenced by the frequency with which it is shown at revival theaters throughout the country.

Kenneth T. Burles

THE STRATTON STORY

Released: 1949
Production: Jack Cummings for Metro-Goldwyn-Mayer
Direction: Sam Wood
Screenplay: Douglas Morrow and Guy Trosper; based on an original screen
   story by Douglas Morrow (AA)
Cinematography: Harold Rosson
Editing: Ben Lewis
Running time: 106 minutes

> *Principal characters:*
> Monty Stratton .... James Stewart
> Ethel Stratton .... June Allyson
> Barney Wile .... Frank Morgan
> Ma Stratton .... Agnes Moorehead
> Ted Lyons .... Bruce Cowling
> Luke Appling .... Dean White

Perhaps because of the popularity of televised sporting events, manifold film scenarios are now centering on athletic competition. In this new wave of sports films, almost every type of athletic competition has been covered, from hockey (*Slapshot*, 1977) to women's track (*Goldengirl*, 1979). Particularly popular have been football films such as *Semi-Tough* (1977) and *North Dallas Forty* (1980) and boxing films, including *Rocky* (1977) and *Raging Bull* (1980). Otherwise unathletic actors and actresses have been eagerly donning sneakers and sweat socks in anticipation of luring the avid sports fan away from television. In addition to actors, professional athletes are themselves turning to acting, most notably O. J. Simpson, Alex Karras, and Muhammad Ali. This new Hollywood phenomenon is something of an anomaly of recent years, as not long ago films focusing on sports (with the exception of prize-fighting) were considered box-office poison. *The Stratton Story*, released in 1949, was a notable exception: it was the sixth-highest-grossing film of its year, earning four million dollars in receipts—a tidy figure for a time when bus rides to the theater in most cities still cost only five cents.

The Stratton Story is strikingly similar to another box-office champion released at the beginning of the decade: *Pride of the Yankees* (1942). Both pictures center on real-life baseball players who are faced with major physical impairments but who are inordinately courageous; they are supported by sweet, loyal spouses and are able to stand tall and firm while in the pit of adversity. *Pride of the Yankees* is the tale of Lou Gehrig, the New York Yankee Hall of Fame first baseman whose career and life were tragically shortened by amyotrophic lateral sclerosis, a mysterious killer now commonly known as Lou Gehrig's disease. *The Stratton Story*, however, focuses on an

athlete not as renowed, Monty Stratton (James Stewart), a pitcher for the
Chicago White Sox who lost a leg in a hunting accident but who managed a
comeback to the professional ranks with an artificial limb.

This story of a rise, fall, then rise again is a formula Hollywood scenario,
a staple in films from the silents to *Rocky*. The plot of *The Stratton Story* was
a cliché even thirty years ago, but as the film is based on fact and is so well
acted, written, and directed, it is a compelling human drama. The unknown
but talented Stratton, a young farmer athlete, plays baseball for a sandlot
team in the Texas boondocks. He is discovered by Barney Wile (Frank Morgan), a has-been catcher barnstorming through the area. Baseball is in Stratton's blood, and, under the tutelage of Wile, he develops into a brilliant
pitcher, but before he can establish himself as a major league star, he badly
injures his leg in an accident. His wife Ethel (June Allyson) must decide for
or against amputation. His leg is cut off above the knee, and the brooding,
self-pitying Stratton refuses to walk with his fake limb. Eventually, however,
with the support and encouragement of his wife and his mother (Agnes Moorehead), he and his young son take their first steps together. He learns how
to use his artificial leg, regains his pitching prowess and finally plays—and
wins—in the East Texas League.

In this saga of triumph over overwhelming odds, screenwriters Douglas
Morrow and Guy Trosper (Morrow spent three weeks in Texas with the
Stratton family before writing the original story, and received an Oscar for
his effort) effectively play to the viewer's emotions. Their screenplay is spirited, perceptive, and inspirational in its depiction of the real-life drama whose
highlights are Stratton's initial attempt to walk with his son and his success
as a one-legged pitcher in an All-Star game. *The Stratton Story* is, of course,
sentimental, but it never becomes syrupy or mawkish.

The role of Monty Stratton is custom-made for Stewart, and the gangly
actor is thoroughly believable as the crippled ballplayer . Stratton is not his
most famous part—perhaps his Jefferson Smith in Frank Capra's *Mr. Smith
Goes to Washington* (1939) is his most memorable—but Stewart *is* Monty
Stratton, and the role is a solid, colorful portrait in the gallery of Stewart
characterizations. Curiously, most critics dubbed this role his best since the
end of World War II, his George Bailey in Capra's *It's a Wonderful Life* (1947)
notwithstanding. *It's a Wonderful Life* received decidedly mixed notices when
previewed for the press, but at the time, Capra felt it was his best work to
date, and Stewart was nominated for an Academy Award, an honor he did
not receive for *The Stratton Story*. Stewart is not just a Hollywood star, but
a skilled actor equally adept as a dramatic, romantic, or comedy lead in these
films as well as in *The Philadelphia Story* (1940), *You Can't Take It with You*
(1936), *Call Northside 777* (1948), *Anatomy of a Murder* (1959), and *The
Mortal Storm* (1940), to name but a few of his numerous successes.

The film is Stewart's initial screen appearance opposite sugary M-G-M contract player Allyson. The pair clicked as a romantic team: their courtship and domestic relationship are as much a part of *The Stratton Story* as the ballplayer's exploits on the diamond. Allyson later played opposite Stewart as Mrs. Glenn Miller in *The Glenn Miller Story* (1954) and as Mrs. Robert Hollander in *Strategic Air Command* (1955). In her most popular roles—and *The Stratton Story* is one of these—Allyson is the wholesome girl next door who marries the hero and is required to do little more than render moral support to her troubled spouses.

Having already been responsible for *Pride of the Yankees*, Sam Wood was the ideal director for *The Stratton Story*. In both films, he infuses the athletic sequences with a feeling of the thrill of realizing one's dream of playing in professional baseball. His handling of the scenes between Stewart and Allyson is no less skilled. Long-time M-G-M character player Morgan, in one of his last films, is appropriately colorful as Stratton's mentor, consistently adding a note of endearing eccentricity to his roles. This is something which he did in many other films for M-G-M in the 1930's and 1940's, most notably in *Boom Town* (1939) and *The Wizard of Oz* (1939), perhaps his most famous role. As Ma Stratton, Moorehead is called upon to do little more than elicit concern for her son, but she renders a solid, slick performance within the confines of the role. Major leaguers Gene Bearden, Bill Dickey, Jimmy Dykes, and Mervyn Shea appear as themselves, while Bruce Cowling and Dean White impersonate, respectively, White Sox stars Ted Lyons and Luke Appling. Stratton himself assisted in the film's production as a technical adviser.

The Stratton Story holds up today as an appealing tribute to its title character, who in 1946 won a phenomenal eighteen games for his Texas League team and was honored as the nation's "Most Courageous Athlete." The real Monty Stratton was justifiably satisfied with the Hollywoodization of his life.

Rob Edelman

STRAW DOGS

Released: 1971
Production: David Melnick for Cinerama
Direction: Sam Peckinpah
Screenplay: Sam Peckinpah and David Zelag Goodman; based on the novel
  Siege at Trencher's Farm by Gordon Williams
Cinematography: John Coquillon
Editing: Paul Davies, Roger Spottiswoode, and Tony Lawson
Running time: 113 minutes

> *Principal characters:*
> David Sumner ....Dustin Hoffman
> Amy Sumner ....Susan George
> Tom Hedden ....Peter Vaughan
> Charlie Venner .... Del Henney
> Scutt ....Ken Hutchinson
> Cawsey .... Jim Norton
> Henry ....David Warner

Sam Peckinpah made his reputation in the 1960's by directing a series of increasingly violent Westerns. Peckinpah's West was truly wild, a land where men were men, and proved it by shooting one another at every opportunity. This phase of Peckinpah's career reached its zenith with *The Wild Bunch* (1969), which featured a multitude of lyrical, almost loving, slow-motion shots of men dying violently. He drew a good deal of criticism for what some critics felt was excessive violence, and *Straw Dogs* was his reply. In *Straw Dogs*, Peckinpah abandons the Wild West and the trick photography. He does not, however, abandon his basic philosophy about violence. Quite the contrary; *Straw Dogs* is a tightly constructed and beautifully crafted argument on behalf of the moral necessity of violence.

Set in the contemporary English countryside, the film's landscape is, at first glance, almost pastoral. David Sumner (Dustin Hoffman), an American mathematician, has moved to a remote farmhouse in Cornwall with his English wife Amy (Susan George). His intent is to get away from the turbulent college life in the United States, where confrontation politics are an everyday occurrence, and find a place where he can pursue his research in peace. Amy's parents' old house seems like the perfect place, and as the film opens, David and his wife have just moved in. Their house, which will come to be an important symbol in the film, is still being remodeled.

As David and Amy go into town for groceries, Peckinpah wastes no time in letting the viewer know that England will not turn out to be the idyllic haven from strife that David seeks. The suggestion of trouble appears in two forms. Peckinpah's first shot of Amy strutting down the village street, obviously braless, swinging her hips, offers a contrast with the shy, inhibited David that is immediate and ominous. Amy's old boyfriend Charlie Venner (Del Henney) turns up immediately and with a lewd grin reminds Amy of their earlier romance. The look on Amy's face during the conversation says that Charlie's attentions are not entirely unwelcome.

Meanwhile David, going into a pub for cigarettes, walks in on the middle of an ugly quarrel by Venner's uncle, Tom Hedden (Peter Vaughan), over the bartender's refusal to sell him a pint of beer. Hedden is a brute of a man and a mean drunk. David also sees the villages heap verbal and physical abuse on Henry (David Warner), a hulking mental defective with (it turns out) an attraction to young girls. With a sexy wife and neighbors who range from surly to psychopathic, David's potential problems are apparent to everyone but him.

Blithely ignoring their sneers of contempt, David hires Venner and two other local bullies, Scutt (Ken Hutchinson) and Cawsey (Jim Norton), to work on his house. Things quickly begin to worsen. Neglected by her husband ("I love you, Amy, but I want you to leave me alone," David says when she interrupts his astrophysical musings), Amy flirts with Venner and his friends. The men grow increasingly contemptuous of David, who is, or at least pretends to be, oblivious to the whole situation. At first, their scorn is expressed merely by casual insubordination. One day, however, the Sumners discover that their pet cat has been strangled and hung by a cord in their bedroom closet. Amy senses the significance of the incident at once: Scutt and/or Cawsey did it "to prove to you that they could get into your bedroom." She insists that David fire the pair. David, however, wants to avoid a confrontation, and declines to do so.

Soon afterwards, the men become inexplicably chummy with David. They invite him to go duck hunting with him, and, eager to win their acceptance, he readily agrees. The hunt turns out to be another of the men's pranks, however, as they leave the hapless David alone on a remote moor, where he blasts unsuccessfully away at passing birds for hours before it dawns on him that he has been deserted.

While David is trudging home on foot, Peckinpah arranges a more sinister fate for Amy. Having disposed of her husband for the day, Venner returns to the isolated house, where he has sex with a mildly protesting Amy. Things grow more complicated when Cawsey arrives unexpectedly. Keeping Venner at bay with his shotgun, Cawsey proceeds to rape Amy brutally. The two men leave, and Amy, confused and humiliated, never tells David about the incident. Peckinpah clearly believes that Amy deserved, and in some way, wanted to be raped. Whatever its merits, *Straw Dogs* is undeniably misogynistic; indeed, the only other significant female role in the film is that of a young girl who is killed by Henry while she is in the process of seducing him.

Peckinpah has thus painted a picture of a completely ineffectual man, scorned by his peers and cuckolded by his wife. David has ignored or avoided every confrontation, and it has not helped him. His cowardice—for that is clearly how the rest of the characters in the film, as well as its director, see it—has only encouraged his enemies. Peckinpah will shortly place an even sterner test of David's pacifism before him, however, and his character will change.

David's house, the site of so many humiliations, becomes the occasion for his change. He abandons his nonviolent attitude when Tom Hedden, along with Venner, Scutt, and Cawsey, invade his home in search of Henry, the village idiot who has (unintentionally, and unbeknown to David) killed a local girl and taken refuge in the Sumners' house. Hedden and the others are armed, drunk, and in a vicious mood. It is clear that, if David surrenders Henry, they will kill him for his crime.

The realization that he must either send Henry to his death or fight, snaps something in David. Shouting "This is *my* house," he pushes the startled invaders out. They regroup outside, but David is determined to defend his home. The final twenty minutes of the film are a maelstrom of violence and terror, as, one by one, using everything from boiling oil to an antique mantrap, David repels his assailants. The film ends as David, surveying the carnage around him, says, in a voice half-amazed and half-delighted, "Jesus, I beat 'em all."

In *Straw Dogs*, then, Peckinpah argues that there are times when violence is the only appropriate and moral response; and, indeed, by the time David is forced to choose between giving up Henry or defending the sanctity of his home, he is left with no meaningful alternative to violence. The film is put together so brilliantly that Peckinpah appears to have proved his point. It is only after the film is over, and there has been time for reflection, that questions arise. What, for example, is a woman like Amy doing with an American astrophysicist? Their relationship seems highly improbable, and can only be seen as an example of Peckinpah's weighting his argument unfairly by basing part of it on a faulty premise. Another question is whether David Sumner is truly representative of a mature, thoughtful person committed to nonviolence. He could have avoided much of his trouble simply by firing Charlie Venner and company earlier for insubordination; his refusal to confront the situation when it could have been resolved peacefully was motivated much less by principled nonviolence than by stupidity and cowardice. Clearly, in scripting his story, Peckinpah and cowriter David Zelag Goodman were loading the dice.

Nevertheless, *Straw Dogs* has its merits, among them the performances of Hoffman and George as David and Amy Sumner. Hoffman is perfect for the part of David. As an actor, he excels at communicating callowness and indecision (more than one critic noted the similarity between David Sumner and Benjamin Braddock, Hoffman's first starring role in Mike Nichols' *The Grad-*

uate, 1967), which are David's only significant character traits until his violent epiphany. George was likewise an apt choice for Amy. A fine actress, she radiates a child-woman's sexuality. Vaughan also deserves special mention for his portrayal of the terrifyingly brutal Tom Hedden. His work in this supporting role is outstanding, and contributes much to the film's general air of menace.

Straw Dogs, then, is a flawed masterpiece. Its flaws—a bone-deep misogyny and an almost mystical reverence for violence—are those of its director. Despite, or perhaps because of, these flaws, *Straw Dogs* remains Peckinpah's best, most coherent work. By withholding the carnage that had become his trademark until the film's climactic denouement, Peckinpah intensifies its impact. Even those critics who find the film philosophically objectionable concede its power, and that, perhaps, is the film's ultimate tribute.

Robert Mitchell

THE STRAWBERRY BLONDE

Released: 1941
Production: Hal B. Wallis for Warner Bros.
Direction: Raoul Walsh
Screenplay: Julius J. Epstein and Philip G. Epstein; based on the stage play
   One Sunday Afternoon by James Hagan
Cinematography: James Wong Howe
Editing: William Holmes
Running time: 98 minutes

Principal characters:

Biff Grimes	James Cagney
Amy Lind	Olivia de Havilland
Virginia Brush	Rita Hayworth
William "Old Man" Grimes	Alan Hale
Hugo Barnstead	Jack Carson
Nicholas Pappalas	George Tobias

The Strawberry Blonde is a charming, leisurely paced Gay Nineties tale, replete with the corner saloon, nickel schooners of beer, horse-and-buggy courtships, barbershop quartets, period tunes, and other nostalgic trappings which summon up an elaborate re-creation of America at the turn of the century. Scripted by Julius J. Epstein and Philip G. Epstein (the brothers who also wrote scripts for the 1942 films *Yankee Doodle Dandy* and *Casablanca*), *The Strawberry Blonde* is based on the 1930 stage play, *One Sunday Afternoon*.

The film's story centers around the misadventures of Biff Grimes (James Cagney), a beer drinker, brawler, and correspondence school dentist. These qualities and more surface in the film's opening moments. For in between games of horseshoes with barber Nick Pappalas (George Tobias), Biff exchanges heated words with neighboring college boys, and he yells angrily toward the nearby bandstand because they keep performing "And the Band Played On," which is not Biff's favorite tune. Biff also confides to Nick that he still has fond feelings for Virginia (Rita Hayworth), the strawberry blonde in his past. He also admits that he holds a grudge against her husband, Hugo Barnstead (Jack Carson)—that, in fact, he would like to kill Hugo. His attentions return to the bandstand, however, the scene of a brawl caused by Biff which nets him a shiner.

The excitement is interrupted when Amy (Olivia de Havilland), Biff's wife, calls him to the telephone. Hugo, whom he has not seen in years, is in severe pain and needs a tooth pulled. When he arrives, Biff plots to carry out his plans by overdosing Hugo with gas. Then the story flashes back to ten years earlier. Biff is working as a saloon bouncer by day and studying dentistry at night. His father, Old Man Grimes (Alan Hale), has been fired from his work with the street-cleaning department because he refused to wear the new uniform. Old Man Grimes now plays guinea pig for his aspiring dentist son, with Biff pulling out his teeth according to Lesson Number One in the correspondence course. In addition to working for a career in dentistry, Biff longs for the love of Virginia, who is as self-centered (a trait Biff fails to see) as she is beautiful. Virginia, however, is smitten with his buddy, Hugo, who has better prospects than Biff. It is through a blind date arranged by Hugo and Virginia that Biff meets Amy. Their meeting on a bench in a picturesque park is one of the film's highlights, as the rather plain-looking girl boldly professes her approval of bloomer girls, cigarettes, and even actresses. "She's fast!," Biff says breathlessly.

The story line takes on serious tones when Hugo proves himself a crook, by sponsoring a rigged ticket-selling scheme. (The Ladies Club of the Fifth Democratic Ward sponsored a boat ride, and Hugo sold three thousand tickets although the boat could hold only 750 .) Despite Hugo's fast-talking con-man stance, however, Virginia elopes with him, leaving Biff heartbroken as he waits for her in the park. Unenthusiastically, he asks to marry the delighted Amy, who has to break the news about the elopement to him.

When Hugo reappears as a successful businessman, Biff is driving a milk delivery truck. Impressed with Hugo's wealth and newfound status, Biff agrees to go to work for him. Hugo makes him vice president of his construction corporation, but as Biff is disappointed to discover, it is a job in name only. He has little to do other than signing occasional paperwork, including some documents that he does not understand. When one of Hugo's buildings collapses during construction, Biff's father, who had been working for the company, is killed, and when an investigation reveals that it was Biff who (unknowingly) signed the fraudulent building specifications, the crafty Hugo never comes forward in his defense, as a result of which Biff is imprisoned. During his imprisonment Biff matter-of-factly reflects on his predicament ("The election's coming up, and the D.A.'s gotta have convictions") and practices dentistry on the warden. When he is at last free, he returns to the faithful Amy, who is waiting at the park bench where they first met.

The story line again shifts to the present, as Biff holds the gas nozzle above Hugo's face. Time and truth have worn away the hatred, however, and now, as Hugo and Virginia bicker, Biff realizes that there is an ugliness to their lives, and Virginia, he is surprised to find, is not as radiant as he once thought she was. In a humorous twist, Biff changes his mind about killing Hugo. Instead, he pulls away the gas and yanks the tooth without benefit of medication. As the film comes to a close, Biff is jubilant to learn that Amy is pregnant. In keeping with his high spirits, Biff kisses Amy, then runs off to brawl at the bandstand. Before the closing credits roll, the film's audience is invited to sing along, as the lyrics to a nostalgic tune make their way across the screen.

A testament to director Raoul Walsh's diversity as well as to his ability to etch a charming period piece, *The Strawberry Blonde* was released during a prolific period for the director. In addition to *The Strawberry Blonde*, 1941 saw the release of Walsh's *High Sierra*, the gangster tale starring Humphrey Bogart, and *They Died with Their Boots On*, the much-romanticized saga of Custer's last stand. Among his many titles, however, *The Strawberry Blonde* is unique for its charm, quaintness, and innocence. A bittersweet thread runs through the film, despite its charm. In fact, for all its enticing looks at American manners and mores in the 1890's, *The Strawberry Blonde* is not without serious moments. The death of Biff's father is as touching as it is tragic, and the love that blossoms between Biff and Amy comes only after Biff has conceded to some of life's bitter lessons—including the fact that appearances can be deceiving (as in the case with the glowing but cold-hearted Virginia) and that society itself is sometimes unfair, as when it causes his imprisonment.

These realistic tones, however, do not detract from the film's gentle and uplifting mood. Adding to the film's polish are the exceptional performances. Cagney, who came to the film following a string of "tough guy" roles, is a natural as the bickering Biff. De Havilland's work has a subtle effectiveness, creating an interplay between her and Cagney which gives the film its most effective moments—particularly during their first encounter, when a bluffing Amy makes Biff believe she is brazen. Moreover, Amy's appearance, a bit mousey and sedate in the beginning, takes on a spirited air as the film progresses, pointing to the beauty within her character. *The Strawberry Blonde* provided Hayworth with her first major screen role, and she makes the most of it, showing her adept skill at portraying a flirt. The rest of the case is equally in control, with Carson most convincing as the occasionally charming, often vulgar Hugo. Hale as Old Man Grimes and Tobias as Nicholas Pappalas are also memorable.

The film, incidentally, was not shot without some behind-the-scenes headlines. Hayworth was a last-minute addition to the cast, replacing Warners' star Ann Sheridan, who had been put on suspension for being rebellious and protesting because she was overworked. Because Hayworth had a similar figure and could wear the costumes fitted for Sheridan, she was given the role. It has also been reported that feuding erupted on the set between Cagney and de Havilland. Cagney purportedly felt he was being upstaged by the actress, and insisted that some footage be reshot, thus trimming down some of de Havilland's work. Once the filming ended, however, any troubles that might have existed disappeared, and in ensuing years both stars have had only kind words regarding each other.

The Strawberry Blonde marked the second filming of the stage play upon which it was based. The first film version, in 1933, starred Gary Cooper,

Frances Fuller, and Fay Wray. In 1948, Walsh directed a musical remake, *One Sunday Afternoon*, which starred Dennis Morgan, Dorothy Malone, Janis Paige, and Don DeFore as the four principals. It is the 1941 version, however, which has garnered the most acclaim. It has held up well through the years, and now stands as a fanciful look at decade's past.

Pat H. Broeske

STREET GIRL

Released: 1929
Production: William Le Baron for RKO/Radio
Direction: Wesley Ruggles
Screenplay: Jane Murfin; based on the story "The Viennese Charmer" by W. Carey Wonderly
Cinematography: Leo Tover
Editing: no listing
Running time: 91 minutes

Principal characters:
Freddie Joyzelle	Betty Compson
Mike	John Harron
Happy	Ned Sparks
Joe	Jack Oakie
Keppel	Joseph Cawthorn
Prince Nickolaus	Ivan Lebedeff
Pete	Guy Buccola

As early as 1921, the studio that was to be the home of RKO-Radio was opened in Hollywood, directly adjacent to the new Paramount Studios. In its early days, it had been known as Robertson-Cole, and was the American home for a British firm distributing the Roamer automobile and exporting its film products from its American branch directly to Europe. The studio sported a distinguished list of contract people including such artists as Pauline Frederick, Bessie Barriscale, Sessue Hayakawa, and others. By 1922, Robertson-Cole was reorganized and its corporated name changed to FBO (Film Booking Office of America). They produced Westerns and "B" features until 1928, when William Le Baron became vice president in charge of production, and the new company president was financier Joseph P. Kennedy. Radio Corporation of America purchased control of FBO, merging with the Keith-Albee-Orpheum Circuit, and by 1930 RKO had also assimilated the Pathe Exchanges. With the advent of talking pictures, RKO/Radio was ready for business, and the first all-talking feature film shot on the new lot for release by the company was a light-hearted comedy romance, *Street Girl*, starring Betty Compson and directed by Wesley Ruggles, both of whom were to play a large part in the destinies of the new RKO product.

During the days of the silents, Betty Compson had risen from Al Christie Comedies to become one of the big stars of Paramount, achieving stardom with her first release for that company, George Loane Tucker's *The Miracle Man* (1919). She married James Cruze, an eminent director, and by the end of the 1920's was starring in features released by nearly every company based in Hollywood and London. *Street Girl*, RKO's first, made her a top star for

RKO/Radio, and she signed a nonexclusive contract with them, appearing over the next years as star of seven talking features.

Compson had begun her career as a vaudevillian, working out of Utah and playing the whole Pacific Coast with an act called "The Vagabond Violinist." Dressed as a gypsy, she proved herself an extremely capable violinist as well as a very pretty performer and actress, sometimes appearing in her own chestnut-colored hair, or, when she was in a more sophisticated mood, a blonde wig. By the time she initiated RKO's feature films, she had already made her debut in talking pictures, appearing with great success in George Fitzmaurice's First National part-talkie, *The Barker* (1928), in which she shared billing with Milton Sills, Dorothy Mackaill, and Douglas Fairbanks, Jr. Her role in *The Barker* won her a nomination by the newly formed Motion Picture Academy as Best Actress for 1928-1929, and although Mary Pickford won the Oscar that year for *Coquette*, Compson's nomination provided an opening for her to all other studios venturing into sound production.

Street Girl might have been especially written for Compson. Based on a W. Carey Wonderly magazine story, "The Viennese Charmer," it had all the ingredients of a successful romantic comedy. It was perfect as the first release of a new studio, for it was charming, it had a European background and a light-hearted story, and it was highlighted by musical numbers and variety offerings. Compson plays Fredericka (Freddie) Joyzelle, a Viennese charmer who earns her living by playing the violin on the Viennese boulevards, hoping that some entrepreneur will take her over as a café or cabaret artiste. Mike (John Herron), a young American musician, saves her from the annoyances of a street bum and introduces her to his three buddies, also musicians— Happy (Ned Sparks), Joe (Jack Oakie), and Pete (Guy Buccola). The four fellows constitute a jazz band known as "The Four Seasons," and they take Freddie in as one of them, working with her as star violinist for a café act which brings them a hundred dollars a week. Almost at once, Freddie's presence works well for them, and the five are elevated to three thousand dollars a week as jazz entertainers in an exclusive Viennese café.

From the moment Freddie is rescued by Mike from the solicitations of a masher, there is a bond between them. Their romance has its problems, but Freddie, installed as the star guest performer of "The Four Seasons," and living with them in their one big room, soon makes herself indispensable. She handles their business affairs, and her knowledge of money soon makes them financially sound. A handsome adventurer called Prince Nickolaus (Ivan Lebedeff) comes to the café and falls in love with Freddie. She is attracted to and flattered by the Prince and Mike is jealous, but eventually Freddie and Mike are reunited and continue on with their successful band.

Oscar Levant, with Sidney Clare, wrote three special songs for the entertainers to perform. "Huggable and Sweet" is the big jazz number for the band, and "My Dream Melody" is the song that Betty Compson, as Freddie, plays on her violin. Critics remarked that "If she's fiddle-faking, it's one of the most skillful jobs of its kind." Compson acknowledged that as a onetime professional violinist herself, she knew how to finger and use the bow, but it had been a long time since she had earned a living as a solo violinist, so although she was seen performing the songs, a working violinist dubbed the actual music performance for her onto a sound track. The third musical number, "Broken Up Tune," is led by Doris Eaton in a café ensemble set, in which she performs with the Radio Beauty Chorus. Gus Arnheim and his Ambassador Band dubbed for "The Four Seasons" when in their success the quartet was augmented into a real jazz band.

Variety praised the film highly, noting that it was a real "coin clicker." Throughout the years, RKO/Radio did not forget the initial success they had scored with *Street Girl*. In 1936 its story formed the basis for a new film version, *That Girl from Paris*, in which not only American jazz and swing were featured but well-staged operatic numbers for Freddie, who becomes a young Parisian opera singer who graduates into the big time. This later version launched opera star Lily Pons as an RKO screen star. Five years later, at the outbreak of World War II, the basic story of *Street Girl* formed the genesis for another remake entitled *Four Jacks and a Jill* (1941).

In *Street Girl*, however, the story's appeal was instant and new. It reintroduced Betty Compson as a talking film star of importance, and it served as the first release for a company that during the next decade was to be home not only for Compson, but also for Richard Dix, Bebe Daniels, Irene Dunne, Katharine Hepburn, Fred Astaire, Ginger Rogers, and finally even Orson Welles.

DeWitt Bodeen

STREET SCENE

Released: 1931
Production: Samuel Goldwyn for Samuel Goldwyn Productions; released by
   United Artists
Direction: King Vidor
Screenplay: Elmer Rice; based on his play of the same name
Cinematography: George Barnes
Editing: Hugh Bennett
Art direction: Richard Day
Music: Alfred Newman
Running time: 80 minutes

Principal characters:
Rose	Sylvia Sidney
Sam	William Collier, Jr.
Abe Kaplan	Max Montor
Mr. Maurrant	David Landau
Mrs. Maurrant	Estelle Taylor
Sankey	Russell Hopton
Easter	Louis Natheaux
Mae Jones	Greta Granstedt
Emma Jones	Beulah Bondi
Willie Maurrant	Lambert Rogers

Elmer Rice was a minor playwright, with only two plays, both of which
were relative failures, to his credit, when *Street Scene* opened at New York's
Playhouse Theatre on January 10, 1929, to restrained reviews. It was not long,
however, into the play's run of 601 performances that Rice's talent came to
be recognized. The author received the Pulitzer Prize for Drama, and the
screen rights to the play were purchased by Samuel Goldwyn as the first
Goldwyn production of King Vidor after the director's six-year sojourn with
M-G-M. Just as Rice had been allowed considerable control of the play's
production, even the casting of all the parts, he was permitted unusual influence in the screen production, adapting his own work and also advising on
casting and participating in rehearsals.

In his filming, Vidor remained reasonably faithful to the original play. He
decided not to use any interior shots, but to contain the action on the one
New York city block. To avoid the dull, static quality that would arise from
the lack of changing sets, however, Vidor decided to let his camera do the
moving. In his autobiography, *A Tree Is a Tree*, he wrote, "In *Street Scene*
we would never repeat a camera setup twice. If the setting couldn't change,
the camera could. We would shoot down, up, across, from high, from low,
from a boom, from a perambulator, and we would move back and include

not only the sidewalk but the street as well." This camera movement, unlike similar work in many late silent films, is not distracting; it is a part of the whole production, not a "flashy," irritating contrivance.

From the original stage production, Vidor brought eight cast members: T. H. Manning, Matthew McHugh, John M. Qualen, Anna Kostant, George Humbert, Eleanor Wesselhoeft, Conway Washburne, and Beulah Bondi, beginning an illustrious screen career as the doyenne of character actresses. Erin O'Brien-Moore, the leading lady of the stage production, was replaced by Sylvia Sidney, who was joined by William Collier, Jr., as the young hero and Estelle Taylor, a prominent silent-screen actress, as Sidney's mother. Vidor rehearsed his players as if they were participating in a stage production and, even before shooting began, had his cast perform a full dress rehearsal for Goldwyn.

Music plays an integral part in *Street Scene*; it emphasizes action, adds additional drama to a scene, and even, at times, almost saucily mimics the human voice. The composer, Alfred Newman, is given complete freedom in the opening, establishing shots of New York, leading to the block in the West Sixties where *Street Scene* is set, with a symphonic poem which is best described as pseudo-George Gershwin and which became a popular hit when arranged by Newman into a piece titled "Sentimental Rhapsody."

Street Scene is a study of the inhabitants of a brownstone tenement. There are the Maurrants, consisting of a drunken father (David Landau), a mother (Estelle Taylor) who yearns for kindness and affection, and a daughter who attempts to escape from the restrictions of her Jewish background by changing her last name to Moran. Then there are the Kaplans, the Jewish socialist father (Max Montor) whom his neighbors brand as a bolshevik, the school-teacher daughter, and Sam (William Collier, Jr.), his law student son, who tries to understand why there is so much misery and unhappiness in the lives of those around him. Constantly spying on the group is Emma Jones (Beulah Bondi), the malicious local gossip who fails to see how unpleasant her own two children are—an overfriendly (as far as boys are concerned) daughter and a rude, vulgar son.

Just as Emma Jones observes the group, so does the audience. We see Mrs. Maurrant perhaps talking a little too much to the milk collector, a married man. We see Rose, her daughter (Sylvia Sidney), fending off the advances of her married employer. We hear the happy sound of a newborn baby crying. We experience the sorrow of another family, visited by a social worker prior to being evicted from their apartment. As the tenants sweat in the stifling and sultry heat of a New York summer, we experience their discomfort. It is perhaps similar to life on any block of any city until tragedy strikes.

As is so often the lot of prying neighbors, Emma Jones is not around to witness the horrors of the next day. Instead, it is Sam Kaplan who sees the milk collector (Russell Hopton) sneak up to the Maurrants' apartment after

Mr. Maurrant has apparently gone out of town for a job interview. It is Sam who watches in horror as Maurrant returns, looks up to the windows of his apartment to see the drawn blinds, and climbs the stoop. It is Sam who hears the two shots ring out and sees Maurrant running from the apartment, a revolver in his hand. If there is any criticism that can be leveled at the film of *Street Scene*, it is, perhaps, that this sequence is a little too frenzied, a little too far removed from reality, but the fault may lie as much with Rice's play as with Vidor's film. The character of Mr. Maurrant is not sufficiently delineated over the one evening and one day period that the audience has gotten to know him, and it is hard to accept—drunken brute though he may be— that he would commit a double murder. It is equally hard to accept that Mrs. Maurrant could be having sexual relations with another man; despite her desire for a warm, emotional relationship, she is all too obviously a woman who knows and accepts her unbreakable ties to her husband.

Rose returns in time to see her mother's body being carried down the stoop on a stretcher. Shirley Kaplan (Anna Kostant) tries to comfort the grief-stricken girl, and together they talk of the double tragedy that has struck the Maurrant household, and Rose tries to explain why she cannot accept the suggestion that she marry Sam, who obviously has affection for her. The shooting evokes the callousness of city life; a newsvendor sells newspapers headlining the crime with photographs of the dying mother, and two nurse-maids, with their charges in perambulators, appear on the scene, anxious for a policeman to assuage their morbid curiosity. As the policeman talks with the two girls, further shots are heard and cries that Maurrant has been caught; he had been hiding in the basement of the building. He begs, and is allowed, to talk to Rose, and sobs his guilt to her, that he did not mean to shoot his wife, that it was the fault of the drinking, and, ultimately, the fault of his surroundings.

Life for most of the inhabitants of the tenements settles down to normal. The apartment of the evicted family has a new tenant. Emma Jones returns from the police station, anxious to tell her neighbors of all that happened there. Rose prepares to leave and make a new life for herself and her young brother, Willie (Lambert Rogers). As in the play, she tells Sam, who asks to go with her, that she must go alone, but, unlike in the play, there is a suggestion that perhaps the two young people will come together at some time in the future. In a final, moving scene, Rose is seen slowly walking down the street past the children happily playing their games to the El station in the distance.

Much of the success of *Street Scene* rests in the playing of the character performers. There are thirty-four speaking parts in the film, and not one can be faulted. Bondi in particular stands out, dominating the film from her first scene where she is seen casually scratching her backside. One critic, in *International Photographer*, rightly compared *Street Scene* to some of the early Biograph productions of D. W. Griffith in its handling of the lives of simple, ordinary people, far removed from the flappers and society types who inhabit so many early talkies. *Street Scene* compares more than favorably with Vidor's later films, such as the pretentious *Our Daily Bread* (1934), which also tried to depict the lives of simple people, and his other Goldwyn productions, *Cynara* (1932) and *The Wedding Night* (1935).

Anthony Slide

THE STUNT MAN

Released: 1980
Production: Richard Rush for Twentieth Century-Fox
Direction: Richard Rush
Screenplay: Lawrence B. Marcus; based on Richard Rush's adaptation of the novel of the same name by Paul Brodeur
Cinematography: Mario Tosi
Editing: Jack Hofstra and Caroline Ferriol
Music: Dominic Frontiere
Running time: 127 minutes

> *Principal characters:*
> Eli Cross ....Peter O'Toole
> Cameron .... Steve Railsback
> Nina Franklin ....Barbara Hershey
> Sam .... Allen Goorwitz (Allen Garfield)
> Jake ....Alex Rocco
> Denise .... Sharon Farrell

Richard Rush's highly acclaimed *The Stunt Man* is one of those rare, superior films like Philippe de Broca's *King of Hearts* (*Le Roi du Coeur*, 1967) that will take many years to find an audience. Arguably the outstanding film of 1980 (with few apologies to the Academy Award-winning *Ordinary People*), *The Stunt Man* was nominated for three Academy Awards, a half-dozen Golden Globe nominations in various categories, and similar honors from the Directors' and Writers' Guilds. Additionally, its star, Peter O'Toole, received a Best Actor Award from the National Society of Film Critics. In fact, film critics placed the film on as many as seventy individual "top ten" film lists across the country. Yet *The Stunt Man*, as a result of what its producers term a "mishandling" of the distribution, has been seen by very few members of the moviegoing public.

The Stunt Man was first announced as a 1971 release to be directed by Richard Rush, who, up to that point, had gained most of his experience in motorcycle and hippie exploitation motion pictures; however, it was not filmed until 1978. When it was finally completed in 1979, some of the potential distributors cautioned that the film was not marketable due to its subject matter, which consisted of what some people viewed as an "inside joke" concerning filmmaking and life as visualized through the eyes of a young stunt man who is trying to contend with an eccentric director. The film opened in 1980 in Seattle without a distributor but played to record crowds for forty consecutive weeks, attracting, in the process, enough critical interest to make a Los Angeles engagement feasible. In Los Angeles, where it played for six weeks, it was the period's top-grossing film. This feat attracted a major distributor, Twentieth Century-Fox, who immediately released the film in Canada and then more quietly at two theaters in New York City. These Manhattan openings were unsupported by any television advertising, and when as a result the film drew disappointing crowds, it was again relegated to less important theaters.

Finally, in another attempt to reach a somewhat wider audience, Twentieth Century-Fox released the film in other cities but, at the same time, in an effort to reduce costs, the studio tampered with much of the film's promotion, cancelling television advertisements and juggling the designs of poster and newspaper ads, with the result that the film again did not draw well, although it was nominated for three Academy Awards. At that point, the studio held up distribution, intending to release it with more ballyhoo if it won an award in at least one of the nominated categories, Best Director, Best Screenplay, or Best Actor. During the voting period, however, it played in only three theaters nationwide, and after it failed to win any Oscars, it virtually disappeared.

De Broca's *Le Roi du Coeur*, known in the United States as *King of Hearts*, had suffered a fate in 1967 which paralleled that of *The Stunt Man*; yet in succeeding years, it managed to acquire a significant following on the art film circuit, and its rapidly increasing status as a genuine cult film finally prompted a number of successful re-releases to neighborhood theaters and cable television, where it has done well. A similar destiny would seem to be inevitable for its 1980 counterpart if it is eventually to gain significant recognition.

The Stunt Man, unlike other films about filmmaking, is a challenging work that merges action with an interplay of ideas. It is a fluid mosaic of incessantly shifting perceptions and characterizations that threatens to leave its viewers stranded unless they are willing to play as fast and loose with the film's premises as its creators do. Throughout the film, its characters are able to perceive only a small segment of every situation's entirety, and thus, since we view the action through their eyes, the audience is able to comprehend each scene only in terms of the individual character's interpretation of it. Unfortunately, each character misinterprets the action in varying degrees relative to the extent of his own paranoid perspective. For example, each person in the film distrusts almost every other person in it. Like a puzzle, the situation is constructed to demonstrate how difficult it is particularly for the central character and for the viewer to discern the truth. Ideas collide head-on in *The Stunt Man*; and just as the viewer sorts out the intellectual traffic jam, the film races ahead, confusing him again.

On the surface, the story is about Lucky Cameron (Steve Railsback), a fugitive from the police who happens upon a film company on location. Its director, Eli Cross (Peter O'Toole), an egomaniacal, hyperactive dictator, offers him protection from the police if he will take over the job of a recently deceased stunt man who may have been a victim of the director's quest for a terrific death scene. Beneath this surface description, however, lurks a rapid-fire chain reaction of paranoid interactions that reveals the essence of the film and instigates the action up to this point.

On a typically peaceful summer day, stirred only by the frenetic music of Dominic Frontiere ricocheting on the sound track, a police car sounds its horn at a dog sleeping in the road. The dog snarls. A telephone lineman watching this occurrence throws a rock at a raven, which darts away, smashing into a helicopter carrying a cameraman and a movie director, Eli Cross. The pilot yells, "That damn bird tried to kill us!" The voice of the unseen director replies, "That's your point of view. Did ya ever think to ask the bird what he thought?" Cross takes a bite from an apple and tosses it out of the helicopter. The apple plunges down onto the roof of a café and rolls off of it to the top of a parked police car, giving its two officers a start. Inside the building, a truck driver attempts to touch a bending waitress' breast and is bitten by the Chihuahua that she is carrying clutched to her bodice. Nearby, a jittery, scruffy-looking young man (Steve Railsback) is playing pinball and becomes terrified when the police enter. They handcuff him, but he knocks them down, runs out the door, and sprints away while they shoot at him.

A short distance away, the fugitive encounters the telephone lineman, knocks him down, and then grabs his tools before disappearing into the woods. Near a river, he uses the tools to separate the handcuffs, and then, sighting a bridge, he bolts across it and tries to hitch a ride in a classic old Duesenberg that happens to be passing. Its driver stops, but when the young man attempts to climb in, he pushes the fugitive out with his foot and speeds away, leaving him sprawling in the dust. Then the old car turns around and aims right at him. Thinking that the driver is intent upon killing him, the escaped prisoner picks up a heavy metal bolt and throws it through the car's windshield. The car does not come near him, however, and when the young man opens his eyes, it has disappeared. In fact it has crashed through the side of the bridge and is now on the bottom of the river. Next, the escapee looks up and sees the helicopter, which comes down close while its occupant, Cross, looks him over. Terrified, the young man runs madly off the bridge and through the countryside until he comes to the ocean. He cuts off the legs of his pants so that he will resemble a vacationer and joins the crowd mingling around a resort watching a film crew staging a war scene on the beach.

The action has moved along up to this point because each character thinks that one of the others is out to get him. The helicopter pilot is afraid of the raven, the falling apple unnerves the police, and the jittery young man panics the moment the police enter, thus giving himself away. He again panics on the bridge, assuming that the driver of the Duesenberg is going to kill him for unknown reasons, so he takes defensive action again and possibly causes the driver's death. Finally, his fear of the helicopter sends him plunging madly on to the ocean resort. The words of Eli Cross now come back to haunt us,

"That's your point of view." No one has, in fact, stopped to get any other character's point of view.

The audience has by now been forced to choose between two possible perceptions of what has occurred. First, since there is a helicopter hovering overhead during the action, the young man might not be a fugitive but actually an actor playing a scene shot from above. On the other hand, the fugitive might have instead intruded on a scene in progress in which the man in the Duesenberg was doing a stunt and had fully intended to drive off the bridge but could not take the time to explain because the camera was rolling. This is, indeed, exactly what happened, as the audience soon discovers. The fleeing prisoner, however, misinterpreted what he saw and thus caused the stunt man's death by drowning when his thrown bolt cracked the car's protective windshield before it plunged into the water. A paranoid reaction that failed to distinguish between reality and fantasy has now brought tragedy.

When the fugitive shows up at the beach filming, Eli Cross recognizes him from the events on the bridge. Yet the director has problems of his own and must cover for him with the police. Cross has a permit allowing him to film at the resort which he could lose if the death becomes known. Therefore, he pretends that the young man, whom he calls "Lucky" Burt Cameron, was actually the driver of the car. This satisfies the police for the moment, particularly when the other actors and crew members, who know perfectly well that Cameron is a stranger, stand behind their director and keep up the charade. Only Cameron has doubts, but once he is cleaned up, clean shaven, and has his hair dyed a sandy color, he becomes Cross's stunt man.

Cameron soon becomes caught up in his new role, and after some basic training in how to fall, he is plunged into his first stunt. The complexities of this stunt would in reality be impossible to photograph in one continuous take the way it appears in the film when Cameron does it; actually, it would require numerous setups and movements of the camera. This scene is constructed as a thematic microcosm paralleling the paranoid chain reactions of the film's opening minutes. As one event quickly sets off another, the new stunt man runs across rooftops pursued by World War I German soldiers and is shot at by airplanes. He leaps from a tower and lands on a balcony and then crashes through a skylight falling on a brothel bed between two people making love. He is finally captured by soldiers carousing in the downstairs bar who become the symbolic counterparts of the camera crew on the beach earlier in the film.

After the scene is concluded, Cameron realizes how much money there is to be made by doing stunts. He is also rather puffed up over his own success and over the fact that he thinks that Nina (Barbara Hershey), the actress who is playing the leading role, is falling in love with him. Between his stunts, he plays love scenes with her. Yet the stunt man's confidence does not last long, as the director like some malevolent god, seeks to redefine Cameron's existence on an almost daily basis and to keep him forever off balance with almost existential cross-examinations. Cameron's paranoid tendencies quickly reassert themselves, and he begins incessantly to reevaluate his own premises, thus forcing the audience, which must share his limited perspective, to do the same. Is Nina, for example, really in love with him or is she toying with on Eli's orders? In fact, what is her actual relationship with Eli? The stunt man distrusts Cross and cannot decide if the director is actually protecting him or if he is merely another expendable bit of equipment to be employed in the director's mad quest to produce a masterpiece.

Finally, Cameron is called upon to repeat the Duesenberg stunt, and he is by now totally convinced that Eli is going to murder him in order to make a perfect realistic scene. The night before it is to take place, he tries to convice Nina to run away with him, but she wants to finish her scenes. Additionally, Eli has security police keeping anybody from leaving the hotel, ostensibly to insure that the crew will be sober and on time for the next day's shooting. Cameron ultimately convinces her to prove her love for him by hiding in the trunk of the Duesenberg. Instead of doing the stunt, he will escape with both the car and her in the morning.

Yet the next day, he cannot get away and must perform the dangerous stunt with the added worry of the passenger in his trunk. Or is she really there? He finally makes a break for it in the Duesenberg, intending to roar across the bridge and down the road, but something goes wrong and the car falls off the bridge into the water. Stunned, Cameron still manages to roll down a window and swim to safety. As his head appears above the water he sees Nina on the shore applauding him along with the rest of the film company. She had been found in the trunk the night before and was told that Cameron had changed his mind and intended to do the stunt after all. Thus, as the film ends, Cameron is giddy with success as both stuntman and lover. The final shots of the film show Cameron demanding more money from Eli and cursing the director's refusals as he departs, almost floating off in his helicopter.

The complexity of the materials that make up *The Stunt Man* could, with a lesser director, have resulted in nothing more than a static puzzle. Yet this film is a virtuoso work of filmmaking that takes its viewers on an intense, mysterious trip to an undefined destination. Beginning with the misunderstood raven and the apple rolling down the roof of the café, the subjects of paranoia and motion pictures are joined in a completely believable manner. O'Toole's Eli Cross, for example, is imbued with the strident, visionary drive of a director who is totally self-absorbed and will do anything to achieve what he wants. Railsback's Cameron brings his own paranoid type of madness with him. The clash of these two mad entities elicits the major suspense in the film. Cameron feels that he is trapped—that if the police do not get him, Eli will. He is totally convinced that the director means to kill him in three days when he must reshoot the stunt of the Duesenberg going off the bridge, and the audience believes this also. The placement of the story on a movie location encourages this paranoid fantasy. It is a world that trades on illusions and different angles of vision.

Cameron is obviously totally deluded and wrong. It was Eli Cross who first states the film's premise: "That's your point of view. Did ya ever think to ask the bird what he thought?" It is actually Cross who ultimately frees Cameron from his paranoia. Yet to Cameron, the flamboyant director is a whimsical god hovering over all in the basket chair of his crane, holding in his hands the power of life and death. He is always lurking overhead, dangling from his crane or his helicopter. He is able to drop into each frame of film seemingly at will, or, when his mood changes, to swing in from the side. Cross is above the world, controlling everything and everyone. He knows what his people are doing and what they are thinking at all times.

Cameron is at the other extreme. He does not even know how to interpret the situations in which he finds himself. He does not realize that Cross has a use for him beyond covering up the fact of Burt's death. The director senses, within Cameron's desperate will to live, something of a kindred madness— the kind that he desires for his film. The director's need, beyond a successful motion picture, is to do something mad and to be worshiped for his accomplishment. In Cameron's fugitive inability to trust anyone, the director has found the foil that his legend requires. At the end of the film, when Cross has accomplished his act of madness and burnished his own legend, the self-centered god appears benign and Cameron need fear no more.

Eli Cross as portrayed by O'Toole may be as definitive a satire of the *auteur* theory as has ever been done. O'Toole's Eli is Captain Ahab with a camera, a monomaniac obsessed with his legend and his film, and he will manipulate anyone to get it made. He plays out his destiny with the passionately crazed strength and sureness of vision of the totally self-centered. O'Toole gives a once-in-a-lifetime comic performance, playing his character as a composite of a crotchety director of the John Huston type and a tough one in the style of the fierce-tempered Sam Peckinpah. He shapes the character verbally through volleys of words and lines that fly like tennis balls, alternately slamming and punching to catch an opponent offguard, or gently rolling to their intended target. He pounces flamboyantly on other characters' lines and creates ideas like a man possessed. His conversations with the screenwriter Sam (Allen Goorwitz) are comic pirouettes marked by style and timing. The fat, earthbound Sam, a practical man and a worrier, is Eli's best friend, but even as such he is an obstacle to Eli's improvised madness. The director repeatedly throws out Sam's uninspired scenes in exchange for his own ideas that never seem to touch the earth and then tries to explain his actions through unequal philosophical exchanges that resemble comedy routines in which Sam always grudgingly admits that Eli is right.

Railsback superbly counterbalances O'Toole's flamboyance with a portrait of a down-and-out, thoroughly beaten loner who is able to survive only through his inability to trust anyone. The audience perceives the film's action largely through his eyes, sharing his misapprehension and his limited perspective. With his head and his eyes to guide us we become caught up in the uncertainty and suspense of the situation, and we fear for what conceivably might happen. We are thus taken in by Eli Cross along with Cameron and everyone else. This is a testimony to Railsback's conviction and believability as an actor. We know nothing about Cameron except that he was in Vietnam for two years and that he is on the run. For all we know, he might be a killer. Yet, he persuades us to share his fears and his uncertainties through the persuasiveness of his will to live. Ultimately, through the sheer physicality of his performance, Railsback makes a deluded, paranoid, self-pitying loser with terrible judgment come across as a superb stunt man and a sympathetic figure.

The mysterious journey toward some kind of truth that comprises *The Stunt Man* winds its way through a veritable circus of exciting stunt scenes. Technically, these scenes designed by director Rush lie somewhere between raw footage and the finished product and in this way are remarkably effective in their contribution to the illusionary quality of the film. Some cases in point are the shooting scenes at the Hotel Del Coronado (the same hotel used in Billy Wilder's *Some Like It Hot*, 1959) near San Diego. Rush's cameras are placed for a dual purpose—to record the scene that Eli Cross is shooting and the one that Rush is making. Consequently, during a scene in which Eli's film crew is photographing soldiers being strafed and bombed on the beach, we also see, in our version, the hotel that will not be visible in Eli's shots. Rush then juggles the perspectives back and forth using Eli's crowd of onlookers like a Greek chorus to react to the camera's alternation of fantasy and reality. First, the crowd cheers and applauds the bombing and strafing, and yet when the smoke clears, the people become hysterical, believing that live ammunition has actually been used as they view the carnage and the bloodshed. They revert again to laughter when the blood-stained corpses get up and walk away. These crowd reactions are magnificently effective because the real audience watching Rush's film also becomes momentarily confused by the bloody bodies.

This type of reality versus illusion paradox recurs throughout the film. The audience sees the camera when it hangs back recording Eli's film being made, but when it closes in on the action in long continuous takes that give the viewers the impression of constantly changing angles and of accelerating speed, we begin to get confused as to which film we are in. Cameron's chase scenes on the rooftop exemplify this confusion. When we see the hotel's structure, parking lots, and palm trees, we are secure in San Diego, but when Rush charges in close with his camera and all we see is a rooftop, Cameron, and some German soldiers running, it is World War I France in 1917. The cameras are located so strategically by Rush that they satisfy the needs of the film being shot as well as of the one being shown, and this also allows for a certain amount of interplay between the two. Behind all of this action is the driving music of Frontiere which lashes the characters on. The melody never completes itself but repeats and accelerates when the characters go into motion or when the mood of the film changes. The music is essential to the action, and we hear it long before we see some of the characters or the stunts. It actually seems to be prodding the action forward.

The Stunt Man is, then, a magnificent mystery that keeps its viewers off balance and constantly revises their interpretation of what they have seen. It is thus fully deserving of a chance to spin its tricks on a larger and more varied audience. If it had been made by Federico Fellini or François Truffaut instead of by Rush, perhaps it would have had more publicity and better distribution, but then it would not reflect the ultimate illusion that is Hollywood. Filmmaking as it is practiced in America, with its emphasis on competition and commercial success, creates the conditions necessary to drive a film crew to the point of lunacy. Movie people can understand this madness, but possibly their executives do not believe the public can share the joke, so *The Stunt Man* remains little seen.

                                                                    Stephen L. Hanson

SUCH GOOD FRIENDS

Released: 1971
Production: Otto Preminger for Paramount
Direction: Otto Preminger
Screenplay: Esther Dale (Elaine May); based on David Shaber's adaptation of the novel of the same name by Lois Gould
Cinematography: Gayne Rescher
Editing: Harry Howard
Running time: 100 minutes

Principal characters:
Julie Messinger .... Dyan Cannon
Dr. Timmy Spector .... James Coco
Miranda .... Jennifer O'Neill
Cal Whiting .... Ken Howard
Mrs. Wallman .... Nina Foch
Richard Messinger .... Laurence Luckinbill

Critic/film historian Andrew Sarris calls Otto Preminger "a director with the personality of a producer" in his much-too-short critical assessment in *The American Cinema: Directors and Directions* (1968). Preminger is the opposite of the classic successful artist who is given free rein over his budget and ends up ruining the film and nearly bankrupting the studio. Josef von Sternberg, Orson Welles, Eric von Stroheim, and more recently, perhaps, Francis Ford Coppola and Michael Cimino are victims of their own success. Preminger, on the other hand, has a reputation as a tyrant on the set with an eye more to the shooting schedule than to the artistry of the film, but he is more than a successful bookkeeper among the producer/directors; he is a courageous artist who takes on some of the most delicate issues of his time. *The Man with the Golden Arm* (1955) is a sensitive study of drug abuse and contains arguably Frank Sinatra's best performance. Preminger openly hired Dalton Trumbo, a blacklisted writer, to write *Exodus* in 1960 when blacklistees were still working under pseudonyms for a fraction of their previous salary. *The Moon Is Blue*, released in 1953, was the first film to be denied a seal of approval by the Production Code Administration of the Motion Picture Association of America (MPAA). Not only did *The Moon Is Blue* do well financially—believed to be impossible without the seal—but Preminger's action (with United Artists) was also an important step in breaking the power, which amounted to virtual censorship, that the MPAA Code Administration held over producers.

Preminger is an *auteur* of considerable reputation. He is best known for his *films noir—Laura* (1944), *Fallen Angel* (1945), *Daisy Kenyon* (1947), *Whirlpool* (1949), *Where the Sidewalk Ends* (1950), and *Angel Face* (1952)—and for his "objective" camera style. He favors long takes and medium shots over highly edited sequences with revealing close-ups; the effect is in the vein of French critic André Bazin's aesthetic of greater realism achieved by maintaining the integrity of space instead of chopping it up. Preminger's films stress character rather than suspense and are rich in the ambiguity that is the goal of Bazin's aesthetic of realism. Preminger's characters are rarely good or evil, but rather live with illusions they must pierce in order to become complete human beings. *Laura* is Preminger's masterpiece. In it, a detective falls in love with a girl he believes to be dead, falling in love with the image of Laura created by the man who "murders" her. Only when he accepts the reality of the live woman instead of the fantasy of the illusion do the two have a future.

Such Good Friends is not really similar to *Laura*, yet it is concerned with many of the same themes. In it, a woman is forced to see the lies of her many illusions and is painfully liberated by the film's end. Instead of a *film noir*, *Such Good Friends* is a black comedy. Like Preston Sturges' *Unfaithfully Yours* (1948) and Billy Wilder's *Kiss Me Stupid* (1964), other black comedies released before the public was ready for their particular brand of irreverence, *Such Good Friends* was not a smashing success. Most reviewers hated it: Richard Schickel called it the "most repellent movie of 1971." Only the *Hollywood Reporter* liked it, with most other reviews citing its vulgarity, bad taste, and lack of redeeming values.

Such Good Friends is about the frivolous, trivial lives, hopes, and illusions of moderately rich, moderately Jewish New Yorkers. Richard Messinger (Laurence Luckinbill), art director of a glossy picture magazine and author of a just-published children's book, *Melancholy Melinda and the Magic Melon Patch*, goes into the hospital to have a mole removed from his neck. Fussily frightened of death, he rejects his wife's sexual overtures, is sarcastically witty with his children and black maid, and overprepares for his one-night hospitalization. His friend Timmy Spector (James Coco), a gluttonous, sexually absurd, and overweight physician, supervises the operation and subsequent treatment, and through a hilarious and criminal series of medical errors, Richard does indeed die. In the removal of Richard's mole, an artery is nicked, necessitating a blood transfusion. Because Timmy neglects to type Richard's blood precisely, he is given Rh positive blood, to which he has a massive allergic reaction which sends him into a coma. He additionally has an adverse reaction to the anesthesia, and even though doctors assure Julie that only in intensive care does medical treatment become adequate and that the mystery is not how they lose so many patients, but rather how so many survive, Richard dies. When she acidly objects to the absurd medical errors, she is told, "Try not to be too bitter, Mrs. Messinger, you'll have plenty of time for that later."

During Richard's hospitalization, his wife Julie (Dyan Cannon) remembers her painful adolescence, teenage lesbian love affair (presented as a reaction to her mother's continual negative assessment of Julie's charms and prospects), and Richard's impotence with her which each seems willing to consider in large measure her fault. Additionally, she learns a great deal about her husband and their friends. Their best friends are Cal Whiting (Ken Howard), a photographer, and Miranda (Jennifer O'Neill), an actress. When Richard slips into a coma, Miranda tells Cal—with whom she lives and whom she expects to marry—that she and Richard have been having an affair. Cal promptly takes Julie out to a drunken lunch and relays the information. Then Timmy lets it slip that there were many others as well, and Julie learns how to decode Richard's "little black book," which is actually a record of women with whom he was making love, how they were doing it, and how many times. Julie and Cal try to have the "good time" they feel Miranda and Richard owe them, but he is impotent, and it becomes a sad, funny mess in which Julie is again somehow to blame. Julie can find no comfort from her so-called friends or even her mother (Nina Foch) as her illusions about her life collapse. When Richard finally dies and everyone crowds around to give advice, Julie walks out, away from the camera, with her two sons. The end credits roll over the long shot of Central Park after she has disappeared in the distance.

The plot may not sound hilarious, but Preminger, screenwriters Elaine May (writing under the pseudonym of Esther Dale) and David Shaber, and novelist Lois Gould take deadly aim at doctors, hospitals, sexual hype, pretentious artists, materialism, and, perhaps most subtle but most scathing, at the attempts of the Jewish bourgeois to blend into WASP "culture." Like Timmy, each character except Julie is wrapped up in himself or herself so completely that they have no sensitivity to anyone, while Julie thinks of nothing but everyone else until the picture ends. They are all too easy on themselves: Cal bitchily tells Julie her marriage is a sham while Richard is in a coma; Miranda explains that she had no qualms about her affair with Richard before now because she did not really know Julie. Now she is upset, because she finds she likes Julie, but she still tells Julie that Richard wanted to divorce her and marry Miranda, and is angry when Julie shows Cal Richard's little black book which shows Miranda was not the only one, and of course Cal promptly shows it to Miranda. Julie, on the other hand, is too hard on herself. She apologizes to the comatose Richard ("Whatever I did, I'm sorry"), and blames herself at every turn. Through the course of the film, she is traumatically liberated from her all-consuming guilt. She gets angry at the doctors, at Cal, at Miranda, at Richard, and finally even at her mother before realizing, as Richard is dying, that none of it matters—only his life is important.

Julie's mother is of course the major source of her problems. She tells the teenage Julie she is "dull and overweight" and the adult Julie that she has no idea how to dress. Mrs. Wallman is a caricature of the carefully whitewashed Jewish matron. She treats the gathering at the hospital to donate blood for

Richard like a party of which she is hostess, and when Julie comes to her (at the Elizabeth Arden beauty salon where Mrs. Wallman is having her thighs waxed) for help, her mother tells her to have a shampoo, a facial, "the whole works. . . . It may sound frivolous to some, but next to prayer, good grooming is the greatest comfort a woman can have." The class aspect to the mother's pretentiousness is made obvious when a clearly lower-class Jewish woman who has been sharing their vigil (and who is treated kindly only by Julie's black maid) refers to a trait as Jewish. "I never thought of that as particularly Jewish," Mrs. Wallman disdainfully answers. "How would we know, Mother," replies Julie. "We've never been particularly Jewish. We've never been particularly anything, except well-groomed."

By the end of the film, the senseless, useless lives full of sexual games and too much money that surround Julie have been exposed as ridiculous. Her illusions are wrenched from her, she is in some sense free as she walks into the park without a backward glance, holding the hands of her two small sons.

Janey Place

SUDDENLY, LAST SUMMER

Released: 1959
Production: Sam Spiegel for Columbia
Direction: Joseph L. Mankiewicz
Screenplay: Gore Vidal and Tennessee Williams; based on the play of the same name by Tennessee Williams
Cinematography: Jack Hilyard
Editing: Thomas Stanford
Running time: 112 minutes

Principal characters:
Catherine Holly .... Elizabeth Taylor
Mrs. Venable .... Katharine Hepburn
Dr. Cukrowicz .... Montgomery Clift
Mrs. Holly .... Mercedes McCambridge
George Holly .... Gary Raymond
Dr. Hockstader .... Albert Dekker

Unlike most film adaptations of well-known plays and novels, the films of Tennessee Williams' works have been fairly successful. That Williams has been involved in many of the adaptations may be part of the reason, but more significant, perhaps, is the innate visual sense with which he colors his plays. Visual metaphors and symbols abound, from the glass menagerie in the play of the same name through the "varsouviana" music in *A Streetcar Named Desire* to the iguana in *The Night of the Iguana*. In addition, Williams' poetic monologues supply a wealth of imagery which any enterprising filmmaker can draw upon and portray cinematically. Even Williams' exaggerated, mannerist characterizations are particularly suited to the mythical dimensions of the cinema. Blanche DuBois and Stanley Kowalski (*A Streetcar Named Desire*), Laura (*The Glass Menagerie*), and Reverend Shannon (*The Night of the Iguana*) are but a few of the archetypal figures to whom Williams has given drama, archetypes which resonate with universal emotions and feelings.

Suddenly, Last Summer reexplores many of the themes which have haunted Williams all of his life: death versus desire, madness, the indifference of nature (God), and sensitivity versus savagery. *Suddenly, Last Summer* is the story of a poet manqué, Sebastian, who, although dead when the film opens, dominates the action and development of the drama. He is the center of all discussions; and the luxurious, Byzantine mansion that he decorated with his mother and the savage tropical garden they cultivated are the central sets. All major characters, except Dr. Cukrowicz (Montgomery Clift), are defined in relation to Sebastian. His mother, Mrs. Venable (Katharine Hepburn), is a domineering, aging Southern belle who lives under the illusion of her son, an illusion that she has created in order to protect him from the savagery of the real world, to foster his poetic nature no matter how little it produced, and, ultimately, to hold him to her. Catherine (Elizabeth Taylor) is Sebastian's cousin and companion. It is through contact with the true Sebastian, as opposed to the lie with which his mother has surrounded him, that she is driven to the edge of insanity. Mrs. Holly (Mercedes McCambridge) and George Holly (Gene Raymond) are Catherine's mother and brother, who hover around Sebastian's corpse like vultures, awaiting their supposed inheritance. Dr. Cukrowicz, the other major character, is the outsider, the only one who is unacquainted with Sebastian and who consequently has been untouched by his magic or his curse. It is because of this detachment, coupled with his concern for the welfare of his patient, Catherine, that the truth of Sebastian slowly and painfully emerges from the darkness.

The central metaphor for the film and the key to understanding Sebastian is the incident of the Encantadas which is revealed at the denouement. Sebastian's mother describes the poet's fascination with the drama of nature enacted on these South American islands: the turtles crawling to shore to lay their eggs only to have themselves and their progeny cannibalized by vultures. In this scene, according to his mother, Sebastian sees the "face of God." He identifies himself with the victims and humanity and nature with the predators. It is exactly this kind of savagery which erupts at different points throughout the film and seems to confirm Sebastian's perception. It is savagery which leads Sebastian's mother to request that a lobotomy be performed on Catherine to "cut this hideous story out of her brain," the story of Sebastian's death which Catherine insists on repeating, to "cut out" the truth that Sebastian's mother is trying so desperately to hide. It is the same savagery which is evidenced in the callous avariciousness of Sebastian's cousins who await the reading of the will. Finally, it is the same savagery which results in the mutilation and cannibalization murder of Sebastian by a band of beggar boys that he has taunted.

The whole issue of Sebastian's homosexuality is handled very subtly in the film. Catherine admits to having acted as a sort of pimp for him, a firefly attracting men for his amusement, much as his mother had done in her youth. The matter is never clearly spelled out, however; his homosexuality remains in the background, acting as a factor of his sensitivity and fragility and as a way of emphasizing his alienation and "difference." It is interesting to note that in another context Sebastian's homosexuality could have been considered his salvation, since it is, in a sense, his only tangible connection with reality, the world of flesh and desire from which he has been so alienated and protected by his mother.

The filming of *Suddenly, Last Summer* can be considered a model of one of the two most common ways of adapting a play. The first is the path chosen by director Kazan in *A Streetcar Named Desire* (1951), that of staying pretty much within the restrictions dictated by the requirements of the stage—in other words, staying within the sets and confines set up in the original dramatic production. Director Joseph Mankiewicz and screenwriters Gore Vidal and Williams took the opposite path in *Suddenly, Last Summer*. The original play takes place entirely within the set of the Venable house and gardens, with all other incidents related in dramatic dialogues and monologues. The film version moves many of the scenes to the sanatorium in which Catherine has been committed and where Dr. Cukrowicz is in residence. In doing this, more time is given to the institution itself. A new character is created, Dr. Hockstader (Albert Dekker), the director of the institution and the one who pressures Cukrowicz to operate on Catherine in order to obtain a sizable donation from Mrs. Venable. The laxity and callousness of the sanatorium is brought to the forefront through the portrayal of the "snake pit" wards, the violence of patient against patient, and the indifference of the staff. What this accomplishes is the addition of a social dimension beyond the film's personal one. The crucial scenes in the Encantadas and in Cabeza de Lobo where Sebastian is murdered suddenly, last summer, as the title foretells, are also visualized with Catherine's dramatic monologue acting as voice-over narration. After her story is given to Cukrowicz there is no need for the lobotomy as the truth has now been told.

The performances in *Suddenly, Last Summer* are brilliant examples of ensemble acting at its best. Hepburn's Baroque, elegant Mrs. Venable; Taylor's neurotic, sensual Catherine; Clift's sensitive Dr. Cukrowicz; McCambridge's avaricious, vulgar Mrs. Holly; and Dekker's opportunistic Dr. Hockstader are all finely drawn individual characterizations. They are far more powerful as a whole, however, interacting with one another like brilliant patterns of light.

James Ursini

THE SUGARLAND EXPRESS

Released: 1974
Production: Richard D. Zanuck and David Brown for Universal
Direction: Steven Spielberg
Screenplay: Hal Barwood and Matthew Robbins; based on an original story
    by Steven Spielberg, Hal Barwood, and Matthew Robbins
Cinematography: Vilmos Zsigmond
Editing: Edward M. Abroms and Verna Fields
Running time: 110 minutes

> *Principal characters:*
> Lou Jean Poplin .... Goldie Hawn
> Clovis Poplin .... William Atherton
> Maxwell Slide .... Michael Sacks
> Captain Tanner .... Ben Johnson

The Sugarland Express exemplifies a new generation of Hollywood film-making in that it borrows both stylistically and thematically from several earlier American masters of the screen to create a unique, compelling work. The story is loosely based upon an actual incident in Texas in 1969. In the film, Clovis Poplin (William Atherton) is serving the last four months of a one-year sentence for petty larceny. His wife, Lou Jean (Goldie Hawn), has already served a shorter term for the same crime. Lou Jean seductively persuades Clovis to escape so that they may reclaim their baby boy Langston, who is in a foster home in Sugarland awaiting adoption because Lou Jean has been deemed an unfit mother as a result of her arrest for petty theft. This premise is revealed in the opening minutes of the film and motivates all of the action that follows. The couple's journey to Sugarland contains an epic quality, exploring both human nature and Americana within the framework of a comic adventure story.

In their attempt to find transportation for their trip, the couple attracts the attention of Patrolman Maxwell Slide (Michael Sacks). Clovis' fear and ignorance motivate him to hijack the police car and force Slide to take them to Sugarland. Police cars are sent out and roadblocks are established to catch them, but with no success. Before long numerous police cars are trailing the Poplins and their hostage, and what started out as a chase turns into a caravan. The parade grows as the news media and private citizens queue up for closer involvement. The visual impact of the growing line carries great comic weight, and by the end of the film, there is an unusual, captivating sight of more than than three hundred cars winding their well-choreographed way through Texas.

Inside Slide's car, another element of the story unfolds. It is here that the film becomes quiet and intimate, providing an opportunity for the audience to get to know the three main characters. Lou Jean is obviously motivated by her love for her baby, as well as by a need to disprove the court's ruling that she is an unfit mother. She is a child-woman, changing from one minute to the next, unstable, strong-willed, and utterly charming. Although Clovis would have been happier finishing his prison sentence, he submitted to his wife's threats of desertion and escaped. A quite likable although rather spineless character, he is forced to play the indulgent father to the little girl in Lou Jean. Slide, too, is a pleasant man, but an inexperienced cop, which has enabled Clovis, with his equally amateurish behavior, to succeed in the hijacking. In fact, all of the main characters are an ignorant, bumbling lot. It is their behavior which gets them where they are and which continues to propel them and enable them to elude the police. This is also true of Captain Tanner (Ben Johnson), the police chief in charge, and of his deputies.

During the course of the journey, barriers are broken down between Slide and the Poplins, and before long they are friends. When we see them sharing laughter and conversation, it is hard to believe that they are on opposing sides of the law. Captain Tanner likes the couple and continually tries to reason with them. Still, the police must do their job to apprehend the criminals, and Tanner plans to prevent the couple from retrieving Langston when they arrive in Sugarland. He is successful in his goal, but it is achieved tragically. Because of the attention given to their plight by the news media, the Poplins have become celebrities and heroes of the common people. They are innocent, childlike good guys in opposition to the police force's methodical armed bad guys. People sympathize with their simple desire to reclaim their child, and well-wishers line the streets of every town through which the entourage passes, providing the couple with food, money, and gifts for the baby. The Poplins have become stars and are receiving treatment befitting such a station. All of the attention is not altruistic, however; opportunists abound, seeking novel ways to obtain free publicity. A fried-chicken stand, for example, offers the trio a free meal if they surrender at their establishment.

These scenes are filled with manic, comic energy, and the people seem like cartoon caricatures in an American dream gone haywire. Here, as well as in numerous other points in the film, director Frank Capra's influence is felt. Although Steven Spielberg gives his film a more pungent twist, it contains the absurd, hysterical forces inherent in Capra screwball comedies. Capra's heroes are also bumbling, likable people pursued by larger forces, and their inherent good fortune allows them to be saved by happy accidents in order to provide fully resolved endings. In *Sugarland Express*, however, Lou Jean and Clovis are not so lucky. The three fugitives are attacked by red-necked would-be heroes with shotguns, an incident which leads the police to them. However reluctantly, Captain Tanner is convinced that he must thwart the rescue of the baby. He therefore evacuates the child and its adoptive (but very sympathetic) parents from their house and places sharpshooters instead in their places. When Lou Jean pushes Clovis out of the car to get the baby, he is brutally murdered by the gunmen.

The film is important as Spielberg's first feature. It received good critical notices, but went unnoticed commercially. Spielberg had previously directed episodes of several television series, as well as the acclaimed television film *Duel* (1971), and after *The Sugarland Express*, he went on to achieve fame with *Jaws* (1975) and *Close Encounters of the Third Kind* (1977). Each of these films are about widely diverse subjects, but, through Spielberg's interpretation, all could loosely be called action or adventure stories. The epic tone of *The Sugarland Express* is present in varying degrees in its director's subsequent successes. Through the course of his storytelling much is revealed about the individual characters and human nature in general, without great attempts at profundity. The three characters are so very human that people respond to them. This is the heart of the film. In this respect, Spielberg resembles John Ford. Ford used the Western milieu, whereas Spielberg uses contemporary settings, but they share the same ability to weave engaging tales.

The three primary players were all relative newcomers to the medium when they starred in the film. Hawn was already a household name for her appearance in the television series *Laugh-In*, and from a handful of previous films including *Cactus Flower* (1969), for which she won an Oscar, but she was still the funny, mindless girl from the television series in the public's mind. Her portrayal of Lou Jean here changed that image, showing the public the full range of her acting ability. Although an experienced stage performer, Atherton made his film debut as Clovis Poplin, a sensitive and well-drawn characterization. Sacks had previously starred in the film *Slaughterhouse-Five* (1972). His role as the hijacked patrolman is perhaps the most demanding in the film, as he gradually and convincingly evolves from being the Poplins' enemy to becoming their friend. It is a realistic, subtle performance.

Although some elements of the film are smoother than others, all its aspects coalesce to form a strong, cohesive unit. Vilmos Zsigmond's beautiful cinematography conveys well the varying moods of the film, which was skillfully coedited by Edward M. Abroms and Verna Fields. The latter then went on to work with Spielberg on *Jaws*, for which she received an Academy Award. Also sprinkled throughout the film are Country and Western songs which add rhythm and flavor to the work. Although the screenplay is perfectly well-written and serviceable, it provides little more than a blueprint for the finished film. It is through the performances and fine direction that the film became what some critics have called one of the best films of the decade.

Debra Bergman

SUMMER AND SMOKE

Released: 1961
Production: Hal B. Wallis for Paramount
Direction: Peter Glenville
Screenplay: James Poe and Meade Roberts; based on the play of the same name by Tennessee Williams
Cinematography: Charles Lang
Editing: Warren Low
Costume design: Edith Head
Music: Elmer Bernstein
Running time: 118 minutes

Principal characters:

Alma Winemiller	Geraldine Page
John Buchanan, Jr.	Laurence Harvey
Rosa Zacharias	Rita Moreno
Dr. Buchanan	John McIntire
Nellie Ewell	Pamela Tiffin
Rev. Winemiller	Malcolm Atterbury
Zacharias	Thomas Gomez
Archie Kramer	Earl Holliman
Roger Doremus	Casey Adams
Mrs. Winemiller	Una Merkel

Glorious Hill, Mississippi, is a sleepy Delta town which, in the stifling summer of 1916, sees the return of John Buchanan, Jr. (Laurence Harvey), from medical school. He arrives ten days later than expected because an extended shipboard card game took him well off his course. One of the icy artisian springs for which Glorious Hill is noted surfaces near the center of town at a fountain graced with a stone angel named Eternity. It is here that Dr. John first stops upon sighting a neighbor and friend since childhood, Miss Alma Winemiller (Geraldine Page). Daughter of the town's Episcopal preacher, Miss Alma has come to the fountain to find a cool drink and to regain her composure after singing "La Golondrina" poorly during the band concert in progress. The fireworks bursting overhead awe and fluster her, but no less so than the sight of long-awaited Dr. John.

Miss Alma, approaching thirty years of age, is now only dimly pretty after wasting her youth as a dutiful daughter to an imperious father (Malcolm Atterbury) and demented mother (Una Merkel). In addition to teaching singing to the young ladies of the town, she has performed as rectory wife, housekeeper, and her mother's nursemaid these years. As a result of this "cross" she bears, she is given to heart palpitations, sleeplessness, and delicate nerves. Her excessive refinement and affected mannerisms have often amused and faintly intrigued John Buchanan as they do now while they speak together at the fountain. As it always has, his teasing provokes and delights her although she feigns ridicule and detachment. Her radiance at his attentions pales to embarrassment, however, when Dr. John relates that he believes she is possessed of a *Doppelgänger*, or another person inside herself who yearns to get free. She is humiliated and hurt and blames her position as a preacher's daughter for her prim and prissy ways.

One of Miss Alma's singing students, Nellie Ewell (Pamela Tiffin), discovers her adored teacher at the fountain with the new Dr. John Buchanan. He takes favorable notice of the childishly pretty girl but later finds an excuse to take leave of Miss Alma only after spying a fiery Cuban beauty in the crowd. Much later he finally arrives at his father's house. Dr. John Buchanan, Sr. (John McIntyre), is the much-loved town physician in whose shadow the son has spent his self-indulgent boyhood. The man is furious at his son's late return from school and denounces him, as he has on previous occasions, as a "drunkard, wastrel and lecher." John seeks refuge at Moon Lake Casino outside of town, which is owned by the father of his new dark-eyed ladyfriend, Rosa Zacharias (Rita Moreno).

From her bedroom window Miss Alma furtively watches the comings and goings of Dr. John during that summer of 1916. He is far too busy to attend an evening meeting of the Glorious Hill Cultural Society to which she has invited him, or to take her riding in his automobile as he had once promised. She quietly endures the long steamy months of her mother's kleptomania and taunting jeers, returning to her nighttime vigil behind her window curtain.

One very early morning, Dr. John returns home badly cut from the spur of a cock on which he gambled at the casino. As he attends to the wound in his father's medical office in the house, he is surprised to find Miss Alma enter the examining room. It seems that she is in search of relief from a nervous heart palpitation which keeps her from sleeping. Since the elder doctor is away at a distant fever clinic, Dr. John must attend her. She receives his cold stethoscope against her skin with shy agitation but accepts his bottle of sedatives with gratitude. In a moment of seeming sympathy, he confides in her that he had always wondered if there might be a chance for them, and she assents to his request to call for her the next evening.

Moon Lake Casino is not where Miss Alma had expected the doctor to begin his courtship of her. It is barely tolerable to her until he takes her into the barn where a cockfight is under way. During the screaming frenzy of the match, blood is splattered on her white bodice, which sends her shrieking from the barn. Outside, John calms her. She accepts his kiss but not his hopeful advances. He is not persuaded by the argument that he must respect any woman who might become the mother of his children. She is sent home in a taxi. She realizes that she must now accept an offer of marriage from another suitor, Roger Doremus (Casey Adams), as his could very well be her last. Roger, also a member of the Cultural Society, is very much his mother's son. Although his touch repulses her, Alma acknowledges him as her last hope.

John throws a loud and sodden party which lasts well into the next night. In its midst, the Reverend Winemiller (Malcolm Atterbury) is asked to solemnize the marriage of John to Rosa Zacharias. It seems that John has lost three thousand dollars to her father during a high stakes card game. Señor Zacharias (Thomas Gomez), who is used to getting his beloved Rosa anything she desires, knows that she wants John for her husband. A bargain is struck. Later, the reverend tells Alma of his refusal to sanctify such a union when she comes in from an evening of viewing slides with Roger. She is stunned at John's choice for a wife. The party continues, and Alma moves from her window observation post to the telephone where she calls the elder doctor, who is still away fighting an epidemic, long distance. Buchanan arrives home much later to a house littered with human and glass debris. Outraged, he orders Zacharias to remove the swine from the house. Zacharias vengefully repays the insult with a shot that kills Buchanan. While his father is dying upstairs, John reviles the meddlesome Alma who, out of spite, called his father home. To Alma's admission he cries, "Dead by the hand of a hysterical old maid terrified of the animal in herself!"

It is now mid-winter, and Miss Alma has seen no one for months. She no longer accepts singing students, and most days does not bother to get dressed. Pale and thinner, she impassively hears the news from her father that Dr. John is returning from months at the fever clinic after finishing the work which his father began and successfully eradicating the resistant fever. Winemiller is disgusted with Dr. John receiving the credit for his father's work. When Dr. John calls on Miss Alma after settling into his father's practice, Winemiller firmly tells him that she is not at home to him and wishes never to see him again. To Alma, who inquires about the reason for the doctor's visit, her father replies that Dr. John did not ask after her.

Nellie Ewell, who is now home on Christmas vacation from a term at finishing school, has matured into a lovely but still childish beauty. Meeting Miss Alma at the fountain, Nellie presents her with a little gift as well as with the news that Dr. John is much indebted to Miss Alma for inspiring him. His reformed and dedicated ways are the direct result of her influence upon him. Startled yet very hopeful, she calls upon him at the medical office under the guise of needing his professional attention. She is able to receive the cold stethoscope against her heart with less composure than the summer before. She soon finds herself confessing her lifelong love of him and offers herself to him, stating that "The girl who said no, she doesn't exist anymore. She was suffocated in smoke from something on fire inside her!"

John resists her importuning as she had once resisted his. He now believes what she had believed, that their love is spiritual, while *she* now wishes it to be much less so. It is now John who attempts to persuade her, with the aid of his anatomical chart, of the presence of the soul within the human body. They are interrupted by a beaming Nellie who comes in and reveals her engagement to Dr. John. Hiding her devastation in expressions of joy, Alma takes her prescription from the doctor and quickly departs. Wandering alone near the fountain later that evening, Miss Alma meets a young and folksy traveling salesman named Archie Kramer (Earl Holliman) with whom she boldly strikes up a conversation. In unaccustomed friendliness, she suggests that they find the only excitement which Glorious Hill has to offer at Moon Lake Casino. Obliging her, Archie takes her arm and escorts her into the night as the film ends.

Originally entitled *A Chart of Anatomy*, *Summer and Smoke* was written by Tennessee Williams in 1948. It is his most complete interpretation of the South, according to critics, and Miss Alma his favorite character. He wrote of her again in a reworked version of *Summer and Smoke* called *Eccentricities of a Nightingale* (1967). Although written before *A Streetcar Named Desire*, *Summer and Smoke* reached off-Broadway later, in 1952, and fared badly because of the inevitable comparison with the hit play. Williams never forgot the failure.

Summer and Smoke marked the turning point in the career of Geraldine Page. She is able to convey Miss Alma's stifled propriety and yet bring warmth and compassion to the characterization. In re-creating the role for the screen almost ten years later, Page finds a greater depth in Miss Alma and succeeds in carrying off the portrayal with renewed conviction.

Predictably, critics found the Hal B. Wallis production to be a pedestrian version of the original, although the Motion Picture Academy approved of it to the point of nominating it for four Oscars. Working with screenwriters James Poe and Meade Roberts, director Peter Glenville was able to bring movement to a play consisting, on stage, of a single tri-scene set. Yet, he is criticized for his studio-bound locale which gives no sense of place or time to the production. For the torpid, redolent mood of prewar Mississippi, art director Hal Pereira suffuses the film in warm pinks, lace curtains, gingerbread moldings, and cluttered interiors. An atmosphere of sensuality pervades every scene; it is heavy and repressed in Alma, blatant in Rosa Zacharias, incipient in Nellie, and calculated in John.

Williams' male characterizations are often not so strong as his Southern women. To the indistinct *persona* of John Buchanan, Jr., Laurence Harvey brings no clarity. We cannot see the fineness of character which originally attracted and sustained the distant adoration of the fastidious Miss Alma. Furthermore, it seems out of character for the redeemed and soulful Dr. John to be marrying a child-woman of such evident physical appeal. Perhaps this irresolution is the playwright's final means to portray the duality of human nature, the interplay of spirit and sex, virtue and depravity. As Alma says upon viewing through the doctor's microscope ". . . a mysterious universe—part anarchy and part order. . . ," her analogy for passion and reason struggling for supremacy within man.

The small role of Alma's deranged mother, played by Una Merkel, is crucial to the understanding of Alma. Mrs. Winemiller's mocking revelations bear truth which might not otherwise be inferred. "How she stares out the window! How she expects him to come over!" Mrs. Winemiller also represents a less strong version of Alma who broke down under the strain of excessive piety and repression. She is the specter of what Alma might become.

Summer and Smoke has been described as a young playwright's naïve discussion of spirituality and sexuality and the tension between these opposites. The screen adaptation retains the essence of Williams' work and, like the play, invites a deeper look at the layers of meaning and the involved symbolism for which he came to be known in later works.

Nancy S. Kinney

A SUMMER PLACE

Released: 1959
Production: Delmer Daves for Warner Bros.
Direction: Delmer Daves
Screenplay: Delmer Daves; based on the novel of the same name by Sloan Wilson
Cinematography: Harry Stradling
Editing: Owen Marks
Music: Max Steiner
Running time: 130 minutes

Principal characters:
Ken Jorgenson .... Richard Egan
Sylvia Hunter .... Dorothy McGuire
Molly Jorgenson .... Sandra Dee
Bart Hunter .... Arthur Kennedy
Johnny Hunter .... Troy Donahue
Helen Jorgenson .... Constance Ford
Mrs. Hamble .... Beulah Bondi

Although the films of Delmer Daves encompass nearly every genre, the director is probably best known for his work with war films and Westerns. Stirring action sequences and memorable characters are the hallmarks of his war films, which include *Destination Tokyo* (1943) and *Pride of the Marines* (1945), while social realism marks his Westerns. In fact, Daves helped to redefine the genre with his ground-breaking 1950 film, *Broken Arrow*, the first Western to deliver a pro-Indian statement. Daves, who went on to direct a string of liberal-minded Westerns in the 1950's—including titles such as *Jubal* (1956), *3:10 to Yuma* (1957), and *The Hanging Tree* (1959)—shifted his attention to glossy, turgid, big-screen soap operas during the latter part of the decade. Replete with sentiment and sermonizing, these films, made for Warner Bros., usually showcased predictable, somewhat scintillating (for their time) story lines against lavish location cinematography. The casts, which often included skilled veterans in supporting roles, were sometimes dominated by young, attractive performers of rather limited range. Most popular of Daves' soap operas is *A Summer Place*, the story of loveless marriages and the breakdown of communication between the generations. Handsomely mounted, the film combines lush Technicolor cinematography, a stirring Max Steiner score, earnest performances, and a teary tale of romance. Because of its story line involving adultery and a teenage love affair, the film was controversial at the time of its release. It also generated considerable press because its young stars, Sandra Dee and Troy Donahue, who appear as the young lovers, were especially popular with teenage audiences; they went on to become major box-office stars of the 1960's.

Produced, directed, and scripted by Daves and based on the best-selling novel by Sloan Wilson (best-known as the author of "The Man in the Gray Flannel Suit"), *A Summer Place* deals with the passions that stir during a summer season on Pine Island, a resort located off the East Coast. Early in the film, the island is called "a perverted Garden of Eden," a description which caused some critics to see the film as a kind of Peyton Place-by-the-sea. Peyton Place was a repressive community, however; in contrast, the Pine Island ocean breeze and pine scent are said to act as aphrodisiacs, and the island seems to welcome passion.

As the film opens, Ken and Helen Jorgenson (Richard Egan and Constance Ford) and their pretty teenage daughter Molly (Sandra Dee) are vacation-bound aboard a yacht headed for the island. Jorgenson, who worked as a lifeguard on the island during his youth, is now returning, a millionaire because of his discoveries as a research scientist. On Pine Island, Bart and Sylvia Hunter (Arthur Kennedy and Dorothy McGuire) are readying their home-turned-inn for the Jorgensons' arrival. The once-wealthy island family is in financial disarray, partly because of Bart's inability to manage money.

By the time the Jorgensons' reach the island, the characters have been clearly identified as either "good" or "bad"—or at least sympathetic and unsympathetic. Helen, who appears cold and irrational, has argued with Molly over the girl's mode of dress. She wants Molly to look "completely modest," which causes Ken to intervene on his daughter's behalf. Ken nobly accuses Helen of trying to "desex" Molly, "as though sex were synonymous with dirt." The Hunter marriage does not appear to be any happier, for Bart has a drinking problem and a cynical outlook, while Sylvia has a kind but defeated spirit. Molly, who nearly bubbles over with innocence and confusion, is obviously a pawn, and Johnny (Troy Donahue), the Hunter's handsome teen-age son, is no better off.

Pine Island soon becomes the setting for a flurry of romantic interludes. As it turns out, Ken and Sylvia were lovers many summers ago, prior to her marriage to Bart, and entrapment in loveless marriages quickly sends them back into each other's arms. Johnny and Molly also become infatuated. In a particularly telling scene during the first night on the island, Sylvia and Ken gaze longingly at each other from their respective bedroom windows, while Johnny and Molly do the same.

Helen, who is immediately alarmed by her daughter's interest in Johnny, does not detect the romance between Ken and Sylvia, but after the island's night watchman tells her of their early morning encounters in the boathouse, Helen telephones her mother. Her mother advises Helen to keep quiet about the situation so that the lovers can continue to meet; thus, a bigger divorce settlement may be in the offing.

It is a sailboat accident involving Molly and Johnny which sets off actions that reveal the tangled Pine Island relationships. After capsizing in a storm, Molly and Johnny spend the night together on a deserted beach. They are immediately subjected to Helen's erroneous suspicions, following their rescue by the Coast Guard. In fact, Molly is forced to undergo a complete medical examination, despite the girl's hysterical pleas that she has been "good." Later, a humiliated Molly tells Johnny of the ordeal, before running away. In turn, Johnny angrily threatens Helen's life. Ken also gets into the disagreement when he confronts Helen about the medical exam, which proved unnecessary. Helen retaliates by revealing that she knows about his affair with Sylvia. The accusations are made in front of a subdued Bart and a devastated Johnny, who storms out of the room. "You seem to have an infinite capacity for hurt," Sylvia tells Helen.

Helen's accusations fuel the Pine Island headlines and gossip mills, and divorce proceedings begin for both couples. Ken and Sylvia plan to marry, but neither receives custody of their children. Both Molly and Johnny feel betrayed by what has ensued. Their own relationship is temporarily stilled by the divorces. Johnny is sent away to a Virginia prep school, and Molly goes to a posh girl's school outside Boston. Ken and Sylvia, each hoping for a reconciliation with their children, marry and move into a luxurious beach house. They invite both Molly and Johnny to spend a spring vacation break with them, hoping to soothe hurt feelings, but Johnny and Molly still feel otherwise. "Let's face it, we're all alone on this earth," Johnny tells Molly during an afternoon on the beach. Their shared feelings of loneliness are impetus for the affair that follows.

After returning to Boston, Molly learns that she is pregnant. Johnny quickly comes to her, and the two weigh their limited options. Helen would become hysterical if she learned of the situation, and the two have yet to forgive Ken and Sylvia for what they perceive as betrayal. In desperation, they travel to Pine Island, hoping Bart will give his consent for marriage. Bart is found in a drunken stupor awaiting the arrival of the Coast Guard for transport to a naval hospital for treatment. He cynically views his son's situation, surmising, "Shirtsleeves to shirtsleeves in three generations—at least you won't have to start where I did, from the top." Refusing to give his approval to the marriage, Bart advises the two to strive for good times, rather than marriage, because "some of the best parts of life are frivolous." He especially angers Johnny when he insists, "Molly is merely a succulent little wench. They're all alike in the dark."

His words drive Molly and Johnny back to the mainland, where they are determined to marry. After a justice of the peace turns them down because they are underage, however, the two realize they must turn to Ken and Sylvia for help. "We live in a glass house. We aren't throwing any stones," says Sylvia, during the final teary reunion. In the film's last scene, newlyweds Johnny and Molly return to Pine Island, where they will refurbish and run the inn and begin their lives together.

Lavishly photographed by Academy Award-winner Harry Stradling, Sr., *A Summer Place* was filmed on the beautiful Monterey Peninsula, which substituted for the Eastern Seaboard. A spectacular Frank Lloyd Wright house (located in Carmel) served as Ken and Sylvia's beach house and proved a scene stealer. Steiner's sumptuous music score provides further embellishment. In fact, the film's romantic theme song, as performed by Percy Faith, went on to dominate record charts for months, and "Theme from a Summer Place" remains a hauntingly beautiful piece of film music.

Melodramatic dialogue aside, the film's performances are also effective. Egan and McGuire, cast as the adulterous lovers, competently etch sympathetic portraits. McGuire, who is gentle and rather teary throughout, elicits a luminous beauty, especially during love scenes. "I'm not pretty anymore. I'm sorry for that," she tells Ken, during an encounter in the boathouse. Her voice is soft but clear, and tears swell in her vibrant blue eyes. Ken's reply, a muffled, "I love you too much to speak," doubtless won audiences over to their cause. As the incompetent Bart, Kennedy has a melodramatic field day, and Ford is appropriately evil as the unfeeling, frigid Helen. Beulah Bondi, cast as a cranky guest at the inn, also has several enjoyable scenes.

As the young lovers, both Dee and Donahue have a fresh, engaging quality. Dee, a pert, brown-eyed blonde probably best-known for her work in teen-oriented films such as *Gidget* (1959) and *Tammy and the Doctor* (1963), also has dramatic abilities, as seen, most notably in *Imitation of Life* (1959). She also starred in a series of light, enjoyable comedies that proved popular in the 1960's, occasionally costarring with her then-husband, the late pop singer Bobby Darin. In 1970 she also appeared in the low-budget but effective horror film, *The Dunwich Horror*. Today she is absent from the screen, but her films remain television staples.

Bolstered by his blond good looks, Donahue appeared in the Warner Bros. television series *Surfside Six* and a series of films for that studio, before turning mostly to low-budget exploitation films. His rapid rise and fall within the industry is well known and the subject of much cruel Hollywood humor. Still, Donahue delivered likable work, which propelled him to fame as a "teen idol." His starring roles in films such as *Parrish* (1961), *Susan Slade* (1961), and *Rome Adventure* (1962), all directed by Daves, are proof that the attractive Donahue was also not without talent. Today, Donahue surfaces occasionally in films, such as *The Godfather* (1972), in which he appeared briefly, and makes television appearances now and then.

Pat H. Broeske

SUMMERTIME

Released: 1955
Production: Ilya Lopert for United Artists
Direction: David Lean
Screenplay: David Lean and H. E. Bates; based on the play *The Time of the Cuckoo* by Arthur Laurents
Cinematography: Jack Hilyard
Editing: Peter Taylor
Running time: 99 minutes

Principal characters:
Jane Hudson	Katharine Hepburn
Renato Di Rossi	Rossano Brazzi
Signora Fiorina	Isa Miranda
Eddie Jaeger	Darren McGavin
Phyl Jaeger	Mari Aldon
Edith McIlhenny	Jane Rose
Lloyd McIlhenny	MacDonald Parke
Mauro	Gaitano Audiero

Summertime occupies a clear middle position in the career of eminent British director David Lean. Between his black-and-white period films of earlier years such as *Brief Encounter* (1946) and his later color and widescreen productions, such as *Lawrence of Arabia* (1962), it stands out as his last contemporary film. While not his initial effort in color, it was his first film photographed entirely on location, a method which Lean has refused to abandon in subsequent work. Also for the first time, both the principal actors, Katharine Hepburn and Rossano Brazzi, and the source material, Arthur Laurents' Broadway play, were non-English. *Summertime* was, in short, Lean's first step away from being the British director of English motion pictures aimed at a predominantly home audience and toward becoming an international filmmaker working with "foreign" producers and stars in the world market, a position with all the attendant increased professional reputation and popular recognition which he has held ever since.

Thematically, however, *Summertime* has much in common with its antecedents in Lean's work. The imaginings of Laura Jesson (Celia Parker) aboard the train in *Brief Encounter* are obvious foreshadowings. The romantic narrative and even the Venetian locale of *Summertime* are anticipated in Laura's dream image of riding with her lover in a gondola on the grand canal. To a considerable extent Jane Hudson (Katharine Hepburn), the main character in *Summertime*, who comes to Venice looking for excitement and adventure, represents a fulfillment of Laura's fantasies in that earlier film. Still, Jane is a more refined and less defined characterization than Laura Jesson, who was basically writer Noel Coward's creation. The blending of opposing qualities makes Jane outgoing yet repressed, eager but ambivalent, brash yet self-conscious, graceful but a bit clumsy. She is sharply delineated and outwardly a more realistic figure than Laura. Few of the events of her past and almost nothing of her personal history are specified. Inwardly she is as much prone to fantasy as any character in Lean's films.

The style of *Summertime* is not as subjective as it was in *Brief Encounter*. Early in the film, as she checks into her *pensione* in Venice, Jane stands exultantly on the balcony silhouetted against the bright, sunlit city below. Later, in her disenchantment, she draws the room's curtains and sits in her white dress amidst the dark furnishings, posed like a figure from a Vermeer painting listening to the selected sounds of isolation: the scrape of slippers on the floor above, the distant toll of a single bell, and the canal water lapping against wooden hulls below. Both scenes, although reflecting radically different moods, are subtly and subjectively expressive.

Throughout Lean drives the narrative forward with small, climactic moments when Jane experiences an emotional peak or low. By restructuring in this manner, he not only moves away from the rhetorical explicitness of the original play but also creates a visual flow between what were originally static acts and scenes. As they are indicators of her emotional flux, her self-consciousness and physical maladroitness plague Jane in many of the film's sequences. There is actually little comic effect derived from these ostensibly humorous conditions, at least in the sense of making her actions laughable. In fact, there is little in *Summertime* to qualify it as a comedy, neither in the traditional sense of a "happy ending" nor through an abundance of amusing incidents. The terrace scenes, for example—particularly the one in which Jane paces back and forth listening to the street singers and amorous couples laughing and then throws a rock into the water to break the tension only to retreat in embarrassment when a gondolier mistakes it for a summons—have more an air of desperate pathos than comedy.

A sequence such as Jane's fall into the canal is more overtly comic but simultaneously fulfills several other functions. It is visually amusing action, a restatement of the stock gag: Jane, the embodiment of an American tourist in Italy, backing up to get a better picture of the shop of Renato Di Rossi (Rossano Brazzi), losing her footing, and tumbling into the water. Narratively, it also provides the necessary excuse for the handsome Di Rossi to call on Jane at her hotel to inquire if she is all right. Lean combines the subjective factor of having the audience share a disconcerting moment with Jane with the ironic presence of her young guide, Mauro (Gaitano Audiero), who is unable to get a word of warning in and resigns himself to watching her slip. Lean even prolongs the pure comedy of the scene by having an unidentified tourist perform a replay for his friends up to and including the fall into the water. Symbolically, this sequence links Jane's camera with her loss of control, both a physical loss of equilibrium in the action itself and an emotional agitation aggravated by the onlookers who crowd around and the proximity of Di Rossi in his store.

Jane's camera is also a key element in her first encounter with Di Rossi on the terrace of a café near San Marco. While idly photographing the passersby, she inadvertently witnesses a "pickup" through her viewfinder. For the first time in the film her control of what her camera records, her selective view, is disrupted; her image of Venice and its romantic idealism are belied. Disturbed, she stops filming; and while she rewinds her camera, a panning movement reveals Di Rossi seated behind her. As she raises the camera to her eye and shoots again, the motor noise distracts him from his newspaper. The camera assumes his point of view as his eyes wander over Jane's legs and up to her waist, until the intensity of his gaze is translated into a traveling movement into the back of her neck. She senses it, turns, fumbles to put on her sunglasses in symbolic concealment, and the incident ends.

From this simple event, Lean sets in motion a series of increasingly sensory experiences for Jane. As he energetically opens up the play through architectural expanses and nocturnal fireworks displays, the viewer coexperiences with Jane the realization of various of her expectations of the "City of Romance." Di Rossi is in a sense the last element in this landscape which encourages her to freer and more instinctive responses.

The subsequent scenes between Jane and Di Rossi are increasingly stylized. To balance the first meeting where her camera catches Di Rossi's attention, her own eye is caught by an antique red goblet displayed in Di Rossi's store window. Lean later exploits two long sequences of theatrical dialogue; he adds dramatic tension by staging them both in long takes and in medium close shots subliminally accentuated by a slow, barely perceptible traveling motion that seems to bring the couple closer together in a diminishing frame as their words reflect growing physical attraction. As Jane's emotional insulation is penetrated by Di Rossi, Lean changes pace again through his composition and editing. The evening concert, the night strolls by the canals, and the overhead long shot of Jane crossing a crowded square are all milestones in Jane's passionate evolution. The couple's final outing to the "Isle Where the Rainbow Fell" where they pose against the fiery colorations of the setting sun, marks the completion of a cycle, the end of Jane's transformation, and the resolution of her inner doubts.

To this point in his work, Jane Hudson is, more than any other figure adapted from a novel or play, Lean's character. Lean alters not simply the name, but, with Hepburn, Jane's whole way of being. Her appearance is radically unlike Laurents' original character, Leona Samish, played on Broadway by Shirley Booth, and so is her attitude. From the first glimpse of her on the train entering the city, she is no longer a cynical, intemperate, slightly overweight, middle-aged woman running away from life, but one who somehow senses that she has missed something and is actively running after it. Leona Samish loses because she can never accept life for what it is; Jane wins because she can. In the character of Renato Di Rossi and in the use of Italian star Brazzi, *Summertime* continues to diverge from the source material. Despite the dialogue in which Di Rossi claims to be an "ordinary man," Brazzi's movie image reinforces the "storybook" aspect of his affair with Jane. The Di Rossi of *The Time of the Cuckoo* is something of a gigolo, careless with money at best, unscrupulous at worst. Lean makes Di Rossi painfully sincere; for Lean's interest is obviously in the fantasy/reality of Jane's world, in the way *she* and no one else deceives herself. Accordingly, Di Rossi becomes an honest and mature figure, not merely an antique dealer who speaks humorously imperfect English ("He is my niece") and challenges Jane's more prudish beliefs with bizarre similes ("You are hungry. Eat the ravioli!"). Because Lean reinterprets the character in this manner, *Summertime* possesses a narrative development in which Jane does separate fantasy from reality, and does realize as Di Rossi runs after her departing train that the perpetuation of the dream is less valuable than the moment of unguarded emotional experience.

Alain J. Silver

THE SUN ALSO RISES

Released: 1957
Production: Darryl F. Zanuck for Twentieth Century-Fox
Direction: Henry King
Screenplay: Peter Viertel; based on the novel of the same name by Ernest
   Hemingway
Cinematography: Leo Tover
Editing: William Mace
Running time: 129 minutes

> *Principal characters:*
> Jake Barnes ....Tyrone Power
> Lady Brett Ashley ....Ava Gardner
> Robert Cohn ....Mel Ferrer
> Mike Campbell ....Errol Flynn
> Bill Gorton ....Eddie Albert
> Romero ....Robert Evans

It is an axiom of film *criticism* that great films are not made from great novels. The best films are usually made from original scripts or from second- or third-rate novels on which the filmmakers can put their own imprint. The best novels, on the other hand, usually use the written word so well that they resist the transformation to another medium. An axiom of the film industry, however, is that a film based upon a work by Ernest Hemingway will be a hit at the box office. *The Sun Also Rises*, the 1957 film based upon Ernest Hemingway's 1926 novel, confirms both these axioms; it is a disappointing work that nevertheless was one of the twenty most popular films of 1957.

The film tells essentially the same story that the novel does. It is set in France and Spain in the 1920's. Jake Barnes (Tyrone Power), impotent because of a war wound, is an American writer working in Paris. He is involved in a torturous relationship with the promiscuous Lady Brett Ashley (Ava Gardner), an Englishwoman whom he met while she was a nurse during the war. Neither can receive satisfaction from their attraction to each other, but neither can sever the bond between them. Also involved is a friend of Jake, Robert Cohn (Mel Ferrer), who becomes obsessed with Brett from the first moment he sees her and before he knows anything about her relationship with Jake. Then Brett tells Jake that she is going to marry Mike Campbell (Errol Flynn) and go away with him.

Jake goes on a fishing trip with another friend, Bill Gorton (Eddie Albert), and then on to Pamplona, Spain, with him for the fiesta and the bullfights. There they unexpectedly find Robert, Mike and Brett, and the next few days the five characters spend together in a round of eating and drinking at the cafés and watching the running of the bulls and the bullfights. It is not, however, a happy group. Brett has not married Mike, who spends most of his time drunkenly telling Robert he is not wanted. Robert, still obsessed with Brett, refuses to leave although she gives him no encouragement.

The group breaks up explosively when Brett, who has told Jake she is sick of the whole scene, becomes interested in a young bullfighter, Pedro Romero (Robert Evans). This angers Jake, Mike, and Robert. When Robert goes to Romero's room and finds Brett there, he beats up the young bullfighter. They all leave Pamplona, Brett going with Romero and Robert back to Paris. Later, Brett cables Jake, who is in Biarritz, France, to come to Madrid. There he finds that she has forced Romero to leave because she would ultimately hurt him. She asks Jake to take her with him, and in the last scene the two are in a cab, where Brett says, "Darling, there must be an answer for us some-where," and Jake replies, "I'm sure there is."

Although the film did receive many favorable reviews at the time, it has now become obvious that Twentieth Century-Fox did not make a film of Hemingway's novel; it made a standard 1950's Hollywood film using some events and some dialogue from that novel. The major flaw that stands out today is that the young Bohemian writers of the novel are made to look like middle-aged businessmen who wear nice clothes and have plenty of money in the film. Lady Brett's appearance is also definitely that of 1950's Hollywood rather than 1920's Paris. The acting and directing are unexceptional; they also remind one more of Hollywood than Hemingway. Flynn as Mike Campbell is perhaps better than the rest, and Evans as Pedro Romero is the weakest of the principal actors. It was not until Evans became a producer many years later that he distinguished himself in the film world with such pictures as *Rosemary's Baby* (1968) and *Chinatown* (1974). Both the filmmakers and some of the critics seem to have believed that a certain faithfulness to the outline of the plot was all that was required. Unfortunately, they ignored the themes and especially the flavor of the novel.

In the book, the fishing in Spain is tremendously important to Jake and to the reader's understanding of his character, but in the film it is only a minor episode. Also, many critics have called the bullfighter Pedro Romero the moral center of the film, and his prowess and art in the ring are described in great detail, with his performance so excellent in one fight that the audience "did not want it to be over." This aspect of the novel could not be conveyed in a Hollywood film in which no bloodletting is shown in the bullfight scenes and in which the fullfighter is portrayed by an actor in the close-ups and by a real bullfighter only in the long shots. Thus the film is like the book in that it has fishing and bullfighting, but it is unlike the book in that it fails to convey the thematic and emotional overtones of these actions. In addition, a slight but significant change was made in the ending for a somewhat more optimistic tone. Instead of assuring Brett as he does in the film that he is sure that there is an answer somewhere, in the book Jake merely says, "Isn't it pretty to

2354   *The Sun Also Rises*

think so," when Brett says they could have had a good time together.

Hemingway himself was seldom satisfied with films made from his books, and *The Sun Also Rises* was no exception. "It's all pretty disappointing, and that's being gracious," he said. Despite Hemingway's reaction, director Henry King and producer Darryl Zanuck continued to insist that they had made a good and faithful adaptation. Their good intentions, however, were not enough. *The Sun Also Rises* must today be viewed chiefly as an example of Hollywood's approach to a "classic" novel in the 1950's rather than as a true filming of Hemingway's novel.

Sharon Wiseman

THE SUN SHINES BRIGHT

Released: 1953
Production: John Ford and Merian C. Cooper; distributed by Republic
Direction: John Ford
Screenplay: Laurence Stallings; based on the short stories "The Sun Shines Bright," "The Mob from Massac," and "The Lord Provides" by Irvin S. Cobb
Cinematography: Archie Stout
Editing: Jack Murray
Running time: 90 minutes

Principal characters:

Judge William Pittman Priest	Charles Winninger
Lucy Lee Lake	Arleen Whelan
Ashby Corwin	John Russell
Jeff Poindexter	Stepin' Fetchit
Doctor Lewt Lake	Russell Simpson
Herman Felsburg	Ludwig Stossel
Buck Ramsey	Grant Withers
Horace K. Maydew	Milburn Stone
Lucy's Mother	Dorothy Jordan
U. S. Grant Woodford	Elzie Emanuel
General Fairfield	James Kirkwood
Amora Ratchitt	Jane Darwell
Uncle Pleasant Woodford	Ernest Whitman
Mallie Cramp	Eve March

In the 1930's, John Ford made three films starring Will Rogers: *Doctor Bull* (1933), *Judge Priest* (1934), and *Steamboat Round the Bend* (1935). All three were warm, nostalgic re-creations of small-town America, and in 1953, Ford returned to that milieu to remake *Judge Priest*. This time the film was titled *The Sun Shines Bright*, and Ford would later call it his favorite film. Considering that it immediately followed his celebration of the Irish in *The Quiet Man* (1952), and that his affection for his ancestral homeland is palpable in the earlier film, it is most surprising that Ford would prefer this modest little film set in Kentucky, a work that won no awards and passed unnoticed at the time of its release by audiences and critics alike. Ford scholars have rediscovered it, however, and most critics now concur with Ford's estimation of the film. Certainly it is a superb example of the reworking of many of the themes that concerned the director throughout his career, a film that illustrates some hard moral lessons in a sugar-coating of gentle, easygoing humor.

The film begins at the turn of the century with a shot of a steamboat approaching the wharf in Fairfield, Kentucky. A banner attached to the upper deck urges citizens to vote for Judge Priest. When the boat docks, Judge

Priest (Charles Winninger) and his black retainer, Jeff Poindexter (Stepin' Fetchit), watch a dashing young man unload his horses and ride through the town. His friend Dr. Lake (Russell Simpson) recognizes the man as Ashby Corwin (John Russell) and introduces him to his ward, Lucy Lee (Arleen Wheeler), who is attracted to the young man, but the doctor tries to discourage her interest. Judge Priest leaves to go to the Courthouse to oversee a trial which becomes quickly disrupted when a young black man, U. S. Grant Woodford (Elzie Emanuel), plays "Marching Through Georgia" on his banjo. The judge convinces him to play "Dixie" and arranges for him to find work on a friend's plantation.

Later that night, Judge Priest pays a visit to a friend, General Fairfield (James Kirkwood), to urge the reclusive old man to attend the meeting of the Veterans of the Confederate Army. The general refuses, as he has apparently done for years, but reassures the Judge that "Little Billy Priest looms large in my memoirs." At the meeting of the veterans, they conduct an elaborate ritual, saluting the United States flag and reciting a highly patriotic ode to the Confederate flag. The meeting is interrupted by the commander of the G. A. R. veterans seeking to borrow the United States flag since someone has once again stolen their flag. When Priest orders the Sergeant-at-Arms to carry the flag to the G. A. R. meeting, he refuses, saying he had "never returned a captured Yankee flag, and was too old to start now." Priest himself returns the flag to the G. A. R. meeting room. When he returns to the Southern veterans, they agree to remove a portrait of a man in a Confederate uniform and a woman dressed as a nurse from the lodge wall.

At the end of the meeting, Lucy Lee returns the Doctor's carriage to the livery stable. On her way, she stops briefly to flirt with Ashby, who is slightly drunk. At the stable she encounters Buck Ramsey (Grant Withers), who suggests she take a ride with him. When she refuses, Ramsey insults her. Ashby overhears the remark and challenges him to a fight with buggy whips. In the harness room, they strip to the waist and begin the fight, only to be stopped by Judge Priest. After Ramsey leaves, Priest explains to Ashby that Lucy Lee's past is the town secret, and he must not make it worse for her, explaining that Lucy's father was the son of General Fairfield and was killed in a duel over Lucy's mother. Lucy's mother has disappeared, and General Fairfield has refused to accept Lucy as his granddaughter. Lucy, on the other hand, knows that Dr. Lake is not her real father, but she knows nothing about her true heritage.

When the steamboat next arrives several days later, a lone female passenger (Dorothy Jordan) disembarks. When she refuses help from the black porters and starts toward the saloon district, the porters suggest that a white lady should go another way. She responds that she knows the town and begins her walk, only to collapse after a few steps. Ashby Corwin sees her fall, picks her up, and carries her to Dr. Lake's house. Dr. Lake recognizes her immediately and begins to examine her only to be interrupted by Lucy Lee just as the woman awakens to see her and murmur, "I want to see my baby." Recognizing Lucy Lee as her lost baby, the woman faints again. Ashby tells the Doctor that he saw her going to Mallie Cramp (Eve March), the madam of the local brothel. Doctor Lake replies that "it doesn't matter as she will not last long."

Later, Doctor Lake goes to tell Judge Priest that he has moved the mysterious woman to Mallie Cramp's and that he will go back to see her even though it may cost the election. Lucy Lee also comes to see the Judge in order to find out about her real parents. When she sees the portrait the veterans had removed from the lodge, she understands the story. As she leaves, the sheriff drives up in a buggy to tell the Judge he has arrested U. S. Grant Woodford for the rape of a white girl. U. S. Grant swears his innocence, and the Judge promises him a fair trial. The next day a lynch mob forms, and the sheriff runs away. Judge Priest is left alone to face the mob led by Buck Ramsey. He draws a line in the dust in front of the jail and threatens to shoot anyone who crosses it, which disperses the mob but may have cost the judge a chance at reelection. That evening, as the judge attends a ball considered vital to his campaign, the family of the raped girl arrives to announce that she has regained conciousness and has identified Buck Ramsey as her attacker. Ramsey attempts to escape in Lucy Lee's buggy but is shot by one of the Confederate veterans.

When the Judge returns home, Doctor Lake tells him Lucy's mother has died. Mallie Cramp arrives and tells Priest that she has promised the dying woman a church funeral and asks Judge Priest to help her keep the promise. Priest is obviously disturbed by the effect his actions will have on the election, but he agrees to help Mrs. Cramp, saying that "the Lord will provide."

On Election Day, the Republicans are giving campaign speeches when they are interrupted by the funeral procession. Judge Priest walks behind the hearse and is followed by Mallie Cramp and the other prostitutes in a buggy. The crowds gathered for the election begin to jeer, but slowly, one by one, the bystanders join the procession. The commander of the G. A. R. joins the Judge, then the blacksmith, then the department store owner, the social arbiter Amora Ratchitt (Jane Darwell), Lucy Lee, Ashby Corwin, and Doctor Lake, until the cortege is quite large when it passes General Fairfield's home on the way to the black church on the edge of town. In the church, Lucy Lee takes her place as chief mourner, Ashby on one side, Mallie Cramp on the other. As Judge Priest begins the funeral sermon, General Fairfield enters the church and tells Ashby that he is standing in the General's place, thereby publicly acknowledging Lucy Lee as his granddaughter. Priest asks Ashby to offer the concluding prayer. Ashby, the reformed scoundrel, can only remember a childhood prayer, "Gentle Jesus, meek and mild".

The film then cuts to a raucous election parade to the polling place where the tally clerk announces that Horace Maydew (Milburn Stone) is leading.

Voters from the Tornado district, the same men who had earlier formed the lynch mob, arrive and cast their ballots. When their votes are counted the two candidates are tied. Judge Priest remembers that he has not yet voted and tells Maydew that he is not too modest to vote for himself.

The victory parade passes by the Judge's home, and Priest stands on the steps acknowledging the cheers of the various factions in the town—the G. A. R. members, the Temperance Ladies, the Confederate veterans, the men of the Tornado district (who carry a banner that says "He saved us from ourselves"), and the black people. When the parade has passed, Judge Priest enters the house. Lucy Lee and Ashby arrive to express their gratitude, but seeing the Judge alone, they respect his privacy and walk on as the film ends.

Ford critics Joseph McBride and Michael Wilmington have pointed out that the film touches "every Ford base: the film is simultaneously a work of nostalgic Americana, a raucous comedy, a caustic social protest, and a Christian parable." Ford's view of small-town life at the beginning of the twentieth century is dreamlike and essentially false. It is also charming and compelling. Even as we recognize the unreality of the depiction, we yearn to return to that time and place. Ford makes the town even more appealing through his use of comedy in the film. The humor of many of the situations, and our delight in seeing so many familiar faces from Ford's stock company of actors— Darwell, Simpson, and Jordan—giving new twists to some of their old routines, enhances the film's warm, nostalgic aura.

Playing against that cozy and amiable vision are the darker strains of prejudice, violence, and hypocrisy. Judge Priest's funeral oration is based on the Biblical parable of the woman taken in adultery. Priest knows the weaknesses of his fellow citizens, and he teaches them to be tolerant of one another, extending that toleration to the black people of the town. Modern audiences are uncomfortable with the stereotyped servility of Fetchit's performance, but placed in the context of the film, in which the most dignified characters are the blacks, Fetchit's "shufflin' darkie" routine is less offensive. Fetchit was, interestingly, playing the same role he had played in *Judge Priest* in 1934. Ford imbues the black community with a sense of decency and compassion that the white community lacks until they can learn from Judge Priest. Ford also demonstrates for his audiences the need for racial toleration in a period when most parts of the country were still segregated.

The film justifies Ford's affection; it is an immensely rewarding work that attests to the creative genius of its director and his love of his native land. Like the Irish, Americans are human, with many frailities, but they are also capable of great generosity and kindness, qualities that Ford celebrates in so many of his films, but never in a more rewarding and satisfying manner than in *The Sun Shines Bright*.

Don K Thompson

SUN VALLEY SERENADE

Released: 1941
Production: Milton Sperling for Twentieth Century-Fox
Direction: H. Bruce Humberstone
Screenplay: Robert Ellis and Helen Logan; based on an original story adapted
  by Art Arthur and Robert Harari
Cinematography: Edward Cronjager
Editing: James B. Clark
Choreography: Hermes Pan
Music: Mack Gordon and Harry Warren
Running time: 86 minutes

Principal characters:

Karen Benson	Sonja Henie
Ted Scott	John Payne
Phil Corey	Glenn Miller
Nifty Allen	Milton Berle
Vivian Dawn	Lynn Bari
Receptionist	Lynne Roberts
Miss Carstairs	Joan Davis
Jack Murray	William B. Davidson
Jimmy Norton	Melville Ruick
Agents	Eddie Kane and Edward Earle
Process server	Chester Clute
Doorman	Ralph Sanford
Nurse	Almira Sessions
Sleigh driver	John "Skins" Miller

Sonja Henie, the Norwegian-born winner of three consecutive Olympic women's figure skating championships (1928, 1932, and 1936), made ice-skating a film art. Although she appeared in only eleven Hollywood features between 1936 and 1948, their success made her a star. Many athletes have been able to capitalize on their prowess in films—for example, swimmers Esther Williams, Buster Crabbe, and Johnny Weismuller; boxer Max Baer; football star O. J. Simpson; and others—but skating naturally lends itself to lavish production numbers and gives skaters an advantage. The majority of Henie's films were musical in nature, although, strangely, only one was in color. Her success led to the emergence of Belita, Vera Hruba Ralston, and child skater Irene Dare as film stars, although the first two became dramatic actresses and Dare and her contemporary, Twinkle Watts, retired rather young.

All but two of Henie's films were made for Twentieth Century-Fox not counting a Swedish silent, *Syv Dager for Elisabeth*, in 1927, and a British color travelogue, *Hello London*, in 1958. Under the auspices of producer

Darryl F. Zanuck, her Hollywood debut, the tune-filled comedy *One in a Million* (1936) with Don Ameche was a total success. The Ritz Brothers and Borrah Minevitch's Harmonica Rascals—all making their feature debuts— provided the comedy and music, while Adolphe Menjou, Jean Hersholt, Ned Sparks, Montagu Love, Arline Judge, and Dixie Dunbar provided solid support. The formula was established in this film that would be used for the rest of Henie's Fox career: a top male lead, either established or up-and-coming; veteran supporting players; a musical group (later amended to a top orchestra); and as many comics as could be fit into the cast. Joan Davis and others also made token appearances to steal a scene and a few laughs.

Tyrone Power costarred in two Henie films, *Thin Ice* (1937) and *Second Fiddle* (1939), with songs by Irving Berlin. Ameche was on hand again in *Happy Landing* (1938) with Ethel Merman, Cesar Romero, and Hersholt repeating as Sonja's father. *My Lucky Star* (1938) featured Richard Greene, Joan Davis, Romero, Gypsy Rose Lee (then Louise Hovick), Arthur Treacher, and Buddy Ebsen in the cast. For a change of pace, *Everything Happens at Night* (1939) concentrated on plot, with two reporters, played by Ray Milland and Robert Cummings, investigating the anti-Nazi writings of Sonja's supposedly dead father, Maurice Moscovich. Henie's leading man from *Sun Valley Serenade*, John Payne, followed that film with *Iceland* (1942), also with Jack Oakie, Osa Massen, and Sammy Kaye and his orchestra. The final Fox feature, *Wintertime* (1943), used Cornel Wilde, Carole Landis, S. Z. Sakall, Oakie, Romero, and Woody Herman and his band.

After leaving the safety of Twentieth Century-Fox, Henie made her only color film, *It's a Pleasure* (1945), costarring Michael O'Shea as a hot-headed ice hockey player in love with skating star Henie, for RKO release. The film featured one original song, "Romance," by Edgar Leslie and Walter Donaldson. The next and last Henie vehicle was a remake of *The Countess of Monte Cristo* (1948) for Universal-International, with Olga San Juan, Treacher, and Henie's skating partner, Michael Kirby.

Henie was given top directors and songwriters to help her films, although few memorable songs came from these productions. If *One in a Million* was one of her best, *Sun Valley Serenade* was certainly the last good film and possibly the very best she ever did. Few musicals are as thoroughly entertaining, and even fewer from the early 1940's are as fondly remembered. In addition to an outstanding cast, the Glenn Miller Orchestra shines with a number of their old standards. The Miller band appeared in one other film, *Orchestra Wives* (1942), made two years before Miller's death in World War II. "At Last," a song instrumentalized in *Sun Valley Serenade*, is also featured in *Orchestra Wives*. Henie and Miller can both be seen at their best in *Sun Valley Serenade*.

As the film opens, the Miller band is seen in shadow performing "The Kiss Polka" during the credits. Producer Jack Murray (William B. Davidson) is in New York looking for a band to book at Sun Valley, Idaho, as a snow resort attraction. Singer Vivian Dawn (Lynn Bari, with vocals dubbed by Pat Friday) and the Jimmy Norton (Melville Ruick) band have the inside track. Meanwhile, Phil Corey's (Glenn Miller) Dartmouth Troubadours arrive at the audition, but the receptionist (Lynne Roberts) tells them they have little chance to be heard. Onstage, however, Vivian does not like Jimmy or his arrangement of "It Happened in Sun Valley," which she is trying to sing, and Ted Scott (John Payne), a pianist with Phil's group, agrees with her. He is immediately smitten with the temperamental star and plays "I Know Why" as Vivian sings, accompanied by a male quartet (The Modernaires) and then by Ted himself.

The Troubadours' manager, Jerome K. "Nifty" Allen (Milton Berle), tries to butter up Murray, beating two anxious agents (Eddie Kane and Edward Earle) to lighting the producer's cigar. Murray agrees to book the Troubadours with Vivian, but first tests them, giving them a job performing at the Lido Terrace, following Carmen Miranda. Things soon become complicated when a process server (Chester Clute), whom Nifty Allen thinks is Ted's "Uncle Sam," presents the pianist with an order from the immigration department giving him responsibility for a refugee. This is the result of Nifty's publicity stunt, which got the band half of gossip columnist Walter Winchell's column some months earlier.

Ted is dismayed at the prospect of caring for a young child, but he and the band go to the boat to greet their new arrival. The band plays a jazz version of "Farmer in the Dell" until they realize that Ted's charge is a lovely young woman, Karen Benson (Sonja Henie), from Norway. Nifty quips that her number, thirty-six, must be her chest measurement. Karen attempts a speech of thanks and later, in a taxi, tells Ted that she is a good housekeeper. Suddenly, she mistakes an ambulance siren for an air raid warning and clings to Ted, causing both to tumble out of the cab in front of a hotel and a bewildered doorman (Ralph Sanford). A nursery and a nurse (Almira Sessions) are in waiting for Karen in Ted's room but the nurse walks out upon seeing how old she is.

The refugee explains that she had lost her father, a schoolmaster, in the war and is looking for a husband. At the Lido, Karen applauds enthusiastically for the Troubadours and then tells Ted she has decided to marry him. Although Nifty plans to send her to his Aunt Rose in Weehawken, New Jersey, Karen winds up accompanying the band to Sun Valley. "It Happened in Sun Valley" is sung by a sleigh driver (John "Skins" Miller), the Troubadours, Nifty, Karen, Ted, and Vivian over skiing scenes and a shot of a swimming pool. When Karen shows her skating skill (to the song "I Know Why"), Nifty insists that Ted—who is unaware that she is there—take a look. He is distracted by a call from Vivian and goes to her room, unable to convince her to ski with him or to marry him. Nifty meanwhile is distracted by wacky

Miss Carstairs (Joan Davis), a hotel worker.

Using ski lifts, Ted goes to an elevation of nine thousand feet before skiing down the slopes. Playful Karen whizzes past him four times, including once between his legs, and finally Ted chases after her to the music of "It Happened in Sun Valley" and "The Kiss Polka." When he finally catches up with her, Karen says that she admires his skiing ability. Rehearsal is held up for Ted, so the Troubadours—with Chummy MacGregor on piano—perform "Chattanooga Choo Choo." Trombones are thrust right at the camera, and the vocal is performed by sax man Ted Beneke, The Modernaires, and Paula Kelly. Dorothy Dandridge and the nimble Nicholas Brothers sing and dance the number.

On the slopes, Nifty is literally pushed down the hills (to "Comin' Round the Mountain") as Ted and Karen laugh. At an inn high above the main lodge, the sextet does "The Kiss Polka," and Karen and Ted join in the dancing. A jealous Vivian announces that she has decided to accept Ted's proposal. Nifty, under the delusion that Karen prefers him, suggests a double wedding. When Ted and Karen choose to ski back after the last lift leaves, Karen decides to sabotage the romance. She causes Ted to lose his skis and then limps to the cabin so that he has to stay with her until help comes. Ted finds the broken part of one ski, then rips open a pants leg to massage vigorously Karen's "injured" knee. He is angry as he prepares to sleep on two chairs.

When the others come, Ted and Karen are singing and dancing to "I Know Why." Vivian gets mad and walks out, and Ted decides that he will wed Karen. An ice ballet starring Karen and a skating chorus is performed as the Troubadours play "It Happened in Sun Valley," "At Last," and "The Kiss Polka." She dances with partner Harrison Thompson, soldiers take to the ice, and "I Know Why" is heard before the finale. On the slopes, Karen and Ted happily chase each other.

As with all of Henie's films, this was a great financial success. During one period of the late 1930's, Henie was not only Fox's highest-paid star, but also rumored to be the highest-paid woman in the United States. Although she skied and even danced in her films, it is the skating numbers for which she is best remembered. Not rivals of the extravagant Williams' aquatic numbers produced by M-G-M perhaps, they still remain well staged, excellently skated, and aesthetically pleasing sequences.

After *The Countess of Monte Cristo*, Henie retired from feature films and became more active as producer and star of her own ice show for many years. Eventually she retired and returned to Norway, where she died in 1969.

John Cocchi

SUNDAY, BLOODY SUNDAY

Released: 1971
Production: Joseph Janni for United Artists
Direction: John Schlesinger
Screenplay: Penelope Gilliatt
Cinematography: Billy Williams
Editing: Richard Marden
Running time: 110 minutes

Principal characters:
Alex Greville .... Glenda Jackson
Dr. Daniel Hirsh .... Peter Finch
Bob Elkin .... Murray Head
Mrs. Greville .... Peggy Ashcroft
Mr. Greville .... Maurice Denham
Alva Hodson .... Vivian Pickles
Bill Hodson .... Frank Windsor
Businessman .... Tony Britton
Operator .... Bessie Love

Sunday, Bloody Sunday is a very British movie, a kind of *Brief Encounter* for the 1970's. Whereas David Lean's 1945 masterpiece dealt with an illicit relationship between a married woman and a young doctor, John Schlesinger's film, in keeping with its more sexually explicit decade, concerns a bisexual triangle involving middle-aged doctor Daniel Hirsh (Peter Finch), a divorced business consultant Alex Greville (Glenda Jackson), and the young artist they both love, Bob Elkin (Murray Head). The real similarity between the two films lies in the approach of screenplay and direction to these fraught situations. Noel Coward's screenplay and Lean's direction in the earlier film maintain a discreet, matter-of-fact distance from the affair, which becomes passionate only for one short, final moment. In *Sunday, Bloody Sunday*, Schlesinger, working from a sparse and extremely literate screenplay by novelist and movie critic Penelope Gilliatt, similarly avoids dramatic confrontations in favor of a cool, affectionate, but equally dispassionate view of the triangular relationship. Nor does he even allow himself the climax: the drama is repeatedly defused, and, at the end of the film, the relationships are simply dissolved by the departure of the young artist.

Plans for the film began in conversations between producer Joseph Janni and Schlesinger during the shooting of *Far from the Madding Crowd* (1967). By the summer of 1969, it was at the preproduction stage, and Penelope Gilliatt, who had expressed an interest in working with Schlesinger, was busily adjusting her screenplay in the course of transatlantic telephone conversations with Schlesinger. *Sunday, Bloody Sunday* started shooting in February, 1970,

with Jackson, Head, and Ian Bannen as Dr. Hirsh. Bannen fell ill with pneu-
monia, however, and was replaced the following month by Peter Finch—an
inspired replacement, as it turned out, since he gives one of his finest screen
performances. The film was released in Britain early in 1971 to virtually
unanimous praise—John Russell Taylor in the London *Times* called it a "continuing triumph of observation"—and in the United States in October of the
same year. In America it was somewhat less successful, partly because of its
very British background, and partly because it is a talk film rather than an
action movie. Its completely straightforward, sensitive treatment of a homosexual relationship won it a great deal of acclaim, however, although ironically
the fact that the film was not commercially successful has often been cited as
proof that there is no market for honest films about gay relationships. The
fact that one of the relationships in the triangle is a homosexual one, however,
is almost incidental to the tone of the film: it is about the tensions that exist
within relationships of any kind, and about how the people concerned deal
with them. As Alex's mother (Peggy Ashcroft) tells her, "Darling, you keep
throwing in your hand because you haven't got the whole thing. There *is* no
whole thing. One has to make it work."

Daniel Hirsh is a successful Jewish doctor, well-established in his career
and largely free from the pressures of a demanding family. Alex Greville,
daughter of a wealthy business executive (Maurice Denham) whose priorities
lie more with his tickertape machine than with his wife ("being married for
a course or two at mealtimes" is how Alex describes it), is recently divorced,
thirty-four, and currently working without much enthusiasm as a business
efficiency expert—somewhat anomalously, since she is absentminded and
hates "thrusters." Daniel and Alex are both in love with Bob Elkin, a young
designer of trendy art objects ("plastic rubbish" is how he disparagingly
describes it, although he is by no means unaware of his talent).

Sunday, Bloody Sunday covers a ten-day period (the days are indicated by
screen captions) at the end of the relationship. We do not know how it began,
nor how Daniel and Alex became aware of—and came to accept—each other's
existence. In fact, they have never met, and do not do so until one brief,
awkward scene, beautifully written, directed, and acted, at the end of the
movie. We pick up the triangle at what Schlesinger calls "a deliberately static
time," and we build our picture of it through close observation of the gestures
of the three principal actors, all of whom are magnificent, and from discerning
the half-admitted needs and fears that lurk between the lines of what Daniel
and Alex actually say. As Daniel puts it at the end, after Bob has gone, in
what is virtually a soliloquy: "I want his company and people say, what's half
a loaf, you're well shot of him; and I say, I know that, I miss him, that's all.
They say he'd never have made me happy and I say, I am happy, apart from
missing him."

Sunday, Bloody Sunday is a carefully constructed mosaic of a film, slotting together scenes with the three main characters which accurately reflect the environment from which they come and to which, to a certain extent, they are reacting. Daniel is seen in his consulting room with a self-obsessed hypochondriac patient to whom he is nevertheless attentive and sympathetic. Alex consoles a middle-aged businessman client (Tony Britton) whose world and temporary face-lift have both just collapsed, even to the extent of taking him home to bed with her. Bob is shown alone on the London Underground. In addition to these scenes, there are two beautifully economical scenes of Alex at home with her mother, and Daniel performing with grace but total detachment his expected family role at a vast *bar mitzvah*. To complete the panorama, there is a series of wonderful vignettes, perhaps a little too specifically British for American audiences, of a trendy, left-wing academic family, the Hodsons (Frank Windsor and Vivian Pickles), complete with a dog called Kenyatta, famine relief posters on the kitchen wall, and marijuana-smoking preteen kids who turn up in the bedroom at dawn and announce to Bob and Alex that "We always come here first thing. Then we watch Mummy and Papa have a bath together." The nearest thing to a thematic link in the film is a pair of incidental details: the recurring newspaper headlines and radio newscasts that detail Britain's economic crisis, and the telephone answering service to which all three subscribe (operated by a comfortably curious Bessie Love, former D. W. Griffith actress) and which from time to time fails to put each in touch with the other.

Sunday, Bloody Sunday is not a message film about either the parallel collapse of Britain's moral and economic values, or the failure of human communication in an age of proliferating electronic networks. Taking its title from the feel of a British Sunday on which everything is closed down and nothing ever seems to happen, it simply observes the end of the triangle. It is not a sensational movie, despite a long, on-the-mouth kiss between Finch and Head. It is not even particularly bleak, despite the fact that, at the end, Bob leaves for America where he appears to be convinced that, somehow, things will be better: one almost believes Daniel when he observes that, at times, nothing is better than just anything.

Sunday, Bloody Sunday sometimes seems a surprising movie to come from John Schlesinger, whose previous three films—*Darling* (1965), *Far from the Madding Crowd*, and *Midnight Cowboy* (1969)—had tended to overdevelop their material. In *Sunday, Bloody Sunday*, he achieves a tender and disciplined compassion for his three characters. As Daniel puts it in his final soliloquy: "Something. We were something. You've no right to call me to account." A large measure of the credit must obviously go to Penelope Gilliatt's wonderfully controlled screenplay, never stating what it can merely suggest and never developing a scene further than is strictly necessary. An even larger share of the credit must go to the outstanding performances, especially those of Glenda Jackson (in, for example, her tearful, fudge-eating scene in the Hodsons' kitchen) and Peter Finch (in his final monologue), and equally from a select company of supporting players (particularly Vivian Pickles and Frank Windsor as the Hodsons). Finally, however, it is Schlesinger's film, relying as it does so heavily on the precise, minute observance of the people and their environment, and on the muting of emotions that keeps the movie firmly away from the melodrama that the subject could so easily have elicited.

Nick Roddick

THE SUNDOWNERS

Released: 1960
Production: Fred Zinnemann for Warner Bros.
Direction: Fred Zinnemann
Screenplay: Isobel Lennart; based on the novel of the same name by Jon
  Cleary
Cinematography: Jack Hilyard
Editing: Jack Harris
Music: Dmitri Tiomkin
Running time: 133 minutes

> *Principal characters:*
> Paddy Carmody .... Robert Mitchum
> Ida Carmody .... Deborah Kerr
> Venneker .... Peter Ustinov
> Mrs. Firth .... Glynis Johns
> Jean Halstead .... Dina Merrill
> Sean Carmody .... Michael Anderson, Jr.

An appropriate choice for a traditionally family-oriented premiere, *The Sundowners* opened in New York as Radio City Music Hall's 1960 Christmas holiday film offering and met with enormous success there, and eventually worldwide. The appeal of the sentimental story about a family of itinerant Australian sheep drovers is readily apparent from its early scenes, and the film remains appealing today. The film is a staple at motion picture revival houses and on television and finds a new audience at each showing. The title refers to a particular breed of Australian nomad who is known to "make his home where the sun goes down." A 1950 Eagle Lion release starring Robert Preston and Robert Sterling bore the same title, but holds no relation to the Warner Bros. picture of a decade later.

The novel from which this screen story was drawn was brought to the attention of producer-director Fred Zinnemann by Mrs. Oscar Hammerstein II, who had long urged her friend to consider a film project dealing with Australia. Upon deciding to adapt the story to film, Zinnemann began the meticulous and long-range planning of location shooting which resulted in the superb look if not verisimilitude to the Australian outback of 1925. Six months ahead of schedule, he required that forty acres be planted with a special grass seed in order that the proper hue of green be ready for the color cameras on time. He ordered two flocks (2,500 head) of sheep to be brought a distance of five hundred miles (each sheep had a stand-in) since the local breeds were not the proper whiteness. His painters and carpenters transformed the sleepy and shabby town of Nimmitabel from a remote outpost of the 1960's to a lively sheep town of the mid-1920's.

It is this town, renamed Cawndilla for the film, which provides the setting
for the brawling pub scenes which flavor the downhome, folksy saga. The
story, although villainless, is abundant with conflict. Robert Mitchum plays
the burly Irish-Australian, Paddy Carmody, who is at once protagonist and
antagonist. He has, during fifteen years of marriage, resisted his wife's and,
later, his adolescent son's pleas to settle down and make a home for themselves. Ida and Sean Carmody (Deborah Kerr and Michael Anderson, Jr.)
long for a farm of their own and recently have located a small, vacant one
near the dusty village of Bulinga. Paddy, however, prefers to wander about
the plains of Australia as jobs and family economics dictate. He fends off his
family's petitions, as their story begins to unfold on the screen, by taking on
a long-distance sheep drive, thus keeping them on the move. His vagabond
ways also hold them precariously close to poverty, as the specter of the
emptying glass money jar continually reminds them.

The trek to Cawndilla requires that Paddy Carmody hire another drover
to manage the vast herd for several hundred miles. The drover is a crusty old
Englishman named Venneker (Peter Ustinov), who, despite his aristocratic
pretensions and claims to wealth, agrees to join the three as the hired man.
Venneker, too, is committed to the gypsy life, which is occasionally imperiled
by marriage-minded ladies of his acquaintance.

During the expedition, Ida Carmody devises a plan whereby her family can
earn the down payment for the beckoning farm. Rather than moving on after
depositing the sheep at their destination, Wattle Run Sheep Station, the three
will take jobs there for the season: Paddy as a shearer, Sean as a tarboy, and
herself as the cook. The close of the several weeks' work will coincide with
the passing of six months, at which time her husband has promised to reconsider his son's needs for proper schooling and friends his own age. These
needs, persuades Ida, can only be met once a permanent home is made for
him. The boy is bright but shy as a result of having known only his parents
and his dog. Staying on at Wattle Run appeals to Venneker too, as does the
attractive widow Firth (Glynis Johns) who owns the nearby hotel and would
appear to be a good match for him.

Ida is very happy as the station cook. At last she has a real stove on which
to cook, rather than her accustomed camp fire, and can make women friends
with the wife of the station owner, Jean Halstead (Dina Merrill), and the wife
of the station's union representative. Not surprisingly, Paddy chafes at the
routine work and resents his wife and son who spend time with their newfound
friends. He prepares to leave before the station work is completed. Ida and
Sean must acquiesce, but Venneker steps in with the proposal of a shearing
contest between Carmody, reputed to be the fastest shearer within miles, and
the best man of the rival Mulgrue station. Carmody is temporarily distracted
from his wanderlust, but he does not win the contest. He seeks consolation
by getting drunk with the boys in town, where he wins two hundred pounds

and a young race horse in a card game.

At the close of the season, the down payment is at last in hand, and the horse, which Sean has named Sundowner, is ready for entry into back country races. Sean has become a fine jockey with Venneker as his trainer. As Ida yearns for the farm, Paddy looks forward to making the rounds of the small bush tracks, while Sean is torn between his parents. Once at Bulinga, Paddy yields to his wife, but on the eve of buying the farm, he loses their savings during a bad gamble in town. Sober and contrite the following morning, he agrees to take the winnings from Sundowner's first victory, combined with money from the sale of the horse, in order to come up with the second down payment. Ida will hear of no such sacrifice, however. In the story's pivotal last sequence, Sundowner wins the race and is about to be sold when the track announcer reveals that the horse has been disqualified for interference. The buyer immediately cancels the sale. "There," smiles Ida, "goes both our chances to be noble!" In the last scene, the Carmody family, the horse, and Venneker continue their wanderings, resolute in their roles as Sundowners.

The film's strong suit lies not in the simple story, but in the splendid capturing of the Australian countryside at the hands of British cinematographer Jack Hilyard. His camera shows the ceaseless distances of the hostile yet beautiful regions which are unfamiliar to the nonnative eye. Isobel Lennart's sensitive interpretation of the Jon Cleary novel cannot be faulted, nor can Zinnemann's skilled execution of her screenplay.

The choice of players, however, could have been better. In the harsh and glaring Australian bush country, light-complexioned Kerr seems out of place. The sight of a woman of Kerr's beautiful and delicate appearance hanging out a wash in the blistering sun seems slightly ridiculous. Her efforts at erasing her patrician British diction with a downunder twang are not entirely successful, although her acting, as usual, is first rate. Mitchum is not able to rise above his seedy detective reputation in order to bring about a persuasive country boy character. His urban look and heavy-handed accent seem wrong.

The supporting players, Ustinov and Johns, deserved far greater screen exposure. It is not difficult to imagine them as the Carmody pair, roles which might have fared better in their capable hands. Although possessed of a daintiness not unlike Kerr's, Johns sports a boisterous earth-mother quality far better suited to the toughened Carmody woman. Had Ustinov played the Paddy role, he might have been more likable, and perhaps more persuasive, than Mitchum is. Yet it would be difficult to feel great affection for the self-indulgent, drinking, gambling drifter who prizes his unfettered ways over the well-being of those who love him, no matter what actor played the role.

Dmitri Tiomkin's swelling title theme rivals the beauty if not the popularity of his earlier "High Noon." Yet the light and cheerful touch his compositions lend to many scenes undermine their impact. Perhaps his intention is to lessen the severity of Carmody's mean temperament and the often stinging exchanges between husband and wife. At this he succeeds, the net effect being the transformation of a heavily dramatic scene to one of little consequence.

The major asset of the film may be its capturing of the flavor of the Australian back country, while its major flaw is the lack of conviction of the main characters. Despite its flaws, however, the film made a fine showing among award-winning films of 1960: Kerr won the New York Film Critics' Award for Best Actress of the year; several small organizations of critics singled out its excellence; and the Academy of Motion Picture Arts and Sciences nominated it for four top categories.

Nancy S. Kinney

SUPERMAN II

Released: 1981
Production: Ilya Salkind and Pierre Spengler for Warner Bros.
Direction: Richard Lester
Screenplay: Mario Puzo, David Newman, and Leslie Newman; based on an
  original story by Mario Puzo and the comic strip characters by Jerry Siegel
  and Joe Shuster
Cinematography: Geoffrey Unsworth
Editing: John Victor Smith
Music: Ken Thorne; based on original material by John Williams
Running time: 127 minutes

Principal characters:
Superman/Clark Kent	Christopher Reeves
Lois Lane	Margot Kidder
Lex Luthor	Gene Hackman
General Zod	Terence Stamp
Perry White	Jackie Cooper
Non	Jack O'Halloran
Ursa	Sarah Douglas
Otis	Ned Beatty
Eve Teschmacher	Valerie Perrine
The President	E. G. Marshall

By the time *Superman II* finishes all of its theatrical runs, re-releases, sales
to television, and videocassettes it will probably rank as the top moneymaking
film of all time, a feat that could say as much about the American society of
the 1980's as it does about contemporary filmmaking. In the film's first nineteen
days of release in the summer of 1981, it tallied $46,506,653, a truly remarkable
showing even considering inflation as a factor. This popularity at the box
office is not surprising, considering the trend set by 1979's *Superman The
Movie*.

Although Superman has become established as perhaps the preeminent
American hero, he was actually born in the writings of German author Johann
Wolfgang Goethe in the eighteenth century and became formally established
a century later under the philosophical concept *Ubermensch* (Overman) by
Friedrich Nietzsche in *Also Spake Zarathustra* (1883). Superman, according
to Nietzsche, would not be a product of long evolution but would emerge
when a man with superior potential mastered himself and struck off conventional Christian "herd morality" to create his own code of values rooted in
life on this earth. This superior being would possess mental and moral strength
but would never use that strength to do violence or to force his code of

behavior upon others. In 1903, this concept, under the name of Superman, became generally popularized in the English-speaking world by George Bernard Shaw in his play *Man and Superman*.

The idea languished in the United States, however, until the 1930's, when it was revived through the phenomenon of the comic strip. Comic strips, which had been featured in newspapers for many years, underwent a major change in the Depression years with the emergence of a new category: the continuous-action adventure strip. The earliest adventure strip featuring a larger-than-life hero was *Tarzan*, created by Harold Foster in 1929. The strip broke completely with the caricatural style of previous comics and adopted cinematic techniques featuring picturesque documentary realism. The idea caught on, and the rapidly increasing demand for adventure stories spawned a new, highly lucrative medium for the comic strip—a cheap, 7½ by 10¼-inch staple-bound format which became popularly known as the comic book. By 1935 such titles as *King Comics*, *Tip Tap Comics*, and *Famous Funnies*, which had started as reprints of newspaper strips, were selling in large enough quantities to create a demand for original stories. Specialization set in two years later with the advent of *Detective Comics* in 1937 and *Action Comics* in 1938.

Jerry Siegel and Joe Shuster, two Cleveland teenagers, had adopted Nietzsche and Shaw's Superman figure in 1933, modified it, and had been trying to market the idea unsuccessfully as a comic strip until the birth of *Action Comics* finally gave them the forum they sought. The modern legend of Superman as constructed by Siegel and Shuster and as employed in *Superman The Movie* describes how the infant Kalel comes to earth in a tiny spaceship, the only survivor of a cataclysm that destroyed his native planet, Krypton. He is found on a prairie in the American Midwest by a farm couple, Jonathan (Glenn Ford) and Martha Kent (Phyllis Thaxter), who adopt him and rear him to manhood. As the boy grows to maturity, he astounds his new parents with feats of superhuman strength, gradually revealing that he is not an earthman at all but a being from outer space who happens to be endowed with an array of awesome powers far beyond human conception. These powers include the ability to fly through the air at speeds faster than light, X-ray vision, and strength far beyond that of an ordinary mortal. Reaching maturity, Superman (Christopher Reeves) embraces the fateful mission of becoming the guardian and protector of his adopted planet. Hidden inside his secret identity of the timid and fumbling Clark Kent is the all-powerful avenging giant who, with his miracles, becomes the embodiment of all childhood dreams.

Although the actual comic-book character evolved through the years, Superman was "super" chiefly because, being a nonmortal from an alien world, he was acted upon by the less rarefied atmosphere of earth with a resulting enhancement of his attributes. His flying ability, for example, was first attributed to enormous leaps made possible by the earth's relatively weak gravity. Another explanation attributed all of the "man of steel's" powers to the proximity of atoms within his body. According to this theory, the atoms composing Superman's body have greater density and are packed more closely together than our own, thus giving him super strength and invulnerability.

The Superman adventure formula is really quite simple. Superman does not, for example, have the deductive or enlightened powers of reason of a Sherlock Holmes. Instead, his forte is swift action and overpowering force. This is normally sufficient to solve the problem at hand since the typical 1938 vintage villain, as featured in *Action Comics*, was usually somewhat below Neanderthal man in basic intelligence.

Superman moved from comic books to radio on February 12, 1940, as a three-day-a-week program on the Mutual Network. The role was played by Clayton "Bud" Collyer. The radio drama was significant in that it introduced Superman's Achilles' heel in the form of Kryptonite, the green remnant of his native planet that could kill the normally indestructible "man of steel." The program also brought together Superman and his multimedia sponsor, Kelloggs Cereals, in a relationship that would last until 1957.

In 1941, Superman made the inevitable leap to the movie screen, appearing in the first of seventeen expensively produced, fully animated color cartoons intended to challenge the Walt Disney market. These short features, beginning with *Superman* (also titled *The Mad Scientist*), were produced by Fleischer Studios and Paramount and were noted for high production values. Collyer was again employed as the voice of the superhero. As a result of his radio experience, Collyer had developed the art of shifting his voice several octaves in range—low for Superman and higher for Clark Kent. Some of the titles in this series were *Destruction, Inc.* (1942), *Terror on the Midway* (1942), and *Secret Agent* (1943). A great many of these films, such as 1942's *The Japateurs*, were superpatriotic in nature, portraying Superman as the great American national epic hero, comparable to Rome's Aeneas, England's King Arthur, and Greece's Odysseus, who, like his predecessors, defended his country in its climactic struggle with external enemies. During World War II, Superman's emblem became practically synonymous with the American flag and did so much for the morale of the American fighting man that German propaganda minister Joseph Goebels leveled a massive counterattack against the "man of steel," referring to Superman as a "Jewmonger," among other things. The war department was unfazed, however, and stepped up its program of making Superman comic books standard issue for all GI's.

The "man of steel" became flesh and blood after the war when Columbia cast Kirk Alyn in two fifteen-chapter motion picture serials: *Superman* (1948) and *Atom Man vs. Superman* (1950). The serials and their star, Alyn, made some small revisions in the Superman character. His giant leaps of earlier years finally became actual flight, prompting him to boast "two thousand miles away? I can be there in thirty seconds." The serials also took issue with *Action Comics'* explanation of the character's powers, saying that Superman's feats on earth were no mere accident or geographical phenomenon. They suggested that Krypton, his birthplace, was, in fact, a planet of superhumans, no doubt akin to Greek mythology's Mount Olympus.

Columbia was extremely careful and protective concerning the Superman image. Alyn, for example, was made to shave after he had auditioned for the part wearing a beard. He was subsequently kept under the watchful eye of the legal department, which supervised and screened all of his personal appearances.

In 1951, the role was given to George Reeves (no relation to the current Superman, Christopher Reeves) for the film *Superman and the Molemen*. George Reeves would be Superman until his death in 1969, and for a generation of Americans he will remain the only real "man of steel." Kirk Alyn and Christopher Reeves are, perhaps, more handsome and dashing, but George Reeves is more trustworthy and inspires greater confidence in the audience. Alyn had been faithful to the 1940's interpretation of the character, and Christopher Reeves plays the role with the irreverence and reevaluation characteristic of the 1980's, but during the Cold War, and with the world situation of the 1950's, Americans felt more comfortable with a grandfather in the White House and a father figure in the red cape and blue tights. After all, didn't Christopher Reeves actually drop Lois Lane from fifteen thousand feet in 1979's *Superman The Movie*?

The aerial flying sequences presented problems in all of the films, particularly *Superman and the Molemen*, because the technical expertise evident in the later films was not yet in existence. In the film's first rushes, the viewers could actually see the actor's cape become entangled in the lines to his lift wires. Consequently Reeves was fitted with a special harness which left his cape free to fly in the wind. He would take four or five strides toward the camera and then jump while a crew of technicians pulled on the wires to lift him into the air over the camera. Occasionally, however, a wire would break, sending Reeves plummeting to the earth like a wounded duck.

Superman and the Molemen was, on the whole, quite successful and prompted some critics to place it also well within the patriotic tradition established by the earlier cartoons. With its plot revolving around a species of alien subterranean beings invading the surface world, it was a reflection of its time. The molemen are not unlike infiltrating Communists, and many critics found parallels between the film and a Pentagon paper entitled "The Red Menace." Superman, of course, saved the day, and the success of the film prompted a television series, again featuring George Reeves.

On television, Reeves made less of a distinction between Superman's two identities than had Alyn in the 1940's. Alyn had disciplined himself to keep Clark Kent totally distinct from his Superman identity, but Reeves seemed to blur that distinction; yet in many respects, his Clark Kent is a much stronger personality in his own right. The show's writers, Robert Maxwell and Whitney Ellsworth, constructed Kent as a competitive investigative reporter who was as much feared by criminals as was Superman. Consequently, the shows relied more heavily on dialogue than on super feats of action.

The television series also made some revisions in the powers of Superman, granting him attributes far beyond those of his predecessors in radio, serials, and comic books. For example, Reeves's Superman separated his molecules to walk through walls, split in two, traveled through telephone lines, and become invisible, in addition to exercising his normal powers of superstrength, superhearing, X-ray vision, flying, microscopic vision, and supertyping (perfect for an investigative reporter).

As a result of the success of the television series, *Superman and the Molemen* remained the only full-length theatrical Superman motion picture until 1979. Two other feature scripts were written for Reeves, *Superman and the Ghost of Mystery Mountain* (1954) and *Superman and the Secret Planet* (1957), but they were never produced. Although no one seems to know the reason for this, it is probably due to the fact that the producer did not want to risk the success of the television series with a flop at the box office.

In the late 1970's a new set of producers, Alexander Salkind, Ilza Salkind, and Pierre Spengler, and a new studio, Warner Bros., decided that Superman was long overdue for a return to the large screen. Encouraged by the success of films such as *Star Wars* (1977) and *Close Encounters of the Third Kind* (1977), they planned a medium-budget spectacle along the lines of the James Bond films with plenty of special effects. The producers were, in fact, counting upon one special effect that would be crucial to the success of their efforts. In *Star Wars*, the viewer wanted to see space ships and talking robots, while in *Close Encounters of the Third Kind*, the attractions were the flying saucers and extraterrestrial beings. *Superman The Movie* and *Superman II* would succeed or fail based on whether modern film technology could make the characters fly convincingly.

Superman The Movie and *Superman II* are essentially parts of the same film. They were, for the most part, filmed together, although estimates concerning the amount of *Superman II* completed by the release of its predecessor varies from sixty-five to eighty-five percent. The project as a whole is schizophrenic in other respects as well. In one sense, the films are science fiction, beginning as they do with Superman's escape from the planet Krypton. Yet, while projecting into the near future with the Metropolis segments, the films also reach deeply into the American past and into the pages of the original Superman comic books in other instances. This is done to resurrect Superman as the American Odysseus from a simpler era in which one individual could make a difference, and in which the evils confronting a hero were less complex and more black and white in their delineation. Thus, while the appeal for the young viewer is one of fantasy, for the older viewers it is primarily nostalgic in nature.

The irony of this approach is that, while the comic-book Superman is still the character with whom audiences identified in childhood, he, too, has come of age in the 1970's. There is more conflict between Superman and his Clark Kent identity than any film actor was ever asked to portray. The comic-book character of the 1970's wonders why he must maintain the charade of weakness and suffer the scorn of those he loves. At the same time, Superman's heroic efforts are increasingly foiled because legal restrictions prevent him from intervening. Also, when he does commit himself to action he is hounded by the thought that his intervention might rob others of the initiative to solve their own problems. The comic-book Superman has become a product of the 1970's with the same problems common to all of us—a fact ignored by the current cinematic treatments of the superhero. Pauline Kael noted this problem in her review of *Superman The Movie*, suggesting that it would be more fun "to see him putting out a fire while kids threw stones at him or arresting a mugger and being surrounded by an angry booing crowd."

Superman The Movie appears to have been made in something of a panic in 1977-1978, and the product on the screen shows that it has passed through many hands. The script originally written by Mario Puzo was rewritten three times by other pens which took the screenplay from the extremes of tragedy to slapstick. Although the script sticks for the most part to the traditional Superman legend, the finished product resembles almost three films (even before we look at *Superman II*).

The early scenes in Krypton and Kansas reflect the legend and are totally earnest. Marlon Brando as Jorel, father of Superman, projects a God-like image of fatherhood as he sends his son to earth with the injunction "We shall explore various concepts of immortality. . . . Earthlings can be a great people, they only lack the light. For this reason I've sent them you, my only son." This statement, of course, falls well within Nietzsche's admonition that the "Superman must create his own code of values rooted in life on this earth." Superman, according to this film, is the son of a secular God taking his gospel to the Americans, an image that is reinforced when Superman raises Lois Lane (Margot Kidder) from the dead at the end of the film. In other words, one of the great revelatory myths is, in the person of Superman, making a comeback into the modern collective consciousness in the most effective manner in which our civilization can reproduce it—through the movies.

The tone shifts sharply when the action moves to Metropolis. Although the first part of the film contained intriguing questions about the possibilities inherent in the boy Superman, questioning the need to keep his powers under wraps and his identity a secret when all of his teenage compatriots are flaunting their athletic prowess, the Superman of the middle years is content with comedy, sight gags, and fast backchat as he pursues his career at the *Daily*

Planet and a romance with ace reporter Lois Lane.

A pervasive subplot in which Lex Luthor (Gene Hackman) maneuvers to destroy Superman and explode a bomb which will separate California from the North American Continent comprises still another film tone, that of high camp with an obvious reference to television's old *Batman* series. Taken alone, Luthor's scenes are admittedly humorous, but they constitute a film in themselves and serve only to fragment further an already awkwardly plotted film.

Superman The Movie suffered from a fear on the part of the writers of tampering with the legend. For example, Brando is rumored to have wanted to play the part of Jorel as a green suitcase projecting his voice from the center of the screen. Reminded by the producers that even his own children would take offense at this abuse of their legend, the actor succumbed and conformed to tradition in his portrayal of Superman's father.

Superman II, however, is free of such limitations. After paying homage to the legend in the first film, the writers and director Richard Lester decided to let their imaginations run wild, unfettered by historic restraints. The result is a better film if only because it is a cohesive, unified effort. There are even some rudimentary attempts to depict Clark Kent's identity crisis in a realistic manner. A paradox exists because Clark Kent is not real. He does not represent Superman's actual identity in the manner that Don Diego is Zorro's or Bruce Wayne is Batman's. Clark Kent is, in fact, the sham; the glasses and the business suit are the costume, not the red and blue cape and tights. As Clark, he can pretend an interest in Lois Lane or any other woman, but as Superman with an identity to protect, he naturally cannot keep up with what Clark started. He is a perennial celibate who must feign a weakness to which he cannot fully reconcile himself.

In *Superman II*, the man of steel renounces his heritage in order to break his celibacy and go to bed with Lois, whom he wants to love. In doing so, he loses the powers that set him apart from his mortal comrades. Unfortunately, as if the humiliations of a human existence are not enough, the new "man of the flesh" is threatened by the release of three Krypton villains, previously imprisoned in a prism by Jorel in *Superman The Movie*. The three supervillains have powers equal to Superman's own, but lack his conscience and sense of moral integrity; they are vain psychopaths who attempt to rule the world by taking over the United States. They strut their stuff first in a small town and then in Washington, destroying the White House before going ultimately to Metropolis, where they ransack the offices of the *Daily Planet* itself in a successful attempt to kidnap Lois Lane. The trio, in their black vinyl costumes and their "Thou shalt kneel before me" posturing, are an embodiment of 1980 America's seeming love affair with sadomasochism (as epitomized in television advertising, particularly blue jeans commercials). They appear somewhat ludicrous, however, in the light of day with predictable

antics borrowed from the James Bond films and with production values reminiscent of the low-budget Vic Savage epics of the 1950's and 1960's such as
The Creeping Terror and Bela Lugosi's abortive *Plan 9 from Outer Space*
(1956). There is even one unforgettable scene in which General Zod (Terence
Stamp) throws a small-town citizen through the air, and the unfortunate victim
comes to rest upon what is obviously a brown mattress disguised as a clump
of earth.

Obviously the filmmakers thought that *Superman II* and its predecessor
Superman The Movie would sell on their special effects: Superman's flying,
his rescues, and the disasters and cataclysms. While the films' effects, such
as the imprisonment of the three Kryptonian criminals in the prism and their
subsequent escape in an H-bomb blast, are spectacular, most of the scenes,
particularly those of Superman flying in daylight, are crude superimpositions
and not much advanced over the television series or the early cartoons. The
editing is rushed, jerky, and uneven and even the most significant scenes,
such as Superman (in the first film) zipping up the San Andreas fault, are
somewhat truncated. The epic concluding battle in *Superman II* is marred by
an "overkill" of trite action sequences, obviously borrowed from *Moonraker*
(1979), *The Spy Who Loved Me* (1977), and other James Bond epics. It is
indicative that in the midst of this chaos, human characters examine their
wrecked cars, make phone calls, buy hamburgers, and pursue other humdrum
activities as if not realizing that the fate of the world lay in the outcome of
the epic battle of the four supertitans. The special effects appear, on the
whole, to be patched together, highly variable, grainy, bleached, and, more
often than not, poorly framed.

The strength of *Superman II* lies in the performances of Reeves, Kidder,
and Hackman and in the cinematography of Geoffrey Unsworth. The good-
looking Reeves makes a sharp distinction between the shy, bumbling Clark
Kent and the all-powerful Superman. Although the character renounces his
powers too easily for love, Reeves does create the overall impression of a
man attempting some kind of very real reconciliation between the two aspects
of his personality. Although Superman's experiment with mortality fails and
he must regain his superpowers (by what means, we are never told), the
merging of gallantry and innocence is believable. Kidder as Lois Lane is too
easily dismissed by most critics. She is, in fact, as is Reeves, too good an
actress for this type of film. Kidder performs an amusing satire on hot-shot
journalism, presenting an all-too-accurate picture of contemporary reporters
who casually and repeatedly misspell key words. She is alternately humorous,
raunchy, and tender, particularly in the scene in the Niagara Falls hotel room
with Clark when she confronts him with his true identity.

Hackman may have had a better writer for his scenes than did the other
three villains. His Lex Luthor is an effective counterpoint to the unbelievable,
often ludicrous strutting of the three villains from Krypton: General Zod

(Terence Stamp), Ursa (Sarah Douglas), and Non (Jack O'Halloran in an obvious theft of Richard Kiel's "Jaws" in *The Spy Who Loved Me*). Hackman portrays a man who loves to be bad and who easily manipulates all of the supervillains through his irrepressible wheedling, sniveling, and bargaining. His comedy brings, incredibly, some sense of sanity and reality to the unearthly plot twists concocted by director Lester and writer Puzo.

Unsworth, who participated to a great degree on both Superman films before his death, sweeps and radiates the screen with light, from the stark barren glow of the Krypton sequences through the panoramic scope of the Kansas plains to the vertical, diamond-studded projections of Metropolis at night. His Metropolis sequences explode and radiate in shrapnel-swift bursts of action countered only by the Krypton-like, barren white expanses of the North Pole when the action shifts to Superman's fortress of solitude.

All of this is directed by Lester in the same tongue-in-cheek vein employed in his earlier *The Three Musketeers* (1973), *The Four Musketeers* (1974), and *Robin and Marian* (1976). He loves sneaky details, chaos, and juicy comedy which blends at a moment's notice into pathos. All are present in abundance, except, perhaps, genuine introspection, and this reflects the major critical failure of *Superman II*. When Superman flies through the air at the film's end carrying the American flag, it is obvious that there remains a serious statement about us as a nation that has not been explored in sufficient detail or in the manner that it might have been. There is a fascination among Americans for the myth of Superman that makes him a semideity in our minds and places him on a plane with King Arthur, Odysseus, and even, perhaps, Jesus Christ. This mystique is hammered at the audience but never explored. Unfortunately, as the greatest moneymaking film of all time, history will not let us compare *Superman II* as entertainment to *Superman The Movie*, *Star Wars*, or *Close Encounters of the Third Kind*. Its very financial success must make us consider it in terms of *Citizen Kane* (1942) or *Gone with the Wind* (1939) for a possible message about America. The answer that we find must be more than simply the plaintive cry of "Superman! Superman Save Us!"

Stephen L. Hanson

SUPPORT YOUR LOCAL SHERIFF

Released: 1969
Production: William Bowers for United Artists
Direction: Burt Kennedy
Screenplay: William Bowers
Cinematography: Harry Stradling, Jr.
Editing: George Brooks
Running time: 96 minutes

Principal characters:
Jason McCullough	James Garner
Prudy Perkins	Joan Hackett
Pa Danby	Walter Brennan
Olly Perkins	Harry Morgan
Jake	Jack Elam
Joe Danby	Bruce Dern
Henry Jackson	Henry Jones
Fred Johnson	Walter Burke
Luke Danby	Dick Peabody
Tom Danby	Gene Evans

Support Your Local Sheriff, an affectionate, well-acted spoof of the Old West, derives its comedy from poking fun at myriad familiar genre clichés— the mysterious stranger who rides into town; the beautiful, brave heroine; the town derelict-turned-deputy; and the community under siege of a tyrant and his no-account sons. These and other familiar traits of the sagebrush saga get comic treatment in this 1969 film. *Support Your Local Sheriff* can be viewed on several levels, including that of the broadly funny, G-rated family film. The film also delivers ribald humor, however, through countless *double entendres*. That the film so deftly deals this double-edged humor is one of its greatest strengths, as is the understated performance of its star, James Garner. In a role reminiscent of his famed television character, Bret Maverick, Garner portrays roguish Jason McCullough, the smooth-talking stranger who rides through the trouble-ridden town of Calendar and dares to put on a badge.

As the film opens, a small group of Calendar residents, including Mayor Olly Perkins (Harry Morgan), preacher Henry Jackson (Henry Jones), and Olly's headstrong daughter, Prudy (Joan Hackett), are burying a transient on Boot Hill. All reverence for the occasion ceases after Prudy spies the glint of gold in the open grave, however, and, pushing the coffin aside, jumps in and claims it as her stake. A near-riot follows, as does the inevitable gold rush fever. In no time at all (a matter of minutes on the screen), the once-quaint Calendar brims with lawlessness. Generating much of it is the ruthless Danby clan, led by Pa Danby (Walter Brennan). Because the Danbys own the ranch blocking the road out of town, Calendar's miners must allow the Danbys to skim twenty percent off every mine shipment. Thanks to the Danbys, there is little semblance of law and order remaining. In fact, of the town's last three sheriffs, two were killed and the third left only ninety minutes after accepting the job.

Then, into town rides McCullough—by his own admission, "passing through" on his way to Australia (a running gag throughout the film). After a chance meeting with accident-prone Prudy, McCullough witnesses a saloon gunfight involving Joe Danby (Bruce Dern). It is a case of cold-blooded murder, but only McCullough will say so. The town council immediately signs him to the post of sheriff—although McCullough insists the position will only be temporary, since he is heading for "real pioneer country." "But we're pioneer country," counter the officials.

After pinning on the badge, McCullough sets about to calm the wild town. A brawl is under way on Main Street, and the inventive McCullough uses the fire hose to disperse the crowds. He also sends Jake, the town drunk (Jack Elam), to tell Joe Danby that he will soon be charged with murder. He also arranges room and board for himself at the home of Olly Perkins. While there he again bumps into Prudy, who was among those hosed down on Main Street. Wearing red long johns, with her hair dripping wet, she is so embarrassed that she runs outside and takes refuge in a tree.

McCullough next arrests Joe Danby in the aftermath of another shoot-out which sees Jake coming to the new sheriff's defense. The reluctant Jake is now deputized. Together, he and McCullough escort Danby to the new jail. Although the jail is yet without bars (as Perkins explains, "the iron bars ain't arrove yet"), McCullough has spilled red paint around the edges of the cell. His "psychological" bars work—for Danby believes that the "bloodstains" on the floor belong to the last jail occupant who attempted to escape. When Pa Danby arrives in town and sees his son inside an open jail, he is irate. He pulls a gun on McCullough, who promptly sticks his finger in the barrel. Stunned, Danby and his sons decide to bring in outside help. McCullough outshoots the succession of gunfighters who storm into town, however, and even gets rid of one by throwing rocks at him. Meanwhile, Prudy has taken to husband-hunting, and handsome McCullough is her target. Her tactics literally go up in smoke, however, when her dress catches fire as she is cooking a meal for him. In desperation, Mayor Perkins tells McCullough that the man who marries Prudy will become a wealthy man, since he will become coowner of her mine, "shaft and all."

Still outraged over Joe Danby's arrest and the fact that Joe even helped to install the new jail bars, the Danbys ride into town, fifteen abreast. Only Jake and Prudy stand with McCullough in the shoot-out, which parodies—among other things—the classic confrontation at the O. K. Corral. At one point during the melee, McCullough shouts, "Hold it! Hold it!" The shooting dutifully stops until McCullough scurries to better cover. When McCullough signals "okay," the bullets resume.

McCullough gets the best of the Danbys when he spirits Joe out of the jail cell and ties him to the front of the town cannon. After he threatens to light the fuse, the Danbys throw down their rifles. Later, after all the Danbys are jailed, McCullough tells Prudy that the cannon could not really have gone off, and, to back his words, he lights the fuse. The blast destroys Madame Orr's House, and as the walls collapse in rubble, members of the town council are viewed wearing long johns. As the film comes to a close, McCullough is saluted by the town. He of course agrees to marry Prudy—although he is still "passing through" on his way to Australia.

A superlative cast, most of them veterans of countless Westerns, effectively underplay their roles, giving *Support Your Local Sheriff* an affectionate stance. For Brennan, the role, which spoofs his portrayal in *My Darling Clementine* (1939), marks his one-hundred-and-tenth film. Hackett, who previously appeared in serious films such as *The Group* (1966) and *Will Penney* (1968), proves herself a charming comedienne, and Garner reenforces his image as one of the industry's most amiable and engaging leading men. With his wry sense of humor and easygoing delivery, he is one of the Western genre's funniest, most likable heroes. The script itself pays fond homage to the genre through countless plays on words as well as situations. When Garner sticks his finger in Brennan's gun, Brennan says, "Why, if I'd pulled the trigger, the danged thing would have blowed up in my face." Garner smoothly retorts, "Well, it wouldn't have done my finger a bit of good, either." At another point, when Morgan discusses his daughter with Garner, he notes, "She looks just like her dear departed mother." When Garner says he is sorry her mother is dead, Morgan offers, "Not dead, just departed."

Support Your Local Sheriff was made by Cherokee Productions, Garner's own production company. With its exceptional cast and script, it remains one of the best films from director Burt Kennedy. Originally a radio writer, Kennedy directed for television before turning to feature films. Known mostly for his Westerns, he has had critical and commercial success with such films as *The Rounders* (1965), *Return of the Seven* (1966), and *The War Wagon* (1967). Recent efforts from Kennedy, such as *Hannie Caulder* (1971) and *The Train Robbers* (1973), have been less satisfying. In 1971, he also directed *Support Your Local Gunfighter*, a weak sequel (or remake) of *Support Your Local Sheriff*, with Garner and Elam again in the lead roles. Garner also capitalized on *Support Your Local Sheriff*'s success when he starred in the short-lived television series *Nichols*, whose lead character was, essentially, McCullough.

With its hilarious demythologization of the West, *Support Your Local Sheriff* joins a relatively small group of titles to parody the horse opera effectively. Of these films, Mel Brooks's *Blazing Saddles* (1974) is perhaps the most outrageous, while Lee Marvin offers a vivid characterization as the drunken gunfighter in the offbeat *Cat Ballou* (1965). The *Destry* films also offered satire, coupled with gentle messages. In fact, *Destry Rides Again* (1939), which starred James Stewart and Marlene Dietrich, helped to popularize the Western satire. In 1954, Audie Murphy starred in *Destry*, a remake that is surprisingly considered by many to be an improvement over the original.

Pat H. Broeske

SVENGALI

Released: 1931
Production: Warner Bros.
Direction: Archie Mayo
Screenplay: J. Grubb Alexander; based on the novel *Trilby* by George du Maurier
Cinematography: Barney McGill
Editing: no listing
Running time: 76 minutes

Principal characters:
Svengali	John Barrymore
Trilby	Marian Marsh
Little Billee	Bramwell Fletcher
The Laird	Donald Crisp
Taffy	Lumsden Hare
Honori	Carmel Myers
Gecko	Luis Alberni

Although John Barrymore died in 1942, he is still celebrated in many quarters as the greatest American actor of the twentieth century. The "Hamlet" he played in New York in 1922 has assured him theatrical immortality, and his cinema *persona* conjures images of "The Great Profile," a flamboyant matinee idol. Indeed, no actor thrust a rapier so dashingly as did Barrymore in *Don Juan* (1926), or made love so beautifully as he did with Greta Garbo in *Grand Hotel* (1932), or played comedy with such madcap glee as he did in *Twentieth Century* (1934). Yet Barrymore's greatest screen performances were not as lovers and dandies but as villains and madmen: the screen's most maniacal *Dr. Jekyll and Mr. Hyde* (1920), the peg-legged, vengeance-crazed Ahab of *The Sea Beast* (1926), and a nightmarish Richard III in a special sequence of *Show of Shows* (1929). Such grotesque characters were Barrymoore's favorite and most intriguing delineations, and he played such a scoundrel in the climax of his cinema career in *Svengali*.

Although George du Maurier named his richly romantic 1894 novel after its tragic heroine, *Trilby*, it was the wicked, hypnotic, Jewish musical genius Svengali who mesmerized the readers. When a stage version promptly followed, ladies in the gallery sighed as Svengali employed his seductive hypnosis and wicked *chutzpah* to transform the tone-deaf milkmaid Trilby into Europe's most sensational concert singer.

Barrymore was aware of the villain's impact and of the great stage success that Beerbohm Tree enjoyed with the role in England and that Wilton Lackaye savored in America on both the stage and screen (1915, under the title of *Trilby*). There had been a British one-reeler version in 1922, and in 1923 a second Hollywood production was filmed with Arthur Edmund Carewe. Barrymore was therefore quite eager to undertake the first talking screen version of the story, especially since the title was to be changed to be *Svengali*. Although Jack Warner preferred to employ his $76,250-per-picture attraction in lighter fare, he had faith in the picture. Production began in January of 1931, with Archie Mayo directing, blonde newcomer Marian Marsh assigned the role of Trilby, and Barrymore as Svengali exulting in the makeup of curled beard, lanky, pompadoured wig, glass eyeball covers, and the cultivation of a Polish/Jewish accent.

Svengali wastes no time in establishing the villainy of its title character. The film opens in the rascal's studio, where his lovesick pupil Honori (Carmel Myers) arrives for a lesson. After she screeches her vocal exercises (accompanied by some furtive and hilarious eye-rolling by Svengali), she informs her lover that her cuckolded husband refuses to pay her a settlement. Svengali fixes his evil eye upon her, Honori goes wailing into the streets, and Svengali's familiar Gecko (Luis Alberni) soon rushes in with the news that Honori's body has been found in the river.

This does not bother Svengali's conscience; he is hungry, so he visits the studio of the English artists, the Laird (Donald Crisp), Taffy (Lumsden Hare), and Little Billee (Bramwell Fletcher, who would wed Barrymore's daughter Diana in 1942) to snare a meal. Instead, they dunk the vulgarian into a tub. There later enters the studio a lovely milkmaid, Trilby (Marian Marsh), who is a part-time model. Soon the sensitive Little Billee and the milkmaid are in love; but the tone-deaf girl also becomes fascinated by the musical Svengali, who cures her headache through hypnosis. The Englishmen try to warn her to be wary of Svengali, but the evil genius soon summons her to his lair by his hypnotic powers, which, in a splendid scene, travel over the Caligariesque rooftops to summon the helpless Trilby. Not long after, Trilby and Little Billee have a misunderstanding when the innocent artist discovers her posing nude for fellow artists; Trilby subsequently disappears from the town and Svengali disappears with her.

The artists later hear that a musician named Svengali is becoming the rage of the European continent, and that his wife, Madame Svengali, is blessed with the most beautiful of voices. The artists all attend a concert, and discover Madame Svengali to be Trilby. While Svengali has been able to improve Trilby's voice through hypnosis, he has never been able to win her love, and now, terrified that Trilby may run to Little Billee, he cancels the concert. Stricken by heart disease and increasingly fearful of the presence of Little Billee, who vows to follow their trail and win back the girl he loves, Svengali soon becomes unreliable and erratic, and his fortunes plummet.

Finally, Little Billee catches up with Svengali and Trilby in a dingy Cairo nightclub. As Trilby sings "Ben Bolt," Svengali suffers a heart attack, and Trilby, no longer under his hypnotic power, shocks the grimy patrons by suddenly singing outrageously off-key. As Svengali dies, he prays, "Oh God, grant me in death what you denied me in life—the woman I love." To Little Billee's anguish, Svengali's final prayer is heard, and Trilby joins her demonic lover in death.

Released in April of 1931, two months after Universal's great success with *Dracula*, *Svengali* captivated a large audience. Director Archie Mayo effectively mixed the humorous aspects (particularly Svengali's early badinage with the Englishmen) with the sinister ones (Svengali's hypnotic spells, when his eyes appear to be only gaping white orbs). Marsh as Trilby and Fletcher as Little Billee both possess a picturesque innocence that serves the fantasy well. Naturally, however, the film belongs completely to Barrymore, who is magnificent. *The New York Times* opined that he ". . . surpasses anything he has done for the screen," and as such, he presents the viewer with a full repertoire of marvelous memories. Nevertheless, Barrymore, the only one of the Barrymore family of Lionel, Ethel, and John never to win or even to be nominated for an Oscar, was not cited for *Svengali* in a year when the Motion Picture Academy awarded not one, but two Best Actor prizes to Wallace Beery for *The Champ* and Fredric March for *Dr. Jekyll and Mr. Hyde*. Still, *Svengali* was so successful that Barrymore happily chose *The Mad Genius* (1931) as his next picture, completing his Warners' contract. This film presented Barrymore as a club-footed madman who inspires his adopted son (Donald Cook) to become a great ballet star. It was similar to *Svengali* and included Marsh in the female lead.

Sadly, Barrymore's *Svengali* is rarely seen today, although many television stations do play the 1955 British *Svengali* starring Hildegarde Neff and Donald Wolfit. In no way can that version compare to the 1931 classic containing the masterful performance of a gloriously theatrical, deeply touching John Barrymore.

Gregory William Mank

SWEET BIRD OF YOUTH

Released: 1962
Production: Pandro S. Berman for Metro-Goldwyn-Mayer
Direction: Richard Brooks
Screenplay: Richard Brooks; based on the play of the same name by Tennessee
   Williams
Cinematography: Milton Krasner
Editing: Henry Berman
Makeup: William Tuttle
Costume design: Orry-Kelly
Running time: 120 minutes

Principal characters:
   Alexandra Del Lago
   (Princess Cosmonopolous) .... Geraldine Page
   Chance Wayne .... Paul Newman
   Tom "Boss" Finley .... Ed Begley (AA)
   Heavenly Finley .... Sandra Knight
   Miss Lucy .... Madeleine Sherwood
   Aunt Nonnie .... Mildred Dunnock
   Tom Finley, Jr. .... Rip Torn
   George Scudder .... Phillip Abbott

   Screen interpretations of successful Broadway plays rarely fare well with
critics. Should the stage story be adapted intact for the screen, the motion
picture is dismissed as a filmed play. If the play is reworked for the screen,
its writer or director is charged with ruining the original. The filmed version
of *Sweet Bird of Youth* was a victim of the latter criticism. The New York-
bred conviction which views film as the bastard offspring of the theater is at
work here, but never more wrongly so. Each version of *Sweet Bird of Youth*
utilizes the strengths of its respective medium: the play has the impact of
immediacy, while the film benefits from evocative camerawork, variety of
setting, and deft movement back and forth in time. On stage or on film,
however, the Tennessee Williams drama is incorrectly regarded as one of his
minor works, despite wide acceptance by audiences and a fine box-office
showing.
   Chance Wayne (Paul Newman) is a local boy who, contrary to expectations,
has not made good. The handsome, athletic, but poor pride of the Florida
Gulf Coast island town of St. Cloud left home to make a fortune on the only
commodities he possessed, his youth and good looks. His plan was to return,
an accomplished actor, and to wed his sweetheart Heavenly Finley (Sandra
Knight) once he was able to support her in her accustomed style as the

daughter of the state's political boss Tom Finley (Ed Begley). Fame, however, was as elusive in New York as it was in Hollywood. Nor was fortune to be found as an escort to show-business doyennes or Back Bay socialites. With each return to St. Cloud, once on a freight car, Chance brought Heavenly greater promises for their future and more entreaties for her patience. The townspeople and her father were not fooled, however, and Chance Wayne has come to be the topic of chuckling conversation at the St. Cloud Hotel bar which he once tended.

At his most recent homecoming, on which the film opens, Chance trails what he believes to be clouds of glory. Arriving sharply dressed and at the wheel of a new Cadillac convertible, he checks in at the St. Cloud Hotel. He is not alone. His lady friend, semiconscious for the last several hundred miles, requires assistance out of the back seat. Alexandra Del Lago (Geraldine Page), a faded screen actress, is traveling incognito as the Princess Cosmonopolous. The memory of her recent catastrophic film comeback attempt is only partly relieved by consumption of oxygen, Benzedrine, vodka, contraband from Tangier, and young men.

At the hotel, meanwhile, preparations are under way for an important televised political rally upon which Boss Finley's next election depends. Chance's unexpected presence in town threatens the Boss's tenuous hold on the support of some factions which have not forgotten Heavenly Finley's involvement with the ne'er-do-well. Rumors have circulated that Heavenly had required an illegal abortion, which was performed by young Dr. George Scudder (Phillip Abbott), recently made chief-of-staff at Finley Hospital. Boss Finley therefore attempts to prevent Chance's further association with his daughter. Although he enlists the Finley Youth, a group of vandals which includes his son Tom, Jr., (Rip Torn) and which he retains for such assignments, to keep Chance from Heavenly, the two meet with the help of a Finley sister-in-law, Aunt Nonnie (Mildred Dunnock). It is at their meeting that Chance learns of Heavenly's ill-fated pregnancy, which was precipitated during his last visit home.

At the hotel, meanwhile, Alexandra is frantic at Chance's frequent absences from her, and to find him, she unwisely ventures from their room. In the hotel bar, she is rescued from falling on her face by another resident of the hotel, Miss Lucy (Madeleine Sherwood), Boss Finley's longtime mistress. The women strike a friendship born of mutual desperation. Later confronting each other back in their room, Chance and Alexandra have it out. With renewed conviction, she evades the promises she made to him recently about signing a film contract for him. His unavailability at her time of need has inflamed her. He, however, has just succeeded in reaching columnist Walter Winchell in New York, to whom he is touting Alexandra Del Lago's young talent discoveries, Chance Wayne and Heavenly Finley. Winchell is much less interested in hearing from the brash self-promoter than he is in bearing the news to Alexandra of her smash comeback. Alexandra, it seems, had misread the audience's response at the premiere and had fled the theater in terror before realizing her victory.

Once off the telephone, Alexandra hastily prepares to leave for New York and her public, with Miss Lucy as her driver. She no longer needs Chance, but begs for a reconciliation. During their final showdown, they hear the violent turn taken by the Finley rally outside the hotel. Boss Finley's political opponents had been tipped earlier by an anonymous caller who confirmed the rumors of Heavenly's abortion and who outlined in slanderous detail certain of Finley's political stratagems. The caller was a vengeful Miss Lucy who had been viciously beaten and discarded by the Boss the night before in retaliation for her kiss-and-tell revelations about his sexual inadequacies. Chance hears hecklers taunt Heavenly, who has been forced by her father to appear at the rally "in the white of a virgin." Abandoning his last slim hope for a future in Hollywood, he leaves Alexandra in search of Heavenly, acknowledging the actress's prophecy: "Each of us has his own private hell to go to."

At the Finley estate, Chance is accosted by Heavenly's brother and his Finley Youth cronies. While Chance calls out for her, he is reviled and beaten by them. Tom, Jr., takes a cane to his face, calling it his "meal ticket." When Heavenly appears and discovers Chance, bloodied and semiconscious, they laugh and cry over his shattered dreams and manage to flee before Boss Finley can stop them, speeding away to Finley's exhortations to come back and Aunt Nonnie's whispers, "Go, go."

Producer-director Richard Brooks was universally damned for tampering with Williams' themes of racism, venereal disease, and castration. Indeed, he did soften the racist elements of the Finley story and likewise substituted Heavenly's venereal disease and resulting sterility with a pregnancy and abortion. Also, Chance's castration was replaced with a mere face-smashing. Brooks' final sin, according to critics, was ending the film happily. Hollywood in the early 1960's, however, still had die-hard vestiges of Production Code standards to be met. Coupled with the demands of the box office, these exigencies left Brooks with little choice but to cool the steamier aspects of the Williams original. The performances retain their original power, however, as Page, Newman, Sherwood, and Torn repeat the brilliant performances they had delivered on the New York stage two years earlier.

On stage or screen, the drama was acknowledged to belong to Page. Far from the neurasthenic, lazy character for which she came to be known on the stage, however, Page here is transformed into a film glamour queen by make-up man William Tuttle, hairstylist Sydney Guilaroff, and dress designer Orry-Kelly. She is quoted as wanting to "drown herself" upon first seeing her character on screen, so great was the change. Alexandra Del Lago's beauty and self-possession in the motion picture production is so great that believing her to be a Hollywood has-been requires a considerable exercise of the imagination.

The strength of her screen showing netted Page an Academy nomination for Best Actress of 1962, but she lost to Anne Bancroft for her performance in *The Miracle Worker*. The Best Supporting Actor award, however, was won by Ed Begley for his characterization of the vile and despicable Boss Finley, a compelling departure from Williams' more familiar Big Daddy patriarch/despot character in *Cat on a Hot Tin Roof* (1958). A third Academy nomination placed newcomer Sandra Knight in the running for Best Supporting Actress. Her delicacy and refinement as Heavenly Finley provided a much-needed balance and relief from the debased and rancorous populace of St. Cloud. Also noteworthy in the production are art directors George W. Davis and Urie McCleary, who expertly manipulate mood with their hot and tawdry interiors and colors which were alternated with cool, sea-swept exterior locations in which sea gulls wheel and cry.

Sweet Bird of Youth is a timeless study of the corrupt Deep South. The film survives viewing decades after its release because the truths it imparts remain of immediate concern for what they reveal about the human condition.

Nancy S. Kinney

SWEET SMELL OF SUCCESS

Released: 1957
Production: James Hill for United Artists
Direction: Alexander Mackendrick
Screenplay: Ernest Lehman and Clifford Odets; based on a novelette of the same name by Ernest Lehman
Cinematography: James Wong Howe
Editing: no listing
Running time: 96 minutes

Principal characters:
J. J. Hunsecker .... Burt Lancaster
Sidney Falco .... Tony Curtis
Susan Hunsecker .... Susan Harrison
Steve Dallas .... Martin Milner
Harry Kello .... Emile Meyer
Rita .... Jeff Donnell

In some ways *Sweet Smell of Success* broke away from traditions under which Burt Lancaster, Tony Curtis, and Lancaster's production company had labored. Lancaster plays an unredeemable villain for the first time in his career, and Curtis strays away from his usually glamorous image to play a slimy yes-man. The film was the first box-office failure for Hecht-Hill-Lancaster Productions, causing the company to produce as their next effort a more commercially successful film called *Run Silent, Run Deep* (1958), starring Lancaster and Clark Gable. *Sweet Smell of Success* does, however, illustrate Lancaster's and Curtis' broad acting abilities and is a good example of veteran cinematographer James Wong Howe's excellence and Clifford Odets' own peculiar style of dialogue.

Curtis plays Sidney Falco, a struggling press agent determined to scratch his way to the top "where everything is balmy" and he "can smell his favorite perfume—Success." He curries favor with a powerful columnist named J. J. Hunsecker (Burt Lancaster), who wields much influence over anyone who wants to get anywhere, including budding actresses, jazz club owners, and highly placed politicians. J. J. secretly assigns Sidney the task of breaking up the romance between his younger sister Susan (Susan Harrison) and a jazz musician named Steve Dallas (Martin Milner) and refuses to print any of Sidney's items when he fails to keep the lovers apart. Sidney, in trouble with his clients because he promised them publicity in J. J.'s column, smears Steve with a false item planted in another column which says the musician is a Communist and smokes marijuana.

In observing this and other incidents, we find that Sidney manipulates those who care about him and degrades himself before those whose favors he needs.

The smear item succeeds in influencing Steve's boss to fire the jazz quintet in which Steve plays and eventually breaks up the young couple when Steve accuses J. J. of planting the item. J. J. becomes angry at Steve for confronting him and denigrating him in front of Susan and others at the television studio and therefore bribes Sidney to plant marijuana in Steve's overcoat and contact a corrupt cop named Harry Kello (Emile Meyer) to arrest him. Sidney balks at first at completing this particularly unscrupulous task but cannot resist J. J.'s bribe: to write J. J.'s column for three months while J. J. takes Susan on an extended cruise to help her recover from her broken romance. Harry arrests Steve and according to J. J.'s unspoken directions beats him severely, sending him to the hospital.

Susan hears about Steve's hospitalization and attempts to visit him, only to be turned away. She realizes that J. J. and Sidney were behind the beating and calls Sidney at the restaurant where he is celebrating his newfound success and leaves a message that J. J. wants Sidney to drop by his apartment. When Sidney arrives looking for J. J. he finds Susan prepared to leap from the balcony, claiming that her brother will punish Sidney for allowing her to jump. Sidney pulls her back into the room and during the struggle, J. J. walks in, assumes Sidney is raping Susan, and punches him several times before calling Harry and telling him that Sidney planted the marijuana on Steve and that he should be arrested. Sidney vows "to tell the world" about J. J.'s smear campaign although "that fat cop will break every bone in my body." J. J. confronts Susan about her attempted suicide but she has realized that he was behind the whole plan to separate her from Steve and leaves him to go to Steve, doing the very thing that J. J. wanted to prevent. As she leaves, the day dawns, hinting that she will find happiness finally and J. J. and Sidney will receive their just punishments.

Despite the positive conclusion, the bulk of the film is an unrelieved view of the diseased side of life. This film has many elements of *film noir*, an appropriately moody genre which focuses on seamy urban society rather than on glamorous fantasy. This postwar phenomenon in film usually had several characteristics which were reactions against the light-hearted, upbeat musicals of the 1930's. One *film noir* characteristic in this film is the story of corruption, diseased love, and a disturbing lust for power. The dialogue reflects the artificial world of press agents and columnists with its slick manner and twisted jargon permeating all the characters' conversations. An example of this is J. J.'s remark when Sidney reveals his plan to discredit Steve: "I'd hate to take a bite out of you. You're a cookie full of arsenic." The more this type of language enters a character's conversation, the greater his involvement in the sordid world. Even the innocent Susan shows her contamination when she tosses out a bit of slang in a conversation with J. J. which foreshadows her break-up with Steve to prevent a conflict with J. J. Odets and Lehman worked well together on the script to delineate a synthetic society filled with people who can never say anything but warped phrases which reflect their corrupt outlook.

J. J. and Sidney completely overwhelm the more ethical characters although no one is totally honest. We see another columnist refuse to print Sidney's smear item about Steve although Sidney threatens to reveal his fling with a cigarette girl named Rita (Jeff Donnell) to his wife. We also sympathize with Sidney's secretary and Rita, who both feel affection for Sidney, who manipulates them and then discards them when they are of no further use. Despite these more sympathetic characters, we remember only J. J. and Sidney. Steve and Susan, the unfortunate lovers, seem out of place in this sordid life: they are too good and too innocent about the world around them to have survived this long. Susan especially is too innocent and unbelievably weak-kneed although she realizes that her brother adores her with an incestuous passion and will do anything to keep her with him. For her not to take advantage of this situation and manipulate J. J. to her benefit seems incongruous with the rest of the characterizations, but since the focus is on J. J. and Sidney, this weakness is not serious.

Lancaster and Curtis are excellent in their roles as the two unscrupulous men who abuse power. Lancaster handles the vitriolic dialogue well as he stares malevolently through spectacles which seem incongruous with his usual image of athletic hero. Curtis' performance is excellent: his oily manner is suitably repulsive. Milner is the straight-laced, self-righteous "average Joe," while Harrison sometimes overplays the snivelling Susan who flutters at every move her brother makes.

This film is not only a departure from Lancaster's and Curtis' usual roles but also marks a change for director Alexander Mackendrick. He did comedies with social comment such as *Man in the White Suit* (1951) in England before coming to the United States to direct his first American film. He has done well in capturing the atmosphere of an American locale, in eliciting breezy delivery of lines, and in presenting larger-than-life characters. He has taken the distinctly American film subject of gangsters and crime and translated the same feeling into the more subtly corrupt themes of dirty journalism and unethical public relations.

The main thrust of *film noir* technique lies in Howe's cinematography. Every face is lit with unglamourously bright lights which harshly etch out every line and every smirk. This shocking illustration of corruption lit in every face causes us to cringe at J. J.'s first appearance in the restaurant "21." His glasses cast ominous shadows on his cheeks, and his face has a ghastly pallor as if he never saw the sun but spent all his time in noisy restaurants engaging in slurs about passing celebrities and collecting items for his column. Besides the harsh lighting which gives a gritty look to everyone's face, dark bands of shadows are constantly cast over characters' eyes, causing an alienated feeling between audience and characters. The large number of low-angle shots of

J. J. and Sidney also emphasize their threatening or at best unattractive personalities. One especially effective low-angle shot is one of the police car which barrels down the street after Steve only seconds before he is arrested and beaten. The film was shot on location on Broadway and Times Square in New York, which adds to the realism of big-city hustling. The streets are wet as if it had recently rained (a classic *film noir* touch), and the neon lights glisten on the streets and on the cars, giving a glittering, hard-edged look to the story. As in other *film noir* works, the action takes place at night. People escape from the night into garishly lit nightclubs full of bleak characters and stale cigarette smoke.

Although the film is well done and displays versatile abilities on the part of all concerned, its lack of sympathetic characters and its completely cynical outlook caused it to be shunned by film audiences. Despite the film's depressing look at powermongers and manipulators, however, the excellent acting, Mackendrick's astute direction, and Howe's admirable cinematography combine to produce a well-made film.

Ruth L. Hirayama

THE SWIMMER

Released: 1968
Production: Frank Perry and Roger Lewis for Horizon
Direction: Frank Perry and Sydney Pollack
Screenplay: Eleanor Perry; based on the short story of the same name by John Cheever
Cinematography: David L. Quaid
Editing: Sidney Kats, Carl Lerner, and Pat Somerset
Running time: 94 minutes

Principal characters:

Neddy Merrill	Burt Lancaster
Shirley Abbott	Janice Rule
Betty Graham	Kim Hunter
Howard Graham	Charles Drake
Julie Hooper	Janet Landgard
Peggy Forsburgh	Marge Champion
Mrs. Hammar	Cornelia Otis Skinner
Joan	Joan Rivers
Mrs. Halloran	Nancy Cushman
Mr. Halloran	House Jameson

Works of literature hold a particular attraction to filmmakers. They often serve as a temptation, since the adapter of a best-selling novel is guaranteed an instant audience, and the filmmaker looking for prestige might be assured of a new reputation by adapting a literary classic to the screen. Yet more often than not, the masterpiece of literature fails to become a masterpiece of cinema. There are problems which immediately come to mind for each separate literary genre. The novel generally covers either a large expanse of time and a large number of characters, or a limited time and characters investigated in depth. The numerous superficial incidents which the author must explore to illuminate one facet of a character's personality are difficult to capture in a film of limited length. An undistinguished work of literature which neglects development of characters and motivations and favors telling a one-dimensional tale is often more successful as a film. Film can present visual images to fill in the deficiencies of the story, attracting readers to the book who come to it with established images in mind. This procedure can be seen carried to the extreme in the process of "novelization": a book created from the screenplay of a film in order to capitalize on the film's success.

The short story, while presenting a different set of problems, offers the filmmaker a manageable sequence of events related in a limited time frame. Character development is also restricted, making it possible to present the story in the limited number of scenes available in a feature film. John

Cheever's story *The Swimmer* serves as an interesting case of the short story being faithfully adapted to the screen. Neddy Merrill (Burt Lancaster) is an athletic, successful man reaching middle age—a perfect WASP. He decides one day to swim from his neighbor's home to his own, using the backyard swimming pools along the way as a river, which he names Lucinda after his wife. As he makes his way from one pool to another, he encounters his friends, that odd assortment of affluent suburban people who share much with Neddy. Each one, however, has distinct, idiosyncratic characteristics. Some insist he have a drink with them; the Hallorans (Nancy Cushman and House Jameson), an elderly couple who enjoy their radical reputation, always sunbathe and swim nude; at another pool, the host and hostess talk about money all the time and are not completely accepted in this WASP world; Shirley Adams (Janice Rule), Neddy's former mistress, does not welcome him and already has another lover.

As Neddy's journey advances, it becomes apparent that something is wrong. He is greeted as someone who has been absent from this scene. Frequent references are made to his bad luck, the job he has lost, and the money he wants to borrow. Gradually, virile, athletic Neddy begins to show signs of strain, not only physically, but also emotionally. By the time he reaches the last leg of his journey, he can no longer spring from the pool without the aid of the ladder. In fact, he is not even able to swim the length of the pool without resting. When he finally completes his journey, he looks tired, drawn, and older. Suddenly, as he attempts to enter his own home, it becomes evident that Neddy's world has collapsed. The house is empty, appearing to have been that way for some time. Neddy's world is no more, a fact he has been unable to accept.

Neddy Merrill is a typical Cheever character, boasting, drinking, and socializing. When his youth goes, so does his success. His drinking increases, and his productivity fails. He loses job, friends, and family. The story effectively conveys this feeling of the failed American dream through language. The film, while using much of the story's language, takes advantage of the medium to capture the tone through visual images. Neddy, as played by Lancaster, shows the physical strain as his journey progresses. He also shows detachment, alienation, and an inability to accept the reality of his failed life. The supporting characters play a larger role in uncovering the true situation in the film. Their comments benefit from their expressions and gestures, becoming more telling than words alone. This proves neither more nor less effective in the total construction of the story, but it clearly points out the strengths and weaknesses of the respective media.

Lancaster both succeeds and fails as Neddy Merrill. His hearty, robust manner makes Neddy's athletic past credible, as well as his slap-on-the-back cordiality. His fatigue and disorientation are also believable since Lancaster was the appropriate age at the time of filming. Lancaster, however, is not completely convincing as the embodiment of the aging WASP. His broad style of acting and his physical appearance seem better suited to the stupid but emotional Alvaro Mangiacavallo of *The Rose Tattoo* (1951) or the huckster Bill Starbuck of *The Rainmaker* (1956).

The additional performances in *The Swimmer* are distinctly supporting roles, filled by a strong cast portraying the stereotypes of WASP society. Particularly notable is the performance by Rule; her scene was refilmed with Rule under the direction of Sydney Pollack, giving it a noticeable difference from the rest of the film. Also of interest is a rare screen appearance by Cornelia Otis Skinner as Mrs. Hammar.

The screenplay, written by Eleanor Perry, remains remarkable in its faithfulness to the original and successfully maintains the gradual revelation that not all is in order in Neddy's life. One obvious addition has been made which allows Neddy to talk about life, youth, and family: a teenage girl accompanies him part of the way. Offering merely an obvious encounter with youth, the scene seems to add little to the original story.

The Westport, Connecticut, locations mesh well with other production values to create the tone of the story. Although the cinematography at times falls into a stylized romanticizing of the autumn landscape, looking more like a sentimental greeting card than a film illustrating an autumnal point in a man's life, overall the film succeeds both as cinema and as an adaptation of a short story. The single incident around which the story revolves and the twist which reveals that everything is not as it seems are well captured. The film is small and subtle, not so explicit and magnificent in scope as to capture a wide audience. It is interesting to compare *The Swimmer* to the dramatization of several Cheever stories for the PBS television series *The American Short Story*. The low-keyed presentations in these shorter versions seem in some ways more appropriate than a full-length film. Perhaps *The Swimmer*, too, would benefit from such treatment.

Kenneth T. Burles

SWING TIME

Released: 1936
Production: Pandro S. Berman for RKO/Radio
Direction: George Stevens
Screenplay: Howard Lindsay and Allan Scott; based on an orginal story by
    Erwin Gelsey
Cinematography: David Abel
Editing: Henry Berman
Art direction: Van Nest Polglase and John Harkrider
Song: Jerome Kern and Dorothy Fields, "The Way You Look Tonight" (AA)
Running time: 105 minutes

>   *Principal characters:*
>   John "Lucky" Garnett .... Fred Astaire
>   Penny Carrol .... Ginger Rogers
>   Pop Cardetti .... Victor Moore
>   Mabel Anderson .... Helen Broderick
>   Mr. Gordon .... Eric Blore
>   Margaret Watson .... Betty Furness
>   Ricardo Romero .... Georges Metaxa
>   Mr. Watson .... Landers Stevens

The teaming of Fred Astaire and Ginger Rogers produced a series of musicals for RKO in the 1930's which are a landmark in cinema history. These films possess a special appeal which goes beyond the excellence of the dancing, singing, and acting in them. Astaire and Rogers complement each other to create a style and a mood which are still remembered, and many would say unequaled, more than forty years after the two made their last film for RKO together.

In an Astaire-Rogers musical the characters played by Astaire and Rogers are usually strangers who meet by accident: he nearly always falls in love with her right away, but she is antagonistic to him or annoyed by his advances and tries to escape or evade him until finally, persuaded by a romantic dance number, she succumbs. In these films the dances communicate and deepen the emotion and moods expressed in the stories surrounding them, revealing the nuances of the characters' relationship more dramatically than words. Through the dances the audience can identify the moods of the characters played by Astaire and Rogers and the depth of their involvement with each other.

Even though it is not reflected in the screen credits, Astaire was involved in virtually every stage of the development of each of his dance numbers, from its conception through the final editing of the sound and picture. He was especially concerned that the camera and editing techniques not detract from the natural progression of the dance. His basic method, therefore, was to film a dance straight through with the entire body of each dancer always in the camera frame. He thought that reaction shots (views of people watching the dancers) interrupted the flow of the dance and tried to avoid them. He also avoided close-ups because he felt that the movement of the upper part of the body was as important as that of the feet in any dance, even tap. As a result the audience sees his dances from an ideal perspective without being distracted by the camera technique.

Swing Time, the fifth in the series of Astaire-Rogers films, is one of the best. Its lovely settings, outstanding dances by Astaire and Rogers, and the Jerome Kern score ("The Way You Look Tonight" won an Oscar for Best Song) make it one of the greatest of dance musicals. Astaire plays Lucky Garnett, a dancer who thinks his talent is gambling. "Hoofing is all right," he tells his friend Pop Cardetti (Victor Moore), "but there's no future in it." At the opening of the film he is planning to quit dancing and marry his hometown sweetheart, Margaret Watson (Betty Furness). The rest of the dancers in his troupe, however, not wanting his marriage to interfere with their careers, devise the ruse of telling him that his formal trousers for the wedding should have cuffs and that they have taken them away to be altered. Through this ruse they make him hours late for the wedding, so that when he arrives the guests are gone and the wedding has been called off. He pacifies Margaret and her irate father (Landers Stevens) by saying that he is going to New York to make money and leaves with the understanding that he will come back and marry Margaret as soon as he has $25,000.

Lucky goes to the railroad station to buy his ticket, but he has lost all his money because he had bet the troupe that his marriage would take place. Undeterred, Lucky, still in formal morning dress, hops a freight for New York, followed by his faithful sidekick, Pop. One of the memorable images of the film is Astaire in top hat and swallow-tailed coat, waving good-bye to his friends as he clings with one hand to the side of the moving freight car.

Pop and Lucky arrive in New York broke except for Lucky's good-luck quarter and the clothes on their backs. The quarter is very important to Lucky, but Pop becomes so desperate for a cigarette that Lucky decides to get change for it. As fate would have it, the person he asks is Penny Carrol, the character played by Rogers. She gives him the change, and that would be the end of the encounter except that when Pop gets his cigarettes, dozens of coins spill out of the machine. Lucky then runs after Penny to retrieve his good-luck piece. Penny, thinking he is trying to strike up an acquaintance, ignores him until he accidentally knocks the packages out of her arms. While Lucky helps her pick up her packages, Pop takes the quarter from her purse, but before he can replace it, Penny snatches the purse away, and when she finds the quarter gone summons a policeman. The policeman takes one look at the impeccably attired Lucky, however, and tells Penny to run along.

Wanting to apologize, Lucky follows the fuming Penny into Mr. Gordon's Dance Studio.

Penny is furious when she finds that Lucky has followed her and that the manager, Mr. Gordon (Eric Blore), wants her to give Lucky a trial dance lesson. The two begin the lesson, but Lucky clumsily slips and slides around the floor, finally falling down. This cleverly leads into the first song, "Pick Yourself Up," in which he vows to learn and she encourages him to try again. They try the step again, and this time they both slip and fall. "No one could teach you to dance in a million years," Penny tells him disgustedly, "save your money." Gordon, overhearing, fires her on the spot, but Lucky attempts to get her job back for her by demonstrating how much she has really taught him. He astonishes both Penny and Gordon with a burst of intricate tap steps and then leads her into a dazzling routine to "Pick Yourself Up." The dance builds gradually, with the two swinging each other back and forth over the low railing that rings the dance floor until the tempo picks up and the two, in a perfectly timed effortless leap, glide over the railing and walk casually out the door. An amazed Gordon is so impressed that he arranges a tryout for Lucky and Penny at the Silver Sandal night club. Lucky's problem, which he does not tell Penny, is that he does not have a dinner jacket for the tryout. Having no money, he tries to win a suit of evening clothes by gambling but only succeeds in losing most of his own clothes and the chance for the audition. Penny is so disappointed that she refuses to speak to Lucky; so, like striking factory workers, Lucky and Pop picket the hall outside Penny's room, wearing signs proclaiming "Penny Carrol Unfair to John Garnett."

Penny's friend, Mabel Anderson (Helen Broderick), however, is on Lucky's side and, suspecting Penny is in love with him, persuades her to invite him inside. Penny stubbornly refuses to see him, however, and goes off to wash her hair, which leads into the lyrical ballad, "The Way You Look Tonight." As Lucky sings and plays the song, extolling her loveliness and charm, Penny—drawn into the room by the music—comes closer until her hand rests on Lucky's shoulder. Just as he finishes the song with the words "the way you look tonight," he looks up and is startled to see Penny in an old bathrobe with her head covered with shampoo.

Penny and Lucky's second chance to audition is frustrated by the orchestra leader, Ricardo Romero (Georges Metaxa), who is in love with Penny and does not want her to dance with anyone else, but Lucky finally manages to coax him into playing "Waltz in Swing Time." The music begins, and Lucky and Penny are off into the flowing movements of the number. It is one of the most intricate, graceful, and watchable of all the dances of Astaire and Rogers. Rogers, in a beruffled white evening dress, whiter than the white, gleaming set, and Astaire in tuxedo and floppy Bohemian tie, seem to glide across the floor. The waltz has no lyrics and no special story to tell; it gives the impression of being danced in moonlight.

Later, one of the cleverest songs in the film, "A Fine Romance," dramatically expresses the frustration and ambivalence of Lucky and Penny's romance. Penny has gotten over her initial dislike of Lucky and is puzzled because the romance does not seem to be making any headway. Indeed, she never sees him alone. Lucky, as we know but she does not, is in a dilemma: he is in love with Penny but engaged to Margaret. One snowy day when Lucky and Penny go with Pop and Mabel to the country, Lucky tells Pop to leave him alone with Penny. The setting is a beautifully stylized winter fantasyland of falling snow, ice-covered bushes, and snow-laden trees. Penny and Lucky wander off alone to a snow-covered gazebo. Lucky resolutely stares straight ahead with his hands in his pockets as Penny snuggles closer to him, but when Lucky helps her flap her arms to keep warm they end up almost embracing. "Funny how we met and all that's happened to us since," she muses. Still trying to encourage him, Penny says that it is sort of like a romance. As the strains of "A Fine Romance" are heard in the background and they prepare to kiss, however, Pop yells a warning to Lucky, who backs away and deflates the romantic mood by telling Penny she should be wearing galoshes. She stalks off disgustedly, then turns to Lucky and sings "A fine romance, with no kisses." She goes on to accuse him, among other things, of being as cold as yesterday's mashed potatoes.

Stung by her sarcastic accusations, Lucky decides to forget his engagement to Margaret, but again, just as they embrace, Lucky is hit by a snowball thrown by Pop. When Lucky retaliates, his missile hits Mabel instead, and he rushes off to apologize. Meanwhile, Pop tries to explain to Penny about Lucky's engagement to another woman, so when Lucky returns, she pushes him away. It is now his turn to reproach her in song. By the end of the song both are again unhappy and dissatisfied.

Later, however, backstage at the Silver Sandal, they finally do kiss for the first time in the film, but they are interrupted when Lucky is called for his solo dance. Exhilarated, Lucky begins applying his makeup for the number, "Bojangles of Harlem." "Bojangles" is in three parts: at the opening of the number two large panels slide diagonally apart to reveal the members of the chorus—half in white, half in black—who sing the lyrics. Then another pair of panels opens to reveal a huge black *papiermâché* head. This becomes the soles of two gigantic feet connected to long legs stretching from the camera back to Lucky, who is perching atop a cardboard model of Harlem. After the chorus removes the legs, Lucky jumps down and begins dancing his way toward the camera, tapping his feet and clapping his white-gloved hands in two rhythms that are different from the rhythm of the music. He does several dances with the chorus before chasing them off stage as if they were a flock of chickens. Another pair of panels now opens to show a screen on which three huge shadows of Lucky are seen. He turns, sees the shadows, and begins to dance with them, in unison at first, then in counterpoint. As he taps and spins faster and faster, the shadows eventually give up and walk off, flapping their hands disgustedly. All alone now, Lucky taps frenziedly around the stage, then stops and shuffles slowly off stage, waving good-bye.

The number is a complex and inventive one. Conceived as a tribute to the great black dancer, Bill "Bojangles" Robinson, it is a homage rather than an impersonation, and Astaire remains distinctively himself, even in blackface. It is also the first time Astaire used trick photography in one of his dances. The imaginative use of a few props to create an illusion, the controlled and inventive dances Astaire does with the chorus, the effective use of trick photography, and the varying tempos and moods of the number make this one of his unforgettable solo dance numbers.

As Lucky takes his bows after the "Bojangles" number, he is startled to see his fiancée, Margaret, in the audience. When she comes backstage, he tells her he will see her the next day and goes off to find Penny, who has found them together and is now sure that Lucky is going to marry Margaret. In a setting as lovely, sparkling, and shimmering as the one for "Waltz in Swing Time," and "A Fine Romance," the audience sees Penny and Romero standing close together on the deserted dance floor of the Silver Sandal night-club. Then we realize that we are seeing a reflection in a mirror when Lucky, dressed in white tie and tails, opens the glass doors and enters. He asks to see Penny alone even though she tells him she is going to marry Romero.

The stage is now set for the great dramatic dance of the film, the plaintive "Never Gonna Dance." Seemingly the end of Penny and Lucky's romance, it is a pensive song of frustration, parting, and defeat. As Penny slowly climbs one of the glistening black staircases, Lucky sings that if he cannot dance with her he will not dance at all. One of the most beautiful images of the film is Penny in a shimmery white evening gown standing on the black staircase against a starry background while Lucky sings to her of his frustration and heartbreak.

The song ends, she comes slowly down the stairs to meet him, and they walk side by side, reflectively, not touching, around the deserted dance floor, until they are not just walking but gliding into a dance step. The story of their whole relationship is then recapitulated in the dance. Suddenly she turns to leave. With a sudden sideways leap he stops her. They face each other. He pleads dramatically, arms outstretched but still not touching her. Face to face, then side by side, they continue dancing, still not touching each other. Then to "Waltz in Swing Time" they whirl and pirouette for a few moments as they remember happier times. Steps from the "Pick Yourself Up" dance lesson are repeated, and the melodies of "The Way You Look Tonight" and "A Fine Romance" are interwoven with the dance to recall their previous encounters. Gradually they stop dancing together and slowly dance separately up the two staircases flanking the stage. At the top they meet for one last fiery and dramatic series of pirouettes and turns until Penny exits alone, leaving Lucky behind in an attitude of despair. This great duet deepens and expands our awareness of Lucky's and Penny's relationship, representing their feelings more poignantly and more vividly than any dialogue.

After "Never Gonna Dance" the rest of the film is anticlimactic as the story lines are untangled and Lucky and Penny are reunited. The scriptwriters rely on the same device used in the beginning of the film—Lucky and Pop take Romero's trousers to have them altered because they have no cuffs and fail to return them in order to prevent his marriage to Penny. Then, after everyone laughs helplessly because Penny and Romero are not going to get married, Lucky and Penny sing to each other in counterpoint as the sun shines through the falling snow.

Even the nonmusical portions of *Swing Time* are highly entertaining. Astaire and Rogers are adept light comedians and are ably supported by Broderick as Penny's friend Mabel and Moore as Pop. The Astaire-Rogers musicals are widely regarded as one of the high points of dance in film, and *Swing Time* is arguably the best of the series. In addition to one of Kern's best scores, beautifully designed settings by Van Nest Polglase and John Harkrider, and the able direction of George Stevens, the film features Astaire and Rogers at the peak of their powers in a film carefully designed to display their charm, humor, and talents.

Julia Johnson

SYLVIA SCARLETT

Released: 1935
Production: Pandro S. Berman for RKO/Radio
Direction: George Cukor
Screenplay: Gladys Unger, John Collier, and Mortimer Offner; based on the novel *The Early Life and Adventures of Sylvia Scarlett* by Compton MacKenzie
Cinematography: Joseph H. August
Editing: Jane Loring
Running time: 97 minutes

> *Principal characters:*
> Sylvia Scarlett .... Katharine Hepburn
> Jimmy Monkley .... Cary Grant
> Henry Scarlett .... Edmund Gwenn
> Maudie Tilt .... Dennie Moore
> Lily .... Natalie Paley
> Michael Fane .... Brian Aherne

Sylvia Scarlett was a failure at the box office when it was first released and has since been made famous—or notorious—by its director, George Cukor, who often tells the story of its preview. As he describes it, the experience was a "nightmare." The audience obviously did not like the film, and many people left during the showing. When Katharine Hepburn, who attended the preview with Cukor, went into the women's restroom, she found a woman lying down. Hepburn asked if the picture was that bad, and the woman merely rolled her eyes. Cukor and Hepburn then went to the producer, Pandro S. Berman, asked him not to release the film, and offered to do another one free; Berman replied, "I never want to see either of you again." This story unfortunately too often obscures the virtues of the film and the fact that it has gained a number of devoted followers. Today it is quite successful whenever it is shown.

The film begins as an almost picaresque tale of three adventurers and ends as an unusual romantic comedy. Also, an intriguing twist throughout is the fact that the Hepburn character is a young woman who usually masquerades as a boy. The film explores many facets and implications of this pretense without being exploitative or unduly contrived. The reason for the masquerade is established in the first scene, which is unfortunately one of the weakest in the film. According to Cukor, the scene, a sort of prologue, was added almost as an afterthought, and he was never satisfied with it. In it we see a young woman in Marseilles, Sylvia Scarlett (Katharine Hepburn), mourning the death of her mother. Then she finds that her father, Henry (Edmund Gwenn), has embezzled money from his employer to pay his gambling debts and faces prison if he does not leave the country immediately. Sylvia gives him the money for passage to England, but he does not want her to go with him because a father and daughter traveling together would be too easy to trace. She solves that problem by cutting her hair short, dressing in boys' clothes, and changing the label on her luggage from Sylvia to Sylvester.

On the boat to England they meet Jimmy Monkley (Cary Grant), a carefree young man with a Cockney accent who claims to be "nobody's enemy but my own." Henry soon warms to Jimmy (after first suspecting him of being a policeman) and boasts to him about the valuable lace he is going to smuggle into England. This proves to be a mistake because Jimmy informs the customs officials. Henry loses the lace and nearly all his money. "We're all fools sometimes," Sylvia tells him, "only you choose such awkward times." They have not, however, seen the last of Jimmy. When they board the train for London, he is in their compartment. He explains that he alerted the customs officials to divert them from his own more lucrative smuggling, and he shows them a handful of diamonds hidden in the heel of his shoe.

Jimmy gives Henry one hundred pounds, which more than covers his losses, and the animosity is forgotten. Indeed, Jimmy asks them to team up with him. He thinks "Sylvester" will be a good pupil and can learn to be a hawk rather than a sparrow. Jimmy explains that a person is either a sparrow or a hawk, prey or hunter—although he uses more euphemistic phrases to explain his idea. Once Sylvia penetrates Jimmy's Cockney accent, she understands his idea, and she and her father agree to join Jimmy in making money from sparrows.

Thus is established the premise of the middle section of the film: Jimmy devises schemes to obtain money and the three attempt to carry them out. The first scheme is truly ingenious. Sylvia pretends to be a French boy who cannot speak a word of English and has no money. Jimmy and Henry separately "happen" to notice the wailing youngster and soon convince the gathered crowd to donate money to the unfortunate child. The scheme works perfectly until Sylvia momentarily forgets and speaks English. She then begins laughing, and the three have to escape quickly.

After another scheme that does not work, the group adds one more member, Maudie Tilt (Dennie Moore), who was to have been an unwitting pawn in a scheme to steal the jewelry of her employer. The four then set out to give shows in seaside towns, and the scene shifts to the Cornish coast where we see the new life of the group. They travel from town to town in two old wagons and, dressed in clownlike costumes, perform a song, dance, and comedy act.

It would seem to be a simple life, but it soon becomes extremely complicated. Henry has married Maudie, but she is far from being the faithful and devoted wife he wants. Then they are all invited to a party at the studio of a Bohemian artist, Michael Fane (Brian Aherne). The party is a fiasco for the troupe, Maudie disappears, and Henry—encouraged by Michael's girl friend Lily (Natalie Paley)—makes a spectacle of himself with his pitiful jealousy. The party does have one fortunate outcome, however: Sylvia meets Michael. Their relationship becomes the most complex and subtly delineated one in the film. Since it begins while Sylvia is masquerading as a boy, many of the actions and events have a different and deeper meaning to her than they do to him. Indeed, their first real conversation takes place in his bedroom and ends with him—perfectly innocently—offering to let her share his bed for the night. Twice Sylvia begins to tell him that she is not a boy, but each time she is interrupted.

Finally, Sylvia must let Michael know who she is so that he will take her seriously as a woman; so she changes to a dress and goes to see him. The scene is an excellent one, full of moments of awkwardness and moments of grace. When she arrives, Sylvia is unable to make an impressive entrance because Michael is in the bath and asks her to bring him his clothes. Before too long, however, she is able to talk to him more openly than she has ever talked to anyone. Then, just as she is beginning to relax and think Michael likes her, Lily returns, and Sylvia finds herself almost ignored.

A series of melodramatic events then lead to the ironic happy ending. One night Henry is again betrayed by Maudie and ventures out in a rainstorm, nearly demented by grief, to find her. When Sylvia finds her father gone, she starts out to find him. Jimmy first tries to dissuade her; then he helps her. After searching through the night, they find the next morning that Henry has fallen to his death on the rocks below a cliff. Next, not long after her father's funeral, Sylvia sees Lily drowning in the surf. Without a moment's hesitation, she jumps in the water and saves her rival for the affections of Michael. After a few quick twists and turns of the plot, we find that Jimmy has run off with Lily and Sylvia is helping Michael find them. When Sylvia and Michael do find the escaping couple on a train, they realize that they are more interested in each other than in any reunions with the "fugitives." They stop the train by pulling the emergency cord and leave together quietly without confronting Lily and Jimmy. The final scene, which shows Jimmy and Lily in their train compartment, adds an ironic touch: Jimmy has seen the couple leave together, so when Lily threatens to leave him and go back to Michael, Jimmy bursts into uproarious laughter as the film ends.

Not only is the performance by Grant one of the main strengths of the film, but the film was also an important milestone in his career. It was the first time he had worked for a top-flight director, the first time he played a comic character role rather than that of a handsome leading man, and the first time he was costarred with Hepburn. Two later notable pairings of Grant and Hepburn, both directed by Cukor and both classic films, are *Holiday* (1938) and *The Philadelphia Story* (1940). Hepburn's performance in *Sylvia Scarlett* is also outstanding, especially in the scenes with Aherne, who plays Michael.

She expressively conveys her feelings, both before and after she reveals that she is a woman. Cukor's direction is an additional strength. As usual, he elicits superior performances from the actors and contributes such touches as the fact that after Hepburn disguises herself as a boy, he hides her face from us for several shots by photographing her from behind or in shadow. Although *Sylvia Scarlett* is not a masterpiece, it is a generally well-crafted and well-acted entertainment that has now found the audience it could not attract in 1936.

Timothy W. Johnson

TABU

Released: 1931
Production: F. W. Murnau and Robert Flaherty; distibuted by Paramount
Direction: F. W. Murnau
Screenplay: Robert J. Flaherty and F. W. Murnau; based on their story *Turia*
Cinematography: Floyd Crosby (AA) and Robert J. Flaherty (uncredited)
Editing: no listing
Running time: 80 minutes

Principal characters:
Reri .... Herself
Matahi .... Himself
Hitu .... Himself
The policeman .... Jean
The captain .... Jules
The Chinaman .... Kong Ah

After a debacle over *City Girl* (1930, originally titled *Our Daily Bread*) the relationship between F. W. Murnau and Fox studios had reached a breaking point. Dissatisfied over the studio's interference in his latest film, Murnau found a kindred spirit in the documentarist Robert Flaherty, who was similarly at odds with the studio over a film he was making on the Acoma Indians. In Hollywood, Murnau had become acquainted with the filmmaker's brother, David Flaherty, who had inspired Murnau with tales of the South Seas (Flaherty had previously made two films there—*Moana*, 1926, and *White Shadows of the South Seas*, 1928, the latter film having been taken out of his hands). Arrangements for financing a new film, at first called *Turia* and later released as *Tabu* were made with an independent group, Colorart, and in April of 1929, Murnau and David Flaherty set out for Tahiti on the former's newly acquired yacht, the *Bali*.

Robert Flaherty left one month later on a steamer but would arrive in Tahiti first. Murnau's cruise was a leisurely one, and when he finally arrived, he received the disheartening news that Colorart had not followed up on its obligations and was in fact near to bankruptcy, Flaherty himself having lived for some time on credit. Since Flaherty had little money, Murnau decided he would finance the film out of his own pocket. Thus from the start, Murnau assumed the dominant role in the partnership; he would direct as well as produce the film, and Flaherty would write the story.

It would be difficult to imagine two personalities more strikingly different. Flaherty was an instinctive artist whose works grew out of a costly process of trial and error. Murnau was almost his exact opposite, requiring careful preplanning for his films, of particular importance here since he would be shooting on his own money. Originally Flaherty was to have photographed the film, but when his camera began to have difficulties Murnau brought in Floyd Crosby, who had previously worked on Flaherty's documentaries. Flaherty's role in the film diminished, but he and Murnau already reached a disagreement over the shape it was going to take. Flaherty had wanted to do the film the studio had not allowed him to do on *White Shadows of the South Seas*, depicting the corruption of the natives by the white man, which is, to some extent, in the film. Murnau had discovered an ancient legend, no longer observed, of certain maidens thought of as sacred virgins who become taboo to any of the men, upon pain of death. The breach between the two men was completed when Flaherty finally sold his half-interest in the film to Murnau. It is necessary to recount the events behind the production because some uninformed confusion arose later as to the role that each of these men played in the making of the film.

The story of *Tabu* is very simple and can be easily summarized. A boy (Matahi) and a girl (Reri) are in love. She is chosen by a high priest, Hitu (played by himself) to join the ranks of the sacred virgins, thereby becoming tabu to all men. Together, they escape by canoe to another island where Western culture has made some inroads and the old beliefs do not hold so strongly. Matahi supports himself and Reri by diving for pearls, but his naïveté leads him into debt with a Chinese merchant (Kong Ah). A ship bearing Hitu arrives, and he discovers the couple. Their attempt to leave the island is foiled when Matahi must give up his pearls to the merchant to pay his debt. Reri agrees to leave with Hitu if he will spare Matahi's life. Unaware of this, Matahi dives in an area marked as tabu for a priceless pearl. After killing the shark which guards this spot, Matahi returns to find Reri gone. He then swims out to the boat carrying Reri, but as he grabs onto a line, Hitu cuts it and he is left, perhaps, to drown.

This story of virtuous love thwarted by some greater force is a strain running throughout Murnau's work. Thus *Tabu* bears remarkable similarity to such earlier films as *Nosferatu* (1922), *Faust* (1926), *Sunrise* (1927), and *City Girl*. In each of these films, the male protagonist is somehow flawed or weak, while the woman emerges as the stronger figure. The force which represents the danger is personified through different characters: In *Nosferatu*, a vampire; in *Faust*, the devil; in *Sunrise*, the city woman; in *City Girl*, the father; and in *Tabu*, the priest, but in each they can be seen as symbolic of death. In the first two films especially, this outside force is less personally malignant than it is the agent of even greater forces. Hitu, who is also this type, is perhaps the most sympathetic since his motives are the least personal—he is as much under the influence of the tabu, perhaps even more so, as any of the other characters.

There is a strong mythic element present in nearly all of Murnau's work, and in *Tabu* this is markedly so. Murnau has been criticized for what many believe to be a Teutonization of these characters with Matahi at one point assuming the position of the statue *The Dying Gaul*. In the simplicity of its drama, *Tabu* does lend itself to allegorical interpretation, but in actuality Murnau's models were more along the lines of Herman Melville and Joseph Conrad than the German romantics. If anything, the simplicity of the story makes it Murnau's most universal film.

Murnau has been lumped together with Fritz Lang and G. W. Pabst as representative of a particular school of creative thought, German expressionism. This academic pigeonholing works well enough to demonstrate certain surface similarities, but it is at the expense of certain vital differences. Murnau's one famous example of the *kammersspielfilm*, *The Last Laugh* (1924), is an uneasy mixture of Murnau's collaborator Carl Mayer's deterministic and rather trite scenario and Murnau's more tenative direction. A comparison with Lang, however, is useful. In the latter's films, such as *Metropolis* (1926) and *Spione* (1928), each composition is a complete entity unto itself. In Murnau's films, as well as those of Carl Dreyer, space is never limited by the frame, but leads outward from it. In Murnau, the visual frame is in a continually changing state of readjustment. Movement within the frame assumes great importance with Murnau. Perhaps the most poetic moment in *Nosferatu* is when the ghostly ship bearing the vampire slowly enters and gradually dominates a hitherto empty frame. A similar moment occurs in *Tabu* when the ship carrying Hitu arrives. In one moment the film shifts from an ambience of joyful celebration to one of ever-increasing dread.

It is impossible to separate meaning from method in Murnau, and *Tabu* is perhaps his most difficult work with which to grapple because its technique is also the most subtle. The film's emotional tone is conveyed through a carefully graded use of light and shadow. This is particularly true in the film's last half, most importantly in the use of shadows in the hut shared by the lovers, which casts a subtle menace that has to be seen to be fully appreciated. The film's final act carefully orchestrates the opposition of Matahi and Hitu in a carefully edited sequence of increasing tensions. As Matahi swims farther out to sea to catch up with Hitu and Reri, nature itself, through water and wind, works against him. Finally he is able to grasp a rope, symbolic of his tenuous tie to Reri. Then Hitu takes out a knife which seems to cut through the air as it severs the rope, casting Matahi adrift presumably to drown. It is possible to describe this moment, but only Murnau's camera can elevate it almost to poetry.

After finishing the film, Murnau planned making similar pictures in the Pacific. Paramount, which eventually released the production, had been pleased with the film, and Murnau seemed on the verge of continuing his career at the studio most likely to encourage him. Unfortunately this was not to be the case, as Murnau was killed at age forty-two in an automobile accident only a few days before *Tabu*'s premiere. The film was a critical success, with Floyd Crosby's cinematography honored with an Academy Award. The film and Murnau were forgotten quickly, however, kept alive mainly through the efforts of film societies. Seen today, *Tabu* can be viewed as the culmination of a career sadly cut short at its height. *Tabu* rightfully takes its place alongside *Sunrise* at the top of cinematic art.

Mike Vanderlan

THE TARNISHED ANGELS

Released: 1957
Production: Albert Zugsmith for Universal
Direction: Douglas Sirk
Screenplay: George Zuckerman; based on the novel *Pylon* by William Faulkner
Cinematography: Irving Glassberg
Editing: Russell Schoengarth
Running time: 91 minutes

> *Principal characters:*
> Burke Devlin .... Rock Hudson
> Roger Shumann .... Robert Stack
> La Verne Shumann .... Dorothy Malone
> Jiggs .... Jack Carson
> Matt Ord .... Robert Middleton

Director Douglas Sirk made most of his best films for Universal working in the generally despised (but profitable) "woman's film" genre of melodrama. Since 1970, he has been "rediscovered" by critics of the *auteur* school. There is now a fair amount of literature published on his films, including *Sirk on Sirk*, a book-length interview with Jon Halliday, *Douglas Sirk*, also by Halliday, and a special issue of *Screen* (Summer, 1971). At least one retrospective of his films has been shown at a major film festival (Edinburgh, 1972), and there are now university courses devoted to his films. His critical reputation is perhaps at its zenith, yet his films require a context if they are to be fully appreciated by today's audiences.

The Tarnished Angels is one of Sirk's two most significant films (the other is *Written on the Wind*, 1956, also produced by Albert Zugsmith) and was a favorite project of his long before 1957. Based on William Faulkner's novel *Pylon*, the story takes place in the charged atmosphere of New Orleans at Mardi Gras time during the Depression. Beautiful, erotic, and frightening images of the Mardi Gras celebration intrude into the film and provide an emotional backdrop (through Irving Glassberg's glittering black-and-white cinematography) to the instability of the characters' lives, loves, and fates.

In the film, Roger Schumann (Robert Stack) is a former World War I hero who is now an ace pilot obsessed with flying and with death. His wife, La Verne (Dorothy Malone), had fallen in love with his picture on a liberty bond poster and followed him from one air circus show to another, becoming pregnant in the process. Roger rolled dice with Jiggs (Jack Carson), his mechanic who loved La Verne with a resigned futility, to decide which one would marry her. Shumann won and becomes the father of a son. Their boy Jack is taunted by other children throughout the film about his paternity and will not go to school as a result. He can sleep anywhere except in a bed because "They remind him of hospitals."

This melodramatic situation catches the attention of Burke Devlin (Rock Hudson), an alcoholic newspaper reporter who offers them his apartment when they cannot get a hotel. He falls in love with La Verne and helps Roger get another plane when his breaks down. Burke sums up what the Shumanns represent, calling them "visitors from a strange, faraway planet, fantastic creatures and monsters." He is eventually fired from his paper for his drunkenness and for his refusal to take another assignment when the editor decides that his "human interest" story of the barnstorming flyers is not good enough. Burke continues to follow the air show and ultimately delivers his story in the form of a drunken speech to his editor after Roger is killed.

Burke provides a perspective on the flyers and also serves as a listener for La Verne's highly charged and tawdry story. Yet Burke's speeches are among the most melodramatic and overly romantic in the film, making our identification with him as the audience's stand-in observer rather tenuous at times. Through him, however, we can fully appreciate La Verne and her ill-fated love for Roger as well as Roger's love affair with flying and with death. Roger and La Verne themselves are so exotic as to be nearly beyond the audience's identification, yet the primarily poor reviews the film received when it opened and the difficulty modern audiences have in understanding it are a result of Burke's verbal excess rather than the excesses of Roger's and La Verne's lives.

The forces of love and death are elaborately delineated in *The Tarnished Angels*. Sirk has a classical background which undoubtedly contributed to the symbols—often perversely mixed—of sex and death which pervade the film. La Verne's parachute jump, lovers in clown costumes kissing as a funeral procession passes by, and death masks which burst from the sides of the camera frame are examples of this preoccupation. The camera swoops and sweeps through the air, defining a visual space of precarious instability. Most of the film takes place at night, giving Sirk occasion to use enticing shadows, lush velvety patterns, and dangerously highlighted interiors, making *The Tarnished Angels* an ideal example of a particular visual style.

Sirk's characters are always partially blind, blind to themselves, to their world, and to their lovers. Roger is a man seeking the idealized identity that he lost after the war, an identity based on danger, excitement, glory, and death. Like a man who can only confront his fear by constantly challenging it, he continues to race planes, taking greater and greater risks for smaller rewards. It is both characteristic of the film genre and in keeping with the character's self-destructive personality that Roger tells La Verne that he loves her (for the first time) and promises that they will "settle down, just the three of us," after this one last race. He then dies in a crash. His death is a needless sacrifice in one sense; he must land in the ocean (and therefore drowns) instead of on the landing strip because the audience runs out on the field to get a better look at the impending crash and forces him to avoid hitting the crowd. Yet this absurd cruelty is not the deepest meaning of his death. His obsession with daredevil flying could have ended in no other way.

La Verne has a better chance at self-perception. Burke gives her his copy of Willa Cather's *My Ántonia*, the only book she has read since leaving Iowa to follow Roger. It is a book of attachment to the earth, of return to roots. La Verne lets Burke put her and Jack on a plane for the Midwest at the film's end. This is, of course, not the usual ending for a film of this genre. There is perhaps an implication that Burke and La Verne will see each other again, but it is very subtle. The "love at first sight" that led her away from home was based on nothing more than a picture on a poster, and her gypsy life since then has been a series of humiliations and illusions. The frenzy of eroticism, festivals, and death was its result. While Sirk in no way undercuts the intensity of La Verne's love for Roger, it is clear that such a basis will never offer a future, especially when the other person is as blind as she is.

Children are often the "hope for the future" in melodrama, a reason for life to go on and a compensation for tragedy. Sirk does not use them in this way, however; he sees children as "tragedies which are starting over again, always and always." When Roger dies, his son Jack is going around and around in a carnival airplane ride. The connection with his father is both direct (the planes from which neither can escape) and indirect (the endless circle from which there is no release).

The Tarnished Angels is a beautifully visual, fully realized film. The dialogue is sometimes awkward and overly melodramatic, but most of the film contains the rawness, imagery, and basic emotions of passion and destruction that give the genre of the "woman's film" its power.

Janey Place

A TASTE OF HONEY

Released: 1961
Production: Tony Richardson for Bryanston Films
Direction: Tony Richardson
Screenplay: Shelagh Delaney and Tony Richardson; based on the play of the
  same name by Shelagh Delaney
Cinematography: Walter Lassally
Editing: Antony Gibbs
Music: John Addison
Running time: 102 minutes

Principal characters:
Jo .... Rita Tushingham
Helen .... Dora Bryan
Peter .... Robert Stephens
Geoffrey .... Murray Melvin
Jimmy ....Paul Danquah
Shoe Store Proprietor .... Herbert Smith
Landlady .... Margo Cunningham
Schoolteacher ....Eunice Black
Bert ....David Boliver
Doris .... Moira Kaye

From the early 1960's, Britain's "Angry Young Men" period on the stage
and screen, emerged such film classics as *Look Back in Anger* (1959), *Saturday
Night and Sunday Morning* (1961), and at least one "Angry Young Woman"
offering, Shelagh Delaney's *A Taste of Honey*. While not as outspoken as
some of its contemporaries, the film version of the play was still considered
frank enough to warrant an X-rating from the British censors. Although the
story of a tough but sensitive young woman who is alienated from her promiscuous mother, is pregnant through an interracial love affair, and is maintaining a close relationship with a homosexual might seem tame by today's
standards, it is still powerful and touching. Only nineteen when she wrote
the play, Delaney saw her smash London production become a Broadway
success and then a well-received film. Through it all, Tony Richardson, who
had also directed *Look Back in Anger* and *Saturday Night and Sunday Morning*, directed each production and finally collaborated with her on the screen
adaptation, which he also produced and directed. Critics agreed that the film
version was better than the play, since the constant use of actual locations
gives the work a more realistic feeling. Few if any of the scenes betray their
origins on the stage, with the action constantly shifting from indoors to outside.

The British Film Academy was generous in bestowing honors: the pro-

duction was named Best British Film of 1961, Dora Bryan won the Best
Actress Award, Delaney and Richardson captured the Best Screenplay prize,
and Rita Tushingham was singled out as Most Promising New Star. Tushingham, also only nineteen, is brilliant in her first film, giving a totally unaffected and assured performance as a teenager who learns to fend for herself
out of necessity. Ironically, none of the stars really capitalized on their excellence in the film. Singer-comedienne Bryan and young Paul Danquah, who
made his film debut as the black lover, were seldom seen on screen again.
Murray Melvin, repeating his London stage role as Geoffrey, made other
films, but they lacked the impact of this performance. More than one observer
felt that Robert Stephens was miscast as the oafish boyfriend of the mother,
since he was too young for the part. Stephens later went on to more sophisticated roles quite unlike the part of Peter. Although Tushingham also had
other good films, notably Richardson's *The Girl with Green Eyes* (1964) and
Richard Lester's *The Knack* (1965), she never became the star she might
have. Although still active in cinema, she has made too few film appearances
in her maturity.

The popular song "A Taste of Honey," recorded by Herb Alpert's Tijuana
Brass, is not heard in the film, but was merely inspired by it. The score,
composed and conducted by John Addison and played by the Virtuoso
Ensemble, is a surprisingly happy one for such a dramatic story. Richardson
opens and closes the film with a children's song and focuses on young people
in every possible instance in order to emphasize Jo's impending delivery. A
few scenes feature rock-and-roll, which hardly seems out of place in such an
atmosphere centering on youth. There is a good deal of comedy to offset the
almost tragic events, and although some of the relationships seem too casually
developed and the ending is a bit contrived, there is some hope for Jo's future
even in her resignation to her situation.

Before the credits begin, some schoolgirls are playing ball on a field. The
most inept of them is Jo (Rita Tushingham), who has no real interest in the
game. She tells a school chum that she is no good at it. She has little interest
in anything else and says that she never goes anywhere. At seventeen, she
looks forward only to getting out on her own. Home is a dingy flat in which
her self-centered mother Helen (Dora Bryan) relaxes between dates. Her
latest boyfriend has given up supporting her, so she argues with the landlady
(Margo Cunningham) about the rent. When the landlady leaves, Helen has
Jo help her pack their clothes, and they exit through a basement window,
carrying Helen's birds.

The titles begin as the two head for a new flat by bus. Children are heard
singing a happy song, "On the Last Day of September," while the bus passes
a sign reading "God washes whitest of all." When they arrive at the new
location, a young black man (Paul Danquah) helps Jo off the bus with her
luggage. No sooner are they in their new place than Helen and Jo start arguing

again. Despite her cold, Helen pretties herself up to meet a new beau, a much younger man named Peter (Robert Stephens), and later, at a pub, she sings "Why, Because He Loves Me" with several other patrons gathered around a piano. Peter, bringing her a beer, looks around, a bit embarrassed at Helen's lack of inhibition. As the two are saying goodnight on the stairs of Helen's new place, Jo interrupts them, and it is at this point that Peter first learns of Helen's daughter. Jo is tired of her mother's low-class lovers and merely wants her to come to bed. As Helen prepares to retire, Jo talks of the darkness and reveals that she is not frightened of the darkness outside, only the darkness inside. Stating that she and Peter may get married, Helen goes to the bed that she shares with her daughter.

The next day, Jo emphasizes that she is looking forward to the end of school and the opportunity to get a place of her own and find a job. Helen looks disapprovingly at Jo's drawings, but studies the somewhat unflattering portrait of her that Jo has done. In class, Jo playfully acts out a dramatic piece for the benefit of her schoolmates as the teacher (Eunice Black) reads. Jo gets caught at this and has to stay after school. Later, leaving school, she falls on some steps and cuts her knee and then walks by a canal in the North Country slum that she calls home. Once again, she runs into the black man from the bus, who turns out to be a ship's cook named Jimmy. He attends to her knee onboard his almost deserted ship. While Peter and Helen dance at a dance hall, Jimmy and Jo get more than playful.

During a slow dance, Peter asks Helen to live with him. When she declines, he teases her about her age and refers to their "mother and son" relationship. Jimmy and Jo discuss their own interlude, and he mentions marriage, saying that his ancestors were from Liverpool and not from Africa; then he beats her bag as if it were a tom-tom and she reciprocates with a dance. Jo tells him that she loves him because he is "daft." Returning home, she finds Helen in the tub and learns of her mother's plans to marry Peter. Jo talks about her sailor. At their next meeting, by a canal, Jimmy gives Jo a ring which she wears on a ribbon.

Peter comes for Helen while she is still dressing and is forced to talk to Jo for a bit. Despite their mutual dislike, Jo admits to Peter that she and Helen do not have much love between them. Although uninvited, Jo joins the lovers and Peter's friends, Bert (David Boliver) and Doris (Moira Kaye), for a day at a Blackpool fair. On the way, Peter shows her a photo of the cottage that he has bought for Helen and himself, and the day ends for Jo when Peter states that she cannot live with them after they wed. Jo leaves, avoiding even Jimmy because she is so upset. Later, Jo spends the night with Jimmy, making love. The next morning, she watches him leave, possibly forever, as he walks along a moving bridge to his ship.

Jo develops a cold and stays in bed for the rest of the day. She asks Helen about her father and she replies that he was "simple" and is now dead. He was the first man with whom she had ever made love. You never forget the first time, she says. Finally, with Helen leaving, Jo gets a job as a shoe saleswoman and rents a large apartment. During a children's parade, she runs into Geoffrey (Murray Melvin), a young homosexual who had been a customer. Jo invites the homeless Geoffrey to stay with her, platonically, although she is curious about his love life. He keeps the place tidy and acts "like a big sister" to Jo. He is also artistic and paints her portrait. One day, under an arch, Jo confirms to him that she is pregnant. As they visit a cave, Geoffrey forces her to kiss him and asks her to marry him so that he can continue to care for her and for the baby. Jo says her lover is a black prince, and Geoffrey admits that he would rather be dead than away from her. In a cemetery, Jo sees a retarded boy and voices fears about her child to Geoffrey. Helen arrives at her daughter's new place, accompanied by a drunken Peter. Some time later, she returns for good, having been kicked out by her husband. Geoffrey leaves because of her, and Jo sadly watches Helen take over. Jo tries to participate in a children's bonfire while Geoffrey silently departs from the shadows.

The last scenes are somewhat depressing, as is most of the film. Yet this depressing aspect was taken as realism in the "Angry Young Men" era and was frequently used in plays and films. The episodic nature of the film seems to reinforce another theme of this genre, that life simply continues on rather than improving. While not in any sense an uplifting film, *A Taste of Honey* is still highly regarded by critics for its unglossed realism and its fine performances.

John Cocchi

TEA AND SYMPATHY

Released: 1956
Production: Pandro S. Berman for Metro-Goldwyn-Mayer
Direction: Vincente Minnelli
Screenplay: Robert Anderson; based on his play of the same name
Cinematography: John Alton
Editing: Ferris Webster
Running time: 122 minutes

Principal characters:
Tom Robinson Lee .... John Kerr
Laura Reynolds .... Deborah Kerr
Bill Reynolds .... Leif Erickson
Ellie Martin .... Norma Crane
Ralph .... Tom Laughlin

In 1958, when Brick (Paul Newman) refused to go to bed with his wife Maggie (Elizabeth Taylor) in the film *Cat on a Hot Tin Roof*, the implications of his avoidance were strongly homosexual, if still allusive. The Tennessee Williams drama had raised the issue of Brick's sexuality on the stage, and the same implications (although obliquely implied) were allowed to stand in the film. In 1956, however, all reference to homosexuality was carefully excised from *Tea and Sympathy*. The problem faced by the adolescent boy in the stage play became a much more ambiguous and generalized sense of confusion on the screen. The actors who played the leads in the play, Deborah Kerr, John Kerr, and Leif Erickson, re-created their roles for the film, which was directed by Vicente Minnelli. Robert Anderson also stayed with the production, writing the screenplay adaptation of his stage success. Together, the creative talents of *Tea and Sympathy* had to work to create a new version of the romance between a schoolboy and headmaster's wife, one which need not mention specifically why that romance involved the solicitious care referred to by the title.

One of the interests of the film *Tea and Sympathy* lies in what it does not say. The problems of manhood faced by Tom Robinson Lee (John Kerr) at the boys' school are phrased with an unspoken alternative providing an important background context. What is not mentioned—homosexuality— must be as important to the boy's efforts to prove his manhood as what is mentioned—insecurity. With the censors' refusal to allow any direct reference to homosexuality, the problem of sexual identity faced by Tom is expressed within a repressive absence of reference which mimics just the sort of hushed avoidance faced by the character in the play. At least in the spirit of its censorship of the play, the film remains true to the dread felt by the boy in the play regarding the possibility that he may be homosexual.

Anderson, of course, watched over the removal of all "topical" references to sexual "perversion" and rewrote his play around the issue. That he was able to do so reflects upon the central issue of the drama, which revolves about problems of persecution, tolerance of difference, the definition of manhood, and the courage required to put oneself on the line for another person in trouble. It treats the problems of identity faced by an adolescent in a more general manner, examining the difficulties of "coming into being" of an adult. The drama is also very strongly concerned with the responsibility of older adults to those who, uncertain of who they are, look to their elders not only for guidance, but also for a willingness to exhibit a real involvement. Again, film morality altered the message of the play to some degree by altering the fate of Laura Reynolds (Deborah Kerr), the wife who does risk giving herself to help the boy. The Breen office, then responsible for overseeing and safeguarding the moral quality of Hollywood films, insisted upon a prologue and epilogue in the film in which the wife would be punished for sleeping with someone other than her husband. Thus in the film some believe that Laura dies as a recompense for her sins, although her fate, as revealed in the letter which her husband gives the boy, seems to point more to a life of loneliness rather than death.

The play had been a very durable success with a long stage run. By the time the film was made, the principals were very familiar with their roles, and Minnelli had little to do in shaping their characters. Minnelli had often been concerned with problems of the realization of desire for characters attempting to integrate their idea of what they would like to be with what they were. So the problems of the boy Tom in *Tea and Sympathy* were well suited to Minnelli's interests. Once the major alterations were made on Anderson's play by the Breen office, the play remained largely intact under Minnelli's careful direction.

Tea and Sympathy is the story of a young man who is enrolled in a boys' school where he does not fit in. Tom is interested in pursuits which are not always regarded as "manly"—music, poetry, and the fine arts, things which the other boys do not like. Although Tom is interested in sports (he likes tennis), the common consensus at the boys school is that baseball is the proper sport for boys. The other boys accuse Tom of being homosexual because he does not share their interest in conventionally "manly" pursuits.

At one point, Tom decides to prove his manliness with the town prostitute, Ellie Martin (Norma Crane). From the moment he decides upon this plan, it is clear that he lacks the confidence to carry it out, and the actual encounter with Ellie is a failure which "proves" what Tom has suspected all along, that he is impotent. Tom thinks that when his classmates learn of his failure with the prostitute, the shame will be unbearable. He is determined that the other boys have taunted him for the last time, and so, in desperation, he attempts suicide.

Clearly, what Tom needs is some sympathetic understanding rather than a competitive relationship of "one upmanship" with the schoolboys. He finds that sympathy in Laura, the headmaster's wife, who shares Tom's interest in music and poetry. What is more, her husband Bill (Leif Erickson) may himself be a latent homosexual, although on this point the film, like the play, remains ambiguous. Laura understands Tom's unhappiness, even understanding his brutalizing attempt to prove himself with Ellie. She therefore takes the risk of helping a boy she likes in a way which is dangerous for her as a wife, but important to him. She sleeps with Tom in the woods, proving to him that he is not impotent with women. Laura understands at what personal cost she has rescued Tom. She risks not only her own reputation as the headmaster's wife, but she also risks the changes that Tom will continue to go through as he grows up. She asks remarkably little in return for her "tea and sympathy." As she is about to make love with Tom, Laura says the lines which are well known from the play, "Years from now, when you talk about this—and you will—be kind."

One small problem with the characters in the film reflects indirectly upon the success of the play. Kerr, playing Tom, had stuck with the long run of the play, and in doing so had gotten older. By the time he made the film, he was looking a little bit old to be enrolled in the boys' school, and this detracted slightly from his effectiveness. A short footnote to the film production involves the head bully, Ralph. Tom Laughlin, who persecuted the boy throughout the film, would much later direct and star in another movie about persecution, the box-office hit *Billy Jack* (1971).

One of the questions addressed by *Tea and Sympathy* is the definition of manliness. Tom has an internal manliness based on character. It is not dependent upon conventional manly pursuits to be operative—that is, to permit relations with women. Gentleness, consideration, and sensitivity are qualities which *Tea and Sympathy* is willing to admit as manly ones. The love story between Tom and Laura stresses the importance of respecting differences in character, differences which develop out of strong needs in a character. Even in its altered cinematic form, the message of tolerance is well developed. It could be said that the film's idea of tolerance survives even the intolerance surrounding its production.

Leslie Donaldson

TELL THEM WILLIE BOY IS HERE

Released: 1969
Production: Philip Waxman
Direction: Abraham Polonsky
Screenplay: Abraham Polonsky
Cinematography: Conrad Hall
Editing: Melvin Shapiro
Running time: 97 minutes

Principal characters:
Willie Boy	Robert Blake
Coop	Robert Redford
Lola	Katherine Ross
Dr. Elizabeth Arnold	Susan Clark
Calvert	Barry Sullivan

Abraham Polonsky's first directorial effort after twenty years of blacklisting would seem, at first glance, a far cry from the big city "crime melodramas" which established him in the late 1940's as a powerful filmmaker and social critic. *Tell Them Willie Boy Is Here* can be fitted into the category of a Western, and yet it cannot be confined totally within the limits of that particular genre. Like all his work, this film concerns the corruption of ideals— the attempt by some to live a good and meaningful life and somehow remain untainted by the corruption around them, and the decision by others to choose the easier way through compromise, while the majority continue to live, unaware and unconcerned, interested only in their self-serving ends.

Willie Boy (Robert Blake), a Paiute Indian, regards the American Dream, an illusion that earlier Polonsky heroes were willing to do anything to attain, as a bitter joke. By the early part of the twentieth century, the period of the film, his people are captives of the whites and have been murdered, robbed, and driven onto reservations. The disenfranchised Indian has seen his people robbed of their land and denied their heritage. Even the girl he loves, Lola (Katherine Ross), has been tainted by the teachings of the Indian school and taught to think like the whites. Thus, although she loves Willie, she is unwilling to join him because she feels that to do so would be beneath her.

Willie Boy nevertheless returns to the reservation for Lola and is determined not to leave without her. In an argument with Lola's father, Willie is forced to kill him in self-defense and flee with Lola as his captive. Coop (Robert Redford), the sheriff of Banning, California, is presented with the unenviable job of tracking the fugitive for whom he has a great measure of respect. Clearly, many members of the posse, fired by the dreams of old Indian-fighting days and encouraged by the lurid stories of Calvert (Barry Sullivan), would just as soon see Willie returned dead as alive. Only Coop perceives Willie's actions in a truer light. He is aware that according to Paiute custom of courtship by capture Willie Boy is not the murderer and kidnaper the whites regard him to be. He, Willie, is obeying another set of laws.

Throughout the film we are presented with a study in contrasts in the relationship of Sheriff Coop and his lover, Elizabeth Arnold (Susan Clark), the well-meaning Indian agent from Boston who has little knowledge of Indian custom and thus wants to see Lola, her protégée, rise above the squalor of reservation life. Coop is a far more complicated figure. Director Polonsky has said that he chose the character's name for its irony. Gary Cooper, who was nicknamed "Coop," never faltered in his films; he always did the right thing instinctively. For him the issues were never muddied and there was no other side to the question. This Coop, however, is like a fish out of water. There exists between Coop and Willie Boy an odd relationship. Both men respect values which have begun to disappear, and they are like mirror images of each other. Although Coop is naturally called upon to lead the posse to bring Willie Boy to justice and rescue Lola, he does so with little enthusiasm but the utmost professionalism. Unlike Willie, professionalism is all that he has. Tradition for Coop exists only in the nostalgic boasts of Calvert, who had fought Indians with Coop's father and who regards the hunt for Willie Boy as a kind of glorious last hurrah.

The posse itself is composed mostly of ineffectual storekeepers, drunks, and bullies from nearby towns such as Banning and Twenty-Nine Palms. Coop is the brains, the solidifying force which manages to keep them on the right trail. Willie respects Coop and rightly regards him as the only worthy adversary among his trackers. Again, the mutual respect of hunter and hunted heightens the sense of their being opposite sides of the same coin. Willie is running toward an uncertain future with Lola, and Coop chasing the past, chasing ghosts in fact, as Willie has by this point donned his Ghost-Shirt which his heritage has taught him will serve as protection against his enemies.

As the posse moves into the desert, Willie leads them in circles. He ambushes them, choosing to shoot the horses instead of the men. Yet gradually he begins to realize the futility of the flight. The posse hears a shot, and soon they come upon the body of Lola. Many curse Willie, assuming that he has killed her, but Coop believes that Lola, realizing that she was slowing Willie up, took her own life. Whatever the truth, Willie's reason for running, for remaining free, and for living, has been taken from him. When Coop eventually tracks him down, Willie allows him to believe that his rifle has a round in the chamber. Rather than be taken alive by his enemies, Willie chooses death. Coop, stunned at having been tricked into murdering the adversary for whom he has had so much respect, is enraged. He allows the Indians to burn Willie's body over the angry protestations of the mob. The last words of the film belong to Coop: "Tell 'em there'll be no more souvenirs."

Tell Them Willie Boy Is Here is a complex film which is only a Western on the surface. Although the story itself is essentially factual, there is a feeling of allegory which pervades the film. The whites, even the best of them such as Coop, lack the tradition which sustains Willie and makes possible his superhuman run. In killing Willie, Coop kills that part of himself which he had previously kept safe from the corruption and exploitation of civilization.

Elizabeth, the Indian agent, is regarded as a well-meaning but finally dangerous individual. Her subtle corruption of Lola by introducing her to the white world is partially the cause of Willie's irrevocable act. Had Lola possessed the same sense of herself as Willie did, she would have gone with him willingly. Lola is portrayed as a confused girl torn between both worlds. What Elizabeth does not tell her is that although she has to a large degree abandoned her heritage, she will never be welcomed in white society. As to what fate might await Coop following his unintentional murder nothing is said. His strength will certainly keep him intact, but there is little doubt that he will be haunted by Willie's death for the rest of his days.

For the most part, the acting is top-notch. Ross is surprisingly effective as Lola, a role as far away from her portrayal of Mrs. Robinson's daughter in *The Graduate* (1967) as can be imagined. If she seems too anglicized, one feels this is more the result of her indoctrination by Elizabeth than any shortcomings in Ross's acting. Clark has the stronger woman's role as the Indian Agent. Possessed of a great tenderness and basic good, her job and her need to prove herself equal to men cause her to suppress this side of her nature. She only lets her guard down with Coop, and even then, one feels she regards him as being as savage as the Indians she has made it her life's work to "tame." This distance which she maintains, even with her lover, makes her the loneliest character in the film.

Redford's Coop is close to being a Hemingway type of hero. He does what he must in the face of what he can only regard as an empty and meaningless universe. Unlike his father's friend, Calvert, he has no desire for a return to the "good old days," and yet he is an intelligent man who easily recognizes that, like Willie, he is an anachronism. This knowledge makes his role as leader of the posse a particularly ironic and poignant one.

By far the main character is Willie himself. Polonsky's early successes with John Garfield is repeated here with Blake. Both actors possess a smoldering anger which is manifested in their hatred of the injustice which surrounds and threatens to engulf them, and both project a violence not far beneath the surface. Blake is no cigar-store Indian here. His strength is so palpable that he is able to create a towering figure in Willie Boy working with dialogue which is, for the most part, extremely spare and laconic.

Not one to allow the ironies of the period to slip past, Polonsky anchors the story in time by juxtaposing the manhunt with the imminent arrival of President Taft on a whistlestop tour through the Southwest. Much fun is made of corrupt politicians and the President's enormous girth. At the heart of *Tell*

Them Willie Boy Is Here, however, is the tragedy of what native Americans have suffered at the hands of their usurpers. Cheated, exploited, ridiculed, and murdered, all their hopes, even the simple dream of Willie Boy to find a place where he and Lola might live their lives in dignity, are thwarted at every turn. This important, angry film chronicles with brilliance and compassion an American tragedy.

Michael Shepler

10

Released: 1979
Production: Blake Edwards and Tony Adams for Orion
Direction: Blake Edwards
Screenplay: Blake Edwards
Cinematography: Frank Stanley
Editing: Ralph E. Winters
Music: Henry Mancini
Song: Henry Mancini and Robert Wells
Running time: 122 minutes

Principal characters:
George Webber .... Dudley Moore
Sam .... Julie Andrews
Jenny .... Bo Derek
Hugh .... Robert Webber
Mary Lewis .... Dee Wallace
Bartender .... Brian Dennehy
Reverend .... Max Showalter
Mrs. Kissel .... Nedra Volz
Dr. Miles .... James Noble

In the course of his career, writer/director Blake Edwards has enjoyed commercial and critical success with such diverse films as *Operation Petticoat* (1959), *Breakfast at Tiffany's* (1961), and *Days of Wine and Roses* (1962). In spite of his versatility, however, he is most often associated with a series of films starring Peter Sellers as the outrageous comic character Inspector Clouseau and usually identified by a title reference to a cartoon character known as the Pink Panther. Both Clouseau and the Panther are Edwards' creations, and they saw him through a difficult period in the 1970's. He had achieved artistic maturity, but his films did not find favor, most unfortunately in the case of those starring his wife Julie Andrews, who had been a popular star in the 1960's. As a result, Edwards was exiled to "Pantherland," making three financially successful films in a row about the adventures of the ridiculous French detective, the last of which betrays a certain tiredness. Edwards' distaste for the continuation of the films and Sellers' death in 1980 ended this collaboration, although there has been discussion of a new batch of Pink Panther films with a new star and new director.

10, one of Edwards' finest achievements, has precisely the richness of tone that had necessarily been suppressed in the Panther films which immediately preceded it. At the same time, it demonstrates that Edwards had kept his comic skills sharp with the tireless invention of gags which distinguish his collaboration with Sellers. Among contemporary comedies, *10* stands virtually alone for the hilarity of its physical comedy. Mastery of an art as difficult and specifically cinematic as slapstick should not be dismissed even in works as light as the Panther films. In a film such as *10*, this mastery has uncommon value, the emotional seriousness of the subject remaining consistently fresh and appealing as a result of the delirious comic frenzy which accompanies and complements it.

The story relates the misadventures of George Webber (Dudley Moore), a successful composer of popular songs who has entered a midlife crisis on reaching the age of forty-two. The opening scenes, played straightforwardly, introduce George's girl friend Sam (Julie Andrews), an actress and singer, and his lyricist-partner Hugh (Robert Webber). Driving home from Hugh's beach house, George observes a young woman, Jenny (Bo Derek), who is on her way to her wedding in another car. Entranced by her beauty, he follows her, crashing head-on into a police car in front of the church. He eavesdrops on the wedding, only to be stung by a bee, but his interest in the mysterious young woman is undiminished. In subsequent scenes, he becomes increasingly impatient with both Sam and Hugh. His relationship with Sam is failing to console him, and the two have a fight which circumstances prevent from being readily mended. Hugh, a homosexual, has his own problems with his young boyfriend, and George's unprompted nastiness during a work session strains the friendship of the two partners.

In the meantime, George learns Jenny's identity from the minister who performed the ceremony (Max Showalter), suffering through an example of the Reverend's woefully amateurish songwriting in the process, and has four cavities filled by Jenny's dentist father (James Noble) in an attempt to find out where she is honeymooning. Nursing his swollen and aching mouth with brandy and pain pills, George impulsively decides to fly to Mexico. The nightmarish journey is no help to his physical condition, but some needed sleep and a few more brandys in the quiet of the hotel bar finally restore him. At the hotel, he sees Jenny once more, and the next day on the beach, he saves her young husband, who has fallen asleep on a raft, from drifting out to sea. With the sunburned husband in the hospital, George finally has his chance with Jenny, but her too-casual sexual willingness and emotional superficiality alienate him and he retreats from the encounter. The final scenes show him returning home, doing his part to mend his differences with Hugh and reconciling with Sam. The ending affirms that his love for and appreciation of Sam have deepened and that the relationship is now stronger than ever before.

This relatively simple narrative frame is sustained for two hours by an abundance of captivating situations and characters. The brief exposition which establishes sympathy for George ends with his listening to a tape of Sam singing a lovely, haunting song, presumably one of his compositions, as he drives home from the beach. It is into this mood of tenderness that Edwards daringly thrusts the first gag, the crash into the police car, with hilarious effect. From that point on, he continually varies the tone, thoughtful character development being disarmingly displaced by absurd comic situations at every turn. His visual strategies for the staging of these gags is never predictable. The much-praised sequence of the elderly Mrs. Kissel (Nedra Volz) crossing the length of a room to serve tea to George and the Reverend gains its comic effect from being shot in one long take. The many comic bits involving George's physical discomfort build on one another so that each excruciating moment makes his luckless struggle with physical reality more bizarre. The movie reaches a peak of hilarity when George travels to Mexico, awaking with a startled cry as the plane makes a bumpy landing. Two ensuing sight gags, realized in a contrasting manner, display the director's visual imagination at its most inspired. In the first, the taxi which screeches down the streets of the little Mexican town stops abruptly in front of the hotel in an extreme long shot, and George is barely discernible as he is tossed forward shrieking in agony. The second gag begins with a shot of a band of musicians playing mariachi music, which is then altered by a sudden zoom to a terrified, hungover George, revealing that the musicians are playing directly beneath the balcony of his room.

The humor of *10* is exhilarating, more so for coexisting with the romantic sentiments which Edwards unambiguously endorses. The film is set in an atmosphere of sexual freedom which bedevils the hero, who is essentially a sensitive man ill-suited to the casualness with which much of contemporary life is lived. Jenny has a value for him, but as a fantasy figure rather than as a real person. After saving her husband's life, he sits at the piano in the bar playing his latest composition (which will later be heard as a completed song), visions of romance with Jenny intercut with the actuality of the scene. Absorbed by the intensity with which he interprets his music as much as by the wish-fulfillment of the reverie, he gives the impression of being a man whose romantic impulses require a lover possessing a similar sensibility. Lacking such a lover, he expresses himself most completely through his creative gifts. Walking out of his fantasy life and becoming a real woman, Jenny has nothing to give him. Sam, on the other hand, has the genuine sexual allure of the woman for whom love is passionate and emotional. A cut from the final shot of Derek, alone on her bed and oddly disenchanting in her magnificent nudity, to Andrews performing in period costume reveals through visual contrast an explicit attitude which has the force of a moral. Contrary to its apparent premise, the true *10* of this film is Andrews.

The values the film celebrates are touchingly confirmed by those characters whom Edwards has created from his heart. The Mexico sequences present two such characters, incidental to the plot but essential to the emotional tone of the film. One is the bartender (Brian Dennehy) for whom George feels an instinctive kinship. The other is Mary Lewis (Dee Wallace), an insecure

woman only slightly younger than George, whom he picks up in the bar.
Plagued by melancholy and exhaustion, George is unable to be aroused by
her, and she launches into an endearing account of her romantic misfortunes
("I just don't bring out the man in men"). These two warm-hearted characters
are significantly the only people in the bar when George plays the piano, and
they both give him their undivided attention.

Hugh is an even more memorable character, with Webber's rugged mas-
culinity undermining any possibility of a conventional response to his homosexuality. In his final scene, he speaks with George on the telephone after he
has thrown out his lover (a male counterpart to Jenny), and the two partners
share a moment of communion only partly accounted for by the new song for
which Hugh has now provided lyrics ("It's Easy to Say I Love You"). In this
brief exchange, it becomes evident that Hugh and George are fundamentally
alike, and the success of their collaboration takes on an emotional meaning.

Webber, Wallace, and Dennehy give superb performances in *10*, but Moore
deserves to be singled out for praise. Moore's previous experience in the art
of creating a complete characterization was not considerable, and he was cast
in *10* at the last moment after George Segal left the project on the first day
of shooting. The versatility Moore demonstrates is remarkable. He gamely
earns every laugh, and he is both sympathetic and convincing in the film's
quieter, more serious moments. His performance also benefits from his genuine musical abilities. He plays the piano himself, and at the fadeout, he sings
a duet with Andrews.

Edwards' conception of George as a composer of popular songs is a moving
tribute to Henry Mancini. The bittersweet sophistication of Mancini's best
melodies has been an invaluable element of the director's films over the years.
"Moon River" and "Days of Wine and Roses" are among the haunting and
evocative songs which Mancini has written for those films, and both the
Andrews solo early in the film and "It's Easy to Say I Love You" are beguiling
additions. George is not Mancini, any more than he is Edwards himself, but
George does embody Edwards' profound respect for popular songwriters as
artists. It is just this kind of respect that the creator of popular films such as
10 himself deserves.

Blake Lucas

THE TEN COMMANDMENTS

Released: 1956
Production: Cecil B. De Mille for Paramount
Direction: Cecil B. De Mille
Screenplay: Aeneas MacKenzie, Jesse L. Lasky, Jr., Jack Gariss, and Fredric M. Frank
Cinematography: Loyal Griggs, John F. Warren, and W. Wallace Kelley
Editor: Anne Bauchens
Art Direction: Hal Pereira, Walter H. Tyler, and Albert Nozaki; set decoration, Sam M. Comer and Ray Moyer
Special effects: John Fulton (AA)
Costume design: Edith Head, Ralph Jester, John Jensen, Dorothy Jeakins, and Arnold Friberg
Sound: Loren L. Ryder (AA)
Music: Elmer Bernstein
Running time: 219 minutes

Principal characters:
Moses	Charlton Heston
Rameses	Yul Brynner
Nefretiri	Anne Baxter
Sephora	Yvonne DeCarlo
Dathan	Edward G. Robinson
Sethi	Sir Cedric Hardwicke
Joshua	John Derek
Lilia	Debra Paget
Bithia	Nina Foch
Memnet	Judith Anderson
Aaron	John Carradine
Baka	Vincent Price
Yochabel	Martha Scott
Miriam	Olive Deering
Jannes	Douglas Dumbrille
Pentaur	Henry Wilcoxon
Amminadab	H. B. Warner

The Hollywood Biblical epic is most often associated with the name of Cecil B. De Mille, although he did not originate the genre. D. W. Griffiths previously had filmed *Judith of Bethulia* in 1913, and his *Intolerance* (1916) dramatizes the Old Testament story of the fall of Babylon and the New Testament Life of Christ. Another quasi-Biblical epic, the 1925 *Ben-Hur*, directed by Fred Niblo, was an immense hit. Although De Mille made a great many other films, he directed four Biblical pictures and one other dealing with early Christianity which made his name synonymous with that type of film. His first was *The Ten Commandments* (1923), most of which dealt with a story of 1920's decadence in which the Ten Commandments are broken by one brother, who comes to a bad end, while his good brother keeps the Commandments and triumphs. De Mille decided to precede his cautionary tale with a prologue dramatizing the Book of Exodus, however, showing the liberation of the Hebrews from Egyptian bondage, their trek across Sinai, the parting of the Red Sea, and Moses' receiving of the Ten Commandments. The modern story has long been forgotten; what audiences remember is the spectacle of the Egyptian scenes. A consummate showman, De Mille realized that if he was to film parts of the Bible, he must not merely preach but provide spectacle, dramatic excitement, and the sin (including liberal amounts of sex) that preceded salvation.

De Mille provided all these ingredients again in *King of Kings* (1927), a retelling of the life of Christ. Although he dealt reverently with the gospels and used only Biblical texts for his titles, he worked in a lurid romance between Judas and Mary Magdalene before her repentance and portrayed Magdalene's harlotry on a scale to rival Cleopatra's. Setting a model for all subsequent Biblical films, De Mille produced an epic, with vast hordes of extras, immense sets, and a spectacular earthquake following the Crucifixion.

In 1932, De Mille made another epic of early Christianity, *The Sign of the Cross*; this film does not have any Biblical scenes but deals with the persecution of the Christians under Nero. Along with its uplifting religious elements, it also portrays the decadence of a homosexual Nero and his promiscuous empress Poppea, extravagant orgies, carnal temptations, torture chambers, gladiatorial combats, and other horrors of the arena.

Thereafter, De Mille departed from religious themes; his *The Crusades* (1935) has a touch of religiosity, but otherwise he devoted himself to epics of American history for the next seventeen years, during which no one else made Biblical films either. De Mille did not return to a Biblical story until 1949, when he made *Samson and Delilah*, with Victor Mature and Hedy Lamar. Paramount's executives were skeptical about a film derived from the Book of Judges, but De Mille quickly pointed out the possibilities for eroticism, violence (Samson fighting a lion, bashing the Philistines with the jawbone of an ass, being blinded), and spectacle (the destruction of the temple), and they were convinced. Despite its almost laughable acting and story, *Samson and Delilah* was such an immense commercial success that it ushered in a nineteen-year-revival of the Biblical film, from 1949 to *The Bible* (1968). In the first half of the 1950's, the genre flourished with *Quo Vadis* (1951), *David and Bathsheba* (1952), *The Robe* (1953), *Demetrius and the Gladiators* (1954), and *Salome* (1954).

De Mille therefore decided to get back into Biblical epics with the biggest of them all, a remake of *The Ten Commandments*, this time with sound, color, and the new wide screen, plus more sophisticated special effects. This version would not have a modern story prefaced by the Exodus of the Israelites but would deal entirely with the life of Moses form infancy to imminent death. De Mille decided to film the Exodus on location in Egypt and Sinai. The logistical problems were formidable, but he persevered. The company went to Egypt in October, 1954, and studio filming finished on August 13, 1955.

The screenplay alone took three years to complete and was the work of four writers. Jesse Lasky, Jr., and Fredric M. Frank had worked on earlier films for De Mille; to them he added two writers new to him—Aeneas MacKenzie and Jack Gariss. For the early part of Moses' life, which the Old Testament leaves largely blank, they drew in part from the novel *Moses, Prince of Egypt* by Howard Fast.

De Mille said that he never had any doubt who would play the lead. For Moses, he picked Charlton Heston, who had played the owner of the circus in De Mille's 1952 Best Picture Oscar-winner, *The Greatest Show on Earth*. Heston's other films to that time consisted mostly of formula adventure fare, but he had a solid background of stage and television work, had done a good deal of Shakespeare, and had played Marc Anthony in a 1950 film of *Julius Caesar*. He had the stature and voice for heroic roles, and bearded and in costume, he bore a striking resemblance to Michelangelo's Moses. (Later he was to play Michelangelo himself in *The Agony and the Ecstasy*, 1965.) For Rameses, De Mille cast Yul Brynner after seeing him on stage in *The King and I*. Brynner had not yet appeared in a film (he would win the Oscar for his first, *The King and I*, released shortly before *The Ten Commandments*), but De Mille found him capable of portraying the regal arrogance required for the role. Cornel Wilde, the trapeze artist in *The Greatest Show on Earth*, was offered the part of Joshua but declined it, and it went to John Derek, the star of numerous "B"-class swashbucklers. The voice of God in the Burning Bush was Heston's; a different voice (De Mille would not reveal whose) was used for God when He gives the Ten Commandments.

The film opens with the birth of Moses to a Hebrew slave (Martha Scott), who then places the infant (Heston's own son Fraser, now a screenwriter) adrift on a raft of bullrushes. He is found by the Egyptian princess Memnet (Nina Foch), who rears him as her own son, with his real mother as nursemaid. Thus Moses grows to manhood as a prince of Egypt. Pharoah Sethi (Sir Cedric Hardwicke) favors him over his own son, the arrogant and vicious Rameses. The two princes are rivals not only for the Pharoah's throne but also for the hand of the sensual princess Nefretiri (Anne Baxter). She also favors Moses. The apocryphal part of the drama deals with the conflict between the two young, haughty princes. Rameses is the warlike one. To compete with him for the Pharaoh's favor, Moses builds an immense new city. During its construction, he unwittingly saves the life of his mother, now a slave greasing the blocks upon which the monolithic building stones are being hauled. Her robe catches in the machinery, and she is about to be crushed to death, as the foremen are not about to stop the work for the life of a miserable slave, but Moses intercedes to save her. He also finds himself becoming involved with another Hebrew slave, Joshua (John Derek), when the latter incurs the wrath of the vicious overseer Baka (Vincent Price), who lusts after Joshua's beloved Lilia (Debra Paget).

Meanwhile, Rameses is doing his best to discredit Moses. As he becomes more involved with the Hebrews, Moses discovers the truth of his ancestry, realizing that he belongs to the tribe of despised slaves. Yet he is the same person, of no less worth as a human being, and he therefore comes to recognize the worth of the Hebrews. Without revealing his Jewish identity to the Egyptians, he tries to help the Israelites. When Baka, who has ordered them to perform the nearly impossible task of making bricks without straw, drives Joshua to the breaking point, Moses kills him.

Meanwhile, Princess Nefretiri has also learned of Moses' identity, but loving him and fearing Rameses, she murders the spy who has discovered that her lover is Jewish. Her crime is of no avail, however, for Rameses has also made the discovery. When the Pharaoh asks him what he has done to match Moses' gift of the treasure city, he responds by producing Moses in chains and denouncing him as a traitor and a murderer. Heartbroken, Sethi is forced to condemn his favorite; he turns him over to Rameses for punishment but forbids the vindictive prince to take his life. Accordingly, Rameses turns him loose in the desert, expecting him to die there. Moses survives the agonizing ordeal in Sinai and arrives, more dead than alive, at a community of Jewish shepherds. There he recovers, marries a Midianite shepherdess Sephora (Yvonne DeCarlo), and lives for years as an obscure shepherd himself. One day, however, he sees a burning bush on a hillside, and from it the voice of God commands him to return to Egypt and to set his people free. Together with his brother Aaron (John Carradine), Moses returns to Egypt.

In the interval since his departure, Sethi has died, his last words being of Moses. Rameses is now the Pharaoh and rules with an iron tyranny. When Moses reappears, Rameses greets him with scorn, but even he is awed when, at Moses' command, Aaron's rod performs miracles that seem feats of magic stronger than any that the Egyptian magicians can accomplish. When the latter produce serpents to attack the Jewish ambassadors, Aaron's rod turns into a serpent that devours the others. When he touches his rod to a pool of water in the court, it turns to blood that spreads through all the waters of Egypt. Still the Pharaoh refuses to let the Hebrews go. Meanwhile, his queen Nefretiri, still in love with Moses and despising her evil husband, goes to see Moses, but he now rebuffs her. Her love turns to hatred when the final plague of Egypt—the death of all the firstborn sons—kills her son as well. This plague breaks Rameses' spirit, and he finally lets the Hebrews go.

His now vengeful queen taunts him with weakness and persuades him to pursue the departing Israelites and kill Moses, who, she feels, has killed their son. The Egyptian army comes in sight of the Hebrews just as they seem trapped on the shores of the Red Sea. Moses raises his staff, however, and to everyone's amazement parts the waters of the Red Sea. The fearful Israelites proceed onto the sea floor and cross between towering walls of water that threaten to engulf them. Just as they reach the other side, the Egyptian chariots dash into the sea in pursuit. When they are all racing across the sea floor, Moses again raises his staff, and the walls of water crash down and drown the Egyptians. Rameses returns to his queen in impotent rage.

The Hebrews then cross the Sinai peninsula, where Dathan (Edward G. Robinson), a Jewish traitor who had collaborated with the Egyptians but was expelled to go reluctantly with his people, corrupts them with his demagoguery. To save Joshua's life back in Egypt, Lilia had become Dathan's mistress. Now, while Moses goes up into Mount Sinai, Dathan persuades the fearful Israelites to deny their god and worship a golden calf with depraved heathen orgies. Angered at their falseness, God engraves the Ten Commandments on two stone tablets that Moses carries down with him from the mountain. When Moses sees his followers reveling in worship of the golden calf, he dashes down the tablets in rage. The ground then opens in an earthquake that swallows up Dathan, the golden calf, and some of the revelers. Restored to their faith, the remaining Hebrews now follow Moses until they are in sight of the promised land. Moses himself is not to enter it; he turns over the leadership to Joshua and prepares to die, and the film ends as he watches the now free Hebrews march off to the promised land.

After premiering in Salt Lake City, Utah, *The Ten Commandments* opened in New York on November 9, 1956. The critical reception was luke-warm; intellectuals objected to De Mille's blending of straightforward Biblical drama with some ingredients of sex and sadism, accused the work of lacking subtlety, and were supercilious at De Mille's middlebrow taste. Despite some sophisticated technology, it was basically an old-fashioned piece of filmmaking, stronger on melodrama than subtlety, but reviewers conceded that it was an energetic and robust film, with vigorous if not particularly complex performances. It did receive six Academy Award nominations, including Best Picture, and won two of them, for Sound and Special Effects.

The churches and churchgoers loved *The Ten Commandments*, and it won the Torah Award from the League of United Synagogues. It was immensely popular; by 1959, it had grossed $83,600,000 and had been seen by some 98,500,000 people. As sheer spectacle, it dwarfed most of the competition. Particularly impressive were the building of the new city, the plagues of Egypt, the Exodus, and the parting of the Red Sea. For the angel of death, De Mille devised a sinister cloud that reaches down with clawlike fingers, from which a greenish pestilence spreads. Perhaps the best sequence is the Exodus, for despite the cast of eight thousand, the episode concentrates on individual human details—families packing their belongings, anxieties over what or whom might be left behind, pet animals rounded up, and the sheer joyfulness of the release. The Hebrews depart through the 107-foot-high city gates of Per-Rameses and progress through an avenue of sphynxes (all with the face of Brynner) a quarter of a mile long. The parting of the Red Sea is awesome but not altogether believable, for as *The New York Times* critic Bosley Crowther observed, the sea bottom looks "as smooth and dry as a race track," and the threatening walls of water occasionally seem like the work of animators. Nevertheless, De Mille got his money's worth. The production cost $13,282,712.35, making it at the time one of the most expensive movies ever made.

The cast is fine; Heston is stalwart as Moses, Brynner regally tyrannical as Rameses, Baxter seductive as Nefretiri, Hardwicke urbane as Sethi, and the rest play their roles with conviction. The only problem is that Heston was made to age far too rapidly; by the end, he is a white-haired patriarch, while Joshua and Lilia are still young people who have not aged perceptibly.

The Ten Commandments launched Heston into a string of epics and led to his Oscar-winning role as Ben-Hur. It also gave added impetus to the Biblical spectacle and was followed by *Solomon and Sheba* (1959), *Ben-Hur* (1959), *King of Kings* (1961), *Barabbas* (1962), *The Greatest Story Ever Told* (1965, with Heston as John the Baptist), and *The Bible* (1968), plus other ancient-world epics such as *Spartacus* (1960) and *Cleopatra* (1963). Eventually prohibitive cost plus several fiascoes brought the genre to an end, except in the form of an occasional television movie.

The Ten Commandments was the last film De Mille directed; he lent his name to a remake of *The Buccaneer* (1958), but it was produced by long-time De Mille actor Henry Wilcoxon and directed by De Mille's son-in-law, actor Anthony Quinn. De Mille suffered a heart attack while filming *The Ten Commandments*; another attack killed him in January, 1959. Although his works have been criticized for lack of subtlety, he was a pioneer filmmaker in many areas and one of the few directors whose name was enough to sell a picture to the public. Aimed at popular tastes, his films were immensely successful according to the terms by which he created them. *The Ten Commandments* sums up everything he accomplished and is perhaps his most lasting monument.

Robert E. Morsberger

THE TERROR

Released: 1928
Production: Warner Bros.
Direction: Roy del Ruth
Screenplay: Harvey Gates; based on the play of the same name by Edgar Wallace
Cinematography: Chick McGill
Editing: Thomas Pratt and Jack Killifer
Running time: 80 minutes

Principal characters:
Olga Redmayne	May McAvoy
Mrs. Elvery	Louise Fazenda
Ferdinand Fane	Edward Everett Horton
Doctor Redmayne	Alec B. Francis
Joe Connors	Matthew Betz
Goodman	Holmes Herbert
Alfred Katman	John Miljan
Soapy Marks	Otto Hoffman
Narrator	Conrad Nagel
Cotton, the butler	Frank Austin

The Lights of New York, released by Warner Bros. in the summer of 1928, became the first all-talking film. It is only important for that historical reason, because it did little else but talk for a total of fifty-seven minutes; in terms of action, it was the crudest kind of gangster movie. It could not compare, for example, with Sternberg's splendid silent, *Underworld*, released the previous year. It appeared that if movies were going to talk, everything that had been learned during the silent days which had made films an important art form was going to be dismissed in favor of nothing but dialogue.

In August, a month after the disastrous premiere of *The Lights of New York*, Warner Bros. presented its second all-talking feature, *The Terror*, based on an Edgar Wallace play that had been highly successful in London, but had never even been produced on Broadway. *The Terror* boasted a vast improvement over its predecessor. There were still many technical flaws, but at least there was talk *and* action advancing the story. There were no expository subtitles, but the voice of Conrad Nagel (uncredited) was used both to give the credits for the film, and to speak the narration that bridged certain sequences. For the audiences of 1928, it worked, and *The Terror* is legitimately all-talking, and in every sense of the word a moving picture.

It is not a good film, however, for it has more faults than virtues. Its actors recite their lines more often than they speak them naturally, but there is an attempt made by those who had experience on the stage to give characterization to their dialogue. Both in the United States and in England, where audiences even hooted at some of the speech anachronisms, there were certain actors who were singled out for the professional way in which they delivered their lines—in particular, Edward Everett Horton and John Miljan.

The Terror is a mystery that evokes a degree of suspense and danger. It is about a maniacal criminal known as "The Terror" who is at large in the English countryside; he haunts an old tavern where strange things occur such as the playing of music on the organ at night. A hooded figure in black seen prowling around the house terrifies its inhabitants, especially the heroine, Olga Redmayne (May McAvoy), who spends most of the film retreating in silent terror or screaming hysterically when she is attacked.

The old tavern seems to have been selected as the meeting place for "The Terror" and two ex-convicts, Soapy Marks (Otto Hoffman) and Joe Connors (Matthew Betz), recently released from prison, who plan vengeance upon "The Terror" (whom they call "Shea") for having framed them for the robbery that brought them a ten-year prison sentence and allowed him ten years to enjoy the money stolen in the bank robbery.

Living in the tavern is an eccentric old lady, Mrs. Elvery (Louise Fazenda), a spiritualist who tries to conjure up contacts from the world beyond who can explain the ghostly happenings. A heavy storm, typically complete with rain, thunder, and lightning, descends upon the countryside, and in the midst of it a man, Ferdinand Fane (Edward Everett Horton), arrives, complicating everything by his own peculiar conduct. He is only pretending to be weird, however, for he is really a detective with a lead on the real identity of "The Terror." The climax comes when "The Terror" corners Olga, and is on the verge of killing her when he is attacked by Fane, then unmasked, and apprehended.

There is about as much subtlety in the story as there is in a comic strip, but audiences flocked to attend the film everywhere it was shown. In New York it played a twice-daily engagement with top tickets selling for two dollars, and capacity audiences revealed that the all-talking feature was more than a novelty; it was a form of entertainment audiences really wanted and would pay to see.

Dialogue benefited some of the players. Horton, an accomplished stage comedian in Los Angeles who staged his own productions of the best in Pacific Coast theater, immediately found himself in great demand as a talking film comedian. During the rest of the 1920's and all of the 1930's, he worked constantly in talking films by day and on the local stage at night.

For McAvoy, on the other hand, the advent of the talking feature meant the end of her career as a film actress. Her voice was not really bad, and she certainly did not lisp, as certain commentators later carelessly said she did. She had not, however, been a trained stage actress. Few women had voices to which the early Vitaphone was kind. Even accomplished stage stars such as Pauline Frederick and Doris Kenyon suffered in their initial appearances as recorded by the Vitaphone. McAvoy had been one of Hollywood's best silent leading ladies, in features such as *Sentimental Tommy* (1921), *The Enchanted Cottage* (1924), *Lady Windermere's Fan* (1925), and M-G-M's colossal *Ben Hur* (1926). She was also leading lady to Al Jolson in *The Jazz Singer* (1927), although she had almost no dialogue in that film.

Now, after her first all-talking feature, she found herself a target for critics both in America and England. Following *The Terror*, she made only three more motion pictures for Warner Bros., all routine part-talkies, and then she retired. Years later she returned to films under contract to M-G-M on a stock deal awarded several silent players regarded as dependable who could play bits. She survived all her colleagues, and then retired again. She at least found her own happiness apart from that real terror, the microphone, which had really destroyed the careers of established stars such as Norma Talmadge, Vilma Banky, and Corinne Griffith, who, like McAvoy, were attacked by critics because of their inability to handle dialogue with any distinction.

Meanwhile, the all-talking feature, with dialogue and sound recorded on Vitaphone discs, only continued for a short time at Warner Bros. Soon all studios, including Warners, recorded on optical sound tracks. None of the early Vitaphone all-talking features has survived. Silent versions were released simultaneously for viewing in foreign countries and the American hinterlands, wherever there were theaters that had not yet installed expensive talking equipment. Even those silent versions, however, are now rarities.

DeWitt Bodeen

TEST PILOT

Released: 1938
Production: Louis D. Lighton for Metro-Goldwyn-Mayer
Direction: Victor Fleming
Screenplay: Vincent Lawrence and Waldemar Young; based on a story by
  Frank Wead
Cinematography: Ray June
Editing: Tom Held
Running time: 118 minutes

Principal characters:
Jim Lane .... Clark Gable
Ann Barton .... Myrna Loy
Gunner Sloane .... Spencer Tracy
Drake .... Lionel Barrymore
Landlady .... Marjorie Main

The Hollywood studio system has received a good deal of abuse, much of
it deserved, but it did produce a number of the classics of cinema as well as
a greater number of lesser works with definite virtues of their own. A prime
example of the latter type of film is *Test Pilot*, for which M-G-M brought
together three stars, excellent supporting actors and actresses, a strong and
knowledgeable script, and a first-rate director.

At the very beginning of the film we meet two of the three main characters
and learn what sort of men they are and what the relationship between them
is. Jim Lane (Clark Gable) is a test pilot who enjoys his dangerous work and
also enjoys women and drink when he is not working. In contrast to the
reckless Jim is his friend and mechanic, Gunner Sloane (Spencer Tracy).
Gunner, we learn, is Jim's caretaker; he tries to see that Jim's off-duty indul-
gences do not interfere with his ability to do his work well. He has taken upon
himself the thankless task of attempting to get the daring pilot to bid good-
bye to women and drinks in time to get enough sleep for the next day's
demanding job.

The third main character comes into the film when Jim's try for a coast-to-
coast flight record goes awry because he has engine trouble over Kansas and
makes an emergency landing at the farm where Ann Barton (Myrna Loy)
lives. In the usual pattern of romantic comedies, Jim and Ann are two quite
different people unexpectedly thrown together who fight at first but finally
fall in love. In this film, however, the process is speeded up, and the film
then goes on to other matters. They find in each other something missing
from their previous lives. Ann is unexcited about the life she sees before her
of being a farmer's wife in Kansas, and Jim says that sitting on her front porch
he has found peace for the first time since he was born. When they go to a

baseball game together, he finds that this college-educated farm girl is just as enthusiastic and knowledgeable a fan as anyone.

There is some confusion about what they mean to each other, and when Jim takes off in his airplane the next morning, they do not expect to see each other again. When she finally breaks into tears, Gunner, who has come to help repair the airplane and who knows the difficulty of being with Jim, says to her, "You'll be glad in the end." When Jim flies over the baseball field, however, he realizes that he cannot leave her. He returns, picks up Ann, and the two are married when they stop in Indianapolis, less than two days after their first meeting.

The focus then shifts to the attempts of the three to adjust to being together and especially to Ann's endeavor to cope with being married to this undisciplined man with an extremely dangerous job. Gunner says that now he is going to be "associated with two nuts instead of one," and Ann says to Gunner, "Help me make you like me," but it is Jim who is the major concern for both of them. They watch him fly in an airplane race in Cleveland. When his airplane catches on fire and he will not stop, Ann becomes afraid. Not at all calm himself, Gunner calls Ann a sucker for marrying Jim without even thinking about his work, which is "death every time you move." Despite the fire, Jim wins the race and the $10,000 prize, but another flier is not so lucky: we see him carried off in an ambulance as his wife fruitlessly tries to catch up with it and his children cry for their mother.

When Jim then disappears for a five-day drunken spree during which he spends or loses all the $10,000, Ann finally realizes what she is up against. She sees that he must be the kind of man he is and that the road they are on will end in his death. Gunner understands exactly; he has been on the same road for ten years: "He gets you—there's no fun being with anyone else." Ann says she does not want to love him that much and that she is leaving him. Jim, who has never asked anyone for anything, asks her to stay, and finally she is unable to leave. "Your life is yours," she tells him, but he resolves to settle down. After his next job, a test for the Army in which the wings of the aircraft come off and he has to parachute to safety, he gives the $4,000 check to Ann and takes her to a show instead of going drinking.

Unfortunately, that does not solve all their problems. When Jim and Gunner test a large airplane for the Army, the craft goes into a spin after reaching the altitude Jim was trying to reach. Then the load in the airplane shifts, pinning Gunner in his seat. Jim refuses to parachute out; instead he crash-lands the airplane and pulls the wounded Gunner from the burning wreck before it explodes. Gunner is mortally wounded, however, and dies after telling Jim that at least he will never have to go home and break the news to Ann.

When Ann learns of Gunner's death, she is unable to remain stoical. Even though Jim's attitude is that Gunner died at his trade and that his (Jim's) memory of his friend is beautiful, Ann says she will go crazy waiting for Jim to suffer the same fate. "Why don't you die and leave me alone?" she explodes. Soon afterward Jim discusses the matter with his boss, Mr. Drake (Lionel Barrymore). Jim admits to him that being with Ann will make Gunner's death easier to accept, so Drake advises him to tell her that.

The scriptwriters then fashion an ending which is reasonably happy even though not entirely in keeping with the rest of the film. Drake telephones Ann and tells her that he will arrange for Jim to work on the ground, without his ever exactly realizing what is happening, and next we see an obviously uncomfortable Jim training a group of young pilots. Then Ann arrives with their young son, and the film ends with a shot of the child's face with the departing airplanes of the young pilots superimposed over it.

The screenplay by Vincent Lawrence and Waldemar Young is based upon a story by Frank "Spig" Wead, who was a pilot in World War I and later became a screenwriter. He was himself the subject of a film, *The Wings of Eagles* (1957), directed by John Ford. The *Test Pilot* script intermixes three elements: romantic comedy, exciting aerial drama, and the human drama of the three characters' relationships with one another and with the danger of flying. One particularly amusing scene finds Jim buying a nightgown for Ann while she watches from a discreet distance. He cannot even pronounce the word *lingerie*, but does carry out the task.

The next year, 1939, saw the release of another film on pilots and a woman's attempt to come to terms with one, *Only Angels Have Wings*. Instead of either domesticating or killing the pilot, however, the later film merely ends with the flier (Cary Grant) asking the woman (Jean Arthur) to stay after she has been made fully aware of the life she can expect.

Gable had, by the time this film was made, virtually perfected the role of the dashing adventurer, and he conveys superbly that facet of the character of Jim Lane. Gable had also demonstrated a flair for romantic comedy in *It Happened One Night* (1934), a flair that is evident in many of his scenes with Loy. Loy herself had worked for nearly a decade in near obscurity in Hollywood before the Thin Man films (beginning in 1934) made her a star comedienne. She saw *Test Pilot* as a chance to show that she could play dramatic scenes as well as comedy, and she did so quite convincingly. Tracy had proven in *San Francisco* (1936) that he could play the quiet friend of the irrepressible Gable and he did so again in *Test Pilot* and *Boom Town* (1940), but he let it be known that he did not want to be stuck in the shadow of Gable, and they made no additional films together. The supporting actors and actresses are excellent in *Test Pilot*, most notably Barrymore as Mr. Drake and Marjorie Main as the landlady.

Much of the credit for bringing together the separate elements of *Test Pilot*, which was one of the fifteen most popular films of the year, should probably go to the director, Victor Fleming. He had begun his career in the film industry in 1910, had directed Gable in two early 1930's films, and was to have his greatest year in 1939 when he directed *The Wizard of Oz* and was one of the directors of *Gone with the Wind*, for which he won an Academy Award.

Clifford Henry

THAT'S ENTERTAINMENT

Released: 1974

Production: Jack Haley, Jr., for Metro-Goldwyn-Mayer; released by United Artists

Direction: (new segments) Jack Haley, Jr.

Screenplay: (narration) Jack Haley, Jr.

Cinematography: (new segments) Gene Polito, Ernest Laszlo, Russell Metty, Ennio Guarniri, and Allen Green

Editing: Bud Friedgen and David E. Blewitt

Running time: 127 minutes

That's Entertainment is the most popular compilation film ever made. Compilation films, in which parts of many different films are brought together, have been made for almost as long as the film industry has existed. Most, however, have been documentaries consisting of parts of newsreels, and few have been popular with the general public. In the early 1970's the Metro-Goldwyn-Mayer studio decided to produce a lavish assemblage of the highlights of its famous musical films made between 1929 and 1958. M-G-M was generally acknowledged to have been the source of most of the great musicals of the 1940's and 1950's, but a method of presentation had to be devised that would present the parts of separate films in a unified and aesthetically pleasing manner while still doing justice to the individual numbers.

Jack Haley, Jr., who at the time was head of creative affairs at M-G-M, became producer, director, and writer. Under his general supervision nineteen months of intense effort began. The overall format established was that the film would be divided into many separate segments, each of which would be introduced and narrated by a star connected with the films of that period. Eventually eleven stars were enlisted: Fred Astaire, Bing Crosby, Gene Kelly, Peter Lawford, Liza Minnelli, Donald O'Connor, Debbie Reynolds, Mickey Rooney, Frank Sinatra, James Stewart, and Elizabeth Taylor. Minnelli, of course, was too young to have participated in the glorious days of M-G-M musicals, but as the daughter of Judy Garland and director Vincente Minnelli, her credentials were impressive.

It was found that musical numbers that were effective and appropriate in the context of the film for which they were created usually seemed much too long when shown as part of a series of separate selections. The length of most of the numbers, therefore, was reduced by one-half or more. It was a delicate aesthetic and technical task to make these reductions unnoticeable. Indeed, it is the technical staff—headed by Bud Friedgen, supervising film editor, and David Blewitt, co-film editor—that deserves a great deal of the credit for the success of *That's Entertainment*. It was confronted with a herculean task: to take more than two hundred films, many of which had physically deteriorated or were made with now out-moded materials and methods, excerpt and shorten the principal musical numbers, and combine them all so that they would satisfy the modern viewer who is accustomed to sound and picture quality undreamed of in the early days of the film musical. The staff succeeded. The eighty-four musical sequences finally chosen for the finished film had not looked better since they were first shown, some of them more than forty years before. In addition, the sound editors were frequently able to apply sophisticated technical equipment and procedures to the original soundtracks to make them sound better than they had when they were new.

The film opens with a title announcing that M-G-M is "beginning our next 50 years." Then, after the roar of the famous lion that is the emblem of the studio, a series of clips showing the use of the song "Singin' in the Rain" in four separate films appears. Then, after the titles, Sinatra appears on the steps of the Thalberg building on the M-G-M studio lot to introduce the first segment. This establishes a pattern that continues throughout the film: a star from the old days appears in a contemporary setting at the studio and introduces the next group of numbers. Astaire and Lawford, for example, speak their introductions from the now decaying settings of one of their famous musicals—the train station from *The Band Wagon* (1953) for Astaire and the college setting from *Good News* (1947) for Lawford.

Because it would take several pages merely to list the eighty-four separate selections, only some highlights, groupings, and themes can be described in this essay-review. Besides the group of clips of "Singin' in the Rain," there is a series of excerpts from Esther Williams numbers that show that her swimming ability became little more than a pretext for aquatic extravaganzas, with colored smoke and outlandish choreography by Busby Berkeley. There is also a series of excerpts from the "backyard musicals" starring Rooney and Garland. The plots of these films involved the young characters deciding to put on a show. As the segment reveals, these shows became more and more elaborate as the pair became more and more popular, but the theme was always the same. Another group with a theme, which is introduced by Stewart, shows such non-musical stars as Cary Grant, Jean Harlow, Clark Gable, and Stewart himself singing in various films.

Three performers are presented in long segments—Astaire, Kelly, and Garland. The Astaire segment is introduced by Kelly and naturally begins with "The Babbitt and the Bromide" from *Ziegfeld Follies* (1946), their only appearance on film together, up to that time. Also seen are Astaire's film debut in *Dancing Lady* (1933) and his last appearance with Ginger Rogers, in *The Barkleys of Broadway* (1949). Since the best of the Astaire-Rogers films were made at the RKO studio, they are not represented. In addition, three numbers are shown in which Astaire uses various gimmicks because he disliked doing the same routines over and over. He dances with a hatrack and then with seemingly disembodied feet; then, in a famous sequence from

Royal Wedding (1951), he dances on the walls and ceiling as well as on the floor. Kelly says that film buffs are still arguing about how this sequence was filmed, but actually it was explained in a *Life* magazine article at the time the film was made. A special room that could be turned sideways or upside down was constructed. The camera and the room were then turned upside down during the filming while Astaire remained upright. Because the viewer sees the film from the camera's viewpoint, it appears that the room is upright and Astaire upside down. The segment ends appropriately with Kelly remarking that Astaire needed no gimmicks and was most impressive in simple settings. As a perfect example we see his dance with Cyd Charisse in an unadorned park setting—"Dancing in the Dark" from *The Band Wagon.*

Astaire returns the favor and introduces the Kelly segment. Kelly is seen in what may be the best-known number in film musicals, "Singin' in the Rain" from the film of the same name (1952). Other examples of his dancing come from *The Pirate* (1948), *On the Town* (1949), and *Anchors Aweigh* (1945). In the last he dances with Jerry the Mouse (of the Tom and Jerry cartoons, also produced by M-G-M) in a celebrated combination of animation and live action. The segment is a good demonstration of Kelly's athletic dancing style and outgoing screen *persona.*

Near the end Minnelli appears to introduce and narrate a segment on her mother, Garland. We have already seen several Garland numbers in other segments, but this one shows such items as a rare color short in which she is merely one of the singing Gumm sisters. Also seen are such numbers as an early duet with Deanna Durbin, "The Trolley Song" from *Meet Me in St. Louis* (1944), and—naturally—"Over the Rainbow" from *The Wizard of Oz* (1939).

The film concludes with the ballet from *An American in Paris* (1951), featuring Kelly and Leslie Caron followed by credits that list the composers and lyricists for all the songs. It must be noted that the great majority of the best of the M-G-M musicals came from one unit within the studio—the Freed unit, a talented group of performers, writers, directors, choreographers, and designers headed by Arthur Freed, a lyricist who became a producer in the late 1930's.

That's Entertainment was well-received by both critics and the public. Part of its appeal was frankly nostalgic; many people wanted to be taken back to what seemed a simpler time when musicals offered a delightful escape from the ordinary world. The film offered more than nostalgia, however; it offered a sampling of a popular art form at its best. Indeed, one of the most common criticisms of *That's Entertainment* was that it did not include enough of the classic numbers that many knew so well. It was also faulted for taking the numbers out of their context, but the film was never intended to replace the original films.

That's Entertainment contains many individual masterworks, and overall it is a reminder of a sad fact. As Sinatra remarks in the film about what is arguably its best single number—Astaire and Eleanor Powell tapdancing to "Begin the Beguine"—"You can wait around and hope, but I'll tell you, you'll never see the likes of this again."

Timothy W. Johnson

THAT'S ENTERTAINMENT, PART II

Released: 1976
Production: Saul Chaplin and Daniel Melnick for Metro-Goldwyn-Mayer
Direction: (new sequences) Gene Kelly
Screenplay: (narration) Leonard Gershe
Cinematography: (new sequences) George J. Folsey
Editing: Bud Friedgen and David Blewitt
Title design: Saul Bass
Running time: 130 minutes

As a result of the great success of *That's Entertainment* in 1974, Metro-Goldwyn-Mayer decided to do another anthology of selections from their great films of the 1930's, 1940's, and 1950's. Producers Daniel Melnick and Saul Chaplin conceived a new format for the second film. Instead of using a number of narrators as did the first compilation, *That's Entertainment, Part II* is presented and narrated by only two—Gene Kelly and Fred Astaire. Special sets were built and special visual effects used for the interludes between the sections of the film. These interludes are directed by Kelly and usually feature both Kelly and Astaire occasionally singing and dancing as well as speaking. One—an introduction by Kelly to a segment on M-G-M films set in or connected with France—was actually photographed in Paris. The other significant difference between the two films is that the second includes nonmusical as well as musical selections.

Although critical reaction overall was quite favorable, *That's Entertainment, Part II* provoked another round of criticism of the idea of presenting musical numbers out of the context of their original films. While it must be admitted that a few of the selections do suffer from this treatment, in most instances the criticism is unwarranted; indeed, in some cases an excellent production number is rescued from an otherwise subpar film. In many other cases the number excerpted is not part of the plot of the original film, and thus an appreciation of it does not require an understanding of the entire film. For example, in *The Band Wagon* (1953) the main characters are stage performers and are seen several times in the film performing musical numbers on stage; the novelty number "Triplets," which is shown in *That's Entertainment, Part II*, is one of these stage numbers and therefore is nearly as effective in the anthology film as it is in the original. There are numbers presented in the anthology that have some connection to the plot of the film from which they have been taken, but these have been chosen carefully so that those in the audience who do not know the plot connection can still appreciate the number on its own.

Although the most famous numbers from M-G-M musicals were used in the first *That's Entertainment*, the second compilation is not a collection of second-rate efforts. Indeed, for several films a number shown in *That's*

Entertainment, Part II is actually as good as or better than the more famous one selected for the previous anthology. For example, the first film shows Kelly's almost too-familiar performance of the title song of *Singin' in the Rain* (1951), while the second one shows his artistic and exciting dance with Cyd Charisse to "Broadway Melody" from the same film. The first film presents the formal "They Can't Take That Away from Me" performed by Astaire and Ginger Rogers in *The Barkleys of Broadway* (1949), while the second film shows the joyous informal rehearsal number "Bouncin' the Blues" from the same film also performed by Astaire and Rogers.

One of the most noticeable new features of the second film are the opening titles. Saul Bass, who had designed the famous title sequences for such films as *The Man with the Golden Arm* (1956) and *Anatomy of a Murder* (1959), was given the large number of names to present and responded with a sequence that displays or parodies a multitude of styles of titles. There are names seen on the pages of a book (with a pressed rose on Greta Garbo's page), names written in the sand, names in a bottle washed up on shore, names spelled out in flower petals, and a word spelled out by a band.

It would take an article much longer than this one to note every selection that appears in *That's Entertainment, Part II*, since approximately sixty musical numbers are represented as well as parts of many nonmusical films. Several highlights and themes, however, deserve special notice.

The film affectionately pokes fun at two types of films that flourished in the 1930's—the Jeanette MacDonald-Nelson Eddy operettas and the James Fitzpatrick travelogues. The "Lover Come Back to Me" number from *New Moon* (1940) displays MacDonald and Eddy, and more than one dozen short excerpts from different travelogues clearly demonstrates the Fitzpatrick style, including the narrator continually noting the sun sinking in the West. Another humorous sequence shows the process of composing a song as envisioned in the films of M-G-M. Among these scenes we see the words for the song "Three Little Words" (from the film of the same title, 1950) being suggested by an angry remark by one of the songwriters, and "Tales From the Vienna Woods" (*The Great Waltz*, 1938) being inspired by the sounds of nature during a carriage ride.

Of the nonmusical elements, which naturally suffer much more from being taken out of context than do the musical ones, three are especially memorable. One is a sequence of selections from the films of Katharine Hepburn and Spencer Tracy that shows the talent of each as well as the special chemistry produced when they worked together in such films as *Adam's Rib* (1949) and *Pat and Mike* (1952). Another is the series of scenes in which Garbo says that she wants to be alone. The third is the famous stateroom scene from *A Night at the Opera* (1935), featuring the Marx Brothers. In this scene not only Groucho, Chico, Harpo, and a large steamer trunk are placed into a small stateroom, but also eight or nine other people, including an engineer, a manicurist, and a maid, before the door bursts open.

Other musical highlights abound. Doris Day appears singing "Ten Cents a Dance" from *Love Me or Leave Me* (1955), her first film for M-G-M and one of the two or three best she ever made. A somewhat fictionalized story of the singer Ruth Etting, the portrait of a determinedly ambitious woman who becomes the mistress of a gangster (played by James Cagney) to further her career, was quite a change for Day at that time.

Eleanor Powell's numbers display her marvelous dancing talent, but they also demonstrate M-G-M's unfortunate tendency to submerge that talent in huge production numbers in which she almost became lost. Judy Garland is well represented in a variety of roles, and Maurice Chevalier and Hermione Gingold perform "I Remember It Well," one of the few numbers from *Gigi* (1958) that is able to stand on its own. Nearly all the other songs in *Gigi* are so well integrated into the plot that they suffer greatly when they are seen out of context.

Only one singer has an entire section devoted to himself—Frank Sinatra. Six numbers from five separate films are presented in this section, which seems a bit excessive in view of the fact that no other star is given such a treatment in the film.

Astaire and Kelly, as the premier male musical stars at M-G-M during the 1940's and 1950's, are appropriately represented by approximately ten numbers each. Besides the ones already mentioned, we see such highlights as the title number from Kelly's first film, *For Me and My Gal* (1942), "I Love All of You," with Astaire and Charisse, from *Silk Stockings* (1957), and Leslie Caron and Kelly in "Our Love Is Here to Stay" from *An American in Paris* (1951).

In the last part of *That's Entertainment, Part II*, the number "That's Entertainment" from *The Band Wagon*, performed by Astaire, Charisse, Nanette Fabray, Oscar Levant, and Jack Buchanan, is combined by split screen techniques with the 1976 Kelly and Astaire dancing to and singing the same song. It is a fitting finale for this album of Metro-Goldwyn-Mayer highlights.

Timothy W. Johnson

THEM!

Released: 1954
Production: David Weisbart for Warner Bros.
Direction: Gordon Douglas
Screenplay: Ted Sherdeman; based on Russell Hughes's adaptation of an original story by George Worthington Yates
Cinematography: Sid Hickox
Editing: Thomas Reilly
Running time: 93 minutes

Principal characters:
Robert Graham	James Arness
Sergeant Ben Peterson	James Whitmore
Dr. Harold Medford	Edmund Gwenn
Dr. Patricia Medford	Joan Weldon
Little Girl	Sandy Descher
Crotty	Fess Parker

By the mid-1950's, America was completing its first decade in the atomic era. With the Korean War still fresh in everyone's memory and the Cold War at its height, the testing of nuclear weapons continued in the Southwestern deserts of Nevada and New Mexico. At the same time (and probably not coincidentally), there was a resurgence of interest in science fiction, both in print and on film. Movies from the sublime (*The Day the Earth Stood Still*, 1951) to the ridiculous (Japanese-made *Godzilla Vs. the Smog Monster*, 1972) reached for a piece of the audience's psyche at the dawn of the nuclear age. Gordon Douglas' *Them!* uses one of the staple themes of this genre—nature gone beserk from atomic mutation—but adds something extra. For *Them!* is no mere parade of monsters. In addition to the chills of a horror film, Douglas offers the audience the tension of a good mystery, as the film's protagonists desparately sift through clues in an effort to stop "Them" before "They" take over the earth.

The film begins in the desolate desert of New Mexico, near Alamagordo, the site of many nuclear tests. A little girl (Sandy Descher), obviously in a state of shock, trudges down a dusty road, staring blankly ahead. When she is picked up by Sergeant Ben Peterson (James Whitmore) of the New Mexico State Highway Patrol, she is virtually catatonic, offering no response whatsoever to those trying to help her. Something devastating has obviously happened out on the desert, although as yet we do not know what. Douglas offers us more clues. Sergeant Peterson and a fellow patrolman find an abandoned house trailer and a deserted general store. Both have been ransacked by a seemingly superhuman force—walls have been torn down and furniture demolished, and the store's proprietor has been crushed to death, the barrel of his shotgun twisted like a pretzel—that eliminates mere vandalism as a possibility. Robbery is not a motive either; no money is missing, only sugar. The only other clue is a strange footprint in the sand outside the trailer. At this point, the patrolmen, like the audience, are baffled.

Director Douglas heightens the tension even more, without revealing the nature of the marauders, when one of the patrolmen is murdered by the mysterious killers. Left to guard the store while Sergeant Peterson goes for help, the patrolman hears an eerie chittering sound, such as a bird or an insect might make, only much louder. While the camera remains inside the store, the patrolman walks offscreen to investigate. He sees what remains hidden from the audience. The chittering grows louder, as gunfire and the patrolman's dying scream end the scene.

Sensing that they are out of their depth, the New Mexico authorities bring in outside help. The first to arrive is FBI agent Robert Graham (James Arness), who hears the bizarre medical report on one of the dead men: "There was enough formic acid in him to kill twenty men." Graham is as baffled by the evidence as are the New Mexico police. He and Sergeant Peterson will supply the brawn necessary for the extermination of "Them," but the brain-power is supplied by two United States Department of Agriculture biologists. Dr. Harold Medford (Edmund Gwenn) is the quintessential 1950's film scientist, old, myopic, stubborn, and eccentric, and seeming to wear his hat and topcoat at all times. He also has a beautiful daughter, Pat (Joan Weldon), who has a doctorate in biology as well as good looks. Medford persists in calling her "doctor" throughout the film, although her main function appears to be to provide a low-key romantic interest for FBI man Graham.

The Medfords examine the evidence, finding the formic acid and the casting of the unusual footprint particularly significant. The catatonic girl is brought in, and when Medford waves a vial of formic acid under her nose, she comes to life, shrieking "Them! Them!" It quickly becomes apparent that the Medfords have a pretty good idea what is going on. Maddeningly, however, they refuse to explain their theory to Graham and Peterson. They do not want to start a panic, they say, but instead, they scour the desert, asking the two confused lawmen to help them look for large conical structures.

The group finds the structures and the bizarre killers all at once. The eerie chittering again fills the soundtrack, but this time the attack occurs on camera. "Them" turns out to be ants, grown to enormous size through atomic mutation. The attack is repelled, but there are untold numbers of ants still on the loose. Douglas ends the scene with a background of ominously chittering ants, over which the dour Dr. Medford intones a biblical prophecy about beasts ruling over the earth. "We haven't seen the last of *them*," he says, "we've only had a close view of what may be the beginning of the end of *us*." The mystery of the killers' identity solved, Douglas replaces the "whodunnit" with a "howdunnit": how will Medford, Graham, and Peterson save the world from Them? The second phase of the film begins when Medford discovers that two mutated queens have escaped from the desert around Alamagordo.

Medford and his team fly to Washington, D. C., where Douglas uses the briefing they give to the President and the Joint Chiefs to make sure the audience understands the full horror of the situation: ferocious warrior ants, each ten feet long and able to lift twenty times its own weight, are breeding somewhere in the United States. They must be found and destroyed without causing a national panic.

A wave of UFO sightings sweeps the country. Finally, however, a massive forty-ton theft of sugar from a freight train in Los Angeles tells Medford that the giant ants have relocated in Southern California. Douglas adds a subplot involving two missing children whose father was killed by the ants: if they can locate the children, Graham and Peterson (who finally have an investigative job for which their training has prepared them) will have a pretty good idea where the ants are. A bit of conventional, if thoroughly professional, policework follows, and the children are traced to a Los Angeles viaduct. They, and thus the ants, appear to have taken refuge in the sewers. The army is called in (residents having been, at long last, alerted to the nature of the emergency and warned to stay indoors) and, led by Graham and Peterson, undertakes an armed sweep of the entire Los Angeles sewer system. In the film's climactic scene, Peterson finds the children unharmed but in imminent peril from advancing ants. He helps them escape, but is killed in the process. Graham leads a team of soldiers armed with bazookas and flamethrowers into the ants' stronghold, where they finally exterminate the monsters in a burst of flame.

Dr. Medford provides the film's cautionary epitaph: We have seen, he suggests, only one of the fruits of nuclear testing. "When man entered the atomic age, he opened the door to a new world. What we'll eventually find in that world nobody can predict." As Medford speaks, Douglas ends the film with a pessimistic bit of symbolism. The camera slowly pulls back from the burning ants' nest, leaving Medford silhouetted against a terrifying wall of fire.

Them! is far from a perfect film. Douglas had a terrific story and a good script, but he was saddled with a pedestrian cast. In a film where no single character dominates, Gwenn as the brilliant but uncommunicative Dr. Medford and Whitmore as Sergeant Ben Peterson turn in workmanlike performances. Weldon, however, has little to do as Pat Medford, and Arness (who was soon to become a major star as Matt Dillon in *Gunsmoke*, one of television's most enduring and popular series), is particularly wooden as Robert Graham. Only Fess Parker (whose fortunes would also soon take a sharp turn for the better as the star of Walt Disney's *Davey Crockett* films) in a bit of comic relief as a man who was sent to a asylum when he reported seeing flying ants shows any real spark of life.

Douglas nevertheless saves the film by deemphasizing the acting and concentrating on telling his story effectively. He accomplishes this by focusing not, as in conventional science-fiction thrillers of the era, on special effects, but on pacing the film properly—by playing down the horror and playing up the mystery. If anything, the scenes in which the ants actually appear are deemphasized; instead, Douglas holds the viewers' attention by making the ants mysterious. Clues, first to the identity of Them and then to their whereabouts, are added logically, one at a time, and the plot moves along nicely to its ominous conclusion.

Had Douglas concentrated on the horrific aspects of the film, *Them!* would doubtless have enjoyed a moment of popularity and then vanished without a trace, like so many science-fiction films of the 1950's. Instead, emphasizing the mysterious as well as the horrific, he transcends the boundaries of the science-fiction genre, and in the process, manages to tell what remains a very timely tale about the unknown perils of the nuclear age.

James P. Girard

THEODORA GOES WILD

Released: 1936
Production: Everett Riskin for Columbia
Direction: Richard Boleslawski
Screenplay: Sidney Buchman; based on a story of the same name by Mary McCarthy
Cinematography: Joseph Walker
Editing: Otto Meyer
Costume design: Bernard Newman
Music: Morris Stoloff
Running time: 94 minutes

Principal characters:
Theodora Lynn .... Irene Dunne
Michael Grant .... Melvyn Douglas
Ted Waterbury .... Thomas Mitchell
Arthur Stevenson .... Thurston Hall

The essence of screwball comedy was expressed by Preston Sturges in 1941 in his *Sullivan's Travels*: "There's a lot to be said for making people laugh! It isn't much, but it's better than nothing in this cockeyed caravan. . . ." The screwball comedy films emerged out of a Depression-ridden America to poke fun in the face of deprivation which at times seemed hopeless and insurmountable. These frothy yet cogent films may have largely ignored the reality of the world off the movie screen, but there was more truth to their madcap zaniness than many imagined. Americans went to the movies to get away from the drudgery of everyday life and to be entertained. Early comedies had relied mostly upon slapstick and visual comedy, but talking pictures brought dialogue, and when it sparkled, when it was bantered back and forth at a rat-a-tat-tat speed as in this genre, audiences loved it.

The key to screwball comedy was its depiction of real characters. That is not to say they could not be glamorous, but they were identifiable characters, from the runaway heiress (Claudette Colbert) and her down-to-earth reporter (Clark Gable) in Frank Capra's screwball breakthrough *It Happened One Night* (1934), to Gary Cooper's Longfellow Deeds in Capra's *Mr. Deeds Goes to Town* (1936). The characters were, as Capra insisted, "human and do the things human beings do—or would do if they had the courage and opportunity." Another staple ingredient of screwball comedy was poking fun at the rich—a device that said, "Sure, there's a Depression, but look, the rich aren't happy either." Even if they did not do it wholeheartedly, film audiences took delight in seeing the rich as targets of ridicule.

Thus Capra spawned a whole new film genre which went on to include directors such as Leo McCarey, George Stevens, and Gregory La Cava;

actresses such as Carole Lombard, Myrna Loy, Claudette Colbert, and Jean Arthur; and actors such as Cary Grant, William Powell, and James Stewart.

Theodora Goes Wild is one of the most delightful pictures of the screwball genre, and it was a pivotal film in the careers of its two stars, Irene Dunne and Melvyn Douglas. Dunne had made her screen debut in 1930 and gained a popular following by starring in romantic women's pictures such as *Back Street* (1932) and *Magnificent Obsession* (1935) and glamorous operettas and musicals such as *Roberta* (1935) and *Show Boat* (1936), in which she displayed a melodious soprano singing voice. In 1931, she had been nominated as Best Actress for *Cimarron*, in which she played Edna Ferber's heroine, Sabra. Her plans for her professional future took a decidedly dramatic bent, and when she was asked to star in *Theodora Goes Wild*, she was on her way to Europe to meet with relatives of Madame Curie in hopes of starring in a filmed biography of that famous scientist. Columbia insisted she appear in the picture, however, and it proved a turning point in her career which led to *The Awful Truth* (1937), *Joy of Living* (1938), *My Favorite Wife* (1940), and others.

Douglas had debuted in motion pictures in 1931, and while he had played the suave, handsome leading man to numerous screen beauties, such as Gloria Swanson, Claudette Colbert, Greta Garbo, and Joan Crawford, *Theodora Goes Wild* was, as he put it, singlehandedly responsible for earning him "an international reputation for being one of the most debonair and witty farceurs in Hollywood . . . and a saleable commodity." The sparkling screenplay for *Theodora Goes Wild* was written by Sidney Buchman based upon a story by Mary McCarthy and involves a sweet, level-headed small-town girl named Theodora Lynn (Irene Dunne).

Theodora is a resident of Lynnfield, Connecticut, where she has been the church organist since age fifteen and a Sunday school teacher for ten years. She is the personification of small-town, prim and proper femininity, except that she has a secret. She has penned a titillating sex novel à la English novelist Elinor Glyn under the pseudonym Caroline Adams. It is a secret she must keep not only from her spinster aunts but also from the entire town, whose moral guardians and members of the Lynnfield Literary Society have labeled the best-seller "unmoral and not fit to print." The only one in Lynnfield who defends the book is the irascible newspaper editor, Jed Waterbury (Thomas Mitchell), who thinks Lynnfield should learn "how people live and love in the wide awake world. You can't keep civilization out of Lynnfield forever."

Theodora goes to New York City to meet with her publisher, Arthur Stevenson (Thurston Hall), with whom she can barely discuss the risque novel. She also meets dashing Michael Grant (Melvyn Douglas), the illustrator who designed the cover for the book. Grant is immediately smitten by the lovely Theodora, and after becoming inebriated and going back to his own apartment, he attempts to reenact the seduction scene in Theodora's book. Unfortunately for him, Theodora does not respond like her free-spirited heroine;

instead, she admonishes him with, "Don't you dare!"

Grant is now challenged to free Theodora from her repressive behavior and follows her back to Lynnfield, getting himself hired by her aunts as a gardener. In his attempts to defrost her inhibitions, he exclaims, "I'm going to break you out of this jail and give you the world." Theodora resists, but does go fishing with him on a Sunday, an activity which the local townspeople find so shocking that Theodora's aunts insist Grant leave town. He does so, but before leaving, he writes her a note, saying, "You're free, baby. Step out and be yourself. There are big things ahead and you'll travel faster alone."

Now angry as Lynnfield's small-mindedness, Theodora does rebel. She follows Grant to New York and "goes wild." She becomes an ardent champion of women's rights, speaking out in press conferences. She is named a correspondent in two divorce suits, one, her publisher's and the other Grant's, which threatens to ruin the political career of Grant's father-in-law. At the finale, Theodora arrives back in Lynnfield at the railroad station with a baby (which belongs to a friend) in her arms. The love-smitten Grant is waiting for her there, and when he jumps to the obvious but wrong conclusion, she saucily snaps, "It isn't mine, stupid."

Theodora Goes Wild premiered at Radio City Music Hall on November 12, 1936, and was an instant hit. Critical reaction was surprisingly mixed, with many complaints that the script was too lightweight. Dunne, who was extremely popular, was criticized for being too mannered at times but her role did get her an Academy Award nomination for Best Actress. Douglas received universally excellent reviews, reviews so good that he was type-cast for a time as a witty farceur, which he later resented. All in all this is one of the 1930's memorable screen comedies, deftly written and directed, fast-paced, and well-edited by Otto Meyer, whose editing received an Oscar nomination.

Ronald Bowers